# From the Dust of the Earth

# From the Dust of the Earth

*Benedict XVI, the Bible,
and the Theory of Evolution*

Matthew J. Ramage

The Catholic University of America Press
Washington, D.C.

The paper used in this publication meets the minimum requirements
of American National Standards for Information Science—
Permanence of Paper for Printed Library Materials,
ANSI Z39.48–1984.

∞

Library of Congress Cataloging-in-Publication data.

Names: Ramage, Matthew J., author.

Title: From the Dust of the Earth: Benedict XVI, the Bible,
and the Theory of Evolution / Matthew J. Ramage.

Description: Washington, D.C.: The Catholic University of America Press, 2022.
Includes bibliographical references and index.

Identifiers: LCCN 2022006263 (print) | LCCN 2022006264 (ebook)
ISBN 9780813235141 | ISBN 9780813235158 (eISBN)

Subjects: LCSH: Creationism. | Cosmology. | Bible and evolution.
Evolution—Religious aspects—Catholic Church. | Benedict XVI, Pope, 1927-
Catholic Church—Doctrines.

Classification: LCC BS651 .R33 2022 (print) | LCC BS651 (ebook)
DDC 231.7/65—dc23/eng/20220314
LC record available at https://lccn.loc.gov/2022006263
LC ebook record available at https://lccn.loc.gov/2022006264

"I am the Alpha and the Omega, the first and the last, the beginning and the end."

—*Revelation 22:13*

# Table of Contents

# Acknowledgments

As Professor Joseph Ratzinger once wrote in the foreword to his seminal text on St. Bonaventure's theology of history, a book is never the exclusive work of a single author. The present volume is no exception to this rule. It has been in the works for many years, and it would never have come to fruition if not for many people—living and dead—who deserve my gratitude.

It has been a joy to collaborate on four projects now with the outstanding staff of The Catholic University of America Press. I am grateful in particular for the hard work of John Martino, Brian Roach, Laureen Gleason, Jaymie Stuart Wolfe, and the anonymous peer reviewers who greatly strengthened the manuscript by supplying crucial comments on the book's penultimate draft.

Among the many individuals who made consistent contributions to this project informally, pride of place goes to my students and colleagues at Benedictine College whose conversations over the years have helped me to develop many of the ideas that now see the light of day here. I wish to thank my assistants Raphael Imgrund, Sarah Newbolds, and Victoria Rogers for their copyediting, as well as the students of my Pentateuch courses and honors seminars on Genesis, Faith, and Science who were among the first to engage the text. What is more, my grand plan was made possible by the diligence of our college's library staff who handled a constant stream of obscure and foreign-language inter-library loan requests from my desk.

A number of individuals outside of my institution also contributed to this text either through conversation or by taking a critical eye to it at my request. This long list includes Christopher Baglow, John Gavin, SJ, Jordan Haddad, Martin Huss, Robert Imbelli, the late Joseph Koterski, SJ, Nicholas Lombardo, OP, James Madden, John Martino, Aaron Pidel, SJ, James Prothro, Piotr Roszak, Brett Salkeld, Mark Schramp, Nicholas Sparks, Daria Spezzano, and Giuseppe Tanzella-Nitti.

Important refinements were made thanks to the keen work of Mariusz Tabaczek, OP, who edited an earlier version of Chapter 3 published in *Scientia et Fides*.[1] Portions of Chapters 1, 4, and 6 were improved by the editorial team at *Review for Religious*; they helped me polish an essay on this topic that now appears in that journal.[2] Chapter 9 benefited from revisions suggested by Andrew Hofer, OP, Roger Nutt, and Michael Dauphinais, who edited an early version of the essay for the volume

---

1. Matthew J. Ramage, "Machine or Melody? Joseph Ratzinger on Divine Causality in Evolutionary Creation," *Scientia et Fides* 8, no. 2 (2020): 302–21. https://doi.org/10.12775/SetF.2020.023.

2. Matthew J. Ramage, "Does Evolution Undermine Christianity? Joseph Ratzinger on the Bible and Humanity's Evolutionary Origins," *Review for Religious: New Series* 1, no. 2 (2021): 159–77. doi:10.1353/rfr.2021.0026. The content has been revised for publication in this book and is reprinted here with permission.

*Thomas Aquinas and the Crisis of Christology.*[3] Parts of Chapters 9 and 10 appeared in the journal *Religions*, where they were enhanced by the editorial expertise of Piotr Roszak and Sasa Horvat.[4] The Epilogue will also appear in a forthcoming volume from Emmaus Academic edited by Michael Dauphinais and Roger Nutt.[5] All the above individuals are to be thanked for eliminating many infelicities in the present text, and any that remain are solely mine.

Among my fellow academics, two seasoned Ratzinger scholars deserve a special word of gratitude. It was in meeting Fr. Santiago Sanz of the Pontifical University of the Holy Cross at a 2019 conference at the Angelicum that I was first introduced to the unpublished lecture notes of Professor Ratzinger's 1958, 1964, and 1976 courses on creation. As these remarkable manuscripts deal extensively with the themes at the heart of this volume's inquiry, I have translated many of them into English for the first time and deployed them throughout the text alongside insights from Fr. Sanz's commentaries on them in Italian and Spanish. Even though on certain points we differ in our interpretations of Ratzinger, my thought has been greatly enriched by Fr. Santiago's wisdom, and I am deeply grateful for our friendship.

What is more, around this same time, Fr. Emery de Gaál published his own surveys of Ratzinger's 1957 Mariology course, his inaugural lecture on natural theology in 1959, and his 1958–59 class on fundamental theology. I am indebted to Fr. Emery's willingness to share his research for a number of insights in this volume. While there is certainly enough material in Ratzinger's published writings for a book on the relationship of Scripture, doctrine, and evolution, having these sources from the beginning of Ratzinger's career provided the final puzzle pieces I needed to paint a full picture of this theological giant's career-long reflection on the subject. I apologize to Fr. Emery in advance for any deficiencies in my translations or understanding of Ratzinger's texts.

Last and above all, I thank my wife, Jen Ramage, for her instrumental role in the composition of this volume. Beyond her full-time job of mothering and educating our six children, the text has benefited directly from Jen's literary and theological expertise. She has patiently talked through these matters with me for more than a decade, relentlessly called me to clarify my thought, carefully edited the first draft of the manuscript, and helped to formulate a number of the more lucid thoughts that appear in its pages. If readers only knew half the contributions she made and the things she had me change, they would be very appreciative indeed.

---

3. Matthew J. Ramage, "Putting the Last Adam First: Evolution, Suffering, and Death in Light of Kenotic Christology," in *Thomas Aquinas and the Crisis of Christology*, eds. Michael A. Dauphinais, Andrew Hofer, OP, and Roger W. Nutt (Ave Maria, FL: Sapientia Press, 2021), 279–302.

4. Matthew J. Ramage, "Ratzinger on Evolution and Evil: A Christological and Mariological Answer to the Problem of Suffering and Death in Creation," *Religions* 12, no. 8 (2021): 583. https://doi.org/10.3390/rel12080583.

5. Matthew J. Ramage, "Evolution and Eschatology: Jesus Christ, the Alpha and Omega of All Creation in the Thought of Joseph Ratzinger," in *Hope and Death: Christian Responses*, eds. Michael Dauphinais and Roger Nutt (Steubenville, OH: Emmaus Academic, forthcoming).

*Part I*

# Preliminary Philosophical Questions

# Chapter 1

# In the Beginning

*Evolution's Challenge to Christian Teaching on Human Origins*

"The LORD God formed man of dust from the ground, and breathed into his nostrils the breath of life; and man became a living being."

—*Genesis 2:7 RSV*

"Like a 'universal acid,' evolutionary theory 'eats through just about every traditional concept, and leaves in its wake a revolutionized world-view.'"

—*Daniel Dennett*[1]

"Before Darwin came along, it was pretty difficult to be an atheist, at least to be an atheist free of nagging doubts. Darwin triumphantly made it *easy* to be an intellectually fulfilled and satisfied atheist."

—*Richard Dawkins*[2]

"[The words of Genesis] give rise to a certain conflict. They are beautiful and familiar, *but are they also true*? Everything seems to speak against it. . . ."

—*Joseph Ratzinger*[3]

## ON (NOT) SEEING THE PROBLEM

The claim that evolution undermines Christianity—that it renders the "God hypothesis" unnecessary—is standard fare in our culture these days. It is an assertion that I encounter often in my work as a Catholic educator, typically in the context of trying to help students who come to me struggling because somewhere along the line they had been told that the theory of evolution is incompatible with their faith. Sometimes, the challenge takes the form of the allegation that the science of evolution renders Christian faith unsustainable. At other times, it is the

---

1. Daniel Dennett, *Darwin's Dangerous Idea: Evolution and the Meaning of Life* (New York: Simon & Schuster, 1995), 63.

2. Richard Dawkins, comment of December 29, 2008, in response to Madeleine Bunting, "Darwin Shouldn't Be Hijacked by New Atheists—He is an Ethical Inspiration," *The Guardian* (December 28, 2008). Dawkins adds, "That doesn't mean that understanding Darwin drives you inevitably to atheism. But it certainly constitutes a giant step in that direction." See also Dawkins, *The Blind Watchmaker* (London: Penguin Books, 1991), 6.

3. Joseph Ratzinger, *In the Beginning: A Catholic Understanding of the Story of Creation and the Fall* (Grand Rapids: Eerdmans, 1995), 3–4. Emphasis added.

opposite: that a commitment to one's faith means precludes the acceptance of evolutionary theory.

Individuals who find themselves in this situation—university students and others—have often been well catechized. They know the story of salvation history. They love Jesus Christ and are committed to living as his disciples. However, they often struggle in vain to find sane answers to their questions due to the widespread assumption that faith and evolutionary theory are incompatible. Regrettably, one reason that seekers often run into this difficulty is that would-be apologists for the faith too often respond to the challenge of evolution simply by referencing verses from Genesis that are assumed to be historical but in reality, contradict the known facts of our universe's history. In the case of Catholics, one also encounters two spurious claims: first, that evolution must be rejected because many Church Fathers held the Adam and Eve narrative to be historical; second, that magisterial documents preclude the acceptance of evolutionary theory. These claims are made despite the fact that the Fathers were neither literalists nor primarily interested in scientific questions and that the Church has never condemned evolution.[4]

That some Christians reply to scientific discoveries in this way is only natural. The modern theory of evolution is less than two centuries old, while the Christian faith has endured for two millennia. Moreover, much of the most compelling evidence for Charles Darwin's original theory has only surfaced in recent decades. When I was studying biology as an undergraduate, the human genome—which provides breathtaking confirmation of the gradual evolution of *Homo sapiens*— had not even been completely mapped. The same holds true in other areas like the fossil record, which is being filled in better and better with each passing year. Indeed, as I write this book, just last week my family and I trod a path in Utah alongside fossilized dinosaur footprints from the Jurassic Period (almost two hundred million years ago) that were discovered by humans just twenty years ago. That said, the reality is that the conclusions of genetic and paleontological science are not any more obvious to most people today than was it obvious to ancient people that the earth revolves around the sun, that continents drift and collide to form mountains, and that all physical objects are drawn together by a mysterious force called gravity.

The difference between evolutionary theory and such realities is that most people in our society are now used to them, yet it must be remembered that they were not immediately obvious without modern science and were unknown to the

---

4. On the Catholic Church having never condemned the theory of evolution, see Society of Catholic Scientists, "Did the Catholic Church ever condemn Evolution in the past?," https://www.catholic-scientists.org/common-questions/a-does-catholic-church-accept-evolution-b-did-catholic-church-ever-condemn-evolution-in-past. As this source notes, key theological sources from 1874, 1909, and 1929 confirm this observation. See also John O'Brien, *Evolution and Religion: A Study of the Bearing of Evolution upon the Philosophy of Religion* (New York: The Century Co., 1932), 15. On the Fathers and Medievals not being literalists, see Paul O'Callahan, *God's Gift of the Universe: An Introduction to Creation Theology* (Washington, D.C.: The Catholic University of America Press, 2021), 142–44, where the author discusses Augustine and Aquinas specifically.

writers of the Bible. Add to this the fact that nonspecialists seldom have the occasion to study the vast body of evidence in favor of human evolution but that they *do* have some knowledge of the Christian tradition, and it is easy to see why the modern scientific theory is at times perceived as a threat to faith and rejected accordingly.[5]

Although there is certainly merit to consulting ancient texts for wisdom on how to illumine present issues, unfortunately Christians who reject evolution on the basis of nonscientific authorities often fail to see the point at issue when someone is struggling with their faith over a perceived conflict between faith and evolution.[6] If my experience is any indication, replying with nonscientific sources to someone versed in evolutionary theory is not likely going to cause him to dismiss conclusions that he has arrived at through his God-given use of reason. Indeed, to one who has encountered powerful evidence of man's gradual evolutionary origin, it may give the impression that one has to choose between his faith and reason—a battle that reason will rarely lose.[7] In the words of Henri de Lubac, a dear friend and theological mentor of Joseph Ratzinger: "To one who has seen a problem, the

---

5. The number of believers who reject evolution today is significant. A 2017 study from Georgetown University's Center for Applied Research in the Apostolate found that just 56% of Catholics agreed that humans and other living things evolved over time, and only about 25% thought that the Catholic Church allowed to accept human evolution. https://cara.georgetown. edu/wp-content/uploads/2018/06/CARA_Fall2017_Special-Report_FaithScience-FINAL.pdf. For earlier data concerning the public at large, see Pew Research Center. "Public's Views on Human Evolution" (December 30, 2013), https://www.pewforum.org/2013/12/30/publics-views-on-human-evolution/.

6. The last official papal encyclical to treat evolution was Pius XII's 1950 *Humani Generis*, which cautiously opened the door to evolution. That this was the last encyclical to weigh in on evolution can easily give the impression that the Church has not developed her thought on the topic over the past seventy-plus years. However, this conclusion rests on the failure to recognize that the Church has since wisely changed her mode of addressing evolution, preferring not to take it up in high-level magisterial documents. In the case of the *Catechism of the Catholic Church*, the reason for this is given by Ratzinger and Cardinal Christoph Schönborn who oversaw the text's composition: "It cannot be the task of the Catechism to represent novel theological theses which do not belong to the assured patrimony of the Church's faith." *Introduction to the Catechism of the Catholic Church* (San Francisco: Ignatius Press, 1994), 71. Nowadays, the Church's approach has been to treat evolution through making it the subject of research by pontifical commissions, by hosting conferences on the topic, and by having popes who have frequently addressed it and sought to incorporate its insights. These more recent works remain in harmony with the principles handed on by Pius, yet advance well beyond what he envisioned due to the vastly improved understanding of evolution that has emerged in recent times. I have listed some of these works in the appendix.

7. For helpful thoughts on the growing anti-evolution movement within the Catholic Church, see Nicanor Austriaco, OP, "Reading Genesis with Cardinal Ratzinger," *Homiletic and Pastoral Review* (January 1, 2009) and Brett Salkeld, "Catholic Creationism as a Conspiracy Theory," *Church Life Journal* (May 13, 2020). For an accessible, up-to-date, and scientifically rigorous textbook to introduce faith and science topics to young adults, I cannot recommend highly enough Christopher Baglow, *Faith, Science, & Reason: Theology on the Cutting Edge*, 2nd ed. (Downers Grove, IL: Midwest Theological Forum, 2019). For another accessible introduction to the Church's teaching on faith and science, see Stacy Trasancos, *Particles of Faith: A Catholic Guide to Navigating Science* (Notre Dame, IN: Ave Maria Press, 2016).

most beautiful and true things, uttered by someone who has not seen it, are but words and yet more words."[8]

As a Christian disciple, educator, and father, I deeply appreciate the concerns of traditional believers who are cautious when it comes to evolutionary theory, and I do not think that their wariness of the scientific community is entirely unfounded. After all, scientists and biblical scholars are fallible mortals who can have their own prejudices and agendas, a phenomenon Pope Benedict XVI identified in commenting, "Science has opened up major dimensions of reason that previously had not been accessible. . . . But in its joy over the greatness of its discoveries, it tends to confiscate dimensions of our reason that we still need."[9]

Further, it is admittedly difficult to explain why some things are considered essential to the Christian tradition (e.g., the Incarnation and Resurrection of Christ, to name just two) while others that were once typically assumed to be such (e.g., geocentrism, the direct creation of two first humans, etc.) are today generally regarded not to be. Noting this understandable concern, Cardinal Ratzinger writes of our current situation:

> [T]here is an almost ineluctable fear that we will gradually end up in emptiness and that the time will come when there will be nothing left to defend and hide behind, that the whole landscape of Scripture and of the faith will be overrun by a kind of "reason" that will no longer be able to take any of this seriously.
>
> Along with this there is another disquieting consideration. For one can ask: If theologians or even the church can shift the boundaries here between image and intention, between what lies buried in the past and what is of enduring value, why can they not do so elsewhere—as, for instance, with respect to Jesus' miracles? And if there, why not also with respect to what is absolutely central—the cross and the resurrection of the Lord?[10]

---

8. Henri de Lubac, *Paradoxes of Faith* (San Francisco: Ignatius Press, 1987), 54. For an illuminating article that surveys the influence of de Lubac and other renowned thinkers upon Ratzinger, see Tracey Rowland, "Benedict's Intellectual Mentors and Students," *Crisis Magazine* (February 19, 2013). In his final book-length interview, the retired pontiff replied to the question about which theologians he trusted the most quite simply: "I would still say Lubac and Balthasar." Benedict XVI and Peter Seewald, *Last Testament: In His Own Words* (London: Bloomsbury, 2016), 125.

9. Benedict XVI, *Creation and Evolution: A Conference with Pope Benedict XVI in Castel Gandolfo* (San Francisco: Ignatius Press, 2008), 145. Esteemed evolutionary biologist Stephen Jay Gould likewise captured this point well in Gould, "Evolution as Fact and Theory" and Stephen Jay Gould, "Nonoverlapping Magisteria," in *Leonardo's Mountain of Clams and the Diet of Worms* (New York: Harmony Books, 1998), 269–83.

10. Ratzinger, *In the Beginning*, 6–7. On the subject of how to deal with fear in matters related to faith and certitude, I find myself largely agreeing with Peter Enns when he writes, "If I had to name the most common obstacle for Christians to a life of true trust in God, it would be fear—mainly the fear of being wrong about the Bible, which is often equated with being wrong about God." Enns, *The Bible Tells Me So: Why Defending Scripture Has Made Us Unable to Read It* (San Francisco: HarperOne, 2014), 239. For a brief but interesting piece on why conservatives should not fear evolution that also includes a critique of progressives who reject the findings of evolutionary science, see Razib Khan, "Conservatives Shouldn't Fear Evolutionary Theory," *National Review* (May 13, 2019).

I find it remarkable how lucidly this quote captures the worry of a slippery slope so frequently felt by Christians when broaching questions at the intersection of Scripture, science, and doctrine.

That said, what concerns me more than a potentially slippery slope is that our Church's brightest people (especially the young) will increasingly abandon their faith if we let our worries get the best of us and back them into the corner of having to defend the indefensible by forcing them to reject evolution.[11] Following Ratzinger's lead, I would say that the question ought not to be how we can defend the faithful against the advances of this science but rather how we can engage in dialogue with it so as to more deeply penetrate the mysteries of the Christian faith and, in turn, illumine the science with our faith.[12]

This task is described well when Joseph Ratzinger (Pope Benedict XVI) deploys a scientific metaphor to speak of the need for believers to make "the experiment of faith."[13] As in any experiment, no outcome is guaranteed in advance, so Benedict writes that the experiment of faith involves an existential "risk"—the possibility that we may have to revise certain preconceptions in light of what we end up discovering. On this point, then, I like to bear in mind the words of Henri de Lubac who offers us this warning and an exhortation: "The fear of falling prey to error must never prevent us from getting to the full truth. Love of truth never goes without daring. And that is one of the reasons why truth is not loved."[14] Indeed, Ratzinger has said that one incurs great "risk" by *not* being bold in our pursuit of truth, for it prevents us from realizing for ourselves that the Christian faith is strong enough to stand up to any challenge that modern science may appear to throw at it:

> It seems to me that we quite often run a particular risk: that of not wanting to see these things. We live with shades down over our windows, so to speak, because we are afraid that our faith could not stand the full, glaring light of the facts. . . . *But a faith that will not account for half of the facts or even more is actually, in essence, a kind of refusal of faith, or, at least, a very profound form*

---

11. Indeed, by some accounts, the seeming incompatibility of science and faith is the top reason young Christians leave the faith. For a discussion of this point, see Dennis Venema and Scot McKnight, *Adam and the Genome: Reading Scripture after Genetic Science* (Grand Rapids, MI: Baker, 2017), 104.

12. I appreciate how William Cavanaugh and James Smith frame this point: "What if ours is not a Galileo moment but a Chalcedonian opportunity?" Cavanaugh and Smith, *Evolution and the Fall* (Grand Rapids, MI: Eerdmans, 2017), xvii.

13. This book at times refers to the one man Ratzinger/Benedict by his surname and at other times by his papal name in the effort to distinguish writings composed during his pontificate from those preceding it. When not referring specifically to a text, the name Benedict or "emeritus pontiff" is employed since this volume was written during the period of his retirement. For a thorough account of the role played by the expression "experiment of faith" in Benedict's thought, see Matthew Ramage, *The Experiment of Faith: Pope Benedict XVI on Living the Theological Virtues in a Secular Age* (Washington: Catholic University of America Press, 2020). He may have been influenced here by Luigi Giussani's description of the "risk of education." See Luigi Giussani, *The Risk of Education: Discovering Our Ultimate Destiny* (Montreal: McGill-Queen's University Press, 2019).

14. Lubac, *Paradoxes of Faith*, 101.

*of skepticism that fears faith will not be big enough to cope with reality. . . .* In contrast to that, true believing means looking the whole of reality in the face, unafraid and with an open heart, even if it goes against the picture of faith that, for whatever reason, we make for ourselves."[15]

The reality is, though, that many Christians find it too daunting to take up this challenge when it comes to engaging evolutionary theory. There is a temptation to retreat into perceived safe havens like strict biblical literalism (a wooden reading of the Bible as if it were a history and science textbook) or what Cardinal Ratzinger called "a positivistic and rigid ecclesiasticism" (an overly simplistic and exclusive reliance on documents of the Church).[16]

Although it is tempting to turn to authorities like the Church Fathers and ecclesial documents of times past for quick answers to the problems that evolutionary theory poses for Christian belief, I suggest that that we all would do well to continually reflect on G.K. Chesterton's classic quip that "Catholic doctrine and discipline may be walls; but they are the walls of a playground."[17] In other words, while doctrine is indispensable and tradition a perennial source of wisdom, we should be wary of hastening to the judgment that there is only one way to address a new scientific development or that recourse to sources that preceded it are sufficient unto this end. In this regard, we might thus bear in mind what de Lubac wrote on the subject of evolution: "There is more truth in the complex attitude of the Church

---

15. Ratzinger, *What It Means to Be a Christian*, trans. Henry Taylor (San Francisco: Ignatius Press, 2006), 19–20 (emphasis added).

16. Ratzinger, "Biblical Interpretation in Crisis: On the Question of the Foundations and Approaches of Exegesis Today," in *Biblical Interpretation in Crisis: The Ratzinger Conference on Bible and Church* (Grand Rapids, MI: Eerdmans, 1989), 1–23 at 6. Jeremy Holmes has recently diagnosed this attitude well in noting that believers today sometimes fall into a trap of disregarding any domain of inquiry less lofty than theology or philosophy. Though often motivated by the sincere desire to defend the faith, Holmes finds that their overconfidence may mask the fear of letting a given line of questioning "take them anywhere scary." Holmes, *Cur Deus Verba: Why the Word Became Words* (San Francisco: Ignatius Press, 2021), 222–23. As he adduces principles to help readers avoid doing violence to the meaning of Genesis, Holmes nevertheless has no pretensions that all will be able to overcome their mistaken presuppositions about its relationship with science: "There will always be some population of readers who, wishing to submit themselves to the text, conclude that they must accept a geocentric cosmology or something else not really taught by the text." For other incisive discussions of the phenomenon of believers writing off evolutionary science and a warning about how our approach to Scripture can unwittingly become ideological, see Venema and McKnight, *Adam and the Genome*, 100–101; Kenton Sparks, *God's Word in Human Words: An Evangelical Appropriation of Critical Biblical Scholarship* (Grand Rapids, MI: Baker Academic, 2008), 303–308; Enns, *How the Bible Actually Works* (San Francisco: HarperOne, 2019), 166, 268.

17. G.K. Chesterton, *Orthodoxy* (New York: John Lane Company, 1909), 269. Also worthy of consideration is Chesterton's line on the madman's habit of oversimplifying things: "His mind moves in a perfect but narrow circle. A small circle is quite as infinite as a large circle, but . . . it is not so large. In the same way the insane explanation is quite as complete as the sane one, but it is not so large." Chesterton, *Orthodoxy*, 20. For an interesting book in which I have most recently encountered this line from Chesterton, see Telford Work, *Jesus—the End and the Beginning: Tracing the Christ-Shaped Nature of Everything* (Grand Rapids: Baker, 2019), 47–48.

than in all simplifying philosophies. The practice of the saints is to accept reality rather than impose a system upon it."[18]

This enterprising spirit was also captured well by the late agnostic biologist Stephen Jay Gould, himself always eager to engage people of faith on the subject of evolution, (even contributing to the work of the Pontifical Academy of Sciences alongside fellow renowned agnostic scientist Carl Sagan). Gould suggests that science is most fascinating and promising when it involves healthy debate over new ideas. Scientists, he notes, regard debates on fundamental issues as a sign of intellectual vitality and a source of excitement. As he puts it, "Science is—and how else can I say it?—most fun when it plays with interesting ideas, examines their implications, and recognizes that old information might be explained in surprisingly new ways. Evolutionary theory is now enjoying this uncommon vigor."[19] The reason that I am an academic theologian is that I think the same is true of theology. One of the main things that gets me to work in the morning is the prospect that engaging modern discoveries of all kinds might help us to understand our ancient faith better. And, when working on the subject of faith and evolution in particular, time and again I find myself thanking God with these powerful lines from the pen of Charles Darwin, the father of the modern theory of evolution by natural selection:

> [F]rom the war of nature, from famine and death, the most exalted object which we are capable of conceiving, namely, the production of the higher animals, directly follows. There is grandeur in this view of life, with its several powers, having been originally breathed by the Creator into a few forms or into one; and that, whilst this planet has gone cycling on according to the fixed law of gravity, from so simple a beginning endless forms most beautiful and most wonderful have been, and are being, evolved.[20]

## "JUST A THEORY"?

Many Christians find evolutionary theory itself to be noncontroversial. For these individuals, the main point of interest lies in how to better understand evolution in light of faith and, in turn, how to more deeply probe the mysteries of faith (e.g., human uniqueness, original sin, etc.) through an engagement with the science. At the start of this volume, however, it is also important that we pause to address a nagging difficulty that presses upon many Christians and sometimes keeps them from pursuing the dialogue between faith and evolution in the depth that it deserves. This obstacle consists in the common misperception that evolution—the

---

18. Henri de Lubac, *The Religion of Teilhard de Chardin* (New York, Desclee Co. 1967), 237. For another related and helpful book on Chardin's evolutionary worldview, see Lubac, *Teilhard de Chardin: The Man and His Meaning* (New York: Hawthorn Books, 1965).

19. Stephen Jay Gould, "Evolution as Fact and Theory," in *Hen's Teeth and Horse's Toes* (New York: W.W. Norton & Company, 1994), 253–62 at 256.

20. Darwin, *On the Origin of the Species by Means of Natural Selection* (London: John Murray, 1959), 490.

gradual process by which all life on earth on our planet has emerged from a common ancestor or pool of ancestors—is not a fact but is rather "just a theory."[21]

The nonscientist's confusion over the epistemic status of evolutionary theory has a number of causes. However, it is often connected with an equivocation on the meaning of the word "theory." In colloquial usage today, this term tends to denote an unproven personal view—a person's uninformed hunch, opinion, or pet idea. Perhaps more confusingly still, sometimes it is confused with a hypothesis, which is a proposed explanation for something that perhaps does have some real evidence to support it yet has failed to attain the certainty of a bona fide scientific theory. When we read sensationalist headlines to the effect that a "theory has been overturned" and that we will now "need to rethink everything we thought we knew," it is typically a falsified hypothesis that is in view. Unsurprisingly, for a person who is not well versed in the various branches of science that converge to yield extraordinary confidence in the fact of evolution, it is easy to assume that this long-established science is—like the "proof" in favor of the latest health or wellness trend—uncertain and likely to be overturned at some point in the future.[22]

The problem with this is that it is to fundamentally misunderstand the nature of the theory at hand. For, in science, theory is not a mere conjecture but rather refers to *a well-substantiated explanation of a multitude of facts observed in the natural world that makes predictions whose accuracy has been repeatedly confirmed through testing.*[23]

Some, like Stephen Jay Gould, thus distinguish between evolution as a fact and evolution as a theory.[24] Among the key the facts or real-world data points of evolution outlined shortly below, we find innumerable fossils in the geological record, remarkable similarities across species at both the anatomical and genetic levels, and the phenomena of vestigial structures and genetic material in creatures. Like the rest of biology, these *facts* make no sense apart from evolutionary *theory* and

---

21. Nicanor Austriaco offers a lucid summary of the two major claims that define evolutionary theory: "First, evolution posits that every living species is descended from a common ancestor or a pool of common ancestors. In other words, according to evolutionary theory, every living organism is a distantly related cousin of every other organism, living or dead. Second, it proposes that the diversification of life that has occurred in history has been driven primarily by a process of natural selection, whereby the composition of a population of living organisms is altered from one generation to the next because of the differing abilities of the individuals in that population to survive in a given environment. Over time, this process of descent with modification led to the appearance, the transformation, and in most cases, the disappearance of numerous species of life." Austriaco, "A Theological Fittingness Argument for the Evolution of *Homo Sapiens," Theology and Science* 17:4: 539–50 at 542.

22. For a discussion of this unfortunate confusion over the meaning of the word theory in connection with notions (e.g., dietary fads) that are not bona fide scientific theories, see Venema and McKnight, *Adam and the Genome*, 4–8.

23. For helpful discussions on the meaning of theory in the scientific sense, see Tia Ghose, "'Just a Theory': 7 Misused Science Words," *Scientific American* (April 2, 2013); Alina Bradford, "What Is a Scientific Theory?," *Live Science* (July 29, 2017); Kenneth Angielczyk, "What Do We Mean by 'Theory' in Science?," Chicago Field Museum (March 10, 2017).

24. This is the very subject of Gould's essay "Evolution as Fact and Theory" mentioned above.

will not go away even as the scientific method requires that the framework for explaining them be always open to refinement.[25] Indeed, atheist biologist Richard Dawkins highlights the astounding confidence we have in the fact of evolution by pointing out that the discovery of even a single fossil in the wrong geological stratum would constitute significant evidence against evolutionary theory—and yet no such evidence has turned up after two hundred years of digging.[26]

Contextualizing the certainty of life's evolutionary history on our planet, Dominican priest and biologist Nicanor Austriaco summarizes the epistemic status of evolutionary theory as follows:

> I am often asked if evolution is a fact. If gravity is a fact, then evolution is a fact as well. The evidence [i.e., facts, in Gould's language] is so overwhelming in favor of evolution that there really is no rival explanatory theory of repute for the origin and diversity of life on our planet, in the same way that there is no rival explanatory theory to the theory of gravity for the attraction of bodies.[27]

Well aware that every relevant domain of inquiry points to the evolutionary history of life and none against it, Gould offers a clear explanation of why the attempt by some Christians to capitalize on people's confusion over the word "theory" is a red herring:

> Yet amidst all this turmoil no biologist has been lead to doubt the fact that evolution occurred; we are debating *how* it happened. We are all trying to explain the same thing: the tree of evolutionary descent linking all organisms by ties of genealogy. Creationists pervert and caricature this debate by conveniently neglecting the common conviction that underlies it, and by falsely suggesting that evolutionists now doubt the very phenomenon we are struggling to understand.[28]

All this is to say that, for those like Gould, Austriaco, and others who are competent in this scientific field, the debate is not over *whether* evolution occurred—i.e., whether every living species on our planet descended from a common ancestor or a pool of common ancestors through incremental change across the ages—but rather *in the details of how precisely it happened.* Like the theories of general relativity, plate tectonics, the Big Bang, heliocentrism, and many others, evolutionary theory is—precisely because it is a theory in the *second* sense of the word (i.e., *not*

---

25. The point that nothing in biology as a whole and in evolution in particular makes sense apart from evolution is explored in Theodosius Dobzhansky's famous essay "Nothing in Biology Makes Sense Except in the Light of Evolution," The American Biology Teacher 35.3 (1973): 125–29.

26. Dawkins, *The Greatest Show on Earth: The Evidence for Evolution* (New York: Free Press, 2009), 146.

27. Nicanor Austriaco, OP, et al., *Thomistic Evolution: A Catholic Approach to Understanding Evolution in the Light of Faith*, 2nd ed. (Tacoma, WA: Cluny Media, 2019), 138–39. For detailed discussion of the words "fact" and "theory" as used in science, see Richard Dawkins, *The Greatest Show on Earth*, 8–18.

28. Gould, "Evolution as Fact and Theory," 256.

an individual person's unfalsifiable pet idea)—always fundamentally open to refinement and even rejection from any new evidence that emerges.

Yet this intrinsic openness of natural science should not be misconstrued as a
lack of confidence in its repeated, time-tested discoveries. For example, one may
acknowledge that it is *technically possible* that one day heliocentrism (i.e., the theory
that the planets of our solar system revolve around the sun) will be shown to be
wrong and geocentrism (i.e., the view that the sun revolves around the earth as
assumed for the first 1600 years of Christianity) will be rehabilitated as the better
account of why it is the sun streaks across our sky every day. Yet to admit the latter
scenario as being a technical possibility does not typically cause modern Christians
to seriously consider that we will one day return to thinking that the sun revolves
around the earth. Similarly, those well studied in the arena of evolutionary theory
are not very worried that all of the evidence in its favor will one day be overturned
and we will go back to maintaining such views as that the world is only several
thousand years old, that humans were the first creatures to appear and came from
dust, that every species on our planet arose directly by divine intervention, and that
all of these species were once aboard a single marine vessel at the same time.

What is more, the scientific community's remarkable confidence in evolutionary
theory has been confirmed by recent popes. For instance, Pope St. John Paul II
famously called evolution "more than a hypothesis," adding, "The convergence in the
results of these independent studies—which was neither planned nor sought—
constitutes in itself a significant argument in favor of the theory."[29] For his part, Professor Ratzinger described the evolutionary history of life on our planet as a discovery
that "for practical purposes already lies behind us as self-evident."[30] As Benedict XVI,
he further remarked that "there are so many scientific proofs in favor of evolution
which appears as a reality that we can see and enriches our knowledge of life and
being as such."[31] Speaking of how Christianity envisions the created universe, Cardinal
Ratzinger said, "The Christian picture of the world is this, that the world in its details
is the product of a long process of evolution (*Evolutionsprozeß*) but that at the most
profound level it comes from the Logos."[32] As pope, Benedict rightly rejected the
notion that our world's marvelous tree of life is the product of a "blind and irrational
evolution," yet in the same breath he underscores the correct approach: "[E]volution
reflects the creative will of the Creator and his beauty and goodness."[33]

The Church's International Theological Commission (ITC), which studied the
topic from the years 2000–2002, published a document entitled *Communion and
Stewardship* that explains in more detail:

---

29. John Paul II, Message to the Pontifical Academy of Sciences on Evolution (October 22,
1996), §4.

30. Ratzinger, *Introduction to Christianity* (San Francisco: Ignatius Press, 2004), 66.

31. Benedict XVI, Meeting with Clergy of the Dioceses of Belluno-Feltre and Treviso (July 24, 2007).

32. Ratzinger, *God and the World* (San Francisco: Ignatius Press, 2002), 139.

33. Benedict XVI, Address to Students Taking Part in the Meeting Promoted by the Sorella Natura
Foundation (November 28, 2011).

[T]here is general agreement among them that the first organism dwelt on this planet about 3.5–4 billion years ago. Since *it has been demonstrated* that all living organisms on earth are genetically related, it is *virtually certain* that all living organisms have descended from this first organism. *Converging evidence from* many studies in the physical and biological sciences furnishes mounting support for some theory of evolution to account for the development and diversification of life on earth, while controversy continues over the pace and mechanisms of evolution.[34]

Articulating a point that we will unfold in more detail below, the document wraps up its summary of man's evolutionary history by noting that, while the precise narrative "is complex and subject to revision, physical anthropology and molecular biology combine to make a convincing case for the origin of the human species in Africa about 150,000 years ago in a humanoid population of common genetic lineage."[35] That said, the above narrative will almost certainly never be explicitly declared as Church teaching. After all, the issue of all life on this planet having arisen through evolution is a matter of science and not of faith or morals.[36] However, I hope that the above sampling of statements suffices to show what her overall stance is toward the subject given the astonishing amount of evidence that has amassed in its favor in recent times.

---

34. International Theological Commission, *Communion and Stewardship: Human Persons Created in the Image of God*, §63 (emphasis added). For a helpful treatment of the general point that converging lines of evidence can yield certitudes even as an individual person may not be able to exhaustively prove every single one, see Thomas Dubay, S.M., *Faith and Certitude* (San Francisco: Ignatius Press, 1985), 107–115. Newman referred to the certainty that comes through such converging lines of evidence as resulting from a "cumulation of probabilities" by which a person perceives the fittingness of a whole without being able to exhaustively prove it in strict logical form. As Dubay notes, Newman was thus deploying the word "probability" in a technical sense, i.e., not in contrast with certitude as we do in common parlance, but with the ability for a conclusion to be well-founded yet not immune to objection from one who does not see the whole. In the effort to help modern readers avoid confusion regarding Newman's meaning, Dubay suggests "convergence of evidences" as a substitute for Newman's "cumulation of probabilities." Dubay, *Faith and Certitude*, 109.

For another helpful treatment of the type of certitude that is obtainable through the various empirical sciences (e.g., physics, biology, psychology) as distinct from one another and philosophy, see Jacques Maritain, *The Degrees of Knowledge* (Long: Geoffrey Bles, 1937), especially 181, 235–36. In these pages, Maritain affirms that biological science yields real knowledge, yet one (which he calls "empirico-schematic") that is distinct from that of physics (which he terms "empirico-mathematical"). In Maritain's understanding, biological science is descriptive and inductive in nature and "is not thought out or rationalised according to the laws of mathematical conceptualisation, but in accord with the schemas which have themselves been experimentally discovered by the reason in phenomena." Maritain, 181n1.

35. International Theological Commission, *Communion and Stewardship*, §63.

36. As the website of the Society of Catholic Scientists notes, papal statements supporting evolution are not intended to represent official endorsements of evolution, for "The popes and bishops have made clear repeatedly in recent decades that it is not the role of the Church, nor within her competence, to pass judgment on questions that belong to the empirical sciences." Society of Catholic Scientists, "Did the Catholic Church ever condemn Evolution in the past?" https://www.catholicscientists.org/common-questions/a-does-catholic-church-accept-evolution-b-did-catholic-church-ever-condemn-evolution-in-past.

## A BRIEF SCIENTIFIC NARRATIVE OF EVOLUTIONARY HISTORY AND THE EVIDENCE FOR IT

Magisterial statements and details over minutiae aside, some readers may find it helpful to review the broad narrative of evolutionary history that is the fruit of two centuries of research on the subject from various scientific fields. For starters, it is worth recalling that the universe is much older than we once thought. Although some Christians continue to maintain that the Bible demands our universe to be roughly six thousand years old, science has revealed that it is roughly 14 billion years old, Earth having been around for about 4.5 billion of those years. According to the most up-to-date evidence from the fossil record, the first life on our planet arose around 3.7 billion years ago. It is from a common ancestor or pool of common ancestors living at this time that all life on this planet has evolved, gradually diversifying into myriad and increasingly complex forms: multicellular worm-like creatures, soft-bodied jellyfish, jawless and then jawed fish, amphibians, reptilians, birds, and finally mammalians.

The order of primates came on the scene roughly 65 million years ago. Around 6 million years ago, our species' direct ancestral line split from that of the chimpanzees (our great ape ancestors split from monkeys millions of years earlier than that—and thus no scientist claims that humans came from monkeys). From *Australopithecine* fossils, we know that our ancestors were bipedal by at least 4 million years ago. By 2 million years ago, *Homo erectus* was making stone tools (and possibly possessed a capacity for symbolic thought that enabled its members to sail across large bodies of water).[37] Just a couple hundred thousand years later, *Homo ergaster* was crafting increasingly sophisticated teardrop hand axes and may even have begun making fire. Over the next two million years, many other hominin (protohuman) species came on the scene, including those that currently go by the names *Homo heidelbergensis*, *Homo antecessor*, and *Homo neanderthalensis*. These gradually perfected the ability to make fire, blade tools, wooden spears, and clothing. All this was prior to 200,000 years ago, when at last that strange and remarkable creature we call *Homo sapiens* first emerged in Africa.

The evolution that has occurred since modern humans first arose constitutes its own story within the story of evolutionary history. These earliest *anatomically*

---

37. Given the distinct likelihood that the capacity for rational thought was present in Neanderthals and Denisovans (and possibly even in earlier hominins as far back as *Homo erectus*), some have suggested that bona fide intelligence may have been present on this planet as far back as two million years ago. On *Homo erectus* making multi-purpose stone tools and possibly even possessing a capacity for symbolic thought that allowed them to have language and sail, see Daniel Everett, *How Language Began: The Story of Humanity's Greatest Invention* (New York: Liveright, 2017), 48–64, 94–98, 116–18, 186–88 and William von Hippel, *The Social Leap: The New Evolutionary Science of Who We Are, Where We Come From, and What Makes Us Happy* (New York: Harper Wave, 2018). For a discussion of the strong evidence that *Homo erectus* was cooking with fire by 1.9 million years ago (a period during which tooth and gut size correspondingly decreased dramatically), see Richard Wrangham, *Catching Fire: How Cooking Made Us Human* (New York: Basic Books, 2009).

modern members of *Homo sapiens* did not seem to have enjoyed the quintessen-tially *behaviorally* human capacities for language, symbolic thought, art, religion, culture, and collective learning that allow us to innovate and better our species from generation to generation. Yet, eventually, evidence of features that we associate with the *imago Dei* appear to have come online in *Homo sapiens* about 100,000 years ago. Meanwhile, a subset of the human population migrated East out of Africa about 60,000 years ago, breeding with and eventually replacing other closely related species such as the Neanderthals and Denisovans. It is around this timeframe that we find evidence of cave art in South Africa (from around 75,000 years ago) and in France (as early as 40,000 years ago) along with an interesting twist: Neanderthals were apparently doing it as well, (e.g., making jewelry from eagle talons 130,000 years ago). All the while, scientists have been able to determine that the vast genetic diversity that we see among human beings alive today necessitates that modern humans arose not directly out of nothing but gradually within an ancestral inter-breeding population ("humanoid population," as the ITC calls it) that never shrank below approximately 10,000 individuals.

Why are scientists convinced that the above account is true? Why is human evolution a theory along the same lines as the theory of gravity? Many converging lines of evidence agree upon this same conclusion. I have included an appendix at the end of this book where readers can find clear and detailed summaries of the data, but I will briefly recap some of it here.

For starters, there is, of course, the fossil record. It is common for those skep-tical of evolution to allege that there are no "transitional fossils," and that each of earth's species was created instantaneously a relatively short time ago. That sort of claim is hard to sustain nowadays when we have evidence of this sort for all manner of species. For example, the evidence of our species' ancestral lineage just discussed comes from fossils and the artifacts that accompanied them. Further, the fossil record allows us to witness the evolution of such creatures as horses, snakes, and birds. We can also trace the gradual development of specific structures such as wings and lungs. We have solid evidence that informs us of when amphibians first moved from water to land (e.g., *Tiktaalik*), and we now even possess a series of fos-sils that show how land animals resembling hippos returned to the water 375 mil-lion years ago. It is not that the fossil record of humans, whales, or any other species is perfect. Since evolution happens gradually and on a massive time scale, a "skep-tic" of evolution will always be able to observe that there are missing links or gaps in the record. Yet, given the very specific conditions required for living things to fossilize and how rarely it happens, in truth it is astounding that the record is as complete as it is.[38]

---

38. Expressing his reasonable frustration with those who constantly demand more and more "transitional forms" before they will accept evolutionary theory, Dawkins compares this demanding a complete frame-by-frame cinematic record of a murderer's steps leading up to his crime before being willing to convict him—and, when one gap in the record is filled in, proceeding to declare that there are now twice as many gaps! Dawkins, *The God Delusion* (Boston: Houghton Mifflin, 2006), 153.

Contrary to popular opinion, it is not just the fossil record that shows us evolution.[39] Amazing and important as it is to be able to visualize the progressive origin of species, many other lines of evidence converge on the same conclusion. One such line, *comparative anatomy*, offers equally compelling evidence for the same conclusion. From the fossil record, for example, we know that our human anatomy is astoundingly similar to that of our hominin ancestors (we can trace how hominins gradually grew taller, began to walk upright, and grew larger brains. However, evidence also comes from comparing our anatomy to that of other creatures alive today. To take one example, human arms have remarkably similar structures (called homologies) to bat wings and whale flippers. That sharks do not have hand remnants in their fins, but whales do have them is a strong indicator of the latter being more closely related to us—a comparison reinforced by other lines of evidence, including the sometimes-forgotten fact that whales are mammals and not fish!

Comparative anatomy also studies the phenomenon that creatures' bodies sometimes possess useless features, called vestigial structures. Why do whales have pelvises, as palentology has now shown, if their ancestors did not walk on land at some point? (In fact, they did, as paleontology has now shown.) And what about humans? Why do we have an appendix, wisdom teeth, tonsils, goosebumps, and ears that at least some of us can move? And why do women have vitellogenin DNA that is used in other animal mothers to transfer nutrients to their egg yolks when our species does not reproduce by egg-laying? These oddities make no sense apart from evolution, but the mystery of their presence is unlocked once we grasp how the science works.

Vestigial structures are interesting, but perhaps my personal favorite line of anatomical evidence for evolution lies in the bizarre phenomenon of atavisms, or traits of distant ancestors that occasionally reappear when long-dormant DNA suddenly reactivates a trait that a species possessed earlier in its evolutionary history. For instance, we all know that humans have tailbone vertebrae, but what many people do not know is that our genes still retain their ancient genetic program for making tails and that sometimes human babies are actually born with them. The

---

On the reasons we are lucky to have fossils in the first place given just how specific the conditions have to be for a fossil to be formed, along with an overview of evidence for alleged "missing links" in the evolutionary process, see Dawkins, *The Greatest Show on Earth*, Ch. 6. Anti-evolutionists often point to the Cambrian Explosion from approximately 541 million years ago as evidence that life's many species were created directly by God, seeing as most of the great animal phyla (the main divisions within the animal world) begin to appear in the fossil record over a span of about 20 million years during this period. The jury is still out on precisely why this is, but Dawkins argues that it is consistent with most creatures prior to the Cambrian being soft-bodied like modern flatworms. Dawkins, *The Greatest Show on Earth*, 149–50.

39. Dawkins compares the fossil record to evidence from a camera in a murder trial. The jury would have plenty of evidence to make a conviction without the camera, and so it is best to see the camera as a bonus. "Similarly," he says, "there is more than enough evidence for the fact of evolution in the comparative study of modern species and their geographical distribution. We don't need fossils in order to demonstrate that evolution is a fact." Dawkins, *The Greatest Show on Earth*, 145.

same sort of thing happens in other animals, too. Sometimes you find chicken embryos with teeth or a snake with a leg. Again, this makes no sense unless we know—as we now do—that humans evolved from primate ancestors that had tails, that snakes are lizards that lost their legs, that whales used to resemble hippos, and that birds are descended from dinosaurs even though they have not had teeth for 60 million years!

But evolutionary science is not just about looking at bones, living or dead. We can also pan out to the largest of scales and consider *biogeography*—the study of species distribution across space and time. Now that biologists have canvassed the globe in the effort to catalog as many of its many life forms as possible, it has been discovered that species are not randomly spread across our planet. That is, creatures that are most similar and most closely related tend to be found in the same regions. This is because evolutionary change is often caused by geographical change (e.g., species diverge when they became isolated from one another by barriers like oceans, rivers, and mountains that themselves come and go over time). Interestingly, sometimes highly similar species are found on different continents. Yet now that we have the science of plate tectonics and understand the phenomenon of continental drift, this oddity is relatively straightforwardly explained: our present continents were joined together in the supercontinent Pangaea until 170 million years ago.

If evidence for evolution can be found at the largest of levels, so too is it present at the smallest. The field of *embryology*, for example, also provides remarkable evidence for evolution. For instance, we now know that humans in the womb temporarily have pharyngeal arches, structures that derive from ancestral gills. It does not seem to be the most efficient way to make a human but knowing that we have evolutionary ancestors who had gills unlocks a compelling reason for their presence.

Yet, arguably the most astounding display of human evolution's explanatory power comes at a microscopic level: from the field of *molecular biology*. It is worth observing something that we all now take for granted but which is often overlooked as evidence that all life on our planet evolved from a single ancestor: we all share the same genetic code. It was not necessary that all things living have the same language of life, and for all we know there is life elsewhere in the cosmos with a different chemical basis. Knowing this becomes all the more powerful when we consider *comparative genomics*, which studies affinities between our DNA and that of other species. As research in this field has revealed, the similarities between humans and other species alive in the world today and in the fossil record are also present at the molecular level. The more closely related species are, the more genetic information they share.

As one would expect, our closest genetic relatives are chimpanzees, with whom we share approximately 98% of our DNA. But it is not just that we have the vast majority of our genetic material in common with other great apes. The parallels run down to the minutest of levels. In recent years, scientists have been able to map out genetic trees for individual genes, and the result is that they all bear approximately the same phylogeny (family tree). Thus, in order of increasing similarity, we know that humans as a whole *and* our individual genes are closest to orangutans, then gorillas, and finally chimpanzees. Tracking these genetic changes is like tracing the evolution of a language over time; for example, the changes in English from Beowulf to Chaucer to Shakespeare to contemporary American English (or, perhaps even more accurately, tracing the origin of each Romance language from their common ancestor language, Latin).

To illustrate: by comparing olfactory (smell) receptor genes among these species, one can see that the sense of smell among these creatures gets worse the farther one gets from orangutans and the closer one gets to man. The reason for this is that we used to depend more on our sense of smell for survival, whereas more primitive apes still do. Over time, human olfactory genes were rendered less and less effective by the same sort of mutations that are constantly occurring in nature and which—when detrimental—usually get eliminated because they render the creature with them incapable of surviving and reproducing (natural selection). However, since *Homo sapiens* eventually ceased to depend on this sense for survival, individuals who acquired these mutations continued to pass along their defective DNA—which piled up ever more and more, turning its code into gibberish. As a result, we who are alive today bear pseudogenes or "genetic fossils" of once-functional olfactory receptors in our genome (Personally, I am glad that these genes are no longer active—I can only imagine the dread I would have at changing diapers if my sense of smell were many times stronger than it already is.)

At any rate, the above observation raises a crucial question: if God really did create man apart from evolutionary processes, as some claim, why did he go to the trouble of inserting non-functional DNA in our genome at the precise locations that evolutionary theory predicts we would find it? In other words, why would God design so many of our genes to look like less well-made versions of the same thing that we find in species closely related to us if we are not genetically related to them? As Christian biologist Dennis Venema says, such a designer "seems oddly constrained to designs that have the strong appearance of having evolved."[40]

Of course, it is always possible to confront the evidence of evolution and claim that God has planted it in the world to trick our intellects and test our faith, as I have heard a few Christians say. Yet, one thing that strikes me as odd about this assertion is that it reflects a sort of Gnosticism in which only a select few prophets know that truth about the natural world and are to be believed over those who are learned in the relevant domain of inquiry. Another problem is that it seems scarcely compatible with a religion whose God is the *Logos*, the Word that orders the universe, creates rational persons in his image, and spent millennia of salvation history trying to make the truth known to them. To most Christians, God designing a world that was unintelligible to our minds would appear to be the opposite of reason and love.

Returning to DNA, what will perhaps surprise one most to learn is that comparative genomics has enabled us to compare modern human DNA with that of extinct hominins, and the science has found that most of us on this planet are not "pure" *Homo sapiens*. Non-Africans have inherited 1.5 to 4 percent of their genomes

---

40. Venema and McKnight, *Adam and the Genome*, 74.

from their Neanderthal ancestors, while others among us (e.g., the Melanesians) have inherited between 1.9 and 3.4 percent of their genome from another extinct species of archaic humans called Denisovans. The fact that our ancestors bred with other hominins and we have inherited their DNA should cause us to reconsider whether it is effective to insult someone by calling them a Neanderthal!

Finally, I would just briefly mention one last body of evidence that converges on evolution: we can see it happening through *direct observation* today in organisms with short lifecycles, as we see in mosquitos whose genetic mutations gives them resistance to pesticides and bacteria that become resistant to antibiotics. These changes are instances of what is often called microevolution, or evolutionary changes that happen across short time spans and in small populations. Macroevolution, meanwhile, is just microevolution over a longer time scale, and is easier to observe directly in flies than in humans. This is not to say that science has yet yielded a comprehensive understanding of every step in the process by which new species arise. Yet, by understanding the relationship (or, really, identity) of the two and that evolution always occurs in populations, the Christian begins to see why it is not tenable to say, as some do, that one will accept microevolution but not macroevolution. As a friend of mine once pointed out, this is rather like saying that is okay to recognize minutes and hours but not days or weeks.

## OUR CONCERN: NOT DEFINITIVE SOLUTIONS, BUT A COMPELLING APPROACH TO SCRIPTURE AND CATHOLIC DOCTRINE IN AN EVOLUTIONARY CONTEXT

We can count on the details of the above narrative (i.e., the theory of evolution) being hammered out for as long as humans keep doing science. Dates will be refined, percentages will be altered, and empirical gaps will be filled. Yet the great mass of evidence that converges upon the theory of evolution (i.e., the fact of evolution) will not go away, and one who has seen it cannot unsee what he has seen.

Meanwhile, our concern in the present book is what the *implications* of it all are. On this score, in a document penned under the direction of its then-president Cardinal Joseph Ratzinger, the Vatican's International Theological Commission charged theologians with "the responsibility to locate modern scientific understandings within a Christian vision of the created universe."[41] The present volume is a response to this

41. International Theological Commission, *Communion and Stewardship*, §66. In other words, if the natural sciences give us persuasive reasons to hold that evolutionary theory best explains the development of life on this planet, then it is imperative that we take up the sacred responsibility to creatively and faithfully rethink some fundamental theological issues in dialogue with this newfound scientific knowledge. Describing this task as a "sacred responsibility," Peter Enns writes that it is modeled after a parallel process that runs throughout the entire Bible itself and is "an expression of responsible faith . . . not evidence that our faith is weakening." Enns, *How the Bible Actually Works*, 15, 123–26. For a fascinating book that reflects on the need for traditions to engage in this sort of creative and faithful rethinking, see Jonathan Lear, *Radical Hope: Ethics in the Face of Cultural Devastation* (Cambridge, MA: Harvard University Press, 2006). As Lear argues, it is necessary that cultures and religions (or "practices")

call—one especially to the point, seeing as the major scientific concern that this document had in mind was human evolution.

Incidentally, I think it is worth recalling that now is not the first time that the Church has had to do some serious rethinking along the above lines. The Galileo affair (which concerned the then-novel heliocentric theory) has many affinities to our situation today (where the emerging science is that of evolutionary theory). As Catholic physicist Stephen Barr notes, theology in Galileo's time had unfortunately become too wedded to scientific ideas from an earlier era that turned out to be false.[42] Similarly, Cardinal Ratzinger noted that prior to Galileo, the Christian tradition tended to assume that "the geocentric world picture was inextricably bound up with the revealed message of the Bible, and that champions of the heliocentric world picture were destroying the core of Revelation."[43] Writing as pope, Benedict XVI later went so far as to lament "the Church's error in the case of Galileo Galilei"—a mistake that had damaged the Church's credibility and which he clearly wished to avoid repeating in the case of Darwin.[44] I hope that the above survey of the evidence of evolution shows why the search for a fresh and robust interpretation of Scripture is so needed today—one that always bears in mind the principle that perceived errors in Scripture are not God's fault but rather that of the interpreter who misapprehends what he has read.[45]

That said, a person might of course respond to everything said above (as I have seen some Christians do) by arguing that all of this evidence nevertheless does not amount to a definitive *proof* of evolutionary theory. To this, I believe that a balanced thinker must indeed admit that it is indeed always *conceivable* that all the scientific evidence of evolution is wrong or that it has been globally misinterpreted. In fact, as I have heard a few Christians suggest, it is even *technically possible* that God made it look like things evolved in order to test our faith. Significantly, St. John Henry Newman—just a year after the publication of Darwin's *On the Origin of Species*— wrote to a friend who held just such a view.

Having been told that God placed the fossils in the rocks so as to give species the *appearance* of having evolved, Newman simply laughed and drew this notion to its logical conclusion:

---

continually lay to rest certain of their old ways, yet without abandoning their tradition entirely and naively replacing it with a foreign one. Although one may find that there is no way to continue living the old ways precisely in the way people used to do, Lear suggests that learning from what is new while drawing upon the tradition's own inner resources may serve to deepen and renew that same tradition. To my mind, it is not difficult to see how this logic applies to the issue of Christian faith and evolutionary science: an authentic engagement with evolution should not lead the Christian to abandon the faith but rather to penetrate it more deeply.

42. Barr, *The Believing Scientist*, 139.

43. Ratzinger, "Exegesis and Magisterium of the Church," 134.

44. Benedict XVI, Address to the Parish Priests and Clergy of Rome (February 14, 2013).

45. Augustine, *Letter 143*, trans. J.G. Cunningham, in *Nicene and Post-Nicene Fathers*, First Series, Vol. 1, ed. Philip Schaff. (Buffalo, NY: Christian Literature Publishing Co., 1887), §7. Galileo Galilei cites this text in his "Letter to the Grand Duchess Christina," in *The Galileo Affair: A Documentary History* (Berkeley: University of California Press, 1989), ed. Maurice Finocchiaro, 87–118 at 96.

There is as much want of simplicity in the idea of the creation of distinct species as in that of the creation (of) trees in full growth (whose seed is in themselves), or of rocks with fossils in them. I mean that it is as strange that monkeys should be so like men, with no historical connection between them, as the notion that there should be no course of history by which fossil bones got into rocks. . . . I will either go whole hog with Darwin or, dispensing with time and history altogether, hold, not only the theory of distinct species but that also of the creation of the fossil-bearing rocks.[46]

It is remarkable that, at a time when Darwin's theory was brand new, Newman already recognized it as rather obvious that some form of evolutionary explanation was needed to account for phenomena like the presence of fossils in rocks and physical similarities between humans and other species. At the very least, he says, there is as much "want of simplicity" in the notion that God for some strange reason created things to look as if they evolved when, despite all the evidence pointing in the other direction, they in fact did not.

Yet, seeing as it is always conceivable that our discoveries in the field of evolutionary science are illusory and that Newman's friend is correct, this reveals the need to reflect more deeply on how it is that humans come to know truth more generally—especially when it comes to navigating apparently contradictory truth claims from the domains of faith and science. Newman's principles reveal that, when weighing the evidence for rival accounts of reality, the real question should not be whether a given explanation is technically possible, but rather whether it is *plausible*. In other words, we must ask: is this a *believable* and *compelling* account of the way things happened? We might also pose the question in this way: does a putative explanation fit coherently into the overall story of how we know God works in the world?

To illustrate this point, I find it helpful to recall some epistemological insights from classic Catholic authors. For instance, Newman himself said, "I have not absolute demonstration that my father was not a murderer, or my intimate friend a sharper, but it would not only be heartless, but irrational, not to disbelieve these hypotheses or possibilities *utterly*."[47] Similarly, G.K. Chesterton quipped that the possibility that cows might start fasting on Fridays or bending their knees in prayer is no good reason to suppose it will ever be the case.[48] For Josef Pieper, meanwhile, a true philosopher ("lover of wisdom") must have a critical attitude, which "does not primarily mean accepting only what is absolutely certain, but being careful not to suppress anything."[49] This last point is especially apropos when it comes to addressing evolution. It is tempting for the believer to write off the immense scientific evidence in its favor on the

---

46. John Henry Newman, Letter of December 9, 1863, in *Sundries*, 83, cited in Dwight Culler, *The Imperial Intellect* (New Haven: Yale University Press, 1955), 267.

47. John Henry Newman, Letter to William Robert Brownlow, in vol. 25 of *The Letters and Diaries of John Henry Newman*, eds. C.S. Dessain and T. Gornall (Oxford: Clarendon Press, 1978), 324.

48. G.K. Chesterton, *The Everlasting Man*, in *The Collected Works of G.K. Chesterton*, vol. 2 (San Francisco: Ignatius Press, 1986), 181.

49. Josef Pieper, *In Defense of Philosophy* (San Francisco: Ignatius Press, 1992), 51.

grounds that it is not "absolutely certain." Yet, if Pieper is right, this is not the way a lover of wisdom approaches reality, for such an individual is concerned less with keeping out new ideas that would challenge his point of view than with making sure not to miss anything that might require him to refine it.

Building on insights from the above authors, I would suggest that, while it is admittedly technically possible that all our scientists are wrong about evolution while nonscientist biblical literalists are right about this same science, we need to seriously consider whether this claim is truly compatible with our Catholic under-standing of God. God not only authored Scripture but also gave us the gift of reason by which to understand the other "book" that he authored: the natural world.[50] This, then, gives rise to some other questions that we need to ponder in embarking on a dialogue between faith and evolutionary science: Does faith elevate our God-given gift of reason so that the two work together, or do faith and reason compete against each other? Is nature intelligible to human reason through research into the various scientific fields, or is the natural world better understood through revealed sources regardless of what human reason has discovered in those fields?

On this score, I have found that well-intentioned Christians who face the sort of evidence we have outlined above sometimes remain skeptical of the evolutionary narrative. This is fair enough, for the Catholic faith does not require a person to affirm specific scientific propositions, even extraordinarily strong ones like evolu-tionary theory, gravity, and heliocentrism. In situations like this, rather than con-tinually playing defense and merely answering objections to evolutionary theory, I find it helpful to ask my interlocutors a question of my own: "If the evolutionary narrative of human origins is not correct despite all the evidence in its favor, then what, pray tell, is *your* narrative? How do *you* account for the evidence?" I have found that some people have a difficult time answering this question, for they do not want to accept evolution, but they also tend to recognize that a strictly literal reading of Genesis is unsustainable if they actually engage the scientific data that supports evolutionary theory.

In other words, many are aware that acknowledging the antiquity of the uni-verse (roughly 13.7 billion years and counting) is already not to read the Bible in a strictly literal manner, as doing so would yield an age more to the tune of a mere six to ten *thousand* years. Further, to correctly recognize that plants and animals predated *Homo sapiens* is already not to read Genesis as consistent with science, for in chapter two, Adam is described as being molded from the dust of the ground and *before* all other creatures (Gn 2:7ff).[51] In this book, all I can reasonably hope

50. For an in-depth exploration of the notion of "God's two books" and its application to debates in early modern science, see Kenneth Howell, *God's Two Books: Copernican Cosmology and Biblical Interpretation in Early Modern Science* (Notre Dame, IN: University of Notre Dame Press, 2002).

51. As another illustration of this point, Stacy Trasancos mentions Gn 3:7 wherein the eyes of Adam and Eve are opened after sinning: "A literal interpretation of this sentence would compel us to sbelieve that Adam and Eve had walked around up to that point with their eyes closed. A real interpre-tation allows us to believe that Adam and Eve's biological eyes were open all along, but that their mental vision, their perception, changed." Trasancos, *Particles of Faith*, 133.

to do is help readers think more deeply about such things and whether the narrative they have in their own minds aligns with the actual data of science and properly interpreted Scripture. My hope is that a deep dive into both of these sources will reveal that far from contradictory, they mutually illumine one another.

## POPE BENEDICT XVI'S EMBRACE OF FAITH AND SCIENCE AS AN *APOLOGIA* FOR THE CATHOLIC CHURCH

As the reader has probably already gathered from the title of this book, my goal in this work is to develop an intellectually compelling theological approach to questions at the intersection of faith, evolutionary theory, and human origins with the thought of Joseph Ratzinger / Pope Benedict XVI as our guide. While there are a number of recent good texts out there on the theme of Christianity and evolution, none has endeavored to provide a systematic book length treatment of Ratzinger's extensive contributions on the subject. In the following pages, we will be examining the emeritus pontiff's thought on how to understand the science of evolution in light of the Catholic faith and how, in turn, our own understanding of divine revelation might be deepened in conversation with evolutionary science.

Our biblical scholar pope left us with two pivotal resources for navigating a dialogue between faith and evolution. First, Benedict articulated clear principles that can help us to discern the meaning of both Scripture and magisterial teachings. For example, he tells us, "We cannot say: creation or evolution . . . we are faced here with two complementary—rather than mutually exclusive—realities."[52] Second, and especially apropos for the present project, the emeritus pontiff also *applied* his principles to numerous concrete topics at the intersection of theology and evolution (for example, the meaning of man's special creation and original sin).

Even before being elected pope, Joseph Ratzinger was an eminent theologian who served as the right-hand doctrinal chief of Pope St. John Paul II. He always had the uncanny ability to cut right to the heart of the most demanding questions, endeavoring to understand them in light of science, Scripture, and the entire Christian tradition. In his writings, we find a keen awareness that Christians in our modern age need more than a mere acquaintance with the Bible's stories and acceptance of the Church's teachings. To compellingly re-propose the faith in today's world, Ratzinger insists on an intelligent faith that is conversant with the discoveries of modern science. In the emeritus pontiff's words, today's disciple must

---

52. Ratzinger, *In the Beginning*, 50. John Henry Newman, himself remarkably open to evolution when it was a new theory, has something similar to say of the Catholic in relation to science: "He is sure, and nothing shall make him doubt, that, if anything seems to be proved by astronomer, or geologist, or chronologist, or antiquarian, or ethnologist, in contradiction to the dogmas of faith, that point will eventually turn out, first, not to be proved, or, secondly, not contradictory, or thirdly, not contradictory to anything really revealed, but to something which has been confused with revelation." Newman, *The Idea of a University* (London: Longmans, Green, and Co., 1907), 466. For an excellent essay on Newman and evolution, see Berta M. Moritz, "A Patron Saint of Evolution?," *Church Life Journal* (October 16, 2019).

have the willingness to "enter into the debates of our time," armed with "[t]he courage to engage the whole breadth of reason."[53]

This courage is on full display in Ratzinger's unrivaled readiness to confront the truth question with sincerity and rigor whenever and wherever it presents itself. Yet, remarkably, few people are aware this scholar-pope wrote extensively on faith and evolution. In fact, this was one of the issues he considered most important to get right if the integrity of the faith is to be preserved and the Gospel made accessible to modern men. Reflecting on the captivating literary masterpiece that is the Book of Genesis's creation narrative, then-Archbishop Ratzinger thus raised the following poignant question with which this volume opened: the words of Genesis are beautiful, but *are they true*? Alongside the atheists that I also cited at the start of this chapter, Ratzinger acknowledges that "[e]verything seems to speak against" the truth of the Bible's creation narrative and that "science has long since disposed of the concepts" that are bound up with it. Indeed, asking yet again whether these words are true, Ratzinger proceeds to supply the skeptic's next line: these lines have, "along with the entire Word of God and the whole biblical tradition, come out of the reveries of the infant age of human history, for which we occasionally experience homesickness but to which we can nevertheless not return."[54]

As the above passage illustrates, Ratzinger understands well that the opening chapters of Genesis, more than any other portion of Scripture, bring into focus the pivotal question of how we ought to construe the relationship between faith and reason in light of modern scientific discoveries. It also affords us a first glimpse at a characteristic of the emeritus pontiff's thought that makes him such an extraordinarily lucid thinker. It has been said that the mark of an educated mind is to be able to entertain an idea without holding it. Whereas it can be discomfiting to sincerely ponder the possibility that a position other than one's own might be true, Ratzinger does this all the time. In my view, this ability to grasp all points of view is what makes him a singularly effective apologist for the Christian faith—as well as for human reason.

Ratzinger's above observation raises some crucial questions: Does the Book of Genesis present a true account of mankind's origins, or is it simply a relic of mankind's naïve past that ought to be relegated to the dustbin of history? What ought to be our response when findings from converging fields of science contradict the letter of the Bible? And, perhaps even more importantly for a Catholic, what if the sound conclusions of science contradict how Christians have read Genesis over the ages? What are we to make of our longstanding traditions that were inspired by this portion of the Bible when science appears to render them untenable?

Bearing these questions in mind, I frequently counsel people confused in these matters to bear in mind St. Thomas Aquinas's twin principles for interpreting the creation narratives in Genesis: First, hold the *truth* of Scripture without wavering.

---

53. Benedict XVI, "Faith, Reason and the University: Memories and Reflections" (September 12, 2006).s

54. Joseph Ratzinger, *In the Beginning*, 3–4.

Second, be ready to abandon a particular *explanation* of Scripture if is proven to be false, lest Scripture be exposed to the ridicule of unbelievers and obstacles posed to their believing.[55] Echoing Augustine, Galileo said as much in the debate over heliocentrism that raged in his day:

> For how can [outsiders] believe our books in regard to the resurrection of the dead, the hope of eternal life, and the kingdom of heaven when they catch a Christian committing an error about something they know very well . . . things they have been able to observe or to establish by unquestionable argument?[56]

Aquinas, Augustine, and Galileo were all concerned to avoid making the faith look ridiculous to outsiders by insisting upon strictly literal interpretations of Genesis

---

55. Aquinas, *Summa Theologiae* trans. Fathers of the English Dominican Province (Westminster, MD: Christian Classics, 1981), I, q.68, a.1. Desiderius Erasmus (1466–1536) wrote poignantly along the same lines, "By identifying the new learning with heresy, you make orthodoxy synonymous with ignorance." These words are cited in John O'Brien, *Evolution and Religion*, 5. Although this book is clearly out-of-date in relation to the vast scientific data we now have in our possession, it remains an illumining read, for nearly a century ago a serious Catholic scholar like Fr. O'Brien already considered evolutionary theory to be persuasive. Rather than disputing the work of scientists in their own field, O'Brien sought to understand the philosophical and theological implications of the many lines of converging evidence that support it. In so doing, he levied many incisive criticisms on Christians of his day such as the following, "The real enemies of the Christian faith are not the evolutionary biologists; they are those who insist on setting up artificial adhesions between Christianity and outgrown scientific opinions and proclaim that we cannot have the one without the other." O'Brien, citing R.S. Lull, *Christianity and Modern Thought* (New Haven, CT: Yale University Press, 1924), 84.

56. Galileo Galilei, "Letter to the Grand Duchess Christina," 103, 112. Augustine's lengthy exposition on this point merits to be cited at length: "Usually, even a non-Christian knows something about the earth, the heavens, and the other elements of this world . . . the kinds of animals, shrubs, stones, and so forth, and this knowledge he holds to as being certain from reason and experience. Now, it is a disgraceful and dangerous thing for an infidel to hear a Christian, presumably giving the meaning of Holy Scripture, talking nonsense on these topics; and we should take all means to prevent such an embarrassing situation, in which people show up vast ignorance in a Christian and laugh it to scorn. The shame is not so much that an ignorant individual is derided, but that people outside the household of faith think our sacred writers held such opinions, and, to the great loss of those for whose salvation we toil, the writers of our Scripture are criticized and rejected as unlearned men. If they find a Christian mistaken in a field which they themselves know well and hear him maintaining his foolish opinions about our books, how are they going to believe those books in matters concerning the resurrection of the dead, the hope of eternal life, and the kingdom of heaven, when they think their pages are full of falsehoods and on facts which they themselves have learnt from experience and the light of reason? Reckless and incompetent expounders of Holy Scripture bring untold trouble and sorrow on their wiser brethren when they are caught in one of their mischievous false opinions and are taken to task by those who are not bound by the authority of our sacred books. For then, to defend their utterly foolish and obviously untrue statements, they will try to call upon Holy Scripture for proof and even recite from memory many passages which they think support their position, although they understand neither what they say nor the things about which they make assertions." Augustine, *The Literal Meaning of Genesis*, trans. J. H. Taylor, *Ancient Christian Writers*, Vol. 41 (New York: Newman Press, 1982), 42–43.

For a similar text in which Augustine warns believers ignorant of the physical universe against making misguided claims in the name of defending the faith, see his *Confessions* (Oxford: Oxford University Press, 2008), V.3.9 at 76–77.

1–11 when those outside the Christian fold already know well that this approach is intellectually untenable. Accordingly, if we hold that the truth about the world can be known by human reason apart from special divine revelation, then we should be wary when someone asks us to side with the letter of Scripture *over and against* what we have arrived at through our God-given intellect. Galileo captures the matter well when he writes:

> I do not feel obliged to believe that the same God who has endowed us with senses, reason and intellect has intended us to forego their use and by some other means to give us knowledge which we can attain by them. He would not require us to deny sense and reason in physical matters which are set before our eyes and minds by direct experience or necessary demonstrations.[57]

Yet today it is not just that scientifically untenable interpretations of the Bible place obstacles to Christian belief in the path of non-Christians. It does the same for those who already believe and yet are questioning their faith over the seeming incompatibility of science and doctrine (e.g., man's special creation, original sin, etc.). Rather than fighting evolutionary theory and focusing on the danger it poses for traditional Christian doctrine, Benedict's overarching concern is to build people up in their faith by getting to the truth of things, even when that truth is difficult—cognizant of his predecessor John Paul II's teaching that "truth cannot contradict truth" and Aquinas's conviction that all truth, no matter what its source, is of the Holy Spirit.[58] It is in this spirit that Ratzinger stated in a talk prepared for Cardinal Joseph Frings on the eve of the Second Vatican Council, a speech that would go on to significantly impact the council's proceedings: "Today's man must be able to recognize again that the Church is neither afraid of nor need be afraid of science, because she is sheltered in the truth of God."[59] In other words, even if the truth of nature is propounded by a non-Christian, the believer ought to embrace and illumine his insights with the light of faith. We ought to, as Church Fathers like Augustine would say, "plunder the Egyptians."[60]

---

57. Galileo, "Letter to the Grand Duchess Christina," 102.

58. John Paul II, Message to the Pontifical Academy of Sciences Plenary Session on "The Origins and Early Evolution of Life" (October 22, 1996), 2. See also Leo XIII, *Providentissimus Deus*, §23; Aquinas, *De Veritate*, trans. James McGlynn (Chicago: Henry Regnery, 1953), q. 1, a. 8. Galileo also expresses this principle well when he says that science cannot contradict "properly interpreted Scripture." Galileo, "Letter to the Grand Duchess Christina," 91.

59. Josef Frings, "Das Konzil und die moderne Gedankenwelt," *Herder Korrespondenz* 16 (1961–1962): 168–74, at 174. For an enlightening discussion of this speech, see Emery de Gaál, *O Lord, I Seek Your Countenance: Explorations and Discoveries in Pope Benedict XVI's Theology* (Steubenville, OH: Emmaus Academic, 2018), 149. For the English translation of an abridged version of the speech, see Jared Wicks, SJ, "Six texts by Prof. Joseph Ratzinger as *Peritus* Before and During Vatican Council II," *Gregorianum* 89 (2008): 233–311 at 258–59. On this topic, see also Aquinas, *Summa Theologiae*, I-II, q.109, a.1 ad 1; Aquinas, *De veritate*, q. 1, a. 8.

60. For instances of this Patristic interpretation of Exodus 12:36 that capture its "loftier meaning," see Augustine, *On Christian Doctrine* (New York: Bobbs-Merrill, 1958), 40.60; Gregory of Nyssa, *Life of Moses* (New York: Paulist Press, 1978), 81.

John Paul II set forth this balanced stance perfectly in teaching that the knowledge we glean from evolutionary science can help to refine our understanding of the faith, while the light of faith in turn can help us to situate the findings of science within the grand scheme of things: "Science can purify religion from error and superstition; religion can purify science from idolatry and false absolutes. Each can draw the other into a wider world, a world in which both can flourish."[61] Rather than writing off or disputing scientific findings related to evolution, he and his successor maintain a healthy critical awareness of science's limits while rejoicing in the knowledge we ascertain through it. Both pontiffs believed that embracing this posture is crucial for addressing the pressing questions of what evolution means for understanding the nature of the soul, the uniqueness of mankind, the reality of original sin, and so on. As John Paul himself suggested, it puts us in a position to ask such questions as: "Does an evolutionary perspective bring any light to bear upon theological anthropology, the meaning of the human person as the *imago Dei*, the problem of Christology—and even upon the development of doctrine itself?"[62]

Of course, it is also worth calling out people if they caricature most evolutionary scientists as secularists. A number of my devout Catholic colleagues and friends (including some clergy) are professional evolutionary biologists. Important figures within the history of the field also have been believers—like Gregor Mendel, the Austrian monk who is widely considered the father of genetics, and Francis Collins, who headed the Human Genome Project. In essence, the emeritus pontiff's core concern is the same as these other Christian thinkers: to establish a virtuous approach to creation by steering clear of the opposite pitfalls of naturalist atheism on the one hand and creation*ism* (i.e., which seeks to interpret the Bible according to a strictly literal reading—a task that Benedict describes as impossible to consistently do) on the other.[63]

This vision that we find in Benedict is not brand new. It often goes by the name of *theistic evolution*, qualified to indicate that God authored and guides the process

---

61. John Paul II, Letter to George Coyne, SJ, Director of the Vatican Observatory (June 1, 1988). This approach of our recent pontiffs echoes that advised by Galileo. When it comes to disputes about natural phenomena, he insists, biblical passages ought not to be cited authoritatively. Rather, in the realm of science we must follow the lead of the evidence and demonstrations attained through the study of nature and let our interpretation of Scripture be purified through this engagement. Galileo, "Letter to the Grand Duchess Christina," 93. Around the same time, Cardinal Robert Bellarmine would write, "[I]f there were a true demonstration that the sun is at the center of the world . . . then one would have to proceed with great care in explaining the Scriptures that appear contrary; and say rather that we do not understand them than that what is demonstrated is false." Robert Bellarmine, Letter to Foscarini (April 12, 1516), in Maurice Finocchiaro, *The Galileo Affair: A Documentary History* (Berkeley, CA: University of California Press, 1989), 67–69 at 68.

62. John Paul II, Letter to George Coyne, SJ, Director of the Vatican Observatory (June 1, 1988). For further discussion on this question, see Christopher Baglow, "Does the Extended Evolutionary Synthesis Shed New Light on Theological Anthropology?," *Church Life Journal* (January 10, 2020).

63. "There should be no particular need to demonstrate that on the one hand it is useless to take refuge in an allegedly pure, literal understanding of the Bible." Ratzinger, "Biblical Interpretation in Crisis," 6.

of evolution. Even better, it has been described as *evolutionary creation*, with "evolutionary" as the modifying term to make it clear that God's creation of the world out of nothing is the more fundamental truth and that evolution is the means by which he guides and sustains it. In a wonderful and accessible book on the subject, some Dominicans have worked out this relationship under the heading of *Thomistic Evolution*.[64] Yet another helpful Thomistic approach reserves the word "creation" for the origin and continued dependence of the cosmos on God while describing the processes at work in evolution as God's "evolutionary governance of the universe."[65] As this book focuses on the thought of Benedict XVI, we might even dub this approach *Benedict-ine* or *Ratzingerian Evolution*. However, for the sake of simplicity and clarity, in this volume I will be referring to God's evolutionary governance of the universe as "evolutionary creation"—a term that is especially appropriate given that Ratzinger himself deployed it.[66]

As we will see throughout this book, Ratzinger laid the foundations of his theology of creation over two decades as an academic theologian, part of which time he served as a theological expert (*peritus*) at the Second Vatican Council, on which he exercised an unrivaled influence in setting its agenda, shaping its documents,

---

64. For the term "Thomistic Evolution," see Nicanor Austriaco, OP, et al., *Thomistic Evolution: A Catholic Approach to Understanding Evolution in the Light of Faith*. Francis Beckwith has also used the expression *Thomistic Design* (TD) as a robust alternative to the problematic philosophy of nature that undergirds the Intelligent Design (ID) movement. See Beckwith, "How to Be an Anti-Intelligent Design Advocate," *University of St. Thomas Journal of Law & Public Policy* 4.1 (2009–2010): 35–65. For more on the term *Evolutionary Creation*, see Dennis Lamoureux, "No Historical Adam: Evolutionary Creation View," in *Four Views of the Historical Adam* (Grand Rapids, MI: Zondervan, 2013) 37–65; Lamoureux, *Evolutionary Creation: A Christian Approach to Evolution* (Eugene, OR: Wipf & Stock, 2008). Understood in its fullness, the expression "evolutionary creation" also distinguishes Christians who recognize the reality of evolution from the interpretations of theists in general and of deists in particular who do not believe that God continues to play a role in the world after he created it. For its part, the expression "theistic evolution" is cited approvingly by Francis Collins, longtime head of the Human Genome Project, in his book *The Language of God: A Scientist Presents Evidence for Belief* (New York: Free Press, 2006), 209–10.

65. This point regarding the phrase "evolutionary governance of the universe" has recently been made well by Mariusz Tabaczek, OP. Whatever term one prefers, it is worth bearing in mind the Thomistic distinction that Tabaczek draws between *creatio ex nihilo* (creation out of nothing—God's giving existence to the universe along with its continual and total dependence on him) and *productio* (production—God's governance of the universe by means of evolution and the innumerable creatures in our world that do not have the power to "create" in the full sense of the word). Tabaczek, "Does God Create through Evolution? The Aristotelian-Thomistic Perspective," Public lecture for the Thomistic Institute at Blackfriars, Oxford, UK (February 5, 2020). https://soundcloud.com/thomisticinstitute/does-god-create-through-evolution-fr-mariusz-tabsczek. For a more developed treatment of this point, see Mariusz Tabaczek, "Does God Create Through Evolution? A Thomistic Perspective?" (forthcoming).

66. The term *Schöpfung evolutionistisch* ("evolutionary creation" or, technically, "creation evolutionarily") is found in the lecture notes of Professor Ratzinger's 1964 *Schöpfungslehre* course at 122, 173. Selections from this text are reproduced in Santiago Sanz, "Joseph Ratzinger y la doctrina de la creación. Los apuntes de Münster de 1964 (II). Algunos temas fundamentales," *Revista Española de Teología* 74 (2014), 201–48 at 238n122. More information about this and other lecture notes from Ratzinger's courses on creation will be provided further below.

and authoritatively interpreting it.[67] Remarkably, it remained one of Ratzinger's main concerns during his five-year tenure as Archbishop of Munich and Freising, over the course of his twenty-four years as cardinal-prefect of the Congregation for Doctrine of the Faith, and even throughout the eight years of his pontificate as Benedict XVI. Not only can few people claim to have pondered a topic consistently for so many decades, no one can boast to have played so central a role as Ratzinger in the Catholic Church's teaching and governing office over the past fifty-plus years. For this reason, Cardinal Christoph Schönborn once said that no one is more qualified or better positioned than Benedict to say what exactly the Church's teaching on the subject of evolution is.[68] This—along with the fact that no one else has sought to collect his corpus of writings on the subject of how to think through the relationship of evolutionary science and Christian belief—is why I have chosen Benedict to guide our endeavor in the following chapters. Of course, I will also be marshaling dozens of other thinkers to accompany us on our journey and who will help to demonstrate how Benedict's thought interfaces with that of other ancient and modern insights. However, in many instances I had to make an executive decision and leave brief references to their contributions in the footnotes. Otherwise, I calculated that this book would have ended up well over 600 pages long. Even *I* do not even want to read a book that long, let alone expect my readers to endure me over such a lengthy span!

One final word about my decision to focus on Benedict's writings. A few pages ago, I was recounting how a number of my students over the years had nearly lost their faith over the seeming incompatibility between evolution and the Christian faith. What I did not note at that juncture is that, for many of these individuals, it was thanks to engagement with the thought of Pope Benedict XVI that they were able to finally find a foothold for their faith. Reading Benedict enabled them to

---

67. On Ratzinger's pivotal role at Vatican II and his contributions to its constitution *Dei Verbum*, see Peter Seewald, vol. 1 of *Benedict XVI: A Life* (New York: Bloomsbury, 2020), 406–407, 427–31, 441, 469, 506–509.

68. Christoph Schönborn, Foreword to *Creation and Evolution*, 7. I have encountered some people who try to draw a sharp distinction between Benedict's thought on evolution before versus after becoming prefect of the CDF and pope. Having extensively read his corpus and what I take to be everything he has written on evolution, I simply do not think this is the case. To be sure, Ratzinger discussed more controversial theological topics at length before his tenure as a high-ranking Vatican official tasked with the responsibility of safeguarding the faith rather than engaging in speculative theology. Accordingly, it should not be surprising that, while he brought up the subject of evolution frequently even as pope, Benedict never rendered an official magisterial declaration on specific issues related to evolution (for example, the monogenism/polygenism debate) which he saw fundamentally as scientific in nature and therefore not within the competence of the Magisterium to adjudicate. Despite this, Benedict never renounced his older writings in which he did weigh in on such questions, and indeed he often referenced their fundamental insights throughout his pontificate. In this book I am therefore going to take the simplest approach and treat all writings from Ratzinger/Benedict as a unified body of thought while continuing to distinguish which were and were not written while pope. On Ratzinger's own assessment of his intellectual development over the years, see Ramage, *Jesus, Interpreted* (Washington, D.C.: The Catholic University of America Press, 2017), 43–44.

realize that they did not have to abandon the truth they had discovered through the sciences in order to remain a Christian.

This happens to be the same thing I have experienced in my own life, having been persuaded of the truth of evolutionary theory more than two decades ago. Like many of my readers, I have undergone many trials over these years (e.g., spiritual darkness, ever-present grave illness, and the death of loved ones). I have also studied widely (across the fields of contemporary biblical scholarship, philosophy, classical languages, comparative religion, the empirical sciences, atheist thought, and so on). Most significantly, I have constantly been on the search for Catholic thinkers and peers who grasped the beauty of evolution and its potential for helping us to understand our own faith better. By the grace of God, I have found many such individuals over the past several years. In all of this, it has been my companionship with Benedict through his writings—and with peers who share a similar appreciation of them—that solidified my conviction that evolutionary science is in profound harmony with the teachings of the Catholic faith. I am therefore immensely grateful for the blessing of having been able to dedicate the greater part of two decades to gaining greater acquaintance with the thought of Benedict XVI and to making it known to my readers and students.[69]

In sum, having studied Benedict's thought for so many years, I am convinced that no one has better exemplified how to advance the faith in light of new scientific developments all while remaining steadfastly faithful to Scripture and tradition. The beauty of his theological synthesis, his courage to engage every area of inquiry, his love for the liturgy, his steadfast search for the face of Christ, his holiness and humility—these qualities and more like them are what make the thought of this extraordinary man a veritable *apologia* for the Christian (and especially Catholic) faith.[70]

## WHO WILL BENEFIT FROM THIS TEXT?

I have designed this volume to be as accessible as possible to the same wide audience that I have sought to reach in my other writings. It will thus be right in your wheelhouse if you are a college or graduate student, a member of the clergy, one of my fellow academicians, a lover of Benedict XVI, or just someone interested in engaging the relationship of Christianity and evolution in an intellectually rigorous manner. Because of this envisioned scope, the reader may occasionally wonder: is the present volume a piece of focused scholarship on Ratzinger and evolution that seeks to synthesize this great thinker's thought on the topic and document

---

69. Beyond the present volume, I have especially sought to do this through my monographs *Jesus, Interpreted*, *The Experiment of Faith*, and *Dark Passages of the Bible* (Washington, D.C.: The Catholic University of America Press, 2013). Other articles and talks on Ratzinger's thought can be found through my website matthewramage.com.

70. Ratzinger himself made a habit of emphasizing that the greatest argument on behalf of the faith's truth lies in the beauty and saints that the Church has produced over the ages. For an in-depth exploration of this theme, see Ramage, *The Experiment of Faith*, especially Ch. 12.

how he incorporates an evolutionary worldview into his theology of creation? Or, is it a book on faith and evolution more generally that seeks to address unresolved theological problems in this arena by engaging the best of contemporary Catholic thought on the subject? In a word, the answer to this query is: both.

This being the case, I have no doubt that the following pages will require the non-specialist to sometimes stretch beyond his comfort zone and the specialist to exercise some patience as I establish some things that are not common knowledge and put Ratzinger into conversation with other thinkers who help to spell out points that Ratzinger addresses only briefly or without the precision that one might desire. I also ask the non-specialist pardon in advance for all the footnotes and foreign-language terms that I include to let experts know what precise word is being used in the original language of the text being cited and where to go for more detail on a given topic.[71] The reader need not read these languages to grasp the book's argument. However, this is important from a scholarly perspective because in this volume I am also translating many of Ratzinger's texts—including his unpublished German lecture notes from his time as a professor—into English for the first time.[72]

---

71. Original-language terms from works that have already been translated into English will be bracketed, while original-language terms that I am translating into English for the first time will be parenthesized

72. For a summary and discussion of the importance of Professor Ratzinger's unpublished lecture notes (*Vorlesungsmitschriften*) housed at the *Institut Papst Benedikt XVI* in Regensburg, see Santiago Sanz, "The Manuscripts of Joseph Ratzinger's Lectures on the Doctrine of Creation," trans. Matthew J. Ramage (forthcoming in *Nova et Vetera*). I owe an immense debt of gratitude to Fr. Sanz for putting me in touch with these extraordinary notes. Unless otherwise noted, translations of Ratzinger's unpublished texts (and other texts not published in English) throughout this volume are mine.

Ratzinger offered three courses on the doctrine of creation (*Schöpfungslehre*) over the course of his academic career. I will refer to these three here respectively as *Schöpfungslehre* (1958), *Schöpfungslehre* (1964), and *Schöpfungslehre* (1976). In-depth analyses of these manuscripts along with reproductions of selections from the German originals and translations into Italian and Spanish can be found in Santiago Sanz, "La dottrina della creazione nelle lezioni del professor Joseph Ratzinger: gli appunti di Freising (1958)," *Annales theologici* 30 (2016): 11–44; Sanz, "Joseph Ratzinger y la doctrina de la creación. Los apuntes de Münster," *Revista Española de Teología* 74 (2014): 31–70; Sanz, "Joseph Ratzinger y la doctrina de la creación. Los apuntes de Münster de 1964 (II)," 201–48; Sanz, "Joseph Ratzinger y la doctrina de la creación. Los apuntes de Münster de 1964 (y III). Algunos temas debatidos," *Revista Española de Teología* 74 (2014): 453–96; Sanz, "La dottrina della creazione nelle lezioni del professor Joseph Ratzinger: gli appunti di Regensburg (1976)," *Annales theologici* 30 (2016): 251–83.

For a discussion of the weight that ought to be accorded these unpublished works along with a helpful comparison to the value we duly accord to Aristotle's lecture notes, see Emery de Gaál, "Mariology as Christology and Ecclesiology: Professor Joseph Ratzinger's Only Mariology Course," in *Joseph Ratzinger and the Healing of Reformation-Era Divisions*, eds. Emery de Gaál and Matthew Levering (Steubenville, OH: Emmaus Academic, 2019), 93–120 at 82. Fr. de Gaál emphasizes that, strictly speaking, these are secondary sources, i.e., student notes based upon Ratzinger's lectures that were typed, mimeographed, and even sold to assist other pupils in preparing for oral examinations with Father Ratzinger. While it is safe to assume some differences between what Ratzinger lectured and what his students recorded, de Gaál judges that these lectures grant us authentic insight into Ratzinger's thought. Indeed, he observes that the value of Ratzinger's lecture notes may be considered much in the same way that scholars regard some of Aristotle's most crucial writings (e.g., *De Anima*)—that they authentically

Finally, let the reader be forewarned: I do not pretend that this book will provide definitive answers to all of the problems that it raises. Engaging questions that surface at the intersection of faith and science requires us to acknowledge that there is often more than one intelligent, orthodox way to address a given problem, and Benedict's overall approach has merely stood out to me as the most compelling among these. As Thomas Aquinas says, some things must be believed by the faithful, while in the case of others there is latitude for debate—and indeed "in such matters *even the saints* at times view things differently."[73]

Accordingly, I do not expect this account to change the minds of many who reject evolution (though I would be delighted if it did help some to do this, and I highly encourage those who do not understand the science to consult the sources in the appendix).[74] Nor is my aim to convince the non-Christian to follow Jesus (though I hope it at least helps one to see that Christianity is consonant with evolutionary theory and offers important ways to help ground it in the full truth of the human person and of existence itself). Rather, this book is primarily for those who have "seen the problem" of affirming both the science of evolution and the Christian faith and who are in search of more deeply satisfying answers than they have thus far received. It is for those who understandably may have some apprehensiveness about how the Christian faith will be impacted by a deep engagement with evolution yet who are willing to accompany a great thinker like Benedict as he faces the tough questions head-on.

## STRUCTURE OF THE BOOK

Evolution poses a number of crucial challenges for our understanding of the Christian faith which, when approached with Benedict XVI as guide, simultaneously offer great potential for understanding our faith more deeply. I have no pretensions of tackling every such problem in this book, so I have decided to hone in on those

---

reflect the professor's thought despite being transmitted to us exclusively by way of student scripts. de Gaál, "Mariology as Christology and Ecclesiology," 82. Finally, it must be recognized that, when we do not find a point within these notes repeated later in Ratzinger's career, it is always possible that he changed his mind on the issue. Nevertheless, I have not discovered any instances in Ratzinger's later work that contradicts what he had said as a professor. On the contrary, the content of his lecture notes is often later reprised (sometimes verbatim) in his published works.

73. Aquinas, *In II Sent.*, Lib. 2, d. 12, q. 1, a. 2 (my translation).

74. The father of modern evolutionary theory said it best: "Although I am fully convinced of the truth of the views given in this volume under the form of an abstract, I by no means expect to convince experienced naturalists whose minds are stocked with a multitude of facts all viewed, during a long course of years, from a point of view directly opposite to mine. It is so easy to hide our ignorance under such expressions as the 'plan of creation,' 'unity of design,' etc. and to think that we give an explanation when we only restate a fact. Anyone whose disposition leads him to attach more weight to unexplained difficulties than to the explanation of a certain number of facts will certainly reject my theory." Darwin, *On the Origin of Species*, 481–82. Writing on a different subject, Newman nevertheless makes a point that is apropos here (and can apply not only to those who reject evolution but also to those who reject God), "Men go by their sympathies, not by argument." John Henry Newman, *Apologia Pro Vita Sua* (New York: Longmans, Green, and Co, 1908), 134.

issues that emerged as most dear to the emeritus pontiff throughout his entire career from professor to pope. Given the character of Joseph Ratzinger, some readers will not be surprised that these topics are central to any dialogue between faith and science as they touch on core Christian doctrines.

In his famous 1985 interview *The Ratzinger Report*, then-Cardinal Ratzinger expressed the wish to one day retire quietly and write a book on the topic of original sin and the "necessity of a discovery of its authentic reality."[75] Fortunately or unfortunately, that desire never came to fruition as he was elected supreme pontiff instead. As we will see, Benedict said many interesting things about the Bible's creation stories during his time as cardinal and pope. Humble man of the Church that he was, Ratzinger did not however see it as his job (or that of the *Catechism* that he edited) to offer official statements on the nature of the soul or original sin in light of evolutionary science. In other words, he did not believe it correct in his capacity as cardinal and pope "to represent novel theological theses which do not belong to the assured patrimony of the Church's faith."[76]

This, then, raises the question: what further might Benedict have said about the Fall in relation to evolution had he be given the chance? The same could be asked of the other topics related to evolution that Ratzinger treated off and on throughout his career: reading the Bible's creation narratives in their original context, the meaning of man's special creation, the relationship of sin and death, the interplay of the Old Adam and New Adam, how Jesus Christ brings evolutionary history to its climax and transforms the entire cosmos in the process, and more topics that we will explore in this book.

While it is impossible to know the final judgment of Ratzinger on each of these topics with absolute certainty, it is indeed possible to acquire a very good sense of what it would be by bringing together in one place everything the emeritus pontiff said about them throughout his career. In the end, then, I hope that my reconstruction of Ratzinger's thought in this book will read somewhat like a theological mystery novel. For, the following chapters are an endeavor not only to synthesize everything Ratzinger said on the subject of faith and evolution. It is also one theologian's tentative attempt to apply his thought and so complete the book that the emeritus pontiff might have written on the many mysteries that remain in this exciting and timely area of inquiry.

To this end, in Chapter 2 we will dig down to the foundations of the faith-evolution debate, outlining the deep questions that undergird it and seeking to remove obstacles to understanding the topic aright. A holistic approach to the topic of human origins begins not with any particular biblical passage or doctrine but with consideration of more foundational issues that govern everything else that a person does in sitting down to think about the Bible in relation to science. Specifically,

75. Ratzinger and Vittorio Messori, *The Ratzinger Report: An Exclusive Interview on the State of the Church* (San Francisco: Ignatius Press, 1985), 79.

76. Ratzinger and Christoph Cardinal Schönborn, *Introduction to the Catechism of the Catholic Church* (San Francisco: Ignatius Press, 1994), 71.

we will consider here what Benedict has to say about the different ways atheists and theists approach evolution, in particular the importance of the believer's conviction that a divine intellect underwrites the entire history of evolution. But we will also consider the very different mindsets that Christians themselves have toward evolution, differences which revolve largely around the question of authority. In short, when it comes to the details of how man first emerged, are believers to trust the Bible more than science and thereby reject evolution? Privilege science over Scripture and reject the Church's dogmas? Or is there another approach that might do better justice to both? It is essential to pause and ponder these issues before continuing our journey, for the answers to these questions will have dramatic consequences for how to address the complex issues raised later in the book.

In Chapter 3, we will continue laying our groundwork for a proper understanding of the Bible in relation to evolution by discussing what Benedict thinks on the subject of how God works through evolution in our world. One often hears the claim that evolution does away with the need for God because genetic mutations occur randomly without the need for special divine action and apparently with no preordained design. Like their atheist counterparts, unfortunately some Christians also think that the presence of random events within nature is incompatible with God's existence. In contrast with atheists, though, their response is to reject not God but instead the science of evolution. Here, then, we will also explore questions that divide Christians in their construal of God's action within evolutionary history: Does God cause evolutionary change entirely through natural and even random processes? Through frequent miraculous interventions in the world? Is God's existence manifest through "gaps" in the scientific record, or is his existence compatible with a natural unfolding of evolution regardless of whether it includes gaps or not?

Chapter 4 marks the start of a new section in our book. Having cleared up some fundamental issues surrounding evolutionary theory, here we will turn our attention to the question of how to read Genesis's creation narratives, surveying the core principles needed to read the text (and, by extension, any other biblical passage) with both faith and reason. The framework of our exegetical vision lies in Ratzinger's "Method C" exegetical synthesis, wherein the emeritus pontiff approaches Scripture in concert with the broader Catholic tradition and at the same time through a serious engagement with the best of modern science and biblical scholarship. To understand Genesis 1–11 aright, we will also develop a robust and up-to-date understanding of biblical inspiration and inerrancy with the help of Ratzinger. Crucial to applying these concepts to concrete biblical passages is the meaning of Scripture's literal sense and how to ascertain the sacred writer's intention in crafting his creation accounts. To this end, we will spend some time discussing which questions the Bible answers, and which it does not. Finally, we will reflect on why it is important to situate Genesis within the broader canon of Scripture and the part it plays in the divine pedagogy wherein God gradually led his people toward Christ, whose revelation offers the fullness of truth about God and man.

With these principles in place, in Chapter 5 we will explore what Benedict takes to be the implications of locating Genesis 1–11 in its native Ancient Near

Eastern cultural milieu by revisiting what the opening narrative of Genesis meant to say to its original audience, through its figurative genre. A pivotal prelude to this endeavor will consist in explaining what Benedict means by describing the genre of these chapters alternatively as symbolic, figurative, and even mythical. We will also investigate how modern biblical scholarship has shed light on Genesis by comparing and contrasting it with other stories that were circling in Israel's ancient Near Eastern context. Finally, we will delve into many concrete illustrations of how Benedict applies his principles to ascertain what the Bible *is* and *is not* teaching on the subject of creation—and thereby how it is that faith and evolution are compatible. In so doing, we will ascertain what precisely Benedict takes Genesis to intend with such images as creation through divine speech, its seven-day timeframe, God's "rest," and the garden of Eden where he placed man to dwell.

Our exploration of Genesis's teaching on human origins continues in Chapter 6 as we apply our principles to the figure of Adam. Here, I will contend that Scripture does not intend to make claims on the when, where, or how the first human arose any more than it sought to enumerate how long it took for God to create the world as a whole. Indeed, we will see that the Bible's opening narrative is first a story about Israel and God's covenant with his people. As for Adam, he is not only relevant to Israel—he *is* Israel. After meditating on the meaning of this image, we will then be able to see that Adam is not just Israel: he is all of us. After pondering this connection, we will explore how Benedict arrives at these conclusions through his exegesis of Adam's origin from the dust of the earth, his receiving of God's breath, and Eve's birth from Adam's rib.

Having established the meaning of man's origin from the "dust" and his possession of God's "breath" in the previous chapter, in Chapter 7 we explore how Ratzinger builds on this exegetical approach to engage issues related to the human person that arise from an engagement with evolutionary theory: the meaning of man as God's image, man's special creation, the origin of the soul and its relationship with the body, and the question of how many original humans there were. Unfolding the anthropological implications of Benedict's exegetical approach here will help us to engage evolutionary biology's account of gradual human origins without compromising fundamental principles of the faith handed on to us by the tradition.

A final series of challenges that evolution raises for the faith revolves around the doctrine of original sin, the meaning of which we will consider in Chapter 8. Is original sin tenable in an evolutionary context? If so, what does it mean? By exploring Ratzinger's answers to these questions, the aim here is to arrive at some insights that leave us better positioned to see the harmony between this constant dogmatic teaching of the Church and the knowledge we have attained through modern scientific discoveries.

Chapter 8 will begin by clarifying what the doctrine does *not* teach (how many people first sinned and how precisely it happened). Next, we will unfold Benedict's understanding of what this doctrine *does* teach: through the various figures of Adam, Eve, the serpent, the garden, and the fruit, Genesis tells the story of Israel and provides the reason for the nation's exile. In turn, we will see that this inspired myth extends beyond its original context and speaks of the interior "exile" of every human from God. From here, Benedict unfolds how the biblical Fall narrative provides a "phenomenology of sin" which applies to every human's experience, not just that of Israel or the first member of *Homo sapiens*.

Further, in this same chapter we will see that Ratzinger characteristically articulates his understanding of original sin in a relational key, a rupture in humanity's relationship structure that has accompanied our history from its beginning—a broken relationship with God that has had tragic and inevitable consequences for all other relationships. Finally, we will discover that an important dimension of Benedict's thought revolves around the question of why St. Paul discusses Adam's sin in the first place. According to the emeritus pontiff, the Apostle's point in mentioning it was to highlight the immeasurable gift of grace in Christ. Thus, we will make the claim that the doctrine of original sin is, in reality, more about the Last Adam than the First, a reality that opens up fruitful possibilities for a dialogue with evolutionary science.

In Chapter 9, we turn our attention to some important problems that evolutionary science raises with regard to original sin. Advances in modern biology strongly suggest that humans—like all other organic life forms—have been subject to suffering and death from our species' very origin by virtue of their having descended from hominin ancestors who had been dying for millions of years before our species arrived on the scene of history. This modern narrative clearly challenges the classical theological synthesis assumed by most Catholic theologians until the mid-twentieth century according to which man suffered neither pain nor death before his fall from grace—that human sin either lies at the origin of death itself or that (as Aquinas holds) it precipitated the phenomenon among humans. So, the question is: Were humans immune to suffering prior to sinning, as the tradition at large assumes? Or were we meant to experience pain and death as part of God's plan from the beginning? In short, can the evolutionary story about suffering and death coexist with Catholic doctrine of human origins?

Here, I will argue that the key to a reconciliation may be found in examining how Ratzinger's kenotic Christology informs his anthropology. That is, we will explore how a renewed focus on Jesus Christ as the definitive Adam—he who fully reveals man to himself—can help the Church to think through the place of suffering in God's plan for man. My main contention here will be that looking to Christ's *kenosis* (self-emptying) through his Incarnation and Cross in conjunction with our contemporary knowledge of evolution can serve to deepen our understanding of man's nature made according to Christ's image—particularly our experience of suffering and death. Toward this end, I will chart a path forward by undertaking an *aggiornamento* of the tradition with the help of Ratzinger's keen work at the intersection of Christology and human origins. In particular, we will explore what it means for Christ to be the true Adam and how his *kenosis* is the key that unlocks the mysterious relationship of sin, suffering, and death that so characterize our evolving world.

In the end, Ratzinger finds that the Cross of Jesus Christ reveals a most profound mystery: that virtuous suffering and even death can coexist with sinlessness.

Our Lord's earthly life therefore gives us the perfect picture of what suffering before the Fall would have looked like. While suffering still would not have been a desirable experience for its own sake, it nevertheless would have been the occasion for a synergy of wills in which man handed himself over to God, saying, "Not my will, but thine be done!" (Lk 22:42).

With this in mind, Ratzinger notes that Christ was not the only individual to live a sinless earthly life. Importantly, the emeritus pontiff's corpus includes important material devoted to unfolding what sinless suffering would have looked like in the life of a mere creature: that is, in the sorrows and dormition of the Immaculate Conception. Chapter 10 will reflect on what Ratzinger has to say about the Blessed Virgin Mary's embrace of suffering—and possibly also death—and how this may serve as a privileged lens into the origin of these realities and a guide to help us face them in a more Christ-like manner in our own lives.

I will bring this book's reflections to a close with an epilogue that ties the beginning of the Bible to its end. Here, we will consider Benedict's thought on what the evolutionary beginning of human life has to do with man's last end of eternal life in heaven. In other words, we will ask: what is the connection between *protology* (the study of origins) and *eschatology* (the study of the last things)? Stating the matter plainly, Ratzinger declares that the world's origin is ultimately understood rightly only in light of creation's end—that the Alpha is only truly to be understood in the light of the Omega. In light of this revelation, I will survey Ratzinger's thoughts on the eschatological fulfillment of everything we have discussed in this volume. For example, what happens when the creative process of evolution comes to an end on the Last Day? What will human life look like once we have made—as Benedict calls it—our last "mutation" and greatest "evolutionary leap"? What does it mean to say that there will one day be a new heaven and a new earth (Rv 21:1), and that creation itself will one day be set free from its bondage and obtain the glorious liberty of the children of God? (Rm 8:21–22)

Having surveyed Benedict's sage responses to these questions, this book will have achieved all that it can hope to do: propose the thought of our emeritus pontiff as one promising path by which to make sense of the many challenging questions that evolutionary theory poses for Christian faith. Yet my sincere hope is that readers find that Benedict's thought not only helps to resolve apparent contradictions between faith and evolutionary science. The following pages endeavor to showcase Benedict's conviction that modern scientific discoveries are not merely to be tolerated but rather welcomed as *gifts* that may enable the Church to penetrate the mystery of Christ and the deposit of faith in ever greater depth.

# Chapter 2

# On What Grounds?

*Debates at the Heart of Our Inquiry*

## DIGGING DOWN TO THE FOUNDATIONS

In Chapter 1, we reflected on the challenge that modern evolutionary theory poses to traditional Christian narratives of human origins and proposed the thought of Pope Benedict XVI as a model for how to enter deeply into the debates of our time. Further, we surveyed the narrative of evolutionary history and the evidence for it, insisting with Benedict that all truth is of the Holy Spirit and that the Christian faith is therefore strong enough to stand up to any challenge that modern science may appear to throw at it.

In this chapter, our aim is to dig down to the foundations of the faith-evolution debate, exploring the deep questions that Benedict considers to lie at its heart. The emeritus pontiff's interpretative approach to faith and evolution begins not with any particular passage or doctrine but with a consideration of presuppositions that underpin the different ways people think about the topic. It is essential that we pause and ponder these ideas before continuing on our journey, for each one of us—believer and nonbeliever alike—brings first principles to the table when we sit down to engage matters like evolution. In other words, we all wear "glasses" that color our intellect's perception of reality—including what we think the Bible is and is not teaching or competent to teach in the first place.[1] While Benedict recognizes that none of us can ever be completely objective in our stance on the world, we can at least learn to be aware of our own biases and think deeply about which assumptions best position us for an accurate understanding of the Bible and of the nature of things in general.[2]

To this end, we will begin by considering the two primary and dramatically contrasting ways people approach evolution, which turns on the question of

---

1. Drawing from the physical sciences, Ratzinger argues that Heisenberg's uncertainty principle has an analog in this arena: "Pure objectivity is an absurd abstraction," he says, for "the observer's perspective is an essential determinant of the outcome of an experiment." Ratzinger, "Biblical Interpretation in Conflict," 9. In saying this, of course, Ratzinger does not mean that no certainty at all is available to us in this life. As prefect of the Congregation for the Doctrine of the Faith, he was after all the man in charge of promulgating and defending Catholic doctrine for more than two decades. His intention is to encourage us to be self-critical about our (often unconscious) assumptions when arguing about topics at the intersection of faith and science—biases which inform our thinking despite the noblest of intentions.

2. For another illustration of this exercise, examining the assumptions we bring to our interpretation of the gospels, see Ramage, *Jesus, Interpreted*, Ch. 7.

whether or not a divine intellect (*Logos*) underwrites the universe and thereby evolutionary history. After drawing out the contrasts between theistic and atheistic perspectives on evolution, we will turn our attention to two contrasting mindsets that Christians themselves have toward evolution, differences which revolve largely around the question of authority. In short, when it comes to the details of how man first emerged, are believers to trust the Bible more than science and thereby reject evolution? Privilege science over Scripture and reject the Church's dogmas? Or is there another approach that might do better justice to both? How we answer this question will have dramatic consequences for how we address the complex issues raised later in this book.

## THE FUNDAMENTAL QUESTION: IS NATURE GROUNDED IN REASON, OR NOT?

The first key issue that must be investigated before we embark on a detailed exploration of faith and evolution is something so fundamental that many of us Christians take it for granted. Put simply, the issue is whether God exists and governs the universe, or not. In other words, which of the following approaches to the subject of evolution is true to reality: Is it that of the atheist who denies that divine power is at work in nature, or rather that of the believer who holds that divine intelligence created the evolutionary process and governs it even today? In contrast with what some prominent atheists assume, Ratzinger is adamant that the question posed here is not actually scientific in nature. In other words, we are not going to be able to determine its answer on the basis of the empirical disciplines of physics, biology, and the like. Rather, we are dealing here with a philosophical matter, and so the conversation needed to adjudicate it must take place at the level of philosophical thought.[3]

While Christians have at times been guilty of subordinating science to theology by seeking to predetermine its conclusions, Ratzinger notes that today the opposite tendency is more common: the attempt to explain the whole of reality—including God—in terms of evolution. In this sense, science for many in our day has become a substitute for metaphysics and theology—a sort of universal "first philosophy." That is to say, some who are enamored by the explanatory power of science unfortunately can be led to embrace what Benedict and his predecessor Pope John Paul II called scient*ism*—an ideology that refuses to admit the validity of any form of knowledge other than that which comes from the empirical sciences, thus relegating

---

3. Ratzinger, Preface to *Evolutionismus und Christentum*, viii. For helpful commentary on this point, see Christoph Schönborn, "The Reflections of Joseph Ratzinger Pope Benedict XVI on Evolution," in *Scientific Insights into the Evolution of the Universe and of Life*, 12-21. On questions within biblical exegesis also boiling down fundamentally to a philosophical debate, see Ratzinger, "Biblical Interpretation in Conflict: On the Foundations and the Itinerary for Exegesis Today," in *Opening Up the Scriptures: Joseph Ratzinger and the Foundations of Biblical Interpretation*, eds. José Granados, Carlos Granados, and Luis Sánchez-Navarro (Grand Rapids, MI: Eerdmans Publishing Co., 2008), 19. For an atheist who thinks that science renders the "God hypothesis" unnecessary, see Richard Dawkins, *The God Delusion* (Boston: Houghton Mifflin, 2006), especially Chapters 2 and 4.

religious, theological, ethical, and aesthetic knowledge to the realm of the subjective.[4] In my experience, most Christians who take issue with evolutionary theory are ultimately most concerned with avoiding this widespread error. Though they may not even be able to articulate it, for many believers the issue is not evolutionary science per se but rather that they unwittingly grant atheists the supposition that evolutionary theory, if true, does away with the need for God.

In this vein, Ratzinger insists that the Christian faith stand its ground against totalizing "mythical philosophies" which allege that evolutionary theory can explain everything while failing to acknowledge that many details of the theory (e.g., when and how life first originated, when and how our hominin ancestors finally became truly human, etc.) remain at the level of hypothesis and will continue to be refined as research progresses.[5] Indeed, while he rejoices in the insights that science brings to our understanding of the natural world, Ratzinger notes that evolutionary theory is unable to answer the most fundamental question of whether evolution is grounded by meaning [*Sinn*] or rather meaninglessness [*Sinnlosigkeit*].[6] Neither can it inform us of where everything ultimately comes from, how we ought to live in the world, or what our ultimate destiny is.[7] To recall Galileo's famous words, science teaches us how heaven goes, not how one goes to heaven.[8]

---

4. Ratzinger, Preface to *Evolutionismus und Christentum*, vi–viii; Ratzinger, *Truth and Tolerance*, 178–83. See also John Paul II, *Fides et Ratio*, §88.

5. Ratzinger, *Salt of the Earth* (San Franciso: Ignatius Press, 1997), 31 [*Salz der Erde: Christentum und katholische Kirche an der Jahrtausendwende* (Stuttgart: Deutsche Verlags, 1997), 26]. Here we find a parallel with Ratzinger's famous call for a "criticism of the criticism" within the field of biblical studies. On this subject, see Ratzinger, "Biblical Interpretation in Crisis: On the Question of the Foundations and Approaches of Exegesis Today" in *Biblical Interpretation in Crisis: The Ratzinger Conference on Bible and Church* (Grand Rapids, MI: Eerdmans, 1989), 6.

6. Ratzinger, *Truth and Tolerance*, 181 [*Glaube—Wahrheit—Toleranz: Das Christentum und die Weltreligionen* (Freiburg: Herder, 2003), 146].

7. Benedict XVI, Meeting with Clergy of the Dioceses of Belluno-Feltre and Treviso (July 24, 2007). Benedict's division of labor between science and theology and his recognition of their mutual autonomy is similar to that of John Henry Newman, who writes, "Theology is the highest indeed, and widest, but it does not interfere with the real freedom of any secular science in its own particular department." Newman, *Discourses on the Scope and Nature of University Education Addressed to the Catholics of Dublin* (Dublin: James Duffy, 1852), 152–53. It also has points of contact with the late agnostic evolutionary biologist Stephen Jay Gould's concept of *Nonoverlapping Magisteria* (NOMA) which upholds the mutual autonomy of inquiry within religion and science, respectively. Gould, "Nonoverlapping Magisteria," 269–83.

That said, Kenneth Kemp has observed that Gould's approach is not simply to be equated with that our popes. See Kemp, *The War That Never Was: Evolution and Christian Theology* (Eugene, OR: Cascade Books, 2020), 16–17. For another treatment of the proper domains of theology and science, see John Walton, *The Lost World of Genesis One* (Downers Grove, IL: IVP Academic, 2009), 167. Walton urges neo-Darwinists to stop promoting dysteleology as if it were an essential corollary to evolutionary science, while he asks creationists to concede that traditional interpretations do not always constitute faithful readings of the biblical text.

8. Galileo, "Letter to the Grand Duchess Christina," 91, 96.

For Ratzinger, the fundamental issue ultimately comes down to a very specific question that empirical science cannot answer: *whether or not divine reason stands at the beginning of all things*. Pope Benedict threw down the gauntlet on this matter in an Easter homily:

> Here we are faced with the ultimate alternative that is at stake in the dispute between faith and unbelief: are irrationality, lack of freedom and pure chance the origin of everything, or are reason, freedom and love at the origin of being? Does the primacy belong to unreason or to reason? This is what everything hinges upon in the final analysis.[9]

Articulating this point with a slightly different nuance, Professor Ratzinger once said that there were really only two alternatives: "materialism" and "chance" on the one hand or "meaning" and a "spiritually defined world view" and on the other. The choice between these two boils down to this question:

> ... whether one regards spirit and life in its ascending forms as an incidental mold on the surface of the material world or whether one regards spirit as the goal of the process and, conversely, matter as the prehistory of the spirit. If one chooses the second alternative, it is clear that spirit is not a random product of material developments, but rather that matter signifies a moment in the history of spirit.[10]

These two passages demonstrate that, for Ratzinger, the question of all questions is whether or not the universe originated purely by chance on the one hand or is grounded in spirit or mind on the other.

We might pose the question in another way: Did intelligence come online in humans only after evolution had been blindly unfolding for billions of years? Or, on the contrary, is the Christian tradition right to affirm: "In the beginning was the Word" (Jn 1:1)? Benedict's response is straightforward and unsurprising:

> As believers we answer, with the creation account and with St. John, that in the beginning is reason. In the beginning is freedom. Hence it is good to be a human person. It is not the case that in the expanding universe, at a late stage, in some tiny corner of the cosmos, there randomly evolved some species of living being capable of reasoning and of trying to find rationality within creation, or to bring rationality into it.[11]

One of the then-pontiff's core concerns here and throughout his corpus is to make it clear that Christianity is committed at its very core to the priority of reason over

---

9. Benedict XVI, Easter Vigil Homily (April 23, 2011).

10. Ratzinger, "Belief in Creation and the Theory of Evolution," in *Dogma and Preaching* (San Francisco: Ignatius Press, 2011), 140–41 ["Schöpfungsglaube und Evolutionstheorie," in *Dogma und Verkündigung* (Munich: Erich Wewel Verlag, 1973), 158–59].

11. Benedict XVI, Easter Vigil Homily (April 23, 2011).

the irrational. It is therfore directly antithetical to the faith to hold either that the cosmos popped into existence without a first cause or that man's gift of reason evolved *solely* through an entirely blind and random process.[12]

In place of such a view, Benedict teaches that the evolutionary dynamic itself originated from the divine mind (*Logos*) and has carried rationality within itself from the very start. In fact, this he takes to be the "central message" of the creation narrative in Genesis: "The world is a product of creative Reason. Hence it tells us that, far from there being an absence of reason and freedom at the origin of all things, the source of everything is creative Reason, love, and freedom."[13] This, in fact, is what Genesis 1 teaches when it symbolically depicts God creating by speaking his word (Hebrew: *dabar*; Greek: *logos*). Although God "speaking" creation into existence may seem like a trivial anthropomorphic detail within Genesis's larger creation narrative, Benedict notes that it contains a revelatory truth that runs directly counter to the worldview of other ancient Near Eastern creation narratives. That is, by describing creation as occurring through God's speech, Genesis teaches that it issues forth from God's mind and not by chance or through a cosmic struggle between different deities. And, in case this reading of Genesis is not clear enough, it is made explicit in the prologue to John's gospel, which Ratzinger identifies as "the conclusive and normative scriptural creation account." In other words, when John writes, "In the beginning was the Word," he confirms what Genesis teaches about the origin of the universe from God's mind and reveals the fullness of truth that the opening chapters Genesis foreshadow: that the pre-incarnate Word by which God "spoke" creation into existence is none other than his Son, the second person of the Trinity.[14]

Decades before his tenure as pontiff, Ratzinger wrote a paper arguing along the same lines in which he summarizes what he takes Christianity's doctrine of creation to mean:

> [Belief in creation] expresses the conviction that the world as a whole, as the Bible says, comes from the Logos, that is, from creative mind [*schöpferischen Sinn*] and represents the temporal form of its self-actuation [*die zeitliche Form seines Selbstvollzugs*]. . . . To believe in creation means to understand, in faith, the world of becoming revealed by science as a meaningful world that comes from a creative mind.[15]

---

12. I emphasize the word *solely* here, for we will see further below that Benedict is not denying the presence of chance events like genetic mutations within creation, but rather that they are the only or ultimate cause at work in the universe.

13. Benedict XVI, Easter Vigil Homily (April 23, 2011).

14. Ratzinger, *In the Beginning*, 15.

15. Ratzinger, "Belief in Creation and the Theory of Evolution," 139–40 ["Schöpfungsglaube und Evolutionstheorie," 157–58]. Ratzinger continues: "The recognition of the world of becoming as the self-actuation of a creative thought (*die Anerkennung der Werdewelt als Selbstvollzug eines schöpferischen Gedankens*) includes also its derivation from the creativity of the spirit, from the Creator Spiritus." See also Ratzinger, *God and the World*, 114. For a reflection on the world as the temporal form of divine self-actuation that has some points of contact with Benedict's understanding, see Mark Johnston, *Saving*

For Ratzinger, the teaching that creation issues from God's mind and is inherently rational distinguishes a Christian approach to evolution not only from atheism but, as we will see in later chapters, from other ancient and modern understandings of the universe's origin. Moreover, as we will discuss below, Christians view the universe as grounded not only in reason but also in *love*. Thus, Ratzinger's insistence that creation represents the Word's incursion in time should cause us to think about just what that "self-actuation" looks like. His answer is that it looks like Jesus Christ and sacrificial love on the cross.

## THE SELF-REFUTATION OF EVOLUTIONARY NATURALISM

While geneally very reserved when it comes to the question of how much about God we can prove through reason alone, Ratzinger makes some pointed critiques of the naturalist view of evolution—that is, the atheistic outlook according to which nature is the only thing that is and that therefore no *Logos* underpins evolution. One such argument assumes the form of a question: "[C]an reason really renounce its claim to the priority of what is rational over the irrational, the claim that the *Logos* is at the ultimate origin of things, without abolishing itself?"[16] What I take then-Cardinal Ratzinger to be suggesting here is that our rationality itself would be unreliable if an an infinite Mind did not exist. In other words, there is no reason to believe that any of our reasoning gives us access to the truth if our reason itself is *merely* the product of subrational evolutionary processes.

Considered purely from an evolutionary perspective, our intellect's raison d'être is to help us to survive—which does not necessarily mean producing *true* beliefs. It turns out, then, that an approach to evolution which fails to ground our intellect's origin in the divine *Logos* ends up undermining the very credibility of its own truth claims. While this does not amount to proof for God's existence, it does reduce to the absurd the notion that we can make valid truth claims while denying a divine grounding to the universe. Alvin Plantinga writes on this score:

> What evolution guarantees is (at most) that we behave in certain ways—in such ways as to promote survival, or more exactly reproductive success. The principal function or purpose . . . of our cognitive faculties is not that of producing true or verisimilitudinous (nearly true) beliefs, but instead that of contributing

---

*God: Religion after Idolatry* (Princeton, NJ: Princeton University Press, 2009), especially 120, 187, 125. Johnston speaks of "the outpouring of Existence Itself by way of its exemplification in ordinary existents for the purpose of the self-disclosure of Existence Itself." From the other side, "This world, properly seen, is the outpouring and self-disclosure that is the Highest One," and "this kenosis or self-emptying of Being that envelops everything, is the site of the sacred." In saying this, Johnston, like Benedict, is ascribing great sanctity to the most ordinary things and events in life. As such, in daily life we are "already on holy ground." As for us humans, he writes, "Salvation . . . is a new orientation, a new form of life, which finds itself as the expression and the subject of Divine self-disclosure. . . . A saved human being is just a finite manifestation of the kenosis, filled with an awareness of itself as such, an awareness made manifest in that human being's turn toward reality and the real needs of others."

16. Ratzinger, *Truth and Tolerance*, 181.

to survival by getting the body parts in the right place. . . . Our beliefs *might* be mostly true . . . but there is no particular reason to think they *would* be: natural selection is interested, not in truth, but in appropriate behavior.[17]

C.S. Lewis articulates this point in more familiar language, it is a "flat contradiction," he says, for the atheist to ask Christians to believe that reason "is simply the unforeseen and unintended by-product of mindless matter at one stage of its endless and aimless becoming," for in so doing we would be accepting a conclusion by way of "discredit[ing] the only testimony on which that conclusion can be based."[18] To this point, it is also worth recalling that Darwin himself once expressed "horrid doubt" over whether we can trust our claims to the truth when our minds have evolved from lower, irrational life-forms. After all, he recognized, nobody would trust the convictions of a monkey's mind.[19]

In one of his rare public pieces penned after retiring, Benedict adds that two other things would be undermined if evolution were somehow to occur apart from God. First, a world not grounded in God is a world without any standards of good and evil. It is thus one in which power—in evolutionary language, survival of the fittest—is the only guiding principle. If this and the randomness of natural selection really are the exclusive basis of life, then it turns out that all moral imperatives (Christian or otherwise) are just moralistic coping mechanisms that humans concoct to shield ourselves from those more powerful than us.[20]

---

17. Alvin Plantinga, *Where the Conflict Really Lies: Science, Religion, and Naturalism* (New York: Oxford University Press, 2011), 315. For further discussion of how viewing evolution apart from God is self-defeating in that it undermines man's ability to make any claims to truth in the first place, see Ramage, *Jesus, Interpreted*, 245–49. In that section I draw from the thought of C.S. Lewis, Plantinga, and others to make this point. Alvin Plantinga, who writes the following of a universe evolving without out God. See also Michael Hanby, *No God, No Science: Theology, Cosmology, Biology* (Malden, MA: Wiley-Blackwell, 2013), 150 and Conor Cunningham, *Darwin's Pious Idea: Why the Creationists and the Ultra-Darwinists Both Get It Wrong* (Grand Rapids, MI: Eerdmans, 2010), 59, 161, 173, 213, 282, 365, 421. Michael Augros has likewise written: "Those who see natural selection as the sole author of intelligence must see intelligence as a mere tool. It is for survival (albeit in a weak and nonpurposive sense of *for*). . . . Only the understanding that produces survival results can be of any 'interest' to it." Michael Augros, *Who Designed the Designer?: A Rediscovered Path to God's Existence* (San Francisco: Ignatius Press, 2015), 151.

18. Lewis, "Is Theology Poetry?," in *The Weight of Glory, and Other Addresses* (New York: Macmillan, 1980), 135.

19. "With me the horrid doubt always arises whether the convictions of man's mind, which has been developed from the mind of the lower animals, are of any value or at all trustworthy. Would any one trust in the convictions of a monkey's mind, if there are any convictions in such a mind?" Darwin, Letter to William Graham, Down, July 3, 1881, *The Life and Letters of Charles Darwin Including an Autobiographical Chapter*, ed. Francis Darwin, London: John Murray, Albermarle Street, 1887), 1:315–16. We read likewise in Darwin's autobiography: "But then arises the doubt, can the mind of man, which has, as I fully believe been developed from a mind as low as that possessed by the lowest animal, be trusted when it draws such grand conclusions?" Charles Darwin, *The Autobiography of Charles Darwin* (Cambridge: Icon Books, 2003), 149.

20. Benedict XVI, "The Church and the Scandal of Sexual Abuse," *The National Catholic Register* (April 10, 2019), III, 1. Stephen Barr develops this same point in more length in *The Believing Scientist:*

Second, Benedict emphasizes that a world without God—a world in which man is merely the product of chance mutations—would be a meaningless universe: "Only if things have a spiritual reason, are intended and conceived—only if there is a Creator God who is good and wants the good—can the life of man also have meaning."[21] Yet, as we have seen above, the question of whether or not the universe is purposeful—whether it is has meaning grounded in the divine *Logos*—is a question that the empirical sciences cannot answer.[22]

In a nutshell, the above texts reflect Benedict's understanding that maintaining God's nonexistence while making claims to truth or morality is itself not rational. On the contrary, it is an unprovable premise that arguably involves more "faith" than the Christian conviction that the universe proceeds from the *Logos* of God.[23]

## KNOWING THE TRUTH OF CREATION THROUGH THE "EXPERIMENT OF FAITH"

So much for the "negative" side of the argument in favor of a Christian evolutionary vision which consisted in pinpointing the serious shortcomings of a naturalistic worldview. For Benedict, the "positive" side of this account is actually more important. For, in his view, the real "proof" for the Church's approach to the universe

---

*Essays on Science and Religion* (Grand Rapids: Eerdmans, 2016), 32–38. Barr's specific target is Richard Dawkins, who fails to embrace the logical conclusions of his own atheistic version of evolutionary theory, choosing instead to "rebel" against them when it comes to politics and how we conduct our human affairs. Barr insightfully observes that there is a contradiction between Dawkins the atheist (who holds than man is made entirely of the same mindless stuff as everything else in creation) and Dawkins the humanist (who holds that man is exceptional in the universe). In short, Dawkins's atheism is incompatible with an objective moral order, yet he insists on morals anyway. The atheist lacks a coherent account of why we ought to "rebel" against what we know to be true in nature, whereas the Christian view I am presenting here holds that morality is grounded in reality and flows from nature, not against it.

21. Benedict XVI, "The Church and the Scandal of Sexual Abuse," III, 1. This rare post-retirement comment echoes his earlier reflection as pope: "If man were merely a random product of evolution in some place on the margins of the universe, then his life would make no sense or might even be a chance of nature." Benedict XVI, Easter Vigil Homily (April 23, 2011). See also Benedict XVI, *Jesus of Nazareth: From the Baptism of the Lord to the Transfiguration* (San Francisco: Ignatius, 2007), 166, in which the emeritus pontiff tells us that, if we lose God, we also lose ourselves and are then "nothing more than a random product of evolution." Benedict made this very point in his inaugural homily as pope: "We are not some casual and meaningless product of evolution. Each of us is the result of a thought of God. Each of us is willed, each of us is loved." Benedict XVI, Homily (April 24, 2005).

22. This point was captured well by Étienne Gilson when he explains in Thomistic language that natural science neither disproves nor establishes final causality. As Gilson has it, holding final causality to be beyond *science* is one thing, but to put it beyond *nature* is something completely different. According to Gilson, if one brackets final causality in his scientific inquiry, his science is not false, just incomplete. However, if he denies final causality in nature, he is being arbitrary. Gilson, *From Aristotle to Darwin and Back Again: A Journey in Final Causality, Species, and Evolution* (San Francisco: Ignatius Press, 2009), 20, 31. On this point, see also John Haught, *God After Darwin: A Theology of Evolution* (Boulder, CO: Westview Press, 2000), 166–78.

23. For more on the argument that claims to truth and morality without belief in God are baseless, see Ramage, *Jesus, Interpreted*, 243–45, 261–63.

cannot come from arguments alone: the truth of the faith is ultimately discovered in the *laboratory of life* when we embrace Christ and embark on what he calls (in an analogy deliberately drawn from the sciences) "the experiment of faith."[24]

As Ratzinger sees it, the doctrine of creation on which we are reflecting in this book really is just that: *belief* that the world originated from God's mind and not from sheer nothingness. Christianity is by no means unreasonable, but adherence to it does require an existential decision on our part:

> Christian faith represents the choice in favor of the priority of reason and of rationality. This ultimate question . . . can no longer be decided by arguments from natural science, and even philosophical thought reaches its limits here. In that sense, there is no ultimate demonstration that the basic choice involved in Christianity is correct."[25]

It may sound rather odd for a man who considers reason so important to say this, but Ratzinger is not as sanguine as many when it comes to how much they are able to definitively prove. Although he is obviously a theist and a Christian, Ratzinger is typically reticent to pursue definitive proofs for the Christian approach to reality in general and to the doctrine of creation in particular. However, as we have already seen, this is by no means to say that he despairs of the possibility of knowing the truth about God here below or that he is too shy to poke holes in materialism. Indeed, Benedict notes that science "presupposes the mathematical structure of matter, its intrinsic rationality."[26]

Picking up on this crucial point, Catholic physicist Stephen Barr eloquently explains that, whereas materialists allege that the universe has no rational ground, the actual discoveries of modern physics point in precisely the opposite direction:

> As we turn to the fundamental principles of physics, we discover that order does not really emerge from chaos . . . it always emerges from greater and more impressive order already present at a deeper level. It turns out that things

---

24. For an extensive treatment of this thought in Benedict's corpus, see Ramage, *The Experiment of Faith.*

25. Ratzinger, *Truth and Tolerance*, 181 [*Glaube—Wahrheit—Toleranz*, 146]. Ratzinger's discomfort with adducing failsafe "proofs" for God is evident in this passage and the passages surrounding it. It seems that Ratzinger views traditional proofs for the rationality of the universe and the Christian approach to reality as generally unsatisfactory. However, he does think that there are good arguments for God's existence. Indeed, in this section we have seen him point to the absurdity of holding to our human reason's very rationality and positing moral standards in the absence of belief in God. That said, providing arguments for the existence and attributes of God would take us far afield from the task at hand. For a thorough approach to these matters, see Aquinas, *Summa Contra Gentiles: Book One: God*, trans. Anton Pegis (Notre Dame, IN: University of Notre Dame Press, 1975).

26. Benedict XVI, Address at the University of Regensburg (September 12, 2006). For another description of matter's intrinsic rationality, see Benedict XVI, *Creation and Evolution*, 145. In his university lectures on creation, Professor Ratzinger countered materialism's claim that mind arose only recently in the evolutionary process by teaching, "Spirit is not a mere epiphenomenon of matter. On the contrary, matter is the prehistory of the spirit." Ratzinger, *Schöpfungslehre* (1964), 176.

are not more coarse or crude or unformed as one goes down into the foundations of the physical world but more subtle, sophisticated, and intricate the deeper one goes. . . . [The history of physics] illustrates a general trend in modern physics: the more deeply it has probed the structure of matter, the greater the mathematical order it has found. The order we see in nature does not come from chaos; it is distilled out of a more fundamental order.[27]

All this is to say that, contrary to what the atheist may claim, rationality is not a latecomer to the universe. The divine *Logos* has been there all along, and indeed would exist even if there were no physical universe. Yet, seeing there is in fact a universe, the very rationality of this world's laws at every level stongly suggests that they are grounded not in pure chaos or chance but in a greater Reason of which they are but a reflection.

## CREATION, THE WORK OF *LOGOS* AND *AGAPE*

In Benedict's view, an accurate understanding of the natural world requires wedding two dimensions of reality that are all too often separated: love and reason. Importantly, the Trinity and Incarnation reveal a reality that other theists may not perceive: that the *Logos* who stands at the beginning of all things is also *Agape*—that God is not only the Word (John 1:1) but also Love (1 Jn 4:16). Love and reason, then, are together the fabric that structures reality. Or, as Benedict put it in one of his papal audiences, "The beginning of all things is creative wisdom, and this wisdom is love."[28] Cardinal Christoph Schönborn, one of Ratzinger's former students who along with him oversaw the Catechism's composition, describes this unified vision as "the very thing that most profoundly determines Joseph Ratzinger/Pope Benedict's statements on the topic of creation and evolution."[29]

---

27. Barr, *The Believing Scientist*, 160–62. See also page 119, where Barr writes, "But modern physics gives us eyes to see down to the very roots of the world's structure, to the deepest layers of physical law, and what is seen there is an orderliness of the most pristine mathematical purity." For an illuminating discussion of this principle in relation to there being a deeper structure in the universe that governs the precise forms of life that evolution is able to produce, see Simon Conway Morris, *Life's Solution: Inevitable Humans in a Lonely Universe* (Cambridge: Cambridge University Press, 2003), 310 and this summary of his findings in Christopher Baglow, *Creation: A Catholic's Guide to God and the Universe* (Notre Dame, IN: Ave Maria Press, 2021), 48–51: "[T]he general forms that life can develop and adapt are not haphazard but follow definite chemical, genetic and environmental pathways that were largely 'predetermined from the Big Bang.' In other words, there is a deeper structure that makes the adventure of biological life not utterly random but orderly, somewhat like jazz music in which basic tunes (such as 'When the Saints Go Marching In') are recognizable when played, but are always played with innovation and creativity, so that they are also a little different each time."

28. Benedict XVI, General Audience (November 9, 2005).

29. Christoph Schönborn, "The Reflections of Joseph Ratzinger Pope Benedict XVI on Evolution," in *Scientific Insights into the Evolution of the Universe and of Life*, 20. To this the cardinal adds a beautiful reflection on the person of Ratzinger: "Inherent to Joseph Ratzinger, besides his immense conceptual clarity, is always a very true-to-life and existential approach to the questions he addresses. It is perhaps this close interrelation of high intellectuality, deep piety and close bond with real life that account for the sustained success of his lectures, speeches and sermons."

If both truth *and* love are the foundation of creation, then we creatures are going to make a successful "experiment of faith" only by committing our lives to the twofold vocation of pursuing the truth wherever it may be found *and* pouring ourselves out in love to the other.[30] As I will discuss much more in later chapters, Benedict believes that the universe has a cruciform (or cross-shaped) logic written into it. For us, this means that we mortals enter into the rhythm of creation by pouring ourselves out to God and others while expecting nothing in return, sacrificing our lives in suffering and death in imitation of our God who emptied himself to us. In turn, believers manifest the glory of Jesus Christ to the world by bringing together what Ratzinger calls "two pillars of reality" in our way of life— i.e., that "true reason is love, and love is true reason."[31] In other words, we believers need not just orthodoxy (right teaching—truth) but also orthopraxy (right practice—love).

In sum, Christian faith certainly involves an intellectual dimension. However, it is not true faith—and it will scarcely convince anyone else of its truth—unless it flows into life, transforming our entire existence. Benedict thus issued this exhortation in another one of his rare public statements as emeritus pontiff: "[God] is more than understanding because He creates—and is—love. To once more make people aware of this is the first and fundamental task entrusted to us by the Lord."[32]

## AT THE FOUNDATION OF THE DEBATE AMONG CHRISTIANS: THE AUTHORITY QUESTION

Thus far, we have been considering the fundamental question of whether or not reason underwrites evolutionary history, and our findings have been twofold. First, an atheistic approach to evolution is self-defeating in that it undermines the very reliability of our truth claims and moral laws. In other words, if the world is to have meaning, it must be structured by a *Logos* that precedes and sustains it. Second, we have discovered that a uniquely Christian vision of reality affirms something that a merely theistic worldview lacks: this *Logos* that structures our world is also *Agape*, which in turn means that the whole cosmos has a cruciform or paschal structure.

As we recalled in the introduction to this chapter, though, this is not to say that Christians—even Christians who accept evolution—are unified in their stance

---

30. Ratzinger, "Man between Reproduction and Creation: Theological Questions on the Origin of Human Life," in *Joseph Ratzinger in* Communio: *Anthropology and Culture*, vol. 2 (Grand Rapids: Eerdmans, 2013), 82.

31. "The attempt, in this crisis for mankind, to give back an obvious meaning and significance to the concept of Christianity as the *religio vera* must, so to speak, be based in equal measure upon orthopraxy and orthodoxy. At the most profound level its content will necessarily consist—in the final analysis, just as it did then—in love and reason coming together as the two pillars of reality: true reason is love, and love is true reason. They are in their unity the true basis and the goal of all reality." Ratzinger, *Truth and Tolerance*, 183.

32. Benedict XVI, "The Church and the Scandal of Sexual Abuse," III.1

on it. Indeed, the believer who would approach evolution must consider yet another choice between rival ways of thinking. And, again, it consists of a philosophical debate that cannot be adjudicated on the basis of science—or solely by reference to the Bible and Church documents.

The fundamental issue for a Christian approaching the subject of faith and evolution is clearly not about whether or not divine reason grounds the universe. Rather, the pressing question for people within the Church has to do with a different structural reality: the means by which we come to know truth and the role of *authority*. For some time now, the scientific guild has enjoyed a broad consensus on evolution by natural selection through multiple converging lines of inquiry. But the Christian may understandably find himself confused as to how much epistemic weight this evidence ought to be accorded. Are we to adhere to the letter of Scripture and two thousand years of Christian tradition regardless of what the science says? Or are we to revise particular features of our understanding of creation in light of the scientific consensus that has emerged over only the last two hundred years? Put simply, when it comes to the details of how man first emerged, how we are supposed to know which experts to trust: the theological experts who guide our faith, or the experts of science?

Christians in our world today have various and often overlapping ways of answering the above question, which include the following. One approach is to dispute the science itself, pointing to gaps in the fossil record or contending that some features of life are so complex that they are inexplicable by evolutionary theory. This is the tack taken by the "Intelligent Design" (ID) movement that I will discuss more in the next chapter. A second consists in raising philosophical objections, e.g., asserting that evolution cannot produce more from less, or that species-to-species change violates Aristotelian principles.[33] A third envisions the scientific evidence for evolution as irrelevant, pointing either to the letter of Scripture or the antiquity of the ecclesial tradition that God created human beings and other species directly and relatively recently. Some people of this last persuasion insist that the faith should not be in the business of making what it sees as concessions to science, for it emphasizes that knowledge gained through divine revelation is more certain. Finally, there is the *evolutionary creation* perspective adopted by scholars like Benedict which I introduced in the last chapter. According to this stance, it is best to embrace the overwhelming scientific evidence that God created all life by means of evolution. From there, this perspective asks how

---

33. Thus Ratzinger, in one of his university courses on the doctrine of creation, said that "much of the resistance to the question of evolution does not actually stem from Christian motives, but from attachment to the [Aristotelian-Thomistic] material-form-schema and its essentialism." Interestingly, he further suggests that "in evolution a Christian principle—being as becoming—can appear more clearly than in the traditional matter-form scheme." For our purposes here, it is particularly interesting that he then adds that Christian debate about evolution frequently "is not about the struggle between science and faith . . . but rather is a struggle between two theories." Ratzinger, *Schöpfungslehre* (1964), 74; Sanz, "Joseph Ratzinger y la doctrina de la creación. Los apuntes de Münster de 1964 (II)," 477n67.

knowledge of the natural world can help us to refine our understanding of the Scriptures and how Christian doctrine can illumine the meaning of discoveries in evolutionary science.

In addition to the specific things he says about the relationship of evolution and doctrines like human uniqueness and original sin, Benedict's overall attitude toward evolutionary theory is itself instructive and worth pondering here. Fundamentally, the emeritus pontiff's approach is respectful of the modern sciences as independent disciplines of inquiry. Like the Second Vatican Council and his predecessor John Paul II, he advocates a "principle of autonomy" which allows sciences to operate according to their respective methods without theology seeking to fix their conclusions in advance,[34] or, as C.S. Lewis warns, "to prescribe what God must have done."[35] Ratzinger believes that this is the right approach given that evolutionary theory itself neither invalidates not corroborates the faith, but rather challenges us to understand the faith more profoundly.[36] Or, as he once memorably said in a homily, "We cannot say: creation or evolution . . . we are faced here with two complementary—rather than mutually exclusive—realities."[37] As Benedict would later put it, the antithesis

---

34. For the "principle of autonomy," see John Paul II, *Fides et Ratio*, §13 and §77. See also Second Vatican Council, *Gaudium et Spes*, §36, wherein we read that the council "cannot but deplore certain habits of mind, which are sometimes found too among Christians, which do not sufficiently attend to the rightful independence of science and which, from the arguments and controversies they spark, lead many minds to conclude that faith and science are mutually opposed." Citing the First Vatican Council's constitution *Dei Filius*, ch. 4, §5, it adds, "Therefore if methodical investigation within every branch of learning is carried out in a genuinely scientific manner and in accord with moral norms, it never truly conflicts with faith, for earthly matters and the concerns of faith derive from the same God." These more recent formulations are consonant with the Angelic Doctor's classic statement, "It is impossible that the truth of faith should be opposed to those principles that the human reason knows naturally." Aquinas, *Summa Contra Gentiles*, trans. Anton C. Pegis (Garden City, New York: Hanover House, 1955), 7, §1.

35. The following meditation of C.S. Lewis on Scripture finds a timely application here. Moreover, his lumping together of the Catholic Church and fundamentalism is particularly poignant; for, even if it is not fair to apply this to the Church herself, it is an accurate portrayal of the mentality I have often encountered among some Catholics: "We might have expected, we may think we should have preferred, an unrefracted light giving us ultimate truth in systematic form—something we could have tabulated and memorized and relied on like the multiplication table. One can respect, and at moments envy, both the Fundamentalist's view of the Bible and the Roman Catholic's view of the Church. But there is one argument which we should beware of using for either position: God must have done what is best, this is best, therefore God has done this. For we are mortals and do not know what is best for us, and *it is dangerous to prescribe what God must have done*—especially when we cannot, for the life of us, see that He has after all done it. We may observe that the teaching of Our Lord Himself, in which there is no imperfection, is not given us in that cut-and-dried, foolproof, systematic fashion we might have expected or desired. He wrote no book. We have only reported sayings, most of them uttered in answers to questions, shaped in some degree by their context." Lewis, *Reflections on the Psalms* (London: Harvest Books, 1964), 112.

36. Ratzinger, "Belief in Creation and the Theory of Evolution," 142; Ratzinger, Preface to *Evolutionismus und Christentum*, viii.

37. Ratzinger, *In the Beginning*, 50 (emphasis added). St. John Henry Newman, himself remarkably open to evolution when it was a new theory, has something similar to say of the Catholic in relation to science: "He is sure, and nothing shall make him doubt, that, if anything seems to be proved by

between creation and evolution that he saw in Germany and the United States is "absurd," for "there are so many scientific proofs [*tante prove scientifiche*] in favor of evolution, and it enriches our knowledge of life and being as such."[38] Accordingly, in Benedict's view, the question of whether the Christian ought to privilege the authority of science or that of the faith turns out to be a red herring. Put simply, his view is that we should render judgments in science by the standards of science, and judgments in theology by the standards of theology. The findings of the two can never contradict one another if we are clear on what lies within the purview of each and if we are open to letting them mutually enrich one another.

## CONCLUSION

In sum, Benedict's philosophical disposition is to let the sciences speak for themselves in the realms in which they are competent. Further, he reminds everyone that theology is not competent to judge the validity of scientific findings nor are the sciences qualified to weigh in on theological or philosophical matters. As Christians, then, our work is that of "plundering the Egyptians," as the Fathers of the Church would say. That is, the knowledge we glean from these disciplines can help to refine our understanding of the faith, and in turn the light of faith can help us to situate the findings of science within the grand scheme of things. Or, as John Paul II put it, "Science can purify religion from error and superstition; religion can purify science from idolatry and false absolutes. Each can draw the other into a wider world, a world in which both can flourish."[39]

Rather than writing off or disputing scientific findings related to evolution, our recent popes maintain a healthy critical awareness of science's limits while rejoicing in the knowledge we ascertain through it. This openness allows us to pursue the pressing questions of what it all means for how such issues as the nature of the soul, the uniqueness of mankind, the reality of original sin, and so on. As John Paul II suggested, it puts us in a position to ask, for example: "Does an evolutionary perspective bring any light to bear upon theological anthropology, the meaning of the human person as the *imago Dei*, the problem of Christology—and even upon the development of doctrine itself?"[40]

---

astronomer, or geologist, or chronologist, or antiquarian, or ethnologist, in contradiction to the dogmas of faith, that point will eventually turn out, first, not to be proved, or, secondly, not contradictory, or thirdly, not contradictory to anything really revealed, but to something which has been confused with revelation." Newman, *The Idea of a University* (London: Longmans, Green, and Co., 1907), 466. For an excellent essay on Newman and evolution, see Berta M. Moritz, "A Patron Saint of Evolution?," *Church Life Journal* (October 16, 2019).

38. Benedict XVI, Meeting with Clergy of the Dioceses of Belluno-Feltre and Treviso (July 24, 2007).

39. John Paul II, Letter to George Coyne, SJ, Director of the Vatican Observatory (June 1, 1988).

40. John Paul II, Letter to George Coyne, SJ, Director of the Vatican Observatory (June 1, 1988). For further discussion on this question, see Christopher Baglow, "Does the Extended Evolutionary Synthesis Shed New Light on Theological Anthropology?," *Church Life Journal* (January 10, 2020).

Before tackling those issues, however, there is one more fundamental question on which Christians find themselves divided when it comes to evolution, one which might make a believer hesitant to follow our recent popes in their approach to evolution. This concern is expressed by believers who emphasize the incomplete nature of evolutionary science itself—that certain features of the universe seem just too complex to be explicable by natural causes apart from direct divine intervention.

# Chapter 3

# Machine or Melody?
## *How God Creates through Evolution*

## INTRODUCTION

In the last chapter, we contrasted Benedict XVI's approach to evolution both with that of atheists and with believers who reject the science for one reason or another. We have seen that Benedict thinks Christians should let the natural sciences speak for themselves and from there plunder the wisdom of these "Egyptians" in service of better understanding the faith. Now, we must consider a specific issue raised by those whose concerns with evolutionary theory are expressed by pointing to the incomplete nature of the science itself. The fact that we do not currently have a full grasp on how certain biological mechanisms originated leads some to insist that it is because they are too complex to have arisen through natural causes apart from special divine intervention or planning. This raises another series of questions that the Christian has to consider: Does God cause evolutionary change entirely through natural and even random processes? Through frequent miraculous interventions in the world? Is God's existence manifest through "gaps" in the scientific record, or is his existence compatible with a natural unfolding of evolution regardless of whether it includes gaps or not?

As we are about to see, Benedict and other notable Christian thinkers find significant problems in the insistence on God intervening in nature in order for it to achieve its end. In fact, I will cite thinkers who find that this mindset ironically resembles the atheist's way of thinking about God. In this chapter, we will explore how Benedict's thought can help us chart a path that eschews such a faulty understanding of how God operates through evolution in our world.

In the following sections, it will become clear that Ratzinger has a deep respect for the integrity of nature, as he rejects the notion that God is a "craftsman" who "tinkers" with the world. According to Ratzinger, evolutionary developments occur "precisely *in* the processes of a living being" even as human beings are "not the mere product of development." Finally, we will discuss what the emeritus pontiff means by insisting that creation is an ever-present act that unfolds "in the manner in which thought is creative," a dynamic that he describes analogously as the composition of a story, drama, melody, and symphony. Wedding these and other key insights, I will bring this chapter to a close by submitting that Ratzinger's thought on evolution should lead us to conceive of creation less along the lines of an intelligently designed machine and more as a masterpiece story that is continually being told as its plot unfolds naturally over time.

## DIFFERENT MEANINGS OF THE EXPRESSION
## "INTELLIGENT DESIGN"

Any satisfactory account of how God creates new life forms through evolution must seek to address the role that contingency or chance plays in the natural world. Many people assume that divine providence is incompatible with an evolutionary process that operates through natural selection and random genetic variation.[1] Indeed, atheists frequently base their rejection of God on the supposed incompatibility of chance and purpose—that a system driven by chance has no room for God. This leads some Christians to seek refuge in the notion of "Intelligent Design" (hereafter ID). Not to be confused with the more firmly grounded affirmation that evolution is guided by God and integral to his plan for the universe, ID is a specific intellectual movement that answers the challenge of evolution by searching for steps in the history of life that cannot be explained through natural processes alone. ID advocates thus take Darwin at his own word when he said while authoring evolutionary biology's foundational text: "If it could be demonstrated that any complex organ existed which could not possibly have been formed by numerous, successive, slight modifications, my theory would absolutely break down."[2]

With an eye to meeting Darwin's challenge, ID advocates argue that certain of life's amazingly complex structures indeed could not have arisen naturally over time and that they therefore would not exist today without the intervention or special preplanning of a higher power. In ID language, these marvels of nature are said to exhibit "irreducible complexity" (hereafter IC). A few examples of such complexity that have been said to require direct divine intervention or special divine planning include eyes, wings, and the bacterial flagellum.[3]

---

1. For an excellent discussion of the word "random" as used in science in contrast with how non-specialists commonly understand the term, see Stephen Barr, "Chance, by Design," in *The Believing Scientist: Essays on Science and Religion* (Grand Rapids, MI: Eerdmans, 2016), 54–63.

2. Charles Darwin, *On the Origin of Species*, 189. It is worth noting that Darwin's theory is truly scientific in that it is open to falsification, for example if fossils were discovered in layers of the geological record where they were not predicted to be. However, despite two centuries of work, no such counter-evidence has arisen.

3. Throughout this text, I will be referring frequently to ID proponents or advocates without specifying individual authors. While the constraints of this work do not permit me to explain their arguments in further detail, these thinkers share a common approach. However, I would note that, while they have a basic emphasis in common, this is not to say that all ID proponents hold precisely the same views or that they necessarily deny the fact of species-to-species evolution across time. For example, Michael Behe does not dispute the evolutionary history of life per se but rather takes issue with Darwin's precise account of *how* it happened. Thus, to be attracted to ID is not necessarily to deny evolution, even as some Christians appeal to it for this purpose.

With that caveat in place, the following are some representative works of the ID community: William Dembski, *The Design Revolution: Answering the Toughest Questions about Intelligent Design* (Nottingham, UK: Inter-Varsity Press, 2004; Michael Behe, *The Edge of Evolution* (New York: The Free Press, 2007); Behe, *Darwin's Black Box: The Biochemical Challenge to Evolution* (New York: Free Press, 1996); Stephen Meyer, *Signature in the Cell: DNA and the Evidence for Intelligent Design* (New York: HarperOne, 2009); Meyer, *Darwin's Doubt: The Explosive Origin of Animal Life and the Case for*

For his part, Benedict concurs with ID to the extent that he recognizes the incompleteness of evolutionary science—that at least currently we cannot give a naturalistic account of how every major evolutionary transition throughout history occurred.[4] Further, the emeritus pontiff deploys the words "evolutionary leap" [*Evolutionssprung*] and "breakthrough" [*Durchbruch*] to describe the origin of life, of man, and the Incarnation, respectively.[5] Yet here, we must also be clear where Benedict's approach sharply diverges from that of ID: he does not look to instances of causal discontinuity or gaps within the order of nature to locate the presence of God's causal hand in evolutionary history. Indeed, Benedict once said to his former graduate students at a meeting on evolution, "[It is n]ot as if I wanted now to cram the dear Lord into these gaps: He is too great to be able to find lodgings in such

---

*Intelligent Design* (New York: HarperOne, 2013); Meyer, "Intelligent Design," in *Four Views on Creation, Evolution, and Intelligent Design*, ed. J.B. Stump (Grand Rapids, MI: Zondervan, 2017), 177–230. Further, Michael Chaberek, OP, has endeavored to make the case that the Angelic Doctor would have been attracted to the ID project in his *Aquinas and Evolution* (British Columbia: The Chartwell Press, 2017), 161–212. I have found that the latter's approach is refuted well by the various authors I will cite in this chapter. For the most direct response to Chaberek from other Thomists, see "A Thomistic Response to the Intelligent Design (ID) Proposal" and "In Defense of Thomistic Evolution," in Austriaco, *Thomistic Evolution*, 183–188 and 195–208.

4. For instance, in 1999 Cardinal Ratzinger gave a speech at the Sorbonne in which he observed that evolutionary theory still has not fully explained the process of transition from micro to macroevolution (*le problème se signale lors du passage de la micro à la macro-évolution*). The English translation of the address reproduced here is taken from Ratzinger, *Truth and Tolerance*, 180. To bolster this point, Ratzinger refers to a seminal article by Eörs Szathmary and John Maynard Smith—both biologists who espouse an all-embracing theory of evolution. In their work, these authors proceed to detail eight major transitions in evolutionary history (e.g., eukaryotic cells, multicellular organisms, DNA, chromosomes, sexuality, human language) and how each involves important changes in the way information is stored, transmitted, and translated—changes that have yet to be fully understood and which they seek to explain through their work. See Eörs Szathmary and John Maynard Smith, "The Major Evolutionary Transitions," *Nature* 374 (1995): 227–232. See also their coauthored books *The Major Transitions in Evolution* (Oxford: Oxford University Press, 1995) and *The Origins of Life* (Oxford: Oxford University Press, 2000), 16. In contrast with proponents of ID, these biologists hold that the major transitions in question are still to be explained through natural mechanisms without need for an appeal to divine intervention or an extraordinary instance of design. Indeed, they specifically take up the topic of the "extremely sophisticated complex of organs" that is the visual system, i.e., the eye, the optic nerve, and associated brain regions. Szathmary and Smith, *The Origins of Life*, 152–53.

5. Ratzinger, *Introduction to Christianity*, 238–39 (*Einführung in das Christentum*, 225). For more on Ratzinger's appropriation of Teilhard de Chardin's language of life in Christ as mankind's definitive evolutionary "leap," see Ramage, *The Experiment of Faith*, 106–108, 123, 147n28 and Benedict XVI, *Jesus of Nazareth: Holy Week: From the Entrance into Jerusalem to the Resurrection* (San Francisco: Ignatius Press, 2011), 246–47. See also Benedict XVI, Easter Vigil Homily (April 15, 2006). The Vatican text of this homily translates both of the above German terms, each of which appears twice within the same homily, with the English word "leap." In the German, both *Sprung* ("leap") and *Durchbruch* ("breakthrough") are employed. In the Italian in which the homily was delivered, the word *salto* ("leap") is used four times as "leap" is in English. It may interest some readers to notes that Benedict describes the Resurrection itself as something of a "radical evolutionary leap" (*eine radikalen Mutationssprung*) in Benedict XVI, *Jesus of Nazareth: Holy Week*, 274 [*Jesus von Nazareth: Vom Einzug in Jerusalem bis zur Auferstehung* (Freiburg: Herder, 2011), 299].

gaps."[6] This view is consistent with that of his predecessor John Paul II, who also deployed the language of an "ontological leap" to describe the "moment of transition to the spiritual." According to this pontiff, the "ontological discontinuity" that separates us from our prehuman ancestors (e.g., our capacity for metaphysical knowledge, self-awareness, self-reflection, moral conscience, freedom, aesthetic and religious experience) does not negate the "physical continuity" by which we arose from them—signs of which are discernable at the empirical level through the various "sciences of observation [that] describe and measure the multiple manifestations of life with increasing precision and correlate them with the timeline."[7]

We can gain further understanding of papal thought in relation to the design question by taking a look at the one place where he uses the actual expression "intelligent design." In a powerful homily inspired by St. Basil the Great's lambast of atheists in his day who imagined the universe to lack guidance and order, Benedict has this to say:

> How many these "some people" are today! Deceived by atheism they consider and seek to prove that it is scientific to think that all things lack guidance and order as though they were at the mercy of chance. The Lord through Sacred Scripture reawakens our reason which has fallen asleep and tells us: in the beginning was the creative Word. In the beginning the creative Word—this Word that created all things, that created this intelligent design [*progetto intelligente*] which is the cosmos is also love.[8]

However, the fact that Benedict uses the expression "intelligent design" here should not lead us to equivocate on the meaning of this expression and jump to the conclusion that he would be very interested in the ID movement's specific endeavor. For, in contrast with ID advocates, Benedict demonstrates no interest in pursuing arguments for the universe's intelligent basis based on instances of immense complexity in the created order.[9] While well informed in the sciences, the emeritus pontiff is content to follow the consensus of scientific inquiry over the past two centuries, leaving study of the precise mechanisms behind evolution's "leaps" to the competence of the scientific community. This approach is echoed in the 2002 work of the ITC, *Communion and Stewardship: Human Persons Created in the Image of God.* Stamped with the seal of approval of its then-president Cardinal Joseph Ratzinger, this document echoes the emeritus pontiff's thought that, while scientific debate will inevitably ensue at the level of particulars, the important thing is that the whole

---

6. Benedict XVI, Comments of September 2, 2006, in *Creation and Evolution: A Conference with Pope Benedict XVI in Castel Gandolfo*, ed. Stephan Horn (San Francisco: Ignatius Press, 2008), 144.

7. John Paul II, Message to the Pontifical Academy of Sciences Plenary Session on "The Origins and Early Evolution of Life" (October 22, 1996), §6.

8. Benedict XVI, General Audience (November 9, 2005).

9. To borrow an expression from Michael Augros, Benedict takes what one might call an "an unusually undetailed approach" to the science of evolution. Augros, *Who Designed the Designer?* (San Francisco: Ignatius Press, 2015), 18.

dynamic of evolution is guided by God. While a statement of the ITC like this cannot be taken as perfectly representative of Ratzinger's mind, like Benedict, this document employs the word "design" to speak of a more fundamental order than that envisioned by the ID movement: the providential design of creation *as a whole*.[10]

Consistent with the Christian tradition at large, Benedict and those of us who are compelled by the framework of evolutionary creation perceive God's hand in the glorious power, beauty, and harmony of nature that we all experience everyday—even in those areas where science is able to provide a thorough natural explanation of life's intricate mechanisms.[11] In this, the emeritus pontiff's understanding of how we know that the universe is intelligently ordered is much the same as St. Paul's when he said that all people ought to be able to know God's existence by simply looking at the things he has made: "Ever since the creation of the world his invisible nature, namely, his eternal power and deity, has been clearly perceived in the things that have been made" (Rm 1:20). Or, to take a page from the Old Testament text from which Paul is drawing in Romans, evidence of the Creator is to be found not in complex minute structures but instead in very common phenomena for which we now have good scientific explanations: "fire," "wind," "swift air," "the circle of the stars," "turbulent water," and "luminaries of heaven" (Wis 13:2).[12] In sum, it should not take an advanced degree in biochemistry or physics to conclude that the universe is governed by divine providence. Our faith tradition rationally affirmed the truth of God's existence from its beginnings—long before the advent of modern science with its ability to examine the universe's complexity at the microscopic level.[13]

---

10. International Theological Commission, *Communion and Stewardship*, §68.

11. Early in his *Summa Theologiae*, Thomas Aquinas addresses the challenge that God need not exist since "everything we see in the world can be accounted for by other principles." In other words, the objector alleges that providing a streamlined natural explanation of things in this world that allows for no physical explanatory gaps would seem to do away with the need for God. In reply, it is telling that Aquinas does not challenge the possibility that a completely natural explanation of the workings of nature might be given. Rather, he emphasizes that, regardless of the answer to this question, the fact remains that "whatever is done by nature must needs be traced back to God, as to its first cause . . . for all things that are changeable and capable of defect must be traced back to an immovable and self-necessary first principle." Aquinas, *ST* I, q. 2, a. 3, obj. 2 and ad 2

12. Wisdom continues: "And if men were amazed at their power and working, let them perceive from them how much more powerful is he who formed them. For from the greatness and beauty of created things comes a corresponding perception of their Creator" (Wis 13:4–5).

13. Aquinas's "fifth way," for instance, has nothing to do with proving God's existence through unique instances of complexity in the universe that have emerged over the ages. Rather, his is an argument from the universe's teleology as a whole—that all things lacking intelligence must be directed to an end by another. The entire universe, not just its most complex regions, is radically contingent upon God for its very existence as well as order and development within it in every age. See Aquinas, *ST*, I, q. 2, a. 3. For another helpful articulation of the above point in response to ID advocate Stephen Meyer, see BioLogos president Deborah Haarsma, "Response from Evolutionary Creation," in *Four Views on Creation, Evolution, and Intelligent Design*, 226. I have also drawn here from an excellent articulation of the matter in Stephen Barr, "The End of Intelligent Design?," *First Things* (February 9, 2010). In an essay that is at once very respectful and critical of ID, Francis Beckwith also discusses ID's claims in relation to the Christian tradition at large. Francis Beckwith, "How to Be an Anti-Intelligent Design Advocate,"

To be sure, we ought to marvel at the stunning complexity of nature, but Catholic spirituality teaches us that we also ought to marvel at the ordinary. As G.K. Chesterton remarked, "We should always endeavor to wonder at the permanent thing, not at the mere exception. We should be startled by the sun, and not by the eclipse. We should wonder less at the earthquake, and wonder more at the earth."[14] For, if we seek God's presence above all in the exceptional or miraculous, this has the ironic effect of denigrating the goodness of the ordinary way God operates in the world and in our daily lives. Jeremy Holmes poignantly diagnoses this problem as follows:

> If we think of God as one being among other beings, then we incline toward mechanistic deism: we suppose that God made a universe which now stands on its own without him, we imagine that God intervenes in this free-standing universe only occasionally, and we assume that when he does intervene it is from the outside, like a car mechanic working on an engine. We limit God to the spectacular, like miracles, and we divorce him from everyday things like rocks falling, plants growing, and people riding bicycles. We suppose that a rock flying up would be God's action while a rock falling down would just be the rock's action.[15]

Such disenchantment of nature has also been called "spiritual materialism," for in the name of devotion it unwittingly sets God aside from everyday life.[16] On the other hand, the idea that the evolutionary dynamic has an internal integrity that does not require God to tweak it at certain points is one of the most beautiful contributions that evolutionary biology has made to Christian theology. Such an approach is to my mind deeply Christian, for it confirms that God is present and active everywhere, even in its most ordinary, simple, and seemingly mundane aspects. In other words, it reminds us that we do not need to go looking for God in great signs or travel across the globe to find him. He is here, already present in everyday things which, when properly approached, can lead us to contemplation of their almighty source.

---

*University of St. Thomas Journal of Law & Public Policy* 4.1 (2009–2010): 35–65 at 52–53, citing Stephen Meyer, "DNA and Other Designs," *First Things* (April 2000).

14. G.K. Chesterton, *Illustrated London News* column "Fanaticism in the Suburbs" (October 21, 1905), in Vol. 27 of *The Collected Works of G.K. Chesterton* (San Francisco: Ignatius Press, 1986), 41. See also Chesterton, Letter of July 8, 1899, in Maisie Ward, *Gilbert Keith Chesterton* (New York: Sheed and Ward, 1943), 97, where the literary giant urges us by his own childlike example of wonder to be intoxicated by the "startling wetness of water . . . the fieriness of fire, the steeliness of steel, and the unutterable muddiness of mud."

15. Jeremy Holmes, *Cur Deus Verba?*, 88. For a similar critique of an approach that thinks of God mechanistically as intervening in the universe from the outside as one (albeit higher) phenomenon that produces other phenomena, see Henri de Lubac, *The Discovery of God* (Grand Rapids, MI: Eerdmans, 1996), 63–64n17.

16. Mark Johnston, *Saving God: Religion after Idolatry* (Princeton, NJ: Princeton University Press, 2011), 51, 121–22.

# GOD VERSUS NATURE?

As we have just seen, the Church's International Theological Commission did not demonstrate much interest in the ID endeavor when it had the occasion to address the topic under the leadership of then-Cardinal Ratzinger. The commission did, however, take notice that a growing number of Christians have been focusing their efforts against consensus evolutionary theory on seeking out physical structures that exhibit such intricacy that they cannot have arisen through the processes of natural selection and random genetic variation. The ITC offers the following response to this viewpoint:

> Many neo-Darwinian scientists, *as well as some of their critics*, have concluded that, if evolution is a radically contingent materialistic process driven by natural selection and random genetic variation, then there can be no place in it for divine providential causality. . . . But it is important to note that, according to the Catholic understanding of divine causality, true contingency in the created order is not incompatible with a purposeful divine providence. Divine causality and created causality radically differ in kind and not only in degree.[17]

The ITC here insists that divine providence and contingency within creation are not in competition with one another, because the causality at work within each occurs at a radically different level of being. Andrew Jaeger explains this point well with the help of a light-hearted analogy:

> God is not something that *tinkers around* in the world, but rather what gives rise to the existence of things *other than him* that can tinker around in the world. Therefore, God the Creator is not a "God of the Gaps." God is not a thing to search for to explain an event as one would search for a baseball upon seeing a broken window. Broken windows are explained by the activity of creatures not the activity of God. God gives rise to the *existence* of baseballs, he doesn't do baseball actions, he leaves that to baseballs! However, he does give rise to baseballs being able to do baseball actions, but once again he doesn't do the baseball action himself. What we are seeing is that to talk of God doing something and to talk of creatures doing something is to talk about two completely different manners of "doing" which are so different that they cannot even possibly compete with each.[18]

Indeed, divine and creaturely causality are of such different orders that we must always remain cautious even when envisioning God's causality as occurring as a different kind or on a different plane than that of creatures, for the temptation inevitably arises to picture God as just another, albeit higher, cause within creation (a point we will examine more deeply below with the help of an analogy from the arts).

---

17. International Theological Commission, *Communion and Stewardship*, §69 (emphasis added). See also Aquinas, *Summa Theologiae*, I, q. 22, a. 4 ad 1.

18. Andrew Jaeger, "To-Be or Not-To-Be? The Existence and Non-Existence of God," Lecture at Ashland University (October 19, 2020).

Ironically, the ITC notes, some Christians miss this point and thereby share some of the same problematic assumptions with the philosophy they are trying to combat. Brad Gregory aptly diagnoses this issue: "Insofar as proponents of intelligent design posit normally autonomous natural processes usually devoid of God's influence, they share important assumptions with the New Atheists."[19] The mistaken assumption here is that divine and creaturely causality are mutually exclusive. In other words, on this view, *anything explainable by natural means is not caused by God, and what nature causes, God does not.* Catholic physicist Stephen Barr describes this regrettable scenario as a "zero-sum game between God and nature" in which "[s]cience must fail for ID to succeed" (and *vice versa*), adding that this conception of design "plays right into the hands of atheists."[20] Because they lack a robust appreciation of God's omnipresent causality within creation, Brad Gregory adds, "intelligent design proponents scramble to find remaining places for supernatural intervention," mistakenly assuming that "God, conceived in spatial and quasi-spatial terms, needs 'room' to be God—which is precisely what traditional Christian theology says God does not need."[21] To this, Nicanor Austriaco adds:

> In the end, from the Thomistic perspective, the ID proposal is a misguided distraction. ID proponents claim that irreducible complexity is a sign for intelligent design. It is a sign of God's creative hand. However, like their counterparts pushing an atheist and a naturalist account of the world, they mistakenly

---

19. Brad Gregory, "Science v. Religion? The Insights and Oversights of the 'New Atheists,'" *Logos: A Journal of Catholic Thought and Culture* 12.4 (Fall 2009): 17–55 at 17.

20. Stephen Barr, "The End of Intelligent Design," in *The Believing Scientist*, 72.

21. Brad Gregory, "Science v. Religion?," 41. For another iteration of this point, see Conor Cunningham, *Darwin's Pious Idea: Why the Ultra-Darwinists and Creationists Both Get It Wrong* (Grand Rapids, MI: Eerdmans, 2010), 276. This "room" that Gregory mentions is conceived in different ways by Christians who are drawn to the ID approach. Some think of God intervening within creation by moving its various parts around in order to create complex mechanisms that would not be able to develop through natural means. Others like Michael Behe have moved away from having God intervening or tinkering with the cosmos, holding instead that the universe develops largely via natural processes, only that the whole universe was fine-tuned from the beginning in such a way that it would produce certain nonrandom mutations. Behe, *The Edge of Evolution*, 229–32. This is a step in the right direction and may seem that it alleviates the problem of interventionism within ID, but the concern raised by Bradley and others is that this version of ID's designer ends up looking more like the god of Deism rather than of orthodox Christianity. On this score, incisive criticisms of Deist tendencies within ID have been offered by Conor Cunningham and Edward Feser. See Feser, *The Last Superstition: A Refutation of the New Atheism* (South Bend, IN: St. Augustine's Press, 2008), 110–15 and Cunningham, *Darwin's Pious Idea*, 275–79. Related to the above, ID proponent William Dembski has endeavored to distance himself from a demiurgic picture of God moving particles around, instead locating instances of IC in particular arrangements of genetic information imparted directly to creatures by the divine designer. William Dembski, *The Design Revolution*, 152–53. Similarly, ID advocate Stephen Meyer argues that an intelligent cause must be directly responsible for certain "complex, specified information" within the cosmos, insisting that ID does not challenge evolution's findings regarding life's common ancestry but only the atheistic assumption that the cause of biological change over time is wholly blind and undirected. Meyer, "Intelligent Design," 180.

assume that God works in his creation primarily by pushing and pulling atoms and molecules like a force, generally, and by assembling and disassembling living systems, more specifically. This god of ID is a small and puny god!"[22]

Like the authors I have just cited, Austriaco does not deny ID's observation that the world is breathtakingly complex. His point is that overemphasizing this point unfortunately leads many to conceive of God as just another physical force operating in the world, and moreover that the issue of complexity in nature is irrelevant to the question of God's existence.

Not only does looking to isolated aspects of creation as proof for divine intelligence miss the point, to make matters worse, it can actually backfire. If God's action is confined to phenomena we cannot explain, then his existence is held hostage by every new discovery we might make. It is as if our having the ability to explain the process of photosynthesis, for example, means that God is not involved in causing it. Indeed, atheist scientist Stephen Hawking makes this very argument in alleging that God is not necessary since, in principle, we could give a completely natural account of causation within the universe. Yet, from a Catholic perspective, the need for divine causality is in no way diminished just because God acts through creatures and does not need to "intervene" in the universe's natural processes. For, even in a scenario where God never intervenes in the world and all its rules are preprogrammed, *we would still have to account for the provenance of the program—* as well as explain why it continues to run even now. In this respect, the Catholic therefore need not entirely disagree with atheist biologist Richard Dawkins, who writes that—if God exists—what he made was more like a "recipe" or a computer program for controlling the universe's development which, once operational, works through self-assembly and whose continued maintenance does not require interventions from the outside.[23]

Contrary to Dawkins, however, the God of Christian metaphysics would still be God even if we could give an account of every step of our universe's evolutionary recipe. Indeed, this would be true even if the "program" were all that existed—that is, if the Big Bang never occurred and all that existed were a collection of physical laws and quantum states but no physical universe. For, even then, we would still have to account for why there are any laws or states—any *anything*—in the first place. Herbert McCabe captures the above point and other issues we have discussed when he states:

22. Austriaco, "A Thomistic Response to the Intelligent Design Proposal," in *Thomistic Evolution*, 186. See also Austriaco, "How Does God Create through Evolution?," in *Thomistic Evolution*, 152: "When God acts as an efficient cause in creating a creature, he does not 'make it move' as creaturely agents like human engineers make the things that they "create" move. Rather God makes the creature movable by nature so that it can move itself." On ID being a distraction from the real issues at hand, see also David Bentley Hart, *The Experience of God: Being, Consciousness, Bliss* (New Haven, CT: Yale University Press, 2013), 37.

23. Dawkins, *The Greatest Show on Earth*, 213.

[I]t is clear that God cannot *interfere* in the universe, not because he has not the power but because, so to speak, he had too much; to interfere you have to be an alternative to, or alongside, what you are interfering with. If God is the cause of everything, there is nothing that he is alongside. Obviously God makes no difference to the universe; I mean by this that we do not appeal specifically to God to explain why the universe is this way rather than that, for this we need only appeal to explanations within the universe. For this reason there can, it seems to me, by no feature of the universe which indicates it is God-made. What God accounts for is that the universe is there instead of nothing.[24]

What is more, if we someday find ourselves capable of proving that the Big Bang was a natural event and that our present universe did in fact spontaneously arise by means of quantum fluctuations as Hawking postulates, even this would not disprove its dependence on God. For, as Stephen Barr notes, the no-universe state envisioned by Hawking is not truly *nothing at all* but rather a very specific *state* of a definite quantum system governed by definite laws. To illustrate, Barr offers an analogy:

There is a difference between my having a bank account with zero dollars in it, and my having no bank account at all. As far as my finances go, they may both be said to be "nothing" or "no money"; but there is a big difference. A bank account, even one with zero dollars in it, is something. It presupposes that there is a bank and that I have some contract with that bank. Those facts presuppose, in turn, that a monetary system and a legal system are in place. . . . In the same way, even to talk about a "state with zero universes" presupposes a great deal.[25]

All this is to say that the atheist's dismissal of the Christian doctrine of creation out of nothing (*creatio ex nihilo*) becomes a lot less attractive once we realize that he has seriously equivocated on the meaning of the word "nothing." Applying Barr's analogy, we may say that Hawking is interested in the observation that money seems to have spontaneously popped into his bank account, whereas the doctrine *creatio ex nihilo* is concerned with how it is that there is a bank account in the first place. Yet, Hawking's grave mistake was by no means unavoidable, for earlier in his career he himself had acknowledged that a theory in physics is "just a set of rules and equations" and that empirical science itself cannot answer what it is that "breathes fire into the equations and makes a universe for them to describe."[26]

---

24. Herbert McCabe, OP, *God Matters* (London: Mowbray, 2000), 6. See also Brian Davies, OP, *Philosophy of Religion: A Guide and Anthology* (Oxford: Oxford University Press, 2000), 199.

25. Barr, *The Believing Scientist*, 134–35. See also Barr, "Attempts to Explain Cosmogony Scientifically," *Church Life Journal* (September 21, 2018). Importantly, in his capacity as a physicist Barr does not quibble with Hawking's science. According to Barr, Hawking's notion of a quantum creation of universes is not without merit, as it is proposed by way of an analogy with the well-understood phenomenon of quantum creation of particles. The real problem occurs when Hawking stops doing science and incorrectly infers materialist philosophy from it.

26. Hawking, *A Brief History of Time: From the Big Bang to Black Holes* (London: Bantam, 1988), 174.

At this point, the reader may be wondering how all this talk of the Big Bang and creation out of nothing relate to evolutionary biology. The connection is this: if even the origin of our physical universe might one day be explicable in natural terms, so too may the entire process of evolution and natural selection (whose natural processes we already know quite a lot about). This being the case, the pivotal truth for our purposes is that the ability to explain evolutionary history without recourse to divine intervention does not diminish the need for God any more than, say, knowing the mechanisms of fetal development makes it untrue that God "knit us together in our mothers' wombs" (Ps 139:13) or that knowing about gravity means that Dante was wrong to conclude *The Divine Comedy* by referring to "the Love that moves the sun and the other stars."[27] To capture this point with an analogy that I will develop in greater detail later in this chapter, the possibility of eventually being able to give a natural account of the Big Bang or evolution would not do away with the need for a Creator any more than acknowledging that the opening sentences of *Hamlet* obey the laws of English suggests that the masterpiece wrote itself.[28] Indeed, Barr observes that neither our universe nor a literary masterpiece would depend any less upon its author if it had a circular plot with no clear beginning or end.[29]

Yet, while providing a natural account of the universe's origin and its continuous evolution would not present a huge problem for the traditional Catholic

---

27. Dante Alighieri, *Paradise*, trans. Anthony M. Esolen (New York: Modern Library, 2003), 359 at 33:145.

28. Thus Barr: "That the Big Bang was very likely a 'natural event,' in the sense of obeying the laws of physics, is not a theological problem. It is like saying that the first sentences of Hamlet obey the laws of English grammar just as do all the other sentences in the play. One would expect nothing else. It is only a problem if one falls into crude anthropomorphism and imagines creation to be a physical process, like God setting a lighted match to a fuse. But that is not the Christian conception of Creation. Creation is the act by which God gives reality to the universe, and makes it not merely a hypothetical or possible universe, but an actually existing universe. He does not supply energy, as a match does to an explosive, he supplies reality. God supplies this reality equally to every part of the universe—all events at all times and places—just as Shakespeare equally brought forth every word of the play Hamlet." Barr, *The Believing Scientist*, 127–28.

29. Barr, *The Believing Scientist*, 124, 127. The implication of this part of the analogy is that, even if it turns out that our universe had no beginning in time, it would still owe its entire existence to God and still rightly be said to have been created "out of nothing." For an excellent treatment of the Big Bang in relation to Aquinas's understanding of *creatio ex nihilo*, see William Carroll, "Thomas Aquinas and Big Bang Cosmology," *Sapientia* 53 (203):73–95. Among other things, Carroll shows how Aquinas eschews the common mistake of confusing the question of the universe's beginning (a temporal event) with the question of its origin (the source of its very existence). Against the atheistic claim that God would not be necessary if the world were eternal, Carroll expounds Aquinas's view that the universe would still depend on God for its very being even if the universe had no temporal beginning. Stephen Barr writes along the same lines: "[T]he existence of the universe must have a cause—namely God—but that does not necessarily imply that the existence of the universe had a beginning. Creation has to do with why something exists at all, not with how long it has existed. One may put it another way: there is a difference between the beginning of a thing and the origin of a thing." Barr, *The Believing Scientist*, 124. See also Hart, *The Experience of God*, 41. For more along these lines, see also Thomas Joseph White, OP, *The Light of Christ: An Introduction to Catholicism* (Washington, D.C.: The Catholic University of America Press, 2017), 88–89.

doctrine of creation, it *would* present a tremendous problem for one whose arguments for God depend upon the presence of IC structures in the universe. Hart thus observes:

> But—and here is the crucial issue—those who argue for the existence of God principally from some feature or other of apparent cosmic design are guilty of the same conceptual confusion; they make a claim like Hawking's seem solvent, or at least relevant, because they themselves have not advanced beyond the demiurgic [i.e., mechanistic and this-worldly] picture of God. By giving the name "God" to whatever as yet unknown agent or property or quality might account for this or that particular appearance of design, they have produced a picture of God that it is conceivable the sciences could someday genuinely make obsolete, because it really is a kind of rival explanation to the explanations the sciences seek. This has never been true of the God described in the great traditional metaphysical systems.[30]

Accordingly, not only is it probably a waste of time trying to prove this or that feature of the created order exhibits IC (and, by extension, evidence for God), it can be positively counterproductive to do so. In other words, trying to save God by finding him in creation's alleged gaps can end up providing fodder to atheists who are happy to show (and in some cases, have shown) that supposedly IC things like the eye, wing, and bacterial flagellum have in fact evolved. In other words, we are now aware of many so-called transitional forms that have filled in prior gaps within evolutionary history, thus illustrating that the stepping-stone of "half" an eye, wing, or the like—while not optimal—can be quite advantageous from a survival standpoint and thus selected for and refined over time.[31] It is probably better, therefore,

---

30. Hart, *The Experience of God*, 41. For another helpful critique of how ID's designer is different from the Creator of traditional Christian metaphysics, see William Carroll, "Creation, Evolution, and Thomas Aquinas," *Revue des Questions Scientifiques* 171 (4) 2000: 319–47. Without identifying ID specifically, Thomas Joseph White likewise observes a serious problem in trying to use gaps in the empirical sciences to prove God's existence. See White, *The Light of Christ*: 88–89.

31. Darwin himself was happy to point out the futility of believers insisting that evolution will never be able to explain a given physical phenomenon whose origin was traditionally understood in a supernatural manner. Though one may be put off by his demeanor, Darwin's words are not without merit: "Ignorance more frequently begets confidence than does knowledge. . . . It is those who know little, not those who know much, who so positively assert that this or that problem will never be solved by science." Darwin, *The Descent of Man, and Selection in Relation to Sex*, Vol. 1 (London: John Murray, 1871), 3. To this end, in a discussion of what he dubbed "organs of extreme perfection and complication," Darwin himself acknowledges that it seems absurd to say that the eye evolved by natural selection— after which he proceeds to outline how the eye evolved by gradual degrees. Darwin, *On the Origin of Species*, 186.

For a more recent narrative of how eyes, wings, bacterial flagella, and the like evolved over the course of life's history, see Dawkins, *The God Delusion*, 148–51. With his usual bite, he remarks: "The fact that so many people have been dead wrong over these obvious cases should serve to warn us of other examples that are less obvious, such as the cellular and biochemical cases now being touted by those creationists who shelter under the politically expedient euphemism of 'intelligent design theorists.'" Dawkins, *The God Delusion*, 150.

to follow the lead of St. John Henry Newman, who said: "I believe in design because I believe in God; not in God because I see design."[32] We might also recall the following words of a Catholic author writing on the subject of religion and evolution almost a century ago but which are as timely as ever:

> If there is any one lesson that the progress of science teaches with convincing thoroughness, it is the positive danger of searching for some weak spot in the scientific scheme and saying, "Here at least is one place where you must admit the need of God." For, judging from the history of scientific progress, more than likely the next few decades will find the weak spot converted into a veritable Gibraltar.[33]

In sum, this is just another way of stating the truth that atheists and Christians alike are mistaken when they assume that God's action and natural processes are mutually exclusive. In reality, God and nature always work together in evolution, and an absolutely unguided evolutionary dynamic—one that falls outside the bounds of divine providence—could not exist in the first place for the very reason that nothing can exist apart from the governance of God. As the ITC says, "[E]ven the outcome of a truly contingent natural process can nonetheless fall within God's providential plan for creation. . . . Divine causality can be active in a process that is both contingent and guided. Any evolutionary mechanism that is contingent can

---

For a forceful Thomistic refutation of ID and exploration of a mechanism that suggests the bacterial flagellum is not irreducibly complex, see "A Thomistic Response to the Intelligent Design (ID) Proposal," 183–188 and "In Defense of Thomistic Evolution," 195–208. In brief, Austriaco finds it noteworthy that the flagellar motor is a hollow tube rather than a solid whip-like structure that would have made a more efficient propeller. The most logical explanation for a bacterial flagellum being hollow, Austriaco observes, is that it evolved from a pump that was hollow. On this point, see also Brown University biologist Kenneth Miller, "The Flagellum Unspun: The Collapse of 'Irreducible Complexity,'" in *Debating Design: From Darwin to DNA*, eds. William Dembski and Michael Ruse (London: Cambridge University Press, 2004), 81–97; Miller, *Finding Darwin's God: A Scientist's Search for Common Ground Between God and Evolution* (New York: Perennial, 2007). For descriptions of how blood clotting and the flagellum could have evolved through selection, see Kenneth Miller, *Only a Theory: Evolution and the Battle for America's Soul* (New York: Penguin, 2008) and Jerry Coyne, *Why Evolution is True* (New York: Penguin, 2009), 140.

In another article, Austriaco grants the ID movement's observation that great leaps sometimes do occur over the course of evolutionary history, yet he denies that these are due to divine intervention, noting: "Recent research that has uncovered some classes of genetic mutations that do change the body plan quite radically and relatively quickly suggesting that any apparent sudden changes in body form could still be explained by standard biological mechanisms." Austriaco and Michael Loudin, "Understanding the Controversy Over Intelligent Design and the Acceptability of Intelligent Causality in Science," *Forum Teologiczne* 9: 29–39 at 34. For other thorough rebuttals of ID's scientific claims, see Dawkins, *The Greatest Show on Earth*, 355–72 and McKnight and Venema, *Adam and the Genome*, 67–92.

32. John Henry Newman, Letter to J. Walker of Scarborough on Darwin's Theory of Evolution, in *The Letters and Diaries of John Henry Newman*, eds. C.S. Dessain and T. Gornall, Vol. XXIV (Oxford: Clarendon Press, 1973), 77–78.

33. John O'Brien, *Evolution and Religion* (New York: Century Co., 1932), 228.

only be contingent because God made it so."[34] Or, to put it in the words of Francis Collins, the Christian biologist who headed the Human Genome Project, "[E]volution could appear to us to be driven by chance, but from God's perspective the outcome would be entirely specified."[35]

It turns out, then, that the phenomenon of chance's causal role in our world (e.g., the random genetic mutations that drive evolution) is itself willed by divine design. As Michael Dodds puts it, "God's causality acts precisely through the 'non-causality' of chance . . . through the indeterminism of nature in its very indeterminism."[36] Randomness does not exclude the universe's First Cause from the evolutionary dynamic, for, as Catholic biologist Gerard Verschuuren observes well:

> Evolutionary theory cannot even explain why there is evolution to begin with. . . . When scientists removed "purposes" from scientific discourse, they removed them as secondary causes, but they left their reference to the First Cause untouched. So they did not make purposes disappear completely; they just moved them from inside to outside the scientific domain—from the context of secondary causes to the context of the First Cause. . . .
>
> In a nutshell, all organisms may have come through a process of evolution, but ultimately they must come from Creation, or else they couldn't be here at all. Whereas evolution tells us that everything comes from something else, Creation tells us that everything would be nothing if it didn't come from God. An evolutionary world depends on God as much as would a world without evolution. Evolution follows the laws laid out in Creation, but Creation is the origin and destination of evolution. Humanity may have come here through evolution, but ultimately it comes from God."[37]

On this subject, Verschuuren offers an analogy that explains how it is that the randomness of evolutionary change fits within the larger plan of divine design.

---

34. International Theological Commission, *Communion and Stewardship*, §69. See also Aquinas, *ST*, I, q. 22, a. 2. What the ITC is suggesting here aligns well with what Aquinas has to say about the place of contingent events of chance in relation to God's providence. For a helpful discussion of this topic, see Mariusz Tabaczek, OP, "What Do God and Creatures Really Do in an Evolutionary Change? Divine Concurrence and Transformism from the Thomistic Perspective," *American Catholic Philosophical Quarterly* (2019): 445–82.

35. Francis Collins, *The Language of God*, 205.

36. Michael Dodds, OP, *Unlocking Divine Action: Contemporary Science and Thomas Aquinas* (Washington, D.C.: The Catholic University of America Press, 2017), 220. Moreover, as the Angelic Doctor writes, some things can be said to occur by chance when considering them in light of the particular order from which they escape, yet on the more universal level they still fall within God's providential plan and conduce to his higher end for creation. Aquinas, *Summa Contra Gentiles*, II, ch. 94, 11; Aquinas, *ST*, I, q. 103, a. 7 ad 2. Although chance is not a *per se* or full-fledged cause, it does serve as a *per accidens* cause insofar as it occurs in conjunction with a bona fide principle of causation. A more detailed explanation of this can be found in Mariusz Tabaczek, OP, "What Do God and Creatures Really Do in an Evolutionary Change?," 445–82. Pope Francis also captured these points in his Address before the Pontifical Academy of Sciences (October 27, 2014).

37. Gerard Verschuuren, *How Science Points to God* (Manchester, NH: Sophia Institute Press, 2020), 106.

Asking whether the path of evolution that led to humanity was an entirely random process, he responds that perhaps the best we can say is that it was a process that meandered like a river: as a river follows a path of least resistance governed by the topography of the landscape, so too does the 'stream' of evolution follow a path that is regulated by the design of our universe. It therefore does not 'flow' in a purely random manner, for cosmic design created a 'bed' in which the stream of evolution meanderingly found its culminating destination in the rise of humanity."[38]

Another valuable contribution that Verschuuren makes is to explain what it means for mutations to occur randomly or by chance. Mutations are "spontaneous" in the sense that they just pop up. They are "unpredictable," for one does not know where they will next strike in the DNA. They are "arbitrary," because they affect good and bad alike. And, they are "aimless," for they occur without any clear connection to an organism's immediate or future needs. That said, Verschuuren adds, "randomness cannot steer evolution in just any direction. Certain directions are not possible, because randomness is kept in tow by the laws of nature."[39] After saying this, Verschuuren proceeds to detail precisely how it is that a more fundamental order in nature governs the way mutations work:

> [C]hance events occur *within* nature, and therefore must be a secondary cause. The real First Cause can use random secondary causes similar to the way we can use dice to determine who wins a game. So when the outcome of a mutation is considered random, that does not tell us that God has nothing to do with it. Even random events such as mutations are only possible because they depend on a First Cause and were created by a First Cause, God—otherwise, they could not even exist.
>
> This suggests that God and randomness are not in conflict with each other and do not exclude each other. The role of randomness concerns the relationship between secondary causes, whereas the 'role' of God is about the relationship of secondary causes to the First Cause. Therefore, anything that seems to be random from a scientific point of view may very well be related to God at the same time.[40]

All this is to say that chance *versus* purpose is the wrong way of framing the issue of divine causality in relation to evolution. In reality, evolution is a matter of chance *and* purpose.

---

38. Verschuuren, *How Science Points to God*, 102.

39. Verschuuren, *How Science Points to God*, 94.

40. Verschuuren, *How Science Points to God*, 96–97. Summarizing, he states: "Put in an image, natural selection is only the editor, not the author, of evolutionary change." Verschuuren, *How Science Points to God*, 99.

## GOD WORKS THROUGH THE NATURAL WORLD, NOT "NEXT TO" ITS EVOLUTIONARY DYNAMIC

Having discussed the problems with ID's understanding of the relationship of God and nature, we are now in a position to unfold the emeritus pontiff's understanding of how divine action operates in evolution. In what follows, I will suggest that Benedict's principles offer a robust alternative to the ID approach and an outstanding resource for carrying forward the Catholic tradition's theology of creation when it comes to the topic of evolution. The emeritus pontiff is well aware that evolution challenges our existing analogies for how God works in the world, and below we explore what Benedict proposes as alternatives. First, though, we must acquire a sense of his overall view of the matter.

Ratzinger's approach to divine causality in creation starts with a negative: namely, his insistence that we do not conceive of God as creator "according to the model of a craftsman." Moreover, he emphasizes that the creation of man's spirit is "least of all to be imagined as an artisan[al] activity of God, who suddenly began tinkering [*hantieren*] with the world."[41] By using this language, the emeritus pontiff makes it clear that he does not want us to construe God as a demiurge— that is, a divine machinist. One problem with such a picture of God is that it envisions him inhabiting and acting in the cosmos along the same plane of being as creatures, thus making him fundamentally just one being (albeit higher) among other beings. Moreover, a demiurge creates the world and then leaves it on its own, perhaps occasionally dipping into cosmic processes to keep the engine of nature humming. Otherwise, though, this sort of creator is absent from his world.[42] In rejecting this view, Ratzinger's approach resonates with that of Aquinas, who rejected the image of God as a home builder; for, once a home is built (his "creation" completed), the home ceases to have any relation of dependence to him. By extension, creation would cease to exist if God were not continually present to it at all times.[43]

Further countering the view that God generally allows nature to act entirely on its own without his help while sometimes dropping in to interrupt its dynamic, Ratzinger applies his approach to the creation of the first human or humans. What this would have looked like, he argues, can be grasped by looking at what happens in the creation of every human today. It is a marvel, he says, that the infusion of the human soul occurs "not next to" [*nicht neben*] but rather "precisely in" [*gerade in*] the processes of a living being, i.e., the biological process by which a sperm and

---

41. Ratzinger, "Belief in Creation and the Theory of Evolution," 141 ["Schöpfungsglaube und Evolutionstheorie," in *Dogma Und Verkündigung*, 159].

42. I have drawn the "dipping" expression from Abigail Favale, "Does Darwinian Evolution Petrify God's Image?," *Church Life Journal* (October 5, 2018).

43. Aquinas, *In I Sent.*, in *S. Thomae Aquinatis Ordinis Praedicatorum . . . Scriptum super libros sententiarum Magistri Petri Lombardi episcopi Parisiensis* (Parisiis: Lethielleux, 1929–1947), dist. 37, q. 1, a. 1, resp. On this point, see also Carroll, "Creation, Evolution, and Thomas Aquinas," 319–47.

egg come together to form an embryo.[44] This private writing of Ratzinger also coheres well with the Ratzinger-led ITC when it describes God as the "cause not only of existence but also the cause of *causes*," adding that "God's action does not displace or supplant the activity of creaturely causes, but enables them to act according to their natures."[45] Framing the dynamic in this way reflects Aquinas's understanding of God's creative activity, which the Angelic Doctor sees to consist primarily in giving being to creatures and *endowing them with natures*—the specific capacities or source of actions that enable creatures to *move themselves* to their proper ends.[46] In other words, from a Thomistic perspective one might say that God causes new patterns and organisms through evolution "by bringing about the entirety of evolution, in which each particular pattern is a component."[47]

---

44. Ratzinger, "Man between Reproduction and Creation: Theological Questions on the Origin of Human Life," in *Joseph Ratzinger in* Communio: *Anthropology and Culture,* vol. 2 (Grand Rapids, MI: Eerdmans, 2013), 79 ["Der Mensch zwischen Reproduktion und Schöpfung," *Internationale Katholische Zeitschrift* 1 (1989), 68].

45. International Theological Commission, *Communion and Stewardship,* §68. It is likely that Ratzinger himself likely had little to do with the drafting of this document, and there is no guarantee that he agreed with every single aspect of it. Nevertheless, I believe it is valuable to note affinities between the work of the ITC and that of Ratzinger; for, as its president, he would have intervened prior to publication had the draft contained any serious problems.

46. Nicanor Austriaco explains this well when he says that God does not cause a creature to move as creaturely agents like human engineers make the things that they "create" move. Instead, he continues, "The Creator God revealed in the sacred Scriptures creates through evolution primarily by giving existence to his creatures as individual members of a natural kind with specific capacities directed to a final end." Austriaco, "A Thomistic Response to the Intelligent Design Proposal," 247; Austriaco, "How Does God Create through Evolution?," 202. See also Aquinas, *ST,* I, q. 8, a. 3; I, q. 105, a. 5; Aquinas, *On the Power of God,* trans. English Dominican Fathers (Westminster, MD: Aeterna, 2015), 3.7. Accordingly, if we are to understand how God works through evolution, we would do well to steer clear of picturing God as acting upon creation from the outside as just another, albeit "higher," cause. Instead, we must begin to grasp that his transcendent causality works from the inside *precisely through* the natures of his creatures who are entirely dependent on his ongoing causality for their continued existence and ability to be the causes that they are.

47. Patrick Byrne, "Evolution, Randomness, and Divine Purpose: A Reply to Cardinal Schönborn," *Theological Studies,* 67.3 (2006): 653–65 at 663; Bernard Lonergan, *Insight: A Study of Human Understanding,* vol. 3 of *Collected Works of Bernard Lonergan,* ed. Frederick Crowe and Robert Doran (Toronto: University of Toronto, 1992), 688.

Byrne here is summarizing Bernard Lonergan's approach to evolution as evidenced in the above text. Whereas ID advocates attempt to show that this or that intelligible pattern in the natural world can be explained only by postulating the intervention of a divine designer, Patrick Byrne notes that Lonergan's "more fruitful path toward a valid argument from design . . . shifts the focus by asking whether the entirety of the evolving world itself has an explanation." Byrne, "Evolution, Randomness, and Divine Purpose: A Reply to Cardinal Schöborn," *Theological Studies,* 67.3 (2006): 653–65 at 661; Lonergan, *Insight,* 417, 511–12. For helpful summaries of Lonergan's approach to evolution see also Anthony Kelly, "Lonergan, Emergent Evolution and the Cosmic Process." *Quodlibet Journal* 8 (2009); Patrick Byrne, "Lonergan, Evolutionary Science, and Intelligent Design." *Revista Portuguesa de Filosofia* 63.4 (2007): 893–918. We will return to Lonergan again in the next chapter and see that, for him, God's causality in biblical inspiration can be understood along the same lines as his involvement in evolution: in both, God controls each event—the most mundane and extraordinary alike—because he controls all.

Ratzinger ties together the above principles in deeming it "evident that being-in-movement as a whole [*das Ganze der Seinsbewegung*]—and not just the beginning—is creation."[48] The emeritus pontiff is emphatic that God's creative activity does not consist in a one-time event of the remote past or even in periodic interventions within history. Rather, he insists that creation is an ever-present act that encompasses all of space and time, including the history of evolution itself. Thus, he taught in his 1964 course on creation at Münster that to understand creation in an evolutionary manner (*Schöpfung evolutionistisch*) is to understand that creation does not refer to a remote beginning of the world but is rather "a statement that concerns being as such," in other words, "being as temporal and becoming . . . encompassed by the one creative act of God."[49] For its part, then, "evolution is . . . simply the understanding of creation in its temporal actuality."[50] Or, as Cardinal Ratzinger would later write, "The cosmos is not a kind of closed building, a stationary container in which history may by chance take place. It is itself movement, from its one beginning to its one end. In a sense, creation is history."[51] In sum, for Benedict as for his predecessor John Paul II, creation does not denote a one-time

---

48. Ratzinger, "Belief in Creation and the Theory of Evolution," 141 ["Schöpfungsglaube und Evolutionstheorie," 158]. This point finds a nice echo in Hart, who describes God as the "infinite ocean of being that gives existence to all reality *ex nihilo* . . . whose creative act is an eternal gift of being to the whole of space and time, sustaining all things in existence in every moment." Hart, *The Experience of God*, 36–37, 40–41. As for Ratzinger, so for the Thomistic tradition. Accordingly, the classical idea of creation is in Hart's words "a vision of creation's rational order immeasurably remote from the Deist's or Intelligent Design theorist's notion of the world as a wonderful machine, designed and fabricated by a particularly enterprising superhuman intellect." Hart, *The Experience of God*, 58–59. Many people tend to think of God as the *highest* being in the universe, a being so powerful that he can tweak it at will. But in the classical Christian vision of things, God is not the highest being: he is *Being itself*. As such, in a properly Thomistic vision of creation, it is not mind-boggling complexity but rather *existence itself* that is the sign par excellence of God's creative causality.

49. Ratzinger, *Schöpfungslehre* (1964), 122, 173 [Sanz, "Joseph Ratzinger y la doctrina de la creación. Los apuntes de Münster de 1964 (II)," 238n122. Just a few years later, he would publish this very thought, adding that the biblical account of the creation of the cosmos—and of man—"does not designate a remote beginning." Ratzinger, "Belief in Creation and the Theory of Evolution," 141 ["Schöpfungsglaube und Evolutionstheorie," 159].

50. Ratzinger, *Schöpfungslehre* (1964), 174; Sanz, "Joseph Ratzinger y la doctrina de la creación. Los apuntes de Münster de 1964 (II)," 238n122. To this, Ratzinger adds, "But this seems to be the real turning point of the Darwinian view of the world—that the factor of time also becomes constitutive, because being is grasped as becoming. Being and time coincide (*Sein und Zeit fallen so ineinander*), whereas previously only being and space were internally assigned to each other." Ratzinger, *Schöpfungslehre* (1964), 171; Sanz, "Joseph Ratzinger y la doctrina de la creación. Los apuntes de Münster de 1964 (II)," 237n119. Observing consonance between this view and Heidegger's classic work *Sein und Zeit*, Ratzinger stresses that "being and time enter into an inseparable relation" (*eine untrennbare Relation*) and that "temporality now appears as the essential constitution of being itself" (*die wesentliche Verfaßtheit des Seins selbst*)." Ratzinger, *Schöpfungslehre* (1964), 82; Sanz, "Joseph Ratzinger y la doctrina de la creación. Los apuntes de Münster de 1964 (II)," 233n104. See also Ratzinger, "Belief in Creation and Theory of Evolution," 138 ["Schöpfungsglaube und Evolutionstheorie," 156]: "Being *is* time (*Das Sein ist Zeit*), It does not merely *have* time."

51. Ratzinger, *The Spirit of the Liturgy* (San Francisco: Ignatius Press, 2000), 28.

act in the distant past but rather God's one creative act that encompasses all time—the act by which he gives being to the universe and continues to maintain and govern it in existence.[52]

Accordingly, Professor Ratzinger does not find evidence of God's existence primarily in the world's beginning, for God is the source of all creaturely being at *all* times—including, as we now know, everything that happens in evolution. He writes that God's action in the world must not be thought of in a categorical sense, as if he were one among many causes in this world, but rather in a transcendental sense, that is, insofar as he is "the supporting power in and over the whole."[53] Or, as he wrote in an article published just a few years after giving this course, evolution operates at the *phenomenological* level (which "examines the difference between something and something"), whereas creation occurs at the *ontological* level (which "concerns the difference between nothing and something").[54] Given this difference between creation and evolution, Ratzinger concludes that the "dynamic character of being" that we find in evolution is perfectly compatible with the doctrine of creation, and that what the believer claims is outside the realm of biology. As we saw in the last chapter, Benedict identifies the content (*Inhalt*) of the belief in creation with "the decision of faith to understand the whole as an expression of *logos*."[55]

---

52. "Faith in creation and the theory of evolution correctly understood does not present obstacles [to belief]. Indeed, evolution presupposes creation. In light of evolution, creation is seen as an event that extends along time as a *creatio continua* ["continual creation"] in which God is manifested to the believer's eyes as the Creator of heaven and earth." John Paul II, Address to the Symposium "Christian Faith and the Theory of Evolution" (April 26, 1985), my translation. https://www.vatican.va/content/john-paul-ii/it/speeches/1985/april/documents/hf_jp-ii_spe_19850426_studiosi-evoluzione.html. Similarly, a statement from the Pontifical Academy of Sciences reads, "One could see in . . . evolutionary processes a confirmation of the theological concept of *creatio continua* (*creatio* and *conservatio*) which states that creation is a permanent process of participation of being." Pontifical Academy of Sciences, "Statement on Current Scientific Knowledge on Cosmic Evolution and Biological Evolution," in *Scientific Insights into Evolution of the Universe and Life*, eds. W. Arber, N. Cabibbo, M. Sánchez Sorondo (Vatican City: Pontificia Academia Scientiarum, 2009), 586. Interestingly, the notion of *creatio continua* finds biblical grounding in John 5:17 where Jesus says, "My Father is working still, and I am working."

For an outstanding discussion of the two-fold meaning of creation (*creatio ex nihilo* and *creatio continua*) in light of Thomistic principles, see Mariusz Tabaczek, OP, "Does God Create through Evolution? The Aristotelian-Thomistic Perspective," Public lecture for the Thomistic Institute at Blackfriars, Oxford, UK (February 5, 2020). https://soundcloud.com/thomisticinstitute/ does-god-create-through-evolution-fr-mariusz-tabsczek.

53. Ratzinger, *Schöpfungslehre* (1964), 85; Sanz, "Joseph Ratzinger y la doctrina de la creación. Los apuntes de Münster de 1964 (II)," 235n112. Hart captures this notion well in his *The Experience of God*, 38–39 (emphasis added).

54. Ratzinger, "Belief in Creation and the Theory of Evolution," 133 ["Schöpfungsglaube und Evolutionstheorie," 149].

55. Ratzinger, *Schöpfungslehre* (1964), 174; Sanz, "Joseph Ratzinger y la doctrina de la creación. Los apuntes de Münster de 1964 (II)," 239n123. Without identifying ID specifically, Thomas Joseph White ably demonstrates the folly of arguing for God's existence based upon (im)probabilities, that is, of seeking evidence for or against God's existence through the empirical sciences. See White, *The Light of Christ*, 88–90. In these pages of White's volume, one may find an excellent contemporary Thomist discussion of the point that evolution "presents no argument for or against a doctrine of creation."

# CREATION UNFOLDS ACCORDING TO
# THE MANNER OF THOUGHT

Ratzinger's holistic view of God's action in the world is expressed perhaps most intriguingly when he proposes that creation should be understood as unfolding "in the manner in which thought is creative."[56] As I will explain in a moment based on what he says on the topic elsewhere, the idea is intimately connected with the emeritus pontiff's conviction that creation should be thought of less like a static artifact or a machine that has been intelligently designed and more as a *story*, *drama*, or *song* that is continually unfolding naturally according to its own internal plot or score.

Indeed, these are precisely the images that Professor Ratzinger deployed to explain evolutionary creation in his university courses on the doctrine of creation. In his 1964 course, Ratzinger rejected the view that God's creation and governance of the universe are "separate acts of a two-part drama," arguing instead that they comprise "a single comprehensive reality."[57] To drive home this point, he returns to the notion that creation unfolds analogously to the way in which thought is creative by comparing it to a drama, symphony, or "cosmic melody":

> God's eternity is the creative consciousness. . . . If we understand the actuality of the world as a cosmic melody or as a drama, then we can say that the preservation of the world by God means: being enveloped in this symphony or drama through the presence of the divine spirit.[58]

We find a similar image in Ratzinger's 1976 course on creation held at Regensburg.

> The world is not simply the invariant representation of eternal patterns, but rather like the performance of a score, that is, of a structure that can only be played out in a process of inner movement in being itself. Becoming no longer exists on the surface but penetrates into the concept of being. The movement itself is constitutive. However, the performance of the score is not programmed to the last detail, but occasionally goes wrong.[59]

This last text is particularly valuable, as it not only adds a powerful image to our repertoire of analogies for creation but also makes room for an important reality

---

56. Ratzinger, "Belief in Creation and Theory of Evolution," 140 ["Schöpfungsglaube und Evolutionstheorie," 157–58].

57. Ratzinger, *Schöpfungslehre* (1964), 83; Sanz, "Joseph Ratzinger y la doctrina de la creación. Los apuntes de Münster de 1964 (II)," 234n105.

58. Ratzinger, *Schöpfungslehre* (1964), 84–85; Sanz, "Joseph Ratzinger y la doctrina de la creación. Los apuntes de Münster de 1964 (II)," 235n112.

59. Ratzinger, *Schöpfungslehre* (1976), 93; Sanz, "La dottrina della creazione nelle lezioni del professor Joseph Ratzinger: gli appunti di Regensburg (1976)," 275n3. Of course, we as humans, like the rest of creation, also "go wrong" from time to time. In this regard, I find it interesting that Ratzinger not only emphasizes that the entire creative act is thought, but that this applies to the human being in particular: "Every human being is a thought of God" (*jeder Mensch ist ein Gedanke von Gott*). Ratzinger, *God and the World* (San Francisco: Ignatius Press, 2002), 181.

that is inherent to the contingent nature of the evolutionary process: as in the execution of a drama or score, sometimes things in evolution go wrong. Mutations happen. Sometimes these lead to suffering and death, whereas other times they prove beneficial—thus becoming a *felix culpa* that ends up carrying creation to even greater perfection.[60] Either way, creation does not merely follow the preprogrammed instructions of a divine craftsman, nor does God "tweak" his story or score in the middle of its performance as envisioned by some Christians. On the contrary, evolutionary adaptations arise naturally from within the story of creation itself, according to the rules of its nature instilled therein by its divine author. But why would this author allow his own script to seemingly go off the rails at points? In brief, it is because God has bestowed on creatures the dignity of being real causes. And their errors—our errors—are all known to God and allowed as part of his plan.

Before wrapping up these initial comments on Ratzinger's conviction that creation is best thought of as unfolding "according to the manner of thought," I would like to share one more angle that sheds light on this expression. As I briefly discussed above, physicist Stephen Barr has developed precisely the image of God as a playwright with creation as his play.[61] Comparing God's "thinking up" of the universe to an author's conceiving his whole book, plot, and causes within it, Barr argues that this analogy helps us to steer clear of the ID movement's notion of God as a physical "force" who pushes matter around like the characters and causes that operate within a book. As Barr explains, this conception unfortunately drags God down to the level of a creature as if he were just another part of nature, one in which he is "just one thing among things in our universe, one physical cause among other physical causes."[62] Indeed, Barr extends the analogy so as to explain the reality that God does not tweak creation across time any more than an author acts in his own story—except for when he writes himself into the script as God in fact did do in the person Jesus Christ![63]

---

60. This analogy can be extended to our understanding of how evolution operates at the molecular level. An organism's genome (its total genetic material) can be conceived alternatively as computer code or a musical score. The code or score itself is static information, but the game or music played with it is alive and dynamic. Moreover, the same basic language or score can be actualized in a stunning variety of permutations just as instruments in an orchestra can be started and stopped by a conductor to produce all sorts of music. I have drawn this analogy from the PBS documentary *The Gene*, Episode 1: *Dawn of the Modern Age of Genetics*. All analogies fall short, of course, and so too here; for, the idea that God is a conductor intervening to tell different parts of his creation to start and stop is precisely the idea we wish to avoid. Nevertheless, I think this analogy's essential point nicely complements Benedict's image.

61. Barr, *"Chance, by Design,"* 57, 181.

62. Barr, *The Believing Scientist*, 147

63. Barr, *The Believing Scientist*, 126.

## WHICH KIND OF RATIONALITY SUITS THE
## CHRISTIAN FAITH? WHICH IS THE BETTER STORY?

At the start of his tenure at Bonn University in 1959, newly-minted Professor Joseph Ratzinger delivered a lecture that as cardinal he would later describe as containing questions that still remained "the connecting thread of my thought."[64] The address, entitled "The God of Faith and the God of the Philosophers: A Contribution to the Problem of a *Theologia Naturalis*," did not deal specifically with evolution. Yet the question posed by the young academic at the outset of his career ably summarizes the debate that lies at the heart of how one ought to think about the nature of creation given evolution. The question is: "Which kind of rationality suits the Christian faith?"[65] Other ways we might frame the question would be: What kind of world do we live in? or even "What is God like?"[66]

Given the language Benedict uses to describe the unfolding of life through evolution, I suggest that we re-propose the above question in today's evolutionary context with the help of a familiar analogy. If the medievals were right to see Scripture and Nature as God's "two books," and if Scripture is the story of salvation history, then it can be fruitful to conceive of the "book" of creation also as a story. A benefit of conceiving of evolutionary creation in this way is that it opens up an illuminating analogy that can help us to adjudicate what is the most fitting way to think of creation. That is to say, it leads us to ask whether it is better to make our judgments about evolution based not merely on what is technically possible for God to have done (e.g., the direct creation of species) but rather whether it might be helpful to think about evolution in light of our *overall* knowledge of how God works in the world (e.g., how he "speaks" to us through ordinary events, how holiness is often found in the "hidden" life, etc.). Or, to apply a distinction drawn by Reformed theologian Kevin Vanhoozer, to discern what is not merely *logically* consistent but what

---

64. The lecture is published in Ratzinger, *Der Gott des Glaubens und der Gott der Philosophen: Ein Beitrag zum Problem der theologia naturalis*, ed. Heino Sonnemans (Leutesdorf: Johannes Verlag, 2005), 7 (my translation).

65. Ratzinger, *Der Gott des Glaubens und der Gott der Philosophen*, 8 (my translation).

66. Peter Enns, in his book on the need to creatively rethink the biblical text through the lens of wisdom, writes that the question "What is God like?" is "the wisdom question around which all others revolve." Although Enns is not addressing evolution specifically in this book, he has done so at length elsewhere, and in reading both texts it is easy to see how his point applies to our present discussion. Enns, *How the Bible Actually Works*, 124.

Perhaps we might also take a page from Galileo and ask: is God any less excellently revealed through his work in nature than in the Bible? Would he require us to deny things that are set before our eyes in order to side with the letter of Scripture when it may intend a different meaning than what seems obvious? Says Galileo: "I do not feel obliged to believe that the same God who has endowed us with senses, reason and intellect has intended us to forego their use and by some other means to give us knowledge which we can attain by them. He would not require us to deny sense and reason in physical matters which are set before our eyes and minds by direct experience or necessary demonstrations." Galileo, "Letter to the Grand Duchess Christina," 94.

is *dramatically* consistent with "the whole and complete action of God, creating and recreating in Jesus Christ through the Spirit."[67]

Framing the debate with this literary analogy, we may thus find it fruitful to consider: *Who is the better author or scriptwriter—one whose story cannot advance without resorting to authorial interventions to wriggle his way out of a corner he has backed himself into, or on the other hand the author who crafted his story so tightly that the plot resolves naturally in a way consonant with the story's own terms and internal logic?* In everyday life, one of the ways we judge the quality of a novel, a movie, or any other story is precisely whether it is able to achieve what the latter author above has done, whereas the first author—who has to insert unnatural *deus ex machina* interventions into his plot in order to get the story he wants—is correctly seen as cheating.[68]

I find that this analogy of a story is especially well-suited to explain how God causes evolutionary change through the natures of his creatures rather than intervening from the outside. But, of course, we have also seen that another image Ratzinger evokes in this regard is that of the *enacted* story—i.e., a drama or play. Other thinkers have had this idea, too. For instance, Ronald Osborn writes of God's providence, "[C]reation is best seen as an improvisational theater or musical performance in which the director invites the actors—and not human actors alone—to join in the writing of the script, with all of the danger and of the possibility that this implies."[69] Similarly, Stephen Barr notes that, like any dramatist, the divine playwright is the cause of his entire "play" in all its aspects—every character, every

---

67. Kevin Vanhoozer, *The Drama of Doctrine: A Canonical-Linguistic Approach to Christian Theology* (Louisville, KY: Westminster John Knox Press, 2005), 257. Vanhoozer's discussion merits to be cited in greater length: "Fittingness designates a relationship that obtains between a whole and its constituent parts. What is 'fit' is what rightly finds its place in the 'whole.' Judgments about fittingness thus depend on one's prior construal of 'the whole': its kind, its shape. . . . The whole into which all else fits is none other than Jesus Christ, the definitive and comprehensive display of the wisdom of God. . . . Theological fittingness is less a matter of logical than of *dramatic* consistency, for the wholeness in question is a matter not simply of being but of doing. The dogma is the drama: the whole and complete action of God, creating and recreating in Jesus Christ through the Spirit. . . . Christian wisdom is largely a matter of rethinking theology, ethics, and worship in terms of Christo-dramatic fittingness." Vanhoozer, 256–57.

68. Perhaps the most influential Thomist philosopher of the twentieth century, Étienne Gilson thought of divine and creaturely causality largely along the same lines we have been elucidating it. See Gilson, *From Aristotle to Darwin and Back Again: A Journey in Final Causality, Species, and Evolution* (San Francisco: Ignatius Press, 2009), 12–14; Aquinas, *Commentary on Aristotle's Physics*, trans. Richard J. Blackwell, Richard J. Spath & W. Edmund Thirlkel (New Haven, CT: Yale University Press, 1963), Ch. 14, no. 268.

69. Ronald Osborn, *Death Before the Fall: Biblical Literalism and the Problem of Animal Suffering* (Downers Grove, IL: IVP Academic, 2014), 162. Osborn continues: "God's way of creating and sustaining primarily takes the form of divine providence working within history, including natural history, rather than absolute miracle radically interrupting history from without (which is by no means to deny the possibility of what to human eyes might appear as 'intervening miracles' in other contexts, or even as punctuating parts of the creation process/event itself)." Osborn, 163. See also Cunningham, *Darwin's Pious Idea*, 386–87.

event, every word. Barr calls this "vertical causality," which as we argued above would be no less necessary even if the world were eternal or all that existed were quantum states (which, despite Hawking's confusion, is not *nothing*). At the same time, he continues, it is also true that *within* the play there is true "horizontal causality" as its plot has an internal integrity in which things truly cause one another in accordance with the story's own rules as envisioned in the playwright's plan. In this play, the causality of the playwright and that of the characters in his plot are not in competition with one another but rather occur in different orders of reality.

Extending his *Hamlet* illustration, Barr accordingly asks: *Did Polonius die because the character Hamlet stabbed him? Or did Polonius die because Shakespeare wrote the play that way?* To this, he replies:

> The correct answer, of course, is "both." Hamlet stabbing Polonius is the cause within the play of Polonius dying. But Shakespeare is the cause of the whole thing—of the existence of the play Hamlet, of all its characters, all its events, and all the relationships among the characters and events, including where they occur within the play and how they fit into the causal structure of its plot.[70]

Applying this analogy to concrete created things, we can see that it is therefore idle to ask whether a particular part of creation exists because it evolved or because God specially willed it—that is, whether a feature's immense complexity is evidence of a divine designer or whether it is instead just another humdrum part of creation. For, as Barr says, in reality, "the whole universe and all its events and internal relationships only exist because God conceived of them and willed that they should exist and have these relationships to each other."[71] In other words, while some parts of a story may stand out to us as especially ingenious, God's providence is the cause of every single detail of our evolving universe, just as Shakespeare was responsible for every syllable of *Hamlet*.

So, yes, God is especially involved in the evolution of the bacterial flagellum and the eye, but he is equally present in the falling of a sparrow, the hairs of your head, and the very neurons firing in your brain right now that allow you to pursue these considerations. Things like these, most of which we consider rather dull and routine, have evolved through natural processes at the behest of God's will and manifest his glory in the universe. As the Book of Wisdom says, God's wisdom "reaches mightily from one end of the earth to the other, and she orders *all things* well" (Wis 8:1).

If evolutionary science indicates that the innumerable complex structures in our world have arisen naturally rather than by dint of miracles, does this make it any less amazing that they play the integral role they do in the world? Submitting

---

70. Barr, *The Believing Scientist*, 126–27. Barr proceeds to connect this to the Thomistic distinction between primary and secondary causality, wherein causes within nature are "secondary causes" and God is the "primary cause," i.e., the cause of nature.

71. Barr, *The Believing Scientist*, 126.

that evolution *simply is* God's grand design for creating life, biologist Dennis Venema suggests that God using "natural" mechanisms to fill his creation with biodiversity does not make him any less a creator than if he had achieved the same end miraculously. Indeed, Venema contends against the tendency within ID and contemporary atheism unwittingly to view God as a demiurge, i.e., a divine entity who acts on the same plane of existence as creatures: "[M]aking an object that can self-assemble would require a design far superior to that of an object that requires manual assembly. Rather than suggesting that a self-assembling object was evidence that a designer was not needed, we would be convinced that a powerful intellect was behind it."[72]

In other words, consider who would be the more impressive creator—one who builds amazing structures with blocks, or one who was so intelligent that he was able to create blocks that would *themselves* have the capacity to make new structures? Or, to shift images back to our story-writing analogy, we might ask with the help of a comparison made by Nicanor Austriaco: who would be the more powerful author—one who writes an outstanding book, or one who is so wise that he does something no human can do in authoring a book that writes itself?[73] Upon encountering this line of reflection, one of my students recently made me proud by suggesting that from now on perhaps it is better to continue calling the ID movement by its name "intelligent design" and while referring to evolutionary creation as "*even more* intelligent design"!

In light of this chapter's analogy of creation as God's story or play, we may therefore likewise ask: Is God any less the author of creation's script just because his plot unfolds through the action of characters he created?[74] Is he any less present to creation just because he endows creatures with natures so that they move themselves? Or, we could state the matter positively with the words that St. John Henry Newman penned when evolutionary biology was a new field. Newman notes that some people look at what they consider to be "the accidental evolution of organic beings" and assume that this is inconsistent with divine design, whereas Newman says of this same phenomenon: "It is accidental to us, not to God." Accordingly, he suggests, "Mr. Darwin's theory need not, then, be atheistical, be it true or not." To this he adds that, "[I]t may simply be suggesting a larger idea of Divine Prescience

---

72. McKnight and Venema, *Adam and the Genome*, 89–90. See also Charles de Koninck, *The Cosmos*, in *The Writings of Charles de Koninck*, vol. 1, ed. Ralph McInerny (Notre Dame, IN: University of Notre Dame Press, 2016), 278–83.

73. Austriaco, "The Fittingness of Evolutionary Creation," in *Thomistic Evolution*, 144.

74. While I find this to be a most valuable analogy, like all analogies this one too has an obvious limitation: God eventually does appear as an actor in the events of salvation history, culminating in the life and ministry of Jesus Christ. The framework I am developing here does not deny this but rather assumes it. What I am trying to capture with this analogy is the reality that God is ever present as the cause of all creaturely causes as he moves them to their actions through the natures he has bestowed upon them. As I have attempted to show, Benedict's view is that God guides the natural processes of evolution in this way rather than stepping into his play to act as one cause among many on the world's stage.

and Skill" than would shine forth if God had created all of our planet's myriad species independently of one another by divine fiat.[75] This notion has a further pair of implications.

First, if God's wisdom is manifested in his crafting a story so masterfully that its plot is able to unfold naturally, then by the same token discovering interruptions in the created order ironically might suggest that the divine author of creation lacks wisdom or power. In other words, interventions along the lines envisioned by ID might inadvertently make it appear that God is an *unintelligent* designer because his original plan for the universe needs periodic boosts in order to achieve its end. Thus Hart:

> If [as the ID movement aims to do] one could really show that there were interruptions in that order, places where the adventitious intrusions of an organizing hand were needed to correct this or that part of the process, that might well suggest some deficiency in the fabric of creation. It might suggest that the universe was the work of a very powerful, but also somewhat limited, designer. It certainly would not show that the universe is the creature of an omnipotent wisdom, or an immediate manifestation of the God who is the being of all things. Frankly, the total absence of a single instance of irreducible complexity would be a far more forceful argument in favor of God's rational action in creation.[76]

Second, the fact that God achieves his end for the universe by working through the natures of his creatures not only manifests his wisdom and power, it also bespeaks his *goodness*. That is, God's will to rely so deeply on creaturely causation within evolution blesses us creatures with the immense dignity of participating as his coworkers in the governance of creation. As we have always seen in such practices as intercessory prayer to the saints, the Catholic impulse is to magnify the

---

75. Newman, Letter to J. Walker of Scarborough on Darwin's Theory of Evolution, 77–78. In these same pages, Newman writes, "It does not seem to me to follow that creation is denied because the Creator, millions of years ago, gave laws to matter. He first created matter and then he created laws for it— laws which should construct it into its present wonderful beauty, and accurate adjustment and harmony of parts gradually. We do not deny or circumscribe the Creator, because we hold he has created the self acting originating human mind, which has almost a creative gift; much less then do we deny or circumscribe His power, if we hold that He gave matter such laws as by their blind instrumentality moulded and constructed through innumerable ages the world as we see it. If Mr. Darwin in this or that point of his theory comes into collision with revealed truth, that is another matter—but I do not see that the principle of development, or what I have called construction, does. As to the Divine Design, is it not an instance of incomprehensibly and infinitely marvellous Wisdom and Design to have given certain laws to matter millions of ages ago, which have surely and precisely worked out, in the long course of those ages, those effects which He from the first proposed."

76. Hart, *The Experience of God*, 38–39. Professional chemist Stacy Trasancos also has a nice way of making Hart's point. According to Trasancos, what happens in ID is that people end up making themselves the judges of God's intelligence and unintentionally implying that God created some things *unintelligently*. Trasancos, *Particles of Faith: A Catholic Guide to Navigating Science* (Notre Dame, IN: Ave Maria Press, 2016), 74, 126.

creature's participation in God's action rather than be ashamed of it.[77] Indeed, Aquinas says that it is fitting for a God who is the Good itself to ennoble our created state in this way: "[I]t is a greater perfection for a thing to be good in itself and *also* the cause of goodness in others, than only to be good in itself."[78] In a nutshell, it is more perfect and fitting for God to make creatures authentic causes of evolutionary change in virtue of their own natures than for him to remain the sole cause of new life within the universe.[79] Indeed, as Charles de Koninck writes, "[T]he creative power . . . is most profoundly at work where created causes are most causes. The more a creature is capable of acting, the more it manifests the power of its ultimate cause." To this, he adds that the problem with what he calls "creationism" is that "*it is not creationist enough.*" Indeed, he adds, "in the final instance, it is a form of occasionalism . . . a disguised revival of the ancient doctrine of those who rob natures of their proper actions, a doctrine vigorously opposed by St. Thomas, and which suppresses the divine governance by way of secondary causes."[80]

## CONCLUSION

Benedict's approach to evolutionary creation envisions a creator whose work is best described as a melody, symphony, play, or story. This divine author has composed a script that resolves naturally in a way consonant with the story of creation's own terms, following its own inner logic. It is a story in which God is not merely active in the extraordinary but precisely in the daily workings of his providential plan that has been unfolding for billions of years. It is a script which, while entirely proceeding from the mind of its divine author, is not a static artifact crafted from a blueprint that develops along predictable lines. Instead, it is a dynamic universe whose outcomes are in large part contingent upon its characters exercising true causality in their world—characters who would not even be able to exist if not for the pen of the author who creates them, continually maintains them in existence, and gives each the ability to make its unique contribution to creation's plot.

Of course, like all analogies, this one ultimately has its limits. After all, as literary giant J.R.R. Tolkien said, a human author is a mere "sub-creator." His art is only a reflection of Creation in its true sense ("Primary Art," in Tolkien's language), for no human author has the ability to give his characters existence in the "Primary World."[81] Even so, the image of a story or play is as close as I have been able to get to an image that does justice to Ratzinger's fundamental insight that creation is not

77. See *Catechism of the Catholic Church*, §306–308 and Second Vatican Council, *Gaudium et Spes*, §36, wherein the council discusses how God willed all things to be "endowed with their own stability, truth, goodness, proper laws and order."

78. Aquinas, *ST*, I, q. 103, a. 6 (emphasis added).

79. Austriaco articulates this point well in his "In Defense of Thomistic Evolution," 141–48.

80. Charles de Koninck, *The Cosmos*, 290, 292–93.

81. Tolkien, *Tree and Leaf: Including the Poem Mythopoeia* (Boston: Houghton Mifflin, 1965), 49, 71–72.

to be thought of as the work of a divine craftsman who acts on the same plane as creatures but rather as unfolding "in the manner in which thought is creative."

Moreover, I find Ratzinger's notion of creation as a cosmic melody particularly fitting insofar as a song—unlike an artifact or machine that has been engineered—is not dependent on preexisting material outside of oneself but arises directly from the mind of the artist (or "from the Lion's head," in C.S. Lewis's mythopoeic creation narrative).[82] Related to this point, creation is like a song insofar as it would cease to be as soon as its singer ceased to sing—which is very different from a house that continues to exist long after its builder finishes his job.[83] Not only that, our song analogy further suggests that God's creative has an aesthetic element—that the Lord's aim in creation is not just to design something that is practical and efficient but also something that is *beautiful* and *evocative of his own life*. Reflecting on this same analogy, Andrew Jaeger captures the above point well in observing that the "life" of a musical note communicates not just the musician's ideas but indeed his very personality—his loves, joys, sorrows, and the like. In like manner, Jaeger suggests that a creature—the "note" of the divine Musician—"doesn't just come from the musician, but is capable of communicating, sharing, and being an expression of the life of the musician."[84]

That said, it is easy to see why many Christians sympathize with the ID movement's quest to find God's hand directly operative in specific complex structures within creation. For, seeing God in creation's most ordinary "notes"—especially when their timbre is somber or grating—is not always easy. I will return to this theme at the book's climax in Chapter 9, for Ratzinger invites us to see the sufferings of this world less along the lines of absolute evils and more as J.R.R. Tolkien depicted them in his own creation narrative: that is, as temporary *dissonance* or *minor chords* that contribute to the overall beauty of God's perfect symphony.[85]

---

82. Lewis's narrator notes that Polly "felt quite certain that all the things were coming (as she said) 'out of the Lion's head.'" Lewis, *The Magician's Nephew*, 65.

83. Ratzinger, *Schöpfungslehre* (1976), 93; Sanz, "La dottrina della creazione nelle lezioni del professor Joseph Ratzinger: gli appunti di Regensburg (1976)," 275n3. Of course, this part of the analogy also has its limits. It is not as if a singer requires absolutely no preexisting material, as one does need vocal cords and air (at least if his song is to be audible). Related to this topic, it is noteworthy that Ratzinger's image of the cosmic melody for creation reappears in his eschatological thought. Thus, in the very last lines of his book dedicated to the topic, we read: "[T]he individual's salvation is whole and entire only when the salvation of the cosmos and all the elect (*das Heil des Alls und aller Erwählten*) has come to full fruition. . . . In that moment, the whole creation will become song (*Gesang*). It will be a single act in which, forgetful of self, the individual will break through the limits of being into the whole, and the whole take up its dwelling in the individual. It will be joy in which all questioning is resolved and satisfied." Ratzinger, *Eschatology*, 238 [*Eschatologie: Tod und ewiges Leben* (Regensburg: Pustet, 1977), 193].

84. Andrew Jaeger, "To-Be or Not-To-Be? The Existence and Non-Existence of God," Lecture at Ashland University (October 19, 2020).

85. For Tolkien's mythopoeic creation narrative that portrays creation occurring through song, see J.R.R. Tolkien, "Ainulindalë: The Music of the Ainur," in *The Silmarillion* (Boston: Houghton Mifflin, 2001), 15–22. The latter is particularly poignant for how it uses music to depict the reality of how God brings good out of dissonance/evil.

Analogies aside, in this chapter I have sought to show that a significant area of divergence between ID and Ratzinger's more holistic approach to creation lies in the level at which divine design is perceived and in the role creature causality is allowed to play within the world. ID supporters look for evidence of IC at the minute level which in turn is thought to bespeak divine design in the cosmos. Ratzinger, on the other hand, wisely steers clear of getting bogged down in these details, maintaining that God is "too great" to fit into ID-style gaps and therefore warns against construing God as an artisan who "tinkers" with the world or brings about new things "next to" the ordinary processes of nature. Because he emphasizes that the divine *Logos* imbues the whole cosmos, Benedict does not feel the need to appeal to supposed instances of IC or to divine intervention to prove that the divine power is at work in evolution. Instead, he is able to keep his eyes fixed on how God's hand is operative throughout the whole creation as his masterpiece plot unfolds. As a consequence, one who follows the emeritus pontiff's principles need not worry whether the next scientific discovery might fill in a gap that will disprove design in the universe.

In light of the analysis presented in this chapter, I would say that the ID endeavor—while often carried out with the noblest of intentions and without intending to deny the broad evolutionary narrative of life on this planet—is ultimately a distraction from the real pressing questions that stand before us at the intersection of faith and evolutionary science. Later in the book, we will address specific issues such as how human beings arose in evolutionary history, how many of us were there originally, what original sin means, and how engaging evolution might cast light on the realities of suffering and death. This chapter has focused simply on mining the insights of the emeritus pontiff in the effort to unfold a robust understanding of the amazing reality that God operates in evolution by making creatures true participants in his own causal activity.

*Part II*

# How to Read the Bible's Creation Narratives

# Chapter 4

# How to Keep the Faith without Losing Your Mind

*Reading Genesis with Benedict XVI and the Catholic Tradition*

## INTRODUCTION

As we have already witnessed in this book, Benedict XVI's philosophical disposition toward the question of evolution is to respect the legitimate autonomy of modern science, accepting its sound conclusions while situating them within God's plan in the light of faith. It therefore may come as no surprise that the emeritus pontiff takes the same stance toward modern biblical scholarship, for this is the other recent body of knowledge that he harnesses to help the Church penetrate more deeply into the mystery of man's evolutionary origins.

The goal of this chapter is to provide an overview of Benedict's principles of how to interpret the Bible authentically within the heart of the Church, especially with an eye toward how to read Genesis's creation narratives with a hermeneutic of faith and in light of modern discoveries in the fields of ancient literature and the empirical sciences. As we are about to see, this is an approach that at once seeks to uphold the Catholic tradition while at the same time updating it through a serious engagement with evolutionary science and modern biblical scholarship.

## BENEDICT'S "METHOD C" APPROACH TO SCRIPTURE

As some readers will recall from my other writings,[1] I find that the best way to grasp Benedict's exegetical (interpretative) approach is by breaking down how Joseph

---

1. For those who have read my *Dark Passages of the Bible: Engaging Scripture with Benedict XVI and Thomas Aquinas* (Washington, D.C.: The Catholic University of America Press, 2013) or *Jesus, Interpreted: Benedict XVI, Bart Ehrman, and the Historical Truth of the Gospels* (Washington, D.C.: The Catholic University of America Press, 2017), some of what I say in this chapter will be review. I have refined, however, various points and added many others that particularly concern the philosophical underpinnings of our topic and the issue of how to read Genesis given the theory of evolution. For an extended discussion of the four senses, the origin of the canon, and the traditional interpretive principles of "Method A," see *Dark Passages of the Bible*, Ch. 2 and *Jesus, Interpreted*, Ch. 3. Benedict provides excellent summaries of his twofold approach in the foreword to each installment of his *Jesus* series: Benedict XVI, *Jesus of Nazareth: The Infancy Narratives* (New York: Image, 2012), xi. See also Benedict XVI, *Jesus of Nazareth: Holy Week: From the Entrance into Jerusalem to the*

Ratzinger summarized it in a 1988 lecture in New York City. In the discussion that ensued, the then-Cardinal called on Christians to employ a two-pronged process to interpreting the Bible that takes the best from the ancient Christian tradition *and* the discoveries of the various modern sciences, an endeavor he captures with the concise term "Method C" exegesis:

> You can call the patristic-medieval exegetical approach Method A. The historical-critical approach, the modern approach . . . is Method B. What I am calling for is not a return to Method A, but a development of a Method C, taking advantage of the strengths of both Method A and Method B, but cognizant of the shortcomings of both.[2]

In brief, Ratzinger teaches that we should be eager to draw from both the Church's ancient interpretative tradition (which emphasizes the truth of Scripture and how it transforms our lives) and the modern historical-critical method (with its amazing toolbox that helps us to understand the Bible's meaning in its original context). For present purposes, the upshot of Benedict's "Method C" vision is that, even as we employ modern scientific approaches ("Method B") in the effort to ascertain the original meaning of Scripture, we will be doing so in faithfulness to the principles that governed the ancient Church's biblical interpretation ("Method A") and which are put forward by the Magisterium still today as guidelines for authentic Catholic exegesis.

Why is the modern interpretative method or "Method B" so crucial to understanding the origins account in Genesis? As I have been emphasizing, sometimes Christians unfortunately try to deflect the challenges of evolution by relying solely upon traditional sources like the letter of the Bible, the writings of the Church Fathers, the great medieval theologians, and the popes of years past. The problem, though, is that the authors of these sources—giants on whose shoulders we all stand—lacked a lot knowledge that is well established today (like heliocentrism, the Big Bang, the common descent of all species through evolution, and archaeology that has literally unearthed other ancient myths pertinent to Genesis 1–11). Thus, while we always have much to learn from our forebears and they can be

---

*Resurrection* (San Francisco: Ignatius Press, 2011), xiv–xv. See also Benedict XVI, *Light of the World: the Pope, the Church, and the Signs of the Times* (San Francisco: Ignatius Press, 2010), 171–72; Benedict XVI, *Verbum Domini*, §34.

2. Ratzinger's words are taken from a summary and transcript of the discussion following his lecture. See Paul T. Stallsworth, "The Story of an Encounter," in *Biblical Interpretation in Crisis*, 107–108. This is the only place in Ratzinger's corpus where the shorthand expression "Method C" exegesis is deployed, yet he emphasized the need for this same two-pronged approach from many different angles over the years. For instance, he distinguishes a "historical hermeneutic" from a "faith hermeneutic" and speaks of "scholarly" and "scientific" exegesis in contradistinction to *lectio divina*, insisting that "both [are] necessary and complementary in order to seek, through the literal meaning, the spiritual meaning that God wants to communicate to us today." Benedict XVI, Angelus (October 26, 2008).

trusted when it comes to the essentials, it is not the case that the Fathers know best about every subject matter.[3]

In light of this, the Christian who wishes to follow Benedict's interpretative approach will acknowledge the need to set aside certain incidental features and untenable assumptions of *particular traditions* without abandoning the enduring and authoritative principles of *Sacred Tradition*. As we have already seen, Benedict does not think that having a vibrant faith requires the Christian to espouse *all* ancient assumptions. To the contrary, our commitment to the faith may even receive a boost by entertaining positions that are differ in some respects from those held by the faithful of ages past.

For instance, given what science has revealed in the past millennium, it is difficult—if not impossibile—to adhere entirely to certain patristic and medieval interpretations of Genesis according to which God physically molded the first human directly from mud and crafted the first man's wife from one of his ribs. Yet, impious as it may seem to challenge these longstanding interpretations may seem, it can be liberating to realize that is not necessary to maintain all of these positions in the face of overwhelming evidence to the contrary from empirical science and ancient texts. Remarkably, at a time when Darwin's theory was brand new, St. John Henry Newman was already connecting the Church's past need to rethink her biblical interpretation in light of heliocentrism with a similar need in the case of evolutionary science. Asking whether it is possible that the first man was *not* immediately taken from the dust of the earth, Newman replies that, while all of us are dust (Ecc 3:20), it is also the case that "we never were dust—we are from fathers." To this, he humbly proceeds to ask, "Why may not the same be the case with Adam? I don't say that it is so—but if the sun does not go round the earth and the earth stand still, as Scripture seems to say, I don't know why Adam needs be immediately out of dust."[4]

Accordingly, if we wish to tackle matters of science that our forefathers never had the opportunity to tackle and pursue the line of inquiry exemplified by Newman above, we will also need to consult up-to-date sources of wisdom in conversation with the Christian tradition. This is where modern exegesis comes in. If a hallmark of the patristic-medieval or "Method A" approach is that it sees Scripture from a spiritual perspective and seeks to discern the voice of Christ speaking to us from in it, then a strength of the modern historical-critical or "Method B" stance

---

3. It is noteworthy that Aquinas himself was aware of this point, though of course he assumed traditional interpretations were more often correct than Benedict does. In the Angelic Doctor's view, the authority of the canonical Scriptures offer "incontrovertible proof" of the truth of things, whereas the authority of the doctors of the Church is one that may be used, but merely as "extrinsic and probable arguments." Aquinas, *Summa Theologiae*, I, q. 1, a. 8 ad 2. Of course, stating that the Scriptures offer definitive proof on a given point is not as simple as some may think, for every passage of Scripture also requires interpretation within the heart of the Church with the assistance of the best of all the tools and sources at our disposal. For a helpful discussion of how to weigh the Patristic evidence in relation to that of the sciences, see Galileo, "Letter to the Grand Duchess Christina," 102.

4. Newman, Letter to E. B. Pusey (June 5, 1870), in vol. 25 of *The Letters and Diaries of John Henry Newman* (Oxford: Clarendon Press, 1978), 137–38, at 138.

is that it attends to Scripture's original meaning in its native historical context, language, mindset, and culture. While it need not reject the crucial enterprise of applying the message of Scripture to our lives today, this approach is especially important for engaging people (like me) who experience that feeling that Christians often skip a step somewhere in the process of biblical interpretation, failing to acknowledge that this spiritual sense was probably not on the radar of the Bible's human authors. In the foreword to the first volume of his *Jesus* trilogy, Benedict gives the parameters of historical-critical work: "It attempts to identify and to understand the past—as it was in itself—with the greatest possible precision, in order then to find out what the author could have said and intended to say in the context of the mentality and events of his time."[5]

In the quest to ascertain the original meaning of Scripture, modern scholarship employs all the scientific resources at our disposal today, tools that were less developed or even nonexistent in ages past. These include competence in the ancient languages relevant to the Bible, archaeological discoveries that give us knowledge of the ancient Near Eastern cultural milieu in which the Bible was written, the availability of a host of ancient religious texts with mythology germane to the world of the Bible, paleontological discoveries that have brought to light unfathomable knowledge about the age of the earth and the history of life upon it, and the science of genetics that was not even a discipline until the end of the nineteenth century when the Augustinian friar Gregor Mendel discovered the fundamental laws of heredity.[6]

At this point, we should also say a word about the "critical" attitude of historical criticism. Method B is not necessarily critical in the way we tend to use the word today. It comes from the Greek verb κρίνω meaning "to judge," and it specifically entails the endeavor to judge what the intended meaning of a given biblical text was in its original context. To be sure, Ratzinger is aware that the modern method has at times been deployed alongside unwarranted "academic dogmas" with an eye to dismantling the faith. For this reason, he famously called for a "criticism of the criticism" so as to avoid anti-faith presuppositions when using the legitimate tools of modern biblical scholarship.[7]

That said, Benedict insists that the modern interpretative method in itself is by no means antithetical to faith. In fact, in Ratzinger's view, moving *beyond* a

---

5. Benedict XVI, *Jesus of Nazareth: From the Baptism in the Jordan to the Transfiguration* (New York: Doubleday, 2007), xvi.

6. Benedict's successor puts this well when he recommends St. Jerome's approach as a model for authentic exegesis still today. See Francis, *Scripturae Sacrae Affectus* (September 30, 2020).

7. Ratzinger, "Biblical Interpretation in Crisis," 6; Benedict XVI, *Light of the World*, 171. The emeritus pontiff goes so far as to insinuate the presence of the Antichrist in certain areas of modern biblical scholarship. Benedict XVI, *Jesus of Nazareth: From the Baptism*, 35–36. For further critiques, see Ratzinger, "Biblical Interpretation in Crisis," 21; Scott Hahn and Benjamin Wiker, *Politicizing the Bible: The Roots of Historical Criticism and the Secularization of Scripture, 1300–1700* ( New York: Crossroad Publishing Company, 2013), 9; N.T. Wright, *Jesus and the Victory of God* (Minneapolis: Fortress Press, 1996), especially 16–17.

reductionist approach to texts like Genesis 1–11 can happen only if we *go through the problem and tackle it from within* by engaging the modern method. In other words, as I said back in Chapter 1, we will be of no help to struggling Christians if we only respond to modernity by citing ecclesial texts rather than engaging the science of evolution and modern biblical scholarship on their own terms. As I have also said, though, this will require of the reader a willingness to ask certain questions—and entertain some potentially uncomfortable corresponding answers—that the faithful of previous ages simply did not raise or countenance.

In Chapter 1, I discussed the discomfort and fears many experience when opening up to change in the way we interpret the Bible's creation stories. It may prove helpful here to recall that doctrine has been developing in the Church from the beginning—a truth documented powerfully by St. John Henry Newman in the nineteenth century and a principle that the Second Vatican Council canonized many decades ago.[8] Through all of this, the Church's core dogmas remain permanently normative yet at the same time *our understanding of them* is always increasing. As a result, certain things long associated with these dogmas are going to stand in need of emendation as our treasury of knowledge increases. Just to take one clear example from the turbulent yet rich history of interaction between science and theology, we would do well to recall the sixteenth-century Galileo affair. At this time, many in the Church rejected Galileo's heliocentric theory, believing it was incompatible with Scripture and fearing that it would lead to the destruction of the Christian faith. Yet, four centuries later, practically nobody in the Church disputes the theory.[9]

It certainly would be nice if there were an obvious and easy way to plot out the precise trajectory of future doctrinal development with the help of Benedict's exegetical principles, but the reality is that "Method C" is not really a method in the way people usually think of the term—that is, a set of procedural rules that you can systematically apply to obtain a desired result.[10] Or, as Benedict himself poignantly said:

---

8. John Henry Newman, *An Essay on the Development of Christian Doctrine* (Notre Dame, IN.: University of Notre Dame Press, 1989); Second Vatican Council, *Dei Verbum*, §8.

9. For more on the nature of doctrinal development, see Ramage, *Dark Passages of the Bible*, 108–112 and Ramage, *Jesus, Interpreted*, 41–45. On the reality that certain Catholic traditions eventually stand in need of emendation or correction in light of newfound knowledge, see Ramage, *"Extra Ecclesiam Nulla Salus* & the Substance of Catholic Doctrine: Towards a Realization of Benedict XVI's 'Hermeneutic of Reform,'" *Nova et Vetera 14.1* (2016): 295–330 and "Benedict XVI's Hermeneutic of Reform: Towards a Rapprochement of the Magisterium and Modern Biblical Criticism." *Nova et Vetera* 14.3 (2016): 879–917. On the Galileo issue specifically, see Ratzinger, "Farewell to the Devil?," in *Dogma and Preaching*, 198. A concise summary of Ratzinger's argument in this essay can be found in my piece by the same title "Farewell to the Devil?" for the *Gregorian Institute* website (October 25, 2013).

10. For an excellent statement of the point that Benedict's methods A and B are not monolithic entities but instead umbrella terms used to capture exegetes who share common principles, see Gregory Vall, "Psalm 22: *Vox Christi* or Israelite Temple Liturgy?," *The Thomist* 66 (2002): 176. For a recent text that lucidly explains Ratzinger's Method C" and why modern exegesis with its special attunement to the phenomenon of historical change has much to contribute to our under-standing of Scripture, see Holmes, *Cur Deus Verba?* (San Francisco: Ignatius Press, 2021), 201–25. For yet another excellent source

"Christianity is not an intellectual system, a collection of dogmas, or moralism. Christianity is instead an encounter, a love story; it is an event."[11] Instead, like the faith itself, Benedict sees "Method C" exegesis more as a proposal: a summons to rejoice in the full breadth of reason and to harness every resource at our disposal in the effort to illumine the deposit of faith. This is a daunting and demanding task that is at once urgent and will take time, and this book aims only to inch us a little farther along the path. As my beloved professor Fr. Matthew Lamb used to say of the current crisis in theology: "It took us three hundred years to get into this mess, and it will take us another three hundred to get out—so we have not a moment to lose!"

## CHRISTOLOGICAL TELEOLOGY OF HISTORY

Now that we have laid out the broad strokes of Benedict's "Method C" vision, it will be valuable to highlight a few of its main features that pertain to our encounter with the Book of Genesis throughout the rest of this book. Above all, getting the biblical creation narratives right requires us to grasp two key principles: the Christological teleology of history and the Christology of Scripture. We will delve into the first of these here and return to the second shortly below.

The first of these consists in the necessity of reading Scripture in light of Jesus Christ, its Alpha and Omega, a key I am referring to here as the *Christological teleology of history*. Essentially, what it means is that Christ is the unifying principle and goal (Greek *telos*) of the Old Testament and of history itself. Throughout his long career, Benedict often spoke of the need to bear in mind how a given text fits into the overall canon of Scripture that was composed over the span of more than a millennium. According to the emeritus pontiff, understanding this background is the key to understanding why God's holy word contains what from our human perspective look to be defects. That is, it is essential to the endeavor of explaining the presence of what the Pontifical Biblical Commission (hereafter PBC), as part of a project initiated under the auspices of Benedict's pontificate, called "contradictions of a geographical, historical, and scientific nature, which are rather frequent in the Bible."[12]

In line with Benedict's way of phrasing things, C.S. Lewis adds a poignant description of Scripture's all-too-human imperfections and what our takeaway from this acknowledgment should be:

---

that articulates the importance of a twofold approach that draws from the best of ancient and modern exegesis, see Nicholas Lombardo, "A Voice Like the Sound of Many Waters: Inspiration, Authorial Intention, and Theological Exegesis" Nova et Vetera 19.3 (2021): 825–69.

11. Benedict XVI, "Funeral Homily for Msgr. Luigi Giussani," *Communio* 31.4 (2004): 685–87. On the faith not being reducible to a system, see also Lewis, *Reflections on the Psalms* (London: Harvest Books, 1964), 113.

12. Pontifical Biblical Commission, *The Inspiration and Truth of Sacred Scripture* (Collegeville, MN: The Liturgical Press, 2014), 163, 167. This relatively recent document has particular relevance as it was begun during Benedict's pontificate and approved in 2014 by Cardinal Gerhard Müller, Benedict's appointee as the commission's president. It is noteworthy that this subject was taken up during Benedict's pontificate and describes itself as a partial response to the pontiff's exhortation *Verbum Domini*.

The human qualities of the raw materials show through. Naiveté, error, contradiction, even (as in the cursing psalms) wickedness are not removed. The total result is not "the word of God" in the sense that every passage, in itself, gives impeccable science or history. It carries the word of God; and we . . . receive that word from it not by using it as an encyclopedia or an encyclical but by steeping ourselves in its tone or temper and so learning its overall message.[13]

A Christological teleology of history helps us address precisely these sorts of issues. It allows us to admit the obvious—that the Old Testament does not yet reveal the fullness of truth—all while continuing to venerate it as God's word.

Benedict's Christological teleology of history is particularly well laid out in his exhortation on the Word of God which articulates it as follows: "God's plan is manifested *progressively* and it is accomplished slowly, *in successive stages* and despite human resistance." The then-pontiff explains that God patiently and gradually revealed himself to Israel in order to "guide and educate . . . training his people in preparation for the Gospel." Since "revelation is suited to the cultural and moral level of distant times," he adds, the Bible narrates certain things "without explicitly denouncing the immorality of such things," a fact that "can cause the modern reader to be taken aback." What is needed for correct interpretation, therefore, is "a training that interprets the texts in their historical-literary context [another way of saying Method B] and within the Christian perspective [Method A] which has as its ultimate hermeneutical (interpretative) key 'the Gospel and the new commandment of Jesus Christ brought about in the paschal mystery.'"[14]

In a particularly well-developed passage that explains this dynamic in connection with the development of the biblical canon, Benedict writes:

> Modern exegesis has brought to light the process of constant rereading that forged the words transmitted in the Bible into Scripture: older texts are reappropriated, reinterpreted, and read with new eyes in new contexts. They became Scripture by being read anew, evolving in continuity with their original sense, tacitly corrected and given added depth and breadth of meaning. This is a process in which the word gradually unfolds its inner potentialities, already somehow present like seeds, but needing the challenge of new situations, new experiences, and new sufferings, in order to open up. This process is certainly not linear, and it is often dramatic, but when you watch it unfold in the light of Jesus Christ, you can see it moving in a single overall direction; you can see that the Old and New Testament belong together.[15]

---

13. Lewis, *Reflections on the Psalms*, 111–12. Benedict writes along the same lines as Lewis in teaching that Scripture "carries" the word of God and "bears witness" to the Word of God himself, Jesus Christ. For discussion of how Bonaventure's writings influenced Benedict on this point, see Ramage, *Jesus, Interpreted*, 73–75.

14. Benedict XVI, *Verbum Domini*, §42 (emphasis Benedict's). See also Ratzinger, *Biblical Interpretation in Conflict*, 24n37 and 23n35.

15. Benedict XVI, *Jesus of Nazareth: From the Baptism*, xviii–xix.

Without using the precise wording in this particular paragraph, Benedict is advo-
cating here what he elsewhere refers to as a hermeneutic of *divine pedagogy*, an
approach that appears in the work of the Second Vatican Council and the Catechism which spells it out in this way: "The divine plan of revelation . . . involves a
specific divine pedagogy: God communicates himself to man gradually. He prepares him to welcome by stages the supernatural revelation that is to culminate in
the person and mission of the incarnate Word, Jesus Christ."[16]

To further draw out the full meaning of divine pedagogy as Benedict deploys
it, we might also recall what he says in his *In the Beginning*—a book highly relevant
to our book's topic. In this text, Ratzinger describes the Bible as the story of a twofold struggle and ongoing dialogue between God and man. One the one hand, it
narrates "God's struggle with human beings to make himself understandable to
them over the course of time," while on the other hand it also documents Israel's
struggle to "seize hold of God over the course of time." Ratzinger describes this
familiarization between God and man as a "step by step journey," an "advance
toward Christ" in which God's people increasingly grow in their ability to penetrate
the divine mysteries. Ultimately, however, the real meaning of the Old Testament
(and of Genesis 1–11 in particular) becomes clear only in light of Jesus Christ, the
New Adam who is its beginning and end.[17]

Writing in the thirteenth century, Thomas Aquinas had already captured the
central point that Benedict is driving at with his teaching on history's Christological
teleology. In his *De veritate*, the Angelic Doctor compares the education of the
whole human race in divine things to what takes place in the education of a single
person: "Just as there is a progress in the faith of an individual man over the course
of time, so there is a progress in faith for the whole human race. This is why Gregory
says that divine knowledge has increasingly grown over the course of time."[18] In
the same way that an individual believer slowly appropriates the truths of the faith

---

16. *Catechism of the Catholic Church*, §53. For Benedict's use of the term "divine pedagogy," see
*Verbum Domini*, §11, §20. I have cited the Catechism here because of its clarity and conciseness, but
the Catechism itself is summarizing the Second Vatican Council constitution *Dei Verbum*, §15. For
other magisterial statements of the divine pedagogy, see Pius XI, *Mit Brennender Sorge*, §15 and
*Lumen Gentium*, §9. See also Ratzinger, "Sources and Transmission of the Faith," *Communio* 10
(1983): 28.

17. Benedict XVI, *In the Beginning*, 10–11; Benedict XVI, *Jesus of Nazareth: From the Baptism in
the Jordan to the Transfiguration*, xix. Benedict has dozens of lines that could be cited on this topic. For
instance, see Wicks, "Six texts by Prof. Joseph Ratzinger as *Peritus* Before and During Vatican Council
II," 280; Ratzinger, *God and the World*, 151–53; Ratzinger, *Introduction to Christianity*, 116. For a papal
depiction of revelation as a dialogue that predates Benedict, see Paul VI, *Ecclesiam Suam*, §70. In this
regard, René Girard felicitously describes the Bible, especially the Old Testament, as a "text in travail."
Girard, "Generative Scapegoating: Discussion," in *Violent Origins: Walter Burkert, René Girard, and
Jonathan Z. Smith on Ritual Killing and Cultural Formation*, ed. Robert G. Hamerton-Kelly (Stanford
University Press: 1987), 106–48 at 141. For an excellent concise summary of Girard's approach to Scrip-
ture which I find congenial in many ways with that of Benedict, see Brett Salkeld, "René Girard and the
Literal Sense of Scripture," *Vox Nova* (November 12, 2015).

18. Aquinas, *De veritate*, q. 14, a. 11.

into his life, so the Old Testament people of God gradually grew in divine knowledge over the course of salvation history.

Aquinas explains that God had to hand on the faith to our ancestors in piecemeal form not because he is an inept teacher, but because this is the only way we feeble humans are able to take it all in. Thus the general explanation he gives for why Moses (whom Aquinas, unlike Ratzinger and the majority of scholars today, takes to be the sole author of the Pentateuch) penned seemingly erroneous things is that the sacred author had to "accommodate" his teaching to the understanding of his contemporaries. As Thomas says in his treatment of the six days of creation, Moses divided the work of creation into parts because he was trying to make his instruction clear to an uncultivated [*rudem*] people.[19]

Thomas explains this further in the *Summa*, where he adds that God teaches us patiently in the knowledge that we are slow learners: "Man acquires a share of this learning, not indeed all at once, but little by little, according to the mode of his nature."[20] The people of Israel, God's pupils, therefore originally understood the created world similarly to other ancient Near Eastern people. Accordingly, the Old Testament is not perfect in an absolute sense; yet, as Aquinas says, it was indeed perfect *for what the people needed at the time*.[21] Indeed, he adds a further

---

19. Aquinas, *In II Sent.*, dist. 12, q. 1, a. 2. While his principle remains valid, its application almost certainly extends further than Aquinas thought. For, Moses (or whoever wrote Genesis) was *himself* uninstructed in the manner of how and in what order creation occurred. In other words, the Bible's lack of scientific accuracy on this matter is not due to Moses dumbing things down for his audience—it is because *no one* before Christ (and indeed for many centuries after his earthly life) had access to the realm of modern physics that is just a click away for us today. For a discussion of how much the Old Testament's authors knew compared to what Aquinas assumed they did, see Ramage, *Dark Passages of the Bible*, 103–108.

20. Aquinas, *Summa Theologiae*, II-II, q. 2, a. 3; For the language of the Jews in Moses's day being an uncultivated (*rudem*) people, see Aquinas's discussion of creation in his *In II Sent.*, dist. 12, q. 1, a. 2. A similar principle is enunciated by Galileo in writing that the sacred authors "accommodated themselves to received usage rather than to the essence of the matter in regard to subjects which are not necessary for eternal bliss." Galileo, "Letter to the Grand Duchess Christina," 106–107. As Aquinas recalls, Scripture itself likens the people of Israel in the Old Testament to spiritual childhood before God the Father: "The master, who has perfect knowledge of the art, does not deliver it all at once to his disciple from the very outset, for he would not be able to take it all in, but he condescends to the disciple's capacity and instructs him little by little. It is in this way that men made progress in the knowledge of faith as time went on. Hence the Apostle (Galatians 3:24) compares the state of the Old Testament to childhood." Aquinas, *Summa Theologiae*, II-II, q. 1, a. 7 ad 2. For Thomas, as for St. Paul whose theology he invokes, God's firstborn son Israel gradually made progress in knowledge of him in accordance with the divine Teacher's most wise plan. God condescended and taught man in accordance with the way he learns best, which is "little by little."

21. Aquinas, *Summa Theologiae*, I-II, q. 98, a. 2 ad 1. Aquinas explores the divine teaching method elsewhere in commenting on the same text from St. Paul just cited. He argues that God's teaching was perfectly suited to the needs and ability of the people of God at every stage of divine revelation, taking into account the fact that the people would not always fully grasp what he wished to convey. In the words of Thomas: "Nothing prevents a thing being not perfect simply, and yet perfect in respect of time: thus a boy is said to be perfect, not simply, but with regard to the condition of time. So, too, precepts that are given to children are perfect in comparison with the condition of those to whom they are given,

principle that helps us to understand why God allows defects to be present in Scripture: divine providence permits certain defects for the greater good of the world as a whole.

> Corruption and defects in natural things are said to be contrary to some particular nature; yet they are in keeping with the plan of universal nature; inasmuch as the defect in one thing yields to the good of another, or even to the universal good. . . . Since God, then, provides universally for all being, it belongs to His providence to permit certain defects in particular effects, that the perfect good of the universe may not be hindered, for if all evil were prevented, much good would be absent from the universe.[22]

Applying Aquinas's principles to Scripture's defects, we can envision how some immense goods would have been absent had God prevented the sacred authors from exhibiting their own limited understanding of the world. Drawing an interesting parallel with the idea that God creates species through evolution without interventions from above, stepping in and "fixing" their work would have deprived the sacred authors of the dignity of being true collaborators in the work of divine revelation rather as opposed to being mere witnesses of it. Of course, this may not have been the most efficient way that God could have revealed himself, but it was the best way for God to meet us *in a way that befits our human nature.*[23]

To understand what Aquinas is trying to say in these texts, consider what it would be like to "perfectly" proclaim the gospel for the first time to someone who does not even know God. I myself have had the occasion to try it and find that it is a struggle to get a person in this situation to understand even some of the most basic concepts that we Christians take for granted. As a result, the missionary has to be patient not to overload the person with more than he can handle at any given time and accept that the catechumen is going to have in his head a mix of correct and incorrect notions which will be refined and purified only gradually.[24] The same goes

---

although they are not perfect simply. Hence the Apostle says (Gal 3:24): 'The Law was our pedagogue in Christ.'" For Thomas, it is not that God was unable or unwilling to teach Israel the fullness of truth about himself; rather, it was precisely because of his knowledge of our frail human nature that he went about it so slowly. Accordingly, God knew that the creation accounts of Genesis were going to be imperfect. However, these narratives were indeed perfect *in respect of time* because God, the best of all teachers, adapted his teaching to the needs of his disciple Israel at the time the text was composed.

22. Aquinas, *Summa Theologiae*, I, q.22, a. 2. On the "rule of forms" which has applicability here, see also Aquinas, *Summa Theologiae*, I, q.19, a. 6.

23. Thomas's discussion of whether God could have made a better world on the whole are worth recalling on this topic. See Aquinas, *Summa Theologiae*, I, q.25, a. 6 ad 1, ad 3; I, q. 22, a.2.

24. Giovanni Blandino, SJ, offers an illuminating analogy for how God accommodated himself to Israel's weaknesses as he gradually instructed the people in the realities of God's nature, the afterlife, and moral law. Like a missionary teaching a catechumen, God began with a pagan people who knew little about the divine nature or human destiny: "God worked through a gradual revelation: teaching Israel to believe in one God, then revealing man's destiny, the moral law, etc. He used the same method a missionary does: beginning by teaching some simple and important truths, then

for Israel. Eventually, God's people would be ready for Jesus Christ to come and reveal the fullness of truth, yet until then God was patient. The result: now we have reached the goal. God has definitively manifested himself in history, and in the Gospel of John we possess what Ratzinger calls "the normative scriptural creation account."[25] Even so, today in the Church we continue to strive toward more perfect understanding of this revelation in relation to recent scientific developments.

## INSPIRATION, CONDESCENSION, AND THE CHRISTOLOGY OF SCRIPTURE

The second key feature of Benedict's "Method C" vision consists in what I will call here a *Christology of Scripture*, the incarnational nature of God's word. How can it be that the Bible contains defects? One part of the answer that we have already given has to with the reality that the recipients of God's word were imperfect. The other lies in the astonishing reality that God wished to make his creatures true authors of his holy word, humbling himself to speak in a way that appears imperfect from our limited human point of view. We will now explore this dynamic in some depth.

The author(s) of Genesis doubtlessly lacked knowledge of modern evolutionary science, and so they spoke in ways that we today might be tempted to deem crude or childish. For instance, God almost certainly did not create the world over the course of six twenty-four hour days as the letter of the Bible seems to indicate, nor is it likely the case that he physically molded the first man directly from the ground. So the question arises: why did God not simply depict creation in the way it actually happened—with accurate science—rather than through an anthropomorphic story? Why, in short, did God permit such lack of clarity in Scripture when it was clearly within his competence to paint a perfect picture of the the Big Bang billions of years ago and again more recently when human beings came on the scene a few hundred thousand years ago? I appreciate how C.S. Lewis puts it: the very defects we observe in Scripture turn out to be a most significant clue for grasping its true nature and purpose. In a nutshell, for Lewis, "the value of the Old Testament may be dependent on what seems its imperfection."[26]

Along these lines, I have discussed how the rationale behind God's choice to include what we perceive as imperfections in Scripture lies in his desire to ennoble human beings with the dignity of being *true authors* of the Bible. One of the most fundamental points of Catholic teaching with regard to Scripture is its inspiration, which informs us that God is its primary author. Yet Catholic doctrine also emphasizes that the Lord "condescended" so as to achieve his purpose by means of feeble

---

others. The catechumen at first has in mind a mix of exact and inexact ideas. Little by little as the teaching progresses, the exact ideas increase more and more, while inexact ideas gradually get eliminated." Blandino, *La rivelazione e l'ispirazione della Sacra Scrittura* (Rome, Italy: Edizioni ADP, 1998), 9 (my translation).

25. Ratzinger, *In the Beginning*, 15.

26. C.S. Lewis, *Reflections on the Psalms*, 114.

humans as his "secondary"—though still true—causes. The Second Vatican Council tells us that these humble fleshly instruments wrote down everything God wanted them to write, and nothing more.[27] And yet the same council is equally clear in its teaching that the Bible's human authors were not just God's puppets or scribes recording dictations from above. The authoring of Scripture entailed the full deployment of its human authors' faculties and gifts, put to use that God's own ineffable word might be put into human words which his people could understand. In order to describe this dynamic, the council developed what I have called here a *Christology of Scripture*, which means that the nature of Scripture is best understood by way of an analogy with Jesus Christ himself: "The words of God, expressed in human language, have been made like human discourse, just as the Word of the eternal Father, when He took to Himself the flesh of human weakness, was in every way made like men."[28]

Now, if the word of God in Scripture is *truly* human discourse, then like Christ's human flesh it is going to have its defects. Just as Christ the Word of God crucified was a "stumbling block" [*skandalon*] to Jews and "folly" [*mōría*] to Gentiles (1 Cor 1:22-25), so God's word in Scripture also has a "scandalous" or "moronic" element to it. And yet, as in the case of the God-man himself, the foolishness [*morós*] of God's word in true human words is wiser than men, and its weakness is stronger than men.[29] How so? Ultimately, it has to do with something

---

27. Second Vatican Council, *Dei Verbum*, §11. For a traditional Thomistic approach that complements the council's conception of Scripture's dual authorship, see the thorough discussion in Paul Synave and Pierre Benoit, *Prophecy and Inspiration: a Commentary on the Summa Theologica II-II, Questions 171-178* (New York: Desclée Co., 1961), 93–145 and Ramage, *Dark Passages of the Bible*, Chs. 2 and 4.

28. Second Vatican Council, *Dei Verbum* §13; *Catechism of the Catholic Church*, §101; Pius XII, *Divino afflante Spiritu* §37. This incarnational analogy has roots in the patristic period with Origen's comparison of Scripture to the flesh of Christ. Inspired by a distinction drawn from Mary Healy and applying it to our topic, I would note that Christians often take an exclusively "Method A" or "Monophysite" approach to Genesis wherein, as ancient heretics denied Christ's human nature, people downplay or ignore the human factors that went into the composition of the biblical text. On the other hand, Healy notes that a common form of modern ("Method B") scholarship tends to be "Nestorian." According to Healy, just as the ecumenical council of Chalcedon recognized Jesus's true divinity and true manhood, so a "Chalcedonian form of exegesis" seeks to do justice to both the human and divine aspects of Sacred Scripture. Mary Healy, "Behind, in Front of . . . or Through the Text? The Christological Analogy and the Last Word of Biblical Truth," in *Behind the Text: History and Biblical Interpretation*, eds. *Craig Bartholomew*, C. Stephen Evens, Mary Healy, and Murray Rae (Grand Rapids, MI: Zondervan, 2003), 181–95. See also Denis Farkasfalvy's treatment of the incarnational analogy in his *Inspiration and Interpretation: A Theological Introduction to Sacred Scripture* (Washington, D.C.: The Catholic University of America Press, 2010), 230–35.

29. On this subject, I recommend three insightful authors who explore an incarnational model of Scripture: Peter Enns, *Inspiration and Incarnation* (Grand Rapids, MI: Baker Academic, 2005), especially the postscript to its 2015 second edition on "Embracing the Theological Scandal of the Incarnation"; Telford Work, *Living and Active: Scripture in the Economy of Salvation* (Grand Rapids, MI: Eerdmans, 2002); Kenton Sparks, *Sacred Word, Broken Word: Biblical Authority and the Dark Side of Scripture* (Grand Rapids, MI: Eerdmans, 2011); Kenton Sparks, *God's Word in Human Words* (Grand Rapids, MI: Baker Academic, 2008).

that I will be arguing for later in this book: that reality itself has a cruciform or paschal structure—that we are paradoxically fulfilled only when we humble ourselves, like the persons of the Trinity, through a gift of self-emptying *kenosis* (Phil 2:5–11). For now, I think that C.S. Lewis captures the point well when he asks:

> Does this shock us? It ought not to, except as the Incarnation itself ought to shock us. The same divine humility which decreed that God should become a baby at a peasant-woman's breast, and later an arrested field-preacher in the hands of the Roman police, decreed also that He should be preached in a vulgar, prosaic and unliterary language. If you can stomach the one, you can stomach the other. The Incarnation is in that sense, an irreverent doctrine: Christianity, in that sense, an incurably irreverent religion.[30]

Given how boldly and respectfully he addresses the more problematic portions of Scripture, I have no doubt that Benedict would concur with Lewis's analysis: the Bible's weakness is no cause for shame—on the contrary, its humility, vulnerability, and "scandalous" nature is inextricably bound up with its redemptive character.

## THE LITERAL SENSE, INERRANCY, AND "THE ESSENTIAL POINT"

The Christology of Scripture in turn casts considerable light on another important point of Catholic teaching concerning God's word: the doctrine of biblical inerrancy. But how can an inerrant text authored by God—who can neither lie nor deceive—contain the sort of defects and problems that we have just been discussing? To address this point, it is important to ground our thought in the important words of the Second Vatican Council:

> Therefore, since everything asserted by the inspired authors or sacred writers must be held to be asserted by the Holy Spirit, it follows that the books of Scripture must be acknowledged as teaching solidly, faithfully and without error that truth which God wanted put into sacred writings for the sake of salvation.[31]

If the Catholic Church teaches that all of Scripture is inerrant, then even the most apparently unscientific and outdated passages of Scripture must in some way also be inerrant. In other words, if we find that the Book of Genesis states things that are difficult to reconcile with what we know today through philosophy, historical criticism, or evolutionary science, it nevertheless must convey something true. Yet, if everything asserted by Scripture's inspired authors is to be considered without error, then the difficulty arises: how do we know what precisely is being asserted as true in the biblical text? This is where the *literal sense* of Scripture comes in.

---

30. C.S. Lewis, "Modern Translations of the Bible," in *God in the Dock* (Grand Rapids: Eerdmans, 1998), 229–30.

31. Second Vatican Council, *Dei Verbum*, §11.

To be interested in the literal sense of Scripture is not the same thing as sub-scribing to literal*ism*, wherein one assumes that the Bible contains the sort of raw history that would be captured on a video camera (which itself can indeed be quite biased).[32] Contrary to such a literal*istic* approach, the truly literal—or per-haps better, liter*ary* or liter*ate*—sense of Scripture considers not just the bare meaning of the Scripture's words, but what through them its human authors meant to convey to the people of their time by means of their literary craft. In the following passage that I have cited at some length, Kevin Vanhoozer offers perhaps the best explanation of the crucial difference between these two that I have ever encountered:

> [Literalism or 'letterism'] is a wooden, thin interpretation that fails to go beyond the standard meanings of words and expressions (the locutions) or to discern the manner in which an author attends to these meanings (the illo-cutions). Hence *literalism short-circuits the literal sense insofar as it fails to appreciate the author's intention to give his or her utterance a certain kind of force.* It is most important to distinguish literalistic from literal interpretation. The former generates an unlettered, ultimately *illiterate* reading—one that is incapable of recognizing less obvious uses of language such as metaphor, satire, and so forth. By contrast, the latter attends to what authors are doing in tending to their words in a certain way.[33]

To the above, Vanhoozer adds that "the literal sense is the sense of a literary act" and that truly literal or *literate* interpretation of Scripture is therefore attentive to its communicative context and able to identify its authors' communicative acts for what they are in each given instance—whether this be a command, assertion, joke, irony, parable, or some other mode of communication.

With this distinction in place, one can see that the truly literal sense of Genesis 1–11 will look quite different from that of other biblical texts due to the simple fact

---

32. For a lucid articulation of the above point that even a documentary film does not present the "bare" or "uninterpreted" facts of history, see Gerhard Lohfink, *Jesus of Nazareth: What He Wanted, Who He Was* (Collegeville, MN: Liturgical Press, 2012), 4–6, 12–13. As Lohfink notes, such a historian or filmmaker inevitably interprets what he has received, as he must select only a little from the mass of audio and visual information available, seeking to make sense of it all by cutting, pasting, recom-bining, and commenting using all the tools of his craft, for "without interpretation there can be no understanding."

33. Kevin Vanhoozer, *Is There a Meaning in This Text?: The Bible, the Reader, and the Morality of Literary Knowledge* (Grand Rapids, MI: Zondervan Academic, 2009), 311–12. Emphasis added. Expand-ing on this point, Vanhoozer writes, "'Literalistic' interpretation is like a word-for-word translation that yields verbally exact or 'formally equivalent' versions but that also runs the risk of overlooking the main (illocutionary) point. Literal interpretation, on the other hand, is more like a translation that strives for dynamic equivalence and yields the literary sense. . . . Interpreters err either when they allegorize dis-course that is intended to be taken literally or when they 'literalize' discourse that is intended to be taken figuratively." Vanhoozer, *Is There a Meaning in This Text?*, 311. For another helpful diagnosis of a common confusion made by literalists and a clear breakdown of three meanings of the word 'literal,' see *Holmes, Cur Deus Verba?*, 115–19, 167–73. Critiquing literalism, Holmes adds that modern people often have an "almost superstitious belief in 'bare facts'" and "do not like veils around reality."

that the Bible is not just one book, but a book of books—each of which has its own unique literary style (often with different styles present in the same book, as we see comparing Gn 1–11 to the rest of Genesis). Accordingly, the opening chapters of Genesis will read differently from that of a psalm, which itself may differ in style from another psalm, which in turn has quite a different character from what we see in the wisdom literature. What is more, all these differ in nature from the gospels, which Benedict describes as "interpreted history," noting that the latter were never meant to be completely disinterested and purely objective—an effort he identifies as impossible in the first place.[34] In fact, a plenitude of senses is present even within the gospels. There are parables (e.g., The Good Samaritan) and hyperbole ("If your right eye causes you to sin, pluck it out"). These differ still from the apocalyptic genre of the Old Testament prophets ("The sun shall be turned to darkness, and the moon to blood"). It may sound ironic given our culture's use of the term, but the literal (i.e., author-intended) sense of a biblical passage can even be symbolic or figurative, as is the case in the Bible's opening chapters ("God formed man of dust from the ground, and breathed into his nostrils the breath of life," etc.).

On this very point, the Catholic Church offers clear guidance to help us determine what precisely a given passage is asserting:

> To search out the intention of the sacred writers, attention should be given, among other things, to "literary forms." For truth is set forth and expressed differently in texts which are variously historical, prophetic, poetic, or of other forms of discourse. The interpreter must investigate what meaning the sacred writer intended to express and actually expressed in particular circumstances by using contemporary literary forms in accordance with the situation of his own time and culture. For the correct understanding of what the sacred author wanted to assert, due attention must be paid to the customary and characteristic styles of feeling, speaking and narrating which prevailed at the time of the sacred writer, and to the patterns men normally employed at that period in their everyday dealings with one another.[35]

---

34. Benedict XVI, *Jesus of Nazareth: The Infancy Narratives*, 17. For more on this point, see Ramage, *Jesus, Interpreted*, 182–83n98. This understanding is echoed in curial works published during Ratzinger's time as their head. For instance, see Pontifical Biblical Commission, *The Interpretation of the Bible in the Church* (1993), I.C.3; International Theological Commission, *Memory and Reconciliation: The Church and the Faults of the Past* (1999), 4.1.

In an insightful article, Tracey Roland connects the above insight with the work of Hans-Georg Gadamer, who argued that meaning is not an objective property of texts. As such, it cannot be extracted from a position of complete neutrality but rather requires a "fusion of horizons." Hans-Georg Gadamer, *Truth and Method* (New York: Seabury, 1975), 305; Tracey Rowland, "Reading Scripture within the Horizon of Faith," *Evangelization and Culture* 5 (2020): 88–98. In the case of faith, the upshot is that the Bible can only be understood aright when approached in the same Spirit in which it was written or, as Ratzinger says, by having *sympathia* with the biblical text. Ratzinger, "Biblical Interpretation in Crisis," 22–23; cf. Second Vatican Council, *Dei Verbum*, 12.

35. Second Vatican Council, *Dei Verbum*, §12. Galileo shares a similar vision when he applies this understanding to passages in Scripture that appear to contradict science. Arguing that we should not hastily condemn sense experience or the findings of science upon the testimony of biblical passages

In light of the above teaching, it would be a great mistake to think that everything in Genesis's creation accounts is being asserted as historical.[36] For, as the Church teaches, sometimes the genre of a biblical text is intended to convey the truth poetically or symbolically. Matthew Lamb captures the matter perfectly when he writes, "The whole of the Bible must be approached with faith; this does not mean that every sentence is a definable dogma."[37]

The same point Lamb makes with regard to doctrine may be said with regard to history: just because a given biblical narrative *may* be read historically does not mean that the author *intends* it to be read as such. For example, it is not impossible that the parable of the Good Samaritan originated in a historical event, but setting off on a search for inn records would be to entirely miss Luke's (and Jesus's) point. Applying this to Genesis's creation account, someone familiar with many different kinds of texts—folklore, mystery, science fiction, and the like—would be comfortable recognizing that embarking on a quest for the precise chemical composition of the dust that God used to form man (Gn 2:7) or the precise location of the rib from which he formed woman (Gn 2:22) would be an *il*literate move, mistaking

---

"which may have some different meaning beneath their words," he remarks that the Bible is not "chained in every expression to conditions as strict as those which govern all physical effects." To this, he adds, "[N]or is God any less excellently revealed in Nature's actions than in the sacred statements of the Bible. Perhaps this is what Tertullian meant by these words: 'We conclude that God is known first through Nature, and then again, more particularly, by doctrine, by Nature in His works, and by doctrine in His revealed word.'" Galileo, "Letter to the Grand Duchess Christina," 102.

36. On this score, see Germain Grisez, "The Inspiration and Inerrancy of Scripture," in St. Paul Center for Biblical Theology, *For the Sake of Our Salvation: The Truth and Humility of God's Word* (Steubenville, OH: Emmaus Road Publishing, 2010), 181–90 at 186. In a helpful footnote in which he offers illustrations from Aquinas to support his claim, Grisez notes that the fathers of the Second Vatican Council would have been well aware of the difference between a mere *statement* on the one hand and an *assertion* or *teaching* on the other. Grisez, "The Inspiration and Inerrancy of Scripture," 186n15. With different vocabulary from Grisez, Brian Harrison argues that the key lies in distinguishing what is formally taught in Scripture from what is merely "used" (*adhiberi*) by the sacred writers in view of making their assertions. The category of what is merely used, Harrison concludes, may include expressions (*locutiones*) that are "materially" erroneous. Harrison, "Restricted Inerrancy and the 'Hermeneutic of Discontinuity,'" in St. Paul Center for Biblical Theology, *For the Sake of Our Salvation*, 245.

To understand how God can be the primary author of a Bible that contains defects, it is helpful to remember Aquinas's analogy of an injured leg with a limp which he uses to illustrate the respective roles of God and humans in defective human actions. The soul is the first cause of a person's act limping (defective walking); however, the soul does not cause the limp itself, as this defect is the result of physical injury in the leg. Similarly, any defects in Scripture are due to their authors' weak human intellects and not due to God who acts through them. For the analogy I am adapting here, see Aquinas, *ST* I-II, q. 79 a. 2. For a helpful discussion of the analogy with a broader application, see John Rziha, *The Christian Moral Life: Directions for the Journey to Happiness* (Notre Dame, IN: University of Notre Dame Press, 2017), 317n9.

37. Aquinas, *Commentary on Saint Paul's Epistle to the Ephesians*, 256n17. See also Ramage, *Dark Passages of the Bible*, 133. On the reality that not every sentence of Scripture contains a categorical affirmation on the part of its author, see also Farkasfalvy, *Inspiration and Interpretation*, 232 and Synave and Pierre Benoit, *Prophecy and Inspiration*, 134–35, 142.

the mythological genre in which the sacred author is working in this narrative for raw history or science.

As we will discuss in the following chapters, understanding the biblical creation stories in light of other ancient literature provides confirmation that Genesis 1–11 was never intended to serve as a historical or scientific narrative of human origins. However, more challenging to address is the overwhelming likelihood that the biblical authors held incorrect scientific ideas in their minds (e.g., a relatively young and small earth that was the center of the cosmos, the direct creation of all species apart from evolution, etc.) which in turn served as the literary medium of their message. Confronting this issue, Dominican exegetes Paul Synave and Pierre Benoit write:

> [God] certainly cannot prevent [the sacred author] from using in one way or another these erroneous views and, consequently, from letting them show through in his text. For example, no one will deny that the biblical authors had now outmoded cosmological ideas in which they believed, and that they employed them in their writings because they were unable to think apart from contemporary categories. But they do not claim to be teaching them *for their own sakes*; they speak of them for a different purpose, e.g., to illustrate creation and divine providence.[38]

For the sake of argument, let us say that what Synave and Benoit refer to as the Bible's "outmoded cosmological ideas" were indeed held by their authors. C.S. Lewis speaks to precisely this sort of problem in a marvelous chapter of his book *Miracles* entitled "Horrid Red Things." On this score, Lewis says: "Even if it could be shown, then, that the early Christians [and Jews, in the case of Genesis] accepted the Bible's imagery literally, this would not mean that we are justified in relegating their doctrines as a whole to the lumber-room." Indeed, Lewis argues that, just as a little child understands the essential point about the danger of imbibing poison even if she does so while picturing "horrid red things" inside it, so too our faith's core beliefs held from antiquity "would survive substantially unchanged," even after "the falsity of the earlier images had been recognized."[39] As we will see later, this point is incredibly valuable to keep in mind when we encounter passages in Genesis whose worldview is not consistent with the findings of modern science.

For his part, Benedict is well aware that biblical texts often contain statements that, taken in isolation, contradict what we know from science—and even what is stated in other biblical texts: "It is because faith is not set before us as a complete and finished system that the Bible contains contradictory texts, or at least ones that stand in tension to each other."[40] With this in mind, throughout his corpus he is

---

38. Synave and Benoit, *Prophecy and Inspiration*, 142.

39. C.S. Lewis, *Miracles: A Preliminary Study* (New York: Macmillan, 1978), 119. For an application of this to the New Testament, see Ramage, *Jesus, Interpreted*, 208–209.

40. Ratzinger, *God and the World*, 152; See also Benedict XVI, *Jesus of Nazareth: Holy Week*, 106. For an extensive treatment of various biblical texts that ostensibly contradict one another, see Ramage, *Dark Passages of the Bible*, especially Chs. 5–6.

constantly implementing the Second Vatican Council's principles in an effort to discern the revealed message at the heart of thorny biblical texts.

Most importantly for our purposes, he does this frequently in the case of Genesis 1–11 in the effort to draw out the implications of what the Catechism calls its "figurative" (i.e., symbolic, poetic) mode of exposition—its constant use of symbolic images deployed in service of conveying the deepest truths about God and man.[41] Acknowledging that the early chapters of Genesis are written in this genre, Ratzinger emphasizes:

> [T]his does not imply that the individual passages of the Bible sink into meaninglessness and that this bare extract alone has any value. They too, express the truth—*in another way, to be sure, than is the case in physics and biology.* They represent truth in the way that symbols do—just as, for example, a Gothic window gives us a deep insight into reality, thanks to the effects of light that it produces and to the figures that it portrays.[42]

This image of the stained glass window is illuminating, but I also find it helpful to think of the biblical text through the lens of the early Church's iconography. Unlike much of Christian art, icons are intentionally *not* physically accurate, for their purpose is to reveal truths that are *more* real than what the eye can see. Or, to use a more modern example, one might wish to compare the biblical text to Monet's impressionism, or perhaps even Van Gogh's postimpressionism. Many of us love the work of these artists, but it is not because they have simply tried to replicate on canvas what they have seen in the flesh. Rather, they proceed in the manner they do because they are convinced that doing so might reveal something interesting that they have experienced and which a more literal or "realistic" approach might miss.

Similarly, modern interpreters are aware that the Scriptures do not seek to provide believers with a news report or verbatim transcripts of the *ipsissima verba* (the exact historical words) of its all-star cast. In fact, Jeremy Holmes notes that, as a bona fide literary master in the ancient world, an author of Scripture (e.g., St. Luke) would often compose lines and "put them into the mouths of his characters" in order to convey the sense of an event or speech for which he was not present—a dynamic that Holmes notes is obscured when modern translators add quotation marks to the biblical text which itself does not contain them.[43] Along these very lines, Thomas

---

41. *Catechism of the Catholic Church*, §390. Pope Leo XIII already employed this term in his 1893 encyclical *Providentissimus Deus*, §18. Although Leo lacked the knowledge of evolution that we now possess, many of his principles like this one remain valid still today.

42. Ratzinger, *In the Beginning*, 25–26.

43. Holmes, *Cur Deus Verba?*, 181. Holmes's discussion includes helpful citations from Thucydides and Paul of Samosata to illustrate the reality that what we call "actual history" did not mean the same thing for the ancients as it does for us. For excerpts of the above texts referenced by Holmes, see Darrell L. Bock and Gregory J. Herrick, eds., *Jesus in Context: Background Readings for Gospel Study* (Grand Rapids, MI: Baker,2005), 39–40. On this point concerning the gospels' mode of doing history, see Ramage, *Jesus, Interpreted*, 145–47 and 176–82 as well as the Pontifical Biblical Commission's 1964 work *The Historicity of the Gospels*.

Weinandy—a member of the Vatican's International Theological Commission—notes that the Gospel of John, for instance, frequently "has Jesus say" certain things and that its author has "the chutzpa to put his own theological interpretation into Jesus' mouth." The sacred author felt at liberty do this, Weinandy explains, "because he is convinced, by the inspiration of the Holy Spirit, that what he has Jesus say is what Jesus himself truly revealed"—that he had taken on the very mind of Christ through his contemplation of the Incarnate Lord. Accordingly, he continues:

> Thus, given that John is providing his own theological interpretation of the one historical apostolic gospel tradition, the reader may not always hear the *ipsissima verba* of Jesus, his exact historical words, but what the reader does hear is the enriched theological thought, the fuller revelational meaning, contained in Jesus' historical words—Jesus' deeper intended *ipsissima sententia* [his very own thoughts] that John now provides.[44]

While the above analysis had the gospels immediately in view, what is important for our purposes here is that the same dynamic applies to the Old Testament. All the more so is the case for the biblical creation narratives, whose genre is figurative and thus likely not purporting to record the historical transcripts of conversations between the first human being and God at least two hundred thousand years ago. Yet, as discussed above, this is by no means to say that the Bible's opening chapters tell us nothing important. To the contrary: for those willing to read the text in the spirit of faith in which it was written, Genesis casts unfathomable light onto the mystery of God, man, and creation.

To bring us into contact with this deep realism of the Bible, for his part Benedict is always on the lookout to identify its "essential point" [*Das Wesentliche*], "meaning" [*Sinn*], or "kernel"—the message being taught in a given text—while contrasting this with what is incidental to that message—its literary vehicle or "shell."[45] In a document of the International Theological Commission that Cardinal Ratzinger authorized as its then-president, we catch a glimpse of this language along with insight into why it is so important to make use of it. Dogma, it says, must be boiled down to its original sense [*ursprüngliche Sinn*] in order to make it intelligible amidst "new factors" in our present cultural context.[46] As an above quote from

---

44. Weinandy, *Jesus Becoming Jesus: John* (forthcoming The Catholic University of America Press).

45. Ratzinger, "Zum Problem der Entmythologisierung Des Neuen Testamentes," *Religionsunterricht an höheren Schulen* 3 (1960): 11. For an example of this usage in relation to the gospels, see Benedict XVI, *Jesus of Nazareth: Holy Week*, 43. For another instance of this kernel-shell language, see Lewis, "Is Theology Poetry?," 133, wherein he draws the distinction and then proceeds to insist that the "shell" of symbolic language is nevertheless necessary for the articulation of dogma: "The earliest Christians were not so much like a man who mistakes the shell for the kernel as like a man carrying a nut which he hasn't yet cracked. The moment it is cracked, he knows which part to throw away. Till then he holds on to the nut, not because he is a fool but because he isn't. We are invited to restate our belief in a form free from metaphor and symbol. The reason we don't is that we can't."

46. International Theological Commission, *The Interpretation of Dogma* (1989), A.II.1. The Vatican website translates *Sinn* here as "kernel." This fairly captures what is being said by the commission,

Galileo suggested, it is hard to effectively share the gospel with people if we insist that every single aspect of Scripture perfectly reflects the truth of things while the people to whom we wish to proclaim Jesus Christ are well aware that this is not the case. Certainly, one of the "new factors" that affects evangelization today is the knowledge we now have of evolution that was not an issue in centuries past.

Recalling a similar crisis from an earlier age, Ratzinger articulates his crucial kernel-shell distinction in several other, complementary ways. When encountering a biblical passage that seems to contradict science, Ratzinger says that we must do as we had to learn to do back in the time of Galileo and then-emerging heliocentric theory: to discriminate between "fixed stars" and "planets," between "permanent orientation" and "transient movement"; to distinguish "the doctrinal message [glaubensmäßige Aussage] of the Bible" from "what may be only the temporary contingent vehicle [Instrumentierung] for its real theme [eigentlichen Themas]"; to discern "what is and is not necessary for a profession of faith" and make it clear "where faith ends and where worldview [Weltbild] begins"; to know Scripture's "faith testimony" [Glaubenszeugnis] or "framing worldview" [weltbildischen Rahmen] as distinct from the actual "thought" [Gedanke] expressed; or, to distill the core "content" [Sachgehalt] of Scripture from its literary form.[47] To adapt Galileo's famous phrase as John Paul II once did, we should be trying to determine what it is in Scripture that helps us get to heaven, not what it thinks about how the heavens go. To illustrate the above point, we should always be prepared to ask the following of a challenging issue: does this particular matter change who God is and what he is calling us to do? Here is how Ratzinger answers this question when it comes to scientific matters: "The figure of Jesus, his spiritual physiognomy, does not change whether the sun revolves around the earth or the earth revolves around the sun, whether or not the world came to be through evolution."[48]

One way to think about this distinction is by applying it to narratives that we encounter in books or shows in today's society. For instance, having experienced myriad health problems over the years, I can tell you that medical TV dramas—

---

but Ratzinger himself often also uses another word, *Kern*, which directly translates into English as "kernel" to contrast the essential content of Scripture from its "shell" (*Schale*).

47 Remarkably, with the exception of the last, all of the distinctions immediately above are made by Ratzinger within a couple of pages in the same article "Farewell to the Devil?," 198–99 [*Dogma Und Verkündigung*, 226–28]. For other instances of Ratzinger applying these distinctions, see his "Zum Problem der Entmythologisierung Des Neuen Testamentes," 2–11; Ramage, *Jesus, Interpreted*, 44, 46, 227n80, 230n85; Aaron Pidel, SJ, "Joseph Ratzinger and Biblical Inerrancy," *Nova et Vetera* 12.1 (2014): 307–30 at 324–25. For a helpful recent discussion of the worldview of biblical authors and how this must be distinguished from their assertions, see Holmes, *Cur Deus Verba?*, 92–94, 187–97. Holmes echoes Ratzinger in contending that the fingerprints of a geocentric worldview that we find in Genesis does not render it guilty of error when we grasp the text's proper intention. Nicholas Lombardo's distinction between "sense" and reference" discussed at the end of this chapter provides another avenue by which to make this point. God certainly intends the sense of the Bible's ancient cosmology to be in the text, but this does not mean that the author's entire reference (the erroneous scientific ideas that served as the vehicle for his main claims) perfectly aligns with the divine mind.

48. Ratzinger, "Farewell to the Devil?," 202.

much as I enjoy many of them—often do not paint an accurate picture of life (and death) in a real hospital. However, I tend to forgive their creators for these aberrations, because presenting an accurate, detailed account of how kidney transplants work is not their main objective. To be sure, the show's science should not be so imprecise that it detracts from the story, yet the main point of the story is ultimately something about man for which the medical (or, *mutatis mutandis*, crime, firefighting, etc.) setting serves a vehicle. Pivoting genres, consider that the entire point of *Star Trek* with its probing of philosophical questions concerning human nature or *Star Wars* with its drama of good and evil and human relationships would be missed if we were to get hung up on the inaccuracy of this or that aspect of its science. In a similar way, to reject the Bible's creation narratives for having imprecise science (or, on the other hand, to insist that they give us a better scientific account of reality than the actual sciences do) is to entirely miss the purpose of these stories and confuse the essential point with the literary vehicle by which it is conveyed. Such is the nature of man's literary craft, and the fact that the Bible's creation narratives are inspired by God does not prevent them from being true human literature.

Applying these principles specifically to Genesis's creation narratives, Ratzinger gets a lot of mileage out of this notion as he sets out to differentiate the "image" it might employ from "what is intended" or "what is of enduring value."[49] Recalling the Second Vatican Council's teaching on the need to ascertain a given passage's literary form, he adds that the "form of portrayal" deployed in the opening chapters of Genesis was chosen from what was available in the culture at the time, "from the images which surrounded the people who lived then, which they used in speaking and in thinking, and thanks to which they were able to understand the greater realities."[50] We will discuss the specific ways in which he applies this to concrete images within Genesis in subsequent chapters. For now, our task is to finish fleshing out his overall strategy for interpreting Scripture in general and the primeval history of Genesis in particular.

## A CHALLENGE AND RATZINGER'S ARTFUL RESPONSE

I sincerely hope that the reader finds the above distinctions helpful. However, as Ratzinger himself is well aware, it is not evident to everyone how the Second Vatican Council's call to search out Scripture's intentions and the emeritus pontiff's endeavor to enact it is compatible with the Church's traditional way of reading Genesis.

Indeed, it can be confusing when first encountering the idea that we need to distinguish what is essential from what is incidental or the kernel from the shell of biblical texts. Thus, I have been asked: Why the need for such distinctions between content and form? Is it not simpler to simply embrace everything that came before us and not "water down" the faith? Interestingly, Ratzinger himself anticipates this very question, which presumably is something he too had been asked:

---

49. Ratzinger, *In the Beginning*, 7–8.
50. Ratzinger, *In the Beginning*, 4–5.

For when we are told we have to distinguish between the images themselves and what those images mean, then we can ask in turn: Why wasn't that said earlier? Evidently it must have been taught differently at one time or else Galileo would never have been put on trial. And so the suspicion grows that ultimately perhaps this way of [distinguishing the essential from the incidental] is only a trick of the church and of theologians who have run out of solutions but do not want to admit it, and now they are looking for something to hide behind. And on the whole the impression is given that the history of Christianity in the last 400 years has been a constant rear-guard action as the assertions of the faith and of theology have been dismantled piece by piece.[51]

To be sure, it is easy to see how the distinction-making process Ratzinger proposes may look like hairsplitting from the outside. Moreover, Ratzinger immediately proceeds to suggest, it may even appear that the Church has been in a continual retreat the past five centuries, constantly backtracking on earlier teachings through "distinctions" in order to save face in the modern world.

The truth is, though, that purifying the faith through fine distinctions has been a practice of the Church from the beginning (think: Council of Nicea, Council of Chalcedon, etc.). In a speech he wrote for Cardinal Frings on the eve of the Second Vatican Council (a message that would go on to have a major impact on the council itself), Father Ratzinger talked about how important it is that we learn to make these very distinctions and be able to let go of certain incidentals when they are no longer appropriate and hold us back from effectively proclaiming the Gospel. We do this, he says, by distinguishing the "actual belief" (*das eigentliche Glaubensmäßige*) from its "time-conditioned clothing" (*zeitbedingten Einkleidung*).[52]

Detachment from the past can be a painful undertaking. It is doubly challenging to do this in a thoughtful manner that avoids throwing out the baby with the bathwater. In this regard, I find particularly helpful the following description of what the process ought to look like in any of us who would set out on the task of helping the Church to think through matters of faith and science where new distinctions are required:

> The true reformer, therefore, is someone who does not seek to build for himself a Church in his own image and likeness but, rather, eliminates the dross so as to discover beneath it the true face, the one that Jesus intended to imprint on the community founded by him, entrusting then to the apostles and to

---

51. Ratzinger, *In the Beginning*, 6. Further, it must be remembered that, without making fine distinctions, we would never have been able to articulate who Jesus Christ is (true God, true man, consubstantial with the Father, one Person with two natures). Nor would we have the doctrine of the Trinity (three Persons, one nature). In fact, we would not even have been able to nail down the books of the Bible without engaging in what one outside the tradition might construe as sophistic hairsplitting!
52. Joseph Frings, "Das Konzil und die moderne Gedankenwelt," 174 (my translation).

their successors the task of making it grow but also of preserving unchanged its fundamental characteristic traits.[53]

To bolster this point, Ratzinger evokes an image from Michelangelo, who in his turn was drawing on ancient insights of Christian mysticism and philosophy. The Renaissance master saw in the raw marble that stood before him a figure—a "pure image"—just waiting to be set free by his art. In Michelangelo's view, the artist's job is simply to remove the excess that covers his statue. According to Ratzinger, theology is likewise fundamentally a vocation of uncovering and releasing what is superfluous—not of making something new.

Ratzinger extends this analogy even further by adding that some things in the Church are like an artist's scaffolding. They are necessary for a particular purpose and time. "But," he continues, "they may become obsolete" and even "risk setting themselves up as the essence of the Church and thus prevent us from seeing through to what is truly essential. This is why they must always be dismantled again, like scaffolding that has outlived its necessity."[54] Drawing next on St. Bonaventure, Ratzinger summarizes his point as follows: the Church's reforming task, like our work of personal conversion, is a work of *ablatio* or "taking away" what is inauthentic to make way for faith's true form to emerge.[55]

## WHICH QUESTIONS GENESIS ADDRESSES, WHICH IT DOES NOT

With the above distinctions in place, we may now apply them more concretely to the creation narratives in the opening chapters of Genesis. First, let us consider the text's "shell," or what does *not* pertain to the core of their revealed message. Ratzinger gave his take on the matter in a university lecture on this very theme: Genesis's opening narrative "does not inform about details of the past" or "expand our knowledge of history into the prehistoric."[56] Ratzinger later echoes this in writing, "[T]he Bible is not a scientific textbook. . . . One cannot get from it a scientific explanation of how the world arose."[57] Wedding this point to his hermeneutic of divine pedagogy, he adds, "The Bible is not a textbook about God and divine matters but contains images with perceptions and *insights in the course of development, and*

---

53. Elio Guerriero, *Benedict XVI: His Life and Thought* (San Francisco: Ignatius Press, 2018), 358. Guierrero is summarizing Ratzinger, *La Chiesa: Una Comunità Sempre in Cammino* (Cinisello Balsamo: Edizioni Paoline, 2006), 115–37 at 123. The English translation of this piece can be found in Ratzinger, *Called to Communion: Understanding the Church Today*, trans. Adrian Walker (San Francisco: Ignatius Press, 1996), 140–41.

54. Ratzinger, *Called to Communion*, 142.

55. Ratzinger, *Called to Communion*, 141–42, citing Bonaventure, *Coll. in Hex.* 2, 33, in *Doctoris Seraphici S. Bonaventurae Opera Omnia* (Ad Claras Aquas / Quaracchi: Ex Typographia Collegii S. Bonaventurae, 1882), 5:342b.

56. Ratzinger, *Schöpfungslehre* (1964), 31, 253; Sanz, "Joseph Ratzinger y la doctrina de la creación. Los apuntes de Münster de 1964 (y III)," 456n5, 493n126.

57. Ratzinger, *In the Beginning*, 4.

*through these images, slowly and step by step, a historical reality is coming into existence.*"[58] In its work on biblical inspiration begun during Benedict's pontificate, the PBC explains that the creation accounts of Genesis 1–2 do not show *how* the world and humanity began. Indeed, the commission bluntly remarks:

> As "creation accounts," they do not show "how" the world and humanity began but speak of the Creator and his relationship with what he had created. Much misunderstanding results from reading these texts from a modern [read: literalist] perspective, seeing them as affirmations of "how" the world and humanity were formed. To respond more adequately to the intention of the biblical texts, it is necessary to oppose such a reading, but without putting their assertions in competition with the knowledge that has come from the natural sciences of our time.[59]

John Paul II expressed this same point in teaching, "The theological teaching of the Bible, like the doctrine of the Church . . . does not seek so much to teach us the *how* of things, as rather the *why* of things."[60] In greater length, the pontiff explained by way of referencing Galileo:

> The Bible speaks to us of the origin of the universe and its structure—not to issue a scientific treatise, but to identify man's precise relationship with God and with the universe. Sacred Scripture wishes simply to affirm that God created the world, and to teach this truth with the cosmological language that prevailed at the time of the writer. The sacred book also wants to let men know that the world was not created as a footstool of the gods, as other cosmogonies and cosmologies teach, but that it was created in service of man and for the glory of God. Any other teaching on the origin and structure of the universe is foreign to the intentions of the Bible, which does not wish to teach how heaven was made, but how one goes to heaven.[61]

We might summarize recent magisterial teaching by saying that *how* precisely creation happened is a question for physics and astronomy, just as *how, where,*

---

58. Ratzinger, *God and the World*, 151–52.

59. Pontifical Biblical Commission, *The Inspiration and Truth of Sacred Scripture*, 73–74. To this, the PBC adds, "The narrative of Genesis 1–11, the traditions dealing with the patriarchs and the conquest of the land of Israel, the stories of the kings down to the Maccabean revolt certainly contain truths, but they do not intend to propose a historical chronicle of the people of Israel." Pontifical Biblical Commission, *The Inspiration and Truth of Sacred Scripture*, 124. Interestingly, this understanding that we find in the work of Benedict and today's biblical commission shares some deep affinities with the thought of Pope Leo XIII from over a century ago. While Leo exhibits a more confrontational attitude toward the physical sciences than we find in more recent popes, he too emphasizes that the sacred writers of Genesis "did not seek to penetrate the secrets of nature." Leo XIII, *Providentissimus Deus*, §18.

60. John Paul II, Address to Participants in a Colloquium on Science, Philosophy and Theology (September 5, 1986).

61. John Paul II, Address to the Pontifical Academy of the Sciences. October 3, 1981 (my translation). http://www.vatican.va/content/john-paul-ii/en/speeches/1981/october.index.2.html. As Galileo memorably expresses this truth, the intention of Sacred Scripture is to "teach us how one goes to heaven and not how heaven goes." Galileo, "Letter to the Grand Duchess Christina," 96.

and *when* mankind emerged are questions for biology. In other words, important as they may be, scientific questions do not touch the heart of faith. Or, if we prefer Thomistic vocabulary, these matters belong to the faith only acciden-tally.[62] That is, when the Bible says something that appears to pertain to these questions, they are not its main teaching but rather comprise the "shell," "world-view," or "vehicle" by which it conveys its message about God and man to us. Bearing this in mind frees us to grant the rather obvious fact that the biblical authors' scientific understanding is far from perfect, and to make it clear that this sort of account was not necessary for the text to make its central point to its original audience—or to us today.

If the Bible's opening chapters are not concerned with material origins (*how*, *when*, and *where* things in the universe have happened), then what *are* they teach-ing? We might summarize this positive side of the creation narrative as follows. Genesis teaches without error these vital truths that lie beyond the competence of empirical science: *who* God is (the one and only God by whose gift all things have existence), *what* man is (the divine image, created in grace yet fallen and in need of redemption, made male and female who are of equal dignity and given the voca-tion of marriage), *why* he created us (to work and then also "rest" with him so as to be adopted into the divine family), *why* our life includes so much misery (original sin), and *how* we can find healing and redemption (through the grace of Christ).[63] These matters belong to what Benedict refers to as the kernel of divine revelation and reflect the essential point of Scripture.

As a final note on this point, Ratzinger tackles this issue with the help of some philosophical vocabulary in an essay specifically dedicated to faith and evo-lution. Here, he makes his usual distinction by explaining that belief in creation moves on the *ontological* level, addressing questions that are the core concern of

---

62. Aquinas frequently makes this sort of distinction, but the following instance is especially apro-pos in this book as he applies it directly to the creation narratives in Genesis. Some biblical matters, he says, pertain to the substance of the faith (*ad substantiam fidei*). Others, pertain to the faith only acci-dentally (*per accidens*). For instance, Thomas locates the doctrine that the world began to be by creation (*mundum incepisse creatum*) within the substance of the faith, whereas he indicates that many historical matters (*multa historialia*) like how and in what order the world was made (*quo autem modo et ordine factus sit*) pertain to the faith only accidentally. Aquinas, *In II Sent.*, dist. 12, a. 2.

63. For further discussion of this, see Pontifical Biblical Commission, *The Inspiration and Truth of Sacred Scripture*, 74. More recently, William Lane Craig has provided a valuable summary of ten teachings from the Bible's creation narratives whose truth does not depend upon their being historical or scientific accounts. See Craig, "The Historical Adam," *First Things* (October 2021). I mentioned above that theology explains *why* God created things, whereas science provides a physical explanation of *how* they came to be in time. However, one might reply that science too can also explain "why" a thing exists. For example, if we were to ask, "Why are there rainbows?," the scientist could explain that they are an optical illusion caused by the refraction of light in water droplets suspended in the sky. However, this is still a physical explanation of *how* the rainbow came to be there and is not an *ultimate* account of why rainbows exist in the first place. For its part, theology would speak to this question by explaining that rainbows exist in order to be a sign of God's covenant, to reflect God's glory, or some other nonphysical explanation to that effect.

Scripture (e.g., who God is, why God made things, and what they are in their essence). The theory of evolution, on the other hand, does not lie in Scripture's proper domain because it is situated on the *phenomenological* level (the level of concrete physical things studied via the scientific method).[64] The PBC captures this point as follows:

> In the Bible, we encounter many and various themes. An attentive reading, however, shows that the primary and dominating theme is God and his salvific plan for human beings. The truth which we find in Sacred Scripture essentially concerns God and his relationship with his creatures. . . . To respond to the questions that arise in the interpretation of these difficult texts, it is necessary to study them carefully, taking into account the findings of the modern sciences and, simultaneously, the main theme of the texts, namely, God and his plan of salvation. Such an approach shows how the doubts raised against their truth and origin in God can be resolved.[65]

## SCRIPTURE'S THREEFOLD AUTHORSHIP AND THE NEED TO THINK ON THE LEVEL OF THE WHOLE

While Benedict clearly thinks that it is important to identify discrete teachings in Scripture by recourse to their "essential point," he is also aware of how easy it is to fall into the habit of dissecting the Bible in the search for truth nuggets, considering this in tandem with the truth that God allows defects in the Bible in order to more perfectly achieve his overall goal. As a result, Benedict thinks that it is most helpful to locate biblical inspiration and inerrancy on the level of Scripture's whole. Consider the following:

> The plan in which it is possible to perceive Sacred Scripture as a Word of God is *that of the unity of God, in a totality* in which the individual elements are illuminated reciprocally and are opened to understanding.[66]

> It follows straightaway that neither the criterion of inspiration nor that of infallibility can be applied *mechanically*. *It is quite impossible to pick out one single sentence* and say, right, you find this sentence in God's great book, so it must simply be true in itself.[67]

---

64. Ratzinger, "Belief in Creation and the Theory of Evolution," 133.

65. Pontifical Biblical Commission, *The Inspiration and Truth of Sacred Scripture*, xiv (emphasis added).

66. Benedict XVI, Address to Participants in the Plenary Meeting of the Pontifical Biblical Commission (May 2, 2011). Emphasis added. This text dovetails well with the Catechism and *Dei Verbum* in calling on interpreters to always situate texts within "the content and unity of the whole of Scripture." Second Vatican Council, *Dei Verbum*, §12.

67. Ratzinger, *God and the World*, 153. See also this thought-provoking text from James Tunstead Burtchaell, *Catholic Theories of Biblical Inspiration since 1810: A Review and Critique* (Cambridge: Cambridge University Press, 1969), 299, 303–304: "Both by those who accept these claims [of inerrancy and infallibility] and by those who reject them, they have been imagined as some sort of flawless, eternal

Lastly, I would only like to mention the fact that in a good hermeneutic *it is not possible to apply mechanically the criterion of inspiration*, or indeed of absolute truth by extrapolating a single sentence or expression.[68]

Echoing this holistic approach to inspiration, Jeremy Holmes has recently added that it is best to think of inspiration as a dynamic reality—"God's providential guidance of a process"—rather than focusing our attention on the identities of the many discrete authors and redactors who contributed to the formation of the biblical canon:

> Relocating inspiration in God's intention throws the emphasis onto God's providential guidance of a process, which is something we tend to associate with a people more than with an individual person taken alone. The way is opened to seeing the human authors' efforts as contributions to a process, to a tradition, rather than exercises in self-expression. Consequently, we can imagine the subjective experience of inspiration as being as wide as the tradition itself, including both the exaltation of Isaiah 6 and the humble, workaday efforts of the unknown editor who added the introductory line of Isaiah 1:1. When the Pentateuch is discovered to be the work of many authors and editors, this is no problem for a theology of inspiration.[69]

As Holmes shows, locating inspiration on the level of God's providential guidance of tradition itself reveals that God is at work in the most mundane dimensions of Scripture no less than he is in its most lofty verses. And this thought is not only germane to biblical inspiration but is also relevant for the broader subject of our book. How so?

As we have already seen in Chapter 3 and will emphasize again in later chapters, *Benedict's approach to how divine providence operates in biblical inspiration is paralleled in how he understands providence to work within creation itself.* In other

---

ownership of the truth, expressed in formulas that might from time to time need a little translating, but never need replacing. In this sense, there has probably never been an inerrant declaration uttered or book written, nor need we look forward to one. But if inerrancy involve wild, and sometimes even frightening movement, if it mean being pulled to the right and to the left, being tempted constantly to deviate, yet always managing somehow to regain the road, then it begins to sound rather like what the Church has been about. . . . In sum, the Church does find inerrancy in the Bible, if we can agree to take that term in its dynamic sense, and not a static one. Inerrancy must be the ability, not to avoid all mistakes, but to cope with them, remedy them, survive them, and eventually even profit from them. In a distinct selection of faith-leavings from a distinct epoch of faith-history, we have the archives of the process by which our ancestral faith began from nothing, involved itself in countless frustrating errors, but made its way, lurching and swerving, 'reeling but erect,' somehow though never losing the way, to climax in Christ." For more on the biblical concept of truth, or *emeth*, as indicative primarily of God's faithfulness to Israel—that he is true to his word—see Burtchaell, *Catholic Theories of Biblical Inspiration since 1810*, 266–67, wherein he adds: "While the idea is never absent that God's words are true, this never has reference to the Scriptures, as if to imply that they contain no historical error. . . . This attitude confuses the truth of Scripture with faultless historical chronicle."

68. Benedict XVI, Address to Participants in the Plenary Meeting of the Pontifical Biblical Commission (May 2, 2011). See also Aquinas, *Commentary on Saint Paul's Epistle to the Ephesians*, 256n17.

69. Holmes, *Cur Deus Verba?*, 93.

words, in both cases God works not aside from but instead *in* and *through* natural processes. In other words, inspiration does not occur when the Lord tinkers with an individual's created intellect or gives him a "zap" of enlightenment. As Matthew Lamb helpfully articulates with the help of Bernard Lonergan, biblical inspiration is a particular providential instance of God's universal causality in which "God controls each event because he controls all."[70]

And yet, Lamb, Lonergan, and Ratzinger all maintain that there still remains something special about biblical inspiration. In this regard, the dynamic of inspiration echoes something else I introduced in the last chapter: that in creating through us, God is able to bring about something that is "not the mere product of development, even though it comes to light by way of development." Fundamentally, Benedict is trying to do something similar here that we have also seen him do when it comes to God's activity in creation: lead us away from an unrealistic "mechanical" approach that sees God as an engineer who manipulates creation by pushing and pulling atoms and who manipulates authors by tugging on the strings of their intellect and will.

One unique way that the emeritus pontiff goes about achieving this is by retooling the traditional notion of what we mean by an author's intention.[71] Whereas the neo-scholastic model of inspiration sought to qualify the inerrancy of Scripture through a strained effort to nail down discrete intentions of individual biblical authors, Aaron Pidel, SJ, notes that Ratzinger "transfers the locus of intention and affirmation from the human authors of Scripture to Scripture itself."[72] Thus the emeritus pontiff will often use "text" or "Scripture" as a stand-in for "author" when endeavoring to identify the assertion of a given biblical passage. This move comes across especially well in the following: "*Scripture* is and remains inerrant and beyond doubt in everything that *it* properly intends to affirm, but this is not necessarily so in that which accompanies the affirmation and is not part of it."[73]

---

70. Says Lamb: "St Thomas's concept of instrumentality, as Lonergan has demonstrated, affirms that God controls each event because he controls all. Applied to Scripture, this means that each and every part of it is authored by God because he *originated* . . . the whole process of the Bible's formation. . . . The difference between the instrumentality operative in the composing of the Scriptures and the Universal Instrumentality discussed by Lonergan . . . is that the Providence guiding the genesis of the Bible is an essential element in the special Providence concerned with salvation history. . . . Note the affinity this has with K. Rahner's thesis: God's willing of the Scriptures as a constitutive element in his willing of the Church." Aquinas, *Commentary on Saint Paul's Epistle to the Ephesians*, trans. Matthew Lamb (Albany, NY: Magi Books, 1966), 259n22. See also Aquinas, *Commentary on Saint Paul's Epistle to the Ephesians*, 254nn14–15. For a fuller discussion of what precisely inspiration means if not the "zapping" of an author's intellect, see Ramage, *Dark Passages of the Bible*, 119–26.

71. Pidel, "Joseph Ratzinger and Biblical Inerrancy," 308.

72. Pidel, "Joseph Ratzinger and Biblical Inerrancy," 310–11, 314.

73. Wicks, "Six texts by Prof. Joseph Ratzinger," 280 (emphasis added). Ratzinger's shifting of the locus of intentionality to that of Scripture itself is echoed in the work of John Barton when he notes that it is easier to confidently speak of the intention of a *work* then the intention of individual authors. For, while the intention of an author is sometimes less than obvious and difficult to verify, the intention of a work (i.e., why the Church has included it in the canon of Scripture) is generally discernible. John Barton, *The Nature of Biblical Criticism* (Louisville, KY: Westminster John Knox, 2007), 69–116.

Thus, any incorrect ideas that an individual author has (e.g., Ecclesiastes rejecting the afterlife) are not properly part of the inspired text's assertion.

Ratzinger's major innovation here—and what makes it possible for him to shift the locus of intentionality from the individual authors of Scripture to Scripture itself—is his insight that the Bible's authors (and redactors, e.g., the many individuals who contributed to the Pentateuch over several centuries) never acted alone but as believers embedded within the community of faith. Thus in the foreword to his *Jesus of Nazareth*, Benedict departs from the traditional custom of describing Scripture having two (divine and human) authors and instead speaks of there being three "interlocking subjects" of Scripture. First, there is the individual human who wrote the text. Important here is Benedict's recognition that in some cases a "group of authors" likely originated a given biblical text (e.g., Genesis whose composition likely involved multiple authors writing in different historical epochs). This leads to the second, "collective subject," of Scripture: the People of God (Church) whom Benedict identifies as "actually the deeper 'author' of the Scriptures." In other words, it is the *Church's* intention of having a given text in the biblical canon that matters most, and it—not necessarily what goes on in an individual author's head—is to be considered inerrant. Third, as the tradition has always held, God himself is "at the deepest level the one speaking" through men and their humanity.[74]

## A SENSIBLE DISTINCTION

Before drawing this chapter to a close, at this point I would like to spend some time reflecting on a stimulating article that nicely complements Ratzinger's approach to inspiration by drawing a helpful distinction that the emeritus pontiff himself does not make. The distinction in question is inspired by Gottlob Frege's distinction between "sense" (*Sinn*—the plain or ordinary obvious force of words within their particular community and culture) and "reference" (*Bedeutung*—precisely what the author means by deploying these words).

Applying Frege's distinction to the authorship of Scripture, Nicholas Lombardo notes that, while God always intends the *sense* that Scripture's human authors intend (i.e., that these particular words be in Scripture), the biblical authors at times have *references* in their minds that the divine author does not. In other words, God and Scripture's human authors speak the same words, but they sometimes mean

---

74. Benedict XVI, *Jesus of Nazareth: From the Baptism in the Jordan to the Transfiguration*, xx–xxi. Connecting this threefold authorship to the necessity of ascertaining the author's inerrant intention, Pidel notes, "There is, it would seem, a basic agreement between Ratzinger and scholastic theologians that the scope of immunity from error is coterminous with the scope of intentional affirmation. The major disagreement turns on the identity of the bearer of that intention." Aaron Pidel, SJ, "Biblical Inspiration and Inerrancy According to Joseph Ratzinger," Master's Thesis, Boston College (2011), 73. In keeping with his emphasis upon the people of God as Scripture's collective intending subject, Ratzinger affirms that knowledge of what constitutes the core of Scripture is ultimately discernible only by the living community of faith in communion with the Magisterium. Ratzinger, "Zum Problem der Entmythologisierung Des Neuen Testamentes," 11; Wicks, "Six texts by Prof. Joseph Ratzinger," 276–77.

different things by them. Jeremy Holmes has also recently captured this point with different language but in a way that is consistent with what Lombardo has said. Applying this same sort of distinction to the gospels, he writes, "God has attached his own voice to Mark's written words, not to the entire contents of Mark's mind. It might be the case that Mark, if we were to interview him alone, would say a number of things that God does not want to teach."[75]

The distinction is subtle but crucial. For, as Lombardo demonstrates, holding that the Holy Spirit affirms every reference intended by the human authors of Scripture intend would lead to all manner of contradictions. For example, the author of 1 Samuel 15:1-3 seems to think that God wanted Israel to slay every Amalekite (man, woman, and child). Reading this passage, it seems that the human author of this book thought this event really happened, and that God really made this command. While acknowledging this, Lombardo's distinction allows us to say: whatever the human author intended to claim—whether the passage was intended as a historical claim or rather is decidedly not historical and to be interpreted in a spiritual manner—the New Testament's revelation of God's goodness gives us a serious reason to rule out the possibility that he would ever make such a request.[76] By no means does this rule out the inspired nature the passage: it is just that God meant something different than the human authors did (i.e., a different reference) with respect to the issue of whether it actually happened or not.

At this point, however, perhaps some readers are like Aquinas and have no moral qualms about God commanding the slaying of women and children, seeing as he is God and all.[77] Therefore, it is helpful to consider another problem Lombardo raises: that of ancient Jewish liturgical observances which were promised to be everlasting but which are no longer in effect. If all references on the part of biblical authors are correct, the biblical testimony would require us to hold that ancient Jewish ritual observances have indeed endured for all time as the Old Testament's authors predicted (e.g., Ex 12:17; 31:16–17; Lv 16:29–31,34; 24:8), even though they

---

75. Holmes, *Cur Deus Verba?*, 210. Applying this principle to various difficult biblical passages (like Ecclesiastes denying the afterlife and the Book of Joshua describing the Israelites wiping out entire populations in their conquest of the Promised Land), Holmes writes, "As a result, even though the text of Joshua does not actually say anything contrary to right faith or morals, readers can sense that if they could interview the author then he would say things unacceptable to a Christian. He would not, for example, buy into the idea of turning the other cheek." Holmes, *Cur Deus Verba?*, 219. With regard to the former, he likewise states, "Each text in [Ecclesiastes] can be reconciled with the truth—the Bible gets yet another 'not guilty' verdict—and yet one can tell that, if interviewed, the author would not sign his name at the bottom of the Nicene Creed." Holmes, *Cur Deus Verba?*, 213 .

76. Significantly, the PBC writes of passages like 1 Samuel 15:1-3 that "the law of extermination . . . requires a nonliteral interpretation," as does "the command of the Lord to cut off one's hand or pluck out one's eye." PBC, *The Inspiration and Truth of Sacred Scripture*, 146. For a discussion of this and other related curial texts, see Ramage, "How to Read the Bible and Still Be a Christian: The Problem of Divine Violence as Considered in Recent Curial Documents," *Homiletic and Pastoral Review* (July 12, 2015). https://www.hprweb.com/ 2015/07/how-to-read-the-bible-and-still-be-a-christian/.

77. Aquinas, *ST*, I–II, q. 94, a. 5 ad 2; cf. I–II, q. 100, a. 8; II-II, q. 154, a. 2 ad 2. Thomas's approach to the subject in *De malo* is very similar. See q. 3, a.1, ad 17; q. 15, a. 1 ad 8.

clearly have not and in fact Christ freed his disciples from the obligation to keep them (cf. Acts 10:1–11:18; 15:1–29; Rm 14:1-23; Gal 2:12–16). On this subject, Lombardo writes at greater length:

> Every reasonable application of historical-critical methods leads to the asymp-tomatically certain conclusion that the human authors meant for these ritual practices to be understood as permanently required of their fellow Israelites. And yet, for Christians, God could not have meant for them to be understood in that way, because according to near unanimous opinion among Christians, the Holy Spirit teaches the opposite through the New Testament. Unless we hold that God changed his mind, or that Christians have misinterpreted God's revelation in Christ virtually from the beginning and Jewish Christians were not in fact free from the obligation to keep Jewish ritual practices, we must conclude that the human authors of the Pentateuch intended to convey meaning—references—that God did not.[78]

In light of the observation that Scripture's authors sometimes intend references that God does not, Lombardo therefore proposes that the doctrine of biblical inerrancy is better understood by acknowledging that "God's intended reference is what is immune from error, not the human authors' intended reference."[79] While Ratzinger does not draw this precise conclusion, I think that Lombardo's distinction captures what the emeritus pontiff is attempting to convey in cautioning against a "mechan-ical" understanding of biblical inspiration. For, as we have seen above, Ratzinger does not believe that the doctrine of inerrancy requires affirming that every last thing an individual sacred author says need be true. Both Ratzinger and Lombardo are in agreement that God has willed every word that is in Scripture to be present therein (their "sense"), and yet both also agree that not every last thing a sacred author intends to convey about reality (his "reference") need be in accord with

---

78. Lombardo, "A Voice Like Many Waters," 849 . Lest one get the wrong impression, Lombardo then adds: "To be clear, to say that God intended Jewish ceremonial precepts differently than the human authors does not mean he did not intend the ceremonial precepts at all. Nor does it mean that the Jewish covenant has been revoked and superseded by the new covenant in Christ. It simply means that God intended the ceremonial precepts differently from the human authors. While the authors of the Old Testament intended the precepts in a straightforward way, not aware of their provisionality, God intended their observance as a stage of divine pedagogy, fully valid in itself, but imperfect and destined to give way to a deeper fulfillment, as when the sabbath rest finds fulfillment in the everlasting rest of heaven (Heb 4:8–11). God intends to communicate his message precisely through the flawed and limited understanding of the human authors, without positively willing the flaws and limitations of their under-standing." Lombardo, "A Voice Like the Sound of Many Waters," 850

For an example of a medieval master who recognized that a biblical author's intended reference does not always align with a God's eye view of things, see Bonaventure, *Breviloquium*, vol. 2 of *The Works of Bonaventure: Cardinal Seraphic Doctor and Saint* (Paterson, NJ: St. Anthony Guild Press, 1963), 20. Acknowledging that the Jews expected the law of Sabbath to be per-petual, the Mosaic priesthood eternal, the possession of the earth unending, or the pact of circumcision never to be broken, the Ser-aphic Doctor concluded that these "should be understood in no other way than in their spiritual sense."

79. Lombardo, "A Voice Like the Sound of Many Waters," 857

God's mind on the matter (the "reference" that God intends to convey through the sacred author's words.

## CONCLUSION

I am under no illusion that the above analysis offers the definitive path toward explaining the presence of mistakes in Scripture. Yet, by identifying the People of God as the deepest intending "subject" of Scripture and by calling attention to the complex layers of its corporate intentionality, Ratzinger is able to countenance the existence of infelicities in Scripture (e.g., the outdated biology and cosmology of Genesis) as parts of a grander whole that has been handed on to us by the Church for the sake of our salvation. Ratzinger is aware that these imperfections result from the limitations of Scripture's human authors, who have ideas (in Lombardo's language, "references") that sometimes do not perfectly reflect God's own mind on a given subject. Yet, despite periodic discrepancies of this sort, the emeritus pontiff insists that God's teachings (or, his "references") do indeed shine forth on the pages of Sacred Scripture. On the eve of Vatican II, Ratzinger summarized this point well:

> [A]ccording to a practically irrefutable consensus of historians *there definitely are mistakes and errors in the Bible in profane matters of no relevance for what Scripture properly intends to affirm.* . . . *The true humanity of Scripture*, behind which the mystery of God's mercy arises all the more, is now finally dawning on our awareness; namely that *Scripture is and remains inerrant and beyond doubt in everything that it properly intends to affirm* [i.e., God's "reference"], *but this is not necessarily so in that which accompanies the affirmation and is not part of it* [i.e., the sometimes mistaken references of sacred authors].[80]

This small passage ties together a number of key themes we have discussed in this chapter, in particular the true humanity of Scripture and the necessity of distinguishing its core affirmations from what merely "accompanies" them—or, as we will see him call it in the next chapter, their "vehicle." Moreover, as Pidel says, Ratzinger's conviction that undergirds texts like this is that a failure to concede the Bible's imperfections on historical and scientific matters is "to baptize stubborn fideism and to consign the Church to an intellectual ghetto."[81] This very admission is possible precisely because Ratzinger considers individual biblical texts in light of their place within the entire plan of salvation that culminates in Jesus Christ. Accordingly, the canonical books are surely inerrant in their essence, but, as Pidel remarks, "only to the extent that they bear upon the intention of the whole—the mystery of Christ."[82]

---

80. Jared Wicks, "Six texts by Prof. Joseph Ratzinger," 280 (emphasis added).

81. Pidel, "Joseph Ratzinger and Biblical Inerrancy," 312–13.

82. Pidel, "Joseph Ratzinger and Biblical Inerrancy," 329–30. For Ratzinger one of the key principles that has been deployed in the Church over time is the recognition that an Old Testament passage is "not directly true, in its bare literal meaning," but rather problematic passages within it are "valid insofar as they are part of the history leading up to Christ." Ratzinger, "Farewell to the Devil?," 200.

# Chapter 5

# Myth, History, or Something Else?
## *The Message of Scripture's Creation Narratives in Their Native Context*

## INTRODUCTION

Now that we have Benedict XVI's interpretive principles in place, we will explore how to read Genesis 1–11 in its native ancient Near Eastern context. A pivotal prelude to this endeavor will consist in explaining what Benedict means by describing the genre of these chapters alternatively as symbolic, figurative, and even mythical. Next, we will investigate why this is so, and how modern biblical scholarship has shed light on Genesis by comparing and contrasting it with other stories that were circulating in Israel's ancient milieu. Finally, we will delve into many concrete illustrations of how Benedict applies his principles to the text of Scripture to discern what the Bible *is* and is *not* teaching on the subject of creation and human origins.

By exploring the above topics, my hope is that this chapter will illumine why it is that the Christian faith and evolutionary theory are perfectly compatible. Specifically, in this quest, we will ascertain what precisely Genesis intends with such images as creation through divine speech, its seven-day timeframe, God's "rest," and the garden of Eden where he placed man to dwell. In the chapter that follows, we will continue this trajectory by exploring the meaning of man's origin from the dust of the earth, his receiving God's breath, Eve's birth from Adam's rib, and the couple's fall from grace at the instigation of a serpentine adversary.

## THE "CHOSEN MYTHOLOGY"

In the last chapter, we discussed how grasping what an author intends requires us to first be clear on the literary form he deployed to reach his particular audience. One of the things that contemporary people tend to forget is that the circumstances under which an author writes play a pivotal role in how he sets out to convey his message. Thus, like other ancient Near Eastern people, the author(s) of Genesis wrote about creation not through the medium of the scientific method, but rather through the *language of images and myth*.

The importance of modern biblical scholarship's discovery of Genesis 1–11's mythical background cannot be overstated, for *it is not just the empirical sciences that provide serious ground for reconsidering traditional interpretations of Genesis. Modern discoveries about ancient texts and cultures have independently given us compelling reasons for concluding that sticking to a literalist reading of Genesis is no longer tenable.* Indeed, Nicanor Austriaco argues that it is decidedly *these* discoveries and not those of science that definitively rule out a literalist reading of Genesis's creation account:

> As Cardinal Ratzinger has convincingly argued, in the case of the *Hexaemeron* [six days of creation], we have to depart from a reading that is limited to the literalist sense because studies of ancient texts and ancient cultures—and not natural science—have given us good and necessary reasons for doing so. Sticking to a literalist reading of Genesis would do violence to the original meaning of the human author and thus to the truth God wanted to manifest through his words.[1]

To describe the various features of Genesis's creation narrative in a non-literalist fashion, Benedict frequently invokes the word "image" [*Bild*], adding that they are so important because, "[t]he language of images is admittedly the only means of access here to the authentic reality."[2] Elsewhere, Ratzinger refers to the Bible's poetic portions under the banner of "metaphor" [*Bildersprache*], "legend," [*Sage*] and even "myth" [*Mythos*].[3] As ever, Ratzinger is emphatic that describing divine revelation with such words is fitting provided that one understands the terms correctly. For, while Ratzinger may be said to practice "demythologization" to the extent that he constantly distinguishes Scripture's inerrant core from the form by which it was expressed in its native milieu, he also insists that the figurative elements of the creation narratives are the indispensable means by which the sacred author conveyed his message.[4] The importance of clarity with regard to these terms is evident when Ratzinger addresses biblical texts outside the primeval account of

---

1. Austriaco, "Reading Genesis with Cardinal Ratzinger," *Homiletic and Pastoral Review* (January 1, 2009). In answer to those who seek to use the writings of Pope Leo XIII to rule out evolution, Austriaco reminds us that, in enjoining interpreters "not to depart from the literal and obvious sense [of Scripture], except only where reason makes it untenable or necessity requires," Leo XIII did not limit his statement to scientific reasons. Further, as I argued earlier in this volume, the right question is not whether it is *somehow possible* to somehow square biblical literalism with the scientific evidence, but rather what explanation of the evidence is actually *plausible*.

2. Ratzinger, *Volk und Haus Gottes in Augustins Lehre von der Kirche* (München: K. Zink, 1954), 167–68. The translation reproduced here can be found in Aidan Nichols, OP, *The Thought of Pope Benedict XVI: An Introduction to the Theology of Joseph Ratzinger* (New York: Burns & Oates, 2007), 29. Ratzinger is speaking about the term "People of God" in relation to the Church in this particular case, but the point is also consistent with everything we are discussing in these pages.

3. Ratzinger, *Daughter Zion* (San Francisco: Ignatius Press, 2005), 16 [*Die Tochter Zion*, 15–16]. The precise "myth" or "legend" Ratzinger has in mind here is that of Eve's creation from Adam's rib.

4. Accordingly, Matthew Levering and Kevin Vanhoozer insist that the Bible's metaphors should not be discarded but that, on the contrary, reading Scripture "along the grain of the text" requires that we marshal its symbolic language in order to arrive at its message. Vanhoozer, *Remythologizing Theology: Divine Action, Passion, and Authorship* (Cambridge: Cambridge University Press, 2010), 189; Levering, *Engaging the Doctrine of Israel: A Christian Israelology in Dialogue with Ongoing Judaism* (Eugene, OR: Cascade Books, 2021), 261–71. On Ratzinger practicing a very specific form of "demythologization," see Pidel, "Biblical Inspiration and Inerrancy according to Joseph Ratzinger," 89–90.

Genesis 1–11. For example, when asked about the "myth" surrounding the Ten Commandments being "written with the finger of God" (Ex 31:18), the then-cardinal replied:

> Perhaps we ought here to explain the word 'myth' a little further. What is being said to us here is certainly being expressed in metaphor. . . . The fact that this message is conveyed to us in visionary images [*Bildvisionen*] does not necessarily mean that this is merely a dream or a legend [*Sagen*] or a folktale [*Märchen*]. We have here an image [*Bild*] that refers to a real event, a real entering into history by God, to a real meeting between God and his people—and again, through the medium of this people, a meeting with mankind. . . . This is then the essence of the event [*Ereigniskern*] that is depicted in visionary metaphor [*visionärer Bildsprache*].[5]

I find Ratzinger's words on the Decalogue especially valuable because it illustrates the emeritus pontiff's conviction that mythic elements are present throughout the Bible and not just in its opening chapters. Indeed, it is not insignificant that one of Ratzinger's most explicit treatments of this subject is found in a text dedicated to articulating the essence (*Wesen*) of myth such as it appears in the New Testament. Noting that the proper purpose of myth is not to provide an objective empirical account of the natural world, Ratzinger writes that its aim is to illumine human existence (*Daseins*), and that identifying its core (*Kern*) requires an "existential interpretation."[6]

As for Genesis 1–11, Ratzinger teaches that we encounter primeval truths about man in these chapters—the divine origin of the cosmos, the creation of man in God's image, and our fall from grace—even as these fundamental experiences are related in a poetic rather than historical or scientific manner. For example, the Catechism (which Ratzinger coedited) says on the subject of man's fall from grace: "The account of the fall in Genesis 3 uses figurative language, but affirms a primeval event, a deed that took place at the beginning of the history of man."[7] As we will see below, though, there is quite a difference between what Ratzinger thinks and many Christians assume when it comes to the question of whether we today have access to the particular details involved in events that transpired at the dawn of mankind at least two hundred thousand years ago. For, to be sure, we can know *that* there was a first human being at some point in history, and we can know *that* at some point this individual fell from God's grace, saying much beyond this historically or scientifically is probably beyond our ken as humans. Nevertheless, the

---

5. Ratzinger, *God and the World*, 165 [*Gott und die Welt*, 141]. Similarly, when an interlocutor asked him about the "myth" of Our Lady of Guadalupe, Ratzinger replied, "Once again, concerning the word myth: if myth [*Mythos*] means that this is a story that transcends the factual element [*eine über das Faktische hinausreichende Geschichte*], then we can use the word here. It is in any case important that we are not concerned, here, with an invention, but with real history [*realer Geschichte*]." Ratzinger, *God and the World*, 301 [*Gott und die Welt*, 282].

6. Ratzinger, "Zum Problem der Entmythologisierung Des Neuen Testamentes," 3–4.

7. *Catechism of the Catholic Church*, §390.

emeritus pontiff affirms that Genesis 1–11 gives us deep access to the deepest truths about God and man with its trappings of a seven-day creation, garden, talking snake, tower to the heavens, and all.

In this, Benedict echoes his predecessor who applied the word "myth" to Genesis even more freely than he. For instance, in an audience that would later become part of his Theology of the Body, John Paul II wrote that "the language in question is a mythical one [*linguaggio mitico*]," adding that the term "myth" here "does not designate a fabulous content, but merely an archaic way of expressing a deeper content."[8] In a later audience, this pope would proceed to discuss the differences between the Bible's two creation stories, even going into some detail on the scholarly understanding that the second is more ancient and has a figurative character while the first is more systematic, having originated later in a priestly setting. And, amidst all of this, John Paul adds another highly relevant point for our inquiry:

> *Significant elements cannot be sought from the point of view of the natural sciences.* The research on the origin and development of individual species "in kind" does not find in this description any "binding" norm, nor positive contributions of substantial interest. Indeed, with the truth about the creation of the visible world—as presented in the Book of Genesis—*it does not in principle conflict with the theory of natural evolution, when it is meant so as not to exclude divine causality.*[9]

In brief, the reason Pope John Paul II can say that evolution does not invalidate Genesis's creation account is because the text was written in a genre that had "a mainly religious and theological scope"—one that did not have a scientific aim but rather an "ontological character."[10]

While some believers may be reluctant to think of Genesis in the way that our recent popes have depicted it, in fact it is arguably *better* that the Bible's creation narrative is written in a figurative genre than if it were a textbook of history or science. To gain a further grasp on what it means for there to be myth in the Bible and why this is a good thing, we could do no better than to enlist the help of some of the past century's greatest literary masters who knew a thing or two about how stories work.

A good place to begin is by considering some words of Flannery O'Connor on the subject of fiction, for they apply well here to the figurative genre of the Bible's opening chapters: "You tell a story because a statement would be inadequate. When anybody asks what a story is about, the only proper thing is to tell him to read the story. The meaning of fiction is not abstract meaning but experienced meaning." She then immediately adds something that explain well why we write entire books

---

8. John Paul II, General Audience (November 7, 1979).
9. John Paul II, General Audience (January 29, 1986). Emphasis added.
10. John Paul II, General Audience (January 29, 1986).

on Genesis: "[T]he purpose of making statements about the meaning of a story is only to help you to experience that meaning more fully."[11]

When we hear the word 'myth' today, it is often in the context of a headline like "Top 10 Myths about Sugar!" In its current usage, "myth" tends to be deployed as a synonym for "fallacy" or "lie." Yet we have already seen in this book that the popular notion of certain words (e.g., "theory," "literal") is often drastically different from a correct technical understanding of them as used in the academy. Looking at how G.K. Chesterton describes myth in relation to non-Christian traditions can help disabuse us of confusion in this regard. After lamenting that "he who has no sympathy with myths has no sympathy with men," the literary giant adds: "The substance of all such paganism may be summarised thus. It is *an attempt to reach the divine reality through the imagination alone.*"[12] For Chesterton, myth was not equivalent to falsehood—he understood it to be more like a dream that captures glimpses of reality. We might go even further and add with J.R.R. Tolkien: "To say mythology is a disease of language is like saying thinking is a disease of the mind. It would be more appropriate to say languages are a disease of mythology."[13] Ratzinger himself captures this point as well as anyone in echoing the words of the Second Vatican Council on the subject of non-Christian religions and their stories: "In these traditions there is preserved a primordial human knowledge that is open to Christ."[14]

As insightful as these literary greats are, I find that C.S. Lewis is the most helpful writer of all when it comes to explaining the role of myth in Scripture. Like O'Connor, Chesterton, and Tolkien, Lewis was not a biblical scholar or pastor, yet—unlike many of us who are—he was an expert in literature and had intimate knowledge of ancient mythology which allowed him to provide deep insight into why there is story and even myth in Scripture. To put the point in another way, consider: who better than a man of letters and storyteller like Lewis to help us understand the nature of a story? At any rate, this is how Lewis describes the experience of reading the Bible as one traverses salvation history and approaches closer and closer to the New Testament:

> It is like watching something come gradually into focus. . . . The earliest stratum of the Old Testament contains many truths in a form which I take to be legendary, or even mythical—hanging in the clouds, but gradually the truth condenses, becomes more and more historical. . . . "God became Man" should

11. Flannery O'Connor, "Writing Short Stories" in *Mystery and Manners: Occasional Prose* (New York: Farrar, Straus, and Giroux, 1969), 87–106 at 96.

12. G.K. Chesterton, *The Everlasting Man* (Garden City, NY: Image Books, 1955), 128. Emphasis added.

13. Tolkien, *Tree and Leaf*, 48.

14. Ratzinger, *In the Beginning*, 28. For the Catholic Church's teaching regarding the goodness that we find in non-Christian traditions, see Second Vatican Council, *Lumen Gentium*, §16 and *Nostra Aetate*. In the latter, the Church specifically commends Hinduism for its "inexhaustible abundance of myths." *Nostra Aetate*, §2.

involve, from the point of view of human knowledge, the statement "Myth became Fact."[15]

From the above passage, it is clear that Lewis would be in full agreement with our recent popes on the presence of myth in Scripture. Elsewhere, though, he explores this point in more detail and provides a great definition of myth itself:

> Just as, on the factual side, a long preparation culminates in God's becoming incarnate as Man, so, on the documentary side, the truth first appears in mythical form and then by a long process of condensing or focusing finally becomes incarnate as History. This involves the belief that Myth in general is not merely misunderstood history (as Euhemerus thought) nor diabolical illusion (as some of the Fathers thought) nor priestly lying (as the philosophers of the Enlightenment thought) but, at its best, *a real though unfocused gleam of divine truth falling on human imagination.* The Hebrews, like other people, had mythology: but as they were the chosen people so their mythology was the chosen mythology—the mythology chosen by God to be the vehicle of the earliest sacred truths, the first step in that process which ends in the New Testament where truth has become completely historical.[16]

Seeing as Lewis has such a positive take on myth, it ought not to come as a surprise that he applies this specifically to Genesis. We will see how he does this in the case of original sin later in the book, but for now I think that the following quote ably captures how he perceives the relationship between the "Chosen Mythology" of Scripture and the myths of the nations that it built upon and elevated:

> I have therefore no difficulty in accepting, say, the view of those scholars who tell us that the account of creation in Genesis is derived from earlier Semitic stories which were pagan and mythical. . . . Thus something originally merely natural—the kind of myth that is found among most nations—will have been raised by God above itself, qualified by Him and compelled by Him to serve purposes which of itself it would not have served.[17]

In connection with the above, Lewis offers one further insight that helps us to understand that myth is not just a phenomenon that God tolerated in the Scriptures. To the contrary, Lewis is emphatic that myth is precisely the bridge that allows texts like Genesis to transcend their immediate context and be just as powerful for

---

15. C.S. Lewis, *The Weight of Glory, and Other Addresses* (New York: Macmillan, 1980), 129.

16. C. S. Lewis, *Miracles, a Preliminary Study* (New York: Macmillan, 1978), 218 (emphasis added). Another salient line on myth in this book occurs when Lewis sets out to explain why the Old Testament describes God so anthropomorphically: "The crudest Old Testament picture of Yahweh thundering and lightning out of dense smoke, making mountains skip like rams, threatening, promising, pleading, even changing His mind, transmits that sense of *living* Deity which evaporates in abstract thought." Lewis, *Miracles, a Preliminary Study,* 146. For further treatment of these points, see Ramage, *Dark Passages of the Bible,* 177.

17. Lewis, *Reflections on the Psalms* (London: Harvest Books, 1964), 110–11.

us today as they were at their origin: "In the enjoyment of a great myth we come nearest to experiencing as a concrete what can otherwise be understood only as an abstraction. . . . It is only while receiving the myth as a story that you experience the principle concretely."[18] In brief, the reality that Genesis's opening chapters are written in a semi-mythical genre and are not raw history is precisely why we remain still enthralled with these old stories today.

Of course, being aware of myth in Scripture might seem to make the believer's life more complicated. Once a person has learned from the likes of Lewis and the other thinkers we have just surveyed, one can no longer simply nod and say that the creation stories are scientifically true and need no qualification. Instead, we have to make the effort to distinguish the essential message that its various genres (including the symbolic or mythical) are intended to convey. On the other hand, I have talked to many people over the years who have told me that they found this liberating because it freed them from having to defend the indefensible when it comes to the Bible and science. In place of this fear, this knowledge gives us confidence that the Bible's teachings are entirely compatible with—and add necessary depth to—what we know through science.

## GENESIS 1–11 AS MYTH AND ANTI-MYTH

With our knowledge of the world's age and the evolutionary origin of all life, it is rather obvious to us today that our world's innumerable species did not arise immediately with a divine *fiat*, and to most of us the proposition that a snake could talk, or a human be created from another one's rib seems silly. However, there is another important reason that we have this confidence, and it does not have to do with our knowledge of the natural world generally but rather *with the world of Israel at the time of Genesis's composition*. Specifically, one can appreciate Genesis 1–11 as myth—and, as we will see, *anti*-myth—by comparing and contrasting it with other stories that were circulating in the ancient Near East. Knowing this context is not merely a scholarly curiosity. It bears directly upon the meaning and purpose of Genesis's creation narratives, for knowing something about *when* and *where* a text was written is invaluable for understanding *why*.

As a modern interpreter, Benedict is privy to a critically important realization that Christians of previous ages were not: *that Genesis was written with full knowledge of the great epics of the ancient Near East* (in particular, from *Babylonia* or *Babel* in Hebrew) *and took them up into its own narrative*. The Bible's creation narrative is a myth in the most robust sense of the term, and indeed Ratzinger is not shy to speak of "[t]he pagan creation accounts on which the biblical story is in part based."[19] On the other hand, Benedict expends considerable time explaining the

---

18. Lewis, "Myth Became Fact," in *The Grand Miracle: And Other Selected Essays on Theology and Ethics from God in the Dock* (New York: Ballantine Books, 1983), 66. For further insights into the nature of myth, see Lewis, "Myth Became Fact," 41.

19. Ratzinger, *A New Song for the Lord: Faith in Christ and Liturgy Today* (New York: Crossroad Pub., 1996), 86. Ratzinger is of course aware that the PBC's 1909 decree *On the Historicity of Genesis*

many ways in which Genesis 1–11 serves as an *anti*-myth—a polemic that seeks not merely to modify but to *subvert* these stories by unmasking their errors and revealing (literally, "un-veiling") the truth about God and man hidden within them.[20] At every turn, the Bible's inspired images both echo anthropomorphic imagery and counter concepts from Mesopotamian myths from the second millennium BC such as *Enuma Elish, Atrahasis*, and *Gilgamesh*.[21] These are texts whose roots doubtlessly date back far earlier but which have only relatively recently resurfaced thanks to stunning archaeological discoveries over the past two centuries.

Some Christians are uncomfortable with the notion that God's inspired word bears resemblance to these "pagan" stories, but it is important to remember what we said about myths above: they offer a real glimpse of divine truth through the medium of the human imagination. Moreover, as we are about to see, Genesis's

---

*1–3* had prohibited Catholics from maintaining that Genesis contained material derived from other ancient myths or that it does not depict "objective, historical reality." Translations of this and other PBC documents from the time can be found in Dean Béchard, *The Scripture Documents* (Collegeville, MN: The Liturgical Press, 2002), 188, 192–194. Pius XII later emended this view with a helpful corrective: "If, however, the ancient sacred writers have taken anything from popular narrations (and this may be conceded), it must never be forgotten that they did so with the help of divine inspiration, through which they were rendered immune from any error in selecting and evaluating those documents. Therefore, whatever of the popular narrations have been inserted into the Sacred Scriptures must in no way be considered on a par with myths or other such things." Pius XII, *Humani Generis*, 38–39.

Ratzinger would later criticize the PBC's earlier decisions as symptomatic of an "anti-Modernistic neurosis which had again and again crippled the Church since the turn of the century." Joseph Ratzinger, *Theological Highlights of Vatican II* (New York: Paulist Press, 1966), 11; see also Ratzinger, *Theological Highlights of Vatican II*, 23. Writing as prefect of the CDF, he would add that, in issuing these decrees, "the Magisterium overextended the range of what faith can guarantee with certainty and that, as a result, the Magisterium's credibility was injured and the freedom needed for exegetical research and interrogation was unduly narrowed." Ratzinger, "Exegesis and the Magisterium of the Church," in *Opening Up the Scriptures: Joseph Ratzinger and the Foundations of Biblical Interpretation*, ed. José Granados, Carlos Granados, and Luis Sánchez-Navarro (Grand Rapids, MI: Eerdmans, 2008), 126–36 at 133. For similar comments by Ratzinger on the subject of Pius X's 1907 "Syllabus of Errors" *Lamentabili Sane*, see Ratzinger, *Storia e Dogma* (Milano: Jaca Book, 1971), 15–16. Lamenting the anti-historical and defensive character of this document, Ratzinger maintains that its individual articles must not be "over-valued" and should not be taken out of context but instead seen as symptoms of a *Weltanschauung*. That said, the text is not entirely without value, as it is right to condemn a "radically evolutionist and historicist direction" for the interpretation of doctrine, which the Church at the time called "Modernism." For discussion of Ratzinger's comments, see Nichols, *The Thought of Pope Benedict XVI*, 162–63.

For a detailed discussion of Ratzinger's correctives to the Church's anti-modernist approach of the prior century and points of continuity and discontinuity between them, see Ramage, *Jesus, Interpreted*, Ch. 2. For an application of these same principles directly to Genesis, see Ramage, "In the Beginning: Aquinas, Benedict XVI, and the Book of Genesis," in *Reading Sacred Scripture with Thomas Aquinas: Hermeneutical Tools and New Perspectives* (Turnhout, Belgium: Brepols, 2015), 481–505.

20. For a powerful treatment of this point concerning the Bible's "unveiling" of the myths, see René Girard, *I See Satan Fall Like Lightning* (Maryknoll, NY: Orbis Books, 2001).

21. Bill Arnold captures this dynamic well with regard to the Bible's first creation account: "In a word, ancient religion was polytheistic, mythological, and anthropomorphic, describing the gods in human forms and functions, while Genesis 1 is monotheistic, scornful of mythology, and engages in anthropomorphism only as figures of speech." Arnold, *Genesis* (Cambridge: Cambridge University Press, 2009), 46.

creation narrative is not just another myth. Jeremy Holmes puts it well when he says, "Israel's creation story fits neither into the genre of history as understood today nor into the genre of myth as understood then. It is in fact a unique form of literature with no exact precedent and no exact successor"—adding that this character "makes it very hard to interpret."[22]

The points of contact between Genesis 1–11 and the myths that preceded it are so numerous that their being coincidental is scarcely conceivable. Sources documenting this evidence are easy to find, but for the sake of concision I would just note the following parallels.[23] Importantly, I have indicated Genesis's "anti-myth" revisions in italics to highlight that the purpose of the parallels is to deliver these differences. Seeing these parallels and contrasts together is important, for the continuity of the Bible's literary form with that of other ancient myths is precisely what allows us to appreciate the discontinuity and newness of God's word on the subject of creation:

## Genesis and *Enuma Elish*

- Chaos precedes creation in both texts. Before God performs his first creative act in Genesis, we read that in the beginning "the earth was without form

---

22. Holmes, *Cur Deus Verba?*, 188–89.

23. I have drawn from many sources for these lists, but for especially helpful summaries see Enns, *The Evolution of Adam*, 35–60, especially 39, 47, 54–55. For other surveys of parallels with *Enuma Elish* and other texts like Gilgamesh, see Enns, *Inspiration and Incarnation* (Grand Rapids, MI.: Baker Academic, 2005), 23–56; Venema and McKnight, *Adam and the Genome*, Ch. 6; John Walton, "Genesis," in *Zondervan Illustrated Bible Backgrounds Commentary* (Grand Rapids, MI: Zondervan, 2009), ed. John Walton, 5 vols., 1:10–42; Craig Keener and John Walton, eds., *NIV Cultural Backgrounds Study Bible: Bringing to Life the Ancient World of Scripture* (Grand Rapids, MI: Zondervan, 2016), 18–20; Kenton Sparks, *God's Word in Human Words*, 97–99; Alexander Heidel, *The Babylonian Genesis: The Story of Creation* (Chicago: University of Chicago Press, 1963), 82–140; Bernard Batto, *Slaying the Dragon: Mythmaking in the Biblical Tradition* (Louisville, KY: Westminster John Knox, 1992), 76–77; Victor Hurowitz, "The Genesis of Genesis: Is the Creation Story Babylonian?," Bible Review 21 (2005): 37–48; 52–53.

For the ancient texts themselves, see Victor Matthews and Don Benjamin, *Old Testament Parallels: Laws and Stories from the Ancient Near East* (New York: Paulist Press, 1991); Bill Arnold and Bryan Beyer, *Readings from the Ancient Near East* (Grand Rapids, MI: Baker Academic, 2002). For the classic scholarly anthology of these texts, see James Pritchard, *Ancient Near Eastern Texts: An Anthology and Pictures* (Princeton, NJ: Princeton University Press, 2010). For a particularly engaging translation of Gilgamesh, see *Gilgamesh*, trans. David Ferry (New York: Farrar, Straus and Giroux, 1993). Remarkably, archaeologists over the past two centuries have recovered many tablets containing these contexts from Mesopotamian palaces and put them on display in such locations as the British Museum, the Louvre, and the Metropolitan Museum of Art in New York.

For texts that document the associated art of the cultures that produced these stories, see Kim Benzel, Sarah Graff, Yelena Rakic, and Edith W. Watts, *Art of the Ancient Near East: A Resource for Educators*, www.metmuseum.org/art/metpublications/Art_of_the_Ancient_Near_East_A_Resource_for_ Educators; Henri Frankfort, *The Art and Architecture of the Ancient Orient* (Baltimore: Penguin Books, 1955); Walter Kaiser and Duane Garrett, eds. *NIV Archaeologi- cal Study Bible* (Grand Rapids, MI: Zondervan, 2005); James Pritchard, *The Ancient Near East in Pictures Relating to the Old Testament* (Princeton, NJ: Princeton University Press, 1954); Pritchard, *Archaeology and the Old Testament* (Princeton, NJ: Princeton University Press, 1958).

and void" (Gn 1:2). For its part, *Enuma Elish* begins with a theogony, a gene-alogy of the various gods' origin from preexisting matter. While the Genesis passage does not clearly teach that the universe had a beginning in time, *it differs from other myths in affirming that God precedes creation and exists independently of matter, thus implicitly affirming the doctrine of* creatio ex nihilo—the *universe's total dependence on God—through the literary lens of establishing order from chaos.*[24]

- In *Enuma Elish*, chaos is represented by the saltwater monstrous mother goddess Tiamat. *The term* Tehom—*possibly a cognate to Tiamat—is used in Genesis, yet it is demythologized and simply means "the deep"* (Gen 1:2).
- Light preexists the sun, moon, and stars in both (Gn 1:3; 1:14-19).
- In *Enuma Elish*, Marduk becomes Babylon's high god by slaying Tiamat, divid-ing her carcass into two and forging heaven and earth with them. *Genesis demythologizes this story too, as God makes a "firmament" that divides the waters—not demoted to the status of inanimate creation—into two* (Gn 1:6-8).
- The sequence of the days is similar in each, culminating in rest (Gn 2:3). However, whereas in Genesis the world is fashioned as a home for humans to flourish, in *Enuma Elish* Marduk is much more interested in making dwelling places for the gods than for humans, who are not in view at all until much later.
- *Enuma Elish* and the Bible's first creation account climax in the building of a sanctuary (i.e., Eden).
- In *Enuma Elish*, Marduk slays Tiamat's chief warrior Kingu and forms the first humans out of his corpse. These humans are made to do the toil of the lower gods. *By contrast, in Genesis 1:26, God makes man master of creation. In the Bible's second creation account* (which begins in Gn 2:4), *God is now given the covenantal name "the LORD God"* (Yahweh Elohim) *and man* (adam) *symbolically receives his name by virtue of being molded from the dust of the ground* (adamah). *God then breathes into him the breath of life (Gn 2:7).*
- A "bow" appears in both stories but in strikingly different ways. An instru-ment that deities in the ancient Near East (including Yahweh) were often depicted as wielding, a bow makes its appearance in *Enuma Elish* IV: 95–104 as the vehicle by which Marduk releases his arrow that kills Tiamat. When it comes to the Bible, scholars have noted that there may be significance

---

24. On the subject of *creatio ex nihilo* as a doctrine about the universe's total and continued dependence on God as distinct from the question of whether matter had a beginning in time, see Chap-ter 3. On the ancient Near Eastern conception of creation, see John Walton, *The Lost World of Genesis One: Ancient Cosmology and the Origins Debate* (Downers Grove, IL: InterVarsity Press, 2009), 26–27: "I propose that people in the ancient world believed that something existed not by virtue of its material properties, *but by virtue of its having a function in an ordered universe.* . . . Unless something is integrated into a working, ordered system, it does not exist. Consequently, the actual creative act is to assign some-thing its functioning role in the ordered system." Walton continues, "Ancients presumably would have believed that their gods also manufactured the material of the cosmos, but they show little interest in material origins." Walton, *The Lost World of Genesis One*, 35.

in the fact that the same Hebrew word for bow (*qesheth*) can mean both rainbow and the bow as a weapon. In this context, it is possible that Gn 9 contains vestiges of an old myth where Yahweh vanquishes his nemesis Yamm (the Ugaritic sea-god here called "flood"). Likewise, it is evocative that the breaking of a bow was often connected to the enacting of a treaty in the ancient Near Eastern world. Seen in this light, the hanging of Yahweh's bow in the sky may be meant to suggest peace, i.e., that he has pointed it away from the earth and therefore retired it from service. Another suggestion is that the bow is intended to be seen as pulled back and pointing upward toward heaven, signifying that God's covenantal faithfulness is so great that he has threatened himself with a curse should he fail to uphold its terms. Whatever the case may be, it is clear that *Genesis 9:3 has transformed a common ancient Near Eastern mythological symbol of divine bellicosity into a stunning sign of reconciliation, a bond of peace that stretches between heaven and earth from horizon to horizon.*[25]

## Genesis and *Gilgamesh*

- God / the gods dwell in a garden/paradise in the east (Gn 2–3).
- Man (Adam / Enkidu) is created out of dust / clay of the earth (Gn 2:7).
- A plant confers immortality. In *Gilgamesh*, a serpent steals it. *The biblical version has altered this to show that Adam and Eve's loss of immortality was due to their disobedience, not mere bad luck* (Gn 3).
- Man moves from nakedness to a clothed state. Shamhat the harlot clothes the wild man Enkidu in *Gilgamesh*, while God himself makes garments of skin for Adam and Eve in Genesis 3:21.[26]
- Humans become like God / the gods. In *Gilgamesh*, Enkidu acquires a wisdom like the gods, and it comes through the agency of a woman (the harlot Shamhat). In Genesis 3:22, we read that the man—having fallen in connection with the actions of a woman—"has become like one of us, knowing good and evil."
- God / the gods keep immortality from humans (Gn 3:22-23).
- A hero figure (Noah / Utnapishtim) and his family are saved from a flood (Gn 6–8).

---

25. For more information concerning the bow discussed above, Willem VanGemeren, ed., *New International Dictionary of Old Testament Theology and Exegesis* (Grand Rapids, MI: Zondervan Publishing House, 1997), 1004–1006; Scott Hahn and Curtis Mitch, *Genesis: With Introduction, Commentary, and Notes* (San Francisco: Ignatius Press, 2010), 29; Bruce Waltke and Cathi Fredricks, *Genesis: A Commentary* (Grand Rapids, MI: Zondervan, 2001), 146; Victor Hamilton, *The Book of Genesis, Chapters 1–17*, The New International Commentary on the Old Testament (Grand Rapids, MI: Eerdmans, 1990), 317; John Anthony Dunne, "Enuma Elish," in *The Lexham Bible Dictionary*, eds. John D. Barry et al., (Bellingham, WA: Lexham Press, 2016); W. G. Lambert, "Enuma Elish," in *The Anchor Yale Bible Dictionary* (New York: Doubleday, 1992), 526–28.

26. A further "garments of skin" parallel can be found in the *Adapa* tale.

- An ark is built to precise dimensions and sealed with pitch (Gn 6:14).
- The ark is loaded with the seed of all living things. In Genesis's priestly language, this includes both clean and unclean animals (Gn 7:2).
- The ark comes to rest on a mountain (Gn 8:4).
- Birds are sent out (Gn 8:7-12).
- God / the gods smell the pleasing aroma of sacrifices (Gn 8:20-21).
- A sign of an oath is offered (a lapis lazuli necklace in *Gilgamesh*, a rainbow in the Bible (Gn 9:13).

Similar lists have been constructed enumerating the affinities between Genesis and other Mesopotamian myths like *Eridu Genesis* and *Atrahasis*—parallels so numerous and close that some have dubbed Genesis 2–8 "Israel's Atrahasis."[27] The same could be done comparing Genesis with the Ugaritic *Baal Cycle* within Canaanite culture and Egyptian texts like the so-called *Memphite Theology* and the *Instruction of Merikare*.[28] Yet, for our purposes, the point is that, given the sheer number and closeness of Genesis's parallels with the same ancient myth in its various iterations, scholars have little doubt that Genesis is quite deliberately engaging and offering a revealed response to it.

---

27. Venema and McKnight, *Adam and the Genome*, 115. See also Kaiser and Garrett, eds., *NIV Archaeology Study Bible*, 3152, where after discussing parallels between Genesis and *Enuma Elish* they write that the actual process of humanity's creation in Genesis is better paralleled by the Atrahasis myth in which the goddess Mami shaped clay moistened by the spittle of the gods and pinched off pieces to deliver humans from the womb of the earth. Here as in other Mesopotamian myths, the role of humanity was to serve the gods by constructing their temples, working their lands, and offering them ritual service. For a helpful chart that details more than a dozen of these parallels and further parallels not in any of the three major Mesopotamian texts discussed above, see Enns, *The Evolution of Adam*, 54–55. On parallels and contrasts between Genesis's preflood genealogies and Sumerian king lists, see Sparks, "Genesis 1–11 as Ancient Historiography," in *Genesis: History, Fiction, or Neither?*, 117.

28. For more on possible connections of Genesis 1–2 with Mesopotamian, Canaanite, and Egyptian literature, see Arnold, *Genesis*, 33–34; Enns, *The Evolution of Adam*, 40; Keener and Walton, *NIV Cultural Backgrounds Study Bible*, 905, 953–54; Kaiser and Garrett, eds., *NIV Archaeological Study Bible*, 3152–53. In the *Memphite Theology*, the god Ptah conceives the universe in his mind and creates it by his word, after which he is "satisfied" (or "rested"). This text then ascribes the fashioning of humans to the god Khnum, who molded man out of clay and placed the fetus in the mother's womb. In the *Instruction of Merikare*, the deity subdues chaos (or "the water monster") and creates heaven and earth for the sake of humans, breathing life into their nostrils, forming them according to his likeness ("images" from his body), and even creating plants, animals, fish, and birds for them to eat. In the Ugaritic *Baal Cycle*, the storm god Baal seizes kingship by defeating the sea deity Yam and the underworld god Mot. The Yahweh-Baal connection is certainly present in Old Testament texts outside of the Pentateuch, where the dragon is referred to variously as Yam, Leviathan, and Rahab (Ps 74:12-15; 87:4; 89:9-10; Is 27:1; 30:7; 51:9-10; Job 3:8; 7:12; 9:13; 26:12-13; 41:1-34).

Reflecting on all these connections, Keener and Walton note: "All of this demonstrates that even though God was revealing himself to Israel as very different from the gods of the ancient world, he did not hesitate to use similar metaphors and images to do so. His own activity is described in these culturally embedded ways and makes reference to known mythology to engage the Israelite audience through familiar ideas. However, for Yahweh, imagery of defeating chaos creatures constitutes literary allusions rather than cosmic history. Yahweh did not have to battle chaos creatures in order to bring order to the cosmos." Keener and Walton, *NIV Cultural Backgrounds Study Bible*, 954.

Of course, as we have seen in the case of other topics already in this book, a different explanation of the parallels is technically possible—that is, it is always *conceivable* that the parallels are coincidental. Yet, if faith and reason stand in harmony, we ought to be in the business of asking what explanation of reality is the most *plausible* and *believable*. In this vein, Evangelical scholar Kenton Sparks states the matter plainly, "The most *sensible* explanation for the similarities is that the pentateuchal authors borrowed some of their materials from the ancient world."[29]

Why would the Jews have had such a deep interest in borrowing from and confronting myths found among the ancient Babylonians? If we recall our salvation history, it is not difficult to see why. Ratzinger explains, "The moment when creation became a dominant theme occurred during the Babylonian exile. It was then that the account we have just heard [Gn 1:1–19]—based, to be sure, on very ancient traditions—assumed its present form."[30] In this text as elsewhere, the emeritus pontiff echoes the modern scholarly consensus that the Pentateuch (the first five books of the Bible, including Genesis) was redacted (edited) by multiple authors over many centuries, reaching the final form that we have in our Bibles today after Cyrus of Persia defeated Babylon and allowed the Jews to return from exile in 539 BC (see 2 Chr 36:23).[31] Knowing this information is critical to grasping the meaning of

---

29. Kenton Sparks, *God's Word in Human Words*, 97. See also Ramage, *Dark Passages of the Bible*, 23–24. For other essays related to this chapter by Sparks and other scholars, see James Hoffmeier, Gordon Wenham, and Kenton Sparks, *Genesis: History, Fiction, or Neither?* and Wenham, *Rethinking Genesis 1–11* (Eugene, OR: Cascade Books, 2015). Sparks here offers an apt analogy for this borrowing: "As Rembrandt worked in oil on canvas, the authors of Gen 1–11 worked in the motifs and literary forms of the ancient world." Sparks, *Genesis: History, Fiction, or Neither?*, 118. For a traditional theological account that accepts Israel having borrowed from and adapted prior Mesopotamian myths, see Louis Bouyer, *Cosmos: The World and the Glory of God* (Petersham, MA: St. Bede's Publications, 1999), 12–22, 37–50. In a statement that echoes Ratzinger's approach, Bouyer reflects, "[T]he similarities with the biblical account stand out, but the differences are even more striking." Bouyer, *Cosmos: The World and the Glory of God*, 46.

30. Ratzinger, *In the Beginning*, 10–11.

31. Douglas Knight and Amy-Jill Levine, *The Meaning of the Bible: What the Jewish Scriptures and Christian Old Testament Can Teach Us* (New York: HarperCollins, 2011), 13. Gary Anderson writes: "The modern discovery of the sources of the Pentateuch has revolutionized the way in which the Bible is read. Outside of those conservatives who have an *a priori* commitment to the notion of a single Mosaic author for the Pentateuch, the thesis that Gen. 1–3 comes from two different literary sources is accepted by nearly all." Anderson, *Christian Doctrine and the Old Testament: Theology in the Service of Biblical Exegesis* (Grand Rapids, MI: Baker, 2017), 62. Another author writes: "That the Pentateuch is a 'composite' work, that is, a work in which smaller units of different provenance, and length, and era converge, is a fact that today is obvious in the eyes of literary criticism. . . . What seems obvious today, though, has not always seemed so. On the contrary, the weight of the attribution of the Pentateuch to Moses (an attribution external to the Pentateuch itself), has for many centuries conditioned the reading of the first five books of the Bible, to the point of glossing over many pieces of information that should have called that attribution into question." Ignacio Carbajosa, *Faith, the Fount of Exegesis: The Interpretation of Scripture in the Light of the History of Research on the Old Testament* (San Francisco: Ignatius Press, 2011), 25–26, referencing Joseph Blenkinsopp, *The Pentateuch: An Introduction to the First Five Books of the Bible* (New York: Doubleday, 1992), 1–2.

For an accessible explanation of this within the context of an outstanding overview of faith and evolution, see John Baptist Ku, OP, "Modern Biblical Exegesis of the Creation Accounts," in *Thomistic*

Genesis, for its creation stories in their final form reflect the concerns of Israelite culture during *this* period.[32]

It is not that the people of Israel had no interest in creation before the exile, but Ratzinger tells us that it took on a new urgency once God's people had lost everything they knew—family, land, Temple—when in 587–86 BC Nebuchadnezzar II laid waste the city of Jerusalem, carrying its treasures and citizens off to Babylon (2 Kgs 24–25). At this point, all of God's promises had seemed for naught. As the exilic Psalm 89 has it:

> But now thou hast cast off and rejected,
> thou art full of wrath against thy anointed.
> Thou hast renounced the covenant with thy servant;
> thou hast defiled his crown in the dust.
> Thou hast breached all his walls;
> thou hast laid his strongholds in ruins.

Typically, a god in the ancient world who could not even maintain control over his own land and protect his sanctuary was not worthy of devotion and would tend to vanish from history. Yet, as Ratzinger notes, strangely this is not what happened with the Jews: "When Israel went into exile, quite astonishingly, the opposite happened. . . . The faith of Israel at last took on its true form and stature."[33] Ironically,

---

*Evolution*, 160. For a discussion of the traditional ascription of the Pentateuch to Moses, an evaluation of the Documentary Hypothesis advanced by Julius Wellhausen, and evidence that the text has deep roots in a second millennium BC context, see Pitre and Bergsma, *A Catholic Introduction to the Bible: Old Testament*, 16–92 and Umberto Cassuto, *The Documentary Hypothesis and the Composition of the Pentateuch* (Jerusalem: Shalem Press, 2006). Unfortunately, the scholarly consensus regarding the composite nature of the Pentateuch has been obscured through scholarly bias against the tradition and entanglement with political aims. For an extensive historical treatment of how this played out, see Scott Hahn and Benjamin Wiker, *Politicizing the Bible: The Roots of Historical Criticism and the Secularization of Scripture, 1300–1700* (New York: Crossroad Publishing Company, 2013) and Ramage, *Jesus, Interpreted*, 61–62n9, 236n6.

32. For the many of lines of evidence that speak to the Pentateuch's postexilic editing or redaction, see Enns, *The Evolution of Adam*, 9–34, especially 24–26. Some of the clues to its dating include: the Pentateuch's having been written in Classical Hebrew which was the style between 800–500 BC; its geographic point of view being west of the Jordan, where Moses never lived; the presence of frequent anachronisms; Moses being spoken of in the third person; the presence of many narrative tensions, contradictions, and duplications many of which make most sense in light of a long and complex process of redaction; many indications that two distinct scribal schools edited the Pentateuch). Although the lateness of the Pentateuch has been widely acknowledged only in the past two centuries, scholars first challenged Mosaic authorship publicly in the seventeenth century on the basis of evidence such as the above. This motley crew of thinkers included Baruch Spinoza (an excommunicated Jew), Thomas Hobbes (an agnostic), and Richard Simon (a Catholic priest). In his *Theological-Political Treatise* (Cambridge: Cambridge University Press, 2007), 122. Spinoza dedicates considerable space to documenting passages that pose difficulties for Mosaic authorship of the Pentateuch. The author summarizes his findings thus: "From all this it is plainer than the noonday sun that the Pentateuch was not written by Moses but by someone else who lived many generations after Moses."

33. Ratzinger, *Truth and Tolerance*, 148. Benedict also captured this—with a particular focus on the development of monotheism—in a famous papal address: "Within the Old Testament, the process which

it was when God's people seemed most lost that they found God. Indeed, the exile (and later persecution during the Maccabean period) was a crucial catalyst that solidified Israel's understanding of the moral law, monotheism, and the afterlife.[34]

How did the Jewish faith achieve this feat? By asking hard questions of God. As the Psalmist says over and over, "How long, O Lord? Wilt thou hide thyself for ever?" (Ps 89:46) "Return, O Lord! How long?" (Ps 90:13) "They set thy sanctuary on fire. . . . Is the enemy to revile thy name for ever?" (Ps 74:7–10) A list of such passages could go on and on. What this makes plain, in Ratzinger's words, is that "[t]he faith now had to find its own contours, and it had to do so precisely vis-à-vis the seemingly victorious religion of Babylon."[35] Along these lines, Bill Arnold argues that Genesis's creation narrative is not only a polemic against other ancient Near Eastern stories but is ultimately concerned with helping Israel find its bearings in this brave new world: "[T]he author has a positive agenda," Arnold writes. "He is not only interested in showing the *Enuma Elish* (or others) to be false, but in creating for Israel a new way of thinking about God."[36]

Peter Enns has a similar way of summarizing the Jewish concern at the time. In Enns' formulation, the sacred author's concern was not with the origins of the universe and of humans generally, but with *the nation of Israel* and their burning question: "Are we still the people of God?"[37] Expanding upon the matter at length, Enns emphasizes that knowing something about *when* a text came to be has important implications for our understanding of *why* it was produced in the first place, and, in this case, "The final form of the creation story in Genesis (along with the rest of the Pentateuch) reflects the concerns of the community that produced it: postexilic Israelites who had experienced God's rejection in Babylon." This narrative, while undoubtedly rooted in much older material, was shaped as a theological response to Israel's national crisis of exile. Enns thus says that it was "not written to speak of 'origins' as we might think of them today (in a natural-science sense)" but rather in order "to say something of God and Israel's place in the world as God's chosen people."[38] Summarizing this point, he adds:

---

started at the burning bush came to new maturity at the time of the exile, when the God of Israel, an Israel now deprived of its land and worship, was proclaimed as the God of heaven and earth and described in a simple formula which echoes the words uttered at the burning bush: 'I am.' This new understanding of God is accompanied by a kind of enlightenment, which finds stark expression in the mockery of gods who are merely the work of human hands." Benedict XVI, "Faith, Reason and the University: Memories and Reflections" (September 12, 2006).

34. For extensive discussion of these developments, see Ramage, *Dark Passages of the Bible*, Chs. 5–6.

35. Ratzinger, *In the Beginning*, 12.

36. Arnold, *Genesis*, 32. Specifically, Arnold proceeds to suggest that Genesis seeks to offer a positive view of the Torah to those who belittled the role of the Sabbath, the dietary laws, and the image of God in humans.

37. Enns, *The Evolution of Adam*, 28.

38. Enns, *The Evolution of Adam*, 5.

Placing Genesis in its ancient Near Eastern setting strongly suggests that it was written as a self-defining document, as a means of declaring the distinctiveness of Israel's own beliefs from those of the surrounding nations. In other words, Genesis is an argument, a polemic, declaring how Israel's God is different from all the other gods, and therefore how Israel is different from all the other nations. . . . [T]he ancient Israelites, in making this polemical case, freely adapted the themes of the much-older stories of the nations around them.[39]

Not unlike Enns, on the basis of a detailed genre analysis of Genesis 1–11, William Lane Craig for his part concludes that these chapters may be regarded "as a Hebrew mytho-history that serves as a universal foundational charter for the election and identity of Israel over against its neighbors."[40]

Along these lines, Richard Carlson and Tremper Longman write regarding the parallels between Genesis and Mesopotamian myths, "Even though these similarities exist, *the overall teaching differs radically.* . . . And this makes *all the difference.*"[41] To this, they add:

The first two chapters of Genesis, which accurately present two accounts of creation in terms of ancient Hebrew scientific observations and their historical understanding, *are neither historical nor scientific in the twenty-first-century literal sense.* Instead, the underlying message of these chapters applies for all time and *constitutes a complete statement of the worldview of the Hebrew people in the ancient Near East.* They accurately understood the universe in terms of why God created it but not how in the modern scientific and historical sense. This worldview, markedly different from those of their pagan neighbors, articulates the principles underlying their understanding of the relation of God to the universe, their relation to the true God, and their relation to each other and to the created order.[42]

In sum, these authors emphasize something that is rather obvious but which has crucial implications for helping us today to ascertain what claims Genesis's creation account is and is not making: "For ancient Israelites, as well as any other ancient Near Eastern peoples, origin stories are focused on telling their own story, not everyone else's. These stories are about self-definition."[43] When I read these words of Enns on self-definition, it always reminds me of Reb Tevye from *Fiddler on the Roof* saying that following the tradition tells each man not only "who he is" but also "what God expects" from him.

39. Enns, *The Evolution of Adam*, 5–6; For another articulation of this point about Israel's self-definition, see Enns, *The Evolution of Adam*, 26.

40. William Lane Craig, *In Quest of the Historical Adam: A Biblical and Scientific Exploration* (Grand Rapids, MI: Eerdmans, 2021), 522.

41. See also Carlson and Longman, *Science, Creation, and the Bible: Reconciling Rival Theories of Origins* (Downers Grove, IL: IVP Academic, 2010), 113–14. Emphasis added.

42. Carlson and Longman, *Science, Creation, and the Bible*, 14. Emphasis added.

43. Enns, *The Evolution of Adam*, 69.

Perhaps the most relatable way to understand what the above authors are getting at has been provided by Christopher Baglow when he invites readers to imagine themselves as the author of the Bible's creation narrative.[44] As a leader of a nation in exile, he begins, "You are a priest, a duty of religious leadership bestowed by God upon your family line, a duty that you take as the primary purpose of your life." Your responsibility is to lead the people of Israel in this time of tragedy just as Moses led your forefathers out of slavery to the Promised Land. Yet you are no longer living in that land because it has been ravaged by the Babylonian Empire. In these dire circumstances, Baglow writes, "You now have a new duty—you must help your people hold on to their faith in God and to the way of life he gave to them, and you must do so against all odds." Reflecting upon the myths of your overlords, you are struck by how violent and irrational they are. Thus, while the *Enuma Elish* begins in awe: *When in the height heaven was not named*, it then devolves into a chaotic narrative of the birth of myriad gods and the bloody battles between them. This grates against the fiber of your being, for it depicts the divine in precisely the opposite way the one true God, Yahweh, acts. As a result, Baglow eloquently envisions, "Slowly, but surely, a response is growing within you and within the other priests to this dreadfully warped picture of divinity and of the origin of human beings and the universe. Thanks to you, a different story will be heard by the people, a story with a very different beginning." The new beginning: "In the beginning God [*not Marduk*] created the heavens and the earth" (Gn 1:1).

I find that the above descriptions of the Pentateuch as Israel's response to the Babylonian exile provide a nice complement to some very similar things that Ratzinger says about its timing and purpose. For example, already in his 1964 course on creation Ratzinger writes almost poetically, "In the mystery of creation the mystery of the covenant is present, and in the mystery of the covenant the mystery of creation takes on its full meaning."[45] Of Scripture's directionality, he thus declares, "The OT does not go from creation to history, but vice versa."[46] That is, Israel's knowledge of God as creator "developed from the encounter (*Begegnung*) with the God who works in salvation history."[47] As a result, "Creation is not a self-standing history, but is told in terms of covenantal history and has this entry into the covenant at its inner core (*inneren Kern*)."[48] This, Ratzinger says, serves as a "corrective to a popular notion about creation," adding, "Genesis 1 only *appears* to be at the beginning of biblical religion—the beginning and departure of Israel's faith is the

44. This suggestive narrative, which I have cited and summarized for the sake of concision, is found in Baglow, *Creation*, 20–21.

45. Ratzinger, *Schöpfungslehre* (1964), 189; Sanz, "Joseph Ratzinger y la doctrina de la creación. Los apuntes de Münster de 1964 (II)," 209n29.

46. Ratzinger, *Schöpfungslehre* (1964), 11; Sanz, "Joseph Ratzinger y la doctrina de la creación. Los apuntes de Münster de 1964 (II)," 202n2.

47. Ratzinger, *Schöpfungslehre* (1964), 17 (emphasis added); Sanz, "Joseph Ratzinger y la doctrina de la creación. Los apuntes de Münster de 1964 (II)," 204n9.

48. Ratzinger, *Schöpfungslehre* (1964), 188; Sanz, "Joseph Ratzinger y la doctrina de la creación. Los apuntes de Münster de 1964 (II)," 209n28.

historical experience of God, the event of the covenant."[49] Consequently, one may say that "the creation narrative gives no independent cosmology, but is a part of soteriology" and that, in a certain sense, "the Savior God precedes the Creator God."[50] In sum, and contrary to what some Christians tend to assume, the force of the parallel between Genesis and the rest of the Pentateuch moves from Sinai to Eden, from salvation history to creation, not the reverse.[51]

I have found that my students often struggle with this notion of Genesis 1–11 being Israel's story. Seeking clarity, at times they reasonably ask along these lines: "Why doesn't the Bible just come out and tell us that these chapters are primarily about Israel's story instead of being all cryptic and making it look like it's about the creation of the physical world?" Part of the answer to this question is undoubtedly related to the important and rightful role played by tradition in our religion. Believers for many centuries read Genesis's cosmology as being consistent with the science of their day, and it is only natural to assume that the witness of the Church Fathers is reliable. When modern science and the ancient Christian tradition do not coincide, it is natural for the Christian to assume that the more longstanding view is more credible.

Another problem that makes it difficult to provide simple answers in matters of biblical interpretation lies in the complexity of trying to understand the perspective of an ancient time and culture we have never directly experienced. For, to ask why the Bible's proper interpretation is not always more straightforward is to betray our modern bias that everything in Scripture ought to have been written in the same way we write history today. It is easy to forget to account for context when a story is so familiar to us that we scarcely realize that it originated in a distant land and time. As Enns says, reading the Bible "is like reading someone else's mail."[52]

Picking up on this same point, Pope Francis notes in his apostolic letter on St. Jerome that practicing Christians who are aware of this problem often feel unable to interpret Scripture "because they are unprepared for the biblical language, its modes of expression and its ancient cultural traditions" as a result of which "the biblical text becomes indecipherable, as if it were written in an unknown alphabet and an esoteric tongue."[53] Closely connected to this point, our difficulty in understanding the Bible's creation narrative is exacerbated today by the fact that many of us—even though we are not illiterate—have indeed lost our sense of how truth is conveyed through the medium of story and myth. In this age of mass media, we have come to expect the truth (or at least people's claims to it) to be packaged for us neatly and concisely in 280 characters or less. This,

49. Ratzinger, *Schöpfungslehre* (1964), 197 (emphasis added); Sanz, "Joseph Ratzinger y la doctrina de la creación. Los apuntes de Münster de 1964 (II)," 202n4.

50. Ratzinger, *Schöpfungslehre* (1964), 17; Sanz, "Joseph Ratzinger y la doctrina de la creación. Los apuntes de Münster de 1964 (II)," 204n9; Ratzinger, *Schöpfungslehre* (1964), 11; Sanz, "Joseph Ratzinger y la doctrina de la creación. Los apuntes de Münster de 1964 (II)," 202n3

51. For a more developed treatment of this point, see Anderson, "Biblical Origins and the Problem of the Fall," *Pro Ecclesia* 10.1 (2001): 17–30 at 29.

52. Enns, *How the Bible Actually Works* (San Francisco: HarperOne), 254.

53. Francis, *Scripturae Sacrae Affectus* (September 30, 2020).

however, is not the Bible's overall method of revealing truth, and it ought to serve as a lesson for us about the way in which truth in general becomes known. As Francis elsewhere says, "Wisdom is not born of quick searches on the internet nor is it a mass of unverified data."[54]

Thankfully, none of these obstacles is insurmountable. This is where reading great literature and getting to know how masters like C.S. Lewis who understand myth is so helpful. It is also where reading Ratzinger and seeing how he applies his principles to concrete biblical texts is invaluable. It is to this task that we now turn.

## APPLICATION TO CONCRETE "IMAGES"

In Chapter 4, we discussed the importance of discerning the biblical author's intention, seeking out "the essential point." Having added to this a grasp of the figurative genre of Genesis's creation narrative, we are now in a position to examine how Benedict applies this approach in practice. In other words, we know that the Bible's creation stories are both myth (a statement of Israel's faith) and anti-myth (an anti-Babylonian polemic), but what specifically were they intending to say?

### Creation by One God through His Logos

Many believers are so familiar with the Bible's opening lines that their content can seem almost trivial or banal. Yet, according to Ratzinger, the most stunning and central point of Scripture's creation account appears right in its first sentence: "In the beginning, God created the heavens and the earth" (Gn 1:1). The revolutionary teaching conveyed in these words is very simple:

> They do not depict the process of becoming or the mathematical structure of matter; instead, they say in different ways that there is only *one* God.[55]

> Scripture would not wish to inform us about how the different species of plant life gradually appeared or how the sun and the moon and the stars were established. Its purpose ultimately would be to say one thing: *God* created the world. . . . The world is not, as people used to think then, a chaos of mutually opposed forces; nor is it the dwelling of demonic powers from which human beings must protect themselves. The sun and the moon are not deities that rule over them, and the sky that stretches over their heads is not full of mysterious and adversary divinities.[56]

---

54. Francis, *Fratelli Tutti*, 50.

55. Ratzinger, *In the Beginning*, 25.

56. Ratzinger, *In the Beginning*, 5. For a similar explanation of the "essential teaching" (*l'insegnamento essenziale*) of Genesis, see John Paul II, General Audience (January 29, 1986). The pontiff explains: "As a whole, the image of the world is outlined by the pen of the inspired author with the characteristics of the cosmogonies of the time, in which he inserts with absolute originality the truth about the creation of everything by the one God: this is the revealed truth." https://www.vatican.va/content/john-paul-ii/it/audiences/1986/documents/hf_jp-ii_aud_ 19860129.html. As this particular audience is not available in English, the translation above is mine. See also Pontifical Biblical Commission, *The Inspiration and Truth of Scripture*, 74.

Living millennia later in a culture formed by Christianity, most of us have a hard time appreciating how revelatory this core message of Genesis's opening salvo was for its day. For this, we need to read what Ratzinger highlights next when he comments on the *means* by which God creates, i.e., through speaking his word (Hebrew: *dabar*; Greek: *logos*). Although God "speaking" creation into existence may seem like a trivial anthropomorphic detail within Genesis's larger creation narrative, Benedict notes that it contains a true revelation that runs directly counter to the worldview of other ancient Near Eastern myths. That is, by describing creation as occurring through God's speech, Genesis teaches that it issues forth from God's mind and *not* from chaos as other ancient cultures thought. "The universe," Ratzinger declares, "is not the scene of a struggle among dark forces but rather the creation of his Word."[57] Indeed, he remarks that the truth that the universe comes forth from the creative mind of God is "precisely what the belief in creation means."[58] Accordingly, the sun, moon, and other heavenly bodies are not divinities engaged in adversarial relationships with one another. On the contrary, Genesis reveals that "all of this comes from one power, from God's eternal Reason, which became—in the Word—the power of creation.[59] Reflecting on this radical shift, Ratzinger comments:

> Here we see the audacity and the temperateness of the faith that, in confronting the pagan myths, made the light of truth appear by showing that the world was not a demonic contest but that it arose from God's Reason and reposes on God's Word. Hence this creation account may be seen as the decisive "enlightenment" of history and as a breakthrough out of the fears that had oppressed humankind.[60]

Simply asserting that God created the world through his *Logos* may not seem to mean much on its own, but recalling the context of Genesis's redaction makes all the difference. That is, knowing that the Bible's creation narrative served as a polemic against Mesopotamian religion suggests that its claim about creation occurring through the *Logos* of one God was intended as an attack on Babylonian polytheism (belief in many gods) and its belief that creation arose through a struggle among the gods (theomachy).

The "struggle" our emeritus pope has in mind here is depicted in the Babylonian creation epic *Enuma Elish* with which the authors of Genesis would have been intimately familiar. In this story, the god Marduk slays the sea dragon goddess Tiamat, divides her carcass into two, and with them forms heaven and earth. Genesis demythologizes this story when the one true God makes a "firmament" that divides the waters into two (Gn 1:6–8). This time, though, the waters—like the heavenly bodies that the ancients considered divine—are just that: material creations, not gods.

---

57. Ratzinger, *In the Beginning*, 25.
58. Ratzinger, "Belief in Creation and the Theory of Evolution," 139.
59. Ratzinger, *In the Beginning*, 5.
60. Ratzinger, *In the Beginning*, 14.

Moreover, we read in Genesis, "The earth was without form and void, and darkness was upon the face of the deep; and the Spirit of God was moving over the face of the waters" (Gn 1:2). Whereas in the Babylonian epic a theogony (story of the gods' origin) and theomachy (story of their fighting) precedes the creation of the world, the world of the Bible begins with watery chaos—disorder reigns over the earth, and darkness reigns "over the face of the deep [*Tehom*]."[61] However, now the Spirit of God is said to hover over—that is, precede and control—these waters. At this point, God's *Logos* enters the scene as he brings order out of chaos by speaking creatures into being (Gn 1:3). No cosmic battle is necessary, for the one true God has no rival.

It does take God seven days to go about his work (more on that in a moment), but over this timeframe the narrative shows him systematically commanding and controlling all the forces of nature that were considered deities in the ancient world. He begins by effortlessly speaking light into existence (1:3) and then just as easily separates it from darkness (Gn 1:4). Benedict meditated on the original meaning of this text in his last Easter Vigil Homily as pope:

> The creation account begins symbolically with the creation of light. The sun and the moon are created only on the fourth day. The creation account calls them lights, set by God in the firmament of heaven. In this way, he deliberately takes away the divine character that the great religions had assigned to them. No, they are not gods. They are shining bodies created by the one God. But they are preceded by the light through which God's glory is reflected in the essence of the created being.[62]

As Benedict points out, it is telling that God speaks the sun and moon into being— the very entities by which we measure days—three days after light was created (Gn 1:14–18). This fact alone should make one wary of a literalistic interpretation of the days in question as twenty-four-hour periods. In reality, their presence here serves another function. In calling them into being so easily, the one true God has demoted these great lights—supposed gods—to mere creatures hung in the sky to measure time. Moreover, the recurring mention "there was evening and there was morning" suggests that the cosmos is systematically moving from chaos to order through God's governance, an austere and noble alternative to the Babylonian narrative of Marduk imposing order by slaying the chaos symbol Tiamat.[63] These claims in Genesis would

---

61. Many interpreters like Peter Enns also think that the biblical word "deep" (*Tehom*)—itself cognate to Tiamat—adds yet another layer to the polemical demythologizing agenda of Genesis. It should be noted, however, that this particular point is open for debate. For instance: "Although the Hebrew word is the cognate of the Babylonian *tamtu*/*Tiamat*, it is not personified as a being associated with chaos, nor can it be considered a depersonification or demythologization that is dependent on the ancient Near Eastern texts. It is simply used to describe the 'precosmic condition.'" Keener and Walton, *NIV Cultural Backgrounds Study Bible*, 4.

62. Benedict XVI, Easter Vigil Homily (April 7, 2012).

63. As Matthew Levering notes, scholars have argued that the Hebrew for "evening" expresses disorder, whereas that for "morning" expresses order. For a discussion of this point, see Levering, *Engaging the Doctrine of Creation* (Grand Rapids, MI: Baker Academic, 2017), 123–24.

have been viewed as egregious by the Babylonians (or other ancient Near Eastern peoples who share the same myth), which was precisely the point.[64]

## The Seven Days of Creation

To us today, it may not sound particularly revelatory to hear that one God created the world over seven days. In fact, it strikes most of us as obviously wrong. However, if you were an ancient Mesopotamian (or a Jew struggling to maintain faith in the one true God in the face of the prevailing cultural milieu), this would have been monumental—and not because it was teaching us that the universe was created over seven twenty-four-hour days.

In Genesis 2:3, we read, "God blessed the seventh day and hallowed it, because on it God rested [shabat] from all his work he had done." Perhaps it is helpful to preface any discussion of the positive meaning of this verse by recalling that a non-literal(istic) reading of the seven days is not just something that crafty modern interpreters have invented in order to wriggle out of the embarrassing problem of Scripture's unscientific cosmology. For example, Aquinas is also aware that the "days" of which Genesis speaks do not describe a succession of events in time but rather "denote merely sequence in the natural order."[65] At any rate, here is how Ratzinger replied to an interviewer who asked him about the passage in relation to science:

> The theme you have just mentioned—Darwin, creation, the theory of evolu-
> tion—is the subject of a dialogue that is not yet finished and, within our pres-
> ent means, is probably also impossible to settle at the moment. Not that the
> problem of the six days is a particularly urgent issue between faith and modern
> scientific research into the origin of the world. For it is obvious even in the
> Bible that this is a theological framework [theologisches Schema] and is not
> intended simply to recount the history of creation.[66]

---

64. Ratzinger, In the Beginning, 13–14. Setting aside details concerning the precise deities targeted by Genesis, Benedict pivots from the text's original meaning to its meaning for all time: "What is the creation account saying here? Light makes life possible. It makes encounter possible. To say that God created light means that God created the world as a space for knowledge and truth, as a space for encounter and freedom, as a space for good and for love. Matter is fundamentally good, being itself is good. And evil does not come from God-made being, rather, it comes into existence only through denial." Benedict XVI, Homily (April 7, 2012). For more on the connection of the serpent with fertility cults in the ancient Near East and the suggestion that it may have primarily had the Canaanite god Baal in its sights, see Arnold, Genesis, 62–63.

65. Aquinas, ST I, q.68, a.1; cf. ST I, q.69, a.1. It is fascinating to see Thomas attempt to discern which elements of the narrative are to be taken literally and which are not. While the seven days and the breath of God are not, man's creation from the dust of the earth, the creation of Eve from Adam's rib, and the garden of Eden with its trees are considered material entities by Aquinas. For an essay comparing Ratzinger and Aquinas on several aspects of the creation narratives, see Ramage, "In the Beginning," 481–505.

66. Ratzinger, Salt of the Earth, 31 [Salz der Erde: Christentum und katholische Kirche an der Jahrtausendwende (Stuttgart: Deutsche Verlags-Anstalt, 1996), 26].

Noting that Genesis's two creation stories are not the only discussions of creation in the Bible, Ratzinger ups the ante by insisting that "even then believers themselves did not think that the creation account was, so to speak, a photographic depiction of the process of creation." Rather, he continues, "It only seeks to convey a glimpse of the essential truth [*das Wesentliche*], namely, that the world comes from the power of God and is his creation." On the other hand, he says, "*How* the process actually occurred is a wholly different question, which even the Bible itself leaves wide open."[67]

But if the seven days are not there for scientific reasons, then why? First, we should observe that the narrative of the six days has a literary rhythm to it: God creates spaces in the first three days (light/darkness, sea/sky, land/vegetation), and then he fills them over the course of the next three (sun/moon/stars, fish/birds, animals/man). However, the emergence of man on day six is not the climax of God's work. Rather, the sacred author has structured the process of creation through the metaphor of a seven-day week in order that it might enshrine the goal of creation as such: *rest with God in his Temple on the Sabbath*. In Benedict's words: "One can say that, while material creation is the condition for the history of salvation, the history of the Covenant is the true cause of the cosmos."[68] Or, as Ratzinger states in *The Spirit of the Liturgy*, "The goal of creation is the covenant, the love story of God and man," and "The goal of worship and the goal of creation as a whole are one and the same—divinization, a world of freedom and love."[69] By entering into covenant with God, we become his adopted sons and daughters, with all the rights and privileges pertaining thereto. In other words, by grace we take on his own nature—divinity.

---

67. Ratzinger, *Salt of the Earth*, 31 [*Salz der Erde*, 26.]. Emphasis added. On the issue of multiple creation accounts and how their presence demonstrates the gradual process of development by which the Old Testament came into being, see Ratzinger, *In the Beginning*, 14–16. The "normative" creation account is found within the New Testament and its treatment of the *Logos* in John 1. Ratzinger, *In the Beginning*, 15.

68. Benedict XVI, Address (October 6, 2008). The pontiff continues, "The history of salvation . . . is not a minimal thing which happens by chance on a lost planet. It is the motive for everything, the motive for creation. Everything is created so that this story can exist, the encounter between God and his creature. In this sense, salvation history, the Covenant, precedes creation." Further, from a Christian perspective, the goal of creation is Christ himself. Noting that Judaism during the Hellenistic period developed the idea that the Torah preceded the creation of the world which was created to make room for the Torah, Benedict notes, "The mystery of Christ already is mysteriously revealed here. This is what we are told in the Letter to the Ephesians and to the Colossians: Christ is the *protòtypos*, the first-born of creation, the idea for which the universe was conceived. He welcomes all. We enter in the movement of the universe by uniting with Christ. . . . We reach the roots of being by reaching the mystery of Christ, his living word that is the aim of all creation."

69. Joseph Ratzinger, *The Spirit of the Liturgy* (San Francisco: Ignatius Press, 2000), 26, 28. For other discussions of this connection, see Benedict XVI, Homily, 23 April 2011. See also Ratzinger, *A New Song*, 84; *In the Beginning*, 27. This theme appears already in Ratzinger's 1964 course on creation: "The fact that the creation account is squeezed into the weekly schedule and leads to the Sabbath as its goal means that creation and covenant are intertwined. Covenantal history appears as the goal of God's creation. From here one can justify the formula of Barth: creation is the outer ground of the covenant; the covenant is the inner ground of creation." Ratzinger, *Schöpfungslehre* (1964), 42; Sanz, "Joseph Ratzinger y la doctrina de la creación. Los apuntes de Münster de 1964 (II)," 203n6.

All this is to say that the sacred author deployed the metaphor of the seven-day week *in order to show that, just as God has entered into covenant with the cosmos and "rested" on day seven, so we creatures enter into that same covenant by sharing in his Sabbath rest every seven days.* Ratzinger comments on this claim:

> God created the universe in order to enter into a history of love with human-kind. . . . In the creation account the Sabbath is depicted as the day when the human being, in freedom of worship, participates in God's freedom, in God's rest, and thus in God's peace. To celebrate the Sabbath means to celebrate the covenant. It means to return to the source and to sweep away all the defilement that our work has brought with it. It also means going forth into a new world in which there will no longer be slaves and masters but only free children of God—into a world in which humans and animals and earth itself will share together as kin in God's peace and freedom.[70]

Benedict would further explicate this connection in a papal homily:

> For Israel, the Sabbath was the day on which all could participate in God's rest, in which man and animal, master and slave, great and small were united in God's freedom. Thus the Sabbath was an expression of the Covenant between God and man and creation. In this way, communion between God and man does not appear as something extra, something added later to a world already fully created. *The covenant, communion between God and man, is inbuilt at the deepest level of creation. Yes, the Covenant is the inner ground of creation, just as creation is the external presupposition of the Covenant. God made the world so that there could be a space where he might communicate his love, and from which the response of love might come back to him.*[71]

In sum, to understand why the Bible describes creation culminating on the seventh day, we must remember that it is primarily a story about Israel being called into covenant with God, rest with him, and worship in his Temple.

## The Seven Days as Etiology

As a final and crucial angle into understanding the metaphor of God resting on the Sabbath (seventh day), it is beneficial to consider the image as an instance of a common biblical literary device known as *etiology*. An etiology (from the Greek *aitía*, or "cause") is at its most basic level a story that explains origins—often a folk story or popular myth deployed to explain the origin of a particular word, event, custom, cultural practice, or natural phenomenon. To put it another way, an etiology is a literary device deployed across ancient cultures in which a given reality is explained by linking it to something already familiar to an audience. Often, this "cause" posited is not the real historical or scientific one for the reality in question,

70. Ratzinger, *In the Beginning*, 30–31.
71. Benedict XVI, Homily (April 23, 2011).

and the etiology's essential point is not married to it. On the contrary, etiology is a poetic, vivid, and therefore *memorable* way to drive home important points.

The *New Catholic Encyclopedia* provides a balanced analysis of how to think about etiology as deployed in Scripture:

> [T]he factor of inspiration does not change the character of the literary form utilized; there is no reason to believe that etiology in the Bible has greater historical value than etiology outside the Bible. . . .
>
> In the vast majority of cases it will be found (when it is possible to arrive at a definite conclusion—which is not always the case) that the narrative rests simply on the love of word-play so easily observed in the Bible, on the desire to explain a mysterious monument or some feature of the landscape, or on the author's desire to communicate some deeper teaching, rather than on any real historical basis. Yet this is not to be automatically assumed in every case. . . . There are no universal solutions to this problem; each narrative has to be judged on its own merits.[72]

At any rate, it is particularly noteworthy that Benedict himself also recognizes the role of etiology in Scripture, even defining a particular subset of etiology—"cultic etiology"—as "a traditional story that explains the origin and founding of a particular form of worship and serves to legitimize it."[73] Moreover, he makes note of this literary device's presence in Genesis. As we will see in the next chapter, Benedict even says that the creation narrative is an etiology of Israel's "origin" in the eternal mind of God. Moreover, in his lectures on creation, he similarly teaches that the literary unit Genesis 1–11 is best described as belonging to the genre of "historical etiology."[74]

---

72. Hartman, "Etiology (In The Bible)," 408. It is worth noting that Thomas Aquinas already recognized etiology (alongside history, analogy, and parable) as belonging to Scripture's literal sense. See Aquinas, *ST* I, q. 1, a. 10 ad 2. That said, I have been unable to unearth any evidence that Aquinas was aware of the phenomenon of folk etiology wherein Scripture's authors seek to explain a particular reality through a clever word play without seeking to provide a bona fide historical explanation of its origin.

73. Ratzinger, *Jesus of Nazareth: Holy Week*, 313. Benedict applies this notion to the gospels in *Jesus of Nazareth: Holy Week*, 116–17 and 186. For a valuable article on etiology in Scripture along with many illustrations of this literary device, see Louis Hartman, "Etiology (In The Bible)," in vol. 5 of *New Catholic Encyclopedia*, 2nd ed., ed. Thomas Carson (Washington, D.C.: The Catholic University of America Press, 2002), 407–409. See also Ryan Bonfiglio, ed., *A Study Companion to Introduction to the Hebrew Bible*, 2nd ed. (Minneapolis: Fortress Press, 2014), 24 and Adele Berlin, Marc Zvi Brettler, and Michael Fishbane, eds., *The Jewish Study Bible* (New York: Oxford University Press, 2004), 2128. Here, also I find it appropriate to make a related point about the importance of educating young people with good stories, including classical myths. Arguably the main reason that Christians struggle to grasp the etiological nature of elements in Gen 1–11 is the longstanding assumption that a straightforward reading of the creation narratives should be consistent with science and history. However, another reason is that many today are not familiar with the myriad instances of etiology that one finds in ancient literature: from the Greek myth of Arachne to the Hindu myth of Purusha, to Native American folklore that provides creative explanations of why animals have such diverse and seemingly random colors, and the like.

74. Ratzinger, *Schöpfungslehre* (1964), 29; Sanz, "Joseph Ratzinger y la doctrina de la creación. Los apuntes de Münster de 1964 (II)," 455n2.

Thus far, we have considered only the seven days as an instance of biblical eti-ology. However, in wrapping up this point, it is significant to note that it is just one among many such folk explanations in the Old Testament—including many in Genesis's creation narrative to be explored in this book—which are also only under-stood properly in light of this clever literary device. These include but are not lim-ited to: the names Adam/man (Gn 2:7),[75] woman (Gn 2:23), Eve (Gn 3:20, and Cain (Gn 4:1); Eve's creation from Adam's "rib" which is likely not a rib at all (Gn 2:22);[76] man's donning of clothes (Gn 3:7); why snakes crawl on their bellies (Gn 3:14); woman's birth pains and attraction for man in spite of the harsh treatment she received from him in the ancient East (Gn 3:16); why farmers have to eke out a living by the sweat of their brow and have to deal with thorny plants (Gn 3:17); why man must die and turn to dust (Gn 3:19); why there are rainbows (Gn 9:13); the place-name Babel (Babylon); why the land of Canaan needed to be conquered, why Canaanites had aberrant sexual practices, and why non-Israelite slaves did not need to be emancipated (Gn 9:25–26; cf. Gn 12:5; Lv 18:13; 25:39–46); why Babylon is an enemy of God and each nation speaks its own language (Gn 11:9), and many more. And all of these (along with some I have surely neglected to include) are just from the first eleven chapters of the Bible! Indeed, etiology plays such an important role in Genesis 1–11 that ancient Judaism scholars Amy-Jill Levine and Douglas Knight write, "[T]his whole primeval story in Genesis 1–11 amounts to an etiology of all Western etiologies since it defines the nature of life, the character of social living, humanity's relation to the natural world, and the nature of God."[77]

## The Sanctuary of Eden

If all of creation is ordered toward Sabbath "rest," then clearly there needs to be a *place* in which this communion with God can take place, a place to worship—a sanctuary. Enter Eden, an image that in the Pentateuch's final form figuratively points to Yahweh's sanctuary in Israel. In line with fellow modern interpreters, Benedict understands that this paradisiacal garden was not a physical location on this planet where humans first arose. Like the other elements in the creation narra-tive, this too has a symbolic meaning that had to do with providing a cosmic

---

75. Commenting on this folk etymology for the first man's name, Knight and Levine argue that a more poetically fitting translation of Gn 2:7 into English would be to say that the Lord "formed a human from the dust of the humus." Knight and Levine, *The Meaning of the Bible*, 51. Moreover, Knight and Levine note that the etiology of Adam's name "equally explains the reverse—that at death we return to the earth." Knight and Levine, *The Meaning of the Bible*, 211.

76. Knight and Levine present a strong argument that the "rib" deployed to explain Eve's origin may be a euphemistic etiology which seeks to account for why human males lack a baculum (penile bone) that other vertebrates have but that male humans do have a seam on the underside of their phallus. See Knight and Levine, *The Meaning of the Bible*, 299–300.

77. Knight and Levine, *The Meaning of the Bible*, 198. For discussions of some of these particular etiologies and more from outside Genesis, see Knight and Levine, *The Meaning of the Bible*, 64, 211, 224, 303.

78. Anderson, *Christian Doctrine and the Old Testament*, 62.

foundation for the meaning and purpose of human life.[78] Thus, Ratzinger sees the garden and tree of life together as "an expression for a world that bears the imprint of the Spirit" and a metaphorical "image [*Bild*] for the undamaged creation and for secure existence within it."[79] Eden, in other words, is a figurative way of depicting that original state in which prelapsarian (that is, before sin) man was in communion with God and thereby all of creation.

As we will see in more detail later, Benedict believes that this image of the garden and Adam's life in it is about all of us, not just our first parents. Yet in its original context, the narrative was primarily concerned not with either of these but with Israel and her call to worship the one true God. Ratzinger sets the stage for understanding Eden in this light when he says of the story "It is not [written] in a vacuum. It is not some kind of neutral historiography (*neutraler Geschichtsschreibung*) of the past, but concrete, prophetic, demanding words addressed to the Israel of its day."[80] If creation is for covenant, then Eden figuratively points to the land on this earth where it can be lived—the promised land of Canaan where Israel was to dwell in communion with God.

As scholars have now abundantly documented, the building of God's sanctuary at Sinai—and later the Temple in Jerusalem—mirrors the creation of the world. The following comparisons capture some of the most significant parallels between the creation of the world and the construction of God's sanctuary in the final form of the Pentateuch:[81]

- *Seven divine commands.* As the creation of the world occurs through seven divine speech acts in Genesis 1, the story of the tabernacle's construction follows a sevenfold pattern. God gives its plans to Moses in a set of seven addresses culminating in the command to observe the Sabbath rest on the seventh day (Ex 5:1; 30:11,17, 22, 34; 31:1,12).
- *A sevenfold refrain.* Further, the priestly vestments are fashioned with the seven-fold phrase, "as the LORD had commanded Moses" (Ex 39:1,5,7, 21,22,27,30). This same structure underwrites the construction of the tabernacle (Ex 40:19, 21, 23, 25, 27, 29, 32).
- *Rest with God.* In the ancient Near Eastern world, a god was said to "rest" in his temple (literally, "house"). Solomon took seven years to build a temple

79. Ratzinger, *God and the World*, 77; Ratzinger, *In the Beginning*, 64.

80. Ratzinger, *Schöpfungslehre* (1964), 232; Sanz, "Joseph Ratzinger y la doctrina de la creación. Los apuntes de Münster de 1964 (y III)," 457n9.

81. For many of these parallels and the basis for this list, see Anderson, *Christian Doctrine and the Old Testament*, 62–63; Jon Levenson, *Sinai and Zion* (San Francisco: Harper and Row, 1987), 142–45; John Walton, *The Lost World of Genesis One*, 78–86. On the Jewish tradition (and fourth-century Saint Ephrem the Syrian) seeing Eden as a cosmic sanctuary, see Gary Anderson, *The Genesis of Perfection: Adam and Eve in Jewish and Christian imagination* (Louisville: Westminster John Knox Press, 2001), 46–47, 55–57, and 121–23. Ephrem grasped the intent of the sacred author in identifying the Garden of Eden as a mountain sanctuary whose Holy of Holies was the Tree of Life and where the Tree of Knowledge served as the veil separating this inner sanctum from the rest of the cosmic sanctuary.

after which God rested there (2 Chr 6:41). Further, the Temple was dedicated over seven days (1 Kgs 8:65).[82] Likewise, God is described as taking seven days to create the cosmos before taking up residence in the created world as if it were a house designed for him.

- *God "said" ten times.* We see this in the first creation story (Gn 1:1–29) and when God speaks the Ten Commandments on Mt. Sinai (Ex 20). Ratzinger comments that this connection is made to show that God's laws are not arbitrary but grounded in the structure of creation itself.[83] Further, the concord (*Konkordanz*) between the ten creative words and the ten covenantal commandments confirms the intertwining of creation and covenant.[84]
- *The wages of sin: death/exile from Eden.* As for Adam, Israel's permanency in the land is contingent on obeying the commandment(s), and death/exile results from disobedience. This parallel is especially evident in Deuteronomy 30:15–20, as Gary Anderson summarizes: "For in that book God sets life and death before the Israelites and says the choice is theirs: obey my Torah and you shall have life in the land; disobey it and you shall die in exile. Eden is Torah in miniature. . . . Adam and Eve fall at the first and only command given to them. And like the nation Israel, the consequence of their disobedience is exile from a land of blessing"[85]

What is more, creation and God's sanctuary are not only created in similar ways, but their completed structures are also analogous:

- Both are entered from the East (Gn 3:24; Ez 47:1).
- Both are guarded by Cherubim (Ex 25:18; 1 Kgs 6:23–28).
- Waters tamed in both (Gn 1:2; 1 Kgs 7:23–26; 2 Chr 4:2–4). Indeed, the presence of a "bronze sea" in the Temple "may have functioned as a symbolic representation of Yahweh sitting 'enthroned over the flood' (Ps 29:10), signifying his mastery over the ancient Near Eastern symbol of chaos and disorder, the sea."[86]
- Both are adorned with trees (1 Kgs 6:29-32).
- Both contain a tree, i.e., the menorah/tree of life (Ex 25 / Gn 2–3).
- The same colors and cherubim are present in both (Ex 26 / 1 Kgs 7).
- Both are the source of sacred waters (Ez 47:1–12).
- Both are places where God "walks" (Lv 26:12; 2 Sm 7:6; Mt 26:36; Jn 20:15).

---

82. McKnight and Venema, *Adam and the Genome,* 126–27.

83. Ratzinger, *In the Beginning,* 26.

84. Ratzinger, *Schöpfungslehre* (1964), 43; Sanz, "Joseph Ratzinger y la doctrina de la creación. Los apuntes de Münster de 1964 (II)," 203n7. For more on this connection, see also Ratzinger, *Gottes Projekt: Nachdenken über Schöpfung und Kirche* (Regensburg: Pustet, 2009), 39.

85. Anderson, *Christian Doctrine and the Old Testament,* 71. See also Joseph Blenkinsopp, *The Pentateuch,* 66.

86. Keener and Walton, *NIV Cultural Backgrounds Study Bible,* 4, 576.

As if these parallels were not clear enough to establish the connection between Eden and Yahweh's sanctuary, we also find the Pentateuch casting Moses in the role of the Creator when he constructs Israel's place of worship:

- The "Spirit of God" oversaw the work (Ex 31:3 / Gn 1:2).
- Moses "finished [*kalah*] the work" (Ex 39:32; Ex 40:33 / Gn 2:2).
- Moses inspected and "saw" its goodness (Ex 39:43 / Gn 1).
- Moses "blessed the people" (Ex 39:43 / Gn 1).

Finally, the Eden-sanctuary connection will be even further reinforced in subsequent chapters when we see that the story of Adam's creation and fall mirrors Israel's story from exodus to exile.

## CONCLUSION

In this chapter, we have drawn out the implications of locating Genesis 1–11 in its native context and in light of its figurative or mythic genre. Comparing and contrasting Genesis with Mesopotamian creation stories that were circulating in Israel's milieu has allowed the uniqueness of the revealed story to shine through. Finally, we examined concrete illustrations of how Benedict applies his exegetical principles to Genesis, allowing us to grasp through its many symbols what the Bible *is* and is *not* teaching on the subject of creation. In showing that the creation narrative was not intended to provide a scientific account of the world's origins but was rather addressed to Israel and the concerns of its day, we have been able to reaffirm the reality that faith and evolution are compatible. In the chapters that follow, we will continue along this path by exploring the meaning of man's origin from the dust of the earth, his receiving of God's breath, Eve's birth from Adam's rib, and the couple's fall from grace.

# Chapter 6

# Who Is the Man?

## *Adam as Israel, the First Man,*
## *and Every Man*

## INTRODUCTION

In the last chapter, we accompanied Benedict XVI as he situated Genesis's creation narrative in its ancient Near Eastern milieu and drew in other recent interpreters to pinpoint its similarities and profound differences with other origins stories from the ancient world. Having reflected upon the figurative or mythic genre of Genesis 1–11, we concluded by exploring the meaning of the great images of the Bible's first origins narrative in their original Israelite context: creation through God's word, its seven-day duration, God's "rest," and the garden of Eden. Our exploration in the past couple of chapters has illumined both what Genesis's creation narrative is and is not teaching about creation. Accordingly, we saw that describing God's rest on the Sabbath was not a wager on the part of the sacred author regarding how long it took for the universe to emerge. Instead, Benedict concurs with many other modern interpreters in seeing it as a bold proclamation about the purpose of creation (covenant and divinization) and what this meant for the life of Israel (following the commandments and resting with God on the Sabbath).

The same holds true for the figure of Adam. It is highly unlikely that Scripture intended to make claims on the when, where, or how the first human arose any more than it sought to enumerate how long it took for God to create the world as a whole. In other words, as we have already seen, the Bible's opening narrative is first a story about *Israel* and God's covenant with his people. We will now explore how this applies especially to the figure of Adam, who is not only relevant to Israel but indeed *is* a literary cipher for Israel. After meditating on this figure, we will then be able to see that Adam is not *just* Israel: he is *all of us*. In this chapter, we will explore how Benedict arrives at these conclusions through his exegesis of Adam's origin from the dust of the earth, his receiving of God's breath, and Eve's birth from Adam's rib.

## ADAM IS ISRAEL

After God rests from his work and his cosmic sanctuary is complete, we transition from Scripture's first creation story to a second account that begins in Gn 2:4.[1] If

---

1. Following the standard scholarly consensus, Ratzinger identifies this second account as the earlier and the first as the "so-called priestly document." Ratzinger, "Man between Reproduction and Creation: Theological Questions on the Origin of Human Life," 77.

creation's seven-day structure was intended as a metaphor for the Sabbath structure of creation and Eden is a figurative image of the sanctuary where Israel was to worship God in the Promised Land, then it stands to reason that Adam would also have a figurative significance within his original Israelite context. What, then, did Adam symbolize for the sacred author? Ratzinger shows us that, like the other features of the creation narrative, the figure of Adam is deeply bound up with the mystery of Israel and its vocation:

> Creation belongs to Israel's etiology [i.e., causal explanation of the nation's origin]. There is undoubtedly a tremendous claim in this: to understand Israel one must start with creation, for Israel has its place in the world. Therefore the narrative of the world's creation in Genesis does not come from a neutral scientific interest, but because a story arises here between God and men in which Israel shall occupy a central place. That is the meaning (*Sinn*) of the Bible's beginning.[2]

Ratzinger's words find confirmation in the scholarly consensus articulated as follows by Richard Carlson and Tremper Longman: "The setting for Genesis 1–11 is the same as for the rest of the Pentateuch, namely, Israel herself and *not* the first generations of humanity in general."[3] To my mind, no one has articulated this reality in relation to Adam and Eve better than Gary Anderson:

> The story of Adam and Eve in the J source [or, if one prefers, pre-P or non-P] shows a striking number of parallels to Israel's larger national story. We might say that it is the entire narrative of the Torah in a tersely summarized form. . . . By framing the story of creation in this way, the [writer of Gn 2–3] has recast the national experience in universal terms by learned use of familiar mythic themes and structures and placing it at the beginning as a foreshadowing of what was to follow.[4]

For his part, Benedict does not explicitly spell out the many obvious parallels between Israel and Adam that Anderson has in mind here; for, as we will see, the emeritus pontiff is more interested in Adam's archetypal (universal/paradigmatic) significance and its direct implications for understanding the faith in light of evolution. Thus, before proceeding to examine this fertile area of his thought, it will be helpful to elucidate the analogy between Adam and Israel as envisioned in the mind of the sacred author by enlisting the help of some recent experts on the subject.

Scholars have established the Adam-Israel link in great depth, but the following may serve as a helpful summary of how the Adam story in the Pentateuch's final

2. Ratzinger, *Schöpfungslehre* (1964), 40–41; Sanz, "Joseph Ratzinger y la doctrina de la creación. Los apuntes de Münster de 1964 (II)," 203n5.

3. Carlson and Longman, *Science, Creation, and the Bible: Reconciling Rival Theories of Origins* (Downers Grove, IL: IVP Academic, 2010), 112.

4. Anderson, *Christian Doctrine and the Old Testament*, 70.

form serves as an etiology for Israel's story by mirroring the nation's movement from exodus (the nation's "creation") to exile (the nation's "death"):[5]

- God creates a special person, Adam, and chooses him from all creatures on earth to be the priest-king of creation—his representative "image" (Gn 1:27). Israel, God's son, was created at the exodus (Ex 4:23) and set apart from other nations to be God's representative—a kingdom of priests and a holy nation (Ex 19:6).
- In Genesis 1:28, God commands the first humans to "subdue" [*kabash*] the earth—the same term used in Numbers 32:22, 29 when the Hebrews conquer the trans-Jordan lands.
- Adam dwells in the land of Eden, God's special dwelling place—possibly meant to be a different land from his place of origin seeing as we read that God "put him" in the garden (Gn 2:8,15).[6] This reading fits well within Genesis's broader portrait of Adam-Israel. For, just as God appears to have taken Adam from one place and placed him in a special, holy land with a law and associated punishments for breaking it, so, too, God brought Israel from Abraham's place of origin in Mesopotamia (Gn 11:31) to the land of Canaan.
- To govern life in this paradisiacal land of superabundance, God gave Israel a special law with associated punishments that were eventually enacted at the time of exile. In this reading, then, Adam and Eve were not the first biological members of *Homo sapiens* any more than Israel was the first nation on earth. However, they were nevertheless specially chosen or "elected" by God as his own representative people by means of which all others were to brought into communion with himself. Seeing Adam as a representative human-nation becomes all the more interesting in light of Genesis 4:14, wherein Cain is afraid that "whoever finds me will slay me" and from Genesis 4:17 when he takes a wife. This raises the question: where did these humans come from, unless they were already around before Adam-Israel was created and placed in the garden of Eden?[7]
- God places man in the garden in order to "till" [*avad*] and "keep" [*shamar*] it (Gn 2:15)—terms used elsewhere for the liturgical duties of priests serving as

---

5. This list draws from many sources but uses as its base Enns, *The Evolution of Adam*, 66. See also McKnight and Venema, *Adam and the Genome*, 143.

6. God had created Adam out of the dust of the earth in 2:7, and it is apparently after this that he plants a garden and places him there in 2:8. This understanding appears to be confirmed in *Targum Pseudo-Jonathan* to Genesis 2:15: "The Lord God took Adam from the mountain of worship, where he had been created, and made him dwell in the Garden of Eden to do service in the law and to keep its commandments." *The Targum of Jonathan ben Uzziel*, trans. J. W. Etheridge (London: Longman, Green, Longman, and Roberts 1862).

7. For discussion of the view of Adam as one of many humans or the representative head of humanity in authors such as Kenneth Kemp and Karl Rahner, see Matthew Levering, *Engaging the Doctrine of Creation* (Grand Rapids, MI: Baker Academic, 2017), 227–41, 268–69. A Levering notes, the interbreeding of early huamns with non-rational hominins would help explain the origin of Cain's wife. Levering, *Engaging the Doctrine of Creation*, 240.

ministers and guardians of the Tabernacle (Nm 3:7–8; 8:26; 18:5–6). In fact, rabbinic tradition considered Adam a priest.[8]

- In Genesis 2:17, God gives Adam a law (not to eat of the tree of knowledge) as a stipulation of continued communion with him. Adam and Eve's residence in Eden is contingent on obeying it. Israel also has its commandments to keep (the law given to Moses on Mt. Sinai), upon which their permanency in the Holy Land depends.

- Adam and Eve fail in their vocation in Genesis 3, disobeying God's command by breaking a very simple "dietary" law. For her part, Israel continually disobeys this sort of simple law—as well as more flagrantly serious ones. On this score, Bill Arnold suggests that Genesis sought to offer a positive view of the Torah to those who belittled the role of the Sabbath, the dietary laws, and the image of God in humans.[9] Scot McKnight offers a commentary summary: "Adam and Eve represent Israel in its mission and its failure to fulfill that mission by not living faithfully under God's covenant."[10]

- As a result of their disobedience, Adam and Eve are cursed with a metaphorical death—expulsion from paradise to the east in Genesis 3:24. Similarly, Israel's disobedience brings the nation's epic tragedy full circle at the end of 2 Kings when the Mesopotamian power Babylon breaches Jerusalem's walls and burns the house of the Lord to the ground, after which the fleeing King Zedekiah is captured on the plains of Jericho, his would-be heirs slain, and his own eyes blinded. Carted off to Babylon, he and the Israelites reverse the path of Abraham's journey. At this point, all of Israel's achievements appeared to have come to nothing. The people end up back again in the ancient homeland of Abraham—as slaves on the plains of Shinar in the kingdom of Babel (Gn 11:1–2; 2 Chr 36:17-21; Gn 11:2).[11]

- In the wake of exile, the prophet Jeremiah (Jer 4:23) tells us that the Promised Land [ha-aretz] has been left "formless and empty" [tohu wa-bohu]—the same terms used to describe the earth [also ha-aretz] before God brings order from chaos through his word.[12]

- That this exile is the nation's "death" is apparent in Ezekiel, who described the exiled nation of Israel as a valley of dry, dead bones (Ez 37). This parallel is

---

8. Again, *Targum Pseudo-Jonathan* to Genesis 2:15 is interesting here, as it explicitly describes Adam's "work" in terms of keeping the Jewish law: "The Lord God took Adam from the mountain of worship, where he had been created, and made him dwell in the Garden of Eden to do service [labor] in the law and to keep its commandments." For Adam as a priest of God's cosmic tabernacle, see *Genesis Rabbah* 16, 7 as discussed in Gary Anderson, *The Genesis of Perfection*, 122.

9. Arnold, *Genesis*, 32.

10. McKnight and Venema, *Adam and the Genome*, 144.

11. For more on this point, see Anderson, *Christian Doctrine and the Old Testament*, 70–71. Joseph Blenkinsopp likewise emphasizes that, for Adam as for Israel, permanency in the land "is contingent on obeying a commandment, and death is threatened as punishment for disobedience." Joseph Blenkinsopp, *Pentateuch: An Introduction to the First Five Books of the Bible* (New York: Doubleday, 1992), 66.

12. For this connection, see McKnight and Venema, *Adam and the Genome*, 143.

also evident in Deuteronomy 30:15–20, as Gary Anderson summarizes: "[I]n that book God sets life and death before the Israelites and says the choice is theirs: obey my Torah and you shall have life in the land; disobey it and you shall die in exile. Eden is Torah in miniature. . . . Adam and Eve fail at the first and only command given to them. And like the nation Israel, the consequence of their disobedience is exile from a land of blessing."[13]

- Finally, it is significant that Adam and Israel's sins are depicted as occurring immediately after they receive God's law. As Joseph Blenkinsopp notes, the Golden Calf apostasy of Exodus 32 may be seen as the nation of Israel's "original sin."[14] That is, at the very moment God revealed the final instructions for the tabernacle to Moses on Mt. Sinai, Israel was constructing a bovine idol in direct violation of the commandments received just a few weeks previously. Gary Anderson thus comments: "'[I]mmediacy' may be the best way to define 'original sin' in its Old Testament context. As soon as Israel receives the benefaction of election, the people offer not praise and gratitude but rebellion. This pattern defines the narrative not only of Israel's election but of other founding moments in the Hebrew Scriptures as well."[15]

Concerning this last point, one might consider what to make of God's warning that Adam and Eve would die on the very day that they ate of the forbidden fruit (Gn 2:17) when they seem not to have died. Suggestively, Peter Enns observes that they *do in fact die that day*—just not in the way we typically suppose when using

---

13. Anderson, *Christian Doctrine and the Old Testament*, 71.

14. Blenkinsopp, *Pentateuch*, 66.

15. Anderson, *Christian Doctrine and the Old Testament*, 68. Another significant example of this pattern of immediate disobedience occurs at the establishment of the northern kingdom of Israel after King Jeroboam revolted against the Judahite king Rehoboam. Anderson comments: "No sooner has Jeroboam come forth from Egypt and liberated his people than [Jeroboam] erects golden calves and demands that his citizens worship before them rather than at the altar in Jerusalem (1 Kgs 12:25–33). Jeroboam's words of instruction exactly match those spoken about the first golden calf (1 Kgs 12:28, cf. Ex 32:4). . . . The punishment is swift and sudden (1 Kgs 13: 1–2). . . . And certainly not by accident, Jeroboam's two sons, Abiyah and Nadab—recalling the sons of Aaron—die tragic deaths. The entire cycle of Exodus has been relived." Anderson, *Christian Doctrine and the Old Testament*, 68–69.

Another instance of Israel's "immediate fall" leitmotif is located at the moment of the tent of meeting's dedication (Lv 9:24). The lighting of the tabaracle's sacrificial pyre is the apogee of the Torah. As a microcosm of the world at large, the tent of meeting's consecration was supposed to inaugurate a new age of peace and prosperity. As Anderson points out, though, the final form of the story within Scripture does not honor the script found in parallel accounts from other cultures of the ancient Near Eastern world: for, as soon as Israel's sacrificial pyre is sanctified by fire, it is violated: "When the priesthood was consecrated and the altar lit, God's purpose for the world was completed. He had elected the nation Israel and commanded them to draw near to his presence and tend to his daily needs. But no sooner had creation come to a close than its very centerpiece, the tabernacle, was violated." Anderson, *Christian Doctrine and the Old Testament*, 66–67. At its dedication, glorious fire had issued forth from Yahweh which consumed the burnt offering on the altar (Lv 9:24). Yet, just one verse after this glorious event, Nadab and Abihu offer unholy fire on the same altar with the result that "fire came forth from the presence of the LORD and devoured them, and they died before the LORD" (Lv 10:2). As in the case of Adam, so too sin follows here immediately upon the heels of creation—and the result is again death.

the word. On the narrative's own terms, what happened to Adam in the aftermath of their sin is that he was exiled from Eden: "Therefore the LORD God sent him forth from the garden of Eden, to till the ground from which he was taken. He drove out the man; and at the east of the garden of Eden he placed the cherubim, and a flaming sword which turned every way, to guard the way to the tree of life" (Gn 3:23-24). But, in an ancient Jewish context, *this expulsion was itself a death sentence.* Enns summarizes: "Note that denial of access to the tree of life (3:22) is followed immediately by exile from the garden (3:23–4). This suggests that Adam's exile from the garden is the 'death' sentence pronounced in 2:17."[16] Or, as he writes more casually in another work:

> And so they die. Only they don't. . . . But they do. What actually happens is that the unlucky couple is driven out of the garden—exiled, as it were—so that they might be barred from partaking of the tree of life. Having access to the tree of life is symbolic of spiritually being in God's presence. Death means being alienated from God.[17]

All this is to say that, for the ancient writer who crafted this story, the "life" in question was not primarily physical and yet by that fact no less real. It referred to that life without which biological life is vanity: a life of harmony with God and his entire creation. As Gary Anderson writes, "'Life' in this text does not refer to quantity of time but quality of experience. . . . In the sermonic language of Israel's covenantal charter [cf. Dt 30], death was not defined simply as the termination of life. Death meant being deprived of God's blessing and bereft of life within his holy land."[18] Or, in Gordon Wenham's words, "As the garden, the cosmic mountain, is the source of life, expulsion is a death sentence"—which he proceeds to describe as both spiritual (alienation from God) and physical (Israel's exile and all the suffering it entailed).[19]

---

16. Enns, *The Evolution of Adam*, 67.

17. Enns, *How the Bible Actually Works*, 39–40.

18. Anderson, *The Genesis of Perfection*, 121. Anderson also makes the illuminating observation that Israel's exile can be viewed as more than a punishment meted out by the Lord: namely, as a protection from the great evil that would befall Adam and Eve should they—like priests who entered the Temple sanctuary defiled—remain impure within Eden, creation's Holy of Holies. Anderson, *The Genesis of Perfection*, 129.

19. Gordon Wenham, *Rethinking Genesis 1-11*, 30. For another treatment of this topic and a Patristic view of "death" as the loss of Adam and Eve's original angelic nature, see Gary Anderson *The Genesis of Perfection*, 123–29. For Benedict, death-alienation is the opposite of *communio*, itself a central theme in his writing. For the emeritus pontiff, "the ground of being is communion," and the mystery of the Trinity exemplifies the exodus from the self to which we are all called: "The Trinity is *communio*; to believe the Trinity means to become *communio*." Ratzinger, *Principles of Catholic Theology*, 21–23. Ratzinger describes our conversion as "a death-event . . . an exchange of the old subject for another"—which is precisely what sin refuses to undergo. Ratzinger, *The Nature and Mission of Theology* (San Francisco: Ignatius Press, 1995), 51. Salvation, then, "has always been considered a 'social' reality [which] presupposes that we escape from the prison of our 'I,' because only in the openness of this universal subject does our gaze open out to the source of joy, to love itself—to God." Benedict XVI, *Spe Salvi*, §14. For an Orthodox take on this point, see Kallistos Ware, *The Orthodox Way* (Crestwood, NY: St. Vladimir's Seminary Press, 2012), 80–82.

In light of all of this, Enns lucidly summarizes the most logical rationale behind the Pentateuch's linking of Adam and Israel:

> This mirroring can hardly be coincidental. Adam in primordial times plays out Israel's national life. He is proto-Israel—a preview of coming attractions. This does not mean, however, that a historical Adam was a template for Israel's national life. Rather, Israel's drama—its struggles over the land and the failure to follow God's law—is placed into primordial time.[20]

Casting the Adam-Israel connection in this way, Enns shares Ratzinger's cognizance that the analogy has a clear directionality. That is, regardless of the ultimate historical provenance of these mythological images, in the final form of the Pentateuch the seven days of creation, God's "rest," Eden, and even Adam are deployed not as part of a historical account of human evolution but rather as figures for realities in Israel's liturgical life. Accordingly, he concludes, "It is not an exaggeration to say that the backdrop of the entire Old Testament drama is about how keeping or losing the land is dependent on Israel's religious obedience."[21] As Ratzinger puts it, "The OT does not go from creation to history, but vice versa. . . . Genesis 1 only *appears* to be at the beginning of biblical religion—the beginning and departure of Israel's faith is the historical experience of God, the event of the covenant."[22]

## ADAM IS THE FIRST MAN AND EVERY MAN

We have just seen that Scripture's creation narratives were interested first and foremost in the life of Israel, yet that is not the end of the story. For, if Adam is Israel, he is by extension all of us. In other words, by reflecting on their own *particular* national story, the people of God came to see that it is also a *universal* one—i.e., that *everyone's* individual life from the beginning till today mirrors the nation of Israel's concrete historical experience. In Ratzinger's words, "what the Bible shows in the person of the first man is its conviction about every man."[23] As I will now attempt to show, taking this claim to heart can be a significant boon for understanding human nature in our age of evolutionary science. In other words, I believe that Benedict's work in this area offers a resounding yes to John Paul II's question: "Does an evolutionary perspective bring any light to bear upon theological anthropology, the meaning of the human person as the *imago Dei*, the problem of Christology—and even upon the development of doctrine itself?"[24]

20. Enns, *The Evolution of Adam*, 66.
21. Enns, *How the Bible Actually Works*, 233.
22. Ratzinger, *Schöpfungslehre* (1964), 11, 197; Sanz, "Joseph Ratzinger y la doctrina de la creación. Los apuntes de Münster de 1964 (II)," 202n2, 202n4.
23. Ratzinger, "Man between Reproduction and Creation," 77.
24. John Paul II, Letter to George Coyne, SJ, Director of the Vatican Observatory (June 1, 1988). For further discussion on this question, see Christopher Baglow, "Does the Extended Evolutionary Synthesis Shed New Light on Theological Anthropology?," *Church Life Journal* (January 10, 2020).

Seeing Adam as both Israel and every man is eminently sensible given that Scripture deploys the word *adam* both as a proper noun (the first/representative human's actual name) and a common noun ("human being"). Gary Anderson observes on this score, "Adam and Eve, by virtue of the meaning of their names, 'man' and 'life,' respectively, represent the human condition as a whole."[25] Or, as Scot McKnight explains, "Adam and Eve are not just two individuals but representatives of both Israel and Everyone. Hence, Adam and Eve's sin is Israel's prototypical sin, their 'exile' is Israel's exile, and they therefore represent the sin and discipline of Everyone."[26]

Douglas Knight and Amy-Jill Levine beautifully capture the relevance of this insight into the Adam story for all of us today when they write, "[F]ar from being fictional, these myths are true in a fundamental, essential manner. The question is not: Did Adam and Eve really exist? Rather, it is: How are we like Adam, and in what ways does Eve represent us?"[27] That is to say, the important question Genesis bids us to ask concerns what it is in Adam's story that explains us to ourselves in a way that a story set in our own day could not do as effectively. Ratzinger for his part explains this same connection (Adam = Israel = Everyone) by noting that it is not a "mere report on initial events" at the dawn of our species but rather is about Israel while also extending "beyond the framework of this people and beyond its time to men in general" and thus "speaks of our rebellion and fall, not in the past, but in the present. It is addressed to men of all times."[28]

The emeritus pontiff's insistence that Adam stands for every man and applies to people of all space and time is arguably the most consistent theme one finds in his treatment of human origins. Consider the following sampling of texts spanning Ratzinger's career where this conviction shines through:

> With "Adam" the Bible means . . . the beginning and alternatively the whole of mankind, which is a single Adam. . . . [It is] not a documentary history (*Spezialgeschichte*), but the story of man as such (*Geschichte des Menschen überhaupt*).[29]

---

25. Anderson, *The Genesis of Perfection*, 120. For further discussion on the *adam* in Genesis 1 before Eve's creation, see also Knight and Levine, *The Meaning of the Bible*, 210: "Thus, the first human creation was not a male person, but a human of unstated sex. The division between the sexes is not evident until the end of the chapter when God forms a woman from the first human's side."

26. McKnight and Venema, *Adam and the Genome*, 142–143.

27. Knight and Levine, *The Meaning of the Bible*, 198.

28. Ratzinger, *Schöpfungslehre* (1964), 232; Sanz, "Joseph Ratzinger y la doctrina de la creación. Los apuntes de Münster de 1964 (y III)," 457n9.

29. Ratzinger, *Schöpfungslehre* (1964), 195; Sanz, "Joseph Ratzinger y la doctrina de la creación. Los apuntes de Münster de 1964 (y III)," 484n92. In this same course, Ratzinger adds, "The Adam [Scripture] deals with is not once and for all . . . but this Adam is truly in every single person (*in jedem einzelnen Menschen*)," and: "The concept (*Begriff*) *adam*, the ancestral father of men taken from the earth, is a primal experience of being human as such. . . . In this picture (*Bild*) of Adam taken from the clay, a demythologizing enlightenment of human nature takes place at the same time." Ratzinger, *Schöpfungslehre* (1964), 102; Sanz, "Joseph Ratzinger y la doctrina de la creación. Los apuntes de Münster de 1964 (II)," 213n41.

The picture that describes the origin of Adam is valid for each human being in the same way. Each human is Adam [*Jeder Mensch ist Adam*], a new beginning; Adam is each human being [*Adam ist jeder Mensch*].[30]

The Church Fathers put all their love into their exposition of this scene [of the prodigal son]. The lost son they take as an image of man as such, of "Adam," who all of us are—of Adam whom God has gone out to meet and whom he has received anew into his house.[31]

Immediately following this last text, Ratzinger adds that the concept of Adam—all of us—being taken from the earth was intended by the sacred author as a contrast with how humans originated (i.e., as slaves) in other ancient creation narratives as well as to demonstrate that the earth is not divine as those traditions held: "All are *adam*, because all come from the earth, which is not a goddess."[32] Further, the then-professor even connects the notion of Adam as the archetypal human with the covenantal theme that we explored in the last chapter, thereby demonstrating that this key concept within Genesis's original Jewish context has universal ramifications: "All men are one man. All men are under God's covenant. No man, no people live outside the caring goodness of God, but *all humanity* is involved in this covenantal relationship with the Creator God."[33]

With all of this evidence, it is clear that Ratzinger does not view this paradigmatic meaning of Adam as an instance of eisegesis or merely a later moral reading of Scripture. He regards it as the sacred author's intended literary sense, a reality that flows from Adam as an image for Israel. Moreover, the preceding quote offers us a first glimpse into a crucial facet of Ratzinger's theological approach that will be on full display in the following pages: Ratzinger's personalist "anthropology of relation," an approach to man that he marshals to address all manner of delicate theological problems (e.g., special creation as the establishing of man's unique relationship with God, grace as elevation of this relation, sin as its rupture, and redemption as its healing, etc.).[34]

---

30. Ratzinger, "Man between Reproduction and Creation," 79 ["Der Mensch zwischen Reproduktion and Schöpfung," 68].

31. Benedict XVI, *Jesus of Nazareth: From the Baptism*, 205–206 [*Jesus von Nazareth*, Erster Teil (Freiburg: Herder, 2007), 246].

32. Ratzinger, *Schöpfungslehre* (1964), 102; Sanz, "Joseph Ratzinger y la doctrina de la creación. Los apuntes de Münster de 1964 (II)," 213n41.

33. Ratzinger, *Schöpfungslehre* (1964), 112 (emphasis added); Sanz, "Joseph Ratzinger y la doctrina de la creación. Los apuntes de Münster de 1964 (II)," 213n44.

34. Ratzinger, *Daughter Zion*, 69–70 [*Die Tochter Zion*, 69]. For further discussion of Ratzinger's personalist anthropology of relation, see Sanz, "Joseph Ratzinger y la doctrina de la creación. Los apuntes de Münster de 1964 (y III)," 459–76 and Sanz, "Joseph Ratzinger e il peccato originale: riflessioni a proposito di un libro mancato," *Revista española de Teología* Vol. 78.3 (2018): 439–57 at 452–53. Without using this precise expression, I discussed Benedict's application of this personalist, existential approach to such matters as the soul and the afterlife throughout my work *The Experiment of Faith*, especially 125–28, 158. For an autobiographical reflection on his discovery of personalism, especially the emeritus pontiff's fascination with Martin Buber's I—Thou principle and his dialogic understanding of revelation

Finally for now, the following text is particularly insightful given that it comes from an essay specifically dedicated to the subject of faith and evolution:

> [W]ith respect to the creation of man, too, "creation" does not designate a remote beginning but, rather, has each of us in view along with Adam; *every man* is directly in relation to God. *The faith declares no more about the first man than it does about each one of us*, and, conversely, it declares no less about us than it does about the first man . . . *the mystery of creation looms over every one of us*.[35]

This is arguably the strongest among all of Ratzinger's statements on the scope of what Scripture intends concerning the figure of Adam. Because all of us are Adam, Ratzinger insists that we ought not to be looking for historical or scientific information pertaining to the first member of *Homo sapiens* in Genesis. That is, as we have seen Ratzinger say before, Scripture does not seek to "inform about details of the past" and "expand our knowledge of history into the prehistoric."[36] In all of this, Ratzinger does not deny that Genesis speaks to the condition of the first human being. It is just that he takes Adam to be an archetypal image that applies equally to every man. We will see further below that Benedict considers this concept that all people are "under God's covenant" and "directly in relation to God" the defining feature of our species.

## EVE

After speaking of Adam, it is fitting that we next consider what Ratzinger has to say about his wife, given that the two are indeed "one flesh" (Gn 2:24). In line with his overall understanding of Genesis 1–11, Ratzinger characterizes the creation of Eve from Adam's rib as a "myth" or "legend" [*Sage*]. The purpose of this etiological image, he explains, is to express "the most intimate reference of man and woman to each other."[37] In response to an interview question, then-Cardinal Ratzinger expounds at greater length:

> This, too, is one of the great archetypal images [*ganz großen Urbilder*] the Bible gives us, so that through them we can glimpse things that we can scarcely bring into conceptual form. In the first place, the common nature of man and woman is expressed there. They are one being and have one and the same human dignity. At any rate, their equal dignity is depicted here in the most splendid fashion. The other point is their being turned toward each other. This

---

that operated on a deeper level than stagnant philosophies that viewed it too much as a set of propositions, see Benedict XVI, *Last Testament*, 75–76, 99.

35. Ratzinger, "Belief in Creation and the Theory of Evolution," 141 ["Schöpfungsglaube und Evolutionstheorie," 159].

36. Ratzinger, *Schöpfungslehre* (1964), 31, 253; Sanz, "Joseph Ratzinger y la doctrina de la creación. Los apuntes de Münster de 1964 (y III)," 456n5, 493n126.

37. Ratzinger, *Daughter Zion*, 16 [*Die Tochter Zion*, 15–16].

is shown in the wound, which is present in all of us and which leads us to turn to each other.[38]

After describing Eve's creation with her husband's rib as a metaphor that reveals the complementarity and equal dignity of the sexes, Ratzinger proceeds to show how this fulfills the myths of old, noting that the image we encounter here in Scripture is one that runs through the entire history of religions. He notes that Plato, for example, recounts the myth of how man was divided in two halves which became man and woman—the purpose of which was to show that each sex is only a half and hence forever seeking its other half. Ratzinger suggests that a similar picture appears to be being presented in Genesis, namely that each sex is made to fit the other and is incomplete until they find their wholeness together.[39] Once again, not only is Ratzinger comfortable with describing certain biblical elements as mythical, he goes even farther in sharing Lewis's conviction that pagan myths can provide a real but unfocused gleam of divine truth.

As a final point in this brief consideration of Eve in Ratzinger's thought, it is compelling to note how he sees the Bible's symbolic depiction of Eve's creation not as an unfortunate concession to human weakness—much less something unreal ("just a myth")—but rather as an avenue of access to the *eminently* real. As Ratzinger says, there is no opposition between symbolism and realism in the Bible's creation narratives, for the symbolic is precisely "the way reality comes to light." Expanding on this point, he exhorts us:

> We have to learn to leave behind our rationalistic notion of symbols here.... If you leave the text in its original structure and do not drag it into the mindset of rationalism, then one sees that the text itself does not want to answer the question of *how* it came to pass that a woman began to exist. Rather, it wants to answer the question of *what kind of being the woman is* and *what mystery* lies in the relationship between man and woman.[40]

As we have seen in the cases of Adam and the various elements in Genesis 1, so too Eve is intended to be read archetypally. Thus, to look at the Bible's portrait of Eve for empirical data surrounding the physical origin of the first female member of *Homo sapiens* would be futile. However, if we want to know the more pressing questions that science cannot ultimately answer—what woman is and what her relationship with man ought to be—then we could begin in no better place than with how Genesis presents the mother of all the living.

---

38. Ratzinger, *God and the World*, 80 [*Gott und die Welt*, 69].
39. Ratzinger, *God and the World*, 80 [*Gott und die Welt*, 69].
40. Ratzinger, *Schöpfungslehre* (1964), 185 (emphasis added); Sanz, "Joseph Ratzinger y la doctrina de la creación. Los apuntes de Münster de 1964 (y III)," 458–59n12.

## "DUST" AND "BREATH"

Now that we have covered how Ratzinger understands the figures of Adam and Eve in their own right, we can turn to the other images that Genesis deploys to unveil the mystery of mankind. Whereas in Genesis 1 God creates man and woman immediately with a majestic fiat (Gn 1:26–27), the creation of Adam and Eve in Genesis 2 is narrated in more detail and more anthropomorphically. Notably, this second account unfolds in the opposite order of the previous, which itself is a clear indication that its character is not scientific and historical but figurative in nature. In the Bible's first chapter, plants, animals, and the rest of the universe precede man who (as reflecting evolutionary history) emerges last as the crown of creation (Gn 1:26-28). In the second chapter, meanwhile, man comes first—"when no plant of the field was yet in the earth and no herb of the field had yet sprung up" (Gn 2:5). From here, we read of God forming man "of dust from the ground" and breathing into his nostrils the "breath of life" (Gn 2:7).

Ratzinger, of course, does not read these images any more literally than he does Adam and Eve themselves, for doing so would require one to deny established scientific discoveries of the past two centuries (for example, the fact that plants and other animals most definitely preceded mankind in time). Indeed, as we saw in the last chapter, the very name Adam (*adam*) is explained by Genesis in connection to the ground (*adamah*), itself a folk etiology rather than a scientific claim regarding man's biological origin or a historical claim about the name of the first member of *Homo sapiens* who lived hundreds of thousands of years ago. Because these images do not seek to provide a scientific account of human origins, their true teaching is entirely compatible with evolutionary theory:

> We cannot say: creation or evolution, inasmuch as these two things respond to two different realities. The story of the dust of the earth and the breath of God, which we just heard, does not in fact explain how human persons come to be [*wie ein Mensch entsteht*] but rather what they are [*was er ist*]. It explains their inmost origin and casts light on the project that they are. And, vice versa, the theory of evolution seeks to understand and describe biological developments. But in so doing it cannot explain where the "project" of human persons comes from, nor their inner origin, nor their particular nature. To that extent we are faced here with two complementary—rather than mutually exclusive—realities.[41]

So what, concretely, do the images of dust and breath reveal of man's essence? According to Ratzinger, these images are "archetypical for each and every one of us" and portray the fact that "each person stands in direct relationship with God."[42]

---

41. Ratzinger, *In the Beginning*, 50.

42. Ratzinger, *God and the World*, 75 [*Gott und die Welt*, 65]. Emphasis added. On these accounts applying to all of us and not just our first parents, it is fascinating to consider that the Psalmist depicts himself—definitely not the first human person—being "knit" in his mother's womb to being "wrought in the depths of the earth" (Ps 139:13–15). Likewise, Job says to God of himself: "Thy hands fashioned and made me; and now thou dost turn about and destroy me. Remember that thou hast made me of

We discover here that, for Ratzinger, the defining feature that sets man apart from other creatures—what it means to have God's "breath"—is the capacity for intimacy with the divine.

Meanwhile, if having the divine breath unites man to God in a singular way, it is his origin from the earth or ground (*eretz*) that connects Adam (all of us) to the rest of creation:

> I think we have here a most important image [*ein ganz großes Bild*], which presents a significant understanding of what man is. . . . We can even read into this representation [*Darstellung*] something like evolution. But that's not all. There is something more, which does not come from the earth and which has not simply been developed, but which is completely new: and that is God's own breath. The essential point in this picture [*Das Wesentliche an diesem Bild*] is the double nature of man. It shows both the way he belongs to the universe and also his direct relation to God [*Direktheit zu Gott*]. The Christian faith says that what we learn here about the first man is true of every man. That each and every human being has, on the one hand, a biological origin and yet, on the other, is more than just a product of the available genes and DNA, but comes directly from God.[43]

This last quote is especially significant for our purposes, as Ratzinger perceives that the Bible's depiction of man's origin from the dust aligns remarkably well with our knowledge of evolution (i.e., that humans were not created *ex nihilo* but emerged gradually from more humble organisms). In this, he echoes the thought of his friend Henri de Lubac, who writes, "Man, to be sure, is made of dust and clay; or, as we should say nowadays, he is of animal origin—which comes to the same thing."[44] Taking man's evolutionary origins as a noncontroversial given, both of these authors are nevertheless careful not to assert that the Bible is teaching evolution, for to make that claim would be to fall into the same error of those who claim that it does not—forgetting that the how and when of man's biological origin are not the sacred author's concern even if his narrative providentially aligns with science on certain points.

Instead, Ratzinger maintains that the essential point of these images is man's "double origin." That is, man comes from above *and* below, is connected to the earth (dust) and yet transcends it (breath of life). As Ratzinger explained in his 1964 course on creation, "On the one hand, man is *adam*, taken from the dust of the earth, himself a piece of the earth, and on the other hand he belongs at the same

---

clay; and wilt thou turn me to dust again?" (Jb 10:8–9). On this point, see Ratzinger, "Man between Reproduction and Creation," 79.

43. Ratzinger, *God and the World*, 76–77 [*Gott und die Welt*, 66–67].

44. Henri de Lubac, *The Drama of Atheist Humanism* (San Francisco: Ignatius Press, 1995), 21. To this, de Lubac adds that the image of man's dual origin from "dust" and God's "breath" bespeaks man's lowliness and his sublime vocation—realities that seem commonplace today but whose implications (and, I would add, newness in its day) are too often neglected.

time to the sphere of *Elohim*, the sphere of God."[45] Or, as Benedict would teach in his third to last general audience as pope, "[Man's origin from the dust] means that we are not God, we did not make ourselves, we are earth; yet it also means that we come from the good earth through the work of the good Creator."[46]

Ratzinger finds a crucial implication regarding human dignity in the symbol of man's origin from dust:

> This statement is at the same time humiliation and consolation. It is humili-
> ation because this is what we are told: you are not a god. You have not made
> yourself and you do not rule the universe; you are limited. You are a being
> destined for death, like everything that lives. You are just dust. But what at
> first is humiliation, what shows us our limitations, is also consolation. Because
> this is also what we are told: man is not a demon, as up to then he could have
> seemed. And, as so many mythologies say, he is not an evil spirit. Man is not
> made of negative forces, of dragon's blood and dragon's flesh, but he was made
> with the hand of God.[47]

This critique of a certain mythical view of man echoes Ratzinger's discussion of Babylonian mythology in connection with Genesis 1. Just as God's dominion over the waters, heavenly luminaries, and other beings through his *Logos* reveals that the world is not the carcass of the slain sea monster goddess Tiamat, neither was man formed with the blood of her consort Kingu. Thus, even as the dust signifies our mortality, it simultaneously unveils something deeply positive over and against rival views of man.

Moreover, Benedict teaches the Bible's revealed anthropology entails a very significant consequence: "In addition, there is another fundamental reality: *all* human beings are dust, over and above the distinctions made by culture and by history, over and above every social difference; we are one humanity modeled with God's one earth."[48] In other words, the fact that all of us come from the same good earth and share a common evolutionary history (i.e., our races did not arise independently on different continents as was assumed by the polygenism of the 1950s but instead arose from a single population in Africa),[49] any form of racism is contrary to our nature:

---

45. Ratzinger, *Schöpfungslehre* (1964), 107; Sanz, "Joseph Ratzinger y la doctrina de la creación. Los apuntes de Münster de 1964 (II)," 213n41.

46. Benedict XVI, General Audience (February 6, 2013): "The accounts of the Creation in the Book of Genesis also usher us into this mysterious environment, helping us to become acquainted with God's plan for man. They affirm, first of all, that God formed man of dust from the ground (cf. Gen 2:7). This means that we are not God, we did not make ourselves, we are earth; yet it also means that we come from the good earth through the work of the good Creator."

47. Ratzinger, *Gottes Projekt*, 56.

48. Benedict XVI, General Audience (February 6, 2013).

49. In the next chapter. we will return to the issue of polygenism in light of the current state of genetics and magisterial teaching.

Contrary to what the myths of many religions thought and to what certain conceptions of the world assert even now, there are no different men from the beginning. There are no different castes and races in which men would differ in value. We are all one humanity, formed by God with the earth.[50]

Here, then, we come face to face with a very serious reminder of a weighty truth on which evolutionary theory and biblical teaching converge: beyond. Beyond all the differences that have divided our species across the ages, the fact remains that all of us are equal in dignity. Emperor and beggar, master and servant are in the most profound sense Adam: "one and the same man, taken from the same earth and destined to return to the same earth."[51]

## CONCLUSION

In this chapter, we have made a deep dive into the biblical figure of Adam, understanding him as an image for Israel and in turn of all of us. We then walked with Benedict as he exegeted Adam's origin from the dust of the earth, his receiving of God's breath, and Eve's birth from Adam's rib. In the next chapter, we will unfold the anthropological implications of this exegetical approach that can help us to engage evolutionary biology's account of gradual human origins without fear of compromising fundamental principles of the faith handed on to us by the Christian tradition.

---

50. Ratzinger, *Gottes Projekt*, 56–57. Ratzinger, in a blunt rebuke of Nazi ideology, uses its own language to add immediately, "There are no different species of blood and soil." For a discussion of this point which similarly concludes that racism is contrary both to faith *and science*, see Baglow, "Evolution and the Human Soul," *Church Life Journal* (June 23, 2020). As Baglow notes, all humans are 99.9% genetically the same. As a token of just how close we are to one another, he notes that a single population of chimpanzees in West Africa has been shown to exhibit more genetic diversity than the entire human population alive today.

51. Ratzinger, *Gottes Projekt*, 61–62.

*Part III*

# Understanding Man's
# Special Creation and the
# Fall in an Evolutionary Context

# Chapter 7

# Dust and Breath

## *Man's Evolutionary Origins and the Image of God*

## INTRODUCTION

In the last chapter, we explored Benedict XVI's exegesis of the great figures by which Genesis reveals the uniqueness of human beings and our vocation before God. Having established the significance of man's origin from the "dust" and his possession of God's "breath," we will now see how the emeritus pontiff builds on this exegetical approach to address issues related to the human person that arise from an engagement with evolutionary theory: the meaning of God's image, man's special creation, the origin of the soul and its relationship with the body, and the question of how many original humans there were. Ratzinger provides us with ample material to work with on this topic, yet he never wrote a definitive treatise on it. Accordingly, my hope is that unpacking what he says and unfolding the anthropological implications of his exegetical approach will provide a valuable resource for believers seeking to engage evolutionary biology's account of gradual human origins without fear of compromising the deposit of faith.

## IMAGE THROUGH RELATIONSHIP

We could do no better than to begin our inquiry by exploring the meaning of man as the *imago Dei*, the image of God. Ratzinger approaches this question from a two-fold perspective. First, we may note that the Ratzinger-led ITC looks to the meaning of the term in its original ancient Near Eastern context for insight. While *Communion and Stewardship* addresses a number of points that do not precisely overlap with Ratzinger's specific concerns, and the two at times phrase matters in different ways, I find this to be a valuable resource that has many points of contact with the emeritus pontiff's thought on human evolution. In particular, the following passage weaves in a number of themes we have already discussed in this book:

> The Old Testament understanding of man as created in the *imago Dei* in part reflects the ancient Near Eastern idea that the king is the image of God on earth. The biblical understanding, however, is distinctive in extending the notion of the image of God to include all men. An additional contrast with ancient Near Eastern thought is that the Bible sees man as directed, not first of all to the worship of the gods, but rather to the cultivation of the earth (cf. Gn 2:15). Connecting cult more directly with cultivation, as it were, the Bible

understands that human activity in the six days of the week is ordered to the Sabbath, a day of blessing and sanctification.[1]

As this quote shows, Genesis's ancient context reveals something that many believers miss: just how *subversive* God's revelation was. It overthrew the assertion that one man alone (the king) represented God on earth and universalized the image so that all men—from the greatest to the least—are all bearers of the divine likeness in the world.

While aware of that the notion of God's image [Hebrew: *tselem*] was deployed along the above lines in its original Israelite context, Benedict is nevertheless most interested in approaching the *imago Dei* from his characteristic personalist perspective. To be sure, he recognizes that humans enjoy capacities that other animals either do not possess or do so in only a rudimentary manner (e.g., language, abstract thinking, planning, toolmaking, music, art, mourning, religion, morality, vengeance, etc.).[2] Yet, in Ratzinger's view, it is not any single capacity (or even a combination of them) that demarcates humans from other animals. The scientific evidence shows that our species emerged from a population of hominins (proto-humans) that were ontologically still mere animals. What interests Ratzinger is that, even as man "began with strongly animal-like forms," was "very strongly influenced by the animal," and no precise "moment of hominization" can be identified, the fact remains that at some point along this line there arose a creature uniquely endowed with true relational capacity (*Relationsfähigkeit*).[3] This, in

---

1. International Theological Commission, *Communion and Stewardship*, §8. For more on the divine image in the ancient Near East, see McKnight and Venema, *Adam and the Genome*, 129–30.

2. For evidence of animals having rudimentary capacities for such things that we consider uniquely human and how our species differs in their regard, see Jared Diamond, *The Third Chimpanzee: The Evolution and Future of the Human Animal* (New York: HarperPerennial, 2006), 137–204. On the subject of religion in particular, see Matt Rossano, *Supernatural Selection: How Religion Evolved* (New York: Oxford University Press, 2010).

Distinguishing human language from that of other animals, Christopher Baglow for his part acknowledges the "high degree of cognitive ability, what we might call intelligence or brainpower, in non-human animals," a capacity Aquinas called "natural judgment." However, he adds, "Other animals may act intelligently, and make natural judgments, but we human animals have the power of reason— the ability to capture some aspect of a thing in an abstract concept or symbol and to then reason with respect to it to develop a deeper comprehension of both it and how it relates to other things." The human power of reason uniquely allows us to *make judgments about our judgments*, which in turns means that we bear responsibility for our actions. Baglow, "Evolution and the Human Soul," *Church Life Journal* (June 23, 2020). On man's unique ability to pass judgment upon our own judgments, see Aquinas, *De veritate*, trans. James McGlynn (Chicago: Henry Regnery Company, 1953), q. 25, a. 2. For other thinkers who address simultaneous continuity and distinction between humans and other animals on the question of whether the capacity for abstract thought evolved over time, see Kenneth Kemp, "God, Evolution, and the Body of Adam," *Scientia et Fides* 8.2 (2020): 139–72 and Paul Flaman, "Evolution, the Origin of Human Persons, and Original Sin: Physical Continuity with an Ontological Leap," *The Heythrop Journal* 57 (2016): 568–83.

3. Ratzinger, *Schöpfungslehre* (1964), 213–14: "Paleontological findings pertaining to the early history of mankind cannot give the moment of hominization (*Mensch-Werdung*) but can never-theless give a certain picture of the manifestation of the first human being and of his culture. Today this makes

Ratzinger's personalist perspective, is what distinguishes mankind from every other creature on the planet:

> The first Thou that—however stammeringly—was said by human lips to God marks the moment in which spirit arose in the world. Here the Rubicon of anthropogenesis was crossed. For it is not the use of weapons or fire, not new methods of cruelty or of useful activity that constitutes man, but rather his ability to be immediately in relation to God. . . . Herein also lies the reason why the moment of anthropogenesis cannot possibly be determined by paleontology: anthropogenesis is the rise of the spirit, which cannot be excavated with a shovel.[4]

Young Fr. Ratzinger had already captured this point in his courses on creation when he noted that, despite bodily continuity between the first members of *Homo sapiens* and their immediate predecessors, between animals and humans "there is not merely a gradual difference but a leap in essence (*Wesensprung*)" and that "in man's field of relationships, his essential difference (*Wesensunterschied*) from every non-human creature becomes clear."[5]

Cardinal Ratzinger would later develop this line of thought in more detail in a meditation delivered on the theme of creation, noting that being the image of God refers to that capacity for relationship (*Beziehungsfähigkeit*) by which man is able to move "outside of himself, beyond himself, towards the other, towards others and finally towards the completely Other." To the question: "What distinguishes man from the animal? What is the novelty and the peculiarity of man?," Ratzinger thus responds that it is the species' ability to establish a relationship of word and love with God, a union achieved through prayer and by finding ourselves through the giving of ourselves to others.[6] In sum, as this and the other texts surveyed here demonstrate,

---

it certain that mankind began with strongly animal-like forms (*starken theromorphen formen*), and that he was very strongly influenced by the animal (*sehr stark vom Tier her geprägt war*). . . . The skeleton alone does not yet sufficiently let us know which being gave life to this skeleton."

4. Ratzinger, "Belief in Creation and the Theory of Evolution," 142. Fr. Ratzinger earlier explained along the same lines, "Becoming human occurred at the moment when a being was able to grasp transcendence. The peculiar thing about man is not that he uses stones as hunting tools or knows how to start a fire, but that he can rise above his environment to the wholly other. In other words: man is the being capable of forming the idea of God." Ratzinger, *Schöpfungslehre* (1964), 177; Sanz, "Joseph Ratzinger y la doctrina de la creación. Los apuntes de Münster de 1964 (II)," 244n138.

5. Ratzinger, *Schöpfungslehre* (1958), 73.

6. Ratzinger, *Gottes Projekt*, 62. On man as the only creature not "closed in on himself," see also Ratzinger, *In the Beginning*, 47. Concerning man's unique capacity for prayer, see also *In the Beginning*, 48. To the question of what distinguishes man from other animals, Ratzinger writes, "[T]he answer has to be that they are the beings that God made capable of thinking and praying. . . . The image of God also means that human persons are beings of word and love, beings moing toward Another, oriented to giving themselves to the Other and only truly receiving themselves back in real self-giving."

The ITC echoes Ratzinger's relational approach to man as the *imago Dei*: "As a person created in the image of God, he is capable of forming relationships of communion with other persons and with the triune God, as well as of exercising sovereignty and stewardship in the created universe."

Ratzinger's preferred approach to the *imago Dei* throughout his career was to eschew questions about when and how it first arose and to focus instead on the reality that humans alone enjoy religion and the true relationship with God that comes with it.[7]

Before wrapping up this section, some readers may enjoy knowing that C.S. Lewis's understanding of human origins aligns well with Ratzinger's approach that I have just unfolded. Concurring with Ratzinger regarding the likelihood that man's immediate ancestors would have been physically indistinguishable from him, Lewis writes that, "in the fullness of time, God caused to descend upon this organism . . . a new kind of consciousness which could say 'I' and 'me,' which could look upon itself as an object, which knew God, which could make judgments of truth, beauty, and goodness, and which was so far above time that it could perceive time flowing past."[8] Lewis notes that this being—like a young child who has true spiritual experiences before being able to articulate them—may well have been incapable of fully conceptualizing his interior life. He likely would even be considered "savage" from today's point of view. Nevertheless, Lewis maintains that a real acquaintance with this "naked, shaggy-bearded, slow-spoken creature" that was the first man would lead us to "fall at his feet."[9]

## THE TRINITARIAN AND CHRISTOLOGICAL GROUNDING OF RATZINGER'S ANTHROPOLOGY OF RELATION

Before we proceed much further, I would be remiss not to note that the emeritus pontiff makes an even bolder claim with his anthropology of relation: that the humble relational creature man—every man—is ultimately called to enter into the uncreated relationship of kenotic love that is the Trinity itself. This is what Benedict had to say on the matter to a special assembly of bishops in the Middle East:

> God in himself is relationship, and makes us participate in his interior relationship. Thus we are in his being [*siamo nel suo essere*] Father, Son and Holy Spirit, we are within his being in relationship [*siamo nell'interno del suo essere in relazione*], we are in relationship with Him and He truly has created relationship with us.[10]

---

International Theological Commission, *Communion and Stewardship*, §64. In this approach, Ratzinger simply echoes the Christian tradition with its understanding that man alone possesses the ability to know and love God. *CCC*, §356.

   7. On the uniqueness and role of religion in the evolution of *Homo sapiens*, see Rossano, *Supernatural Selection*, 8, 28–29, 198, 208. As Rossano notes, the "adaptation" of religion provides adherents with many benefits (e.g., safety, health, healing, comfort, social cohesion, reproductive success, happiness), but for most people, that which comes from a relationship with God is "what religion is all about."

   8. Lewis, *The Problem of Pain* (New York: HarperOne, 2001), 72.

   9. Lewis, *The Problem of Pain*, 74–75.

   10. Benedict XVI, Meditation (October 11, 2010). http://www.vatican.va/content/benedict-xvi/it/speeches/2010/october/documents/hf_ben-xvi_spe_20101011_meditazione.html. My translation. For more on this topic, see Ramage, *The Experiment of Faith*, 23, 158–59. For an analogical approach to the Trinitarian logic of self-giving as eternal sacrifice or "super-Kenosis," see Hans Urs von Balthasar, *Mysterium Paschale* (San Francisco: Ignatius Press, 2000), viii.

Pope Francis echoes this understanding in his encyclical *Laudato Si'* and makes it clear that the relational life of the Trinity is reflected not just in man but in all of creation: "The divine Persons are subsistent relations, and the world, created according to the divine model, is a web of relationships." To this, he then adds: the reality that "everything is interconnected . . . invites us to develop a spirituality of that global solidarity which flows from the mystery of the Trinity." Or, to put it in another way that all of us could stand to reflect upon more deeply, "The human person grows more, matures more and is sanctified more to the extent that he or she enters into relationships."[11]

Reflecting the traditional doctrine of man's vocation to *theosis* or divinization, Ratzinger grounds man's last end not only in the Trinity but also in Christology. Thus, just as "the step from animal to logos, from mere life to mind" was crossed when a creature of dust and earth looked out beyond itself was able to mirror the Trinity by addressing God as "You," so our "hominization" is complete now that God has become man, wedding himself to our finite nature and inviting us to participate in his own divinity.[12]

In all of this, Benedict grounds his Trinitarian and Christological anthropology in the Old Testament with its understanding that the invitation to share in divine life is answered by entering into covenant with him.[13] We might therefore summarize by saying that Adam (all humans) being "under God's covenant" and "directly in relation to God" is what Benedict considers the defining feature of our race. The concept of God's covenant in its original context expressed God's closeness to Israel, while the notion of the *imago Dei* reveals the Creator's intimacy with all men who are called into this covenant in their own turn.[14]

## MAN'S "SPECIAL CREATION" AND THE SPIRITUAL SOUL

Having treated the notion of the *imago Dei* in some depth, it is time to change angles and consider Benedict's take on another traditional way of describing the uniqueness of our species. Affirming the historicity of Adam in the face of burgeoning advancements in evolutionary biology and biblical scholarship, the 1909 Pontifical Biblical Commission referred to this as "man's special creation" [*peculiaris creatio hominis*].[15]

---

11. Francis, *Laudato Si'*, §240.

12. Ratzinger, *Introduction to Christianity*, 235. Ratzinger continues, "Man's full 'hominization' presupposes God's becoming man; only by this event is the Rubicon dividing the 'animal' from the 'logical' finally crossed for ever and the highest possible development accorded to the process that began when a creature of dust and earth looked out beyond itself and its environment and was able to address God as 'You.' . . . For—let me repeat—that man is most fully man, indeed the true man, who is most unlimited, who not only has contact with the infinite—the Infinite Being!—but is one with him: Jesus Christ. In him 'hominization' has truly reached its goal."

13. *Catechism of the Catholic Church*, §357.

14. Ratzinger, *Schöpfungslehre* (1964), 108; Sanz, "Joseph Ratzinger y la doctrina de la creación. Los apuntes de Münster de 1964 (II)," 213n43.

15. Pontifical Biblical Commission, *On the Historicity of Genesis 1–3*, trans. Dean Béchard, SJ, in *The Scripture Documents* (Collegeville, MN: The Liturgical Press, 2002), 192–194.

Ratzinger's own words sum up the challenge of upholding this position given how much more certain human evolution is now than it was then: "[W]e have reached the point at which we can answer the question of how in fact the theological state-ment about the special creation of man can coexist with an evolutionary world view or what form it must assume within an evolutionary world view."[16]

Using different language but along the same trajectory as the PBC decades prior, Pius XII would later affirm in his 1950 encyclical *Humani Generis* that, while evidence that points to the evolution of man's *body* does not contradict Catholic doctrine, "the Catholic faith obliges us to hold that *souls* are immediately created [*immediate creari*] by God."[17] While the work of Pius and his predecessors would eventually be given further theological precision in the writings of John Paul II and Benedict XVI, the advancement made in Pius's text is especially interesting as he provides important grounding principles that Ratzinger builds upon and nuances in his work.[18] Penned the better part of a century ago when the evidence supporting human evolution was not even close to what it is today, Pius was able to look beyond the then-prevailing antagonistic ecclesial attitude toward evolutionary theory, granting a new latitude for interpreters to explore the possibility that man's body evolved with the proviso that his spirit cannot.[19]

We will tackle the question of what it might mean to say that the soul cannot evolve shortly below, but for now it will be instructive to begin by seeing how Rat-zinger articulates the nature of soul according to his preferred personalist frame-work, i.e., in terms of relationality:

> The distinguishing mark [*Unterscheidende*] of man, seen from above, is his being addressed by God, the fact that he is God's partner in a dialogue. . . . [H]aving a "spiritual soul" means precisely being willed, known, and loved by God in a special way; it means being a creature called by God to an eternal

---

16. Ratzinger, "Belief in Creation and the Theory of Evolution," 141.

17. Pius XII, *Humani Generis*, §36. Writing in 1950, the status of evolutionary theory was not nearly as certain as it is today, yet even at that time Pius opened the door to research in the possibility that "the origin of the human body as coming from pre-existent and living matter," with the caveat that man's soul is "immediately created by God." A few decades later—at a time when genetics was still not sufficiently developed to offer the full support for evolutionary theory that it does today—John Paul II would echo Pius, "There are no difficulties, from the viewpoint of the doctrine of the faith, in explaining the origin of man in regard to the body by means of the theory of evolution. . . . The doctrine of faith invariably affirms that man's spiritual soul is created directly by God . . . the human soul, on which man's humanity definitively depends, cannot emerge from matter, since the soul is of a spiritual nature." John Paul II, General Audience (April 16, 1986). http://inters.org/John-Paul-II-Catechesis-Spiritual-Corpo-real, translation slightly emended.

18. On the need for corrections to certain parts of prior Magisterial teachings, see Ramage, *Jesus, Interpreted*, Ch. 2 and Ramage, "In the Beginning: Aquinas, Benedict XVI, and the Book of Genesis," 481–505.

19. For an illuminating discussion of Pius's encyclical as a development of the then-prevailing ecclesial attitude toward evolution (e.g., in the writings of Ernesto Ruffini), see Aaron Riches, "El misterio del origen humano. Para mantener la tensión entre la doctrina de Adán y la ciencia de la evolución," *Facies Domini* 8 (2016): 265–286 at 272.

dialogue and therefore capable for its own part of knowing God and of replying to him. What we call in substantialist language "having a soul" we will
describe in a more historical, actual language as "being God's partner in
dialogue."[20]

Remarkably, Benedict would later reaffirm this in a new foreword to his *Eschatology*
penned after becoming pope: "Soul is nothing other than man's capacity for relat-
edness with truth, with love eternal."[21] Earlier in that book, he explains this at
greater length that a soul is not "an addition to a being which really might subsist
in an independent fashion" but rather refers to that which "constitutes what is deepest in man's being"—adding that it is not a product of human achievement but
rather given to us by God.[22]

Ever respectful of the Catholic theological tradition's customary dogmatic language, Ratzinger's interpretation of the soul is accompanied by a familiar and wise
warning not to toss out the baby with the bathwater. Indeed, as Santiago Sanz
observes, he urges interpreters to "carefully distinguish what belongs to the faith
from what is simply an explanation with which the ecclesial tradition intended to
defend this faith."[23] With this in mind, Ratzinger says:

> This does not mean that talk of the soul is false (as is sometimes asserted today
> by a one-sided and uncritical biblical approach); in one respect it is, indeed,
> even necessary in order to describe the whole of what is involved here. But,
> on the other hand, it also needs to be complemented if we are not to fall back
> into a dualistic conception that cannot do justice to the dialogic and person-
> alistic view of the Bible.[24]

---

20. Ratzinger, *Introduction to Christianity*, 354 [*Einführung in Das Christentum*, 336–37]. For an
application of this to the afterlife and issues Ratzinger raises with the notion a "separated soul" after we
die, see Ramage, *The Experiment of Faith*, 122–29.

21. Ratzinger, *Eschatology*, xxi; see also 259. Ratzinger continues, "Beginning with our baptism,
we belong to the body of the resurrected one and are in this sense already attached to our future. Never
again are we totally disembodied." For a discussion of moral problems that result when one views the
body as a container for the soul, see Ratzinger, *Eschatology*, 178–80. On man's capacity for dialogue
with God being "the key to understanding the human form of life compared to other hominid forms
of life" which "shows how human thought and existence transcend the body but at the same time
require the body for expression," see Terrance Ehrman, C.S.C. "Anthropogenesis and the Soul," *Scientia
et Fides* 8.2 (2020): 173–92 at 188 and David Braine, *The Human Person: Animal and Spirit* (Notre
Dame, IN: University of Notre Dame Press, 1992), 543.

22. Ratzinger, *Eschatology*, 154: "[The soul is not] an addition to a being which really might subsist
in an independent fashion. On the contrary, it constitutes what is deepest in man's being. It is nothing
other than what we call 'soul.' . . . Such openness is not a product of human achievement. It is given to
man; man depends for it on Another. But it is given to man to be his very own possession. That is what
is meant by creation."

23. Sanz, "Joseph Ratzinger y la doctrina de la creación. Los apuntes de Münster de 1964 (y
III)," 472.

24. Ratzinger, *Introduction to Christianity*, 354–55. For a contemporary introduction to the philosophy of mind that addresses various problems with dualism like this raised by Ratzinger here, see
James Madden, *Mind, Matter, and Nature: A Thomistic Proposal for the Philosophy of Mind* (Washington,

## WHAT IT MEANS TO SAY THAT THE SOUL CANNOT EVOLVE

What does it mean to say that man's spiritual soul cannot evolve? Though appreciative of Pius's openness to evolution, Ratzinger detects a possible trace of body-soul dualism in such an attempt to exempt man's soul from the evolutionary dynamic:

> Now some have tried to get around this problem [of how to continue affirming man's special creation given what we know of evolution] by saying that the human body may be the product of evolution, but the soul is not by any means: God himself created it, since spirit cannot emerge from matter. This answer seems to have in its favor the fact that spirit cannot be examined by the same scientific method with which one studies the history of organisms, but only at first glance is this a satisfactory answer. We have to continue the line of questioning: Can we divide up man in this way between theologians and scientists—the soul for the former, the body for the latter?"[25]

This incisive text does not offer a neat solution to the question of whether the soul can evolve. Instead, by criticizing the attempt "to divide man up" in the name of ensuring his unique dignity, it seems to suggest that something is wrong in the question itself. For, unfortunately, when people think of the human soul, they often picture it as a separate substance that dwells in our bodies like a ghost.[26] Parting

---

D.C.: The Catholic University of America Press, 2013). As ever, Ratzinger is willing to maintain continuity with the tradition even while updating it in light of new discoveries. Thus, he does express the possibility of affirming a certain sort of dualism—not an ontological but rather an existential one. That is to say, a proper biblically-grounded "dualism" is concerned with two modes of existence by which a human being must choose to live: sinful life according to the "flesh" (*sarx*) or the life of grace according to the "spirit" (*pneuma*). Ratzinger, *Schöpfungslehre* (1964), 118–19.

25. Ratzinger, "Belief in Creation and the Theory of Evolution," 135. On this same point, Aaron Riches notes: "The trouble with Pius's new dualistic latitude is that it tended to undermine the traditional sense of the relation of form and matter, how could God directly will a human soul (which is form) to correspond to a human matter that presumably evolved to the point of spirit without such a form. The best response and expansion of the Pian latitude, which nevertheless rejects its dualism, is offered by Joseph Ratzinger in 'Belief in Creation and the Theory of Evolution,' in which he makes a crucial non-dualist defense of *peculiaris creatio hominis*, which resurrects the best of Teilhard de Chardin in a thoroughly orthodox account of how 'spirit' too could have evolved without entailing either the error of materialism or spiritualism." Riches, "El misterio del origen humano," 272.

For another critique of the dual-origin model of human origins found in Pius's document and reaffirmed by John Paul II, see Ehrman, "Anthropogenesis and the Soul," 170–89. Further discussion of this topic is also found in Sanz, "Joseph Ratzinger y la doctrina de la creación. Los apuntes de Münster de 1964 (y III)," 473 and Giuseppe Tanzella-Nitti, ed., "La questione antropologica in prospettiva teologica," in Centro di documentazione interdisciplinare di Scienza e fede, *Conversazioni fra scienza e fede* (Torino: Edizioni Lindau, 2012), 192–95.

26. For a lucid Thomistic critique of the notion that souls "enter" human bodies that are already human or become so upon the soul's entry, see Mariusz Tabaczek, OP, "Does God Create through Evolution? The Aristotelian-Thomistic Perspective," Public lecture for the Thomistic Institute at Blackfriars, Oxford, UK (February 5, 2020). https://soundcloud.com/thomistic institute/does-god-create-through-evolution-fr-mariusz-tabsczek.

ways with such perspective, Ratzinger bluntly declares: "Spirit does not enter the picture as something foreign, as a second substance in addition to matter; the appearance of spirit . . . means rather that an advancing movement arrives at the goal that has been set for it."[27]

In place of a dualism that considers the body and soul as independent entities, the emeritus pontiff puts forward a more holistic understanding of man. Above all, he prefers to treat the person in his totality with the concept of the *heart*: "Heart," he says, "denotes the corporality of the spirit (*das Leibhaftige des Geistes*) and the spirituality of the body (*das Durchgeistigtwerden des Leibes*). According to Ratzinger, Scripture says with 'heart' the same thing that dogma expresses with *anima forma corporis*: "the soul is the form of the body"—a concept we will return to below.[28] This also echoes what the Catechism teaches in affirming that "spirit and matter, in man, are not two natures united, but rather their union forms a single nature."[29]

## THE "DIRECT" OR "IMMEDIATE" CREATION OF MAN'S SOUL

If this is Ratzinger's view toward Pius's notion that man's spiritual soul cannot evolve, then what does he make of his teaching that this soul comes "immediately" from God in light of what we know today? Nuancing the tradition on this point, Ratzinger wisely steers away from associating the human soul's "direct" origin too closely with a particular philosophical framework or a claim to how this occurred in time. In other words, "special creation" does not refer to the *process* of man's creation but rather its *purpose*:

> If creation means dependence of being, then *special creation* is nothing other than special dependence of being. The statement that man is created in a more specific, more direct way by God than other things in nature, when expressed somewhat less metaphorically, means simply this: that man is willed by God in a specific way, not merely as a being that "is there," but a being who knows him . . . who can think about him in return. We

---

27. Ratzinger, "Belief in Creation and the Theory of Evolution," in *Dogma and Preaching* (San Francisco: Ignatius Press, 2011), 141 ["Schöpfungsglaube und Evolutionstheorie," in *Dogma und Verkündigung*, (Munich: Erich Wewel Verlag, 1973), 159]. Robert North makes a similar point: "To ask how the soul was 'brought into existence' is to fall victim to wrong assumptions about what the soul actually is." North, *Teilhard and the Creation of the Soul* (Milwaukee, WI: Bruce Pub. Co., 1967), 232. For an accessible recent treatment of this point, see Baglow, "Evolution and the Human Soul," *Church Life Journal* (June 23, 2020): "Many mistakenly think of themselves as two things, a living body and a mysterious ghost that is the real self. This, however, is to misunderstand the nature of the soul, which is not a separate thing that God makes but, along with the matter from which our body is made, is one of two principles that make a human being a living being."

28. Ratzinger, *Schöpfungslehre* (1958), 79. See also *Catechism of the Catholic Church*, §368. For an introduction to the Greek concept of the soul as the form of the body and the different but compatible Hebrew image of the heart as the center of the human person, see *Catechism of the Catholic Church*, §363–68.

29. *CCC*, §365.

call the fact that man is specifically willed and known by God his special creation.[30]

Ratzinger's words clearly suggest that he sees the concept of man's soul being created "directly" or "specially" by God as a way of denoting man's unique dependence on God—the singular capacity of this incarnate creature to be in a relationship with the divine.

What Ratzinger means here is better grasped by recalling Chapter 3, in which we saw that the Catholic doctrine of creation does not concern the issue of how and whether the universe had a beginning in time, but instead refers to the reality that the world depends on God for its origin and continued governance. Ratzinger simply extends this understanding to the question of the human person's origin. Whereas in human affairs we tend to think of ourselves being more independent than other creatures, Ratzinger sees humans as *specially* or *more* dependent on God for the simple reason that our species *has been given more* than any other creature on earth. As such, the soul's "direct" creation, like the notion of its "in-fusion" (itself spatial language being used to capture something that is nonphysical), essentially concerns not *how* it was created but rather *what* it is that makes us unique and *why* we were created in the first place. The Second Vatican Council would convey the same doctrinal content by removing the potentially misleading expression "special creation" and declaring that man is "the only creature on earth which God willed for itself."[31] Contrary to what some assume, neither the Second Vatican Council nor recent pontiffs have judged human evolution—our species' chronological continuity with its nonhuman ancestors—to be inconsistent with the affirmation of our species' uniqueness.[32] Indeed, it is significant that, while some churchmen prior to the council desired (and even prepared) a statement that would call this

---

30. Ratzinger, "Belief in Creation and the Theory of Evolution," 141–42. This point was already made in Ratzinger, *Schöpfungslehre* (1964), 178; Sanz, "Joseph Ratzinger y la doctrina de la creación. Los apuntes de Münster de 1964 (y III)," 479n59. Robert North offers another take on "special creation" which seems compatible with Ratzinger's interpretation of it as a reference to what God uniquely wills for man: "'Special creation' is applied to the human soul because of the dignity of the end product." North, *Teilhard and the Creation of the Soul*, 239.

31. Second Vatican Council, *Gaudium et Spes*, §24. For this connection, see Aaron Riches, "El misterio del origen humano," 272. A similar understanding of man's creation entailing him being willed in a specific way is reflected in *Catechism of the Catholic Church*, §362: "The human person, created in the image of God, is a being at once corporeal and spiritual. The biblical account expresses this reality in symbolic language when it affirms that then the LORD God formed man of dust from the ground, and breathed into his nostrils the breath of life; and man became a living being.' Man, whole and entire, is therefore *willed* by God."

32. As John Paul II thus said to the Pontifical Academy of Sciences on the subject of human evolution, the "essential point" (*punto essenziale*) of the Catholic tradition in this matter is that, "if the origin of the human body comes through living matter which existed previously, the spiritual soul is created directly by God." John Paul II, Pontifical Academy of Sciences (October 22, 1996). My translation. Or, as the Catechism relates, the Church's teaching that "every spiritual soul is created immediately by God" precludes it having been "produced" by human parents. *Catechism of the Catholic Church*, §366.

compatibility into question, the Church ultimately decided not to weigh in on the subject of evolution in relation to man's soul or original sin—thereby leaving these matters open to further theological investigation (and, arguably, signaling that they will always remain such).[33]

That said, if one were to assert that man's soul is *merely* the product of evolutionary processes, the Church would indeed find this theologically problematic. While he has no quibbles with the mechanism of natural selection (whose details he leaves to the scientists), Ratzinger thus writes that humans "are not the products of chance and error . . . are not a mistake but something willed; they are the fruit of love."[34] Pope Benedict would declare the same in his very first homily in proclaiming that humans are not just "some casual and meaningless product of evolution." Rather, "Each of us is the result of a thought of God. Each of us is willed, each of us is loved, each of us is necessary."[35]

This is consonant with our above discussion of man's twofold origin from the dust of the earth and the breath of God. As we saw, "dust" signifies that our species has a true biological history and did not spring into existence *ex nihilo*. Receiving the divine "breath," meanwhile, indicates that we all have the gift of direct intimacy with God. Approaching this same point from another angle, we can now say that "each and every human being has, on the one hand, a biological origin and yet, on the other, is more than just a product of the available genes and DNA, but comes

---

33. Along with a number of other such schemata crafted by conciliar preparatory commissions, the council fathers wisely decided not to bring to the floor and promulgate a 1962 preparatory text that treated the subject of evolution in a manner that echoed the themes of Pius XII's encyclical *Humani Generis*, which it cited several times. For the Latin of this text, see *Schema Constitutionis dogmaticae de deposito fidei pure custodiendo*, in vol. I/IV of *Acta Synodalia Sacrosancti Concilii Vaticani Secundi* (Rome: Typis Polyglottis Vaticanis, 1971), 653–94 at 660–62 and 680–87. An unpublished English translation prepared by Fr. Joseph Komonchak is available at https://jakomonchak.files.wordpress.com/2012/09/defending-the-deposit-of-faith.pdf.

For further background on the initial working documents prepared for conciliar discussion by Cardinal Ottaviani's theological commission and the bishops' reaction to them, see Ratzinger, *Theological Highlights of Vatican II*, 28. On the matter of evolution remaining open for theological investigation and an end to the anti-modernist approach to the topic as present in such authors as Ernesto Ruffini, see Yves Congar, OP, *My Journal of the Council* (Collegeville, MN: Liturgical Press, 2012), 257. Reporting the "dismemberment" of the schema *De deposito fidei* (which aimed to condemn polygenism, for instance), Congar describes the document's suppression as "the death knell of curialist theology, of the spirit of Pius XII and *Humani Generis*, of the 'Holy Office.'" Henri de Lubac offers a similar appraisal of this would-be constitution in his own journal of the council, forcefully criticizing certain theologians of the Holy Office (e.g., Cardinal Ottaviani) for the "poverty of their doctrine." According to de Lubac, these churchmen tend to be known for their great firmness in doctrine and refusal to make impoverishing human concessions, yet in reality they defend only "diminished truths" and "human theories, most often ones that are recent, puerile, or outdated, to which they are just as much if not more attracted than to dogma, on which they dig in their heels, and which make them forget the essential part of the Christian mystery." Henri de Lubac, *Vatican Council Notebooks*, vol. 1 (San Francisco: Ignatius Press, 2007), 149. De Lubac later notes that the *De deposito* schema had been set aside and some of its contents placed elsewhere. See de Lubac, *Vatican Council Notebooks*, 521.

34. Ratzinger, *In the Beginning*, 56–57.

35. Benedict XVI, Homily at the Mass for the inauguration of his pontificate (April 24, 2005).

directly from God."[36] Or, as Ratzinger explains weaving this point together with
his archetypal view of Adam, "Every man is more than the product of inherited
traits and environment; no one results exclusively from this-world factors; the mystery of creation looms over every one of us."[37] For Ratzinger, the mystery of each
new human person's "immediate" origin is just as marvelous as the first. This affirmation of the human person's irreducibility to his biology alone is what Ratzinger
takes to be the heart of the Church's teaching that our soul comes "immediately"
from God.[38]

## HUMAN PERSONS ARISE THROUGH NATURAL PROCESSES
## YET ARE MORE THAN THEIR BIOLOGY

Pondering some of Ratzinger's thoughts regarding how God works through the
evolutionary dynamic can help to clarify his understanding of the human soul's
special origin that we have just detailed. As we discussed in Chapter 3, for Ratzinger it is especially important that we not conceive of God as a cosmic engineer who is constantly altering the natural processes he created or an author
who is always changing his script. On the subject of the soul's origin, we thus
read:

> The creation of spirit is least of all to be imagined as an artisan activity [hand-
> werkliches Tun] of God, who suddenly began tinkering [hantieren] with the
> world.[39]

> Man is the being who not only comes from an origin, like all things, but also
> is able to look back at it. . . . It is precisely this double relation that character-
> izes men as created in a specific sense. The statement that man was created
> directly by God is not meant to suggest any miraculous tinkering (mirakulöse

---

36. Ratzinger, *God and the World*, 76–77 [*Gott und die Welt*, 66–67].

37. Ratzinger, "Belief in Creation and the Theory of Evolution," 141 ["Schöpfungsglaube und Evolutionstheorie," 159].

38. Ratzinger says precisely this in his preface to Robert Spaemann and Reinhard Löw, eds. *Evolutionismus und Christentum* (Weinheim: Acta Humaniora, VCH, 1986), vii–ix: "The encyclical *Humani
Generis* . . . had left the question of the origin of individual living species to the competence of research
in the natural sciences and had merely stated the anthropological proviso that man cannot be explained
solely in terms of biological factors; as a living being endowed with a soul, each one is a new beginning
that cannot be derived from biological precursors but points to the Creator. This truce, of course, did
not entirely smooth over the argument about man: soon afterward even theologians no longer knew
what to do with the concept of 'soul' and its direct creation by God." I have reproduced here the translation in Benedict XVI et al., *Creation and Evolution: a Conference with Pope Benedict XVI in Castel
Gandolfo* (San Francisco: Ignatius Press, 2008), 8. In *Laudato Si'*, §81, Pope Francis echoes Benedict's
connecting of the soul's "direct" creation with man's unique call to be in relationship with God, noting
that human evolution does not change the fact that humans are endowed with "a uniqueness that cannot
be fully explained" by evolution.

39. Ratzinger, "Belief in Creation and the Theory of Evolution," in *Dogma and Preaching* (San
Francisco: Ignatius Press, 2011), 141 ["Schöpfungsglaube und Evolutionstheorie," in *Dogma und Verkündigung* (Munich: Erich Wewel Verlag, 1973), 159].

*hantierung*) by God, but precisely this double relation: that man not only has the *logos* behind him, but also in front of him.[40]

But, if God does not cause humans to come into being by disrupting the natural order of biological evolution, then what does Ratzinger offer as an alternative? In an essay in which he argues that the creation of the first human(s) can be understood by looking at what happens in the creation of every human today, he points in a clear direction:

> The picture that describes the origin of Adam is valid for each human being in the same way. Each human is Adam, a new beginning; Adam is each human being. The physiological event is more than a physiological event. Each human is more than a new combination of information; the origin of each human being is a creation. Its wonder is that it happens not next to [*nicht neben*] but rather precisely *in* [*gerade* in] the processes of a living being, i.e., the biological process by which a sperm and egg come together to form an embryo.[41]

> [The soul is] not the mere product of development, even though it comes to light by way of development" [*in der Weise der Entwicklung*].[42]

Tying together Ratzinger's above teachings to the effect that the human person comes into being by way of natural processes while not being reducible to them, I find that James Madden captures Ratzinger's meaning well in writing, "[W]hen I assert that the human soul has not evolved, I do not claim that there is some empirical gap that we expect to find in natural history."[43] This runs counter to our usual way of thinking in which we suppose that something can only be unique if it has arisen separately from other things. Yet, as we discussed in Chapter 3, evolutionary

---

40. Ratzinger, *Schöpfungslehre* (1964), 178; Sanz, "Joseph Ratzinger y la doctrina de la creación. Los apuntes de Münster de 1964 (y III)," 475n58. For a similar approach, see Karl Rahner, *Hominisation* (New York: Herder and Herder, 1965), 101 and Ehrman, "Anthropogenesis and the Soul," 182.

Ehrman also cites David Braine in this connection, noting that "a creative act enters into the natural processes of procreation in every such human coming into existence, but such a creative act will not break the order of the world but serve to preserve it." Braine, "Life and Human Life: Their Nature and Emergence," in *The Missing Link*, ed. Roy Abraham Varghese (Lanham, MD: University Press of America, 2013), 132–60. To this, Ehrman adds that, in causing the soul to come into existence, "God does not intervene into the natural order. . . . Intervention implies a prior absence into which one enters, but God as transcendent primary cause is immanent and present in all things already as the cause of their existence. . . . [T]he origin of the soul is not a causal exception of divine intervention but of normative divine and natural causal concursus that illuminates the transcendent nature of the human person." Ehrman, "Anthropogenesis and the Soul," 187.

41. Ratzinger, "Man between Reproduction and Creation," 79 ["Der Mensch zwischen Reproduktion and Schöpfung," 68].

42. Ratzinger, "Belief in Creation and the Theory of Evolution," 141 ["Schöpfungsglaube und Evolutionstheorie," 159]. Ratzinger delivered this very point in his course *Schöpfungslehre* (1964), 176; Sanz, "Joseph Ratzinger y la doctrina de la creación. Los apuntes de Münster de 1964 (y III)," 474n56. For a contemporary source that addresses the rationality and order that is intrinsic to matter from the beginning, see Cunningham, *Darwin's Pious Idea*, 181.

43. Madden, *Mind, Matter, and Nature*, 273.

science challenges us to see the hand of God working in everyday, mundane, and even hidden ways to bring about amazing things that creatures could never effect on their own. Moreover, as we saw in that chapter, God would still be God even if we are someday able to give a natural account of our universe's origins or a complete record of human evolutionary history. For, providing an empirical account of the natural world still does not account for why there is evolution in the first place and why it continues even now.

## THE RECIPROCITY OF SOUL AND BODY:
### *ANIMA FORMA CORPORIS, CORPUS FORMA ANIMAE*

Intriguingly, Professor Ratzinger devoted considerable time in his university lectures to explicating this precise understanding of the soul's creation. For instance, in 1958 he explained the unity of body and soul at its origin as follows:

> The form of the body is of a different kind and different level as the form of the soul.
> The human soul is precisely a "human" soul not simply on its own as an absolutely existing spirit, but it is only in an intentional relationship to its particular body.
> Not only does the soul create the body, the body also creates the soul. Only when the soul becomes the soul of this body does it truly become a "human" soul. The body does not suffice as a *unica causa* for the spirit, but neither can the soul be brought forth without the body. The soul does not come from (*aus*) the body, but with (*mit*) the body. The formula "God creates the individual soul" is imprecise and needs to be supplemented.[44]

At this early date, Ratzinger was especially concerned to cast his conception of the soul in traditional theological language. Thus, he is interested in articulating what the traditional formula "the soul is the form of the body" (*anima forma corporis*) means in an evolutionary context. Ratzinger observes that this teaching found definitive form in the work of Thomas Aquinas, whose thought on the soul and its relationship to the body Ratzinger endeavors to articulate in explaining that the soul is the principle of man's being alive.[45] To this he adds that, for

44. Ratzinger, *Schöpfungslehre* (1958), 76. For discussion of this text, see Sanz, "La dottrina della creazione nelle lezioni del professor Joseph Ratzinger: gli appunti di Freising (1958)," 27.
45. Ratzinger, *Schöpfungslehre* (1958), 72: "The soul is the principle of man's being alive. The soul is the *actus corporis*, the formal principle of human vitality. Soul is the centralizing force that gathers the abundance of substances into an active unity." For deeper understanding of the soul from a Thomistic perspective that reprises the received philosophical framework of classical hylomorphism in light of the present-day field of systems biology, see Austriaco, "The Specification of Sex/Gender in the Human Species: A Thomistic Analysis," *New Blackfriars* 94.1054 (2013): 701–15 at 710: "The soul makes an organism what it is and determines its end. From a physiological perspective, the net of molecular interactions makes the man what he is. . . . [T]he soul unifies and integrates an organism, maintaining its identity through changes."

Thomas Aquinas, soul and body "are realities only thanks to each other," which, while not identical, are nevertheless one and together constitute the single human being.[46]

Notwithstanding the enduring importance of the Angelic Doctor's contribution to our understanding of the human soul, Ratzinger insists on the need for an *aggiornamento* of his work in our evolutionary age.[47] In his university lectures, he therefore adds that Aquinas's formula "the soul is the form of the body" (*anima corporis forma*) should be now balanced with the complementary affirmation that "the body is in some sense the form of the soul" (*corpus quodammodo forma animae*).[48] Or, as he phrases it slightly differently in light of our contemporary knowledge of heredity, "Man is not built unilaterally from above, but in an interdependence of body and spirit. . . . We must supplement the sentence *anima forma corporis* with the formula *corpus format animam* ["The body forms the soul"]."[49] Repeating this teaching in a similar way, Ratzinger adds, "To this formula [*anima corporis forma*] must now be added a supplement: *corpus forma animae*. . . . Both are valid together—not only does the spirit build its own body, the body in turn builds the reality of the spirit."[50]

Along these lines but independently of Ratzinger, James Madden writes that, in a specified sense, "[T]he human soul may said to be emergent: a certain organization of a certain kind of constituents, for example, human DNA structuring an organism—even as these constituents cannot be the ultimate cause of

---

Noting that the human body is in a constant state of molecular flux and that every two years nearly all of its atoms are replaced, Austriaco adds that the *pattern* of the molecular interactions nevertheless remains the same, thereby grounding the substantial unity of an individual across his entire life span. Austriaco elsewhere adds that this substantial unity comes into being at the moment that sperm and egg fuse at fertilization, resulting not merely in an egg taking on a new structure but indeed a new system altogether—an embryo. From the perspective of systems biology, Austriaco remarks that this new network reflects a new soul. Austriaco, "Immediate Hominization from the Systems Perspective," *National Catholic Bioethics Quarterly*, 4.4 (2004): 719–738 at 733. Noting that this systems perspective differs from traditional hylomorphism only in its emphasis, Austriaco adds, "The human soul and every other kind of soul would be conceptualized here not according to their generic powers, but by their specific power to organize the molecular network that drives species-specific development. In other words, from within the systems perspective, what makes a human soul human is neither its power to think nor to will (though it would still have these of course) but its power to organize a human body and to drive human development."

46. Ratzinger, *Eschatology*, 178–79. For an entry point to the Thomistic conception of the soul's relation with the body, see St. Thomas Aquinas, *Summa Theologiae*, I, q. 76.

47. Ratzinger, *Eschatology*, 180–81: "The synthesis which Thomas formulated with such brilliance in the conditions of his century must be re-created in the present, in such a way that the authentic concerns of the great doctor are preserved. Thomas does not offer a recipe which can just be copied out time and again without further ado; nevertheless, his central idea remains as a signpost for us to follow. That idea consists in the notion of the unity of body and soul, a unity founded on the creative act and implying at once the abiding ordination of the soul to matter and the derivation of the identity of the body not from matter but from the person, the soul."

48. Ratzinger, *Schöpfungslehre* (1958), 76.

49. Ratzinger, *Schöpfungslehre* (1958), 75–76.

50. Ratzinger, *Schöpfungslehre* (1964), 180–81.

the soul coming to be."[51] Granted that all analogies are limited, Madden offers that of a painting in the endeavor to glimpse the relationship of soul and body in a way that avoids both materialism and dualism: while the various components and causes of a work of art may be explicable in natural terms, its *meaning* or *content* is not accountable in this way. Similarly, Roger Scruton writes, "The personal eludes biology in just the way that the face in the picture eludes the theory of pigments. The personal is not an addition to the biological: it emerges from it, in something like the way the face emerges from the colored patches on a canvas."[52]

If the point of the creative juxtaposition of soul and body in the above lines is not clear, I believe that the thrust of his argument can be grasped by considering what Nicholas Lombardo independently has to say about the classical formula *anima forma corporis* in light of what we now know through genetic science. While not making precisely the same overarching argument as Ratzinger or applying his observations in the same way I am here, Lombardo helpfully explains:

> According to Thomas Aquinas and the Council of Vienne, "the soul is the form of the body." If we agree, and if we also hold that the human body is intrinsically oriented toward the human soul and vice versa, it follows that the bodies of the first humans must have been different from the bodies of their nonhuman ancestors. The bodies of the first humans could not have been identical to the bodies of their immediate ancestors. There must have been something about their bodies fitted to their souls. And if there was something about their bodies fitted to their souls, there must have been something new

---

51. Madden, *Mind, Matter, and Nature*, 272.

52. Scruton, *On Human Nature* (Princeton, NJ: Princeton University Press, 2017), 41. Another analogy that casts light on the relationship of body and soul consists in comparing a USB flash drive that is blank to one that is identical in every respect except that it has one's autobiography on it. The hardware of both is the same, but the particular pattern or network of connections that tells one's personal life story in the second is quite different. This "form" is not separable from its underlying "matter," and yet it is not reducible to it, either. For this analogy (to which I have likely done violence by trying to frame it in my own words), I am indebted to conversations with Harvard Medical School neuroscientist Michael Ferguson.

For a lecture that explores the question of whether a certain version of emergent hylomorphism "is special enough for a special creation of man," see Andrew Davison, "Aquinas and Modern Evolutionary Theory: An Inquiry," Thomistic Institute Angelicum, January 18, 2019, https://angelicum.it/it/listituto-tomista/videos-it/2019/01/18/aquinas-and-modern-evolutionary-theory-an-inquiry-prof-andrew-davison/. Davison observes that much of what we glory in about being human arose only gradually (e.g., tool use, art, care for the dead, etc.). This leads him to ask whether the soul—while possessing dignity of the highest order—might have arisen through the ordinary order of things across the long history of hominid evolution or human gestation. In the end, Davison proposes an approach that is non-reductive while also non-dualistic, affirming the reality of the soul but exploring whether light may be shed on its origin by looking to the rest of nature and its layered structure of emergence: atoms emerging from subatomic particles, molecules from atoms, larger biological structures from atoms, cells from these, and so on. To my mind, this seems to align well with Ratzinger's thought that, in some way, "the body forms the soul" (*corpus format animam*) even as it also remains true that the soul is the form of the body and makes the whole greater than its parts would be separately.

and different about their genetic traits. If we accept this conclusion—if we accept the idea that the human body and the human soul are intrinsically fitted to each other, and that this intrinsic orientation implies that human bodies are different from all nonhuman bodies—then we must also conclude that the genomes of the first humans were different from the genomes of their immediate ancestors.[53]

As Lombardo makes clear, it is not the case that the human body creates the soul or that the soul is nothing other than bodily processes. Rather, the point is that the human soul and body are so closely united that whatever was new about the first truly human soul was inevitably accompanied by something new (i.e., a genetic change) in the body of the first human person.

## THE ROLE PARENTS PLAY IN THE ORIGIN OF NEW HUMANS

If the body in some sense "forms" the soul, then the parents who give us our genes surely must play an important role in this whole affair. Ratzinger observes as much in a lecture on the topic when he teaches that the mutation leap (*Mutationssprung*) from the biological to the spiritual takes place in every act of procreation, adding that this "is not just the work of the Creator, but also the work of man." As a result, he says, it can be said truly that "parents are co-workers of the Creator"—that their offspring "are their children in a very concrete way, but also children of God."[54] As to the traditional teaching that God immediately causes the existing of the human soul, Ratzinger explains:

> God must be called the *causa prima et immediata* of every new human soul. Nevertheless, he cannot be considered as its *causa unica* in the strict sense, for in providing the body the parents are real co-causes (*reale Mitursache*) of new human souls. The matter provided by the parents is therefore already spirit-shaped matter.[55]

---

53. Lombardo, "Evolutionary Genetics and Theological Narratives of Human Origins," 525.

54. Ratzinger, *Schöpfungslehre* (1958), 76. To this, Ratzinger adds that "parents are not only the *causa occasionalis*, but are *causa coefficiens* of the child."

55. Ratzinger, *Schöpfungslehre* (1964), 181. On the notion that matter is already "spirit-shaped," Benedict speaks of the "rationality of matter itself, which opens a window onto the *Creator Spiritus*," in Benedict XVI, *Creation and Evolution*, 145; see also 155. For a similar approach to the role of parental causality whereby God, the transcendent cause, "causes the operation of the creature which exceeds and transcends its own possibilities," see Rahner, *Hominisation*, 98–101.

For a Thomistic approach to the causality of parents in the origin of new persons, see Tabaczek, "What Do God and Creatures Really Do in an Evolutionary Change?," 472: "Parental organisms (together with other agents in an evolutionary matrix of causes) properly dispose primary matter to receive it. Consequently, although they can be still regarded as secondary causes of the coming into existence, as well as instrumental causes of the existence (*esse*) as such of the first human being, when it comes to his/her essence (*essentia*) they can only be called secondary causes of the proper disposition of primary matter to be actualized by a human soul, which is not educed from the potentiality of primary matter but is directly created by God."

Accordingly, in his most extensive reflections on the subject, Professor Ratzinger saw that a truly holistic understanding of man would accentuate the role human parents play in the procreation of their children—that they exercise true causality and "outdo themselves" in producing not just a human body but a human *being*.

Not directly engaging Ratzinger yet making this very point, Roch Kereszty connects the causality at work in the origin of new human beings to the overall way God continually creates new forms of life through evolution:

> Thus God's continuous creation in this context means that he enabled non-living things to cause something higher than themselves, and enabled our hominid ancestors to engender a being (or beings) whose level of being transcended theirs. In human conception this same 'miracle' happens every time a man and a woman become parents of a new human person. In the process of generation, God's creative intervention allows the parents to transcend themselves.[56]

Duly acknowledging that God alone is responsible for the origin of every human's spiritual soul, Kereszty nevertheless proceeds to emphasize that "God creates the soul in conjunction with and in dependence on the generative act of the parents and elevates it so that the parents become not only parents of their child's body but of the child itself." In a recent article that treats this same topic, Christopher Baglow adds the following note that also complements what we have seen Ratzinger say above:

> Human souls, then, do come from parents; through the fertilization of the female ovum by the male sperm, human parents are the created causes acting according to their sexual natures. What makes human reproduction different is not that God disrupts this process, but rather causes it to produce a life principle that transcends that of the other animals. The human soul, the very life-principle that makes a human body to be a living body of a specific kind, is not a thing God makes separately.[57]

An important implication of the above is that in principle scientists should be able to trace the various material causes that made the first human soul's infusion possible, and we would need not be disturbed to find a seamless line of transformations led to the emergence of *Homo sapiens*. As the Ratzinger-led ITC wrote, the discovery of man's continuity with his evolutionary ancestors poses no real threat to the doctrine of the soul's immediate creation by God:

> With respect to the immediate creation of the human soul, Catholic theology affirms that particular actions of God bring about effects that transcend the capacity of created causes acting according to their natures. The appeal to divine causality to account for genuinely *causal* as distinct from merely

---

56. Roch Kereszty, *Jesus Christ: Fundamentals of Christology* (New York: Alba House, 2002), 70. On this point, see also North, *Teilhard and the Creation of the Soul*, 239: "The soul is not a separate reality, a bird to be put in a cage as Plato thought. . . . The parents produce a human *being*."

57. Baglow, "Evolution and the Human Soul," *Church Life Journal* (June 23, 2020).

*explanatory* gaps does not insert divine agency to fill in the "gaps" in human scientific understanding (thus giving rise to the so-called "God of the gaps"). The structures of the world can be seen as open to non-disruptive divine action in directly causing events in the world.[58]

## HOW MANY FIRST PARENTS?
## THE MONOGENISM-POLYGENISM DEBATE

One final issue remains to address in this chapter that explores Ratzinger's approach to man's evolutionary beginning: how does he weigh in on the notorious issue of whether monogenism (one first parent/couple) or polygenism (multiple first parents/couples of mankind) offers the best account of our species' origin.

Earlier in this chapter, we saw how Ratzinger distills Pius XII's teaching in *Humani Generis* on the "immediate" creation of the human soul in light of what we know about evolution today. While Pius had carefully opened the door to exploring evolution on the part of science and theology, he did issue the caveat that the faithful could not embrace the polygenism of the day—specifically, the proposition that "after Adam there existed on this earth true men who did not take their origin through natural generation from him as from the first parent of all, or that Adam represents a certain number of first parents."[59] In an apparent departure from this teaching, in 2004 the ITC (headed by then-Cardinal Ratzinger) affirmed that both monogenism and a certain form of polygenism are viable theological opinions Catholics may embrace.

The ITC's document begins with a very brief but helpful scientific narrative of our species' origin, noting that advances in the fields of anthropology and molecular biology combine to make a convincing case for the origin of the human species in Africa about 150,000 years ago in a humanoid population of common genetic lineage."[60] Today this summary of man's origin "from the bottom up" remains broadly accurate, though many more details in the story of human evolution have been filled in since it was written.[61] For example, the field of genetics has now revealed

---

58. International Theological Commission, *Communion and Stewardship*, §70.

59. Pius XII, *Humani Generis*, §37. Pius then adds, on a point related to our topic in the next chapter: "Now it is in no way apparent how such an opinion can be reconciled with that which the sources of revealed truth and the documents of the Teaching Authority of the Church propose with regard to original sin, which proceeds from a sin actually committed by an individual Adam and which, through generation, is passed on to all and is in everyone as his own."

60. International Theological Commission, *Communion and Stewardship*, §63. The ITC continues: "However it is to be explained, the decisive factor in human origins was a continually increasing brain size, culminating in that of *Homo sapiens*. With the development of the human brain, the nature and rate of evolution were permanently altered: with the introduction of the uniquely human factors of consciousness, intentionality, freedom and creativity, biological evolution was recast as social and cultural evolution."

61. For a concise description of this process, see Christopher Baglow, "Evolution and the Human Soul," *Church Life Journal* (June 23, 2020). While not making the same overarching argument as I am here with the help of Ratzinger, Nicanor Austriaco likewise provides a helpful, up-to-date scientific

that the approximate size of the hominin population in which our first parents emerged could not have been less than 10,000 individuals—thus rendering more traditional understandings of man's direct creation untenable.[62]

Further, genetics gives us compelling reasons to believe that the critical point in human evolutionary history occurred roughly 100,000 years ago when just one individual within that population—who were anatomically *Homo sapiens* but lacked the last genetic traits necessary to bear the image of God—was (to put it in the biblical terminology of this book's last chapter) "elected" by God to bear his image. Biologically, what this means is that an individual was at long last conceived with a mutation(s) that disposed him or her to receive a suite of cognitive and behavioral capacities that we associate with the spiritual soul (e.g., language, abstract thought,

---

narrative that incorporates recent discoveries. According to the current data, anatomically modern humans—defined by their light-built skeleton, large brain, reduced face, and prominent chin—first evolved in East Africa around 200,000 years ago from a more ancient African hominin population. Noting that this ancestral population of humans never shrank below a number of approximately 10,000 individuals, Austriaco adds that these modern humans eventually spread across Africa and, around 80,000 to 60,000 years ago, out of Africa into Eurasia, replacing Neanderthals in Europe and western Asia as well as other ancient archaic humans in eastern Asia and Oceania. Austriaco, "Defending Adam After Darwin," *American Catholic Philosophical Quarterly*, Volume 92, Issue 2, (2018): 347.

62. For an extensive explanation of the genetics behind our human population having never dipped below 10,000 individuals, see McKnight and Venema, *Adam and the Genome*, especially Ch. 3. The authors summarize the evidence as follows, "Put most simply, DNA evidence indicates that humans descend from a large population because we, as a species, are so genetically diverse in the present day that a large ancestral population is needed to transmit that diversity to us." McKnight and Venema, *Adam and the Genome*, 55. Extending an illuminating analogy between genetic change and language evolution, they write, "No one expects a new language to start because two speakers suddenly start speaking in radically new ways that separate them from their prior population of speakers. Yet this is how many people think speciation works. . . . Rather, the process starts when populations are genetically separated in some way, usually through physical separation (though other mechanisms are known). What matters is that two subgroups of what was formerly a continuous population cease interbreeding. . . . It is technically possible that a species could be founded by a single ancestral breeding pair, just as it is technically possible that a new language could be founded by two speakers. This is not what one would usually expect, however." McKnight and Venema, *Adam and the Genome*, 45–46.

For helpful narratives detailing various possibilities for how the genetic change(s) that gave rise to mankind's first parent(s) within this sizeable population could have gradually spread throughout it (some of which represent legitimate alternatives to the approach I argue for in this chapter), the following article merits a careful read: Nicholas Lombardo, OP, "Evolutionary Genetics and Theological Narratives of Human Origins," *The Heythrop Journal* 59.3 (2018): 523–533. Importantly, Lombardo notes that the genetic evidence does not challenge the tradition that every human today descends from an original pair. Regarding the tradition that every human living today descends from *only* that same human couple, however, he notes that the genetic evidence "not only challenges this view but makes it completely unsustainable," observing that the genetic data demonstrates that our ancestral lineage cannot have passed through the bottleneck of a single reproducing pair. Rather, the first humans emerged in the context of a sizeable population estimated around 10,000 individuals. Nicholas Lombardo, OP, "Evolutionary Genetics and Theological Narratives of Human Origins," 523. Lombardo's piece also helpfully summarizes the history that led to this community of protohumans including our species' common ancestry with chimpanzees, gorillas, and orangutans (from which we split around 6, 10, and 12–16 million years ago, respectively).

and a relationship with God).[63] Quite likely, these advantageous traits then spread gradually throughout that community through interbreeding so that, as Nicholas Lombardo puts it, "Over time, an effective population of 10,000 nonhumans with one or two human anomalies gradually becomes an effective population of 10,000 humans without any nonhuman anomalies."[64] In other words, the most likely scenario is that there was one truly first human being and that humanity was propagated gradually through reproduction within the larger community in which he emerged. As a result, theologians have suggested that we make a distinction between *anatomically* modern humans and *behaviorally* modern humans or between individuals who are "merely biologically human" and those who are "fully human."[65]

---

63. The earliest archaeological evidence we currently have of this uniquely human kind of behavior comes from Blombos Cave in modern-day South Africa from around 77,000 years ago. Christopher Baglow writes of this evidence, "The pieces of ochre found there, which have a cross-hatch pattern, are the oldest known examples of an artifact that can be confidently interpreted as symbolic. There is no way to know whether or not it was the very first. What seems clear is that the humans at Blombos existed on our side of the cognitive breakthrough often referred to as the "Human Revolution"—the emergence of symbolic thought.... Once we see symbolism, we are seeing the work of other human beings like us. Consider such 30,000 to 40,000-year-old artifacts and ask yourself, 'What other animal does stuff like this?'" Baglow, "Evolution and the Human Soul," *Church Life Journal* (June 23, 2020). For a complementary explanation of how our human language is an all-or-nothing reality that could have arisen with a genetic mutation in a single individual that then spread the *imago Dei* across our ancestral population, see Austriaco, "Defending Adam After Darwin: On the Origin of *Sapiens* as a Natural Kind," *American Catholic Philosophical Quarterly* 92.2 (2018): 337–352 at 347–52.

For an argument that language and rationality arose more gradually, see Diamond, *The Third Chimpanzee*, 165–66. According to Diamond, "Human and animal language once seemed separated by an unbridgeable gulf. Now we've identified a possible series of islands and bridge segments that appear to have spanned across that gulf." Diamond, *The Third Chimpanzee*, 166. For a discussion of the "evolution of the language organ," see John Maynard Smith and Eors Szathmary, *The Origins of Life*, 154–56.

64. Lombardo, "Evolutionary Genetics and Theological Narratives of Human Origins," 525. In favor of this narrative, Lombardo adds: "Since new genetic traits do not usually appear in more than one individual in the same place at the same time, the genetic traits necessary for ensoulment probably appear in a single individual and then spread by reproduction (It is theoretically possible that the genetic traits could have appeared in two or more individuals at the same time by purely natural processes. Statistically, however, such an occurrence would have been extremely improbable.)." Lombardo, "Evolutionary Genetics and Theological Narratives of Human Origins," 526.

65. For the former distinction, see Austriaco, "The Historicity of Adam and Eve (Part III: Scientific Data)," in *Thomistic Evolution*, 171–76. For the latter, see Kenneth Kemp, "Adam and Eve and Evolution," Society of Catholic Scientists (2020), 1. https://www.catholicscientists.org/ idea/adam-eve-evolution. Just as a traditional account of human origins must face the potential objection that incest would have been required for the propagation of the species, so this modern narrative must address the objection that true humans mating with merely anatomically modern ones amounts to bestiality. Both Kemp and Austriaco have excellent responses to this objection. For starters, the mating scenario would have been immensely different from a human attempting to engage in intercourse with our closest relatives alive today, the chimpanzees. For, the first individual with fully human genetic adaptations would have been nearly identical both at the anatomical and genetic level to everyone around him. As a result—and this stands in stark contrast when comparing humans and any other species alive today—these ancient unions were capable of being—and indeed were—fruitful. As a result, in the above piece Kemp helpfully notes, "Such relations would be impersonal, to be sure, but that would make them more like casual sexual acts than like bestial ones."

To make matters even more interesting, we also know a fact that no one knew back when polygenism caused such a stir in ecclesial circles: that early *Homo sapiens* interbred with Neanderthals and Denisovans, other archaic hominins whose DNA many of us on this planet share still today.[66] And, as if that were not enough, there is now strong evidence that these other two archaic humans were rational and that bona fide intelligence dates as far back as two million years ago with *Homo erectus*, for this species made sophisticated stone tools and possibly also possessed a capacity for symbolic thought and language that enabled its members to sail across large bodies of water.[67]

Given the heated debate over whether monogenism or polygenism best accounts for human origins, it is interesting that one highly likely scenario that I have just laid out is actually a form of monogenism. In other words, it is scientifically plausible that there was truly one first human—just not the precise version of monogenism envisioned throughout the tradition. All the same, even if a very specific version of biological monogenism might be true, the Church's most recent writings do not deem it wise for us to hang our hats on this point. At the most fundamental level, this is the case for the simple reason that our faith does not depend upon biological findings. More specifically, though, it is because science could eventually demonstrate that the mutation(s) that led to the emergence of modern humans occurred more than once in the early stages of our species.[68]

---

66. For more on this, see Austriaco, "Defending Adam After Darwin," 347: "This replacement was accompanied by interbreeding among these human-like species such that all non-African populations today inherited roughly 1.5–4 percent of their genomes from their Neanderthal ancestors, and all Melanesians today inherited between 1.9–3.4 percent of their genome from another extinct species of archaic humans called Denisovans. Clearly, our history as a biological species is shaped by migration, interbreeding, and unrelenting adaptation that has generated much diversity within the human population."

67. On this last point, see Everett, *How Language Began* mentioned in Ch. 1. On this subject, the work of William von Hippel is especially poignant where he contrasts *Homo erectus*'s capacity for cooperative teamwork and to plan for unfelt future needs (traits that we observe today only among humans) with the absence of these traits in chimpanzees, the Australopithecines, and even *Homo habilis*. See von Hippel, *The Social Leap*, 37–40. For his part, William Lane Craig identifies the first true humans with *Homo heidelbergensis* and dates them to roughly one million years ago. Craig, *In Quest of the Historical Adam*, 522, 540.

68. Nicholas Lombardo lays out this sort of scenario in his "Evolutionary Genetics and Theological Narratives of Human Origins" piece. For example, it is conceivable that such a mutation happened more than once, in which case some humans bred with others who had independently made the transition. Moreover, for all we know, there were humans who independently underwent this transition but died out before ever mating with our ancestors. Thankfully, Ratzinger makes it clear that the Church's faith is not contingent on any one biological scenario for how many first humans there were. In this regard, we may also recall that, in the evolutionary history timeline presented in Ch. 1 of this book, evidence for Denisovans and Neanderthals being rational is strong (e.g., their making of jewelry, complex tools, etc.), and it is quite possible that two million years ago *Homo erectus* already possessed the capacity for symbolic or abstract thought. These observations serve as just one more reason to be grateful to Ratzinger for emphasizing that central truth claims of the faith concerning human dignity are not dependent on how precisely (e.g., where, when, how many times) the leap to rationality was made.

In this connection, it is therefore particularly noteworthy that the ITC, in an apparent departure from Pius XII's teaching, explicitly acknowledges the possibility that polygenism is the best account of our species' origin:

> Catholic theology affirms that the emergence of the first members of the human species (whether as individuals *or in populations*) represents an event that is not susceptible of a purely natural explanation and which can appropriately be attributed to divine intervention. Acting indirectly through causal chains operating from the beginning of cosmic history, God prepared the way for what Pope John Paul II has called "an ontological leap . . . the moment of transition to the spiritual." While science can study these causal chains, it falls to theology to locate this account of the special creation of the human soul within the overarching plan of the triune God to share the communion of trinitarian life with human persons. . . .[69]

I stated above that this approach is an *apparent* departure from that of Pius XII. This is because, contrary to what many Catholics assume, Pius did not intend his comments to definitively resolve the question of how many original humans populated the planet. As Aaron Riches helpfully notes, the larger context of Pius's text is vitally important, for it reveals that its rejection of "polygenism" was "in the first place not directed at the genetic polygenism of a single ancestral population, but rather race-based polygenetic theory that the different human races originated from different original sources."[70] In Pius's day, some had used a multiregional model of our species' origin (which posited that humans arose independently on different continents) to justify their claim that there were multiple human species with Caucasians being the superior one.[71] This, in turn, they used to justify the slave trade of negroes and others who were deemed different, inferior species. To understand how Benedict and other contemporary ecclesiastical sources like the ITC can stand in harmony with Pius's fundamental convictions, it is crucial to understand this context that lay behind the encyclical's antagonism toward a certain version of "polygenism."

One of many eminent theologians to draw a similar conclusion was none other than Professor Ratzinger himself, who in a lecture dedicated to this precise question argued that *Humani Generis* was "very carefully and cautiously worded" on the issue of polygenism so that it "clearly opens a door in principle."[72] Remarkably, this

---

69. International Theological Commission, *Communion and Stewardship*, §70 (emphasis added).

70. Aaron Riches, "El misterio del origen humano," 271. For further discussion of the compatibility of polygenism and magisterial teaching and the concerns of Pius XII, see Austriaco, "The Historicity of Adam and Eve (I: Theological Data)," in *Thomistic Evolution*, 159–62.

71. For discussion of thinkers who held this now-disproven view, see Kemp, "Adam and Eve and Evolution," 1, Appendix.

72. Ratzinger, *Schöpfungslehre* (1964), 190–91; Sanz, "Joseph Ratzinger y la doctrina de la creación. Los apuntes de Münster de 1964 (y III)," 480n75. For more on the magisterial tradition and biological polygenism's compatibility with Catholic doctrine, see Lombardo, "Evolutionary Genetics and Theological Narratives of Human Origins," 528–30 and Simon Gaine, OP, "The Teaching of the Catholic Church and the Evolution of Humanity" (forthcoming). Gaine suggests that the old tradition that the

statement of Ratzinger from 1964 has recently been corroborated by American Catholic philosopher Kenneth Kemp after making a trip to Rome to study archival materials pertinent to the composition of Pius's encyclical. As Kemp discovered, early drafts of the encyclical excluded polygenism categorically, declaring that it absolutely cannot be reconciled with the doctrine of original sin.

As we know, however, the final form of *Humani Generis* took a more supple position wherein it simply states that it is "in no way apparent" (as of 1950, that is) how polygenism and the doctrine of original sin are compatible. Accordingly, Kemp concludes, "The archival records make clear that the non-definitive language was deliberately chosen over the stronger language of early drafts of the encyclical."[73] Or, as Chris Baglow comments, "[T]hanks to this careful investigator, we now know that putting the emphasis on 'not apparent' is accurate."[74] All this is to say that the official language of *Humani Generis* did not at all intend to close the door on the possibility that humans evolved gradually within a large population. What is more, Professor Ratzinger not only argued that the encyclical left open the door to polygenism, he himself was in fact inclined to think that the emergence of man took place within "an entire population."[75]

Drawing all of the above together, Ratzinger offers an intriguing way to harmonize the Church's traditional teaching with modern science on this question. The key, he says, is to make a distinction between *biological* mono- or polygenism (which addresses how many initial humans there were) and *theological* monogenism (which affirms the central truth that the entire human race is one regardless of how it arose). If we make this distinction, he argues, it should be "clear that biological polygenism is largely a theologically neutral theme because it does not overlap directly with the theological poly- or monogenism."[76] Biological

---

first man's body was immediately formed by God has over time given way to formation by evolution. Aware that evolution will unlikely ever be defined as true by the Magisterium, he nevertheless writes, "Thus a position once commonly held, but effectively reduced by Pius XII to the status of a probable opinion, is arguably from the time of John Paul II, I suggest, merely tolerated by the magisterium."

73. Kemp, "Adam and Eve and Evolution," 1. In a similar vein, Yves Congar notes on the subject of monogenism that others at the time (e.g., Fr. Sebastian Tromp and Fr. Augustine Bea) tried to persuade Pius to go further than he had in his drafting of *Humani Generis*, yet the pope prudently refused to do so. Congar, *My Journal of the Council*, 62.

74. Baglow, *Creation*, 69.

75. Ratzinger, *Schöpfungslehre* (1964), 193; Sanz, "Joseph Ratzinger y la doctrina de la creación. Los apuntes de Münster de 1964 (y III)," 481n81. In 1964, we find further evidence that he was wrestling with the question of whether the best account of humanity's beginnings was "monophylism" (from one genetic line/one Adam) or "polyphylism" (from several genetic lines). At this juncture, Ratzinger points out that, even if monophylism is the correct account of human origins, this should not be confused with monogenism (*monophylismus nicht monogenismus ist*) if understood along literalist lines to mean that the first two humans were directly created by God apart from evolutionary processes. For a helpful overview of how these and other related terms have been variously deployed over time, see Kemp, "Adam and Eve and Evolution," Appendix; James Hofmann, "Catholicism and Evolution: Polygenism and Original Sin," *Scientia et Fides* 8.2 (2020): 95–138.

76. Ratzinger, *Schöpfungslehre* (1964), 194; Sanz, "Joseph Ratzinger y la doctrina de la creación. Los apuntes de Münster de 1964 (y III)," 482n84: "[E]ven if it is highly probable that hominization

monogenism, he continues, "can never be the primary intention of a scriptural statement or a dogmatic teaching," for the Scriptures are concerned instead with the theological concepts of sin and grace.[77] Pithily capturing this understanding, Ratzinger writes, "That mankind's first decision was characterized by a 'no' is essential (*Wesentlich*). Whether this beginning was determined by one or more is not so important."[78] All this is to say that the question of whether or not every human who ever lived is a physical descendant of one first man (*biological monogenism*) is incidental to the faith of the Church. Indeed, Ratzinger thinks that biological monogenism is untrue if by it we mean that God created the first human apart from the evolutionary dynamic. To reiterate a classic principle from Thomas Aquinas, some things must be believed by the faithful, while in the case of others there is latitude for debate—and indeed "in such matters *even the saints* at times view things differently."[79]

## CONCLUSION

We have covered a lot of ground in this chapter. Bringing to light important implications of Ratzinger's exegetical approach, we have tackled several anthropological issues related to evolution: the meaning of God's image, man's special creation, the immediate creation of our souls, the relationship of soul and body, the role of parents in it all, and the debate over polygenism vs. monogenism. In so doing, I hope to have shown that Benedict offers a promising hermeneutical path by which to engage evolutionary biology's account of gradual human origins without compromising the fundamental principles of the faith handed on to us by the tradition.

What is essential to the faith when it comes to the topic of human origins? According to Ratzinger, one such truth is the reality that—regardless of how many of us first attained it—all humans share a common nature made in the image of God but which has been stained by sin and stands in need of Christ's redemption (*theological* monogenism). Moreover, as we have discussed above, *Humani Generis* and subsequent popes have made another thing quite clear: irrespective of the precise biological mechanisms by which man evolved, Genesis proclaims that there is a grandeur in the human spirit that no other creature can boast. As Ratzinger says,

---

occurred within a biological population in a polygenic manner, it is possible that the brilliant flash of transcendence occurred for the first time in one or two individuals. Biological polygenism and theological monogenism are therefore not necessarily mutually exclusive antitheses, because the level of their questions does not fully coincide. . . . [I]t is clear that biological polygenism is largely a theologically neutral theme because it does not overlap directly with the theological poly- or monogenism."

77. Ratzinger, *Schöpfungslehre* (1964), 194; Sanz, "Joseph Ratzinger y la doctrina de la creación. Los apuntes de Münster de 1964 (y III)," 483n86.

78. Ratzinger, *Schöpfungslehre* (1964), 252; Sanz, "Joseph Ratzinger y la doctrina de la creación. Los apuntes de Münster de 1964 (y III)," 484n90.

79. Aquinas, *In II Sent.*, Lib. 2, d. 12, q. 1, a. 2 (my translation).

having a soul means being capable of relationship with God, an ineluctable feature of man's mystery that is not reducible to the biological processes by means of which he evolved. That said, important issues could also be raised at this point concerning the upshot of such an approach for another important Christian doctrine: original sin. As we are about to see, Ratzinger devotes considerable time to exploring this belief through the lens of Adam as the archetypal human.

# Chapter 8

# Relationship Rupture
## *What Original Sin Is and Is Not*

## INTRODUCTION

Having treated the topic of man's special creation and the related issue of polygenism, we now turn our attention to what is arguably the most controverted question at the intersection of faith and evolution: Is original sin tenable in an evolutionary context? If so, what does Benedict XVI take it to mean? By exploring Ratzinger's answers to these questions, the aim of this chapter is to arrive at some insights that leave us better positioned to see the harmony between this constant dogmatic teaching of the Church and the knowledge we have attained through modern scientific discoveries.

Our task will involve several components. We will begin with a discussion of what Ratzinger intends by calling "original sin" a "misleading term," ruling out common misconceptions by clarifying what the doctrine does *not* teach (how many people first sinned, how precisely it happened, and how precisely it is transmitted). Next, we will unfold Benedict's understanding of what this doctrine *does* teach: through the various figures of Adam, Eve, the serpent, the garden, and the fruit, Genesis's creation account tells the story of Israel and provides the reason for the nation's exile. In turn, this inspired myth extends beyond its original context and reveals the interior "exile" of every human from God. From here, Benedict unfolds how the biblical narrative of the Fall provides a "phenomenology of sin" which applies to every human's experience, not just that of Israel or the first member of *Homo sapiens*.

Importantly, Benedict has a unique understanding of original sin that he articulates according to his characteristic relational or personalistic perspective. As we saw in the last chapter, the emeritus pontiff locates man's uniqueness as *imago Dei* in his ability to be in relationship with God. Applying this principle to man's fall from grace, we will next see that he conceives of original sin as a disorder in humanity's relationship structure that has accompanied our history since its first generation—a broken relationship with God that has had tragic and inevitable consequences for all other relationships.

Finally, we will discover that a key dimension of Benedict's thought on original sin concerns the question of why St. Paul discusses Adam's sin in the first place. According to the emeritus pontiff, the Apostle's very point in mentioning it was to highlight the immeasurable gift of grace in Christ. Thus, the doctrine of original sin is in reality more about the Last Adam than the First, a reality that opens up fruitful possibilities for a dialogue with evolutionary science.

## A "MISLEADING TERM"

Ratzinger took up the topic of original sin many times over the course of his career, endeavoring to spell out what it means, how it is transmitted, and why it still has a place in Christian doctrine today. As an indication of the challenge that he considers the topic to be, then-Cardinal Ratzinger remarked in one of his homilies:

> Nothing seems to us today to be stranger or, indeed, more absurd than to insist upon original sin, since, according to our way of thinking, guilt can only be something very personal, and since God does not run a concentration camp, in which one's relatives are imprisoned, because he is a liberating God of love, who calls each one by name.[1]

In this same passage, Ratzinger describes original sin as a "certainly misleading [*mißverständliche*] and imprecise [*ungenaue*] term" and then proceeds to ask of the doctrine: "What does original sin mean, then, when we interpret it correctly?"[2]

This sort of crisp questioning, so characteristic of the emeritus pontiff's writing, stands out even more clearly at the beginning of a catechetical address that Pope Benedict delivered on the relation between Adam and Christ. In this text, he specifically addresses the claim that evolution does away with the notion of a Fall that has spread sin across the entire history of mankind. Here the question is framed quite simply: "Does original sin exist or not?" Benedict's response in this catechesis, as elsewhere, is a resounding yes. Although there is "an aspect of mystery concerning the ontological foundation of this event," Benedict insists that the doctrine is not a matter of mere conjecture. On the contrary, there exists an "inner contradiction" within the being of every human—a "second will" or "law of sin and death"—is an "empirical fact" that all of us experience every day.[3] Indeed, on one occasion Cardinal Ratzinger approvingly cited the anecdote of a friend who had said that, though he struggled with many of the Church's beliefs, original sin is the "one doctrine I don't need to believe at all, because I experience it every

---

1. Ratzinger, *In the Beginning*, 72.

2. Ratzinger, *In the Beginning*, 72 [*Im Anfang schuf Gott*, 55].

3. Benedict XVI, General Audience: "The Apostle's Teaching on the Relation between Adam and Christ" (December 3, 2008). On original sin being "evident," see Ratzinger and Messori, *The Ratzinger Report*, 80–81; cf. Ratzinger, *In the Beginning*, 84. The "law of sin and death" is Paul's expression in Romans 8:2. Because of this law, Paul explains, "I can will what is right, but I cannot do it. For I do not do the good I want, but the evil I do not want is what I do" (Rm 7:18–19).

4. Ratzinger, *God and the World*, 77. Pope Francis has written similarly: "[Original sin is] something we know from experience. Our humanity is wounded. We try to follow the path of goodness, but we often fall because of our weaknesses and choose evil. This is the consequence of original sin, which we are fully aware of thanks to the Book of Revelation." Francis, *The Name of God Is Mercy* (New York: Random House, 2016), 42. Concerning the epistemic status of this doctrine's essential content, the Catechism teaches that it is held with the "certainty of faith." CCC, §403. On the authority of this doctrine, see also Congregation for the Doctrine of the Faith, *Doctrinal Commentary on the Concluding Formula of the Professio Fidei*, §5, §11. In this text promulgated under the direction of Cardinal Ratzinger, the existence of original sin is numbered among "those doctrines of divine and catholic faith which the

day."[4] This internal disharmony that renders us unable to avoid sin entirely is what led Chesterton to call original sin "the only part of Christian theology which can really be proved."[5] In the words of Blaise Pascal, original sin is of all Christian mysteries "the most incomprehensible of all," and yet without it "we are incomprehensible to ourselves."[6]

To understand how the emeritus pontiff situates his own understanding of original sin in light of the tradition, it is helpful to consider what then-Cardinal Ratzinger said on the subject in a famous interview published under the title *The Ratzinger Report*. This text helps us to see that Ratzinger understands his approach to original sin as at once in continuity with the tradition while at the same time a development of it:

> It's always very dangerous to change religious language. Continuity here is of great importance. I hold that the central concepts of the faith, which derive from the great utterance of Scripture, cannot be altered; as, for example, "Son of God," "Holy Spirit," Mary's "virginity" and "divine motherhood." I grant, however, that expressions such as "original sin," which in their context are also biblical in origin but which already manifest in expression the stage of theological reflection, are modifiable.[7]

As will become even clearer in the pages that follow, the emeritus pontiff thinks that certain aspects of the traditional account of original sin are now implausible and thus require certain modifications. At the same time, he is adamant that the doctrine's essential message is of the utmost importance and as necessary as ever; for, "The whole structure of the faith is threatened" by failing to grasp the truth that we are all in a state of alienation that cannot be overcome by our own efforts alone.[8] Commenting that he wished one day to commit himself to the task of rediscovering and writing on the "authentic reality" of original sin, Ratzinger poignantly added, "The inability to understand original sin and to make it understandable is really one of the most difficult problems of present-day theology and pastoral ministry."[9] This chapter and the one that follows seek to move the needle at least a little

---

Church proposes as divinely and formally revealed and, as such, as irreformable." Notably, the *existence* of original sin is here deemed nonnegotiable, yet a requisite *interpretation* of it is not provided. The relation between the Fall and death likewise goes unmentioned here, even though the immortality of the soul is given the same doctrinal weight as original sin's existence.

   5. G.K. Chesterton, *Orthodoxy* (San Francisco: Ignatius Press, 1995), 18–19.

   6. Blaise Pascal, *Pensées*, trans. Roger Ariew (Indianapolis, IN: Hackett, 2004), 37.

   7. Ratzinger and Vittorio Messori, *The Ratzinger Report* (San Francisco: Ignatius Press, 1987), 79.

   8. Ratzinger and Messori, *The Ratzinger Report*, 79. For statement to this effect coming from the field of sociology, see René Girard, *I See Satan Fall Like Lightning*, 189 (Maryknoll, NY: Orbis Books, 2001), 189: "To break the power of [violent] mimetic unanimity, we must postulate a power superior to violent contagion. If we have learned one thing in this study, it is that none exists on earth."

   9. Ratzinger and Messori, *The Ratzinger Report*, 79. Ratzinger was never able to do this as he was elected supreme pontiff instead, fortunately or unfortunately! For an excellent article that seeks to fill in some of the details on what Ratzinger's text on original sin might have looked like, see Santiago Sanz, "Joseph Ratzinger e il peccato originale: riflessioni a proposito di un libro mancato," 439–57.

in terms of advancing this understanding by way of piecing together and applying what Ratzinger says on the topic throughout his corpus.

## WHAT THE DOCTRINE OF ORIGINAL SIN DOES NOT CONCERN

As we have seen throughout this book, an important first step to getting our biblical interpretation right is be get clear on what a given passage does *not* intend to teach. In the case of Genesis 1, the concern underpinning its depiction of creation over seven days was not scientific but rather covenantal and liturgical. Likewise, Adam's creation from the dust of the earth and his infusion with the divine breath in Genesis 2 did not speak to the biological processes that led to the dawn of our species but instead revealed such truths as the ineluctable finitude of our condition in this life and at the same time our election as children of God.

The same holds true when it comes to the Fall narrative in Genesis 3. Professor Ratzinger stated the matter plainly:

> The purpose (*Sinn*) of the doctrine of the original state is not to recount a piece of empirical history (*ein Stück empirischer Geschichte*) and thus to expand our knowledge of history into the prehistoric, but to express the difference between the God-willed meaning of the creature man and the historically existing being man.[10]

With this as his starting point, Ratzinger argues that the Church's doctrine of original sin remains essentially the same regardless of discoveries in evolutionary science. For instance, having become aware that our first parents emerged within a hominin population of at least several thousand individuals does not change the fundamental truth that every man has failed to live according to God's plan for him. This leads Ratzinger to say, "This is basically the same answer to the question of monogenism. . . . That mankind's first decision was characterized by a 'no' is essential (*wesentlich*). Whether this beginning was determined by one or more is not so important (*ist nicht so wichtig*)."[11]

In sum, the emeritus pontiff affirms that a first sin was indeed committed at the dawn of our species, and it continues to affect us all still today. Genesis 3 symbolically describes the essential meaning of this primeval event, but it does not authoritatively address questions of when and how this happened or how many people were involved. Echoing this view, Santiago Sanz summarizes, "To speak of the sin of Adam and Eve does not *necessarily* involve the affirmation of a single couple at the origin of mankind, nor that all of mankind has descended biologically from them."[12] As

---

10. Ratzinger, *Schöpfungslehre* (1964), 253; Sanz, "Joseph Ratzinger y la doctrina de la creación. Los apuntes de Münster de 1964 (y III)," 493n126.

11. Ratzinger, *Schöpfungslehre* (1964), 252; Sanz, "Joseph Ratzinger y la doctrina de la creación. Los apuntes de Münster de 1964 (y III)," 484n90.

12. Sanz, "Joseph Ratzinger e il peccato originale," 451–52. For a recent Thomist treatment of the challenge that man's gradual evolution poses to the tradition that a single act of man's will distorted

we saw in the last chapter, a very specific form of biological monogenism is indeed the likely way our race originated, but it is not wise to hang our hats on an uncertain scientific or historical proposition of this sort that could eventually be falsified. This is all the more the case given that the questions of *how* man first sinned and *how many of us* first sinned are incidental to the doctrine of original sin's essential claims. Simply put, Ratzinger does not believe that the gospel is at stake when it comes to empirical questions surrounding human origins, for evolutionary science has nothing to say either in favor of *or* against the doctrine of the Fall.[13]

While we are in the business of identifying mistaken notions surrounding original sin, it is also noteworthy that Ratzinger singles out a pair of opposite interpretations of the doctrine that should be avoided. On the one hand, he echoes the tradition at large in affirming that none of us by nature has the ability to avoid our sinful condition entirely, and thus, no one begins life in a neutral state or a "zero point of nothing." Reaffirming Augustine's teaching contrary to what Pelagius held and echoing the Council of Trent, Ratzinger teaches that Adam's sin extends "far beyond the mere example."[14] Adopting biblical imagery, I like to make this point about the ineluctability of bearing the burden of original sin by comparing its effects to the loss of a family fortune: As believers, our treasure or "pearl of great price" (Mt 13:46) is none other than Christ himself and our covenantal relationship with him. Even though we ourselves are not at fault for the loss of this great good, the fact is that each of us inherits a situation in which we are deprived of it (as Ratzinger says, none of us begins life in a neutral state) and therefore stand in need of a restoration that we cannot achieve by our own power.[15]

---

subsequent human nature, see Daniel Houck, *Aquinas, Original Sin, and the Challenge of Evolution* (Cambridge: Cambridge University Press, 2020), 200–20.

13. This point has also been articulated well in Lewis, *The Problem of Pain*, 44.

14. Ratzinger, *Schöpfungslehre* (1964), 246; Sanz, "Joseph Ratzinger y la doctrina de la creación. Los apuntes de Münster de 1964 (y III)," 486n102. Reaffirming Augustine's teaching, Trent anathematized a number of positions, including the proposition that Adam's prevarication injured himself alone and not his posterity, that original sin is transmitted via imitation rather than propagation, and that it can be remedied by man's natural powers apart from than the grace of Jesus Christ. Council of Trent, "Decree on Original Sin" (1546), §§2–3. On original sin's transmission not being reducible to imitation, see also Aquinas, *Summa Contra Gentiles*, IV, 50.

15. For an illustration of why it be said that all humans in some sense bear Adam's guilt, see Aquinas, *Commentary on the Letter of St. Paul to the Romans*, trans. F. R. Larcher (Lander, WY: Aquinas Institute for the Study of Sacred Doctrine, 2018). Lecture 3, no. 410. Like Augustine before him, Aquinas approached Adam and his sin in corporate terms. For a helpful overview of Augustine's reading of Romans 5:12 and the notion that all of mankind exists corporately in Adam, see Lombardo, "Evil, Suffering, and the Original Sin," 141–42. Lombardo adds that medievals like Anselm and Aquinas harnessed the tools of Aristotelian philosophy to define original sin as "*formally* the privation of original justice and *materially* the internal disorder resulting from this privation." Lombardo, "Evil, Suffering, and the Original Sin," 143; *CCC*, §406; Aquinas, *ST*, I-II, q. 82, a. 3.

Along these lines, the Catechism notes that original sin is called "sin" only in an analogical sense, as it is "contracted" and not "committed"—a state and not an act. *CCC*, §404. The first man committed a *personal* sin for which he was culpable, yet the Catechism affirms that this sin "does not have the character of a personal fault in any of his descendants." *CCC*, §405. Nevertheless, it did affect human nature

Along these same lines, Ratzinger warns against the commonplace mistake of ontologizing original sin:

> A second extreme is also to be avoided: it would also be wrong to reduce original sin to a mysterious ontological defect [*ontologischen defekt*] that mysteriously passes from generation to generation based on an isolated single act of an individual at the beginning of history.[16]

> The transmission of original sin does not occur through an incomprehensible infection (*unbegreifliche Infektion*) of the soul, but takes place in the overall transmission of a human existence shaped by self-rule.[17]

As we will see below, Ratzinger approaches original sin in the same holistic way he conceives of Adam. In his understanding, original sin should not be construed as a one-time event that caused an infection in the human race but rather as a whole and tragic way of life, a web of broken relationships which goes back to our species' first parents and involves all dimensions of human existence. In agreement with Ratzinger, James Smith helpfully adds that, even if we knew the empirical history surrounding the dawn of mankind's moral awareness, it would still be tall order to pinpoint one discrete moment at which "the transgression occurs" and man first consciously rejected God. For, while affirming that the Fall was a historical event, Smith points out that it may also have been an "event-in-process."[18]

---

as such insofar as afterward the human nature transmitted to all of the first man's descendants is "deprived of original holiness and justice" and is "wounded in the natural powers proper to it, subject to ignorance, suffering and the dominion of death, and inclined to sin—an inclination to evil that is called concupiscence." *CCC*, §§404, 405. For more on concupiscence, see the Council of Trent's "Decree on Original Sin" (1546), §5.

16. Ratzinger, *Schöpfungslehre* (1964), 246; Sanz, "Joseph Ratzinger y la doctrina de la creación. Los apuntes de Münster de 1964 (y III)," 487n103.

17. Ratzinger, *Schöpfungslehre* (1964), 250; Sanz, "Joseph Ratzinger y la doctrina de la creación. Los apuntes de Münster de 1964 (y III)," 491n119.

18. James Smith, "What Stands on the Fall? A Philosophical Exploration," in *Evolution and the Fall*, 48–66 at 61. Orthodox Metropolitan Kallistos Ware takes a similar approach to that of Smith, suggesting that the fall of humanity should be thought of as a *process of degeneration* and as having meaning "in pointing to the fact that each of us is born into a world where the accumulated effects of despair and sin have destroyed what is good and have restricted what is possible." Kallistos Ware, *The Orthodox Way* (Crestwood, NY: St. Vladimir's Press, 1995), 143. See also Ware, *The Orthodox Way,* 62 and Ware, "The Understanding of Salvation in the Orthodox Tradition," in Rienk Lannoy, ed., *For Us and Our Salvation*, IIMO Research Publication 40 (Utrecht-Leiden: Interuniversitair Instituut voor Missiologie en Oecimenica, 1994), 107–31 at 113; Celia Deane-Drummond, "In Adam All Die? Questions at the Boundary of Niche Construction, Community Evolution, and Original Sin," in *Evolution and the Fall*, 23–47 at 44. While not denying that human sin traces back to a single origin, Pope John Paul II likewise emphasized its cumulative nature: "[S]uffering cannot be divorced from the sin of the beginnings, from what Saint John calls 'the sin of the world,' *from the sinful background* of the personal actions and social processes in human history." John Paul II, *Salvifici Doloris*, §15 (emphasis in original).

## WHAT THE DOCTRINE OF ORIGINAL SIN DOES CONCERN

If the above is what the doctrine of original sin is *not* about, then what does Benedict think it *is* about? What is the doctrine's purpose, and what can we know concerning the circumstances surrounding man's first fall from grace? To answer such questions, we first must have a proper grasp of the original context and genre of the Fall narrative.

### The Mystery of Adam-Israel

In a general audience on the topic, Benedict begins his response to the above question with the admission that original sin "remains obscure" and is "a mystery of darkness."[19] While not denying that a first sin occurred in human history, he is not concerned about what precisely happened in that fateful moment (if it indeed was a single moment, which he does not seem too interested in maintaining). To put it another way, we do not speak of the Fall accurately if we depict it "as one fact beside another, because it is a deeper reality."[20] Rather than trying to describe the ins and outs surrounding man's first historical sin, the emeritus pontiff finds that we are better off letting Scripture's inspired creation myth lead the way.

Benedict teaches that the "great images" [*grandi immagini*] from Scripture's creation story allow us to "guess, not explain" the tragic events that transpired at the dawn of mankind.[21] Then-cardinal Ratzinger spoke similarly when he said:

> The biblical narrative of the origins does not relate events in the sense of modern historiography, but rather, it speaks through images. It is a narrative that reveals and hides at the same time. But the underpinning elements are reasonable, and the reality of the dogma must at all events be safeguarded.[22]

> [T]he Genesis story is at any rate an image of the way that this disorder has been present in a mysterious way from the very beginning.[23]

In other words, Benedict interprets the Fall narrative in accord with the same hermeneutical principles outlined in Chapter 4. He sees the story fundamentally as figurative in style, and is thus ever ready to distinguish the essential content of the text from the narrative vehicle or "images" through which it is conveyed. And he is not alone in this approach to Genesis's opening chapters. For his part, C.S. Lewis remarks on the Fall narrative in relation to original sin that we should be careful "not to confuse the doctrine itself with the *imagery* by which it may be conveyed,"

---

19. Benedict XVI, General Audience: "The Apostle's Teaching on the Relation between Adam and Christ" (December 3, 2008).

20. Benedict XVI, General Audience: "The Apostle's Teaching on the Relation between Adam and Christ" (December 3, 2008).

21. Benedict XVI, General Audience: "The Apostle's Teaching on the Relation between Adam and Christ" (December 3, 2008).

22. Ratzinger and Messori, *The Ratzinger Report*, 81.

23. Ratzinger, *God and the World*, 85.

adding that the doctrine of original sin that developed based on Genesis 3 is not dependent on the historical existence of 'a magic apple of knowledge.'"[24] Indeed, he notes that "in the developed doctrine [of original sin] the inherent magic of the apple has quite dropped out of sight, and the story is simply one of disobedience."[25]

As we have already seen in previous chapters, Genesis's symbolic images provide unmatched insight into this aspect of the human condition and God's plan for redeeming it *by way of telling the story of one special nation*: the story of Israel from origin to exile. That is, the narrative vehicle that conveys these truths was initially concerned with the concrete circumstances of God's chosen people as the nation sought to solidify its identity and relationship with God in the midst of exile—to answer the questions "Who are we?," "How did we get ourselves into this mess?," and "What does *God* want us to do about it?" Thus, Ratzinger stresses that "the text of Gn 3 was not [written] in a vacuum and is not some kind of neutral historiography of the past but concrete, prophetic, demanding words addressed to the Israel of its day."[26] As Scot McKnight writes, "[The Fall narrative] is far more about Adam and Eve as Israel than about the historical, biological, and genetic Adam and Eve. . . . Adam and Eve represent Israel in its mission and its failure to fulfill that mission by not living faithfully under God's covenant."[27] This is an idea we have already articulated through the lens of authors including Peter Enns as he explained the ways in which the Adam story mirrors Israel's story from exodus to exile. The early chapters of Genesis are first and foremost about Israel's fall, its aftermath, and what God is doing to save them from their own devices: "The recurring focus in the Old Testament is on Israel's choice whether or not to obey God's law—the very choice given to both Adam and Cain."[28]

For his part, in his third to last papal audience Benedict noted that Scripture's second creation narrative contains two "important images" [*immagini significative*]

---

24. Lewis, *The Problem of Pain*, 79.

25. Lewis, *The Problem of Pain*, 42–43. In his own insightful creation account, Lewis—echoing a line of thought within the Eastern patristic tradition—plays on the idea that Adam and Eve eventually would have been granted access to the Tree of Life had they obeyed God's command. In Lewis's story as in the Bible, physical death is not the immediate consequence for those who steal from the tree, but misery or spiritual death certainly is. C.S. Lewis, *The Magician's Nephew*, in *The Chronicles of Narnia* (New York: HarperCollins, 2001), 7–106 at 100. For the patristic basis of the view that the tree of knowledge was originally intended to be only temporarily off-limits, see J. Richard Middleton, "Reading Genesis 3 Attentive to Human Evolution," in Cavanaugh and Smith, *Evolution and the Fall*," 82 and Nicholas Lombardo, OP, "Evil, Suffering, and Original Sin," *The Oxford Handbook of Catholic Theology*, eds. Lewis Ayres and Medi Ann Volpe (Oxford: Oxford University Press, 2019), 139–50 at 141. This view, prevalent still today in Orthodoxy, is articulated well by Metropolitan Kallistos Ware in, *The Orthodox Church* (New York: Penguin, 1993), 222–24. Enns summarizes this Eastern approach as follows: "The command is not a random test of faith to prove obedience but rather about how knowledge is to be pursued. . . . The problem is the illicit way in which Eve tries to attain wisdom—quickly, prematurely, impatiently." Enns, *The Evolution of Adam*, 89.

26. Ratzinger, *Schöpfungslehre* (1964), 232; Sanz, "Joseph Ratzinger y la doctrina de la creación. Los apuntes de Münster de 1964 (y III)," 458n9.

27. McKnight and Venema, *Adam and the Genome*, 144.

28. Enns, *The Evolution of Adam*, 87.

that connect with the life of Israel: the garden with its two trees, and the deceptive serpent (Gn 2:15–17; 3:1–5). We have already observed that he sees the garden of Eden as a figure for God's cosmic sanctuary and an archetypal "image [*Bild*] for the undamaged creation and for secure existence within it."[29] In this text, the then-pontiff adds a key contextual note that, in its original setting, the serpent was not likely thought of as Satan himself—for there is no evidence that Jewish people made this connection between the two until well after Genesis was written.[30] Accordingly, Ratzinger says that, for its original author, "[T]he serpent is a symbol [*figura*] that comes from the Oriental fertility cults that fascinated Israel and were a constant temptation to abandon the mysterious covenant with God."[31] In an earlier homily, Ratzinger spoke similarly of the serpent's sexual overtones in its original cultic context:

> In that religious setting the serpent was a symbol of that wisdom which rules the world and of the fertility through which human beings plunge into the divine current of life and for a few moments experience themselves fused with its divine power. Thus the serpent also serves as a symbol of the attraction that these religions exerted over Israel in contrast to the mystery of the God of the covenant.[32]

---

29. Ratzinger, *God and the World*, 77; Ratzinger, *In the Beginning*, 64.

30. For further discussion of the origin of Satan in Jewish literature, see Ramage, *Dark Passages of the Bible*, 37–39. For Christians, the most famous and forceful connection of Satan with the serpent is in Revelation 12:9 (cf. Rv 20:2), where John speaks of "that ancient serpent, who is called the Devil and Satan." For a survey of Jewish thought with respect to the serpent and its eventual equation with the devil, see Werner Foerster, "Ὄφις," in vol. 5 of *Theological Dictionary of the New Testament*, ed. Gerhard Kittel, Geoffrey W. Bromiley, and Gerhard Friedrich (Grand Rapids, MI: Eerdmans, 1964–), 576–79.

31. Benedict XVI, General Audience: "I believe in God, maker of heaven and earth, creator of man" (February 6, 2013). In a valuable treatment of the serpent's symbolism in Genesis, William Lane Craig notes, "[The snake] makes for a great character in the story, conniving, sinister, opposed to God, perhaps a symbol of evil, but not plausibly a literal reptile such as one might encounter in one's own garden, for the author knew that snakes neither talk nor are intelligent agents." With regard to a different image, he adds, "It is not as though the author thought, what realism requires, that the cherubim remained at the entrance of the Garden for years on end until it was either overgrown with weeds or swept away by the Flood." In sum, he writes: "That Genesis 1–3 is mythic and anthropomorphic is hinted at in the first two chapters of the book," but it becomes "inescapable in chapter 3, where God is described as walking in the garden in the cool of the day and calling audibly to Adam in his hideout." Craig, "The Historical Adam," *First Things* (October 2021).

An interesting point of contact between medieval and modern interpretations can be glimpsed in that Aquinas, following Augustine, holds that "the concupiscence of sin in the sensuality [is] signified by the serpent" and that "the lower reason, by pleasure, [is] signified by the woman." Aquinas, *ST*, II-II, q. 165 a. 2. Contrary to Benedict, however, traditionally many traditional Catholic authors tended to assume that the first two parents of mankind were tempted by the devil acting through an actual serpent. See, for instance, Aquinas, *ST* II-II, q. 165 a. 2 ad 4.

32. Ratzinger, *In the Beginning*, 65–66. The notion that the serpent in some way represented sexual temptation is not textually certain, yet it is interesting that this interpretation can be seen in the Christian artistic tradition. For instance, the façade of Notre Dame in Paris has the serpent wrapping around a pillar with the head of a seductive woman. Overtones of Adam's paradigmatic temptation are echoed or elsewhere in Scripture. For instance, only several verses after God had foretold that Abram would

Genesis itself does not explicitly identify a particular god as its target here—a number would fit the bill, including the *Enuma Elish*'s Marduk and Tiamat—but that is actually part of the point. The final form of this text is probably not concerned especially with what particular deities are to blame but rather to craft an etiology that establishes why Israel has landed in exile: the allure of false religion (the serpent's instigation) that led her to break the covenant by disobeying God's laws (eating the fruit).[33]

## Not a Giant Leap to All Mankind

As we have seen, the Bible's creation narrative as a whole is not just about Israel but also about the fundamental events that happened in the life of the first man and of every man. Accordingly, it will probably come as no surprise that Ratzinger understands the Fall in the same way. The story has perennial value, he writes, precisely because it "extend[s] not only to Israel, but beyond the framework of this people and beyond its time to men in general. It speaks of our rebellion and fall, not in the past, but in the present. It is addressed to men of all times."[34] Flowing from his view of Adam as an archetypal image of the first man and in turn every man, Ratzinger emphasizes that Scripture's portrayal of man's first temptation is a depiction of "the nature [*Wesen*] of temptation and sin in every age [*zu allen Zeiten*]."[35] As Professor Ratzinger taught in one of his lectures, the fall of man concerns not just "some distant past, but it happens now in the temptations of the

---

have his own son as heir (Gn15:6) and swore a covenant to him this effect (Gn 15:18–21), we find his barren wife urging the patriarch to "go into" her Egyptian servant Hagar to obtain children. Abram immediately "hearkened to the voice of Sarai" (Gn 16:2) as Sarai "took Hagar the Egyptian, her maid, and gave her to Abram her husband as a wife" (Gn 16:3). It is telling that the Hebrew expression "hearken to the voice of" occurs elsewhere only in Genesis 3:17 wherein Adam "listened to the voice of" his wife, eating of the tree that had been forbidden him. What is more, the "taking" and "giving" language applied to Hagar in Genesis 16:3 recalls the Fall sequence in Genesis 3:6, in which the woman "*took* of its fruit and ate; and she also *gave* some to her husband, and he ate." Hagar, seen from the perspective that the text itself invites us to consider, is Abraham's forbidden fruit. For further discussion of this connection, see Gordon Wenham, *Genesis 16–50*, vol. 2, *Word Biblical Commentary* (Dallas: Word, Incorporated, 1994), 7–8.

33. As I mentioned above, it is not necessary to identify the serpent with any one particular god of the ancient Near Eastern world. In Mesopotamia, the magical plant that would have rejuvenated Gilgamesh was stolen by a serpent. In Egypt, serpents were associated with death and wisdom, and a number of gods were represented in serpent form. The mythological figure behind the serpent may also have been the Canaanite deity Baal. For further discussion of these possibilities, see Keener and Walton, *NIV Cultural Backgrounds Study Bible*, 12 and Arnold, *Genesis*, 62–63.

34. Ratzinger, *Schöpfungslehre* (1964), 232; Sanz, "Joseph Ratzinger y la doctrina de la creación. Los apuntes de Münster de 1964 (y III)," 457n9. For another archetypal reading of Adam's sin which, like Ratzinger's, emphasizes that it began with concrete human decisions in remote human history that we inevitably prolong today, see René Girard, *A Theater of Envy: William Shakespeare* (New York: Oxford University Press, 1991), 324–25.

35. Ratzinger, *In the Beginning*, 66 [*Im Anfang schuf Gott*, 52]. See also Theological Commission's *Communion and Stewardship*, especially, §§62–70.

present."[36] The fact that every person is a sinner who stands in need of God's mercy is the heart of what original sin means to convey: "This is ultimately the content (*Inhalt*) of the doctrine of original sin: there is no one—not one—who has opposed the sinful form of history and that has used his freedom exclusively for good."[37]

Cast in biblical categories, this means that Jew and Gentile alike are in exile from God. Scot McKnight captures this perfectly when he writes, "Adam and Eve are not just two individuals but representatives of both Israel and Everyone. Hence, Adam and Eve's sin is Israel's prototypical sin, their 'exile' is Israel's exile, and they therefore represent the sin and discipline of Everyone."[38] Gary Anderson makes a complementary point using historical-critical insights into the authorship of the Pentateuch. While he notes that there is debate in the field as to which authors penned specific portions of the Pentateuch, Anderson remarks, "What is agreed upon, however, is that in the final editing of the Torah, there was a conscious decision made to place the P story first. It was intended to introduce the story that followed."[39] The final editor of the Old Testament clearly intended these two stories to be read together, but the question is: how? Anderson replies:

By placing the story of Adam and Eve after the creation account of P [Gn 1], the editor of the Torah has said something very profound about the propensity of human nature toward disobedience. The story of Adam and Eve according to our J source [Gn 2–3] stands in a very awkward relationship to the Priestly narrative that precedes it. And this awkwardness is not to be understood simply as the result of poor editorial work on the part of the editor who stitched together these two sources. On the contrary, there is real and evident literary and theological artistry here.[40]

The following words of Anderson may be taken as a summary statement of the connection between the creation narratives of Genesis 1 and Genesis 2–3, between the story of man as such and the story of Israel in particular:

---

36. Ratzinger, *Schöpfungslehre* (1964), 230; Sanz, "Joseph Ratzinger y la doctrina de la creación. Los apuntes de Münster de 1964 (y III)," 456–57n7.

37. Ratzinger, *Schöpfungslehre* (1964), 252; Sanz, "Joseph Ratzinger y la doctrina de la creación. Los apuntes de Münster de 1964 (y III)," 483n88. Similarly, Ratzinger says, "[E]very person, when he faces God, must confess himself a sinner. In this respect, the O.T. to a great extent had a clear awareness of what is really at issue in the doctrine of original sin." Ratzinger, *Schöpfungslehre* (1964), 235. It is also worth noting here that, while Ratzinger says that "no one" is exempt from original sin, his corpus as a whole makes it clear that the emeritus pontiff affirms the Mother of God as a singular exception to this rule. For Ratzinger's thought on the Immaculate Conception, see *Daughter Zion*, 61–71.

38. McKnight and Venema, *Adam and the Genome*, 142–43. McKnight later adds, "Adam is the *paradigm* or *prototype* or *archetype* of the choice between the path of obedience and that of disobedience, the path of Torah observance and that of breaking the commandments, the path of Wisdom and Mind and Logos and the path of sensory perceptions and pleasure and bodily desires. The Adam of the Jewish tradition is depicted very much as the *moral* Adam." McKnight and Venema, *Adam and the Genome*, 170.

39. Anderson, *Christian Doctrine and the Old Testament*, 61.

40. Anderson, *Christian Doctrine and the Old Testament*, 71.

The Hebrew Scripture has as its primary focus the nation of Israel. The proclivity toward sin is most profoundly illustrated in the rebellion of this elected
nation at Mt. Sinai. But if the elected nation is so prone to sin and those sins
continue to rebound across generations, then certainly it is not a great leap to
extend this insight to humanity at large. If this is what happens to the nation
so highly favored, what could one expect of those shown less consideration?
What is revealed in microcosm through the nation Israel can be extended, in
macrocosm, to all peoples.[41]

## WHO CAME FIRST—ADAM OR ISRAEL?

Before moving on to the next feature of Benedict's theology of original sin, I think
it is important to pause for a moment and consider a methodological issue that often
confuses Christians seeking to grasp the relationship between Adam and Israel.
Having discussed this subject with many people and taught it to students for years,
I have found that it can be difficult to wrap one's head around the dynamic we discussed back in Chapter 6: that in the Pentateuch's final form Adam the literary figure
represents the historical nation of Israel *after* she had already undergone her exile
and "death." We believers are so accustomed to assuming Genesis's opening narrative
is a historical account of human origins at the dawn of our species that learning to
see Adam as a literary cipher for Israel is often achieved only with great difficulty.

Adding to this challenge, it will never be possible to prove infallibly that the
directionality of the Adam/Israel connection I have just laid out. That is to say,
although I hope that the connections drawn make it clear that Adam is a cipher for
Israel in the final form of the Pentateuch that we have before us, it is always possible
to reply that these parallels are to be expected—that the historical experience of
the first members of *Homo sapiens* hundreds of thousands of years ago is depicted
literally in Genesis 1–3, and that God's plan for Israel providentially had them reca-
pitulating these events in distant time. In this way, one might continue to maintain
a historical-scientific reading of the Adam narrative *and* that of Israel's story in the
rest of the Old Testament. The problem, though, is that most of us are not compelled
by an answer that is merely technically possible. As we have seen in the case of
other topics already in this book, a traditional explanation of the Adam-Israel parallel will always remain *conceivable*. After all, the Genesis narrative would look the
same regardless of whether the Adam story happened historically and prophetically
foreshadowed the life of Israel or whether the Adam story was backwritten or at
least significantly redacted after the events in Israel had taken place. Yet, if faith
and reason really do stand in harmony, then we ought to be asking a different question: seeing as the Church does not wish us to read God's word in isolation from
knowledge that comes from the book of nature, what explanation here is the most
*plausible*, the most *believable*?

---

41. Anderson, "Biblical Origins and the Problem of the Fall," 30. Anderson notes that the basic
thrust of this connection can be found in Karl Barth's treatment of original sin in his *Church Dogmatics*,
trans. G. W. Bromiley (Edinburgh: T& T Clark, 1956) 4 / 1, 427.

We arrive here at what I would identify as another disputed question which concerns the nature of biblical inspiration and its implications for understanding the relationship of Adam and Israel. As we have noted earlier in this book, one of Ratzinger's keys to proper biblical interpretation is to become aware of the fact that our prior philosophical presuppositions govern our exegesis and that the real debate in exegesis is about which set of commitments is the one that is true to reality. This principle applies especially here when it comes to how we construe the relationship between Adam and Israel. In favor of the Adam narrative being a retrospective reflection on Israel's later history, Anderson points out that this makes sense since the story of Adam and Eve, in its concision, remarkably provides "an apt and fitting summary of the tragic epic of Israel's national story in the Torah."[42]

While it is technically possible that the author of Genesis had mystical knowledge of events that transpired 200,000 years before him, this literary perspective combined with what we know today about man's evolutionary origins make a serious case that Israel's creation narrative was originally intended to be more about events in the nation's own day than about things that occurred at the dawn of the species. All the more so is this the case when it comes to the question of whether the sacred author had access to scientific and historical information about the origin of the universe nearly 14 billion years before he lived, or on the other hand, whether his story was meant to speak primarily about the world of his time. Again, this is not to say that God, the divine author, is himself unable to manage what humans fail to achieve. Rather, it takes us back to the question that we encountered in Chapter 3: How do we think God works in the world? Did he cause the human authors of Scripture to act as true human authors along the lines we would expect from other humans, with all the limitations inherent to their created intellects? Or did his inspiration supervene upon their minds in such a way that they were able to acquire a detailed account of the remote past or future?

Another way to think about this question is to consider whether it is more appropriate to think of the author of the Adam story as a journalist recording primal events on the one hand or on the other hand as a literary master with all the artistry that it entails. In other words, is the author of Scripture's creation narrative more like a reporter on the evening news or the Shakespeare of Israel's past? Most modern biblical scholars are in agreement on how this question is most compellingly answered. When it comes the matter of whether Adam's story is primarily that of the first man or rather of Israel, Anderson summarizes the dominant view of modern biblical scholars on in stating that "the force of the parallel moves from Sinai to Eden and not the reverse."[43] Like the majority of contemporary interpreters, we have seen that Benedict too finds that the force of the Adam/Israel parallel moves in a chronologically backward direction.

But if the force of the parallel so clearly runs in this direction, then why does Paul not just come out and tell us that Adam is a cipher for Israel? Why not appeal

---

42. Anderson, "Biblical Origins and the Problem of the Fall," 29.
43. Anderson, "Biblical Origins and the Problem of the Fall," 29.

directly to Israel's story to make his case? An important part of the answer is that the Apostle saw the figure of Adam's fall as especially conducive to his purposes in Romans. Anderson explains:

> In order to understand the reason why Paul ignores this tradition, we need to recall Paul's theological task in the Epistle of Romans. He wants to demonstrate that the *orge*, or "wrath" of God (Rm 1:18), extends over all peoples, Jew and Gentile alike. All persons are guilty to such a degree that they merit the punishing hand of God. If Paul were to look solely at the central Old Testament narratives about Israel's proclivity for sin and rebellion, he would not be able to say anything about the state of the gentiles.[44]

Peter Enns captures this point well when he says that Paul got the essential point of the Fall right even if he had mistaken cultural assumptions about the number of our race's first parents: "Paul's Adam as first human, who introduced universal sin and death, supports his contention that Jew and Gentile are on the same footing and in need of the same Savior."[45] Indeed, Romans is overwhelmingly concerned with the twofold truth that all humans are sinners who are unable to save ourselves on the one hand, and that God wishes to redeem us all—Gentiles included (for example, see Rm 1:13; 2:9–15; 3:20-29; 5:12–14; 9:30; 15:16). As deployed by Paul, Adam is not just archetypal Israel: he is the paradigmatic man who represents both Jews *and* Gentiles. As Adam in the Old Testament provided the perfect avenue for diagnosing the cause of Israel's exile, it was not a great leap for Genesis—and Paul in its wake—to extend the story of Israel to humanity at large.

## A PHENOMENOLOGY OF SIN

The next important facet of Ratzinger's approach to Genesis's temptation narrative flows from his understanding that we are all Adam, that all of us are in exile from God. This consists in his development of a *phenomenology of sin* in which the very specific temptation endured by Israel in their own day illumines the essence (*Wesen*) of temptation and sin experienced by all humans.[46] Thus, Ratzinger writes that the "first and fundamental thing" that the Adam story reveals about the "essence" (*Wesen*) of human sin is that it begins not with a direct affront to God but rather with distrust in God's fatherly love for us. That is, it is a failure to accept our covenantal obligations toward the Lord, viewing these as shackles that hold us back from happiness (from being like gods) rather than what they truly are: the conditions for flourishing as God's children. To state the same point from another angle, "the deepest substance (*der tiefste Gehalt*) of sin is that man does not want to be a creature," i.e., he does not want to be dependent on God.[47] Thus, Ratzinger

---

44. Anderson, "Biblical Origins and the Problem of the Fall," 29–30.
45. Enns, *The Evolution of Adam*, 134.
46. Ratzinger, *Gottes Projekt*, 86.
47. Ratzinger, *Gottes Projekt*, 84; Ratzinger, *In the Beginning*, 62. On the distrust of God's covenantal love that underpins all sin, the Catechism states that Adam let his trust in his Creator die,

interprets God's command regarding the fruit (cf. Gn 3:3) as an injunction not to deny one's creaturely finitude, adding that sin in its very essence [*Wesen*] is a renunciation of this truth.[48] Benedict resumed this line of thought near the very end of his pontificate:

> In this light Sacred Scripture presents the temptation of Adam and Eve as the core [*nocciolo*] of temptation and sin. . . . [T]he serpent awoke in them the suspicion that the covenant with God was nothing but a chain that bound them, that deprived them of freedom and of the most beautiful and precious things of life.[49]

Benedict continues by describing the experience of temptation in these same terms. Adam and Eve's temptation, he explains, consisted in the allure of transcending the categories of good and evil, perceiving their dependence on God as a limitation and burden from which to free themselves. As the archetypal man and woman, our first parents reveal that this dynamic is "always the essence [*nocciolo*] of temptation."[50]

Similar insights into Adam's false notion of freedom can be gleaned from other figurative images in Genesis's creation account. For instance, Ratzinger sees the garments that Adam and Eve receive after sinning as a sort of etiology or "symbolic representation [*symbolische Darstellung*] of the attempt to be ourselves, whereby we attempt an external restoration of the personal dignity that has suffered intimate damage."[51] Likewise, the Tower of Babel story (Gn 11:1–9) at the end of the primeval history narrative is particularly instructive. Ratzinger notes that this narrative is "still not altogether free of certain pagan elements" such as a jealous divine council that fears man's challenge to their power (Gn 11:6–7). Even so, the story's "picture language" [*Bildsprache*] accurately depicts the folly of man's efforts to achieve greatness by means of his own technical ability without God's assistance.[52] In his encyclical *Spe Salvi*, Benedict went so far as to teach that this

---

abusing his freedom by disobeying God's command and preferring himself to God. From that point forward, "All subsequent sin would be disobedience toward God and lack of trust in his goodness." *CCC*, §404. The Catechism is also illuminating in this connection for its figurative reading of the tree of knowledge. This primeval tree "symbolically evokes the insurmountable limits that man, being a creature, must freely recognize and respect with trust," in other words, that "man is dependent on his Creator, and subject to the laws of creation and to the moral norms that govern the use of freedom." *CCC*, §396.

48. Ratzinger, *In the Beginning*, 71 [*Im Anfang schuf Gott*, 55].

49. Benedict XVI, General Audience (February 6, 2013). For a deeper exploration of Benedict's conviction that fulfilling our covenantal obligations to God through the Church's teachings is constitutive of true freedom and happiness, see Ramage, "Benedict XVI on Freedom in Obedience to the Truth: A Key for the New Evangelization," *Homiletic and Pastoral Review* (May 12, 2014).

50. Benedict XVI, General Audience (February 6, 2013).

51. Ratzinger, *God and the World*, 88 [*Gott und die Welt*, 76].

52. Ratzinger, *God and the World*, 141–42 [*Gott und die Welt*, 120–21]. For a critique of Francis Bacon and our current culture's attempt to achieve this same ungodly feat, see Benedict XVI, *Spe Salvi*, §16.

account's symbolic portrayal of man's willful refusal of union with God that led to the disunity of the human race is "an expression of what sin fundamentally [*in radice*] is."[53]

## INTERPRETING THE NATURE AND TRANSMISSION OF ORIGINAL SIN IN A RELATIONAL KEY
### Corporate Personality, Corporate Culpability

Benedict's description of disunity and relational rupture as the essence of sin offers a fitting segue into the next major facet of his approach to the doctrine of the Fall. As we discussed above, the emeritus pontiff rejects a Pelagian interpretation of original sin wherein people have the option not to sin but unfortunately follow Adam's bad example and do it anyway. Against this notion, Benedict echoes the tradition in affirming that—absent a singular grace—bearing the stain of original sin is an unavoidable part of our condition in this life. Yet, at the same time, he generally seeks to avoid certain traditional verbiage that might lead one to construe original sin as a sort of infection that we inherit from our parents.[54]

The way that Benedict will attempt to achieve this balance is by applying his characteristic relational hermeneutic to the topic of original sin, an endeavor that Santiago Sanz has described as the emeritus pontiff's most original contribution to the Church's understanding of the topic.[55] Whether for good or for ill, all of our actions have communal implications; for, as Ratzinger has communicated on number of occasions, "no human being is closed in upon himself."[56] In his encyclical on hope, Benedict thus writes:

---

53. Benedict XVI, *Spe Salvi*, §14.

54. By rightly rejecting Pelagianism's reduction of original sin to a matter of mere imitation, this is not to say that imitation or mimesis has no role to play in its transmission. For an "anthropology of mimetic desire" that sees sin as stemming largely from mimetic rivalry and of crowd phenomena, see Girard, *I See Satan Fall Like Lightning*, 38. Girard's approach, which has been described as a modern scientific version of Augustine's approach to original sin, emphasizes that humans are born with an innate propensity to imitate each other which, while morally neutral in itself, inevitably has led to violence after its first abuse at the dawn of our species. On Girard's view, sin stems from desiring what another has without subordinating our mimetic desires to reason and thereby to God. "Choice always involves choosing a model, and true freedom lies in the basic choice between a human or a divine model," he writes. If we choose humans rather than God as our ultimate model, Girard observes, these humans eventually become rivals with whom a violent conflict is almost inevitable. Girard, *Deceit, Desire and the Novel* (Baltimore: The Johns Hopkins University Press, 1988), 58. For an insightful piece that draws some connections between Girard and Augustine, see Jessica Hooten Wilson, "The Unoriginal Augustine," *Church Life Journal* (December 04, 2019). On Girard's approach being a "scientific version of the doctrine of original sin," see Petra Steinmair-Pösel, "Original Sin, Grace, and Positive Mimesis," *Journal of Violence, Mimesis, and Culture* 14 (2007): 1–12 at 6.

55. Sanz, "Original Sin" (entry in a forthcoming *Joseph Ratzinger Dictionary*).

56. This particular rendering of the point comes from Ratzinger, *In the Beginning*, 72. See also Ratzinger, *Gottes Projekt*, 86–87 and Benedict XVI, General Audience: "I believe in God, maker of heaven and earth, creator of man" (February 6, 2013).

[N]o man is an island, complete by himself. Our lives are involved with one another, through innumerable interactions they are linked together. No one lives alone. No one sins alone. No one is saved alone. The lives of others continually spill over into mine: in what I think, say, do and achieve. And conversely, my life spills over into that of others: for better and for worse.[57]

Expounding upon this point in his university lectures, Ratzinger strives to make sense of the traditional notion discussed above according to which all humans in some way bear the "guilt" of Adam's sin. Seeing as we are all Adam, he maintains, it is an unavoidable facet of nature that all of us are impacted by the sin of the first man and the sins of everyone else:

Original sin has a distant beginning in the first human person endowed with self-possession, but it is also in the immediate present as everyone is involved in it in some way. Accordingly, it is Pharisaic to omit attributing Adam's sin to ourselves when we ourselves are its ongoing architects.[58]

Recovering the sense of Adam as a corporate person—that in a real sense the whole human race is one man—helps us to understand how it is not unjust that we all suffer the "punishment" due to our first parents. The truth is that every sin has a cumulative effect and impacts everyone else whether we realize it or not. According to Ratzinger, then, the message of the Fall narrative is "that sin begets sin, and that therefore all the sins of history are interlinked."[59] To reprise the emeritus pontiff's words from above, his affirmation does not require us to conceive of original sin as a "mysterious ontological defect" or an "incomprehensible infection of the soul" that mystically passes through space and time. In Ratzinger's view, rather, original sin is passed on very concretely by means of broken relationships: "The essence of sin can only be understood in an anthropology of relation, not by looking at an

---

57. Benedict XVI, *Spe Salvi*, §48. Orthodox Metropolitan Kallistos Ware writes similarly: "It is here, in the solidarity of the human race, that we find an explanation for the apparent unjustness of the doctrine of original sin. Why, we ask, should the entire human race suffer because of Adam's fall? Why should all be punished because of one man's sin? The answer is that human beings, made in the image of the Trinitarian God, are interdependent and coinherent. No man is an island. We are members one of another (Eph 4:25), and so any action, performed by any member of the human race, inevitably affects all the other members. Even though we are not, in the strict sense, guilty of the sins of others, yet we are somehow always involved." Ware, *The Orthodox Way*, 62.

58. Ratzinger, *Schöpfungslehre* (1964), 250; Sanz, "Joseph Ratzinger y la doctrina de la creación. Los apuntes de Münster de 1964 (y III)," 491n118. To this, he adds, "The Bible does not see man as a detached individual, but in the unity of a story for which he shares responsibility." Ratzinger, *Schöpfungslehre* (1964), 183; Sanz, "Joseph Ratzinger y la doctrina de la creación. Los apuntes de Münster de 1964 (II)," 218n56.

On the truth that the whole human race is one in Adam and thus implicated in his sin, see *CCC*, §404; Aquinas, *On Evil*, trans. Richard Regan (Oxford: Oxford University Press, 2003), q. 4, a. 1, resp. at 197.

59. Ratzinger, *In the Beginning*, 72.

isolated human being."[60] In other words, if original sin's transmission is traditionally understood in terms of propagation by nature, Ratzinger prefers to describe it personalistically in terms of propagation by relationship.[61]

## The Essence of Sin: Relationship Rupture

Just how important Benedict considered the relational dimension of original sin can be grasped by the fact that he dedicated his third-to-last general audience as supreme pontiff to the theme. In this catechetical text, the then-pontiff asks concerning original sin, "What is the meaning of this reality that is not easy to understand?" In response to this query, Benedict begins by declaring plainly, "Being human is a relationship."[62] We have already seen the grounding for this claim in Chapter 7: The capacity for forming relationships is what distinguishes our species from all others, and our individual identities are located fundamentally in our web of relationships—from whom we come and whom we love. Indeed, Ratzinger writes, "Human beings are relational, and they possess their lives—themselves—only by way of relationship."[63]

Man's most fundamental relationship is of course his relationship with God. For this reason, Benedict writes that the essence [*essenza*] of sin is "the distortion or destruction" of this "fundamental relationship" that occurs when we put ourselves in God's place.[64] This relational perspective on original sin dates back to then-Cardinal Ratzinger's 1981 Lenten homily on the subject, where he rehearses the point multiple times:

> [S]in means the damaging or the destruction of relationality. Sin is a rejection of relationality [*Leugnung der Beziehung*] because it wants to make the human being a god. Sin is loss of relationship, disturbance of relationship [*Beziehungsverlust, Beziehungsstörung*], and therefore it is not restricted to the individual. When I destroy a relationship, then this event—sin—touches the other person

---

60. Ratzinger, *Daughter Zion*, 69–70. As I noted in the last chapter, throughout his corpus Ratzinger invokes the notion of relationality to address all manner of delicate theological problems: special creation as the establishing of man's unique relationship with God, grace as the elevation of this relation, sin as its rupture, and redemption as its healing, etc. This approach will presently allow us to understand better the nature and transmission of original sin.

61. On this formulation, see Giuseppe Tanzella-Nitti, "Il coraggio dell'Intellectus fidei: le 'lezioni carinziane' di Joseph Ratzinger su theologia de la creazione," Introduction to *Progetto di Dio. La Creazione: Meditazioni sulla Creazione e la Chiesa* (Venezia: Marcianum Press, 2012), 7–29 and Sanz, "Joseph Ratzinger e il peccato originale," 453.

62. Benedict XVI, General Audience: "I believe in God, maker of heaven and earth, creator of man" (February 6, 2013).

63. Ratzinger, *In the Beginning*, 72.

64. Benedict XVI, General Audience: "I believe in God, maker of heaven and earth, creator of man" (February 6, 2013). The Catechism, whose editing was supervised by Cardinal Ratzinger, also describes sin in relational terms: "To try to understand what sin is, one must first recognize the profound relation of man to God, for only in this relationship is the evil of sin unmasked in its true identity as humanity's rejection of God." *CCC*, §386.

involved in the relationship. Consequently, sin is always an offense that touches others, that alters the world and damages it.[65]

Ratzinger proceeds to emphasize that every one of us is born into a web of relationships that has been damaged from its very start, as a result of which none of us is able to engage in relationships as we ought.[66]

Ratzinger elsewhere expands upon the above dynamic by seeing all the relational damage across human history has stemming from a rupture in the heart of man as a result of rejecting God. Once the foundational bond of man's relationship with God was disturbed through a failure to order his evolved instincts according to reason, it had a cascading effect that damaged all our other relationships in its wake—to such an extent that the ensuing derangement may be called "ontological" and a "hereditary defect."[67] Pope Benedict would later explain this dynamic as follows:

> [O]ur human history has been polluted from the outset by the misuse of created freedom which seeks emancipation from the divine will. . . . It falsifies above all the fundamental relationships: with God, between a man and a woman, between humankind and the earth. We said that this contamination permeates the whole fabric of our history and that this hereditary defect [*difetto ereditato*] has continued to spread within it and can now be seen everywhere.[68]

---

65. Ratzinger, *In the Beginning*, 72–73 [*Im Anfang schuf Gott*, 56].

66. Ratzinger, *In the Beginning*, 73 [*Im Anfang schuf Gott*, 56]: " To the extent that this is true, when the network of human relationships is damaged from the very beginning, then every human being enters into a world that is marked by relational damage [*Beziehungsstörung*]. At the very moment that a person begins human existence, which is a good, he or she is confronted by a sin-damaged world. Each of us enters into a situation in which relationality has been harmed. Consequently, each person is, from the very start, damaged in relationships and does not engage in them as he or she ought. Sin pursues the human being, and he or she capitulates to it."

67. Ratzinger and Messori, *The Ratzinger Report*, 80–81: "A lucid, realistic view of man and history cannot but stumble upon their alienation and discover that there is a rupture of relationships: in man's relationship to himself, to others, and to God. Now, since man is preeminently a being-in-relationship, such a rupture reaches to the very roots and affects all else. . . . If we are not able to penetrate to the depths the reality and the consequences of original sin, it is precisely because it exists, because the derangement is ontological, because it unbalances, confuses us in the logic of nature, thus preventing us from seeing how a fault at the origin of history can draw in its wake a situation of common sin."

For the presentation of a possible scenario for how the original perversion of man's freedom might have happened historically once humans were freed from being entirely controlled by instinct, see Raymund Schwager, *Banished from Eden: Original Sin and Evolutionary Theory in the Drama of Salvation* (Herefordshire: Gracewing Publishing, 2005), 118–19, 153. While not reducing original sin to a matter of imitation that a person could hypothetically avoid, Schwager emphasizes that mimesis plays an integral role in its transmission and indeed is deeply rooted in human nature. See also Schwager, *Erbsünde und Heilsdrama: Im Kontext von Evolution, Gentechnologie und Apokalypse* (Münster, Germany: LIT Verlag, 1997), 174; and a discussion of this proposal in Steinmair-Pösel, "Original Sin, Grace, and Positive Mimesis," 7.

68. Benedict XVI, General Audience: "Theology of the Sacraments" (December 10, 2008). This language of original sin as "inherited sin" is also found in Benedict XVI, Homily (December 8, 2005). Another statement of how the disturbance of man's bond with God affected all our other relationships is found Ratzinger, *Gottes Projekt*, 56. Pope Francis echoes this understanding when he describes

It is significant Benedict would echo this approach at the very end of his ponitifi-
cate, stressing that sin ruins relationships and thereby ruins everything in its wake.
Now, he adds, if man's relationship structure is disordered from the outset and every
human comes into a world marked by this relational distortion, then we can truly
say that "the initial sin tarnishes and wounds human nature."[69]

It is noteworthy that we find Benedict above calling original sin a "hereditary
defect," an "ontological" derangement that "wounds human nature," for this is the
sort of language he typically seeks to avoid. The key to understanding this idio-
syncrasy is to realize that the emeritus pontiff recognizes the value of traditional
theological language even as he finds it helpful to recast it in a relational key. Perhaps this point is best articulated by the Ratzinger-led ITC when it said that "the
*imago Dei* . . . is essentially dialogical or relational in its ontological structure,"
adding that sin is "a rupture of the relationship with God" which causes division
within man himself (e.g., the inability to order our passions according to reason)
and in turn damages all of man's other relationships.[70] Because being is inherently
relational, calling sin an ontological defect for Ratzinger *is* to describe it as a rupture of relationship.

In light of the above, the traditional formulation of describing original sin
being propagated by nature plays a crucial role in helping to eliminate possible mis-
interpretations of what Benedict is saying: by safeguarding the truth that it original
sin not merely a social phenomenon—something that comes to us from the outside
through our relationships in the world. Rather, the disordered relationality in our
lives begins first in ourselves: it is not as if we would be free from concupiscence if
only our families, friends, and society were more holy. Nor, as John Paul II taught,
can we claim that the presence of "structures of sin" or "social sin" compel us as

---

original sin as a rupture of "three fundamental and closely intertwined relationships: with God, with
our neighbour and with the earth itself." Francis, *Laudato Si'*, §66. For another contemporary scholar
who uses relational categories to describe this dynamic, see Mark Smith, *The Genesis of Good and Evil:
The Fall(out) and Original Sin in the Bible* (Louisville, KY: Westminster John Knox Press, 2019), 62.

69. Benedict XVI, General Audience: "I believe in God, maker of heaven and earth, creator of
man" (February 6, 2013).

70. International Theological Commission, *Communion and Stewardship*, §45. The commission
cites Romans 7:15–25 in support of its depiction of the internal division within ourselves that traditionally goes by the name *concupiscence*. For another relational approach to original sin that is germane to this point, see Middleton, "Reading Genesis 3 Attentive to Human Evolution," 77. Speaking
of original's sin's consequences for the world at large, Middleton writes: "The curse is thus not an
ontological change in the *adamah* but rather a *changed relationship* between man and the earth." See
also Celia Deane-Drummond, "In Adam All Die?," in Cavanaugh and Smith, *Evolution and the Fall*,
45: "My own view is that original sin can be reinterpreted to mean that a person is born in each generation into an imperfect community of others, including other creaturely kinds." This statement
does not say enough about man's interiorly disordered proclivity to sin that obtains regardless of his
environment, yet Drummond does helpfully add that this likewise applies in the life of each individual
sinner, "where sin represents a cutting off from relations with God and with each other, leading to
concrete wrongful acts to which each person can be held to account. It is not so much that guilt is
inherited through original sin, but that original sin creates the distorted social context in which it is
impossible not to be a sinner."

individuals to sin. Rather, according to John Paul, the opposite is the case: structures of sin are rooted in personal sin, not the reverse.[71]

A final point before we proceed to our next topic. We have seen that Benedict conceives of original sin primarily as the rupture of man's relationship with God, as a result of which all other relationships are damaged. Yet, we have not yet explored what the emeritus pontiff has to say about the traditional teaching that a primeval Fall led to man's loss of sanctifying grace.[72] What does this defect look like viewed in relational terms? It is not a particular question that Ratzinger often addressed, but he did do so at some length in his interview book *God and the World*. As in all of the other places where he addresses original sin, Ratzinger begins by laying out his archetypal interpretation of Adam and Eve in Genesis 3: "The disruption of the relationship with God, then, immediately sets [Adam and Eve] at odds with each other. For *anyone* who has turned against God has by the same token turned against others."[73] Then, in a characteristically straightforward reply, he directly tackles the question of what the loss of sanctifying grace caused by man's first sin entails from a relational perspective:

> The loss of [sanctifying] grace means the breaking off of a certain relationship. The original trusting, loving relationship with God, which at the same time strengthens and heals the relationships of human beings with each other, is torn asunder. . . . It is this disordered relationship, this world of distorted relationships, into which we are born. . . . What is meant by the idea that the loss of sanctifying grace lies at the heart of original sin is that a certain disruption of relationships has become a part of the texture of human history. Precisely because we are not, as individuals, directly responsible for this, but encounter it as part of the existing situation, we stand in need of the one who straightens the relationship out.[74]

## ORIGINAL SIN AND MAN'S NEED FOR CHRIST
### We Cannot Save Ourselves

Our above glimpse of Benedict's relational understanding to grace leads directly to the next feature of his theological approach to original sin: his insistence that we cannot truly understand the mystery of man's first transgression except in light of its remedy—the grace poured out through the life, death, and resurrection of Jesus Christ, the New Adam.

---

71. Thus, John Paul taught that it is appropriate to speak of "social sin" and "structures of sin" which are "the result of the accumulation and concentration of many personal sins." Nevertheless, the pontiff insists that finding ourselves thrown into tragic situations that we did not choose for ourselves does not exculpate any of us, for "[t]he real responsibility" for these networks of sin "lies with individuals." John Paul II, *Reconciliatio et Paenitentia*, §16; cf. John Paul II, *Sollicitudo Rei Socialis*, §36.

72. For more on sanctifying grace, see *CCC*, §1999–2024.

73. Ratzinger, *God and the World*, 87 (emphasis added).

74. Ratzinger, *God and the World*, 87–88.

As we have already seen, Benedict views the questions of who, when, where, and how precisely man committed his first transgression as incidental to the doctrine of original sin. For the emeritus pontiff, the core of the doctrine is its reminder of the truth that none of us is able to choose the good perfectly and save ourselves—that we all stand in need of the remedy that can only be found in God's immeasurably precious gift of grace. Paul says in Romans 3:23, "[A]ll have sinned and fall short of the glory of God."[75] As Ratzinger frequently professes, the fundamental purpose of the doctrine of original sin is to drive home this very point made by the Apostle: that "only God's love can purify damaged human love and reestablish the network of relationships that have suffered from alienation."[76] Or, as the then-Cardinal put it in an interview, to overcome "the reality of alienation (the 'Fall') . . . a help from outside is necessary . . . in order to be saved, it is necessary to abandon oneself to Love.[77] Pope Benedict would later expand on this in more detail:

> [B]y himself, on his own, man is unable to extricate himself from this situation. On his own he cannot redeem himself; only the Creator himself can right relationships. Only if he from who we distanced ourselves comes to us and lovingly holds out his hand can proper relationships be restored. This happens through Jesus Christ, who goes in exactly the opposite direction to Adam, as is described by the hymn in the second chapter of St Paul's Letter to the Philippians (2:5–11). . . . Jesus, the Son of God, was in a perfect filial relationship with the Father, he emptied himself and became the servant, he took the path of love, humbling himself even to death on a cross, to set right our relations with God. The Cross of Christ thus became the new tree of life.[78]

In short, if disunity and separation (the sundering of relationship) are the essence of sin, then Ratzinger views redemption and salvation as the reestablishment of unity (the healing and restoration of relationship whereby we find our true selves through love).[79] Yet the significance of salvation's good news is lost on anyone who does not yet know the "bad" news: namely, that none of us can enact redemption by our own steam.

To conclude this point, it is instructive to put Benedict's above approach into dialogue with what the Catechism has to say on the topic. While framed in his own

---

75. Lest the reader get the false impression that Ratzinger (or Paul) denies the Immaculate Conception of the Blessed Virgin, note that Mary's sinlessness and its relationship to suffering and death will be explored in the next chapter.

76. Ratzinger, "The Dignity of the Human Person," in Herbert Vorgrimler, ed., *Commentary on the Documents of Vatican II*, Vol. V (New York: Herder and Herder, 1969), 115–64, at 121. To this, Ratzinger adds, "We can only be saved—that is, become ourselves—when we engage in proper relationship. . . . We can be saved only when he from whom we have cut ourselves off takes the initiative with us and stretches out his hand to us."

77. Ratzinger and Messori, *The Ratzinger Report*, 81.

78. Benedict XVI, General Audience (February 6, 2013).

79. On this point, see Benedict XVI, *Spe Salvi*, §14.

unique relational language, Benedict's claim is fundamentally the same what we find in the Catechism: Adam's sin has had tragic consequences for all mankind, yet that is not the only (or main) point that the Apostle was trying to make when he "contrasts the universality of sin and death with the universality of salvation in Christ."[80] Indeed, the Catechism describes original sin as the "'reverse side' of the Good News that Jesus is the Savior of all men and that all need the salvation that is offered through Christ." So strong is the connection that we are then told in no uncertain terms, "The Church, which has the mind of Christ, knows very well that we cannot tamper with the revelation of original sin without undermining the mystery of Christ."[81]

As we have seen throughout this volume, for Benedict this injunction not to "tamper" with a doctrine does not mean that we cannot refine our understanding of it, reformulating dogmatic realities so that their true form and all their contours can be more clearly seen. As ever, the question before us involves how to promote legitimate doctrinal development—arriving at a fuller understanding of what a given teaching means—and avoid "tampering" with its very essence in the pursuit. The Catechism's words remind us that, while we must be bold and courageous in our efforts to bolster our understanding of the faith through dialogue with reason, we must also remain humble and not presume to have provided definitive solutions to daunting challenges like that of trying to understand the meaning of original sin in an evolutionary context.

In light of the above, we would do recall once more the wisdom of Thomas Aquinas to which I have referred more than once in this volume and will return to once again: some things must be believed by the faithful, while in the case of others there is latitude for debate—and indeed "in such matters *even the saints* at times view things differently."[82] How to ascertain whether a given question admits of a legitimate diversity of theological opinions can be a difficult task, though. In this connection, I find that the following question posed by Peter Enns is helpful for identifying the boundary between a legitimate theological opinion and heterodoxy: "What remains and what gets transformed? At what point have we left the tradition by adjusting it to the present, and at what point have we killed the tradition by refusing to change at all?"[83] Pursuing this wisdom question is pivotal for navigating any inquiry at the intersection of faith and science, especially when it comes to the interrelationship of evolution, human origins, and original sin.

As helpful as I find the above question to be, thankfully we as individuals are not left on our own to wonder what an answer to it might look like. For, not only does the Church have parameters that guide us in our quest, we also have the example of an eminent theologian and pope whose work on our topic manages to walk that narrow path of updating the tradition in light of modern discoveries so it can

---

80. CCC, §402.
81. CCC, §389.
82. Aquinas, *In II Sent.*, Lib. 2, d. 12, q. 1, a. 2 (my translation).
83. Enns, *How the Bible Actually Works*, 216.

survive and thrive while not losing sight of the essentials and thereby compromise the tradition beyond recognition. As the reader already knows at this point in the book, I find that Benedict's work is a second to none as an illustration of how pursuing unresolved theological questions need not be a capitulation to modernity that "waters down" the faith but rather a powerful exercise of loving the Church and a declaration that the truth of the faith is worth fighting for.

## It Is More about Christ than Adam

In Romans 5:12–21, Paul writes, "Therefore as sin came into the world through one man and death through sin, and so death spread to all men because all men sinned." Noting that this passage gives the Church "the essential outline of the doctrine on original sin," Benedict issues a stark warning: "[W]e must never treat the sin of Adam and humanity separately from the salvific context, in other words, without understanding them within the horizon of justification in Christ."[84] Similarly, Ratzinger remarks in his interview *God and the World* that, as soon as we speak of this disrupted relationship that goes by the name original sin, we must always go on to speak of God's response to the catastrophe by setting out at once to rebuild the relationship and to make it right. So strongly is he convicted of this that the emeritus pontiff adds, "If we ever talk about the concept of original sin without mentioning God's response, then we pass into the realm of the absurd."[85] The reason for this is that, in the New Testament, the "Adam-figure" and doctrine of man as the *imago Dei* are transferred to Christ, the definitive Adam who is "concerned less with the origin than with the future of man."[86]

Summing up this understanding of original sin's fundamental claim, Benedict emphasizes that, for Paul, the central figure in the human drama is not so much the first Adam as it is the Last Adam. In a Wednesday audience, the then-pontiff thus offers the following explanation of why the Letter to the Romans dealt with the issue of Adam's sin in the first place:

> At the center of the scene it is not so much Adam, with the consequences of his sin for humanity, who is found as much as it is Jesus Christ and the grace which was poured out on humanity in abundance through him. . . . The comparison that Paul draws between Adam and Christ therefore sheds light on the inferiority of the first man compared to the prevalence of the second. . . . [I]t is precisely in order to highlight the immeasurable gift of grace in Christ that Paul mentions Adam's sin. One could say that if it were not to demonstrate the centrality of grace, he would not have dwelt on the treatment of sin"[87]

---

84. Benedict XVI, General Audience: "The Apostle's Teaching on the Relation between Adam and Christ" (December 3, 2008).

85. Ratzinger, *In the Beginning*, 73–74.

86. Ratzinger, "The Dignity of the Human Person," 121.

87. Benedict XVI, General Audience: "The Apostle's Teaching on the Relation between Adam and Christ" (December 3, 2008).

Ratzinger had already developed this view in a remarkable 1964 university lecture, teaching that the Fall narrative is "about much more than telling a story that happened once" and is ultimately "about the fundamental understanding (*das Grundverständnis*) of man, in which it is revealed that the man without grace is a man unsaved."[88] Indeed, he adds that the doctrine of original sin and of man's original state "developed only secondarily as the flip side of the message of the salvific grace of Christ . . . as part of the doctrine of grace." Consequently, he insists that they have a rightful place in Christianity "only as part of the doctrine of grace," which is in reality "the primary theme (*Ur-thema*) to which the doctrine of original sin is subordinate.[89]

All this is to say that, even as he certainly had certain assumptions in this regard, the essential point of Paul's teaching here was not to make historical claims about who committed it, where, when, and how it happened (or, as we will discuss in the next chapter, whether death resulted from it). While the tradition has long had views on these subjects, for Benedict they are peripheral to the core message of the doctrine of original sin, which is ultimately about the necessity and superabundance of Christ's grace with his desire to save all men, Jew and Gentile alike:

> For if many died through one man's trespass, *much more* have the grace of God and the free gift in the grace of that one man Jesus Christ abounded for many. . . . If, because of one man's trespass, death reigned through that one man, *much more* will those who receive the abundance of grace and the free gift of righteousness reign in life through the one man Jesus Christ (Rm 5:15,17).

In concluding this point, I would like to note a line from Conor Cunningham that I believe nicely complements Ratzinger's understanding of the relationship of Adam and Jesus outlined above. While some Christians believe that a nonhistorical reading of Adam would render the life, death, and Resurrection of the historical Jesus devoid of meaning, Cunningham replies, "[T]his claim amounts to a denial (even if unintentionally so) of the centrality of Christ; for it gives the fallen Adam

---

88. Ratzinger, *Schöpfungslehre* (1964), 201; Sanz, "Joseph Ratzinger y la doctrina de la creación. Los apuntes de Münster de 1964 (y III)," 486n101.

89. Ratzinger, *Schöpfungslehre* (1964), 198–99; Sanz, "Joseph Ratzinger y la doctrina de la creación. Los apuntes de Münster de 1964 (y III)," 485nn96, 98. More recently, Isaac Morales has written along similar lines. Summarizing a conclusion drawn by many biblical scholars, he notes that "the primary theme of Rom 5:12–21 is not some theory about the introduction of sin into the world, but rather the abundant gift of salvation brought about by Christ's act of obedience" and that "In light of the discussion of the relationship between sin and death throughout Romans 5–8, Rom 5:12 must mean what the rest of the verses in this passage mean: Adam's sin brought about a kind of spiritual death for the whole human race." Isaac Morales, OP, "What Kind of Death? Romans 5 and Modern Science" (forthcoming).

For a complementary "new Thomist" approach that sees original sin primarily as a lack of sanctifying grace and right relationship that orients one toward Jesus Christ rather than the inheritance of personal guilt or corruption, see Houck, *Aquinas, Original Sin, and the Challenge of Evolution*, 200–220 and Houck, "Toward a New Account of the Fall, Informed by Anselm of Canterbury and Thomas Aquinas," *Pro Ecclesia* 29.4 (2020): 429–48 at 18–19.

of Genesis an interpretative primacy over the Jesus of history that Paul and the Gospel writers do not allow."[90]

## Placing Christ's Grace Front and Center
## Resolves a Pauline Problem

We are now in a position to draw out a crucial implication of Benedict's thought that the purpose of the doctrine of original sin is to highlight the human race's need for Christ's saving grace. As we have just seen, St. Paul deployed the figure of the Old Adam in order to make a point about the New Adam, yet the fact remains that the Apostle rather clearly seems to have held a position that now poses a problem in light of modern scientific discoveries: namely, that physical death entered the world only after sin. Indeed, whereas we have just been discussing Paul's culturally-assumed conviction that the sin of the first human was the cause of all physical death and suffering among our race, at this point it is important to mention that Paul's assumptions in this regard are perhaps even more in tension with nature than they may at first appear. How so?

It turns out that Paul seems to have viewed not just human death but *all* death (i.e., of all other living creatures) as having entered the world only after the first human sinned. As we will discuss in Chapter 11, the Apostle has a majestic vision in which all of creation will one day be "set free from its bondage to decay" (Rm 8:21-22) and what is "sown in weakness [will be] raised in power" (1 Cor 15:43). What is not at first apparent, however, is that in this passage Paul not only sees the fate of Adam and all of creation as intimately connected, he also views the cause of suffering and death as the same in each case. For, Paul speaks in Romans 8:20 of the "subjection" of creation to decay as resulting not from its own will but due to God's—itself most likely an echo of Genesis's depiction of the ground as cursed because of the sin of Adam-Israel (Gn 3:17–19; 5:29; see also Ezra 7:11).[91] With this biblical data in place, the tension between Paul's narrative of human origins and what we know to be the case through evolutionary science is dramatically heightened. For, it is one thing to hold that sin precipitated human death while acknowledging that other animals died before our Fall (a position taken by Aquinas).[92] However, to hold that *no* creature died before the Fall (as Paul seems to have assumed) is scarcely conceivable in light of modern scientific discoveries.

Thankfully, this problem admits of a resolution once we are able to harness Ratzinger's exegetical principles and distinguish the underlying purpose governing Paul's recourse to the Adam story (its content or essential teaching) from the

---

90. Cunningham, *Darwin's Pious Idea*, 164.

91. Recalling that Adam is a cipher for Israel, it is noteworthy that a similar vision is found in Is 24:4–5, where the earth mourns and withers as a result of Israel's breach of their covenant with God.

92. Contrary to some who preceded him, Thomas insists that the nature of animals was unchanged by man's sin. Although they posed no threat to us, a natural antipathy between certain animals has always existed, and there was (nonhuman) death before the Fall. Lions, then, were never herbivores. Aquinas, *ST* I, q. 96, a. 1 ad 2.

Apostle's associated assumptions when conveying his teaching on the salvific grace of Jesus Christ. With this in mind, William Lane Craig notes that, while original sin may be a core Christian doctrine, its core is not dependent on a particular framework that would postulate an initial sin that corrupted human nature.[93] Likewise, Peter Enns draws a similar distinction and concludes that Paul's assumptions about how death and sin entered the world "cannot and should not be the determining factor in whether biblically faithful Christians can accept evolution as the scientific account of human origins—and the gospel does not hang in the balance."[94] Indeed, Enns dedicates considerable time to discussing how the biblical authors' faulty assumptions about the mechanics of human origins no more affect the essence of the Gospel than did their mistaken cosmological views. Enns's primary concern, like that of Benedict, is to ascertain the essential point of Romans 5 and distinguish it from what is incidental to the Apostle's core message, noting that one can believe that Paul is correct theologically concerning the problem of sin and death and its answer in Jesus Christ without also needing to maintain that Paul's assumptions about human origins are scientifically and historically accurate.[95]

A few pages after making his point that the reality of our need for a savior does not hinge upon the precise means by which physical death first entered the world, Enns adds:

> Some will balk, however, insisting that the gospel is at stake with respect to Adam . . . and that Christian orthodoxy requires us not to entertain such a theologically harmful notion, regardless of what "science says." I understand and respect the motivation to preserve the gospel that lies behind this sentiment. I do not grant, however, that the gospel is actually at stake in the question of whether what Paul assumed about Adam as the progenitor of humanity is scientifically true. That is the very assumption we need to examine.[96]

As for Benedict, so for Enns, the centerpiece of Paul's Adam theology is not the first Adam and the issue of how precisely sin and death entered into history but rather the remedy for it wrought by the true and final Adam, Jesus Christ. In this way, Enns surmises that Paul was concerned with three interrelated realities: the universal problem of death, the universal problem of sin, and the historical event of Christ's Resurrection that has saved us from both: "These three remain: what is

---

93. Craig, *In Quest of the Historical Adam*, 24–25.

94. Enns, *The Evolution of Adam*, xix.

95. Enns, *The Evolution of Adam*, 143. Consonant with Enns's approach, James Smith writes that the "Augustinian package" is essential to the doctrine of original sin, yet neither is it altered if the Fall did not take place as a simple, one-time event as traditionally assumed. Smith says that this still allows us to affirm both of original sin's central theses: the priority of the good (humans were not created sinful), and the necessity of grace (humans are incapable of saving themselves). Smith, "What Stands on the Fall?," in *Evolution and the Fall*, 59.

96. Enns, *The Evolution of Adam*, 146.

lost is Paul's culturally assumed explanation for what a primordial man had to do with causing the reign of death and sin in the world."[97]

# CONCLUSION

Although the Church was initially reluctant to embrace historical-critical exegesis and evolutionary theory, Benedict's work is concrete proof that Christians can see advances in these disciplines as positive resources that help us to understand the faith better, not merely as areas to fear or begrudgingly accommodate.[98] In this chapter, we have unfolded Benedict's account that sees original sin primarily as disorder in mankind's relationship structure that is an unavoidable condition of the present life from which none of us can save ourselves—an account that is compatible with the insights of contemporary science and bespeaks a truth that lies beyond its purview. In the next chapter, we will turn to a topic that evolutionary biology has much to say about: the role of death in the development of all life on this planet. Given evolution, what are we to make of the longstanding conviction that that physical suffering and death result from original sin? Tackling this question will help us better ascertain the core of the biblical message and, *mutatis mutandis*, will allow divine revelation to illumine the role of human evolution and death within God's salvific plan.

---

97. Enns, *The Evolution of Adam*, 123–24. The same distinction applies to the episode of Paul's preaching at the Areopagus when the Apostle proclaims that God "made from one every nation of men to live on all the face of the earth." (Acts 17:26). As in Romans, here too the Apostle assumes that the entire human population has been derived from a single initial human being. However, Paul's overarching purpose in this text is very concrete: speaking to a Gentile audience, he emphasizes the unity of all mankind—that we are all sinners in need of repentance, and that God "has fixed a day on which he will judge the world in righteousness by a man whom he has appointed, and of this he has given assurance to all men by raising him from the dead" (Acts 17:31).

98. For a fuller statement of this point that is not directly tied to Benedict's thought, see Lombardo, "Evil, Suffering, and the Original Sin," 149.

# Chapter 9

# Putting the Last Adam First

## *Suffering and Death in the Light of Christ Crucified*

## INTRODUCTION

In the last chapter, we unfolded Benedict XVI's relational account of original sin and have sought to show that it offers a compelling way to affirm this doctrine in today's evolutionary context and in dialogue with modern biblical scholarship. Thus far, we have been focusing our efforts on ascertaining the essence of the doctrine of original sin, especially insofar as it signifies mankind's disordered relationship structure and our inability to heal it apart from Christ's grace. Now, we will turn our attention to some very specific effects traditionally connected with original sin: the experience of suffering and death.

Advances in modern biology strongly suggest that humans—like all other organic life forms—have been subject to suffering and death from our species' beginning by virtue of their having descended from hominin ancestors who had been dying for millions of years before our species arrived on the scene of history. Indeed, not only do we now know this, the theory of evolution by natural selection further reveals that death and the selective pressures associated with it played an essential role in the development of life from bacteria to the myriad flora and fauna that grace our planet today.[1]

This modern narrative clearly challenges the classical theological synthesis assumed by most Catholic theologians until the mid-twentieth century according to which man suffered neither pain nor death before his fall from grace—that human sin either lies at the origin of death itself or that (as Aquinas holds) it precipitated the phenomenon among humans.[2] Faced with this situation, some

---

1. For further reflection on this point, see Gerald Hiestand, "A More Modest Adam: An Exploration of Irenaeus' Anthropology in Light of the Darwinian Account of Pre-Fall Death" in *Bulletin of Ecclesial Theology* 5.1 (2018): 55–72 at 56.

2. For an extensive survey of this classical synthesis in the context of a comprehensive overview of the tradition *vis-à-vis* this topic, see Lombardo, "Evil, Suffering, and Original Sin," 139–50. According to Aquinas, human nature can be considered in two ways. According to our body's structural principles, death is indeed natural to us. However, Thomas does not believe that man was created with purely natural endowments. In other words, he never experienced the state of *natura pura*. Through this grace of original justice that man possessed, divine providence initially prevented man from experiencing suffering and death. Aquinas, *In II Sent.*, d. 30, q. 1, a. 1; see also Aquinas, *Super Rom. 5*, lect. 3, no. 416; Aquinas, *De malo*, q. 5, a. 5, s.c. 2, in *St. Thomas Aquinas on Evil*, trans. Richard Regan (Notre Dame, IN:

scholars conclude that the right approach is to reject the doctrine of original sin, while many ordinary believers respond to the same challenge by rejecting evolution.[3] So, the question is: Were humans immune to suffering prior to sinning, as the tradition at large assumes?[4] Or were we meant to experience pain and death as part of God's plan from the beginning? In short, can the evolutionary story about suffering and death coexist with Catholic doctrine of human origins? In what follows, I will propose that the key to a reconciliation may be found by examining how Ratzinger's Christology (his understanding of Christ) informs his anthropology (his understanding of man).

In this chapter, we will use Benedict's many statements on this topic as a springboard for articulating how a renewed focus on Jesus Christ as the definitive Adam—he who fully reveals man to himself—can help the Church to think through the place of suffering in God's plan for man. My main contention here will be that looking to Christ's *kenosis* (self-emptying) on the Cross in conjunction with our contemporary knowledge of evolution can serve to deepen our understanding of man's nature made according to Christ's image—particularly our experience of suffering and death.[5] In the course of these pages, I therefore hope to offer a positive answer

---

University of Notre Dame Press, 1995). For a lengthy treatment of this point, see Jean-Pierre Torrell, OP, "Nature and Grace in Thomas Aquinas," in *Surnaturel: A Controversy at the Heart of Twentieth-Century Thomistic Thought*, ed. Serge-Thomas Bonino, OP (Ave Maria, FL: Sapientia Press, 2007), 155–87. Building on this foundation, the Angelic Doctor explains in detail the harmonious relationships experienced by our first parents in Aquinas, *Super Rom.* 5, lect. 3, no. 416 and Aquinas, *De malo*, q. 5, a. 5 ad 16. As we will see below, Ratzinger argues for a development of this tradition in which the doctrine of original sin remains intact while the question of whether all physical suffering and death followed upon sin remains open.

3. For Catholic theologians who respond to the data of evolutionary biology by rejecting the doctrine of original sin, see Jack Mahoney, *Christianity in Evolution: An Exploration* (Washington, D.C.: Georgetown University Press, 2011) and John Haught, *God After Darwin: A Theology of Evolution* (Boulder, CO: Westview Press, 2008).

4. According to Aquinas, the sin of Adam led to a series of cascading disorders that affected not just him but in turn all who ever since have partaken in his nature. See Aquinas, *Super Rom.* 5, lect. 3, no. 410. Like an iron sword left to its own, man after turning his mind from God became corruptible, i.e., subject to death from intrinsic sources and to violence from external ones. See Aquinas, *Super Rom.* 5, lect. 3, no. 416. Sin thus understood by Thomas is the accidental or indirect cause of human death. In other words, sin created a circumstance that permitted the direct cause of death (i.e., our bodily nature) to follow its natural course. Or, as Thomas explains in his commentary on the *Sentences*, death and suffering are not in themselves penalties (*poenae*) due to original sin but rather mere natural deficiencies (*naturales defectus*) that are common to every creature. If, however, we consider human nature as it was actually created in a state of grace, suffering and death are indeed rightly understood as penalties. See Aquinas, *In II Sent.*, d. 30, q. 1, a. 1. See also Torrell, "Nature and Grace in Thomas Aquinas," 162–63, 167 and the various texts he references, including Aquinas, *De Malo*, q.4, a.2 ad 1; q.5, a.1 ad 13.

5. St. Paul provides the *locus classicus* for Christ's *kenosis*: "[Though Christ Jesus] was in the form of God, [he] did not count equality with God a thing to be grasped, but emptied himself, taking the form of a servant, being born in the likeness of men. And being found in human form he humbled himself and became obedient unto death, even death on a cross" (Phil 2:6-8). On Christ's *kenosis* as the model for human flourishing and the means of our divinization planned by God from all eternity, see Osborn, *Death Before the Fall*, 159.

to John Paul II's question: "Does an evolutionary perspective bring any light to bear upon theological anthropology, the meaning of the human person as the *imago Dei*, the problem of Christology—and even upon the development of doctrine itself?"[6] In particular, we will explore below what it means for Christ to be the true Adam and how his *kenosis* is the key that unlocks the mysterious relationship of sin, suffering, and death that so characterize our evolving world.

## CHRIST THE TRUE ADAM IN RATZINGER'S BIBLICAL THEOLOGY

Throughout his corpus, Ratzinger variously refers to Jesus as the "last man," "exemplary man," "second Adam," "definitive Adam" and even "Counter-Adam" [*Gegenadam*].[7] However, the emeritus pontiff's most extensive systematic treatment of the relationship between Adam and Christ can be found in a section of *Introduction to Christianity* dedicated specifically to "Christ, the Last Man." Here, Ratzinger teaches that to confess Jesus of Nazareth as the only begotten Son of God is to recognize him as the exemplary man, which in his view is "probably the best way to translate accurately the . . . Pauline concept of the 'last Adam.'"[8] Or, as he says elsewhere, Christ is the "index for how 'person' must be understood in the first place," adding, "Christology was originally meant in this way: in Christ, whom the faith certainly does present as unique, is revealed to be not only a speculative exemption; rather, in him is manifested for the first time the truth about what is meant by the riddle named 'man'. . . . [Christ is he in whom] the orientation of the creature 'man' first becomes fully evident."[9] In another variation on this theme, Ratzinger adds:

---

6. John Paul II, Letter to George Coyne, SJ, Director of the Vatican Observatory (June 1, 1988).

7. Ratzinger deployed this last formulation in his 1957 Mariology course at the Freising Seminary, the notes for which are housed in the *Benedikt XVI Institut* in Regensburg and have been expertly summarized in Emery de Gaál, "Mariology as Christology and Ecclesiology: Professor Joseph Ratzinger's Only Mariology Course," in *Joseph Ratzinger and the Healing of Reformation-Era Divisions*, eds. Emery de Gaál and Matthew Levering (Steubenville, OH: Emmaus Academic, 2019), 93–120. In what follows, I will refer to the manuscript of Ratzinger's Mariology lecture notes as *Mariologie* (1957) and reproduce de Gaál's translations of the text. For the term *Gegenadam* or "Counter-Adam," see de Gaál, "Mariology as Christology and Ecclesiology," 98 and *Mariologie* (1957), 6.

8. Ratzinger, *Introduction to Christianity*, 234 [*Einführung in das Christentum*, 220]. He continues, "Man's full hominization presupposes God's becoming man" and is "only completed when the Logos itself, the whole creative meaning, and man merge into each other. . . . In [Christ], 'hominization' has truly reached its goal." Ratzinger, *Introduction to Christianity*, 234–345.

9. Ratzinger, "On the Understanding of 'Person' in Theology," in *Dogma and Preaching* (San Francisco: Ignatius Press, 2011), 181–96 at 192. The idea of man's true, long-mysterious nature finally being manifest in Christ bears a strong resemblance to the following: "[Jesus of Nazareth is] the last man (the second Adam), that is as the long-awaited manifestation of what is truly human and the definitive revelation to man of his hidden nature" Ratzinger, *Principles of Catholic Theology* (San Francisco: Ignatius Press, 1987), 156. For another articulation of this point, see Ratzinger, *In the Beginning*, 48 [*Im Anfang schuf Gott*, 41]: "In the New Testament, Christ is referred to as the second Adam, the definitive Adam, and as the image of God (cf. 1 Cor 15:44-48; Col 1:15). This means that in him alone appears the complete answer to the question about what the human being is. . . . He is the definitive human being (*der*

[W]hat is disclosed in [Christ] is what the riddle of the human person really intends. Scripture expresses this point by calling Christ the last Adam or 'the second Adam.' It thereby characterizes him as the true fulfillment of the idea of the human person, in which the direction of meaning of this being comes fully to light for the first time.[10]

Ratzinger had already emphasized this union of Christology and *protology* (the study of origins and God's fundamental purpose for man) in his 1964 course on creation at Munster:

Christology has its place in the doctrine of creation, and faith in creation receives its meaning (*Sinn*) in Christology. . . . Christology can only be meaningful and understandable on the basis of the preceding biblical anthropology; and the antecedent biblical anthropology attains its full significance only when passing over into Christology.[11]

Winsomely summarizing this view, he relates: "From the standpoint of Christian faith one may say that for *history* God stands at the end, while for *being* he stands at the beginning."[12] Cast in Thomistic language, Christ the Last Adam is also the "Final Adam" in the sense of being creation's *final cause*: last in the order of execution, yet first in the order of the God's intention.[13] Capturing the heart of Ratzinger's approach,

---

*endgültige Mensch*), and creation is, as it were, a preliminary sketch (*Vorentwurf*) that points to him." This same image of creation as the *Vorentwurf* of Christ the true man also is made in Ratzinger's 1985 lectures in Carinthia, Austria collected in *Gottes Projekt: Nachdenken über Schöpfung und Kirche* (Regensburg: Pustet, 2009), 63. The work is also published in Italian under the title *Progetto di Dio: Meditazioni sulla Creazione e la Chiesa* (Venice, Italy: Marcianum Press, 2012).

10. Ratzinger, "Concerning the Notion of Person in Theology," in *Joseph Ratzinger in Communio*, Vol. 2: *Anthropology and Culture* (Grand Rapids, MI: Eerdmans, 2013), 103–18 at 114.

11. Ratzinger, *Schöpfungslehre* (1964), 22, 120; Sanz, "Joseph Ratzinger y la doctrina de la creación. Los apuntes de Münster de 1964 (II)," 211n38, 215n49 (my translation). Christology being necessary for any adequate anthropology also has significant implications for eschatology and the (im)possibility of a purely secular humanism. For an overview of Ratzinger's thought on this point and the influence of Henri de Lubac upon his making it, see Tracey Rowland, *Ratzinger's Faith: The Theology of Pope Benedict XVI* (Oxford: Oxford University Press, 2008), 32–34, 107–108.

12. For this vocabulary that I have adapted and applied here, see Aquinas, *ST* I-II, q. 1, a. 1 ad 1.

13. Ratzinger, *Introduction to Christianity*, 242 [*Einführung in das Christentum*, 228]. On Christ as the "first" Adam, see CCC, §359.

For a rich medieval understanding of the crucified and risen Christ as the formal cause of our humanity, see Andrew Salzmann, "Bonaventure," in *T&T Clark Companion to Atonement* (New York: Bloomsbury T&T Clark, 2017), 409; Bonaventure, *III Sent.*, d. 19, a. 1, q. 1, concl. [III.401], Bonaventure, *Opera Omnia* (Quaracchi: Ex Typographia Collegii S. Bonaventurae, 1882– 1902): "Christ's passion and resurrection are also the formal cause of our justification in that they are the essential pattern (*exemplaris regulantis*) of human existence as dying to self and rising to newness of life. . . . Christ, in a sense, is the very divine idea of humanity existing in the mind of God, made flesh, revealing God's truest intention for the human race. Christ is the most adequate form of humanity, 'the key that unlocks to us the meaning of all reality." See also Gerald Hiestand, "A More Modest Adam," 58: "Adam's humanity is made according to the image of Christ's humanity, rather than Christ's humanity made according to the image of Adam's."

Francesa Murphy notes that, whereas Catholic theology has traditionally tended to look forward from Adam to Christ—focusing on man's sinfulness which makes Christ's salvation necessary—Ratzinger places the accent on the *telos* of humanity in Christ and from there looks backward to gain insight into man's origins.[14]

But what, precisely, does it *mean* for Christ to be the archetypal or "final" human being? As we have seen, on Ratzinger's view, what distinguishes man from other creatures is that the human mind can think about and relate to God—that the difference between humans and other creatures is that our spirit has the "capacity to relate back to itself but also to the whole of reality."[15] Ratzinger thus says that the Rubicon of hominization was first crossed when mere life became mind, when "clay" remained itself while being raised in such a way that "a creature of dust and earth looked out beyond itself and its environment and was able to address God as 'You'.[16] Moreover, he understands that our *imago Dei* is fully actualized in man only when we abandon ourselves to others in loving relationships. In words that closely parallel *Gaudium et Spes*'s famous teaching that "man . . . cannot fully find himself except through a sincere gift of himself," Ratzinger explains that "man only comes to himself by moving away from himself."[17] This anthropological background will now enable us to appreciate the central role Jesus occupies in Ratzinger's portrait of human perfection.

As the definitive man, Jesus is understood by Ratzinger as "pure relation," the one who empties himself in a complete gift to others. That is to say, "the decisive feature [*Gestalt*] in the figure of Jesus" is that he "oversteps the bounds of [his] individuality" by being "the completely open man in whom the dividing walls of existence are torn down, who is entirely 'transition' (Pasch)" and thereby "binds humanity and divinity into a unity."[18] According to Ratzinger, this dynamism is captured perfectly in the notion of *exodus* (literally, "going out"):

---

14. Francesa Murphy, "Touching the Void: Ratzinger's Soteriology," in *Gift to the Church and World: Fifty Years of Joseph Ratzinger's Introduction to Christianity*, eds. John Cavadini and Donald Wallenfang (Eugene, OR: Pickwick, 2021) 242–54 at 246–47. On Adam being temporally prior but Christ ontologically so, see also Edward Oakes, SJ, *A Theology of Grace in Six Controversies* (Grand Rapids, MI: Eerdmans, 2016), 131. According to Oakes, Augustine erred by stressing our solidarity with Adam more than that which we hold in common with Christ. He argues that this is contrary to Paul, for whom the "heavenly Christ" comes first and thus to look at the world from "the wrong end of the telescope." Oakes, SJ, *A Theology of Grace in Six Controversies*, 132. For this language, see Aquinas, *ST* I-II, q. 1, a. 1 ad 1.

15. "The essence of mind or spirit is being-in-relation. The difference between matter and spirit is the spirit's capacity to relate back to itself but also to the whole of reality." Ratzinger, "On the Understanding of 'Person' in Theology," 193–94. See also Ratzinger, "Gratia Praesupponit Natura: Grace Presupposes Nature," in *Dogma and Preaching*, 160: "It is the 'nature' of the spirit to be beyond all nature by constantly surpassing itself."

16. Ratzinger, *Introduction to Christianity*, 235.

17. Ratzinger, *Introduction to Christianity*, 234; Second Vatican Council, *Gaudium et Spes*, §24.

18. Ratzinger, *Introduction to Christianity*, 234, 236, 239–40. For a rich treatment of Ratzinger's understanding of Jesus as he who is entirely *transitus* and who shares by his cruciform life all that he has received from his Father in order that we might be Christified, see Robert Imbelli, "Joseph Ratzinger's 'Spiritual Christology,'" in *Gift to the Church and World*, eds. John Cavadini and Donald Wallenfang, 228–29.

The *exi* ["go out!"] that begins the revelation to Abraham is the perpetual fundamental law of exodus, which is perfected in the Paschal mystery and is confirmed as the definitive fundamental law of revelation and at the same time the fundamental law of the spirit, the true fulfillment of the yearning cry that arises out of its nature. In this way, the cross is not the "crucifixion of man," as Nietzsche thought, but rather his true healing which saves him from deceptive self-sufficiency in which he loses himself. The Paschal way of the cross, the breaking down of all earthly assurances and their false satisfactions, is man's true homecoming.[19]

In short, man's "exodus" from self leads to self-discovery in Christ, for by ceasing to assert our self-sufficiency, we open ourselves to union with the entirely and infinitely Other.[20]

Ratzinger sees St. John revealing this same truth vividly through his gospel's crucifixion narrative. After his side was pierced with a spear that ends his earthly life, Jesus's "existence is completely open; now he is entirely 'for.'" And what this shows is that Christ is "no longer a single individual but 'Adam,' from whose side Eve, a new mankind, is formed." In other words, "The fully opened Christ, who completes the transformation of being into reception and transmission, is thus visible as what at the deepest level he always was: as 'Son.'"[21] The implication of this for our own lives is that we become truly human only in bearing the cross with Christ: "Only the humanity of the second Adam is a true humanity, only the humanity that endured the cross brings the true man to light."[22]

To those of us who ponder how we might concretely go about becoming truly human and thereby truly reflect the life of the True Adam in the world, Ratzinger replies: "The question about what the human being is finds its response in the following of Jesus Christ. Following his steps from day to day in patient love and suffering, we can learn with him what it means to be a human being and to become a human being."[23] To draw out this point, Ratzinger reminds us of Pilate's infamous words in John 19:5: *Ecce homo!* The irony of the procurator's unwitting prophetic utterance is that, when we behold the crucified and risen Christ, we are beholding the perfection of man himself:

---

19. Ratzinger, "Gratia Praesupponit Natura," 161. For more on how Benedict replies to this line of criticism from Nietzsche, including the notion that Christianity's moral norms "poison *eros*," see Ramage, *The Experiment of Faith*.

20. Ratzinger, *Introduction to Christianity*, 234–35.

21. Ratzinger, *Introduction to Christianity*, 240–41.

22. Ratzinger, "Gratia Praesupponit Natura," 159.

23. Ratzinger, *In the Beginning*, 58. Ratzinger speaks here of following the way of the Cross as the way for a man to become fully himself. For an insightful theological reflection on how Jesus himself "truly becomes Jesus, Son-YHWH-Saves, in the sacrificial act of his death," see Thomas Weinandy, O.F.M. Cap., *Jesus Becoming Jesus: A Theological Interpretation of the Synoptic Gospels* (Washington, D.C.: The Catholic University of America Press, 2018), 357–411 at 383. The overall thrust of Weinandy's interesting book is to bring new vibrancy to study of the gospels by mediating theologically on what it means for Jesus to become "more and more Jesus in act through his saving acts." Weinandy, O.F.M. Cap., *Jesus Becoming Jesus*, xix.

The question 'what is man?' does not find its answer in a theory, but rather the answer lies in the following of Jesus Christ, in living the project [of God] with him. In the steps of this path—and only in this way—can we learn with him day after day, *in the patience of life and pain*, what it means to be man and thereby become men.[24]

The Letter to the Hebrews captures this same point from John's gospel when it tells us that Jesus was "made perfect" only after he "learned obedience through what he suffered" (Heb 5:8–9). Putting these teachings together, we may therefore say that *to be human is to be like Christ, and therefore to attain perfection through suffering.* To add another dimension to this point, Ratzinger says that to achieve perfection as human is to live a Eucharistic existence—when we abandon ourselves to Christ and let him transform us into his own likeness.[25] Or, to return to Hebrews 5:8–9 and the Old Testament meaning of the Greek participle "being made perfect" (τελειωθείς), we may say that to be a perfect human being is to imitate Christ by exercising a sacrificial priesthood of one's life for the sake of God's people.[26] All this is to say that the connection between the nature and perfection of man and the nature perfection of Christ is so tight that, for Ratzinger, Christology *is* anthropology.[27]

## AN EXISTENTIAL ANALYSIS OF DEATH AND THE PURPOSE OF THE FALL NARRATIVE

Perhaps the most important way in which we humans participate in Jesus' exemplarity is by imitating his self-emptying *kenosis* through our own suffering and death. The ineluctable nature of this call is evident to us every day as we experience the myriad sorts of pains that come with inhabiting a fallen world. Though this observation is far from new, the field of evolutionary biology does pose a novel cause for it by challenging a longstanding feature of the Church's thought regarding man's relationship with suffering and death: the ancient tenet that both are present in our lives only as the result of the Fall. Instead of jettisoning the doctrine of original sin on the one hand or discounting evolutionary science on the other, Ratzinger

---

24. Ratzinger, *Gottes Projekt*, 72 (my translation, emphasis added). Ratzinger's idea is moreover that we find our identity in Christ—and thereby the truth of the Catholic faith—only by *living* the faith of the Church. For a full exploration of this theme, see Ramage, *The Experiment of Faith*.

25. "To receive [the Eucharist] means, precisely, to enter into the dynamic of the transformation of Adam's story. To eat of the tree of life means to receive the crucified Lord, his form of life, his obedience and his obedience to being, to creation and to the Creator." Ratzinger, *Gottes Projekt*, 92 (my translation).

26 For more on the usage of this verb in the Septuagint for the consecration of priests, see William Lane, *Hebrews 1–8*, Word Biblical Commentary, vol. 47A (Dallas: Word, Incorporated, 1991), 122.

27. For a discussion of this point within Ratzinger's commentary on *Gaudium et Spes*, see Ratzinger, "The Dignity of the Human Person," 115–64, at 118–19 and remarks on the text in Emery de Gaál, *The Christocentric Shift*, 107–108. As de Gaál observes, one criticism that Ratzinger levels at *Gaudium et Spes* is its failure to begin with revelation in Christ.

holds that evolutionary biology has much to contribute to our grasp of creation and sin by helping us get down to the essentials of the Church's teaching and rendering it "comprehensible again" to modern man.[28]

To understand Ratzinger's position on the relationship of sin, suffering, and death, perhaps the best place to begin is with his commentary on the Second Vatican Council which declined to add any nuance to the traditional teaching that man would have been immune from death had he not sinned. Regarding this text, Fr. Ratzinger—at the time a theological advisor (*peritus*) at the council—remarks that the authors of the document *Gaudium et Spes* were well aware of the various problems germane to this tradition. It is for this reason, he notes, that they rejected a number of proposals to discuss the specifics of the Fall and man's original condition.[29] Agreeing with the fathers' decision, Ratzinger nevertheless expresses regret that the council had punted on a major difficulty: namely, "[T]he thesis [that man would have been immune from death had he not sinned] in its classical dogmatic form is scarcely intelligible to present-day thought."[30] Having said this, he then makes a proposal: this teaching "could be made [intelligible] by means of an existential analysis of the constitutive features of human life which established a distinction between death as a natural phenomenon and death as seen in the personal categories proper to human life."[31]

What is death, then, if we approach it from an existential point of view? Here is Ratzinger's own attempt to provide the sort of existential analysis he suggests is necessary:

> It is only in moments in which man attains or thinks he attains authentic life, that he does not want to see pass away; in them, the inauthenticity of his ordinary life becomes palpable to him; in the light of such moments, it does not really seem like life at all. At the same time, of course, he realizes that an authentic life would have to be eternal and that the passing away of what is authentic is like a wound, a contradiction within himself. On the basis of this phenomenon of absurdity, shown above all in dread, as well as on that of the difference between authentic and inauthentic life, it would have been possible to make clearer the meaning of the statement which appears rather disconnected in the latter half of the article, to the effect that man would have been immune from bodily death if he had not sinned.[32]

---

28. Ratzinger, *Introduction to Christianity*, 239. This particular comment comes after a sustained reflection on the contributions of Teilhard de Chardin's evolutionary Christology: "One can safely say that here the tendency of Pauline Christology is in its essentials correctly grasped from the modern angle and rendered comprehensible again, even if the vocabulary employed is certainly rather too biological." As he does with any thinker, Ratzinger here appropriates whatever truth he can from de Chardin while remaining critical where necessary.

29. Ratzinger, "The Dignity of the Human Person," 141; Second Vatican Council, *Gaudium et Spes*, §18.

30. Ratzinger, "The Dignity of the Human Person," 141.

31. Ratzinger, "The Dignity of the Human Person," 141.

32. Ratzinger, "The Dignity of the Human Person," 141. For an application of this distinction between authentic and inauthentic life in view of what it is that makes us uniquely human and how we

When we familiarize ourselves with the entirety of his corpus on this question, it becomes clear that Ratzinger wants to avoid pigeonholing the doctrine of original sin into so close a connection with biological death that it contradicts what we know through modern science. His personalist, existential approach therefore endeavors to get down to the essence of what it is about death that troubles man: the misery of dread, absurdity, and rebellion.[33]

From there, Ratzinger sets out to explore how we might recast traditional teaching on the relationship between sin and death primarily as an existential rather than historical or chronological proposition. The inspiration for this connection is rooted in the New Testament: If you die with Christ, you gain everything. If you have everything but not Christ, you have nothing. If your life is authentic, it is true life. If it is inauthentic, it is not true life. This is the case regardless of whether man in his natural state would have died or not. Indeed, as we will discuss below in light of his kenotic Christology, Ratzinger seems to think that it would be all the more fitting—more in step with what we know about Jesus, the True Adam—were humans in fact always destined to biological death.

Professor Ratzinger had already spoken of the difficulties that evolution poses for a traditional understanding of the Fall's consequences in his 1964 Munster course on creation. At the outset of his lecture on this topic, he reaffirms the tradition in saying that there can be "no doubt" that the Bible points to "a very close relationship between sin and death" and that this connection is based upon a "massive scriptural foundation."[34] Notwithstanding the weight of this evidence, Ratzinger is well aware that a strict causal and temporal connection between human sin and the onset of our mortality is difficult to square with the scientific data we now have at our disposal. This knowledge, in conjunction with his understanding that the Adam narrative was written in the mythopoetic key that we discussed in Chapter 5, leads Ratzinger to insist:

> The purpose of the doctrine of the original state is not to recount a piece of empirical history (*empirischer Geschichte*) and thus to expand our knowledge of history into the prehistoric, but to express the difference between the God-willed meaning of the creature man and the historically existing being man.[35]

---

ought to go about living within our traditions even while confronting the inexorable need to adapt them, see James Madden, "Artificial Intelligence and Giving a Damn about It: The Anxiety of Not Being a Machine" (forthcoming). On the subject of authenticity in relation to taking responsibility for our traditions by adhering to them even while acknowledging the dread that they might fail and seeing the necessity of adapting them, see Mark Wrathall, "Between the Earth and the Sky: Heidegger on Life after the Death of God," in *Heidegger and Unconcealment: Truth, Language, and History* (New York: Cambridge University Press, 2010), 69–87 and Jonathan Lear, *Radical Hope: Ethics in the Face of Cultural Devastation* (Cambridge, MA: Harvard University Press, 2006).

33. Ratzinger, "The Dignity of the Human Person," 141.

34. Ratzinger, *Schöpfungslehre* (1964), 207.

35. Ratzinger, *Schöpfungslehre* (1964), 253; Sanz, "Joseph Ratzinger y la doctrina de la creación. Los apuntes de Münster de 1964 (y III)," 493n126.

Flowing from his view that Genesis does not yield empirical data surrounding the circumstances of man's first sin, Ratzinger argues that it does not inform us about the when and how of physical death's origin, either. For, when Paul speaks of death in Romans, Ratzinger explains, "[T]his does not mean physical death, but that death must have another meaning. It is about the state of separation from God."[36] At this point, we may now say that, for Ratzinger, the principal "death" that is man's problem is the fate of *spiritual death* that he refers to in his lectures as a "lack of salvation."[37]

Cardinal Luis Ladaria, whom Benedict would eventually appoint secretary of the Church's Congregation for the Doctrine of the Faith (CDF), understands the death that resulted from man's Fall much in the same way as Ratzinger. Indeed, before his appointment Ladaria wrote a monograph that departed from the traditional view that biological death came into human experience only after sin, judging further that the majority of Catholic theologians today hold this interpretation of magisterial teaching. While it should not be assumed that Ratzinger and Ladaria are making precisely the same overarching argument or would concur on every point in this arena, I find that following text accords with and adds further nuance to Ratzinger's argument:

> To understand the biblical notion of immortality we must bear in mind that death has a meaning in Scripture that goes beyond just biological. Death is the sign of the exclusion of the community from the covenant, of the sep-aration of the chosen people. 'Life,' on the other hand, means being in rela-tionship with God and having the possibility of praising Him, thus being in communion with the chosen people. . . . *To choose between life and death is to choose in favor of or against the covenant*. . . . We can say something similar about the Pauline conception of death; This is undoubtedly the fruit of sin. But the word 'death' is, for the Apostle, especially the estrangement of God that follows sin (cf. Rm 1:32; 6:16; 7:5; 8:6; 1 Cor 15:54–57). *On the contrary, physical death may be the means to get closer to Christ.*[38]

These lines confirm what we saw in the last chapter: granting that Paul seems to have assumed all physical death entered the world as a result of the first human sin, Ratzinger and his eventual successor (being appointed the office's Prefect in 2017) nevertheless concur that the Apostle's greatest concern did not lie in the details of physical death's origin. It lay, rather, in the greatest evil of all—spiritual death—and the proclamation of our inability to overcome it apart from the grace of Jesus Christ.

---

36. Ratzinger, *Schöpfungslehre* (1964), 208.

37. Ratzinger, *Schöpfungslehre* (1964), 210. While writing that original sin does "secondarily" result in physical death and thus not making the same overall argument as Ratzinger, Scott Hahn's com-mentary on Romans 5 in relation to spiritual death is also illuminating on this point. Hahn emphasizes that the core of Paul's teaching concerns the spiritual death that has plagued the human race from its beginnings, a tragedy that results in human life being incapable of transmitting divine life. See Hahn, *Romans*, 81–83.

38. Luis Ladaria, SJ, *Teología del pecado original y de la gracia: antropología teológica especial*, 2nd edition (Madrid: Biblioteca de Autores Cristianos, 2001), 45 (my translation).

In a 1981 homily, Cardinal Ratzinger would likewise interpret Adam and Eve's "death" as the existential state that results when they deny the truth of the limitations imposed on them by virtue of their creaturely existence:

> They are living in untruth and in unreality. Their lives are mere appearance. They stand under the sway of death. We who are surrounded by a world of untruths, of unlife, know how strong the sway of death is, which even negates life itself and makes it a kind of death.[39]

In a 1985 conference, the then-cardinal similarly rejected the notion that Adam and Eve's death was physical in nature and argued that it is rather better understood as a "surrender to the rule and power of death."[40] In other words, by disobeying God and flaunting our own freedom, we paradoxically become *less* free, setting ourselves against the truth of things and thereby following a logic that draws us into the "region of death, of non-truth, of non-being."[41] Or, as Benedict interpreted Genesis 3 in his first papal homily on the Immaculate Conception, the "image" or "metaphor" of the Fall reveals that man "sets his sights on power, with which he desires to take his own life autonomously . . . trusts in deceit rather than in truth and thereby sinks with his life into emptiness, into death."[42]

All this is to say that, for the emeritus pontiff, Genesis's Fall narrative is not primarily concerned with man's bodily death but rather with death of a worse kind—what the Book of Proverbs refers to as "folly." As in Genesis 3 the folly of disobedience (following the serpent's "wisdom") leads to the "death" of Adam and Eve, in this text a life of folly is said to bring death, while its opposites *wisdom* and *fear of the Lord* lead to life (Prv 10:27; 14:27; Wis 9:10). In the garden of Genesis, life was to be attained through fear of the Lord manifested in observance of God's command. In Proverbs, meanwhile, personified *wisdom itself* is the tree of life: "She is a *tree of life* to those who lay hold of her; those who hold her fast are called happy" (Prv 3:18). Given the overt wisdom language in Genesis's narrative of the Fall and that the tree of life appears only in these two books within the Old Testament, the connection can hardly be incidental. It is a signal that the story in question is not primarily about events that transpired at least two hundred thousand years ago in human prehistory, but rather about the nature of human flourishing as such. The "death" in question in both Genesis and Proverbs is existential in nature—what Jesus refers to as destruction of the soul (cf. Mt 10:28). Meanwhile, from this New Testament perspective, the tree of life is ultimately none other than the Cross of Christ (Rv 2:7; 22:2,14,19), who through his flesh has given us a share in his deity.[43]

---

39. Ratzinger, *In the Beginning*, 71 [*Im Anfang schuf Gott*, 55].

40. Ratzinger, *Gottes Projekt*, 83–84.

41. Ratzinger, *Gottes Projekt*, 84. For a discussion of this "logic of death," see Tanzella-Nitti, "Il coraggio dell'Intellectus fidei," 7–29.

42. Benedict XVI, Homily (December 8, 2005).

43. Such is a common patristic interpretation of Revelation 22:2, where in the New Creation the tree of life reappears, "with its twelve kinds of fruit, yielding its fruit each month; and the leaves of the

## THE CAUSE(S) OF SUFFERING AND DEATH
## IN THE NATURAL WORLD

As we have seen, Ratzinger does not believe that providing empirical, historical data about events from hundreds of thousands of years ago falls within the purview of Genesis's creation narrative. This hermeneutical stance, informed by our modern knowledge of evolutionary history and advances in biblical scholarship on the original purpose of the creation narratives within their Israelite context, paints a picture of man who was never intended to live indefinitely on this planet and for whom the problem of "death" lies above all in its existential dimension rather than the fact that all our physical lives must eventually reach a terminus.

Ratzinger's emphasis on Jesus as the exemplary man goes hand in hand with his view that the root rationale for human suffering and death is something other than sin: namely, that these trials play an indispensable role in conforming our lives with that of Christ crucified and risen. In other words, we might say that, for Ratzinger, the structure of creation and of our finite creaturely existence within it is and always was intended to be cruciform (cross-shaped) or paschal (structured according to the pattern of the suffering, Death, and Resurrection of Christ—the Lamb who was slain before the foundation of the world (Rv 13:8).[44]

That is to say, to affirm that creation has a cruciform or paschal structure is to rejoice in God having modeled creation after the Incarnation, with all the suffering (and consequent glory) that it entails. Taking Christ's *kenosis* through his incarnation and Paschal Mystery as the key to interpreting reality as such, it stands to reason that the experience of redemptive suffering that characterized the Final Adam's entire earthly existence is constitutive of the human vocation.

Some of Ratzinger's comments on this subject can be interpreted either along the above lines or in a very traditional manner, in which death and suffering only exist because of sin. Consider this text:

> The way human life is, implanted in a world where death is the condition of life, birth is always ambivalent, simultaneously a dying and a becoming. The words of judgment in Genesis 3:16 describe exactly this fate of man, and the ambiguity of the figure of Eve expresses the ambiguity of biological

---

tree were for the healing of the nations." For English translations of instances from Tyconius, Apringius of Beja, Andrew of Caesarea, Oecumenius, and more, see William Weinrich, ed., *Revelation*, Ancient Christian Commentary on Scripture (Downers Grove, IL: InterVarsity Press, 2005), 22–23, 388–391, 402–403.

44. There are two principal ways to translate Revelation 13:8 (identifying either the writing of believers' names or, alternatively, the death of the Lamb as occurring before the creation of the world), but a traditional one is to see it in reference to the sacrifice of Christ as an act decreed in the counsels of eternity. Thus, the Vulgate renders the verse adorabunt eum omnes qui inhabitant terram quorum non sunt scripta nomina in libro vitae *agni qui occisus est ab origine mundi*. For commentary, see for example Robert Mounce, *The Book of Revelation* (Grand Rapids, MI: Eerdmans, 1997), 252.

becoming: birth is part of death, it happens under the sign of death and points to the death that it in a certain sense anticipates, prepares, and also presupposes. To give birth to life always signifies at the same time to open oneself to death.[45]

Based on this text taken on its own, one might infer that Ratzinger views death as essential to life only in *this* world—that is to say, in a postlapsarian (i.e., fallen) one. And, to be sure, he has not closed the door on this traditional conviction.

Having said that, Ratzinger's many other texts on this matter make his mind clearly known. For instance, in his 1985 Carinthian lectures, he read our Lord's words in John 12:24 as teaching that not just man but the entire cosmos has a kenotic or cruciform structure: "Truly, truly, I say to you, unless a grain of wheat falls into the earth and dies, it remains alone; but if it dies, it bears much fruit." Ratzinger understands this dynamic to be a fundamental law of creation, whereby the suffering and death of organisms ultimately makes possible the rebirth and flourishing of life: "[T]he paschal mystery, the mystery of the dying grain of wheat appears before us already among the ideas of creation. Man must become with Christ a grain of dead wheat, to truly rise again and truly be lifted up, to truly be himself. Only then does he attain his real goal."[46] In the words of C.S. Lewis, the reality that one must lose his life to save it, that a seed must die to live, is "the ultimate law."[47]

This cosmic vision traces all the way back to Ratzinger's time in the academy. Indeed, Professor Ratzinger's lecture notes—while early, unpublished, and thus not guaranteed to represent his definitive position—contain his most strongly-worded statements to the effect that the world itself has a cruciform shape. Specifically, Ratzinger's teachings from his 1964 course on creation illustrate this conviction. For instance, noting that the fate of death is not a special destiny of sinful man, he remarks that "the whole creation bears the stamp (*Prägeform*) of the mystery of death."[48] Later in the course, he teaches that suffering and death are the "foundational principles (*Grundprinzipien*) upon which the whole interplay of the world is built" and "are not peripheral, but belong to the structuring principles (*Bauprinzipien*) of the world"—to which he adds the powerful claim that "whoever wanted to take that away would dissolve the world

---

45. Ratzinger, *Daughter Zion*, 77 [*Die Tochter Zion*, 77].

46. Ratzinger, *Gottes Projekt*, 63 (my translation).

47. Lewis, *The Problem of Pain*, 154. Cast in Old Testament language, one might perhaps say that to be adopted as a child of God and brother of Jesus Christ is to be chosen or "elected" by God to die. For more on this point, see Anderson, *The Genesis of Perfection*, 29–30.

The BioLogos foundation captures this dynamic well in its article "Did Death Occur before the Fall?" from May 18, 2020: "Jesus thus pointed to the role of death in a healthy ecosystem as a parable for the importance of His own death. Just as the death of an organism allows for the rebirth and flourishing of life, so the death of Jesus leads to a rebirth and new life for Jesus' followers. Perhaps the biological death in the evolutionary epic was not a purposeless waste, but a hint at the way God redeems the negativity of death for the sake of new life." https:// biologos.org/common-questions/did-death-occur-before-the-fall/.

48. Ratzinger, *Schöpfungslehre* (1964), 211.

as such."⁴⁹ In the end, Professor Ratzinger thus concludes that all the evidence
we have at our disposal today (e.g., from modern biblical studies and evolutionary biology) "makes it impossible to uphold the said teaching (i.e., original sin)
*in the usual way.*"⁵⁰ The emphasis in this last citation is mine, so as it make it
clear that Ratzinger is not denying the doctrine of original sin, but rather questioning common *interpretations* of it.

## WHY THERE IS A "LAW OF BRUTALITY" IN NATURE

The emeritus pontiff does not pretend that his *aggiornamento* of the tradition that
we are outlining here definitively resolves all problems related to the subject of faith
and evolution. Indeed, even with an understanding that the very fabric of the
cosmos is paschal, this humble theological giant still considers the "law of brutality"
or the "riddle of the terrible element in nature" ("Nature, red in tooth and claw," as
Tennyson's poetry has it) to be "one of the great riddles of creation."⁵¹ At a conference on faith and evolution, Pope Benedict expanded upon this point:

> Despite the rationality that exists, we can observe a component of terror,
> which cannot be further analyzed philosophically. Here philosophy calls for
> something more, and faith shows us the Logos, who is creative reason and
> who incredibly at the same time was able to become flesh, to die and to rise
> again. With that, a completely different face of the Logos is manifested from
> what we can manage to glimpse on the basis of a groping reconstruction of
> the fundamental reasons for nature.⁵²

I find this passage noteworthy; for, while not employing the precise word, the then-
pontiff suggests that the fundamental structure of the universe—its rational
nature—is at the same time a cruciform one. As we discussed in Chapter 2, Jesus
Christ's Death and Resurrection reveal that *logos* is *agape*—that "true reason is love,
and love is true reason."⁵³ Because we know the Trinitarian mystery that love and
reason together structure reality and that the dying grain will ultimately rise, we as
Christians also believe that none of the terrible suffering and death in the created
world is ultimately a waste. To return to the analogy of creation as a symphony,
Ratzinger invites us to see the sufferings of this world less along the lines of absolute
evils and more as variations upon a musical theme—as temporary *dissonance* or
*minor chords* that contribute to the overall beauty of God's perfect symphony.⁵⁴

---

49. Ratzinger, *Schöpfungslehre* (1964), 215. Other statements along these same lines could be
adduced. For example: "[T]he world is constructed as a world of death (*die Welt als todeswelt konstruiert
ist*)." Ratzinger, *Schöpfungslehre*, 215.
50. Ratzinger, *Schöpfungslehre* (1964), 215.
51. Ratzinger, *God and the World*, 79; Benedict, *Creation and Evolution*, 115.
52. Benedict, *Creation and Evolution*, 115–16.
53. Ratzinger, *Truth and Tolerance*, 183.
54. O'Brien, *Evolution and Religion*, 10. Already in 1932, John O'Brien had likewise used the
analogy of a symphony to explain why so many species have existed, suffered, and died throughout

In connection with the problem of the "terrible element" in nature that Ratzinger addressed above, it also helpful to bring in some Thomistic insights on the
presence of suffering throughout the history of life on this planet. Asking why God
chose to work via an evolutionary process rather than through special direct creation, Nicanor Austriaco thus argues that the evolutionary dynamic with all the suffering it entails is fitting in that it better reveals the divine glory and power better
than a direct creation of species would have. This is because the diversity of creatures that have graced our planet over the course of evolutionary history (four billion species over a three-billion-year period, compared with the eight million extant
species today) have all manifested God's perfection in unique and unrepeatable
ways. Offering an analogy to illustrate why extinct species are not pointless waste
as God prepared the way for man over billions of years of evolutionary history,
Austriaco writes:

> [N]o one thinks that Michelangelo 'wasted' marble because there were leftover
> marble pieces after he had completed sculpting his masterpiece, *David*. There
> is no waste when the agent fittingly attains his end. Likewise, I propose that
> extinct species are not pointless waste. Rather, they were the necessary 'left-
> overs' from the creative evolutionary process that God used to generate the
> novel and diverse forms of life visible today in a manner most fitting to reveal
> his glory.[55]

I might add that the myriad beings that God has created through evolution over
across the ages not only manifest God's glory as such—they also reveal it to *us*. The
joy of children learning about dinosaurs comes to mind. As a father of six children,
moreover, I have enjoyed rekindling my sense of discovery and awe when it comes
to these creatures who dominated our planet for millions of years. The same goes
for fish, reptiles, trilobites, and even bacteria who had their turns as dominant life-
forms. In our home, we have a fossil cabinet with all manner of specimens, from
mosasaur vertebrae to dinosaur dung to a 5-inch megalodon tooth. I find it good
for my soul to stop every once in a while, pull out a 400-million-year-old trilobite,
and marvel at three things: that so many species have come and gone on our planet
to pave the way for us, that we now know this in the first place, and that we can
even hold this history our hands!

Beyond this aspect of evolution as a revelation of God's glory, Austriaco also
makes an important point regarding the impracticality of a direct creation of so

---

evolutionary history. "Major or minor departures from the ideally generalized condition," he writes,
"remind one of the variations upon a theme in music: no matter how elaborate the variation may be,
the skilled musician recognizes the common theme running through it all." In light of what we now
know about DNA as the common language of all life on our planet, we might thereby see the myriad
creatures that have inhabited our world as so many variations upon a common theme, each of which
manifests a unique quality that no other can.

55. Austriaco, *Thomistic Evolution*, 146–47. For a fuller argument on the fittingness of evolution
as opposed to the direct creation of species, see Austriaco, "A Theological Fittingness Argument for the
Evolution of *Homo Sapiens*," *Theology and Science* 17:4: 539–50.

many species at the same time. This would have been unfeasible in any case, he notes, for "it would have been ecologically impossible for all four billion species to coexist on our planet, because there is only a limited number of ecological niches on the planet at any given moment in time."[56] Beyond the question of where all these animals would have lived and how they would all have enough food to survive simultaneously, just imagine how implausible it would be for the Asian elephant or *Homo sapiens* to fare very well with *Tyrannosaurus rex* haunting the streets!

Related to this point, one might wonder whether God could have simply created a world in which animals would not kill and eat one another. To this question, Charles de Koninck writes that in doing so God would have done violence to the integrity of the natural world that he created: "The maintenance of life is accomplished thanks to death. It is necessary for the animal to be nourished by organic substances. The biosphere eats itself in order to grow; it must destroy itself to the degree that it enriches itself. Tragedy is essential to cosmic life."[57] Try to imagine where lightning strikes but does not kill trees, volcanos do not destroy forests, and vultures do not feed on carrion.

This last thought is not novel in our evolutionary age. The patristic witness of Augustine on death's integral role in the universe is also evocative:

> It is, in fact, the very law of transitory things that, here on earth where such things are at home, some should be born while others die, the weak should give way to the strong and the victims should nourish the life of the victors. If the beauty of this order fails to delight us, it is because we ourselves, by reason of our mortality, are so enmeshed in this corner of the cosmos that we fail to perceive the beauty of a total pattern in which the particular parts, which seem ugly to us, blend in so harmonious and beautiful a way. . . . It is not by our comfort or inconvenience, but by nature considered in itself, that glory is given to its Creator.[58]

Like Augustine, Thomas Aquinas has also much to offer by way of understanding the presence of suffering in the world at large. Contrary to what some Christians today assume, Thomas insists that the nature of animals was unchanged by man's sin. Although they posed no threat to us, he acknowledges that a natural antipathy between certain animals has always existed, and he recognizes the presence of non-human death before the Fall. Lions, then, were never herbivores.[59] Indeed, Thomas offers the lion's predatory nature as an illustration that "God and nature and any other agent make what is best in the whole, but not what is best in every single part,

---

56. Austriaco, *Thomistic Evolution*, 146.

57. Charles de Koninck, *The Cosmos*, 301. For a helpful overview of de Koninck's work, see Thomas Hibbs, "A Place in the Cosmos," *First Things* (February 2009).

58. Augustine, *The City of God, Books VIII–XVI*, ed. Hermigild Dressler, trans. Gerald G. Walsh and Daniel J. Honan, vol. 14, *The Fathers of the Church* (Washington, D.C.: The Catholic University of America Press, 1952), 252.

59. Aquinas, *ST* I, q. 96, a. 1 ad 2.

except in order to the whole, as was said above." The reason for this, he explains, is that "many good things would be taken away if God permitted no evil to exist."[60] Accordingly, Thomas observes that "fire would not be generated if air was not corrupted, nor would the life of a lion be preserved unless the ass were killed."[61] Summarizing the Angelic Doctor's perspective on this matter, Nicanor Austriaco emphasizes the respect Aquinas had for the integrity of nature and adds, "For Aquinas—correctly in my view—a lion that eats grass is not and cannot be a lion. It is something else. A falcon that eats berries is not and cannot be a falcon. It is something else. Sin can deform and disorder nature, but it cannot radically undermine and transform it."[62]

Although Aquinas does not deploy the image of the dying and rising grain of wheat that Ratzinger will to make this point, one can see important common ground between these two thinkers who are convinced that God has always allowed natural evils—even death from the very beginning of creation—in order to bring about greater good. In this regard, I find the following passage of Aquinas illumines this point well:

> Corruption and defects in natural things are said to be contrary to some particular nature; yet they are in keeping with the plan of universal nature; inasmuch as the defect in one thing yields to the good of another, or even to the universal good. . . . Since God, then, provides universally for all being, it belongs to His providence to permit certain defects in particular effects, that the perfect good of the universe may not be hindered, for if all evil were prevented, much good would be absent from the universe.[63]

The Angelic Doctor's great respect for the nature of things evinced here, combined with his openness to respectfully emending the tradition when necessary, makes one suspect that—had he known of their existence—Thomas may well have contended that our hominin ancestors too had died.

As a final word on this point, it is noteworthy that St. John Paul II echoed the above Thomistic approach in his writing, arguing that corruption and death are natural to this world and that they ultimately serve a greater good:

> As for the permitting of evil in the physical order, for example in the face of the fact that material beings (among them also the human body) are corruptible and subject to death, it must be said that it belongs to the very structure [*stessa struttura*] of these creatures' being. On the other hand, the unlimited existence of every individual corporeal being would be hardly conceivable in the present state of the material world. We can thus understand that, if 'God did not create death,' as the Book of Wisdom states [Wis 1:13], he nevertheless permits it, in

---

60. Aquinas, *ST* I, q. 48, a. 2 ad 3.
61. Aquinas, *ST* I, q. 48, a. 2 ad 3.
62. Austriaco, "A Theological Fittingness Argument for the Evolution of *Homo Sapiens*," 545.
63. Aquinas, *ST* I, q.22, a. 2. See also Aquinas, *ST*, I, q.19, a. 6 on how "that which seems to depart from the divine will in one order, returns into it in another order."

view of the global good of the material cosmos. But if it is a question of *moral evil*—that is, of sin and guilt in their different forms and consequences even in the physical order—this evil God definitely and absolutely does not will.[64]

## THE NATURAL PRESENCE OF SUFFERING AND DESIRE IN HUMAN LIFE AND THE NATURALNESS OF ORDERING THEM ACCORDING TO REASON

So much for the presence of suffering and death in the world, but what about in man? As we now know that suffering and death have been integral ingredients in the evolutionary dynamic for billions of years, Ratzinger cautions against insisting that human beings were initially exempt from this experience. In sections of his course dedicated to the preternatural gifts of immortality and impassibility, we thus read that the Church's teaching "does not include the thesis that there was no earthly death without sin."[65]

Elucidating this position in great detail, he then applies it also to the inevitability that humans in this life will always suffer in connection with their physical needs and desires. In the following citations, Ratzinger refers to these under the banner of "concupiscence," which is a word with multiple connotations but here simply denotes those morally neutral evolved desires that incline us bodily creatures toward survival. This term, which has a history in the tradition of being used in this way, should *not* be conflated with the common use of the word that refers to the *disordered* desires that we have thanks to original sin.[66] With that clarification in mind, Ratzinger says of our concupiscible desires:

---

64. John Paul II, General Audience (June 4, 1986). http://www.vatican.va/content/john-paul-ii/it/audiences/1986/documents/hf_jp-ii_aud_19860604.html (my translation).

65. Ratzinger, *Schöpfungslehre* (1964), 208.

66. Ratzinger, *Schöpfungslehre* (1964), 217. While not making precisely the same overarching argument as Ratzinger, Nicholas Lombardo explains this meaning of the term well in noting that it can be used both in a neutral way to denote desire and in a more technical theological sense in reference to sinful desire. See Lombardo, "Evil, Suffering, and Original Sin," 145. For a recent distinction between concupiscence in the sense deployed by Ratzinger (which he calls the "weak" sense of the term meaning man's "temptability"—as understood by Anselm) as distinct from the "strong sense" (as being intrinsically sinful—as understood by Augustine), see Houck, "Toward a New Account of the Fall," 2, 13. Noting that concupiscence is a notoriously polysemous term, Houck adds, "Concupiscence in the weak sense of 'temptability' is not sinful, and neither are the internal temptations that arise from it." Houck, "Toward a New Account of the Fall," 15–16.

Further insight into Ratzinger's linkage of concupiscence with our instinctual desires may be found in the work of Luis Ladaria, prefect of the CDF whom Benedict had previously appointed secretary of that congregation. Ladaria endeavors to show that even the Council of Trent and Pius V recognized that, in addition to its negative side that inclines us to sin, there is a certain "positive" dimension of concupiscence (*una visión hasta cierto punto "positiva" de la concupiscencia*). Ladaria holds that we may speak of a "non-strictly sinful nature of concupiscence" insofar as our desires serve to stimulate us toward victory against evil. Ladaria, *Teología del pecado original y de la gracia*, 48 (my translation). In other words, concupiscence is "not only the desire for evil, but rather every appetitive, undeliberated act that precedes the free decision of man . . . the spontaneous appetite of one good or

Concupiscence is simply part of man's essence (*Wesen des Menschen*) and cannot be taken out without abolishing the whole human being. . . . [It is] an essential constitutive element of the human being. . . . Instinctual desire (*Trieb*) . . . belongs essentially (*wesentlich*) to the constitution of man.[67]

He then applies this understanding of desire to pain and even death, noting: "What applies to desire (*Trieb*) also applies to pain, (*Schmerz*), to the presence of death in our lives. As man is built, pain and suffering are a necessary component (*notwendiges Konstitutiv*) of his physical existence."[68] While it is commonly held that death is a consequence of the Fall, in Ratzinger's view it is "as unavoidable as the suffering from the world."[69]

Following these statements, Ratzinger proceeds to explain that our inevitable desires and the suffering that attends them can lead both to good and to bad—drawing us out of ourselves or isolating us more deeply in our own self-constructed prison—depending on what we decide to do with them.[70] This is the same today for us as it was for the first man, Ratzinger argues: "The freedom of the drive to run ahead, and thus the possibility of getting lost, is integrated into the essential structure of man."[71] In a move that is especially apropos for this book, it is noteworthy that Ratzinger draws on evolutionary science and its knowledge of our hominin ancestry to explain why it is that all humans have these desires and experience suffering. According to Fr. Ratzinger, it is "certain that mankind began with decidedly animal-like forms (*theromorphen Formen*), and that he was very powerfully influenced by the animal."[72] In his view, then, concupiscence is simply "an extension of the conditions we have in common with animals,"[73] an observation that leads him to conclude:

---

another." Ladaria, *Teología del pecado original y de la gracia*, 49 (my translation). Aquinas too acknowledges the difference between concupiscence as a craving for bodily pleasure in itself and the disorder we experience when this appetite rebels against reason. On the passion of concupiscence itself, see Aquinas, *ST* I-II, q. 30, aa. 1–4

67. Ratzinger, *Schöpfungslehre* (1964), 217.

68. Ratzinger, *Schöpfungslehre* (1964), 216, 218.

69. Ratzinger, *Schöpfungslehre* (1964), 216.

70. Ratzinger, *Schöpfungslehre* (1964), 218. Recent discoveries in evolutionary psychology confirm Ratzinger's understanding of the ambivalent nature of many features of our species. As William von Hippel explains, man's uniquely cooperative, relational nature and our vicious propensity to tribalism are opposite sides of the same evolutionary coin, and much is determined by how we respond in situations where group dynamics are at play. See von Hippel, *The Social Leap*, 186–208. Addressing this subject from sociological perspective, René Girard writes that the mimetic desire inherent to human nature is ambivalent in its own right, and what matters morally is what we do with it: "It [mimetic desire] is responsible for the best and the worst in us, for what lowers us below the animal level as well as what elevates us above it. Our unending discords are the ransom of our freedom." Girard, *I See Satan Fall Like Lightning*, 6.

71. Ratzinger, *Schöpfungslehre* (1964), 218.

72. Ratzinger, *Schöpfungslehre* (1964), 213.

73. Ratzinger, *Schöpfungslehre* (1964), 217.

From today's insight into man, we can no longer accept concupiscence as a deviation, but as an inescapable part (*unaufhebbaren Teil*) of the ... underlying constitution of human nature, which of course essentially includes danger. . . . The cosmos would bring pain and death to man even if they were not continually rising from within himself.[74]

This recognition of our species' continuity with our protohuman ancestors leads Ratzinger to ask the key question: can a paradisiacal state be reconciled with an account of man's gradual evolutionary origins? In response, he acknowledges that, according to the scientific data, "There appears to be a direct line between our species and our immediate precursors who were savage creatures (*grausame wesen*). It is therefore not quite clear where one would insert an intermediate paradisiacal state."[75]

That said, Ratzinger's conviction that Eden as traditionally envisioned never existed is not to say that human beings were created sinful or that their concupiscible passions already had the character of fallen desires. I understand Ratzinger to be suggesting here that humans from the beginning, though not sinful, nevertheless likely experienced the temptation to excess in their natural drives (e.g., to lust, gluttony, aggression, etc.). Indeed, we find such behavior—which we rightly consider sinful among humans—in the other extant primate species that are the most closely related to us. As Christopher Baglow helpfully observes, man's *inclination* toward these actions is not in itself sinful provided it is properly directed by reason, a point he makes in a passage that deserves to be cited at some length:

In summary, we receive ambiguous inclinations from our evolutionary inheritance that are not yet moral or immoral, but can become so through our own free choices. The very things that lead us toward bonding and generosity, or toward self-defense and the defense of the innocent, can also tempt us to mistrust, suspicion, and even unjust acts of violence. . . . We find the pursuit of bodily pleasures, aggression, killing, and death among animals for hundreds of millions of years before humans came along.

But when we find these inclinations among humans, we do not know whether or not they are sinful until we ask, "To what kind of free choice— expressed in thought, word, or deed—is this inclination leading me?" As long as they are oriented toward choosing what is truly good, then they are good; the same inclinations that are involved in adultery and murder are also involved in true sexual love and in daring acts of heroism, respectively. And yet, these ambiguous inclinations also reveal that our evolutionary inheritance alone is not sufficient for us to be the virtuous, loving, and sinless human beings God created us to be. As our Catholic tradition tells us, God had more to provide for us.[76]

Telford Work is another thinker who has spoken eloquently on this point, acknowledging that many of the passions our tradition has tended to associate with the fall

---

74. Ratzinger, *Schöpfungslehre* (1964), 218.
75. Ratzinger, *Schöpfungslehre* (1964), 214.
76. Baglow, *Faith, Science, & Reason*, 263.

may be understood as quite natural from an evolutionary perspective and do not "simply follow wholesale from our fall from grace."[77] As Work observes, it is not difficult to see how prehuman struggles would have encouraged and shaped our appetites and self-interest, for we perceive these in other animals all the time—especially in those species that are our closest relatives. Given that some Christian authors may have gone overboard in attributing our passions to the Fall, Work nevertheless emphasizes that their moral advice regarding how to master our passions remains sound. In other words, the essential point behind Scripture's dealings with our disordered passions is not to provide a scientific account of how they arose but rather to offer a response to the question of *what we should do with them.*[78]

All the above is to say that man's concupiscible desires are not intrinsically sinful, because something else belongs to our human nature that all our evolutionary relatives lacked: the rational soul with its uniquely human capacity to do something with them that is not merely instinctual. As a rational and relational animal, it is *eminently natural for man to master his desires,* ordering them to reason so as to live in communion with God and others. In doing precisely this, our first parents experienced true human passions from the beginning, and yet, as Aquinas says, they were free from the passions of sorrow, guilt, unhappiness [*dolor, culpa, miseria*], and affliction [*affligio*] that attended any difficulties they faced.[79] Likewise, having not yet sinned, the Angelic Doctor indicates that they would have been free from the "four wounds" of original sin: weakness, ignorance, malice, and concupiscence.[80] As Daniel Houck explains in an account of the Fall that draws on insights from Aquinas and Anselm, mankind's first parents were endowed with "evolutionarily derived impulses to sin" yet were also created in the state of *original justice,* a

---

77. Telford Work, *Jesus—the End and the Beginning* (Grand Rapids, MI: Baker Publishing Group, 2019), 84. Illuminating the uniqueness and continuity of the human brain in comparison with that of our ancestors, Kenneth Miller, writes, "The circuitry of the brain is in fact a poorly integrated mixture of the truly ancient, the very odd, and the relatively new all working side-by-side." Miller, *The Human Instinct: How We Evolved to Have Reason, Consciousness, and Free Will* (New York: Simon & Schuster, 2018), 131. "Evolutionary history may dictate the pleasures, anxieties, and prejudices of our minds, but we, distinct from other creatures, have discovered that history." Miller, *The Human Instinct,* 145. On the naturalness of ordering our human desires to reason, see also Aquinas, *On Evil,* q. 4, a. 2, ad 1, 1. Aquinas adds, "Things that do not belong to the praise of higher beings can be praiseworthy in lower beings. For example, ferociousness is praiseworthy in dogs but not in human beings." Aquinas, *On Evil,* q. 3, a. 1, ad 10. In short, "[I]t belongs to the human good that the whole composite as such be subject to virtue." Aquinas, *On Evil,* q. 12, a. 1, resp.

78. Telford Work, *Jesus—the End and the Beginning,* 85.

79. For a more in-depth treatment of Aquinas on this point and on the relationship between the First and Last Adam in Scripture, see Ramage, "Putting the Last Adam First: Aquinas, Ratzinger, and Human Origins in Light of Kenotic Christology," in *Aquinas and the Crisis of Christology* (forthcoming from Sapientia Press). Aquinas contends that Adam and Eve experienced all of those passions "that casteth not down" (*non affligens*)—those involving the present good (e.g., joy and love) and those which regard future good to be had at the proper time (desire and hope). Aquinas, *ST* I, q. 95, a. 2. At the same time, he holds that "sorrow, guilt, and unhappiness are incompatible with the perfection of the primitive state" (*perfectioni enim primi status repugnat tam dolor, quam culpa et miseria*). Aquinas, *ST* I, q. 95, a. 2.

80. See Aquinas, *ST* I-II q. 85, a. 3; q. 109, a. 9.

habit by which their desires were subjected to God, and were given the gift of *sanctifying grace* that enabled them to love God above all things and to love all things in God.[81] Noting that "[i]t seems strange to say that God spent hundreds of millions of years guiding the evolution of nonhuman animals in preparation for the human animal, only to supernaturally negate the tendencies the latter would have naturally inherited from the former," Houck proposes that our species' evolutionary heritage can be seen as a boon. For, while Houck does not indicate that he considers suffering and death to be compatible with original sinlessness as Ratzinger does, he does grant that certain imperfections are compatible with this state and that consequently "one can think of the evolutionarily derived impulses to sin as opportunities for the formation of virtue, opportunities to defeat evil."[82]

## TWO REASONS WE SUFFER

While Ratzinger the academic sees desire, suffering, and death as constitutive experiences of the graced condition of human nature in which we were created, it is perhaps even more telling that Benedict XVI continued to write along these lines and add dimensions to his thought throughout his tenure as Supreme Pontiff. In his encyclical *Spe Salvi*, Benedict thus distinguishes two reasons that suffering is present as part of human existence. On the one hand, it stems "partly from the mass of sin which has accumulated over the course of history." This evil trajectory, he adds, "continues to grow unabated today," a problem that "none of us is capable of eliminating." On the other hand, "Suffering stems partly from our finitude" that none of us is able to "shake off."[83] In other words, it seems that a certain pain inevitably results from being an imperfect creature modeled after the image of the Triune God and called to divinization while not yet having achieved it—a thought that C.S. Lewis expresses when he supposes that, even unfallen man probably had "a minimal self-adherence to be overcome," adding that this overcoming and yielding to God's will would have been "rapturous."[84]

Significantly, John Paul II appears to have shared Benedict's thought on this matter, remarking, "Suffering is certainly part of the mystery of man."[85] To this, he adds an interesting twist—that suffering stems from our finitude as well as from our *transcendence*:

[E]ven though man knows and is close to the sufferings of the animal world, nevertheless what we express by the word 'suffering' seems to be particularly

81. Houck, "Toward a New Account of the Fall," 10, 16–18.

82. Houck, "Toward a New Account of the Fall," 18.

83. Benedict XVI, *Spe Salvi*, §36. As is often the case, we can find Ratzinger making a similar point in his prepapal writings and lecture notes. Thus, we read in Ratzinger, *Schöpfungslehre* (1964), 210: "The fate of his suffering and death is given to man not only from the inside out of the limitations of his physical constitution, but also from the outside."

84. Lewis, *The Problem of Pain*, 76.

85. John Paul II, *Salvifici Doloris*, §31.

*essential to the nature of man. . . .* Suffering seems to belong to man's transcendence: it is one of those points in which man is in a certain sense 'destined' to go beyond himself, and he is called to this in a mysterious way. . . . [I]n whatever form, suffering seems to be, and is, almost inseparable from man's earthly existence.[86]

After making this claim, the saint proceeds to expound upon the benefits of suffering, such as its role in eliciting compassion and respect on behalf of others and that it may "serve *for conversion*, that is, *for the rebuilding of goodness* in the subject, who can recognize the divine mercy in this call to repentance."[87] In brief, according to John Paul, "suffering is present in the world in order to release love . . . in order to transform the whole of human civilization into a 'civilization of love.'"[88]

Earlier, Professor Ratzinger had emphasized that not only suffering but trials and temptations of all sorts to the mere fact that we are finite creatures:

> The creature cannot be created from scratch in the finished state of perfection. . . . [God] could not have created a creature that would have come to perfection without testing, without *teleiosis*. Testing is not arbitrary, is not imposed from the outside, but belongs to the nature (*Wesen*) of the created spirit. It goes through the test by nature.[89]

From statements like these, it appears that Ratzinger considers trials to be constitutive of the human experience on this side of eternity, sufferings that are further

---

86. John Paul II, *Salvifici Doloris*, §2 (emphasis in original).

87. John Paul II, *Salvifici Doloris*, §§3, 12. Benedict writes similarly, "Although human beings are weak and frail, [suffering] 'teaches' them a sense of creatureliness and humility, protecting them from pride and arrogance." Benedict XVI, Apostolic Letter Proclaiming Saint Hildegard of Bingen a Doctor of the Universal Church (October 7, 2012). Phillip Rolnick speaks well to the fittingness of man's creaturely struggles when he says, "By providing humanity with a reasonably difficult setting, an evolutionary creation may not be what we want, but it may be exactly what need, a training in meeting the demands of reality." Rolnick, *Origins: God, Evolution, and the Question of the Cosmos* (Waco, TX: Baylor University Press, 2015), 58.

88. John Paul II, *Salvifici Doloris*, §31. It is noteworthy that, while he held that human suffering and death emerged only after sin, Aquinas himself held that our struggles in this life are "suitable for spiritual training," in order that we may be fully conformed to Christ, receive the dignity of being his instrumental causes of our own redemption, and thereby "receive the crown of victory." Aquinas, *ST*, III q. 69, a. 3. Further, for Thomas, the reason that we do not immediately receive an immortal and impassible body immediately after baptism is "so that we might suffer along with Christ," for "if we suffer with him, we may also be glorified with him" (Rom 8:17). Aquinas, *Sup. Rom.* Ch. 8, lect. 3, no. 651. For my knowledge of these two passages, I am grateful to Daria Spezzano who has reflected on it in her forthcoming piece "You Prepared a Body for Me" (Heb 10:5): The Eschatological End of Evolution" to which I was privileged to offer a response at a Thomistic Evolution conference in November 2021.

89. Ratzinger, *Schöpfungslehre* (1958), 87; Sanz, "La dottrina della creazione nelle lezioni del professor Joseph Ratzinger: gli appunti di Freising (1958)," 30n4. Luis Ladaria ties this point into God's command to "subdue the earth" (Gn 1:28). Noting some of the problems that a traditional conception of the original state poses, he writes, "We cannot think of a world . . . which is offered to man without the need for him to exert his creative effort. . . . Already in Gn 2:15, work is a fundamental dimension of human existence. It does not seem to make sense to think that man in 'paradise' had had all his problems solved beforehand." Ladaria, *Teología del pecado original y de la gracia*, 51 (my translation).

exacerbated by the presence of original sin—the interior disorder and damaged network of relationships in which we all find ourselves inextricably enmeshed. As we have already seen, Benedict considers original sin to be primarily about the reality that none of us is able to choose the good perfectly and save ourselves—that we all stand in need of the remedy that can only be found in God's immeasurably precious gift of grace in Jesus Christ. In the context of this discussion, Benedict adds accordingly, "Only God is able to do this: only a God who personally enters history by making himself man and suffering within history."[90]

## EARTH WAS NEVER MEANT TO BE MAN'S FINAL DESTINATION

While suffering is inevitable in this vale of tears, believers look forward to that state in which God will wipe away every tear from our eyes, and death shall be no more (Rv 21:4). In *Spe Salvi*, we thus find Benedict acknowledging that, despite the fact that man does not want to die, "neither do we want to continue living indefinitely, nor was the earth created with that in view."[91] Indeed, in the then-pontiff's existential analysis of the human condition, "To continue living forever—endlessly—appears more like a curse than a gift" and "more of a burden than a blessing," as it would be "monotonous and ultimately unbearable."[92] To this, Benedict adds that another reason we would not wish to live forever in this sphere of existence has to do with bearing the burden of sin. Citing the homily St. Ambrose delivered for his brother's funeral, Benedict speaks of death as a mercy for man in his wretched state, a way of limiting the evils that can be inflicted upon him and, most importantly, a means to our salvation.[93]

Remarkably, already in the medieval period, Thomas Aquinas had already taught similarly in affirming that humans were never meant to live out their eternity on this planet. While many writers prior to Thomas had the notion that Adam and Eve would have lived on perpetually in an earthly Eden, this is not Aquinas's position. Instead, his is that man "was not placed from the beginning in [Heaven], but was destined to be transferred thither in the state of his final beatitude." Though framed in different language, the Angelic Doctor's reasoning is similar to that of Benedict. The need for such a "transfer," he explains, is that "[m]an was happy in paradise, but *not* with that perfect happiness to which he was destined, which consists in the vision of the Divine Essence."[94]

---

90. Benedict XVI, *Spe Salvi*, §36.

91. Benedict XVI, *Spe Salvi*, §11.

92. Benedict XVI, *Spe Salvi*, §10.

93. Benedict XVI, *Spe Salvi*, §10. See also Ambrose, "On the Death of Satyrus," in *Nicene and Post-Nicene Fathers, Second Series*, Vol. 10, eds. Philip Schaff and Henry Wace (Buffalo, NY: Christian Literature Publishing Co., 1896.), II, §§46–47.

94. Aquinas, *ST* I-II, q. 94, a. 1 ad 1; I-II, q. 102, a. 2 ad 1; q. 102, a. 4. Commenting upon Mt 22:20, he likewise writes that humans eventually *transferendi erant in statum gloriae ubi omnino generationis cessat*. Aquinas, *In II Sent.*, d. 20, q. 1 a. 1. See also Aquinas *In IV Sent.*, d. 20, q. 1 a. 5, qc. 4 expos, where he writes: *Christi non reducit ad illum Paradisum; sed ad caelestem.*

Noting that the common confusion people have here has to do with the broad semantic scope of the term "paradise," Piotr Roszak notes that the word has three basic meanings for Thomas: the terrestrial paradise of Eden, in which Adam was; the empyrean heavens where the stars reside; and, finally, heaven where the blessed enjoy the Beatific Vision.[95]

Whichever formulation one prefers, Aquinas and Benedict concur that even sinless man would never have been able to enjoy heavenly bliss in this world. Whether he would have died or not is a question on which these two thinkers seem to disagree. However, much progress is made simply by recognizing that all of us— sinless or not—eventually would have had to undergo a miraculous transformation at the end of our earthly life before we can see God face to face and at last know fully what we now know only in part (cf. 1 Cor 13:12).

## "THERE CAN BE NO LOVE WITHOUT SUFFERING"

Not only does Ratzinger consider suffering integral to our created universe and that heavenly bliss will never be a place on earth, remarkably, the emeritus pontiff goes so far as to insist that suffering and death are necessary for human flourishing in the world here below. So strongly does he hold this conviction that Professor Ratzinger said that one who has never endured suffering is not truly a person: "[A] person without suffering in the world in which we live would be a monster and impossible. . . . Suffering and death are essential to the structure of things" (*wesentlich zur Struktur der dinge*).[96] Along these lines, Ratzinger would later add in *Eschatology*: "Of course, suffering can and should be reduced. . . . But the will to do away with it completely would mean a ban on love and therewith the abolition of man.[97] In his interview *God and the World*, Cardinal Ratzinger spoke similarly while emphasizing the positive role that suffering plays in making us "more human":

> Pain is part of being human. Anyone who really wanted to get rid of suffering would have to get rid of love before anything else, because there can be no love [*Liebe*] without suffering [*Leiden*], because it always demands an element of self-sacrifice, because, given temperamental differences and the drama of situations, it will always bring with it renunciation and pain.
>
> When we know that the way of love—this exodus, this going out of one-self—is the true way by which man becomes human, then we also understand that suffering is the process through which we mature. Anyone who has inwardly accepted suffering becomes more mature and understanding of

---

95. Roszak, "Life in Paradise. Thomas Aquinas on Original Justice and Its Anthropological Significance" (forthcoming). See also Aquinas, *In III Sent.*, d. 22, q. 2 a. 1, qc. 3 ad 3.

96. Ratzinger, *Schöpfungslehre* (1964), 215; Sanz, "Joseph Ratzinger y la doctrina de la creación. Los apuntes de Münster de 1964 (y III)," 493nn125. C.S. Lewis writes on this score, "Try to exclude the possibility of suffering which the order of nature and the existence of free wills involve, and you find that you have excluded life." Lewis, *The Problem of Pain*, 25.

97. Ratzinger, *Eschatology*, 103 [*Eschatologie*, 91].

others, becomes more human. Anyone who has consistently avoided suffering does not understand other people; he becomes hard and selfish.[98]

It turns out, then, that in Ratzinger's view, "suffering is the inner side of love," and it is only in learning how to suffer well that each of us is "reshaped."[99]

In any event, if Ratzinger is correct about the relationship of suffering and love, this sheds important insight into God's will to create life by means of evolutionary processes. For, if man is to be truly conformed to the image of the crucified and risen Christ, we too must give ourselves away in a sincere gift of self through suffering and death. And, as the above citations reveal, this appears to be the case not merely because of sin but rather because of the finite nature of our existence and the cruciform shape of the world that serves as a means to conform us to Jesus Christ. Yet, by conforming us to the True Adam, our suffering does something even further and unfathomable: it enables us to share in the life of the Trinity itself.

Pope Benedict spoke to this point in a discussion with a group of clergy. After affirming that humans are "truly the reflection of creative reason," he explains that our conformity to God's inner life has much to do with how we lovingly bear suffering:

> [I]n suffering there is also a profound meaning, and only if we can give meaning to pain and suffering can our life mature. I would say, above all, that there can be no love without suffering [*non è possibile l'amore senza il dolore*], because love always implies renouncement of myself, letting myself go and accepting the other in his otherness; it implies a gift of myself and therefore, emerging from myself. . . . *The inseparability of love and suffering, of love and God*, are elements that must enter into the modern conscience to help us live.[100]

As I understand him here, the reason that Benedict considers suffering and death so essential to our experience in the natural world is that ultimate fulfillment is only attainable by means of it—that the only path to man's *theosis* comes through *kenosis*.

Moreover, Ratzinger's above comments seem to suggest that he views suffering—like all things in this world—as somehow a reflection of the inner life of God

---

98. Ratzinger, *God and the World*, 322. Other important authors have written eloquently along these lines. For instance, Henri de Lubac declares, "There is only one way to be happy, not to be ignorant of suffering, and not to run away from it, but to accept the transfiguration it brings...True happiness can only be the result of alchemy." 173; de Lubac, *Paradoxes*, 173; see also de Lubac, *Further Paradoxes* (Westminster, MD: Newman Press, 1958), 68–69. Concerning the benefit of suffering, he adds, "Together with prayer and love, suffering is one of three realities that frees us from sentimentality." de Lubac, *Further Paradoxes*, 72.

99. Ratzinger, *God and the World*, 323. While differing from Ratzinger insofar as he held that human suffering arose only after our first sin, it is significant that Thomas Aquinas also speaks of suffering as providential.

100. Benedict XVI, Meeting with the Clergy of the Dioceses of Belluno-Feltre and Treviso (July 24, 2007). Emphasis added.

himself. Indeed, in his encyclical *Deus Caritas Est*, Benedict goes so far as to affirm that, in an analogical sense, *eros*—yearning, need-based, suffering love) may be ascribed to God.[101] For, in the language of Scripture, God wants our good so much that it describes him as a passionate lover who is jealous for our love—and angry and heartbroken when we reject him (see, for example, Hos 1–2; Ezek 16; Is 62; and the Song of Songs).[102] Benedict elsewhere explains that these images metaphorically convey something most profound about God: his compassion and mercy. Recalling that the divine nature itself cannot suffer or change (i.e., have passions), God does have *com*-passion for us: "God cannot suffer, but he can 'suffer *with*.'"[103] Because we are creatures made in the likeness of the one true and compassionate God, Ratzinger says that we humans too are "beings of word and of love, beings moving toward Another, oriented to giving themselves to the Other and only truly receiving themselves back in real self-giving."[104] Accordingly, he appears to view the ineluctability of suffering in this life as a reality that flows from the "logic of self-giving" which is grounded in the inner life of the Trinity and "written into creation and into the hearts of men."[105] As Michael Gorman puts it, "*Kenosis* is the *sine qua non* of both divinity and humanity," adding that "cruciformity is theoformity."[106]

Hans Urs von Balthasar, whose work had a significant influence on the thought of Joseph Ratzinger, referred to this Trinitarian life of eternal self-giving as a "super-Kenosis." For, if Christ is the True Adam and "man" par excellence (Jn 19:5) and simultaneously the image of the invisible God in whom all things were created (Col 1:15–16) such that who has seen him "has seen the Father" (Jn 14:9), then in Balthasar's view it stands to reason that Christ's self-emptying *kenosis* (Phil 2:7) is the historical expression of something that exists analogously at an even more fundamental level in the life of the Trinity—a position that is supported by more recent Pauline scholarship.[107]

From this perspective, Balthasar says, the Trinity's inner life of "renunciation" is the foundation and "ultimate presupposition of [Christ's] Kenosis," while Christ's

---

101. Benedict XVI, *Deus Caritas Est*, §§3-10. At the end of this section, Benedict explains that "God's eros for man is also totally agape."

102. For a more in-depth discussion of the relationship of God's *eros* and *agape* in Benedict's thought, see Ramage, *The Experiment of Faith*, 151–54.

103. Benedict XVI, *Jesus of Nazareth: From the Baptism*, 87.

104. Ratzinger, *In the Beginning*, 47–48.

105. Ratzinger, "Man Between Reproduction and Creation," 82. The emeritus pontiff defines Christian belief in terms of this call to a total abandonment of self as gift to the other, a reality made possible in large part by the phenomena of suffering and death. For an extended discussion of this point, see Ramage, *The Experiment of Faith*, 84–99.

106. Michael Gorman, *Kenosis, Justification, and Theosis in Paul's Narrative Soteriology* (Grand Rapids, MI: Eerdmans, 2009), 2, 118. In a pair of other memorable formulations, Gorman speaks of God's "kenotic, cruciform identity" and, describing *theosis* as having a cruciform character, renders Lv 19:2, "You shall be cruciform, for I am cruciform." Gorman, *Kenosis, Justification, and Theosis*, 106, 162.

107. See for example Brant Pitre, Michael P. Barber, and John A. Kincaid, *Paul, a New Covenant Jew: Rethinking Pauline Theology* (Grand Rapids, MI: William B. Eerdmans Publishing Company, 2019), 212.

*kenosis* itself is a "revelation of the entire Trinity."[108] In this way, suffering in our lives on earth becomes an icon of the Trinitarian super-*kenosis*, a finite glimpse of the inner life of God whose entire being is one of total self-gift. As Balthasar elsewhere says, "[T]he final mystery of the kenosis of God in Christ has an analogous structure in the metaphysical mystery of being."[109]

Like Balthasar, C.S. Lewis grounds the presence of suffering in nature and Christ's *kenosis* in something that exists analogically within the Trinity itself. Declaring that self-giving is "absolute reality" and "the shape of the real," he explains: "For in self-giving, if anywhere, we touch a rhythm not only of all creation but of all being. . . . From the highest to the lowest, self exists to be abdicated and, by that abdication, becomes the more truly self, to be thereupon yet the more abdicated, and so forever."[110] Indeed, so strongly is Lewis convinced of this that he suggests that there might even be a kenotic dimension to life in heaven:

> Each soul [in heavenly bliss], we suppose, will be eternally engaged in giving away to all the rest that which it receives. . . . We need not suppose that the necessity for something analogous to self-conquest will ever be ended, or that eternal life will not also be eternal dying. It is in this sense, that, as there may be pleasures in hell (God shield us from them), there may be something not all unlike pains in heaven (God grant us soon to taste them).[111]

Once again, it is crucial to recall that we are speaking analogically here. Yet, perhaps a little more insight into Lewis's meaning lies in the climactic scene of his *Chronicles of Narnia* series. Lewis here reflects an outlook that can be found in the Patristic tradition wherein eternal bliss is envisioned as an eternal yearning and journey "further up and further in"—an ecstatic movement of happiness so great that Lewis's character Emeth can say upon embarking, "My happiness is so great that it even weakens me like a wound."[112] We would not be amiss to discern in this statement

---

108. Hans Urs von Balthasar, *Mysterium Paschale* (San Francisco: Ignatius Press, 2000), viii, 30, 35.

109. Hans Urs von Balthasar, *Glory of the Lord*, vol. 4: *The Realm of Metaphysics in Antiquity* (San Francisco: Ignatius Press, 1989), 38. To my mind, the above point about creaturely suffering being revelatory of the inner life of God is captured well in a statement of D.C. Schindler when he writes, "The poverty of the creature brings to light in a special way the wealth of the mystery of being." Schindler, *A Companion to* Homo Abyssus (Washington, D.C.: The Catholic University of America Press, 2019), 24. Elsewhere in this text, Schindler speaks of the "gift character of being," which again to my mind ably captures Balthasar's above point. Schindler, *A Companion to* Homo Abyssus, 100. For the inspiration behind Schindler's text, see Ferdinand Ulrich, Homo Abyssus: *The Drama of the Question of Being* (Washington, D.C.: Humanum Academic Press, 2018).

110. C.S. Lewis, *The Problem of Pain* (New York: HarperOne, 2001), 157–58.

111. C.S. Lewis, *The Problem of Pain* (New York: HarperOne, 2001), 157–58.

112. Lewis, *The Last Battle* (New York: HarperCollins, 2005), 207. It is significant that the character Emeth ("Truth" in Hebrew) does not belong to the Kingdom of Narnia, yet Aslan nevertheless welcomes him into his own country. "I take to me the services which thou hast done to [the false god Tash]," Aslan tells Emeth, explaining that anyone who virtuously keeps an oath has sworn by his name

echoes of the rapturous joy of the lovers in Song of Songs and the ecstatic "pain" evoked in Bernini's *Ecstasy of Saint Teresa*.

Lewis's vision here reflects an outlook that was already present in Church Fathers who envisioned heaven in paschal terms, as a place of eternal yearning, seeking, and progress. St. Maximus the Confessor, for instance, tied together the concept of paschal suffering with that of unending divinization: "But in the ages to come, we shall undergo (*paschontes*) by grace the transformation unto deification and no longer be active but passive (*paschomen*), and for this reason we shall not cease from being deified."[113] Clearly, the sort of eschatological "suffering" that these authors have in mind is a sinless one. Indeed, as the above translation makes clear, the Greek verb *pathein* ("to suffer") with its various forms deployed by Maximus also means to undergo, to be receptive, and to experience. For this great theologian whom Benedict called "the great Greek Doctor of the Church," heaven is an experience of "suffering" in the sense that it is a perpetual undergoing divinization made possible through the receptivity of a complete self-surrender to the divine Lover. As the saint says elsewhere, a man who loves "certainly suffers (*paschei*) an ecstasy toward it as an object of love," and does not come to rest until he is "wholly present in the whole beloved."[114]

These captivating speculations aside, if we return to Benedict's thought on the relationship of suffering and love, it is especially poignant when he explicitly casts our experience of suffering in a Christological light. At a General Audience we hear him saying: "The Cross reminds us that there is no true love without suffering, there is no gift of life without pain."[115] In other words, "The world in which we stand is marked by suffering and can grant joy only through the Passion. . . . [T]he grief of death itself carries the final, true joy of man.[116] Given this view, perhaps it will then not come as surprise that Professor Ratzinger called the suggestion that sinless man

---

"though he know it not." While not exhibiting precisely the same soteriology, Lewis's vision has affinities with Catholic teaching on the possibility of salvation for individuals (such as early humans) who lack explicit knowledge of God. For more regarding this subject, see Second Vatican Council, *Lumen Gentium*, §16.

113. Maximus the Confessor, *Ad Thalassium*, 22, in *On the Cosmic Mystery of Jesus Christ* (Crestwood, NY: St. Vladimir's Seminary Press, 2003), 117. For other Patristic witnesses to this vision, see Gregory of Nyssa, *Homilies on the Song of Songs* (Atlanta, GA: Society of Biblical Literature, 2012), 389; Gregory of Nyssa, *The Life of Moses* (New York: Paulist Press, 1978), 239; St. Columbanus, Instruction 13 *De Christo fonte vitae*, 1–3 in *Sancti Columbani Opera* (Dublin: Dublin Institute for Advanced Studies, 1957), translated in *The Liturgy of the Hours: According to the Roman Rite*, Vol. 4 (New York: The Catholic Book Publishing Company, 1975), 167–69 and 172–73.

114. Maximus the Confessor, *Ambigua*, 7, in vol. 1 of *On Difficulties in the Church Fathers: The Ambigua* (Cambridge, MA.: Harvard University Press, 2014), 87-88. For a translation that renders *paschei* as "experience," see *Amibgua*, 7, in *On the Cosmic Mystery of Jesus Christ*, 51. Here, we read that a man "certainly experiences (*paschei*) ecstasy over what is loved," and does not come to rest until his beloved is "embraced wholly." For Benedict's appellation of Maximus as "the great Greek Doctor of the Church," see his *Spe Salvi*, §28.

115. Benedict XVI, General Audience (September 17, 2008).

116. Ratzinger, *Schöpfungslehre* (1964), 211.

would have gently and painlessly fallen asleep at the end of his life "no solution" to the problem of death.[117]

In his encyclical *Spe Salvi*, the emeritus pontiff emphasizes that, while we can try to limit suffering, we cannot eliminate it entirely. If this becomes our goal, he continues, "we drift into a life of emptiness, in which there may be almost no pain, but the dark sensation of meaninglessness and abandonment is all the greater." Offering some sage pastoral advice, he concludes, "It is not by sidestepping or flee-ing from suffering that we are healed, but rather by our capacity for accepting it, maturing through it and finding meaning through union with Christ, who suffered with infinite love." In sum, Benedict teaches that, if we embrace our pain in close-ness with Jesus Christ and his *kenosis*, then our suffering "without ceasing to be suffering becomes, despite everything, a hymn of praise."[118]

## CONCLUSION: SUFFERING, THE RAW MATERIAL FOR LOVE

To drive home Benedict's thought on the relationship of suffering and love, I would like to conclude this chapter by sharing some powerful insights from Bethany Sollereder, a BioLogos author and researcher at the University of Oxford who specializes in evolution and the problem of suffering. Drawing the same conclusion independently of Benedict, Sollereder argues that the mass of suffer-ing and death that has littered evolutionary history does not constitute an argu-ment against the goodness of God but on the contrary bespeaks his loving plan for our sanctification. On the contrary, she echoes Andrew Elphinstone in argu-ing that "the present primacy of pain and unrest in the world is part of the raw material of the ultimate primacy of love."[119] Expounding this claim at greater length, she writes:

> By going through the process of pain, love opens up a new option of finding healing, and turning the pain from the agent of evil to the use of good. . . . [Pain] is the key to understanding our high calling of love. When we are in pain, more than any other moment, our passions are invoked and shaped. When our pain leads us to violence, hate, or revenge, our desires turn to evil. If instead, in the moment of pain, we choose to forgive, the power of pain is broken, it is not passed on in aggression or turned upon the self in shame. Forgiveness is the ultimate defeat of evil and freedom from it. While we may still be in pain, we may also find joy in the transformation of love.[120]

---

117. Ratzinger, *Schöpfungslehre* (1964), 209.

118. Benedict XVI, *Spe Salvi*, §37. In this same article, Benedict interprets Christ's descent into hell along these same existential lines: Christ descended into the "hell" of our own isolation and is "there-fore close to those cast into it, transforming their darkness into light." For more on Benedict's personalist understanding of this article of the creed, see Ramage, *The Experiment of Faith*, 112–19.

119. Bethany Sollereder, "From Survival to Love: Evolution and the Problem of Suffering," *Chris-tian Century* 131.19 (2014): 22–25 at 24–25; Andrew Elphinstone, *Freedom, Suffering and Love* (London: S.C.M. Press, 1976).

120. Sollereder, "From Survival to Love," 24–25.

Developing a helpful analogy that nicely complements those developed above, Sollereder argues in light of the above that the many shades of pain in our world are much like the raw ingredients of a good beer or loaf of bread. Neither of these foods is found in nature, and thus it takes human culture and industry to produce them. More to the point, the sweetness one may find in them is the product of ingredients that are of their own accord bitter and distasteful to us. Sweet beer is made from bitter hops. Savory bread requires sharp salt and foul-smelling yeast. More fundamentally still (and with Eucharistic associations), bread comes from grain that is *ground*, oil from olives *pressed*, and wine from grapes that have been *crushed*. In like manner, suffering and pain of all kinds are the raw ingredients of a rich and holy life. Though certainly not desirable in themselves, the experience of being "ground" and crushed" is the means by which God mysteriously transforms us into something altogether new and glorious.[121]

Further, Sollereder contends that the above analysis applies to the violence we observe in nature as a whole—what Benedict above called the "law of brutality" one of the "great riddles of creation." Contemplating the apparent gratuity of pain and waste throughout the natural world across evolutionary history, Sollereder draws a parallel between the process of spiritual formation just discussed and that of the physical formation of the cosmos. The transformation of a man to the state of being fully alive—that is, becoming ever more conformed to the image of Christ crucified—is a "cataclysmic" process much analogous to the manner in which volcanoes, earthquakes, and meteorites shape our universe's development. Though destructive in one order, such forces are eminently creative in another (e.g., volcanoes destroy life, but in doing so they make possible new forms of life, pruning a vine increases its quality and quantity of its yield, the death and decay of organic matter gives life to bacteria and plants, supernovae result in the destruction of stars but the creation of elements, etc.).

In accord with the new understanding of the natural world that we have thanks to evolutionary science, Sollereder thus proposes revising our narrative of human origins in a way that has many points of affinity with Benedict's approach:

> [I]n place of a perfect couple in a pleasant garden, our nonhuman ancestors were engaged in a long struggle for survival. They moved sharply in response to pain, they were protective of their own and aggressive toward perceived threats. Love was totally absent among them. They had skill, strength, intelligence, even altruism, but not love. Love is a uniquely human attribute—or perhaps we should say it is a divine attribute, imparted to humanity—that

---

121. In the second century, Ignatius of Antioch already evoked this point in Eucharistic overtones, urging his flock: "Allow me to become food for the wild beasts, through whose instrumentality it will be granted me to attain to God. I am the wheat of God, and let me be ground by the teeth of the wild beasts, that I may be found the pure bread of Christ." Ignatius of Antioch, *The Epistle of Ignatius to the Romans*, trans Alexander Roberts and James Donaldson, in vol. 1 of Ante-Nicene Fathers, eds. Alexander Roberts, James Donaldson, and A. Cleveland Coxe (Buffalo, NY: Christian Literature Publishing Co., 1885), Ch. 4.

transcends the evolutionary process and shapes us into hybrids of earthly and heavenly forms. Somewhere along the evolutionary process, nascent humanity acquired the ability to exercise a moral will over our innate desires, and with that came the capacity both to sin and to receive divine love and make it our own.[122]

Building on this analysis, Sollereder sees the experience of suffering and death—indeed, even the tempestuous emotions that we inherited from our evolutionary ancestors—as "the raw ingredients of love, awaiting 'divine alchemy.'"[123] This leads her to a conclusion that is very close to that drawn by our emeritus pontiff: "We therefore cannot object to God's goodness when we see around us a world of violence. This is the means to produce love."[124] Accordingly, this perspective may allow us to see how evolutionary theory works not *against* but *with* the Christian narrative of redemption, as Sollereder explains so well:

> In light of evolution, the existence of violence and hatred in the world appears not as an insoluble theological riddle but the outcome of a long and necessary process that is still in development. The bitter raw products of evolution are slowly being brought to transcend evolution itself. We are, through the painful process of forgiveness, being transformed into the image and likeness of Christ.[125]

Pope Benedict's successor writes along the same lines as Benedict and Sollereder in the above text. Creating a world that unfolds through evolution, Francis remarks that nature is such that "many of the things we think of as evils, dangers or sources of suffering, are in reality part of the pains of childbirth which he uses to draw us into the act of cooperation with the Creator."[126]

---

122. Sollereder, "From Survival to Love," 22–23. Sollereder then adds how such a narrative represents an improvement upon the traditional one not only from the point of view of science but perhaps also from a personalist perspective: "When we think of humans created in a moment by divine fiat, we overlook what a mighty achievement it is to love. In evolutionary terms, love is the very latest addition to life. It took countless millennia to arrive at love, and we stand only on the brink of its emergence. Every journey into new environments has come with massive struggle and great cost. Transformation into the realm of love is no exception." Sollereder, "From Survival to Love," 23.

123. Sollereder, "From Survival to Love," 22.

124. Sollereder, "From Survival to Love," 23. Sollereder's fuller comments on the subject of the emotions are worthy of serious consideration: "The ubiquitous demonstrations in humans of selfishness and violence are not evidence of a world gone wrong; rather, they show the human person ripe for radical transformation. The passions produced by evolution are the raw ingredients of love, awaiting 'divine alchemy.' Love is not the opposite of aggression, or joy the opposite of rage. Rather, love and joy are the transmuted forms of aggression and rage. And the process of change from explosive anger to transformed love is slow and precarious." Sollereder, "From Survival to Love," 23.

125. Sollereder, "From Survival to Love," 25.

126. Francis, *Laudato Si'*, §80.

# Chapter 10

# Sinless yet Sorrowful

## *The Blessed Virgin and the Problem of How to Suffer Well*

## INTRODUCTION

In the previous chapter, we explored Benedict's fundamental convictions regarding the reciprocity of suffering and love, in particular his insistence that we humans only find ourselves through a sincere gift of self in union with the *kenosis* of Jesus Christ. Now we are in a position to catch a glimpse of how this cruciform existence might have been lived out in a sinless world.

As Christians know well, the Cross of Jesus Christ reveals that virtuous suffering—and even death—can coexist with sinlessness. Our Lord's earthly life therefore gives us the perfect picture of what suffering before the Fall would have looked like: while suffering still would not have been a desirable experience for its own sake, it nevertheless would have been the occasion for a synergy of wills in which man handed himself over to God, saying, "Not my will, but thine be done!" (Lk 22:42).[1]

That said, Christ was not the only individual to live a sinless earthly life. Importantly, Ratzinger's corpus includes material devoted to unfolding what sinless suffering would have looked like in the life of a mere creature: that is, in the sorrows of the Immaculate Conception. In this chapter, then, we will consider what Ratzinger has to say about the Blessed Virgin Mary's embrace of suffering—and possibly even death—and how this may serve as a privileged lens into the origin of these realities and a guide to help us face them in a more Christ-like manner in our own lives.

## FULL OF GRACE AND FREEDOM FROM ORIGINAL SIN: A RELATIONAL INTERPRETATION

To begin, it will be helpful to ponder what is unique about the Sorrowful Mother that enabled her to embrace suffering in her life so perfectly. Put simply, it lies in the reality that she alone among creatures is "full of grace" (Lk 1:28) and thereby free from original sin. Yet we must ask: what, precisely, does it mean to affirm these statements? Ratzinger answers in his characteristic personalist language:

---

1. For a brief and clear exposition of Maximus the Confessor's teaching on the two wills of Christ, see Benedict XVI, General Audience: St. Maximus the Confessor (June 25, 2008).

What is grace? . . . We have probably objectified this concept too much in our religious thinking, seeing grace as a supernatural something which we carry in the soul. And since we have little or no feeling of it, it has gradually become meaningless for us, an empty word in the Christian idiom which seems not to relate anymore to the lived reality of our everyday existence. In reality, grace is a correlative idea; it does not concern an attribute belonging to an individual self, but refers to a relationship between an I and a you, between God and a human being.[2]

"You are full of grace" again means that Mary is a person who is totally open, who has made herself wholly receptive, and has placed herself keenly and without limits, *without fear* of her own destiny, in the hand of God. It also means that she lives entirely out of and within her relationship with God.[3]

Building on this relational understanding of grace, Ratzinger finds that the Blessed Virgin's freedom from original sin is likewise understood best through an anthropology of relation:

Preservation from original sin, therefore, signifies no exceptional proficiency, no exceptional achievement; on the contrary, it signifies that Mary reserves no area of being, life, and will for herself as a private possession: instead, precisely in the total dispossession of self, in giving herself to God, she comes to the true possession of self. Grace as dispossession becomes response as appropriation.[4]

The light that shines from the figure of Mary also helps us to understand the true meaning of original sin. Indeed that relationship with God which sin truncates is fully alive and active in Mary. In her there is no opposition

---

2. Ratzinger, "'You Are Full of Grace': Elements of Biblical Devotion to Mary," *Communio* 16 (1989): 54–68 at 59.

3. Ratzinger, "'You Are Full of Grace,'" 60 (emphasis added). For another insightful relational approach to Mary's being "full of grace," see Thomas Weinandy, O.F.M., *Jesus Becoming Jesus: Synoptic Gospels*, 7. Weinandy describes this dynamic as one of "reciprocal relational causality"—because Mary is full of grace, the Lord is with her; and, because the Lord is with her, she is full of grace.

On the fear of death in relation to sin (a fear that Ratzinger above describes Mary as conquering), Hebrews 2:14-15 deserves consideration. The epistle states, "Since therefore the children share in flesh and blood, [Christ] himself likewise partook of the same nature, that through death he might destroy him who has the power of death, that is, the devil, *and deliver all those who through fear of death were subject to lifelong bondage.*" For a reflection on this text and the possibility that it may have envisioned Adam and Eve as being intimidated by the serpent's potentially lethal power, see Scott Hahn, *Kinship by Covenant* (New Haven, CT: Yale University Press, 2009), 284–87 at 287. Hahn notes that the *nahash* of Genesis 3 elsewhere is used in literary parallelism with the dragon Leviathan (Is 27:1) or the sea monster Rahab (Jb 26:13) and is therefore no mere garden-variety snake. While not taking up the same overall position as Ratzinger, Hahn insightfully suggests that Adam's sin was connected with his fear of death: "Knowing the serpent's power, Adam was unwilling to lay down his own life—for the sake of his love of God, or to save the life of his beloved. That refusal to sacrifice was essential to Adam's original sin." Hahn, *First Comes Love: Finding Your Family in the Church and the Trinity* (New York: Image, 2002), 69–70. For a reading along these lines, see also Meredith Kline, "Trial by Ordeal," in *Through Christ's Word: A Festschrift for Dr. Philip E. Hughes* (Phillipsburg, NJ: Presbyterian and Reformed, 1985), 81–93.

4. Ratzinger, *Daughter Zion*, 70 (*Die Tochter Zion*, 69–70).

between God and her being: there is full communion, full understanding. There is a reciprocal "yes": God to her and her to God. Mary is free from sin because she belongs entirely to God, she empties herself totally for him. She is full of his Grace and of his Love.[5]

As Pope Benedict would later say in a homily at the Shrine of Altötting in his native Bavaria, the doctrine of the Blessed Virgin's freedom from original sin captures her "permanent attitude." In this, she demonstrates how a person attains holiness: "not by seeking to assert before God our own will and our own desires . . . but rather to bring them before him and to let him decide what he intends to do."[6]

Ratzinger spoke similarly in his 1957 Mariology course, remarkably the only of its kind that he taught over the course of his twenty-two-year academic career. In the following texts, our professor's personalist approach shines through as he shows how Mary serves as the model for how all of us ought to respond to the divine call:

> Faith means to give up oneself and be pure openness to God . . . she [Mary] is not contrasted to us, rather she appears as the exemplar realization of what ultimately . . . must happen to us all; she is the primordial [i.e., prototypical] representation of the Christian faith par excellence.[7]

> Mary's religious position is not on the side of God over against us, but it is on the side of man as an image of what we should be and can be ourselves.[8]

In these statements, we readily discern another category that pervades Ratzinger's corpus and which is integral to his existential approach to the mysteries of faith: that of receptivity. Echoing the Second Vatican Council's poignant line that man "cannot fully find himself except through a sincere gift of himself,"[9] Benedict insists that Mary's freedom from original sin consists precisely in her ability to make this gift that the rest of us are unable to do because of our lack of receptivity to God's grace.

## MARY'S SELF-GIVING OF LOVE IN DEATH

It is no surprise that a Catholic theologian like Ratzinger holds that Mary experienced a great deal of suffering and sorrow over the course of her earthly life. After all, one of her titles is "Our Lady of Sorrows," and indeed Simeon prophesied to her at Jesus's presentation that a "sword will pierce through your own soul" (Lk 2:35). Because of this, the fact that suffering and sinlessness coexisted in the earthly life of Mary is so clear as to appear trivial.

---

5. Benedict XVI, Angelus (December 8, 2012). See also Ratzinger, *Daughter Zion*, 70: "This correspondence of God's 'Yes' with Mary's being as 'Yes' is the freedom from original sin."

6. Benedict XVI, Homily (September 11, 2006).

7. Ratzinger, *Mariologie* (1957), 25.

8. Ratzinger, *Mariologie* (1957), 39.

9. Second Vatican Council, *Gaudium et Spes*, §24.

What is not so obvious to most Catholics today, however, is something else that Ratzinger holds regarding the Blessed Virgin. While many believers today assume that Mary was taken to heaven without undergoing death, this is a relatively recent view that has never been taught by the Magisterium. Ratzinger, on the other hand, follows the ancient tradition that the Blessed Virgin died before her Assumption (or *dormition* in Eastern theology)—a belief attested in the Fathers and Doctors of the Church, in Renaissance art, by a sepulcher in Jerusalem said to contain the original tomb of Mary, and even in the papal bull in which Pius XII declared the dogma of the Assumption.[10] What I would now like to propose is that this dimension of the emeritus pontiff's Mariology is an extension of his Christology that we have been examining and may therefore be of added benefit in our quest to understand the relationship of sin, suffering, and death.

A number of Ratzinger's statements take for granted that suffering and death were essential features in the life of this creature who, while "certainly . . . free from all sin," nevertheless "knows pain suffering, and death" and even "matured as Mother of God" in such a way that "her merits increased until her death."[11] Mary suffered and died in Ratzinger's view. Unlike the rest of us, though, she made the perfect choice when it came to *how she would respond to suffering and death* with the help of God's grace, that is, *receiving them as gifts that lead to greater conformity to Christ*. Accordingly, Ratzinger taught in his Mariology course that the Blessed Virgin's death was not merely a passive affair but the active bursting forth of love in a final grand *fiat*: "Mary's death is not the answer [*Antwort*] to sin, but the self-giving away of love, or the overwhelming power of love, which broke the outer shell and prepared the way for [its] true form [*Gestalt*]."[12]

To better understand Ratzinger's thought on this matter, it is instructive to begin by pondering his words on the Assumption. In *Daughter Zion*, a book specifically dedicated to explaining the Church's key Marian beliefs, he teaches that

---

10. For the dogmatic declaration that Mary was assumed into heaven "having completed the course of her earthly life," see Pius XII, *Munificentissimus Deus* §44. While Pius wisely leaves open the question of whether Mary died, the witnesses he cites (St. John of Damascus, St. Francis de Sales, etc.) all held the view that "the dead body of the Blessed Virgin Mary remained incorrupt," that Mary "gained a triumph out of death, her heavenly glorification after the example of her only begotten Son," and that it was fitting for the Blessed Virgin to "keep her own body free from all corruption even after death." Pius XII, *Munificentissimus Deus* §§20–44. Some have argued that Pius's bull intended to explicitly confirm the longstanding tradition that Mary died. Even as I do not think that this much can be claimed, a thought-provoking read on the subject, along with an attempt to reconcile two opposing views on this subject, may be found in Charles de Koninck, "La mort et l'Assomption de la sainte Vierge," *Laval théologique et philosophique* 7 (1952): 9–86 at 9–42 [where he argues that Pius teaches Mary's death] and 42–86 [where he argues that, while Mary died, there never was an interval of time in which her soul and body were separated, as the moment that her soul ceased to inform her earthly body coincided with the first instant that it informed her glorified body].

11. Ratzinger, *Mariologie* (1957), 47–48.

12. Ratzinger, *Mariologie* (1957), 51. Pondering Mary "actively con-suffering" with Jesus under the Cross, Ratzinger adds that the *Mater Dolorosa* serves as the model of faith for all of us, her spiritual children. Ratzinger, *Mariologie* (1957), 54.

this dogma is not concerned with the issue of whether Mary died but rather with the veneration of Mary who has "arrived at her goal *on the other side of death.*" To this, he immediately adds a sacramental dimension, "In her, everything still resisting baptism (faith) has been conquered without remainder *through the death of her earthly life*."[13] What is perhaps most telling about the above texts is that Ratzinger does not even feel the need to argue that Mary died. Rather, it appears he assumes a positive answer to the question without even feeling the need to argue for it.

After affirming the historical reality of Mary's Assumption, Ratzinger considers the meaning of death, grace, and the immortality that the Blessed Virgin gained through her Assumption. Addressing what these mean from his characteristic existential perspective, Ratzinger replies:

> Man is not immortal by his own power, but only in and through another, preliminarily, tentatively, fragmentarily, in children, in fame, but finally and truly only in and from the Entirely-Other, God. We are mortal due to the usurped autarchy of a determination to remain within ourselves, which proves to be a deception. *Death*, the impossibility of giving oneself a foothold, the collapse of autarchy, *is not merely a somatic* but a human phenomenon of all-embracing profundity.[14]

For Ratzinger, biological death is one thing, but *true* death is something we bring upon ourselves when we live our life as if we were self-sufficient. The reverse side of this, the good news, is that this more important death can be conquered (as happened with Mary) even as we meet our bodily demise and shuffle off this mortal coil:

> Nevertheless, where the innate propensity to autarchy is totally lacking, where there is the pure self-dispossession of the one who does not rely upon himself (= grace), *death is absent, even if the somatic end is present.* Instead, the whole human being enters salvation, because as a whole, undiminished, he stands eternally in God's life-giving memory that preserves him as himself in his *own* life.[15]

In sum, the above texts strongly suggest that Ratzinger viewed Mary as having suffered and died like the rest of us, with the difference lying in her *response* to these

---

13. Ratzinger, *Daughter Zion*, 74 [*Die Tochter Zion*, 74] (emphasis added).

14. Ratzinger, *Daughter Zion*, 78–79 (emphasis added). See also Joseph Ratzinger, "Thoughts on the Place of Marian Doctrine and Piety in Faith and Theology as a Whole," *Communio* 30 (Spring 2003): 147–60 at 155. This article also appears in Joseph Ratzinger and Hans Urs von Balthasar, *Mary: The Church at the Source*, trans. Adrian Walker (San Francisco: Ignatius Press, 1997), 13–95. See also Joseph Ratzinger, "Die Ekklesiologie des zweiten Vatikanums," *Communio* 15 (1986): 41–52, at 52. I have taken the translation of this piece from Emery de Gaál, *O Lord, I Seek Your Countenance*, 230.

15. Ratzinger, *Daughter Zion*, 79 (first emphasis added). The parenthetical content in the above quote wherein Ratzinger connects his personalist understanding of grace to this topic is in the original German text. It may be also worth observing that the original includes an exclamation point after 'grace' though this is not present in the published English translation. Note too that a literal translation of the first emphasized text would perhaps read even more emphatically: "There is no 'death' (even if there is a bodily end) [*da ist nicht 'Tod' (auch wenn somatisches Ende da ist)*]."

trials. Because she was perfectly receptive to God's gift of suffering, Mary did not experience death as an evil to be dreaded and rebelled against but rather as the definitive path to conformity with her son.

## THE MAIN PROBLEM IS NOT HAVING TO SUFFER AND DIE, BUT HOW TO SUFFER AND DIE WELL

The above texts indicate that Ratzinger considers Mary to have died before being assumed into heaven. This, combined with the fact that he did not even feel the need to argue for this position, confirms Ratzinger's broader understanding that suffering and death are in the world not primarily because of sin but in order to conform us to the image of Jesus Christ. In light of the above discussion, we may now add that redemptive suffering and death also unite us to the New Eve, the Blessed Mother. I would now like to draw out some implications of Ratzinger's approach to the Blessed Mother's immaculate acceptance of suffering and death.

In light of Ratzinger's understanding of Mary combined with the integral role of suffering and death in the evolutionary design of the cosmos, it seems appropriate to conclude that mankind's ultimate problem is not suffering and physical death per se but rather *our resistance to accepting these crosses as our path to sanctification*. This is not to minimize the reality of suffering (Lord knows I have had my share of it having had lupus for over two decades) or to excuse us from working to alleviate suffering in this world. Yet, to put it in Ratzinger's personalist language, the ultimate problem is not pain or death per se through which we all must pass but rather our *orientation toward* or *relationship* with these trials—i.e., whether we rebel against them or instead receive them as gifts.[16] From this perspective, the grace lost by our forebears was not something that would have prevented us from suffering and dying but rather that which *allows us to suffer and die well*—with Christ and like his Blessed Mother in a cruciform gift of self-abandonment to the Father's will.

In accord with the above, Ratzinger's vision is one of a human race that has likely always experienced suffering of many kinds. However, as we have seen, this would not have caused in Mary or our first parents the experience of misery, absurdity, and dread that the rest of us experience because of our inept and rebellious response to trials. I find that C.S. Lewis captures this point well when he, like Ratzinger, speaks to the problem of how to bear suffering well in relation to our fulfillment as human beings: "[T]he proper good of a creature is to surrender itself to its Creator . . . the problem is how to recover this self-surrender. We are

---

16. An insightful treatment of this point may be found in Piotr Roszak, "Imperfectly Perfect Universe? Emerging Natural Order in Thomas Aquinas" (forthcoming). As Roszak observes, "The key to understanding the state of nature before sin is not the existence of something that does not exist after the fall, but a change of order, the relationship to it." Roszak, "Imperfectly Perfect Universe?" He continues, "The original perfection of nature, before the fall, is not absolute—but it is open to fullness. The purpose of human life does not change after sin (the access to heaven remains), but the procedure changes, because the original *rectitudo* was broken." Roszak, "Imperfectly Perfect Universe?. See also Aquinas, *In II Sent.*, d. 23 q. 2 a. 3 co.

not merely imperfect creatures who must be improved: we are, as Newman said, rebels who must lay down our arms."[17] From here, Lewis makes a poignant suggestion that might shed light on how our first parents, Mary, and Christ may have experienced their suffering:

> Even in Paradise I have supposed a minimal self-adherence to be overcome, though the overcoming, and the yielding, would there be rapturous. But to surrender a self will inflamed and swollen with years of usurpation is a kind of death. . . . The self-surrender which he practiced before the Fall meant no struggle but only the delicious overcoming of an infinitesimal self-adherence which delighted to be overcome—of which we see a dim analogy in the rapturous mutual self-surrenders of lovers even now.[18]

Lewis's sublime example may be uniquely illuminating, yet everyday experiences may also serve to illustrate what an unfallen response to pain and suffering might look like. Consider the satisfaction that comes from having completed a hard day's work or gratification that ensues upon completing a demanding workout with all the sweat and toilsome pain it involves. Frequently, the sense of fulfillment we receive from achieving these goals comes not *despite* but precisely *because of* hardships endured and obstacles overcome along the way. Indeed, while the journey was not necessarily pleasurable, it was not miserable and indeed ultimately the source of great joy.

This, then, is the key both for Lewis and for Benedict: even if our first parents suffered physical pain and toil before their Fall from grace, the experience—like that which we ourselves sometimes glimpse in the midst of great trials—would not have been one of misery and despair. For, just as the self-giving that we find in the life Christ and the Trinity itself is one of sheer bliss, so too man in a graced state may have found rapturous joy through his surrender of self in loving suffering. Yet, once the first man sinned, he began to experience that same suffering not as a gift and occasion for love but instead as misery and curse. In this way, a Catholic who gravitates in Ratzinger's direction on these matters can rejoice in the Catechism's teaching that "the overwhelming *misery* which oppresses men and their inclination towards evil and death cannot be understood apart from their connection with Adam's sin."[19]

Taking a step beyond Ratzinger and Lewis, it may be helpful to acknowledge that the writings of Ratzinger's CDF appointee Cardinal Luis Ladaria again appear to shed light on this approach. According to Ladaria, the Church's traditional teaching on original sin can indeed be "integrated into a life that would include death," for death embraced properly is able to serve as a "step towards a fuller communion with God, towards a fuller life, and not as a rupture with the sense of frustration

---

17. Lewis, *The Problem of Pain*, 76.
18. Lewis, *The Problem of Pain*, 76.
19. *CCC*, §403 (emphasis added).

and destruction with which we now live it."[20] In support of this position, Ladaria references a distinction made in Philo's commentary on Genesis 2:17. According to this classic Jewish thinker, God's saying that man will "surely die" [*moth tamuth*— more literally translated "dying you will die"] refers to a very specific kind of death.

On the one hand, Philo says, there is physical death, "which exists by the original ordinance of nature." On the other hand—and this is the death that Philo and Ladaria judge Genesis to have in mind—there is that death "which is inflicted as punishment . . . when the soul dies according to the life of virtue and lives only according to the life of vice."[21] This is the death of which Jesus speaks when he commands his apostles: "[D]o not fear those who kill the body but cannot kill the soul; rather fear him who can destroy both soul and body in Gehenna" (Mt 10:28). Following Jesus and echoing the thought of Philo and Ratzinger, Ladaria teaches that the real kind of death that we need to be concerned about—and the only kind that our first parents too should have feared—is that which results when we refuse to surrender our wills into the hands of our loving Lord. In short, Ladaria's writing confirms that, while the precise relationship of sin and the origin of physical death is impossible to know with complete certainty, the despair-inducing *difficulty* and *misery* that we experience in connection with suffering and death most certainly is the result of a sinful response that traces back to the first members of the human race.

To illustrate the importance of the above principles, we will now apply them to some concrete problems at the intersection of faith and evolutionary science.

Consider the toil (Hebrew *itstsabon*; ESV: "pain"), thorns, and thistles with which Adam is said to be cursed after the Fall (Gn 3:17–18). As we saw in Chapter 5, modern biblical scholarship identifies the account depicting the origin of these phenomena as an etiology—a clever literary device that is not meant to offer strictly historical or scientific explanation but rather a poetic, vivid, and therefore memorable way to drive home an important point. In that chapter, we noted that the opening chapters of Genesis are replete with etiological images that seek to "explain" such things as: the names Adam/man, woman, Eve and Cain; Eve's creation from Adam's "rib" (or phallus); man's donning of clothes; why snakes lack legs; why farmers have to eke out a living by the sweat of their brow and have to deal with droughts and thorny plants; woman's attraction for man in spite of the harsh treatment she received from him in the ancient East; why man must die and turn to dust); the origin of rainbows; the place-name Babel (Babylon); why the land of Canaan needed to be conquered; why Canaanites had aberrant sexual practices; why non-Israelite slaves did not need to be emancipated; why Babylon is an enemy of God and each nation speaks its own language.

Situating the origin of toil, thorns, and thistles within this etiological genre and reading Scripture with an eye to the integrity of the natural world God created,

---

20. Ladaria, *Teología del pecado original y de la gracia*, 46 (my translation).

21. Philo, *Allegorical Interpretation*, I, in *The Works of Philo* (Peabody, MA: Hendrickson, 1993), 25–37 at 37.

we must then ask: Were there not any thorns in our fields or heat waves that threatened their survival before the fall? In spite the abundant scientific evidence to the
contrary, do we really wish to maintain that droughts and thorn-bearing species
sprung into existence after humans? Or, supposing they existed, is it truly fitting to
think that God somehow shielded crops from intense heat and weed seed germi-
nation until a human being came along and sinned? And then there is this arguably
even more fundamental difficulty: are we to assume that the first hunter-gatherer
humans 200,000 years ago would have had these concerns in the first place, when
the scientific evidence shows that the practice of agriculture developed within
roughly only the last 12,000 years?[22] Although he does not address this specific
curse and these specific questions in any detail, it seems safe to say that Ratzinger
would say that the true curse upon Adam was not that he now would have to deal
with weeds but rather that sin makes it impossible for him to deal with the weeds
as he should.

If we follow Ratzinger's principles in interpreting Genesis 3:17–18, then they
equally apply to the next verse's etiology which explains the origin of toilsome sweat
and death: "In the sweat of your face you shall eat bread till you return to the
ground, for out of it you were taken; you are dust, and to dust you shall return" (Gn
3:19). Are we to think that humans never sweated before the first sin was committed? If they did not, we may ask how this would not be a violation of the integrity
of human nature, which is designed to (and indeed must) cool itself in order to
survive in the sort of climate in which *Homo sapiens* first arose. In other words, do
we think that operative human sweat glands—that is, sweat glands doing what they
were designed to do—truly are the result of the Fall?

Along these lines, we might think about the human nervous system which
allows us to feel pain. We might gain some insight into why humans did indeed
original feel pain in their toilsome labor by looking to the tragic consequences that
result when humans today do *not* feel pain, such as in those persons who suffer
from congenital insensitivity to pain (CIP). Similarly, we can imagine the problems
that would ensue if we never felt the appendicitis pain that directs us to the emer-
gency room (I, for one, would not be writing this book right now had I not felt that
pain). C.S. Lewis captures this point well: "If fire comforts that body at a certain
distance, it will destroy it when the distance is reduced. Hence, even in a perfect
world, the necessity for those danger signals which the pain-fibers in our nerves
are apparently designed to transmit."[23] Casting this distinction in a Christological
key, Ladaria explains:

[I]n light of the resurrection of Christ, who makes our hope possible, we can
live death as a participation in the death of Jesus so as also to share in his glorious resurrection. It is not unrealistic to think that death can be lived with

---

22. On the developments of human agriculture in the relation to man's "Great Leap Forward," see
Diamond, *The Third Chimpanzee*, especially 32–58 and 180–91.
23. Lewis, *The Problem of Pain*, 23.

meaning, and therefore that in a world without sin it could have been experienced without the difficulties upon which we now stumble. Francis of Assisi spoke of 'sister death' and praised God for her. . . . The original state of justice could have been less painful (although, of course, we refuse to speculate on the concrete way it would have been experienced). Indeed, even now it does not have to be lived tragically if in baptism we participate in the death and resurrection of Jesus.[24]

Having said this regarding the compatibility of sinlessness and suffering, I would now like to propose that the above reflection might shed light on a particular dimension of Mary's life connected with her freedom from original sin: the question of whether the Blessed Virgin suffered birth pangs in giving birth to the Savior. While Mary's perpetual virginity is a well-known Catholic doctrine, what many Catholics may not know is the longstanding tradition that Mary was free from pain in her labor and indeed miraculously remained a virgin "even in the act of giving birth to the Son of God," also known as *virginitas in partu*.[25] At the origin of the view that Mary was free from birth pangs lies Genesis 3:16: "I will greatly multiply your pain in childbearing; in pain you shall bring forth children." This line may be read as implying that the first woman already would have suffered birth pangs even before the Fall. As Brant Pitre notes, though, the emphasis in this text appears to be on the intensity of the pains and is ambiguous as to Eve's state prior to the Fall. Indeed, he notes that the author is engaging here in a wordplay: whereas Adam and Eve had been commanded to "multiply" their offspring (Gn 1:28) they instead sinned before fulfilling their mission, God will now "multiply" Eve's pain.[26]

Recalling our discussion of the etiological curse of sweat and thorns discussed above, I would add that this childbearing curse reads well as an instance of etiology whereby Genesis offers clever wordplay "explanations" for the origin of phenomena. That is, just as Genesis's narration of the first man's creation from dust, the first female from his rib, sweat, weeds in our fields, and snakes losing their legs is not historical or scientific in nature, taking Genesis 3:16 as conclusive evidence that sinless woman would have been immune from pain in childbirth seems to reflect a misunderstanding of the genre of this biblical text.[27]

As far as I have been able to tell, Benedict never addressed the specific question of whether or not Mary (or the first woman, had she not sinned) suffered birth pangs. While it is impossible to verify that he would concur with Ratzinger on every last point in this arena, perhaps the closest one might come to a guess at what the emeritus pontiff's view might be would be to consult the work of another of his

---

24. Ladaria, *Teología del pecado original y de la gracia*, 47 (my translation).

25. See *CCC*, §499, 510 and *Catechism of the Council of Trent for Parish Priests, Issued by Order of Pope Pius V*, trans. John McHugh and Charles Callan (New York: Joseph F. Wagner, Inc, 1923), 45–46.

26. Pitre, *Jesus and the Jewish Roots of Mary* (New York: Image, 2018), 203–4n8.

27. On the pronouncement upon Eve as an etiology, see Knight and Levine, *The Meaning of the Bible*, 303.

successors at the CDF: Cardinal Gerhard Ludwig Müller, whom he appointed as prefect of that office and tasked with curating his *Opera Omnia*. According to Müller, the doctrine of Mary's *virginitas in partu* ("virginity during birth") is consistent with Jesus being born in the ordinary natural way, that is, by passing through the birth canal. Much like we have seen Benedict do for all manner of questions concerning biblical and magisterial teachings, Müller explains the meaning of this teaching as follows:

> It is not about (*Es geht nicht um*) anomalous physiological peculiarities in the natural process of birth (such as the birth canal not being opened, the hymen not being broken, and the absence of birth pangs), but rather about the healing and saving influence of the Redeemer's grace on human nature, which had been 'wounded' by original sin. . . . The content of the faith statement, therefore, does not refer to physiologically, and empirically verifiable somatic details.[28]

Moreover, Müller affirms that this teaching is compatible with Mary having experienced birth pangs in the same way that practically every human mother does—thus bestowing immense dignity upon birth and motherhood itself:

> In any theological interpretation of Mary's freedom from 'pain' in the salvific event of the Savior's birth, one should also take into account the biblically-based doctrine that Mary followed the way of the cross (Lk 2:35; Jn 19:25). With Mary as model, Christian spirituality recognizes in every birth, accepted by a woman in faith, an experience of the salvation that has come in the end time.[29]

Of course, it is always possible that God did indeed shield Mary from experiencing labor pains, as Catholics have traditionally assumed. Similarly, it is possible that the Lord planned either to anesthetize Eve as she gave birth or to sidestep nature and have her babies pass through their mother's body in the same way Jesus walked through doors after his Resurrection. If we prize the integrity of nature and our knowledge of evolutionary processes, however, it seems rather obvious that human mothers were always going to have more difficult births than other animals given the uniquely large size of human heads in comparison to the birth canal through which they must pass (that is, unless we think that the gradual evolutionary size increase of the hominin brain was the result of sin or that the very nerves designed to send pain signals to woman's brain were somehow rendered nonfunctional during the birthing process before the Fall). However, in my estimation—following the likes of Ratzinger and his doctrinal chief successors Müller and Ladaria—supposing this begs the question of why God created the human birth process with its associated body parts in the first place and whether excepting sinless woman from

---

28. Gerhard Ludwig Müller, "Die Jungfräulichkeit Marias in der Geburt," in: *Katholische Dogmatik. Für Studium und Praxis der Theologie* (Freiburg, 2003), 497–99. This text has been translated by Michael Miller in "Archbishop Gerhard Ludwig Müller and the Virgin Birth," *Homiletic and Pastoral Review* (December 13, 2012).

29. Müller, "Die Jungfräulichkeit Marias in der Geburt," 497–99.

it is fitting given the Lord's esteem for the integrity of the natural world he created and his desire to sanctify us through redemptive suffering.[30]

The same could be said regarding all manner of suffering that our first parents may have experienced in an unfallen world. To be sure, God could have simply sidestepped nature and anesthetized them from feeling the pain of our teeth falling out, fevers from infections, getting bitten by mosquitos, stepping on their kids' prehistoric legos, being devoured by wild beasts, and the like. Yet, one has to ask of this scenario: is this any more fitting than God stopping humans from sweating before the Fall or woman from experiencing true biological birth? It seems to me that the bizarre scenario of God shutting off our nervous system, anesthetizing us, putting a force field around us, or diverting tornados around us would be more of a defect than a feature in the marvelous world he created. Further, it makes one wonder how a person prevented from the aforementioned experiences is truly human and thereby a reflection of Christ crucified and risen. Not only that, it risks potentially compromising Christ's humanity if the Incarnate God shared in every aspect of human life apart from being birthed the way we all are.[31]

Finally, I find it highly significant that this same etiological reasoning by which Genesis "explains" the origin of pain in childbirth, thorns, and sweat (Gn 3:16–18) is followed immediately by the declaration of death's origin: "In the sweat of your face you shall eat bread till you return to the ground, for out of it you were taken; you are dust, and to dust you shall return" (Gn 3:19). This may well lead one to ask: Is Genesis's comment that human death began at this point in time any more historical in nature than that the previous lines' insinuation that humans never would have had to deal with thorns, sweat, and birth pangs if we had not sinned? Seeing as the "origin" of these experiences can be understood well as examples of biblical etiology, may not the same be said of death's origin? As we have seen, Ratzinger and other important ecclesial thinkers lead toward or are at least open to the idea

---

30. For a discussion of the evolutionary mechanisms that led to this situation, see Diamond, *The Third Chimpanzee*, 32–58. See also Chapter 3 of the present volume for a deeper discussion of the importance placed upon the integrity of natural processes in the Catholic intellectual tradition.

31. For an illuminating discussion related to this topic in light of Thomistic categories, see Jordan Haddad, "Modern Biology's Contribution to Our Understanding of Christ's Sufferings," *Church Life Journal* (August 08, 2018). https://churchlifejournal.nd.edu/articles/ modern-biologys-contribution-to-our-understanding-of-christs-sufferings/. In contrast with Ratzinger and Lewis, Aquinas taught that prelapsarian man's flesh, subjected to his intellect, did not endure suffering or illness of any kind. Aquinas, *Super Rom. 8*, lect. 1, no. 608. See also Aquinas, *In II Sent.*, d.43, q.1 ad 6; Aquinas, *ST* I, q.72, a.2 ad 3; Aquinas, *De Malo*, q.5, a.4, ad 7; Aquinas, *De veritate*, q. 25 a. 7. For further detail on Aquinas's view that primal man did not suffer these things, see *ST* I, q. 97, a. 2 ad 4: "Man's body in the state of innocence could be preserved from suffering injury from a hard body; partly by the use of his reason, whereby he could avoid what was harmful; and partly also by Divine Providence, so preserving him, that nothing of a harmful nature could come upon him unawares." According to Thomas, sinless man would have used things in conformity with their design, with the result that thistles and thorns (which in his view already existed prior to man's entry into the world) originally served as food for animals and not to punish man. Aquinas, *ST*, II-II, q. 164 a. 2 ad 1. Likewise, harmful plants and animals did not injure us thanks to God's providential protection. Aquinas, *In II Sent.*, d. 14, q. 1 a. 5 ad 7.

that human beings would have died before being able to attain heavenly bliss regardless of sin. For these thinkers, the real death directly caused by original sin is spiritual in nature: that misery which results when we refuse to accept suffering and death as gifts that unite us to God.

## A HISTORICAL FALL WITH RETROSPECTIVE CONSEQUENCES: ANOTHER WAY TO ARTICULATE THE RELATIONSHIP OF ORIGINAL SIN, SUFFERING, AND DEATH

Having said all of this, I will understand if some readers find the above proposal unappealing or a theological bridge too far. Seeing suffering and death as natural parts of a cruciform world, after all, is just one tentative suggestion for how to make sense of these realities in light of Scripture, Catholic teaching, and the discoveries of modern evolutionary theory. Beyond the approach I have sketched, there are other viable and even complementary frameworks by which to address this topic in a way that respects nature and the discoveries of modern biological science while upholding a causal link between sin and the origin of suffering and death. To echo what I said in this volume's introduction, I do not pretend that this book has provided definitive answers to all the problems that it has raised. Engaging questions that surface at the intersection of faith and science requires us to acknowledge that there is often more than one intelligent, orthodox way to address a given problem.

I find one such proposal to be particularly attractive and possibly even complementary to Ratzinger's approach to original sin. Seventh-century theological giant St. Maximus the Confessor offered a unique way to affirm that suffering and death have been around from the beginning *and* at the same time remain causally connected to sin both in man and in all of creation. One of the options that Maximus puts forward for making sense of original sin in relation to suffering is the possibility that "God created matter in this way from the beginning, according to His foreknowledge, in view of the transgression [i.e., of Adam] He had already seen in advance."[32] A similar way of thinking through a possibility such as that proposed

---

32. Maximus the Confessor, *Ambigua*, 8, trans. Nicholas Constas in *On Difficulties in the Church Fathers: The Ambigua* (Cambridge, MA.: Harvard University Press, 2014), Vol. 1, 145. I am grateful to Nicholas Lombardo, OP, for sharing this reference with me. For a survey of this and other Patristic views on this topic, see his "Evil, Suffering, and Original Sin," 141. See also Maximus, *Ambigua*, 42 and Maximus, *On Difficulties in Sacred Scripture: The Responses to Thalassios* (Washington, D.C.: The Catholic University of America Press, 2018), 59, 61.

For an illuminating discussion of these Patristic texts, see also Henri de Lubac, *Cosmic Liturgy: The Universe according to Maximus the Confessor* (San Francisco: Ignatius Press, 1988), 187. In this text, the great *ressourcement* theologian elaborates on Maximus's suggestion that God created the consequences of disobedience along with human nature. For Maximus, de Lubac explains, man's creation and fall are conceptually distinct but factually simultaneous. While I think that the general thrust of Maximus's attempt proves fruitful for reconciling the presence of sin and death with man's causing them, one aspect of this view that stands in need of emendation is that it still assumes the direct creation of

by Maximus may be found in the theological imagination of C.S. Lewis. Lewis emphasizes that God, who knows all things eternally, accounts for all things—including our prayers—in the very act of creation:

> [I]f our prayers are granted at all, they are granted from the foundation of the world. God and His acts are not in time. Intercourse between God and man occurs at particular moments for the man, but not for God. If there is—as the very concept of prayer presupposes—an adaptation between the free actions of men in prayer and the course of events, this adaptation is from the beginning inherent in the great single creative act. Our prayers are heard—don't say 'have been heard' or you are putting God into time—not only before we make them but before we are made ourselves.[33]

While Lewis is clearly concerned here chiefly with prayer, it is interesting that he also proceeds to ponder the mystery of how—notwithstanding the fact that creatures cannot change God—God's action in the world in some sense seems to be elicited in response to our sins. In light of this, Lewis writes that "before all worlds [God's] providential and creative act (for they are all one) takes into account all the situations produced by the acts of His creatures."[34] It is not a far leap from here to Maximus's suggestion that suffering and death—though not they would not have been God's will for human life if not for his foreknowledge of sin—have nevertheless always been part of it and were in the world even before man himself was.

In sum, for those who are attracted to maintaining the tradition that the origin of suffering and death for all creatures is causally connected to human sin, Maximus's perspective has the benefit of maintaining the connection between these realities on the one hand while also recognizing with Ratzinger the distinct possibility that the suffering and death that have always been part of the human drama. As Maximus proposes, God inscribed these realities into the world in order to help man "come to an awareness of himself and his proper dignity."[35] Thus, as we have also seen Benedict say, suffering and death are in the world to detach man from anything that might separate him from God and thereby conform him fully to the image of Christ crucified. To combine Maximus's insight with Ratzinger's, we might say that, regardless of whether or not God created this cruciform world in foreknowledge of *sin*, he certainly allows suffering and death in view of *love*.

---

man independently of an evolutionary history. Another is Maximus's assumption that sexual reproduction only became a reality after the Fall. On this note, I would add that, if the close connection ancient interpreters saw between sin and the biological onset of sexuality was later rejected, this gives us another good reason to consider the likelihood that they had other faulty assumptions concerning the relationship between sin and the biological facts of human suffering and death.

33. C.S. Lewis, *Letters to Malcolm: Chiefly on Prayer* (London: Geoffrey Bles, 1964), 50–51.

34. C.S. Lewis, *Letters to Malcolm*: 52–53.

35. Maximus the Confessor, *Ambigua*, 8, 145.

# CONCLUSION

Whatever the merits of the above proposal might be, I hope that readers will find much fruit in my attempt over the last two chapters to illumine the presence of suffering and death in our evolving universe. Regardless of whether Maximus and the tradition are right to maintain a causal connection between man's Fall and the onset of suffering and death, I believe that implementing Ratzinger's principles and imitating his practice is invaluable for telling a coherent story about who man is, why he suffers and dies, and in what lies his ultimate vocation. According to this vision, the origin of suffering and death was not a backup plan but rather God's vision for man from all eternity. That is, man in his original graced state may well have endured suffering and death in order that we might be configured to the image of the crucified and risen Jesus.

Perhaps the key difference between the traditional approach to this topic and that offered by Ratzinger is that the latter is attracted to the view that creation has a paschal structure with suffering and death as integral ingredients in the natural world on this side of eternity.[36] Inclined toward the view that humans were always going to be passible and mortal regardless of sin, the emeritus pontiff thus steers clear of speculating about a causal or temporal connection between the Fall and the onset of suffering and death.

Yet, even if suffering and death are natural to man in this world on Ratzinger's view, *sin* is definitely not natural. Indeed, saying that sin is original to man's nature and that there is no fall *from* is precisely what the doctrine of original sin precludes.[37] To be sure, the capacity for sin comes with being a free and rational creature in this world, and the first members of our race—like the rest of us—would have inherited inclinations from their evolutionary ancestors that are rightly considered disordered among humans. However, God did not set us up to fail, and he offered our first parents the grace by which to live truly naturally as humans—that is, by ordering their evolved inclinations according to the faculty of reason and through truly loving relationships which our species alone is blessed to enjoy.[38]

---

36. Some patristic warrant for man's natural mortality is perhaps found in a text of Augustine commenting on 1 Corinthians 15 wherein the Apostle teaches, "Lo! I tell you a mystery. We shall not all sleep, but we shall all be changed" (15:51) and "What you sow does not come to life unless it dies" (15:36). Holding these two lines together, Augustine writes, "*[T]he saints in question will not be 'brought to life' unless they die, however brief this death is to be,* nor will they, therefore, be exempt from a 'resurrection' preceded by a 'sleeping,' however short." Augustine, *The City of God, Books XVII–XXII*, ed. Hermigild Dressler, trans. Gerald G. Walsh and Daniel J. Honan, vol. 24, *The Fathers of the Church* (Washington, D.C.: The Catholic University of America Press, 1954), 303–304.

37. Smith, "What Stands on the Fall?," 63.

38. While his understanding of the relationship of original sin and death is not the same as Ratzinger's when it comes to the question of whether unfallen man would have been immune from suffering and death, Nicanor Austriaco likewise affirms man's continuity with his evolutionary ancestors. Recognizing that the first human beings would have inherited adaptations from their evolutionary forebears that are rightly considered disordered in humans (e.g., inclinations toward promiscuity, violence, cognitive bias, etc.), Austriaco and Ratzinger both affirm in their own way that God gave our first parents

And yet, if we are to believe St. Paul, even that evil that resulted because of our abusing this gift ultimately proves to be an occasion for joy. For, where sin abounds, St. Paul tells us that grace abounds all the more (Rm 5:20; cf. Col 1:24). As the Easter Vigil liturgy proclaims, *felix culpa* (happy fault). Or, in the words of Thomas Aquinas, "God allows evils to happen in order to bring a greater good therefrom."[39]

In the end, our knowledge of the events that transpired at the origin of human history is limited, and it is highly unlikely that we will ever have confidence one way or another whether or not original justice would have entailed human immortality. Indeed, in one of his lectures, Ratzinger interprets the cherubim and flaming sword placed outside Eden (Gn 3:24) as a symbol of the reality that "the empirical (*empirischen*) history of the paradisiacal state is no longer within reach."[40] Lacking direct experience and the ability to demonstrate what a world without sin would look like, I have merely endeavored to propose how Ratzinger's thought as a fitting way for us to think about the realities of suffering and death in light of everything we know about God and nature. Indeed, it must be admitted that everything Ratzinger says about the naturalness of suffering and death may just turn out to be the consequences of sin after all and that his words do not describe the world as originally intended but merely the world in which we live.

Yet, if this is what we are inclined to think is the case, then we must again raise the question I have posed many times throughout this book: Does this account truly cohere with our knowledge of God and his action in the world especially in light of modern scientific discoveries? In other words, is it more likely that man was by a continuous stream of miracles (as indeed it would require) preserved from mosquito bites, thorn scratches, and tornado damage or that he in his original graced state was able to bear these things without sin? Is it more likely that God totally redesigned the human nervous system, birth processes, sweat glands, and the like in response to sin, or that these were always part of the plan for our survival

---

a gift of grace by which they could order their animal inclinations in accord with reason. To explain this dynamic, Austriaco reprises the traditional notion of Adam and Eve's "preternatural gifts" under the banner of the "preteradaptive gifts" (= gifts that enable humans to live beyond their evolved adaptations). Austriaco, "A Fittingness Argument for the Historicity of the Fall of *Homo Sapiens*," *Nova et Vetera* 13 (2015): 651–667 at 63. See also Austriaco, "How Did God Create *Homo Sapiens* through Evolution?," 155–58. In a forthcoming piece on this subject, Robert Barry has likewise written that the presence of evolved proclivities like selfishness is not what constitutes original sin, but rather the lack of grace by which to order these instincts according to reason: "It is not the presence of such tendencies, but the privation of the grace that would temper such tendencies, that constitutes 'original sin.' . . . For humans to exist, live and operate in this manner, just like all other animals but lacking the right order of reason, constitutes the very state of original sin." Robert Barry, "The Transmission of Original Sin in Light of Evolution" (forthcoming).

39. Aquinas, *ST* III, q. 1, a. 3 ad 3. See also *ST* I, q. 2, a. 3, ad 1.

40. Ratzinger, *Schöpfungslehre* (1964), 214. This text also is cited by Sanz, "Joseph Ratzinger y la doctrina de la creación. Los apuntes de Münster de 1964 (y III)," 492n123, but I have emended a typo *empyreischen* with *empirischen* that occurs in the original manuscript. On our lack of experience of a sinless world and consequent inability to know what precisely it would be like, see also Ladaria, *Teología del pecado original y de la gracia*, 47.

and sanctification? That man the capstone of creation was divorced in his very origins from the same creation of which he is the crown, or rather that he was integrated into it? That man was exempt from the processes of suffering and death that have always been integral to the operation of nature, or that he as a graced rational creature was able to suffer these things perfectly and thereby grow to maturity and the stature of Christ's fullness (Eph 4:13)? That the Blessed Virgin is our model by being set apart as the one human who never died or as the one who shows us *how* to suffer and die? In posing these questions once more, I hope that the reader will join me in recalling once again Thomas Aquinas's wise saying: while some things must be believed by the faithful, in other cases there is latitude for debate to such an extent that "in such matters *even the saints* at times view things differently."[41]

Yet, thankfully, the most important thing about our human nature is something not up for debate: that the crucified and risen Jesus is the true and definitive Adam who reveals man to himself, and that our road to *theosis* will come only by way of *kenosis*—that is, through a sincere gift of self in union with our Lord's cross. Seen in this light, the very imperfection of our evolving world with all the suffering it entails affords us creatures the opportunity to become more like Jesus Christ— and thus more like God.

---

41. Aquinas, *In II Sent.*, Lib. 2, d. 12, q. 1, a. 2 (my translation).

# Epilogue

# Evolution and Eschatology

## *Jesus Christ, the Alpha and Omega of All Creation*

## INTRODUCTION

In the last chapter, we reflected on the implications of Benedict XVI's understanding of Jesus Christ as the archetypal human being and how his suffering and death reveals the path by which every person is capable of being conformed to God. Further still, we have seen that Ratzinger seems to have considered suffering and death to be integral to the world itself—that the shape of all creation may be described as paschal or cruciform.

As we have just seen, the sinless lives of Jesus and Mary give us a glimpse of how suffering and death look in the absence of sin. Reflecting on the profound connection between suffering and love—their "inseparability," in Ratzinger's words—we proposed that the phenomena of suffering and death so integral to the evolutionary dynamic were not a backup plan but may well have been the vision God had in mind for human sanctification from all eternity. With that, this volume's exploration of Benedict's thought on human origins would appear to have reached its climax.

That said, our journey is still not quite complete. For, if Benedict's vision is of a cruciform cosmos in which evolution, suffering, and death all play vital roles, these will eventually all come to an end, and one day death will be no more. Indeed, as we saw Aquinas say in the last chapter, even sinless man would not have been able to enjoy heavenly bliss in this world and thus eventually would have had to undergo a transformation at the end of his earthly life. This raises the question: What, if anything, does the evolutionary beginning of human life have to do with man's last end of eternal life in heaven? In other words, what is the connection between protology (the study of origins) and eschatology (the study of the last things)? Stating the matter plainly, Ratzinger declares that the world's origins that we have been exploring in this volume are ultimately understood rightly only in light of creation's end: "[T]he Alpha is only truly to be understood in the light of the Omega."[1] Our final task in this volume is to now unpack the meaning of this statement, especially in light of Benedict's frequent teaching that the end of human life and of the cosmos itself may be described as an "evolution."

---

1. Ratzinger, "The Dignity of the Human Person," 121.

In this concluding reflection, I will be referring to the emeritus pontiff's language of evolutionary transformation as an "anagogy" for the definitive transformation that all created reality will undergo on the Last Day. As understood in the Catholic tradition, the anagogical sense is that which "leads upward" by reasoning from things visible to invisible, raising the minds of believers from the things of earth to the life of heaven.[2] In the following anagogy, we will contemplate Benedict's teaching that the dynamic of evolutionary history on earth (a long story of life and death by which God brought about new and ever greater forms of life, preparing for the advent of man and culminating in the Incarnation of the God-man) has a profound connection to the definitive heavenly transfiguration of the cosmos at the end of time (where, passing through death, all life will be transfigured and conformed to the image of Jesus Christ).

As a final word of introduction to those unfamiliar with this upward-pointing mode of interpreting reality, it may be helpful to consider that what Benedict is endeavoring to achieve with his evolutionary anagogy is comparable to what Jesus seeks to achieve with his words about the grain of wheat that bears no fruit unless it "dies" (Jn 12:24) and St. Paul's teaching that a body "sown" into the ground perishable will one day be raised imperishable (1 Cor 15:42–54). As Jesus and Paul found deep intimations of resurrected life within nature, so too does Benedict find a profound glimpse of this same reality in the long history of evolution in our universe. With these biblical anagogical reference points in place and recognizing that every anagogy has its limits, let us proceed to see what Benedict makes of this connection.

## JESUS CHRIST AS THE ALPHA AND OMEGA OF CREATION AND THE CALL TO SHARE IN HIS "EVOLUTIONARY LEAP"

The close relationship between the beginning and end of creation is abundantly clear in the New Testament, and this link is none other than the person of Jesus Christ. He is the Word who was "in the beginning" (Jn 1:1) and the "first-born of all creation" *through whom* all things were created (Col 1:15–16). At the same time, he is "the first-born from the dead" (Col 1:18), *for whom* all things were created (Col 1:16). Nowhere is this captured more powerfully than in the Bible's climactic words: "I am the Alpha and the Omega, the first and the last, the beginning and the end" (Rv 22:13; cf. 1:8; 21:6). Reflecting on this truth, Pope Benedict writes:

---

2. For a thorough overview of the anagogical sense, see Henri de Lubac. *Medieval Exegesis*, Vol. 2: *The Four Senses of Scripture* (Grand Rapids, MI: Eerdmans, 1998), 179–226. As de Lubac explains, anagogy fosters hope as allegory builds up faith and tropology facilitates charity. On this sense, see also *Catechism of the Catholic Church*, §115–18. The evolutionary comparison developed here has been elsewhere described as an *analogy* for the world to come, yet I have opted for the less familiar term *anagogy* as it more precisely captures the future orientation of the connection. Emphasizing one important dimension of the anagogy that will be developed in detail below, Roch Kereszty judges the Eucharist "indeed the best analogy for the world to come, because it is its initial realization," adding that the renewed universe in which Christ will be all in all (Col 3:11) may be conceived of as "the cosmic extension of an unveiled Eucharist presence." Kereszty, *Jesus Christ*, 428.

Christ is the *protòtypos,* the first-born of creation, the idea for which the universe was conceived. He welcomes all. We enter in the movement of the universe by uniting with Christ. . . . We reach the roots of being by reaching the mystery of Christ, his living word that is the aim of all creation.[3]

One of the remarkable points in the above text is how Benedict draws out the cosmic implications of Christ's incarnation and salvific death. By teaching that our union with Christ causes us to "enter in the movement of the universe," the then-pontiff suggests that not just man, but indeed the whole universe, is in some way moving toward Christ as its *telos.*

This thought is profound enough in its own right, but what makes it especially apropos here at the end of our book is that Ratzinger has consistently described this movement as an "evolution." For instance, in his classic *Introduction to Christianity,* he writes that Christification—the transformation of all in Christ—is "the real drift [*die eigentliche Drift*] of evolution . . . the real goal of the ascending process of growth or becoming."[4] Inspired by the language of Louis Bouyer and Pierre Teilhard de Chardin, the pioneering priest-paleontologist whose thought he frequently draws upon and refines, Ratzinger expands in more detail:

Faith sees in Jesus the man in whom—on the biological plane—the next evolutionary leap [*der nächste Evolutionssprung*], as it were, has been accomplished; the man in whom the breakthrough [*Durchbruch*] out of the limited scope of humanity, out of its monadic enclosure, has occurred.[5]

---

3. Benedict XVI, Address (October 6, 2008). For other discussions of this connection, see Benedict XVI, Homily (April 23, 2011). See also Ratzinger, *A New Song,* 84; cf. *In the Beginning,* 27. For another articulation of this dynamic from an author who had a significant impact on Ratzinger's thought, see Romano Guardini, *The Lord* (Washington D.C.: Gateway, 2016), 483: "In his corporeal reality, in his transfigured humanity he is the world redeemed. That is why he is called 'the firstborn' of all creatures, 'the beginning,' 'the firstborn from the dead' (Col 1:15,18). Through him transitory creation is lifted into the eternal existence of God . . . for all creation is called to share in his Transfiguration."

4. Ratzinger, *Introduction to Christianity,* 236–37 (*Einführung in das Christentum,* 223).

5. Ratzinger, *Introduction to Christianity,* 238–39 (*Einführung in das Christentum,* 225). For a systemic outline of the vision of a "universal evolution" described here, see Kereszty, *Jesus Christ,* 68–71, 374, 381–82. Especially apropos to our present topic, Ratzinger adds here that Teilhard de Chardin, though not without his flaws, provided an "important service" to theology by rethinking this notion within modernity's broader evolutionary understanding of the cosmos. Ratzinger's overall assessment of Chardin's thought is grasped from this statement: "It must be regarded as an important service of Teilhard de Chardin's that he rethought these ideas from the angle of the modern view of the world and, in spite of a not entirely unobjectionable tendency toward the biological approach, nevertheless on the whole grasped them correctly and in any case made them accessible once again." Ratzinger, *Introduction to Christianity,* 236. Elsewhere, Ratzinger seeks to purify a certain "tendency" in Chardin's thought (as well as in *Gaudium et Spes*) by emphasizing that the authentic process of christification that he has in mind is not that of a "technological utopia" that can be achieved in this world. See Ratzinger, *Theological Highlights of Vatican II,* 226–29 and Benedict XVI, *Spe Salvi,* §§16–23. For Bouyer's contribution to understanding Christ as the "Omega Point" of creation, see his *Cosmos* as well as Keith Lemna, *The Apocalypse of Wisdom: Louis Bouyer's Theological Recovery of the Cosmos* (Brooklyn, NY: Angelico Press, 2019).

As we saw in the last chapter, the connection between the nature of Christ and the vocation of man is so tight that, for Ratzinger, Christology *is* anthropology. Moreover, what concerns Christ—the "definitive evolutionary leap" he brought about—in turn applies to the ultimate vocation of *all* human beings. Like Christ, the person who dies having been totally transformed by love transcends the limits of space and time and all the suffering that is part and parcel of existence here below. In the eschaton, all facets of our natural life [*bios*] will be "encompassed by and incorporated in the power of love," which itself is not bound to the material world but lives on perpetually. Accordingly, after departing the present temporal "realm of biological evolutions and mutations," Ratzinger describes the blessed man as undergoing a "last stage of evolution," a "leap" [*Sprung*].

Expanding on how precisely a person goes about making this definitive "leap" with Christ, Ratzinger teaches that this movement of *theosis* (i.e., divinization—"becoming God" while remaining distinct from the transcendent Lord whom we worship) only occurs when we make a free and total offering of ourselves in love and even then will only be complete in heaven:

> Only where someone values love more highly than life, that is, only where someone is ready to put life second to love, for the sake of love, can love be stronger and more than death. If it is to be more than death, it must first be more than mere life. But if it could be this, not just in intention but in reality, then that would mean at the same time that the power of love had risen superior to the power of the merely biological and taken it into its service. . . .
>
> Such a final stage of "mutation" and "evolution" would itself no longer be a biological stage. . . . The last stage of evolution needed by the world to reach its goal would then no longer be achieved within the realm of biology but by the spirit, by freedom, by love. It would no longer be evolution but decision and gift in one.[6]

In sum, Ratzinger agrees with Paul in that, if we do not have love, then we have nothing. For, at that point, we would have achieved no higher calling than any other species on this planet. On the other hand, in having love, we have everything, since "love is the foundation of immortality, and immortality proceeds from love alone."[7] Speaking first of Christ but in turn of all of us called to share in his nature through

---

For more on Ratzinger's appropriation of Chardin's language of life in Christ as mankind's definitive "evolutionary leap" in which the body will no longer be subject to decay (1 Cor 15:44), see Ramage, *The Experiment of Faith*, 106–108, 123, 147n28, 269–70. For his knowledge of Chardin, Ratzinger is at least partially in debt to Henri de Lubac's nuanced treatments of the former's thought. See Henri de Lubac, *The Religion of Teilhard de Chardin* (New York: Desclee Co., 1967) and de Lubac, *Teilhard de Chardin: the Man and His Meaning* (New York: Hawthorn Books, 1965). Like Ratzinger, de Lubac found both strengths and weaknesses in Chardin's theology, yet time and again he staunchly defended the orthodoxy of the latter's Catholic faith. This can be glimpsed periodically in de Lubac's council notebooks, as noted in the preface to vol. 1 of de Lubac's *Vatican Council Notebooks* at 11.

6. Ratzinger, *Introduction to Christianity*, 304.

7. Ratzinger, *Introduction to Christianity*, 306.

grace, Ratzinger goes so far as to make the bold claim that "he who has love for all has established immortality for all."[8]

## MAKING ALL THINGS NEW: THE BIBLICAL VISION OF CREATION'S ESCHATOLOGICAL TRANSFIGURATION

A remarkable feature of Ratzinger's Christological perspective on evolution is that it is not just about the salvation of individual human beings but the glorious transformation *of all creation*.[9] Ratzinger's lofty claim about the destiny of the created world—a hope echoed in the teachings of the Second Vatican Council— finds its basis in multiple New Testament texts. With their exalted expectations for the future of the created universe, these letters clearly share the profound con- viction that the evolving world we inhabit is "very good" (Gn 1:31) and therefore destined in some way—however inscrutable it is to us here below—to share with us in eternal glory.[10]

Perhaps most famously, St. John envisions "a new heaven and a new earth" to be revealed in the fullness of time (Rv 21:1; cf. Is 11:6–9; 25:7–9; 65:17–25; 66:22) and sees the Lord declaring, "'Behold, I make *all things* new'" (Rv 21:5, emphasis added). In the same vein, 2 Pt 3:8–14 informs us that, when the day of the Lord arrives like a thief, "then the heavens will pass away with a loud noise, and the elements will be dissolved with fire"—not in order to abolish cre- ation but rather to *renew* it as a "new heavens and a new earth in which right- eousness dwells."[11] Expanding on this eschatological vision in his own turn, Paul depicts the whole creation "groaning [*systenazei*] in travail" as it waits to be "set free from its bondage to decay and obtain the glorious liberty of the children of God" (Rm 8:21–22).[12]

---

8. Ratzinger, *Introduction to Christianity*, 306.

9. An earlier version of this section on cosmic transubstantiation is found in Ramage, *The Experi- ment of Faith*, 106–109. For another discussion of this dynamism in light of the New Testament witness regarding the effect of Christ's redemptive work upon all orders of creation, see Telford Work, *Jesus— the End and the Beginning*, 67.

10. See Second Vatican Council, *Lumen Gentium*, §48: At the time of the "restoration of all things," the council writes, "the human race as well as the entire world, which is intimately related to man and attains to its end through him, will be perfectly reestablished in Christ." Similarly, *Gaudium et Spes*, §39 teaches that, while the form of this world will pass away (1 Cor 7:31), "all that creation which God made on man's account will be unchained from the bondage of vanity." On this topic, see also *Catechism of the Catholic Church*, §§1042–60.

11. For the Old Testament background of Peter's text and that it is describing the renewal rather than abolition of creation, see Richard Bauckham, *2 Peter, Jude* (Dallas: Word, Incorporated, 1983), 325–26: "The cosmic dissolution described in vv 10, 12, was a return to the primeval chaos, as in the Flood (3:6), so that a new creation may emerge (cf. 4 Ezra 7:30–31). Such passages emphasize the radical discontinuity between the old and the new, but it is nevertheless clear that they intend to describe a renewal, not an abolition, of creation (cf. *1 Enoch* 54:4–5; Rom 8:21)."

12. For more on the theme of "groaning" in Paul and in his writings' Old Testament background, see Moisés Silva, ed., *New International Dictionary of New Testament Theology and Exegesis* (Grand Rapids, MI: Zondervan, 2014), 365–67. In the background of Paul's eschatological vision lies the

It is noteworthy that Paul sees the redemption of believers as a prerequisite for the liberation of the cosmos: "For the creation waits with eager longing for the revealing of the sons of God" (Rm 8:19). Brant Pitre, Michael Barber, and John Kincaid explain this dynamic well in their collaborative work *Paul, A New Covenant Jew*:

> God's saving plan includes even more than that. Christ's work of redemption involves more than reconciling humans. According to Paul, there is a genuinely cosmic dimension to the plan of salvation realized by Christ's work. The apostle affirms the goodness of creation, which points to the Creator (Rom 1:20). The material world will also somehow share in Christ's work of redemption. In Romans 8, creation itself "waits with eager longing for the revealing of the sons of God" (Rom 8:19 RSV). Believers, therefore, entertain a hope that is truly all-encompassing of everything God has made. He tells the Corinthians, "For all things are yours, whether Paul or Apollos or Cephas or the world or life or death or the present or the future, all are yours; and you are Christ's; and Christ is God's" (1 Cor 3:21–23 RSV). At the end of time, all things will be subjected to the reign of Christ "so that God may be all in all [*hina ē ho theos panta en pasin*]" (1 Cor 15:28). Yet . . . Romans 8 also indicates that the dawning of this new creation is explicitly tied to the suffering not only of Christ but of believers as well, who endure affliction not merely as individuals but together as the children of God.[13]

Likewise, Constantine Campbell aptly describes this marvel by when he writes, "The sweep of Paul's eschatology includes the entirety of creation. . . . [C]reation is the arena *and object* of God's restorative work. All things in heaven and on earth will be transformed through renewal and unification around Christ."[14] All this is to say that, while Christ has willed "to reconcile to himself *all things*, whether on

---

Septuagint of Genesis 3:16, which portrays God saying, "I will greatly multiply your pains and your groaning; in pains you will bear children." Noting the verbal connection between Romans and the LXX of Genesis, Scott Hahn comments, "Creation, like Adam and Eve, and because of them, is under divine judgment," adding that "Paul also appears to be indebted to the prophets [Is 26:16–18; Jer 4:31; Hos 13:13; Mic 4:9–10], who used the 'pangs of childbirth' motif to describe the Lord's people in distress." Hahn, *Romans*, 139. Indeed, in Paul's day many Jews expected that a period of intense suffering would come just before the end of the age, sometimes referred to as the "birth pangs of the Messiah." Craig Keener and John Walton, eds., *NIV Cultural Backgrounds Study Bible: Bringing to Life the Ancient World of Scripture* (Grand Rapids, MI: Zondervan, 2016), 1962.

13. Pitre, Barber, and Kincaid, *Paul, a New Covenant Jew*, 212. As Scott Hahn puts it, "The relationship between man and the world is so close that the fate of the one is tied up with the fate of the other." Hahn, *Romans*, 139. The universal character of God's plan appears already in Genesis 9:12, where God tells Noah that he is setting his "bow in the cloud" as a sign of his "covenant which I make between me and you and *every living creature* that is with you, for all future generations." Emphasis added. For a survey and analysis of the biblical view that creation will not be a mere spectator to man's liberation and glorification but rather a participant in it, see Joseph Fitzmyer, *Romans* (New York: Doubleday, 1993), 505–11.

14. Constantine Campbell, *Paul and the Hope of Glory* (Grand Rapids, MI: Zondervan Academic, 2021), 241.

earth or in heaven" (Col 1:20, emphasis added; cf. Eph 1:10), Paul insists that believers have a pivotal role to play in this eschatological drama as they "complete what is lacking in Christ's afflictions" (Col 1:24).

The above notion underlies the Apostle's personification of creation as a woman crying out in labor pains and as a slave yearning for freedom.[15] By dramatically depicting creation as awaiting the redemption of man, Paul reveals that creation's own "exodus" from death and decay is contingent upon the faithful first attaining this freedom in their own lives.[16] Just as the Jewish world of Paul's day held that all of creation had been tragically drawn into Adam/Israel's ruin, so too Paul reveals that the New Adam's glorious redemption is no less cosmic in scope. Indeed, the Apostle envisions creation as the transfigured arena that the coheirs with Christ will inhabit with their resurrected bodies. As Campbell says, "It seems that resurrected human beings will require a new creation in which to live. . . . [T]heir renewed creaturely status will be matched by the renewed creation."[17] Accordingly, the created universe is not merely a means by which we humans reach our end in heaven, but rather a gift that will accompany us on our journey toward beatitude and truly share in the final perfection of heavenly glory.[18]

---

15. The Old Testament image evoked by Paul in this context is Exodus 2:23, where the children of Israel "groaned in their slavery." As N.T. Wright observes, this imagery is part of Paul's larger retelling of the Exodus story in which the Apostle sees both human beings and God's good creation alike as subject to the "slavery" of futility and decay and therefore equally in need of finding freedom through an "exodus." N.T. Wright, *The Resurrection of the Son of God* (Minneapolis, MN: Fortress Press, 2003), 258. For more on the groaning motif in Romans, see also James Dunn, *Romans 1–8*, vol. 38A, *Word Biblical Commentary* (Dallas: Word, Incorporated, 1988), 472–73.

16. James Dunn suggests an anagogy to explain this vision: "The thought [of creation awaiting the *apokalypsis* or heavenly 'unveiling' of the faithful] may be paralleled to that of a play in which the final curtain is drawn back to reveal the various actors transformed (back) into their real characters—creation being, as it were, the audience eagerly watching the human actors play their parts on the world stage." Dunn, *Romans 1–8*, 470. For another treatment of Paul's connecting the transformation of all creation with human sanctification within his larger vision of "the cosmic Christ," see George Maloney, SJ, *The Mystery of Christ in You: The Mystical Vision of St. Paul* (New York: Alba House, 1998), 112–17, 122–23.

17. Campbell, *Paul and the Hope of Glory*, 235; also cf. 217. Whether this renewed creation is strictly speaking *required* for man's beatitude may be a matter of debate, yet one may at least confidently say that it is supremely fitting that man with his risen body will inhabit a world with other transfigured physical things. For a valuable article that explores Aquinas's teaching that nonhuman creation is not necessary for man's final beatitude and yet will provide the saints with enjoyment as its transfigured existence leads them to contemplate the glory of God, see Aquinas, *Compendium of Theology* (St. Louis, MO: B. Herder Book Co., 1947), I, 170 and Bryan Kromholtz, OP, "The Consummation of the World: St. Thomas Aquinas on the Risen Saints' Beatitude and the Corporeal Universe," forthcoming in *Nova et Vetera*.

18. Bryan Kromholtz captures a powerful implication of the above teaching when he writes, "It may even be possible that the very quality of *not* being necessary for human beatitude can make the promised eschatological renewal of creatures act as a salutary reminder that there is a higher purpose to the ontological universe than serving us—for God himself is that purpose. . . . Thomas's sharp insistence that human happiness cannot be achieved through material creation points us rightly toward the

## CHRIST AND COSMIC TRANSUBSTANTIATION

With the above biblical data in place, we may now consider the theology that Benedict unfolds in its light. In the first installment of his *Jesus* trilogy, Pope Benedict described the Bible's grand eschatological vision as having a "great Christological—indeed, cosmic—dynamism."[19] Meanwhile, in the second volume of the same series, he would write even more boldly:

> If there really is a God, is he not able to create a new dimension of human existence, a new dimension of reality altogether? Is not creation actually waiting for this last and highest "evolutionary leap," for the union of the finite with the infinite, for the union of man and God, for the conquest of death?[20]

In his first Easter homily as pope, Benedict preached along the same lines using biological terms like evolution and mutation to describe heavenly life anagogically (as one must always speak when dealing with Last Things):

> If we may borrow the language of the theory of evolution, [Christ's resurrection] is the greatest "mutation," absolutely the most crucial leap into a totally new dimension that there has ever been in the long history of life and its development: a leap into a completely new order that does concern us, and concerns the whole of history. . . . It is a qualitative leap in the history of "evolution" and of life in general toward a new future life, toward a new world, which, starting from Christ, already continuously permeates this world of ours, transforms it, and draws it to itself.[21]

As an indication of just how close this theme was to his heart, it is telling that the emeritus pontiff wished to expand upon it in his rare writings penned in retirement. For instance, in one he writes, "If we really wanted to summarize very briefly the

---

One on whom our attention should be fixed even in this life." Kromholtz, "The Consummation of the World" (forthcoming). To my mind, this eloquent point regarding the transfigured presence of creatures in heaven further bespeaks the gratuity of God's love. For, while man cannot be fulfilled through anything less than God himself and strictly speaking God alone is necessary for our beatitude, the Lord nevertheless allows creatures to contribute in a variety of ways to one another's happiness even now. And, in heaven, Aquinas says, nature is not done away with but rather perfected. Aquinas, *ST* II-II, q. 26, a. 13, sc.; Aquinas, *In IV Sent.* d. 49, q. 2, a. 3, ad 8.

In light of the above, Kromholtz suggests, "The 'joy' that such sensible perception of God's creatures might afford, coexisting with the beatific vision but distinct from it, would likely fall under the category of those delights that follow human reason but do not arise from nature." Kromholtz, "The Consummation of the World" (forthcoming); cf. Aquinas, *ST* I-II, q. 31, a. 3. Also suggestive is Aquinas, *Commentary on Hebrews*, 706–707, where Thomas notes, "In heavenly glory, there are two things which will particularly gladden [*laetificabunt*] the just, namely, the enjoyment of the Godhead and companionship with the saints. For no good is joyfully possessed without companions," adding that an additional joy (*complementum*) in heaven will consist in the company of the saints. If this is true of man as a created being, it might well apply to other creatures as well, as suggested above.

19. Benedict XVI, *Jesus of Nazareth: From the Baptism*, 270.
20. Benedict XVI, *Jesus of Nazareth: Holy Week*, 246–47.
21. Benedict XVI, Homily (April 15, 2006).

content of the Faith as laid down in the Bible, we might do so by saying that the Lord has initiated a narrative of love with us and wants to *subsume all creation* in it. The counterforce against evil, which threatens us and the whole world, can ultimately only consist in our entering into this love."[22] In his landmark volume *Eschatology*, Ratzinger spoke of this state that encompasses all of creation as a "pan-cosmic existence" that leads to "universal exchange and openness, and so to the overcoming of all alienation." Making his own the words of St. Paul, he expounds, "Only where creation achieves such unity can it be true that God is 'all in all' [Eph 1:23] . . . where each thing becomes completely itself precisely by being completely in the other."[23]

In another, even more stunning text—this time a brief post-retirement address given on the sixty-fifth anniversary of his priestly ordination—Benedict went so far as to speak of this transformative dynamic as one of *cosmic transubstantiation*:

> The cross, suffering, all that is wrong with the world: he transformed all this into "thanks" and therefore into a "blessing." Hence he fundamentally transubstantiated life and the world [*fondamentalmente ha transustanziato la vita e il mondo*]. . . . Finally, we wish to insert ourselves into the "thanks" of the Lord, and thus truly receive the newness of life and contribute to the "transubstantiation" of the world [*transustanziazione del mondo*] so that it might not be a place of death, but of life: a world in which love has conquered death.[24]

In this short paragraph, the emeritus pontiff emphasizes that the "transubstantiation of the world" is a reality that has at once already begun and yet which will continue to unfold to the extent that we disciples insert ourselves into Christ's saving work as his co-redeemers.[25]

---

22. Benedict XVI, "The Church and the Scandal of Sexual Abuse," April 10, 2019 (emphasis added), https://www.ncregister.com/news/pope-benedict-essay-the-church-and-the-scandal-of-sexual-abuse.

23. Ratzinger, *Eschatology*, 192; Eph 1:23; Col 1:20. For the background to this text and language of "pan-cosmic existence," see Karl Rahner, *Nature and Grace* (New York: Sheed and Ward, 1964), 41 and Karl Rahner, *On the Theology of Death* (New York: Herder and Herder, 1961), 18–19. In this last text, Rahner writes that our bond with the universe is not broken in death but that on the contrary we enter more deeply into it.

24. Benedict XVI, Address at the Commemoration of the 65th Anniversary of the Priestly Ordination of Pope Emeritus Benedict XVI (June 28, 2016), https://w2.vatican.va/content/francesco/en/speeches/2016/june/documents/papa-francesco_20160628_65-ordinazione-sacerdotale-benedetto-xvi.html. Benedict is not the first pontiff to draw out the role of the Eucharist for the transformation of the cosmos. See for example John Paul II, *Ecclesia de Eucharistia*, 8: "[The celebration of the Eucharist] has a cosmic character. . . . Yes, cosmic! Because even when it is celebrated on the humble altar of a country church, the Eucharist is always in some way celebrated on the altar of the world. It unites heaven and earth. It embraces and permeates all creation. The Son of God became man in order to restore all creation, in one supreme act of praise, to the One who made it from nothing."

25. For an example of a Pauline text in which this theme appears, see 2 Corinthians 5:17 ("Therefore, if anyone is in Christ, he is a new creation; the old has passed away, behold, the new has come") and Philippians 3:20, where Paul says that the true "citizenship" of the believer lies in the heavenly realm even now. For an excellent treatment of the reality that the new creation envisioned by Paul is both

What, exactly, will it look like in the new heaven and new earth when the entire cosmos is transformed in Christ? The truth is that Scripture reveals to us *that* this is the vocation of all creation but comprehending *what it means* is another thing. For instance, the above biblical data strongly suggest that whatever good is present in the Ramage family cat and in our backyard orchard will be present in the hereafter in an even more perfect way than it is now ("set free from its bondage to decay" and having obtained "the glorious liberty of the children of God"). Or, we might consider the countless bacteria that inhabit our digestive tracts and which we now know to play an indispensable role in keeping us healthy. Seeing as they are so important to our lives here below—as are trees, pets, and innumerable other creatures—does this give us reason to think that bacteria will exist somehow in heaven?

In his monograph *The Groaning of Creation: God, Evolution, and the Problem of Evil*, Christopher Southgate argues precisely this: specifically, that the justice of God's stewardship of creation necessitates that the expendable victims of every species must somehow enjoy a share in eschatological perfection.[26] Similarly, in his article on Maximus the Confessor's cosmic vision in relation to evolutionary theodicy, Paul Blowers maintains that, "[f]or Maximus, the incarnation, death, resurrection, and ascension of Jesus Christ have, in principle at least, opened a way for that very possibility, even if the first fruits of the coming eschatological transformation are creatures of reason and free will."[27] Evidence for such an eventuality may perhaps also be what Hosea has in mind when he foresees the heavens and earth being restored to proper relationship in the eschaton, adding, "In that day . . . I will make for you a covenant on that day with the beasts of the field, the birds of the air, and the creeping things of the ground" (Hos 2:18).[28] When pondering these sorts of questions, it is important to remember the words of St. Paul: no eye has seen, no ear heard, and no heart conceived what God has prepared for those who love him (1 Cor 2:9, citing Is 64:4). In an erudite reflection on this matter, Andrew Davison thus speaks of three contrasting ways one may understand the eschatological vision upon that we are reflecting upon here: the universal resurrection of every living thing, that of certain creatures whose lives became interwoven with particular human stories, and the traditional view that heaven will exclude the presence of all nonhuman physical beings. In the end, though, none of these seems to precisely

---

already present and still awaiting its completion, see Pitre, Barber, and Kincaid, *Paul, a New Covenant Jew*, 71–73: "Paul affirms that, in some sense, the end of this world and the beginning of the new creation have already taken place. . . . Through the passion, death, resurrection, and exaltation of Christ, the old world was put to death and the new world began. Because of this, believers who are 'in Christ,' live in a kind of 'in-between' realm, where the old and new creations 'intermingle' with one another."

26. Christopher Southgate, *The Groaning of Creation: God, Evolution, and the Problem of Evil* (Louisville, KY: Westminster John Knox Press, 2008), 16, 78–91.

27. Paul Blowers, "Unfinished Creative Business: Maximus the Confessor, Evolutionary Theodicy, and Human Stewardship in Creation," in *On Earth as It Is in Heaven: Cultivating a Contemporary Theology of Creation* (Grand Rapids, MI: Eerdmans, 2016), ed. David Meconi, 174–90.

28. For further reflection on this text, see Matthew Levering, "'Be Fruitful and Multiply, and Fill the Earth': Was and Is This a Good Idea?," in *On Earth as It Is in Heaven*, 80–122 at 89–90n23.

coincide with Benedict's position, and at any rate Davison wisely concludes, "We may do well to leave the discussion at that: speculative eschatological physiology is best avoided."[29] Summing up this matter, Ratzinger likewise says:

> In conclusion: the new world cannot be imagined. Nothing concrete or imaginable can be said about the relation of man to matter in the new world, or about the "risen body." Yet we have the certainty that the dynamism of the cosmos leads towards a goal, a situation in which matter and spirit will belong to each other in a new and definitive fashion. This certainty remains the concrete content of the confession of the resurrection of the flesh even today.[30]

In sum, it is beyond our ken as finite human beings to know whether and how this or that creature might exist on the other side of this vale of tears. Yet what believers do know is that, while our origin is natural, our end is divine—and what awaits us on the other side of death is not less but infinitely more glorious than we could ever imagine.

## THE EUCHARIST AS ANTICIPATION AND CAUSE OF CREATION'S MOVEMENT TOWARD DIVINIZATION

Given the overt sacramental language with which Benedict describes the transformation of our world into Christological fullness (transubstantiation, thanksgiving, blessings), we might expect the emeritus pontiff to argue that communion in the Body and Blood of Christ plays an important role in this dynamic. Indeed, this is precisely what Benedict does on multiple occasions. For instance, he has connected man's divinization to that of the cosmos and suggested that the bridge between the two lies in Eucharistic communion: "I myself become part of the new bread that he is creating by *the resubstantiation of the whole of earthly reality*."[31] To this, he adds that "the very goal of worship *and of creation as a whole* are one and the same—divinization."[32]

Again invoking evolutionary language in an anagogical manner, Benedict writes, God has drawn his creation ever closer to himself through a series of ontological or "evolutionary leaps" in which the transubstantiated Host becomes the

---

29. Andrew Davison, "Christian Doctrine and Biological Mutualism: Some Explorations in Systematic and Philosophical Theology," *Theology and Science* 18.2 (2020): 258–78 at 270–71.

30. Ratzinger, *Eschatology*, 194.

31. Joseph Ratzinger, *Pilgrim Fellowship of Faith* (San Francisco: Ignatius Press, 2005), 78, 118. Emphasis in original. This line also appears in Ratzinger, *Behold the Pierced One: An Approach to a Spiritual Christology* (San Francisco: Ignatius Press, 1986), 89. The latter translation renders the phrase ". . . by transubstantiating all earthly reality." For the original German term *umsubstanziierung*, see Ratzinger, *Schauen auf den Durchbohrten: Versuche zu einer spirituellen Christologie* (Einsiedeln: Johannes Verlag, 1984), 76. For a citation of this text within a larger discussion of Ratzinger's spiritual christology, see Imbelli, "Joseph Ratzinger's 'Spiritual Christology,'" 232.

32. Ratzinger, *Spirit of the Liturgy*, 28. Emphasis added. Describing the Eucharist as "the extension of the Incarnation," Carmelite priest Wilfrid Stinissen echoes Ratzinger in seeing it as the means of achieving "the goal of the Incarnation," which is "for all of reality, everything created, to become the body of Christ." Wilfrid Stinessen, *Bread That Is Broken* (San Francisco: Ignatius Press, 2020), 63, 66.

first-fruits of the renewed creation—"the anticipation of the transformation and divinization of matter in the Christological fullness" which in turn "provides the movement of the cosmos with its direction; it anticipates its goal and at the same time urges it on."[33] As a final illustration of this point, consider this homily that Benedict gave on the feast of Corpus Christi:

> This little piece of white Host, this bread of the poor, appears to us as a synthesis of creation. In this way, we begin to understand why the Lord chooses this piece of bread to represent him. Creation, with all of its gifts, aspires above and beyond itself to something even greater. Over and above the synthesis of its own forces, above and beyond the synthesis also of nature and of spirit that, *in some way, we detect in the piece of bread, creation is projected towards divinization*, toward the holy wedding feast, toward unification with the Creator himself.[34]

---

33. Ratzinger, *Spirit of the Liturgy*. 29. The full paragraph reads: "Against the background of the modern evolutionary world view, Teilhard de Chardin depicted the cosmos as a process of ascent, a series of unions. From very simple beginnings the path leads to ever greater and more complex unities, in which multiplicity is not abolished but merged into a growing synthesis, leading to the 'Noosphere,' in which spirit and its understanding embrace the whole and are blended into a kind of living organism. Invoking the epistles to the Ephesians and Colossians, Teilhard looks on Christ as the energy that strives toward the Noosphere and finally incorporates everything in its 'fullness.' From here Teilhard went on to give a new meaning to Christian worship: the transubstantiated Host is the anticipation of the transformation and divinization of matter in the christological 'fullness.' In his view, the Eucharist provides the movement of the cosmos with its direction; it anticipates its goal and at the same time urges it on."

Contrasting the blessed in heaven with individuals in hell who have willingly failed to undergo the final evolutionary "mutation" by which they might share in Christ's resurrected life, Christopher Baglow offers a suggestive analogy with the "nasty little creature" that we know as the tapeworm: "The tapeworm has evolved from a much more complex organism to the form it has now. In its evolution it adopted a 'less is more' approach to parasitism, losing its nervous system, its digestive system, leaving nothing but the ability to latch onto its prey and reproduce. Similarly, humans in hell would be those who cling to the lower form of existence rather than opening themselves up to the adventure of a new kind of life, losing their capacity for anything beyond themselves." Baglow, *Creation*, 116.

34. Benedict XVI, Homily for the Mass of Corpus Christi (June 15, 2006), emphasis added. For some other examples of the pontiff's appropriation of Teilhard de Chardin's cosmic liturgy wherein the whole of creation becomes a living Host, see Benedict XVI, Homily (July 24, 2009); Benedict XVI, Homily (April 15, 2006); Ratzinger, *Introduction to Christianity*, 234–45; and Ratzinger, *Eschatology*, 93. Notably, Pope Francis cites this very text as part of his ecological vision in *Laudato Si'* (2015), §236. In the specific text cited above, it is also noteworthy that, while describing the cosmos as being drawn toward Eucharistic transformation in Christ, Benedict also depicts the *telos* of this trajectory as a wedding feast. For indeed, the image of the Eucharistic banquet and wedding feast of the Lamb (which emphasizes less our *becoming* Christ than our *feeding on* and *being with* Christ) is another important and complementary anagogy by which the Christian tradition glimpses the hope of heavenly glory.

On this score, Geoffrey Wainwright notes well that the richness of the Eucharist requires that the reality be represented through a variety of images, for indeed "the confusion of the imagery serves in fact as a salutary reminder" that these things of which we dare to speak are divine mysteries known fully to God alone. Wainwright, *Eucharist and Eschatology* (New York: Oxford University Press, 1981), 106–107. While he does not agree with the Catholic doctrine of transubstantiation or its use as an anagogy for the renewed creation, Wainwright nevertheless speaks eloquently of the Eucharist as "the

Beyond hinting that the Eucharist plays a central role in the movement of all creation toward divinization, Benedict once again does not say much about what the
process might look like concretely. Nor does he suggest how precisely to reconcile
a possible eschatological existence of the created world with the likelihood that
entropy will eventually cause the physical universe to fizzle out—not with a bang,
but with a whimper. Indeed, the reason Benedict does not address these topics is
because, as we saw above, he simply does not consider it possible to speak much
more about what precisely will happen at the end of time. Rather, the only thing
we may be able to do cogently is profess *that* a great cosmic transformation will
happen. Nevertheless, I think that we can piece together some of the details by
drawing on resources across the broader tradition.

There is an abundance of biblical, patristic, and liturgical backing for Ratzinger's theology of divinization or *theosis*. The writings of the Fathers are one of
these resources, where we find this classic formula that runs in many variations
throughout the Christian tradition: The Son of God became man so that the sons
of men might become God.[35] In this line, we glimpse both the great Christian hope
of *divinization* (man's becoming God) along with the reason it is possible: the *hominization* of God—that is, because the eternal Word of God became man. Or, as St.
Maximus the Confessor puts it, "By this blessed inversion, man is made God by
divinization, and God is made man by hominization."[36] Like so many other Patristic
teachings, this majestic teaching is nothing other than an exegesis of biblical texts
like 2 Peter 1:3–4 (we are called to "become partakers of the divine nature"), 1 John
3:1–3 ("when he appears we shall be like him, for we shall see him as he is"), Ephesians 3:19 (a prayer that we will "be filled with all the fulness of God"), and 1 Corinthians 15:28 (in the end, God will be "all in all") which reveal that man's last end is
to be totally conformed to God and share in his very life.

In addition to Scripture and the fathers, the liturgy offers an unrivaled treasury
of insight into divinization. Among the many liturgical prayers that speak and pray
for our divinization that one might recall, consider the words of the offertory rite,
uttered *sotto voce* (under the breath) while the priest pours water into the chalice:
"By the mystery of this water and wine may we come to share in the divinity of

---

vehicle of saving fellowship between God and man" in virtue of which the consecrated bread and wine
"are granted, at least in a hidden way, fulfillment of the destiny after which the whole material creation
groans (cf. Rm 8:19–23)." To this he adds, "What is true of the inanimate creatures of bread and wine
cannot be less true of the body of the man who consumes them at the Eucharist." Wainwright, *Eucharist
and Eschatology*, 149.

35. For instance, see Athanasius, *On the Incarnation of the Word* (Crestwood, NY: St. Vladimir's
Seminary Press, 1993), 93. As I mentioned above, the theme of *theosis* runs throughout the Christian
tradition from authors as diverse as St. Peter, Augustine, Pseudo-Dionysius, John of Damascus, Maximus
the Confessor, Thomas Aquinas, Thomas à Kempis, Francis de Sales, Benedict XVI, and countless others
in between. For a work that surveys St. Augustine's theology of divinization, see David Meconi, SJ, *The
One Christ: St. Augustine's Theology of Deification* (Washington, D.C.: The Catholic University of America
Press, 2013).

36. St. Maximus the Confessor, *Ambiguum*, 7, in *On the Cosmic Mystery of Jesus Christ*, 45–75.

Christ who humbled himself to share in our humanity." In this text, the Church enacts ritually what St. Maximus above described verbally, a dynamic so profound that Benedict characterizes it as the "mutual compenetration between Christ and the Christian" in which we reside in Christ and Christ in us.[37] Or, to draw from another liturgical prayer, it enacts a change so astounding that we are "transformed into what we consume" and become by grace what Christ is by nature.[38]

As we see here, the text of the liturgy reveals the same dynamic that Benedict describes in his writings: in the act of consecration, ordinary bread miraculously becomes Christ, which in turn becomes the vehicle to gradually transform those who receive it into Christ. Benedict refers to this dynamic as "the Eucharistic form of the Christian life,"[39] a mysticism described well by Robert Imbelli in saying that it "leads, mystagogically, to the realization that Jesus Christ's very being is to be Eucharist" and that, "to the extent that we become present to his real Presence, our very self becomes Eucharistic: a living out of gratitude to the Father and generosity towards our brothers and sisters." Concretely, Imbelli adds, living this form of life "entails taking on the heart and mind of Jesus Christ so that Eucharistic spirituality become the measure of our thoughts and actions, and the criterion by which we discern the values and disvalues of a given culture."[40]

So much for man, but what of the emeritus pontiff's point that in some way *all of creation* is to be divinized? I would suggest that insight into this mystery might be found in the words of the Second Vatican Council and its teaching that the faithful are called to unite themselves with Christ in a liturgical existence and so "consecrate the world itself to God."[41] In other words, our reception of the Eucharist endows us with the power to extend the transforming love of God to the whole world so that it achieves its end. In this way, suggests Benedict, we the faithful contribute to the "transubstantiation" of the cosmos, leading all creatures to what Pope Francis describes as "a transcendent fullness where the risen Christ embraces and illumines all things."[42] To be sure, this Catholic vision with its overt language of sacramental

---

37. Benedict XVI, "St. Paul's New Outlook," general audience (November 8, 2006); Rm 8:1–2,10,39; 12:5; 16:3, 7, 10; 1 Cor 1:2-3; 2 Cor 13:5; Gal 2:20. See also Bl. Columba Marmion, *Christ in His Mysteries* (St. Louis, MO: Herder, 1924), 54–55: "All Christian life, all holiness, is being by grace what Jesus is by nature: the Son of God."

38. Roman Missal, Prayer after Communion for the 27th Sunday of Ordinary Time.

39. Benedict XVI, *Sacramentum Caritatis*, §§70–83

40. Imbelli, "Joseph Ratzinger's 'Spiritual Christology,'" 234–35.

41. Second Vatican Council, *Lumen Gentium*, §§ 34, 11; cf. 1 Pet 2:5.

42. "[A]ll creatures are moving forward with us and through us towards a common point of arrival, which is God, in that transcendent fullness where the risen Christ embraces and illumines all things. Human beings, endowed with intelligence and love, and drawn by the fullness of Christ, are called to lead all creatures back to their Creator." Francis, *Laudato Si'*, §83. Citing Colossians 1:19–20 (concerning God's will to reconcile *all things* to himself) and 1 Corinthians 15:28 (dealing with the Lord's plan to be all in all) later in this document, the pontiff adds, "In the Christian understanding of the world, the destiny of all creation is bound up with the mystery of Christ. . . . Thus, the creatures of this world no longer appear to us under merely natural guise because the risen One is mysteriously holding them to himself and directing them towards fullness as their end. The very flowers of the field and the birds which

transubstantiation represents a development beyond what one would gain strictly by adherence to the letter of the Bible alone. Yet N.T. Wright does well to observe:

> It is not difficult, again joining up dots which Paul himself leaves in the realm of implication, to suppose that with the vision of the new creation in Rom 8 Paul would say that, since one day God will be "all in all" (1 Cor 15:28), the sacraments are advance signs of that filling, that suffusing with the divine presence, power and love of the creation which will yet remain other than the creator.[43]

## THE INEVITABLE LIMITATIONS OF THIS ANAGOGY

Of course, all analogies and anagogies fall short of reality at some point, and the ones developed here (like the many others we have explored in this volume) are no exception. To understand their grandeur, we must therefore reiterate that the eschatological transformation of creation or "evolutionary leap" that we are discussing is such by way of an anagogy to that of biological evolution in this world. A number of observations bear this out. For instance, biological evolution transpires across immensely long intervals, whereas creation's definitive leap will only occur at the end of time. What is more, whereas biological evolution concerns the transformation of species into other species over the course of which the biological life of individuals comes to an end, in the graced transfiguration of man and the cosmos, creatures do not pass away but rather attain definitive life and become more truly themselves precisely by being united with God—man remaining completely united to and yet distinct from the rest of creation as its crown and steward.[44] Finally, in

---

his human eyes contemplated and admired are now imbued with his radiant presence." Francis, *Laudato Si'*, §§99–100.

43. Wright, "The Challenge of Dialogue," Christoph Heilig, J. Thomas Hewitt, and Michael Bird, *God and the Faithfulness of Paul* (Minneapolis, MN: Fortress Press, 2017), 711–70 at 760.

44. Without digressing into a deep Thomistic discussion of this topic, it is worth observing that the Angelic Doctor has resources that are helpful in the endeavor to clarify the uniqueness of man in relation to the rest of creation even in its "divinized" state. For instance, Thomas deploys the notion of obediential potency as a way to explain the miraculous glorification of the cosmos and its distinction from the elevation of the rational creature man at the end of time. See for example Aquinas, *In 4 Sent.*, d. 48, q. 2, a. 1, ad 3 and ad 4, in Aquinas, *Commentary on the Sentences, Book IV, Distinctions 43–50*, trans. Beth Mortensen and Dylan Schrader (Lander, WY: Aquinas Institute for the Study of Sacred Doctrine), 2018. Explaining the difference between the transformation of man and that of other creatures at the end of time, Lawrence Feingold explains, "Non-spiritual natures cannot receive spiritual perfections without losing their irrational nature and receiving a new spiritual nature. Spiritual creatures, on the contrary, can receive new spiritual perfections above their nature without losing their nature! This is the most sublime dignity of man. Thus spiritual creatures have transcendent obediential potencies that are unique to them." Lawrence Feingold, *The Natural Desire to See God According to St. Thomas and His Interpreters* (Ave Maria, FL: Sapientia Press, 2004), 112. I am grateful to Aaron Henderson for putting me onto these last pair of texts and for fruitful conversation on the topic. For a penetrating treatment of Aquinas's thought concerning the resurrection and restoration of the cosmos, see also Bryan Kromholtz, OP, *On the Last Day: The Time of the Resurrection of the Dead, according to Thomas Aquinas* (Fribourg: Academic Press Fribourg, 2010).

contrast with earlier stages of evolution, it must be emphasized that this definitive "leap" will not occur naturally or within the present physical universe. It involves, as Ratzinger says, movement to a quite different plane of existence altogether: that of "definitive" life [zoe] where the blessed have "left behind the rule of death."[45] This transformation is therefore neither the kind of thing that will simply happen if we leave nature to itself nor something that we can achieve through technological progress on this side of eternity.

While we are on the subject of this anagogy's limitations, it may also be helpful to recall an emphasis of Benedict that helps to avoid a misunderstanding of creation's "divinization." For, as he and other recent pontiffs have taught, to speak of the divinization of creatures is not to say that man or creation should be worshipped. While extolling the beauty and dignity of God's handiwork, Ratzinger makes it clear that, in being divinized, we are not simply absorbed into the Godhead. On the contrary, the deified creature remains intimately united to but *distinct* from God in a manner analogous to how spouses remain distinct from one another even as they are bound together in an indissoluble, "one flesh" union (Gn 3:24).[46] With regard to the rest of the renewed creation, meanwhile, Benedict emphasizes that it too retains its own (elevated) nature and should ought not to be made into an idol. Indeed, the emeritus pontiff insists that it is part of our vocation as humans to "subdue" (Gn 1:28) and "keep" (Gn 2:15) the earth as its lawful steward, to "collaborate in God's work, in the evolution that he ordered in the world [all'opera di Dio, all'evoluzione che Egli ha posto nel mondo]"—a role we fulfill by protecting creation, developing its gifts, and leading it toward its fulfillment in Christ on the Last Day.[47]

---

45. Ratzinger, *Introduction to Christianity*, 304 (*Einführung in das Christentum*, 286). In this vein, Karl Rahner insisted that the key error to avoid concerning the universe's final "evolutionary leap" into Christological fullness is the assumption that the process is aimless and that "such evolution is an ascent which the world accomplishes by forces which are wholly its own." Seeing as "the world is a unity in which everything is linked together with everything else," he adds, "it would not be extravagant, as long as it was done with prudence, to conceive the evolution of the world as an orientation toward Christ and to represent the various stages of this ascending movement as culminating in Him as their apex." Rahner, *Theological Investigations*, Vol. 1 (Baltimore: Helicon Press, 1960), 165; Maloney, *The Mystery of Christ in You*, 127.

46. Of the relationship of the Church and Christ, Ratzinger thus writes, "[T]he Church is the Body of Christ in the way in which the woman is one body, or rather one flesh, with the man. Put in other terms, the Church is the Body, not by virtue of an identity without distinction, but rather by means of the pneumatic-real act of spousal love. Expressed in yet another way, this means that Christ and the Church are one body in the sense in which man and woman are one flesh, that is, in such a way that in their indissoluble spiritual-bodily union, they nonetheless remain unconfused and unmingled. The Church does not simply become Christ, she is ever the handmaid whom he lovingly raises to be his Bride and who seeks his face throughout these latter days." Ratzinger, *Called to Communion*, 39.

47. Benedict XVI, Meeting with the Clergy of the Dioceses of Bolzano-Bressanone (August 6, 2008); cf. Benedict XVI, *Caritas in Veritate*, §48 and Ramage, *The Experiment of Faith*, 185–89.

## RATZINGER'S ANAGOGY AS AN ENCOURAGEMENT FOR CHRISTIAN HOPE

Despite these misunderstandings to avoid and distinctions that must be made, I have found Ratzinger's evolutionary anagogy to bear immense value for fostering Christian hope in a world so often bereft of it. For instance, it reminds us that eternal life will be a truly incarnate communion between man and God—one that takes place not in the vacuum of space but rather in a real world where our resurrected bodies interact with other transfigured creatures. Further, to riff on a line from C.S. Lewis, pondering the sublime destiny of all creation has a very "practical" implication. Just as pondering our neighbor's divine calling should lead us to recognize his dignity all the more even now, so too should contemplating the dignity of creation impel us to appreciate and care more deeply for the marvelous world in which we live—a theme dear to our recent pontiffs and reflected in the teachings of the Second Vatican Council.[48]

Another tangible consequence of our present reflection is that it offers a powerful motive for Christian hope by helping believers to grapple with the mystery of suffering and death in their daily lives—much of which, I have argued, is integral to the evolutionary dynamic. For, whereas naturalistic accounts of evolution posit that its processes terminate in the death of individuals with no hope of future restoration, Benedict's thoroughly Christian alternative invites us to ponder how glorious our expectation truly is. Like Jesus's image of the grain of wheat that bears no fruit unless it "dies" (Jn 12:24) and St. Paul's teaching that a body sown into the ground perishable is raised imperishable (1 Cor 15:42–54), Benedict's anagogy of creation's final "evolutionary leap" should lift our gaze to the things of heaven, pondering the reality that God has been at work guiding our evolving universe for billions of years with the goal of eventually leading all of his creatures to a state that transcends our existence in this world with all of the suffering and death that it entails—a transformation or "transubstantiation" made possible not *despite* but *precisely by* undergoing these trials in union with Jesus Christ and the rest of creation.

On a personal note, I have long found this imagery of cosmic transubstantiation especially fruitful for navigating all the sufferings of my life over the past two decades that I have been meditating on it. For, as with the bread and wine offered at Mass, the fact that we are being "transubstantiated" into Christ does not cause our daily existence to lose its apparently mundane character. No matter how much we might offer up a hectic day at work, disappointment at school, strife within our

---

48. C.S. Lewis discusses the "practical use" of speculating on the eternal destiny of man in *The Weight of Glory*, 45. As the Second Vatican Council teaches, "[T]he expectation of a new earth must not weaken but rather stimulate our concern for cultivating this one." *Gaudium et Spes*, §39. For more on recent papal teaching on the importance of care for creation and a discussion of Pope Francis's designation of it as a corporal and spiritual work of mercy, see Ramage, *The Experiment of Faith*, Ch. 9.

family, or struggle with an illness, the "accidents" of our suffering do not simply go away. Yet, as I have learned especially through having to deal with myriad sources of pain every day since coming down with lupus half my life ago, the act of offering up such things—bearing the Cross joyfully—does change the inner character of the experience from one of rebellion to one of sanctification.[49]

So it was with the Passion of Jesus Christ, "the pioneer and perfecter of our faith" (Hb 12:2) who "in every respect has been tempted as we are, yet without sin" (Hb 4:15). The victory of our Lord on the Cross did not immediately destroy suffering, but rather what it did was to endow it with redemptive power. In his life, Death, and Resurrection, Christ began the work of transubstantiation. Having changed bread and wine into his Body and Blood, he now wishes to transform us into his nature through grace. And we, in turn, now have the joyful duty of bringing his work to completion by consecrating the world—our joys, our sorrows, our work, our families, our entire being—to God.[50]

## CONCLUSION: THE "SALVATION OF THE COSMOS" AND ITS TRANSFORMATION INTO SONG

I would like to bring this book to a close and tie together all that has just been said by returning once last time to the now-familiar comparison of God's creation to song, now deploying the comparison not as an ana*logy* but an ana*gogy*. Fittingly, in the very last words of his book on the Last Things, we find Ratzinger describing his eschatological vision as one of hope not just for man, but for the *salvation of the cosmos*:

> [T]he individual's salvation is whole and entire only when the salvation of the cosmos and all the elect [*das Heil des Alls und aller Erwählten*] has come to full fruition. For the redeemed are not simply adjacent to each other in heaven. Rather, in their being together as the one Christ, they *are* heaven. In that moment, the whole creation will become song. It will be a single act in which, forgetful of self, the individual will break through the limits of being into the

---

49. While not engaged in the same overall project as I am here, I find that this dynamic of *theosis* through *kenosis* is captured well by David Fagerberg when he speaks of the liturgy having the transformative power to "anchor the substance of our lives" and of the possibility of reaching a point where "the substance of the liturgy becomes the substance of the soul." See Fagerberg, *Liturgical Mysticism* (Steubenville, OH: Emmaus Academic, 2019).

50. Wainwright captures this dynamic through the lens of biblical election—God's habit of choosing of individual, unworthy vessels to accomplish his mission of bringing all people (and all creation) to himself at the end of time: "The Eucharistic celebration and the Eucharistic community are instances of the principle of representative election at work. From the whole of humanity God chooses the Eucharistic community, and from the whole of the rest of creation this bread and this wine, in order to show forth his purpose for the whole universe. At the Eucharist men and matter receive and render the divine glory in token of the fact that God's glory will fill the whole universe when God is everywhere actively present and all his creation bows the knee in obedience to his royal will (cf. Phil 2:10f)." Wainwright, *Eucharist and Eschatology*, 149–50.

whole, and the whole take up its dwelling in the individual. It will be joy in which all questioning is resolved and satisfied.[51]

The crescendo of this climactic passage is especially noteworthy for its audacious hope that the universe will somehow achieve "salvation," which itself is but a variation on the theme of cosmic transubstantiation we have been exploring and an extension of St. Paul's teaching that "the creation itself will be set free from its bondage to decay and obtain the glorious liberty of the children of God" (Rm 8:21).

I find that Ratzinger's words fittingly capture and punctuate a major theme of this book in how they depict the whole creation being destined to "become song." For, as we saw in Chapter 3, the emeritus pontiff sees the image of a melody or symphony as the most fitting image to describe our evolving world. At that juncture, we followed Ratzinger as he deployed this analogy to make his case that the universe is not a machine designed by an engineer who occasionally "tweaks" it but rather that creation has an integrity such that it unfolds naturally over the course of time, following the rules of its nature. In the present context, Ratzinger's anagogical suggestion that the entire cosmos will one day become "song" has a further aim: to capture the truth that the new heaven and new earth will be a "single act" in which all creation rejoices together in perfect harmony (Ps 96:1; Rv 5:8–14).

While he does not expand more on the meaning of this enigmatic musical allusion, it is easy to see how it connects our present evolving universe and its seemingly interminable suffering and death with the world of endless life and perfect joy to come. In this vale of tears, our lives are a mess of suffering, death, and myriad other travails. Our existence is chaotic, and it is at times well-nigh impossible to see how the tragic events in history could possibly be a part of some grand cosmic plan. And, yet, as we discussed in the last chapter, one of the most fundamental Christian convictions is that the troubles we now experience are not just evils to be tolerated but on the contrary occasions of grace which ultimately redound to the good.

Ratzinger's anagogy of creation as a symphony thus invites us to think of the sufferings of this world less along the lines of absolute evils and more as variations upon a musical theme—as temporary *dissonance* or *minor chords* that contribute to the overall beauty of God's perfect symphony.[52] Just as moments of tension and

---

51. Ratzinger, *Eschatology*, 238 [*Eshcatologie*, 193]. John Paul II earlier issued a similar statement concerning the 'salvation' of the cosmos: "Christianity does not reject matter. Rather, bodiliness is considered in all its value in the liturgical act, whereby the human body is disclosed in its inner nature as a temple of the Holy Spirit and is united with the Lord Jesus, who himself took a body for *the world's salvation*. This does not mean, however, an absolute exaltation of all that is physical." John Paul II, *Orientale Lumen*, §11. Emphasis added. Pope Francis references this text in his own turn and adds, "For Christians, *all the creatures of the material universe* find their true meaning in the incarnate Word, for the Son of God has incorporated in his person part of the material world, planting in it *a seed of definitive transformation*." Francis, *Laudato Si'*, §235. Emphasis added.

52. For a profound mythopoeic creation narrative that also uses music to depict the reality of how God brings good out of dissonance/evil, see J.R.R. Tolkien, "Ainulindalë: The Music of the Ainur," in *The Silmarillion* (Boston: Houghton Mifflin, 2001), 15–22. For another mythic portrayal of creation occurring through song, see Lewis, *The Magician's Nephew*, Chs. 8–9.

seeming disharmony in a musical masterpiece (or a great drama) conduce to the overall excellence of the piece, so too with God's good creation. If we were to hit the "stop" button on the score of creation right now, we might think it an awful composition. But, if we let it play out to the end, we will one day see that it was really a "single act" all along—and indeed the greatest of acts. For, in the end, God will destroy death and wipe away every tear from our eyes (Rv 21:4). Then, we will understand fully and see clearly that Face that we now only know in part and see only dimly (1 Cor 13:12).

I can think of no more fitting way to bring this volume to a close than to note one final way in which Benedict XVI extends his music anagogy to illumine the truth of creation. As we await that great day when the symphony of creation will sound its final terrestrial note, he says that the Lord of heaven and earth has left us a most unique gift: the musical "solo" of Jesus Christ, who unites all of creation and enables it to become truly itself by raising it up to himself:

> In this symphony is found, at a certain point, what might be called in musical terminology a "solo," a theme given to a single instrument or voice; and it is so important that the significance of the entire work depends on it. This "solo" is Jesus. . . . The Son of man himself epitomizes the earth and Heaven, the Creation and the Creator, the flesh and the Spirit. He is the center of the cosmos and of history, for in him the Author and his work are united without being confused with each other. In the earthly Jesus the culmination of Creation and of history is found, but in the Risen Christ this is surpassed: the passage through death to eternal life anticipates the point of the "recapitulation" of *all things* in Christ (cf. Eph 1: 10; Col 1:16–18).[53]

---

53. Benedict XVI, Homily (January 6, 2009); cf. Benedict XVI, *Verbum Domini*, §13.

# Appendix

# More Than Just a Hypothesis
## *Sources for the Study of Evolution*

## BOOKS

Austriaco, Nicanor et al. *Thomistic Evolution: A Catholic Approach to Understanding Evolution*. Providence, RI: Cluny Media, 2019.

Baglow, Christopher. *Faith, Science, and Reason: Theology on the Cutting Edge*. Downers Grove, IL: Midwest Theological Forum, 2019.

Barr, Stephen. *The Believing Scientist: Essays on Science and Religion*. Grand Rapids, MI: Eerdmans, 2016.

Coyne, Jerry. *Why Evolution Is True*. New York: Penguin Books, 2010.

Dawkins, Richard. *The Greatest Show on Earth: The Evidence for Evolution*. New York: Free Press, 2009.

Diamond, Jared. *The Third Chimpanzee: The Evolution and Future of the Human Animal*. New York: HarperPerennial, 2006.

McKnight, Scot, and Dennis Venema. *Adam and the Genome: Reading Scripture After Genetic Science*. Grand Rapids, MI: Brazos Press, 2017.

Trasancos, Stacy. *Particles of Faith: A Catholic Guide to Navigating Science*. Notre Dame, IN: Ave Maria Press, 2016.

White, Thomas Joseph. *The Light of Christ: An Introduction to Catholicism*. Washington, D.C.: The Catholic University of America Press, 2017 (Ch. 3, especially 98–104).

## SCIENTIFIC TEXTBOOKS

Futuyma, Douglas. *Evolution*. Fourth Edition. Sunderland, MA: Sinauer, 2017.

Herron, Jon, and Scott Freeman. *Evolutionary Analysis*. Fifth Edition. Upper Saddle River, NJ: Pearson, 2013.

Jobling, Mark, Edward Hollox, Matthew Hurles, and Toomas Kivisild. *Human Evolutionary Genetics*. Second Edition. New York: Garland Science, 2013.

## CATHOLIC/CHRISTIAN WEB RESOURCES

Aquinas 101: Science and Faith
https://aquinas101.thomisticinstitute.org/welcome-to-aquinas-101-science-and-faith

Church Life Journal
https://churchlifejournal.nd.edu/articles/category/science-and-religion/

"Evolution Basics"—BioLogos
  https://biologos.org/articles/series/evolution-basics

Interdisciplinary Encyclopedia of Science and Religion
  http://inters.org/

Pontifical Academy of Sciences
  http://www.pas.va/content/accademia/en.html.

Society of Catholic Scientists
  https://www.catholicscientists.org/ideas/discussions

Thomistic Evolution
  https://www.thomisticevolution.org/

"Faith, Science, and Sin"—Word on Fire Institute
  https://wordonfire.institute/

## OTHER LECTURES, VIDEOS, AND WEB RESOURCES

"Aquinas and Modern Evolutionary Theory: An Inquiry"—Andrew Davison
  https://www.youtube.com/watch?v=Mp3OY3qOj-c

"Defending Adam After Darwin"—Nicanor Austriaco, OP
  https://www.youtube.com/watch?v=3MsJ67qtHYY

"Did Christ Die for Neanderthals?"—Simon Gaine, OP
  https://www.youtube.com/watch?v=NKcwCpWOZhk

"Evidence of Evolution"—Bozeman Science
  https://www.youtube.com/watch?v=cC8k2Sb1oQ8

"Evidence for Evolution"—Khan Academy
  https://www.youtube.com/watch?v=Q-aGAX27SIo

"Evidence for Evolution"—Khan Academy
  https://www.khanacademy.org/science/biology/her/evolution-and-natural-selection/a/
  lines-of-evidence-for-evolution

"Evolution"—PBS
  http://www.pbs.org/wgbh/evolution/

"Evolution: It's a Thing"—Crash Course Biology #20
  https://www.youtube.com/watch?v=P3GagfbA2vo

"Evolutionary Development: Chicken Teeth"—Crash Course Biology #17
  https://www.youtube.com/watch?v=9sjwlxQ_6LI

"The Evolutionary Epic"—Crash Course Big History #5
  https://www.youtube.com/watch?v=92oHNd8vFwo&list=PL8dPuuaLjXtMczXZUmjb3
  mZSU1Roxnrey&index=5

"God After Darwin: Are Christianity and Evolution Compatible?"—Nicanor Austriaco, OP
https://www.youtube.com/watch?v=dyLa_ac6YeA

"Natural Selection"—Crash Course Biology #14
https://www.youtube.com/watch?v=aTftyFboC_M&list=PL3EED4C1D684D3ADF
&index=15

"The Origin of Our Species"—British Natural History Museum
http://www.nhm.ac.uk/discover/the-origin-of-our-species.html.

"Seven Million Years of Human Evolution"—American Museum of Natural History
https://www.youtube.com/watch?v=DZv8VyIQ7YU&list=PL-CgoZz-R2C5DKO
qee07TITPxzPu0z10y&index=35

"Understanding Evolution"—University of California, Berkeley
https://evolution.berkeley.edu/evolibrary/home.php

"What Does It Mean to Be Human?"—Smithsonian National Museum of Natural History
http://humanorigins.si.edu/evidence/human-family-tree

"What Is Darwin's Theory of Evolution?"—Live Science
https://www.youtube.com/watch?v=w56u2gv8XLs

"What Is the Evidence for Evolution?"—Stated Clearly
https://www.youtube.com/watch?v=lIEoO5KdPvg

## DOCUMENTARIES AND DOCUSERIES

*Cosmos: A Spacetime Odyssey* (2014)—especially episodes 2, 6, 9, 11
*The Gene* (PBS, 2020)
*Life* (BBC, 2009)
*When Whales Walked: A Deep Time Journey* (PBS, 2019)

## VATICAN CONFERENCES AND PUBLICATIONS

Beyond the many instances in which Joseph Ratzinger/Benedict XVI dealt with evolution as has been the subject of this book, an impressive number of Vatican-level meetings have been held and documents published over the past four decades on the relationship of faith and evolution. Among these the following are particularly noteworthy:

1984: Pontifical Academy of Sciences study week organized by Carl Sagan and attended by Stephen Jay Gould with the following address by John Paul II on October 2, 1984. http://www.vatican.va/content/john-paul-ii/en/speeches/1984/october/documents/hf_jp-ii_spe_19841002_pontificia-accademia-scienze.html.

1985: Symposium in Rome hosted by the Congregation for the Doctrine of the Faith under the direction of Cardinal Joseph Ratzinger. The meeting's proceedings were published with a preface penned by the office's then-prefect in: Spaemann,Robert, R. Löw, and P. Koslowski, eds. *Evolutionismus und Christentum.* Weinheim: Acta Humaniora, 1986.

1996:     Meeting of the Pontifical Academy of Sciences. On October 22, 1996, Pope John
          Paul II issued his famous message to participants in this gathering in which the
          pontiff addressed scientific developments that had taken place since the time of
          Pius XII and in light of them famously dubbed evolution "more than a hypothesis."
          https://humanorigins.si.edu/sites/default/files/MESSAGE%20TO%20THE%20PO
          NTIFICAL%20ACADEMY%20OF%20SCIENCES%20(Pope%20John%20Paul%2
          0II).pdf

2006:     Benedict XVI's *Schülerkreis* (Ratzinger Circle of Alumni) meeting which resulted
          in the edited volume *Creation and Evolution: A Conference with Pope Benedict XVI
          in Castel Gandolfo*. San Francisco: Ignatius Press, 2009.

2008:     Plenary session of the Pontifical Academy of Sciences, attended by Stephen Hawk-
          ing. Resulted in the book *Scientific Insights into the Evolution of the Universe and
          of Life*. Vatican City: Ex Aedibus Academicis in Civitate Vaticana, 2009.

2013      Meetings of the Pontifical Academy of Sciences resulting in the publication *Evolv-
and       ing Concepts of Nature*. Vatican City: Ex Aedibus Academicis in Civitate Vaticana,
2014:     2015.

2019:     Pontifical Academy of Sciences workshop with its short statement "Who Was
          Who, Who Did What, Where and When" available on the academy's website at
          http://www.casinapioiv.va/content/accademia/en/events/2019/who_was_who.html.

# Bibliography

*Note:* Pope Benedict XVI's encyclicals, homilies, general audiences, etc. listed below are found on the Vatican website at https://www.vatican.va/content/benedict-xvi/en.html.

Alighieri, Dante. *Paradise*. Translated by Anthony Esolen. New York: Modern Library, 2003.

Ambrose. "On the Death of Satyrus." In vol. 10 of *Nicene and Post-Nicene Fathers, Second Series*, edited by Philip Schaff and Henry Wace. Buffalo, NY: Christian Literature Publishing Co., 1896.

Anderson, Gary. "Biblical Origins and the Problem of the Fall." *Pro Ecclesia* 10.1 (2001): 17–30.

———. *The Genesis of Perfection: Adam and Eve in Jewish and Christian Imagination*. Louisville, KY: Westminster John Knox Press, 2001.

———. *Christian Doctrine and the Old Testament: Theology in the Service of Biblical Exegesis*. Grand Rapids, MI: Baker, 2017.

Angielczyk, Kenneth. "What Do We Mean by 'Theory' in Science?" Chicago Field Museum. March 10, 2017. https://www.fieldmuseum.org/blog/what-do-we-mean-theory-science.

Aquinas, Thomas. *Commentary on Aristotle's Physics*. Translated by Richard J. Blackwell, Richard J. Spath and W. Edmund Thirlkel. New Haven, CT: Yale University Press, 1963.

———. *Commentary on the Letter of St. Paul to the Hebrews*. Translated by. F.R. Larcher. Lander, WY: Aquinas Institute for the Study of Sacred Doctrine, 2012.

———. *Commentary on the Letter of St. Paul to the Romans*. Translated by. F.R. Larcher. Lander, WY: Aquinas Institute for the Study of Sacred Doctrine, 2018.

———. *Commentary on Saint Paul's Epistle to the Ephesians*. Translated by Matthew Lamb. Albany, NY: Magi Books, 1966.

———. *Commentary on the Sentences, Book IV, Distinctions 43–50*. Translated by Beth Mortensen and Dylan Schrader. Lander, WY: Aquinas Institute for the Study of Sacred Doctrine, 2018.

———. *Compendium of Theology*. St. Louis, MO: B. Herder Book Co., 1947.

———. *De Veritate*. Translated by James McGlynn. Chicago: Henry Regnery, 1953.

———. *On the Power of God*. Translated by the Fathers of the English Dominican Province. Westminster, MD: Aeterna, 2015.

———. *Summa Contra Gentiles*. Translated by Anton C. Pegis. Garden City, New York: Hanover House, 1955.

———. *Summa Theologiae*. Translated by the Fathers of the English Dominican Province. Westminster, MD: Christian Classics, 1981.

———. *S. Thomae Aquinatis Opera Omnia: ut sunt in Indice Thomistico, additis 61 scriptis ex aliis medii aevi auctoribus*, edited by Robert Busa. 6 vols. Stuttgart-Bad Cannstatt: Frommann-Holzboog, 1980.

————. *S. Thomae Aquinatis Ordinis Praedicatorum . . . Scriptum super libros sententiarum Magistri Petri Lombardi episcopi Parisiensis*. Parisiis: Lethielleux, 1929–1947.

————. *St. Thomas Aquinas on Evil*. Translated by Richard Regan. Notre Dame, IN: University of Notre Dame Press, 1995.

Archivi Concilii Vaticani Secundi. Schema *Constitutionis dogmaticae de deposito fidei pure Custodiendo*. In *Acta Synodalia Sacrosancti Concilii Vaticani Secundi I*, 653–94. Roma: Typis Polyglottis Vaticanis, 1971.

Arnold, Bill. *Genesis*. New York: Cambridge University Press, 2009.

Arnold, Bill, and Bryan Beyer. *Readings from the Ancient Near East*. Grand Rapids, MI: Baker Academic, 2002.

Athanasius. *On the Incarnation of the Word*. Crestwood, NY: St. Vladimir's Seminary Press, 1993.

Augros, Michael. *Who Designed the Designer?* San Francisco: Ignatius Press, 2015.

Augustine. *Confessions*. Oxford: Oxford University Press, 2008.

————. *On Christian Doctrine*. New York: Bobbs-Merrill, 1958.

————. *The Literal Meaning of Genesis*. Translated by J. H. Taylor. *Ancient Christian Writers*, Vol. 41. New York: Newman Press, 1982.

————. *The City of God, Books VIII–XVI*. Translated by Hermigild Dressler, Gerald G. Walsh, and Daniel J. Honan. Vol. 14 of *The Fathers of the Church*. Washington, D.C.: The Catholic University of America Press, 1952.

————. *The City of God, Books XVII–XXII*. Translated by Hermigild Dressler, Gerald G. Walsh, and Daniel J. Honan. Vol. 24 of *The Fathers of the Church*. Washington, D.C.: The Catholic University of America Press, 1954.

Austriaco, Nicanor. "Immediate Hominization from the Systems Perspective." *National Catholic Bioethics Quarterly*, 4.4 (2004): 719–738.

————. "The Intelligibility of Intelligent Design." *Angelicum* 86 (2009): 103–111.

————. "Reading Genesis with Cardinal Ratzinger." *Homiletic and Pastoral Review*. January 1, 2009. https://www.hprweb.com/2009/01/reading-genesis-with-cardinal-ratzinger/.

————. "The Specification of Sex/Gender in the Human Species: A Thomistic Analysis." *New Blackfriars* 94.1054 (2013): 701–15.

————. "A Fittingness Argument for the Historicity of the Fall of Homo Sapiens." *Nova et Vetera* 13 (2015): 651–667.

————. "Defending Adam After Darwin: On the Origin of Sapiens as a Natural Kind." *American Catholic Philosophical Quarterly* 92.2 (2018): 337–352.

————. "A Theological Fittingness Argument for the Evolution of *Homo Sapiens*." *Theology and Science* 17:4 (2019): 539–50.

Austriaco, Nicanor, James Brent, Thomas Davenport, and John Baptist Ku. *Thomistic Evolution: A Catholic Approach to Understanding Evolution in the Light of Faith*. Second Edition. Tacoma, WA: Cluny Media, 2019.

Austriaco, Nicanor, and Michael Loudin. "Understanding the Controversy Over Intelligent Design and the Acceptability of Intelligent Causality in Science." *Forum Teologiczne* 9 (2009): 29–39.

Baglow, Christopher. *Creation: A Catholic's Guide to God and the Universe*. Notre Dame, IN: Ave Maria Press, 2021.

———. *Faith, Science, & Reason: Theology on the Cutting Edge*. Second Edition. Downers Grove, IL: Midwest Theological Forum, 2019.

———. "Does the Extended Evolutionary Synthesis Shed New Light on Theological Anthropology?" *Church Life Journal*. January 10, 2020. https://churchlifejournal.nd.edu/articles/does-the-extended-evolutionary-synthesis-shed-new-light-on-theological-anthropology/.

———. "Evolution and the Human Soul." *Church Life Journal*. June 23, 2020. https://churchlifejournal.nd.edu/articles/evolution-and-the-human-soul/.

———. "Faith and Science: Imperfection, Evil, and Human Nature," *Church Life Journal*. July 22, 2020. https://mcgrathblog.nd.edu/faith-and-science-imperfection-evil-and-human-nature.

Balthasar, Hans Urs von. Vol. 4 of *Glory of the Lord: The Realm of Metaphysics in Antiquity*. San Francisco: Ignatius Press, 1989.

———. *Mysterium Paschale*. San Francisco: Ignatius Press, 2000.

Barr, Stephen. "The End of Intelligent Design?" *First Things*. February 9, 2010. https://www.firstthings.com/web-exclusives/2010/02/the-end-of-intelligent-design.

———. *The Believing Scientist: Essays on Science and Religion*. Grand Rapids, MI: Eerdmans, 2016.

———. "Attempts to Explain Cosmogony Scientifically," *Church Life Journal*. September 21, 2018. https://churchlifejournal.nd.edu/articles/attempts-to-explain-cosmogony-scientifically/.

Barry, Robert. "The Transmission of Original Sin in Light of Evolution." Forthcoming.

Barth, Karl. *Church Dogmatics*. Translated by G. W. Bromiley. Edinburgh: T& T Clark, 1956.

Barton, John. *The Nature of Biblical Criticism*. Louisville, KY: Westminster John Knox, 2007.

Batto, Bernard. *Slaying the Dragon: Mythmaking in the Biblical Tradition*. Louisville, KY: Westminster John Knox, 1992.

Bauckham, Richard. *2 Peter, Jude*. Dallas: Word, Incorporated, 1983.

Béchard, Dean. *The Scripture Documents*. Collegeville, MN: The Liturgical Press, 2002.

Beckwith, Francis. "How to Be an Anti-Intelligent Design Advocate." *University of St. Thomas Journal of Law & Public Policy* 4.1 (2009–2010): 35–65.

Behe, Michael. *Darwin's Black Box: The Biochemical Challenge to Evolution*. New York: Free Press, 1996.

———. *The Edge of Evolution*. New York: The Free Press, 2007.

Bellarmine, Robert. Letter to Foscarini (April 12, 1516). In *The Galileo Affair: A Documentary History*, edited by Maurice Finocchiaro, 67–69. Berkeley, CA: University of California Press, 1989.

Benedict XVI. "Psalm 135:1–9." General Audience. November 9, 2005.

———. Homily for the Immaculate Conception. December 8, 2005.

————. *Deus Caritas Est*. Encyclical Letter. December 25, 2005.

————. Homily for the Easter Vigil. April 15, 2006.

————. Homily for the Mass of Corpus Christi. June 15, 2006.

————. Homily. September 11, 2006.

————. "Faith, Reason, and the University: Memories and Reflections." September 12, 2006.

————. Address. October 6, 2008.

————. "St. Paul's New Outlook." General audience. November 8, 2006.

————. *Jesus of Nazareth: From the Baptism in the Jordan to the Transfiguration*. New York: Doubleday, 2007.

————. *Meeting with Clergy of the Dioceses of Belluno-Feltre and Treviso*. July 24, 2007.

————. *Spe Salvi*. Encyclical Letter. November 30, 2007.

————. *Creation and Evolution: A Conference with Pope Benedict XVI in Castel Gandolfo*. San Francisco: Ignatius Press, 2008.

————. "St. Maximus the Confessor." General Audience. June 25, 2008.

————. Meeting with the Clergy of the Dioceses of Bolzano-Bressanone. August 6, 2008.

————. General Audience. September 17, 2008.

————. Angelus. October 26, 2008.

————. "The Apostle's Teaching on the Relation between Adam and Christ." General Audience. December 3, 2008.

————. "Theology of the Sacraments." General Audience. December 10, 2008.

————. Homily. January 6, 2009.

————. "The Church and the Scandal of Sexual Abuse." April 10, 2009. https://www.ncregister.com/news/pope-benedict-essay-the-church-and-the-scandal-of-sexual-abuse.

————. *Caritas in Veritate*. Encyclical Letter. June 29, 2009.

————. Homily. July 24, 2009.

————. *Light of the World: the Pope, the Church, and the Signs of the Times*. San Francisco: Ignatius Press, 2010.

————. Meditation. October 11, 2010. http://www.vatican.va/content/benedict-xvi/it/speeches/2010/october/documents/hf_ben-xvi_spe_20101011_meditazione.html.

————. *Verbum Domini*. Apostolic Exhortation. September 30, 2010.

————. *Jesus von Nazareth: Vom Einzug in Jerusalem bis zur Auferstehung*. Freiburg: Herder, 2011.

————. *Jesus of Nazareth: Holy Week: From the Entrance into Jerusalem to the Resurrection*. San Francisco: Ignatius Press, 2011.

————. Homily for the Easter Vigil. April 23, 2011.

————. *Address to Participants in the Plenary Meeting of the Pontifical Biblical Commission*. May 2, 2011.

————. *Address to Students Taking Part in the Meeting Promoted by the Sorella Natura Foundation*. November 28, 2011.

———. *Jesus of Nazareth: The Infancy Narratives*. New York: Image, 2012.

———. Homily for the Easter Vigil. April 7, 2012.

———. Apostolic Letter Proclaiming Saint Hildegard of Bingen a Doctor of the Universal Church. October 7, 2012.

———. Angelus. December 8, 2012.

———. "I believe in God, maker of heaven and earth, creator of man." General Audience. February 6, 2013.

———. *Address at the Commemoration of the 65th Anniversary of the Priestly Ordination of Pope Emeritus Benedict XVI*. June 28, 2016. https://w2.vatican.va/content/francesco/en/speeches/2016/june/documents/papa-francesco_20160628_65-ordinazione-sacerdotale-benedetto-xvi.html.

Benedict XVI and Peter Seewald. *Last Testament: In His Own Words*. London: Bloomsbury, 2016.

Benzel, Kim, Sarah Graff, Yelena Rakic, and Edith W. Watts. *Art of the Ancient Near East: A Resource for Educators*. 2010. https://www.metmuseum.org/art/metpublications/Art_of_the_Ancient_Near_East_A_Resource_for_Educators.

Berlin, Adele, Marc Zvi Brettler, and Michael Fishbane. *The Jewish Study Bible*. New York: Oxford University Press, 2004.

Blandino, Giovanni. *La rivelazione e l'ispirazione della Sacra Scrittura*. Rome: Edizioni ADP, 1998.

Blenkinsopp, Joseph. *The Pentateuch: An Introduction to the First Five Books of the Bible*. New York: Doubleday, 1992.

Blowers, Paul. "Unfinished Creative Business: Maximus the Confessor, Evolutionary Theodicy, and Human Stewardship in Creation." In *On Earth as It Is in Heaven: Cultivating a Contemporary Theology of Creation*, edited by David Meconi, 174–90. Grand Rapids, MI: Eerdmans, 2016.

Bonaventure. *Breviloquium*. Vol. 2 of *The Works of Bonaventure: Cardinal Seraphic Doctor and Saint*. Paterson, NJ: St. Anthony Guild Press, 1963.

———. *Doctoris Seraphici S. Bonaventurae Opera Omnia*. Ad Claras Aquas / Quaracchi: Ex Typographia Collegii S. Bonaventurae, 1882.

———. *Opera Omnia*. Quaracchi: Ex Typographia Collegii S. Bonaventurae, 1882–1902.

Bock, Darrell, and Gregory Herrick *Jesus in Context: Background Readings for Gospel Study*. Grand Rapids, MI: Baker, 2005.

Bonfiglio, Ryan. *A Study Companion to Introduction to the Hebrew Bible*. Second Edition. Minneapolis, MN: Fortress Press, 2014.

Bouyer, Louis. *Cosmos: The World and the Glory of God*. Petersham, MA: St. Bede's Publications, 1999.

Bradford, Alina. "What Is a Scientific Theory?" *Live Science*. July 29, 2017. https://www.livescience.com/21491-what-is-a-scientific-theory-definition-of-theory.html.

Braine, David. *The Human Person: Animal and Spirit*. Notre Dame, IN: University of Notre Dame Press, 1992.

———. "Life and Human Life: Their Nature and Emergence." In *The Missing Link*, edited by Roy Abraham Varghese, 132–60. Lanham, MD: University Press of America, 2013.

Burtchaell, James Tunstead. *Catholic Theories of Biblical Inspiration since 1810: A Review and Critique*. London: Cambridge University Press, 1969.

Byrne, Patrick. "Evolution, Randomness, and Divine Purpose: A Reply to Cardinal Schönborn." *Theological Studies*, 67.3 (2006): 653–65.

———. "Lonergan, Evolutionary Science, and Intelligent Design." *Revista Portuguesa de Filosofia* 63.4 (2007): 893–918.

Campbell, Constantine. *Paul and the Hope of Glory*. Grand Rapids, MI: Zondervan Academic, 2021.

Carbajosa, Ignacio. *Faith, the Fount of Exegesis: The Interpretation of Scripture in the Light of the History of Research on the Old Testament*. San Francisco: Ignatius Press, 2011.

Carlson, Richard, and Tremper Longman. *Science, Creation, and the Bible: Reconciling Rival Theories of Origins*. Downers Grove, IL: IVP Academic, 2010.

Carroll, William. "Thomas Aquinas and Big Bang Cosmology." *Sapientia* 53 (203) 1998: 73–95.

———. "Creation, Evolution, and Thomas Aquinas." *Revue des Questions Scientifiques* 171 (4) 2000: 319–47.

Cassuto, Umberto. *The Documentary Hypothesis and the Composition of the Pentateuch*. Jerusalem: Shalem Press, 2006.

Catholic Church. *Catechism of the Council of Trent for Parish Priests, Issued by Order of Pope Pius V*. Translated by John McHugh and Charles Callan. New York: Joseph F. Wagner, Inc, 1923.

———. *The Liturgy of the Hours: According to the Roman Rite*. New York: The Catholic Book Publishing Company, 1975.

———. *Catechism of the Catholic Church*. Translated by United States Catholic Conference. Washington, D.C.: Libreria Editrice Vaticana, 1994.

Cavanaugh, William, and James Smith, *Evolution and the Fall*. Grand Rapids, MI: Eerdmans, 2017.

Center for Applied Research in the Apostolate. "Catholics' Opinions about Faith and Science." *Special Report* (Fall 2017): 1–8.

Chaberek, Michael. *Aquinas and Evolution*. British Columbia: The Chartwell Press, 2017.

Chesterton, G.K. Vol. 27 of *The Collected Works of G. K. Chesterton*. San Francisco: Ignatius Press, 1986.

———. *The Everlasting Man*. Vol. 2 of *The Collected Works of G. K. Chesterton*. San Francisco: Ignatius Press, 1986.

———. *Orthodoxy*. San Francisco: Ignatius Press, 1995.

Collins, Francis. *The Language of God: A Scientist Presents Evidence for Belief*. New York: Free Press, 2006.

Columbanus, St. "Instruction 13 De Christo fonte vitae." In *Sancti Columbani Opera*. Dublin: Dublin Institute for Advanced Studies, 1957.

Congar, Yves. *My Journal of the Council*. Collegeville, MN: Liturgical Press, 2012.

Congregation for the Doctrine of the Faith. *Doctrinal Commentary on the Concluding Formula of the* Professio Fidei. June 29, 1998.

Coyne, Jerry. *Why Evolution is True*. New York: Penguin, 2009.

Craig, William Lane. "The Historical Adam." *First Things*. October 2021. https://www.firstthings.com/article/2021/10/the-historical-adam.

———. *In Quest of the Historical Adam: A Biblical and Scientific Exploration*. Grand Rapids, MI: Eerdmans, 2021.

Cunningham, Conor. *Darwin's Pious Idea: Why the Ultra-Darwinists and Creationists Both Get It Wrong*. Grand Rapids, MI: Eerdmans, 2010.

Darwin, Charles. *The Autobiography of Charles Darwin*. Cambridge, UK: Icon Books, 2003.

———. *The Descent of Man, and Selection in Relation to Sex*. London: John Murray, 1871.

———. *On the Origin of the Species by Means of Natural Selection*. London: John Murray, 1959.

Davies, Brian. *Philosophy of Religion: A Guide and Anthology*. Oxford: Oxford University Press, 2000.

Davison, Andrew. "Aquinas and Modern Evolutionary Theory: An Inquiry," Lecture at the Thomistic Institute-Angelicum. January 18, 2019. https://angelicum.it/it/listituto-tomista/videos-it/2019/01/18/aquinas-and-modern-evolutionary-theory-an-inquiry-prof-andrew-davison/.

———. "Christian Doctrine and Biological Mutualism: Some Explorations in Systematic and Philosophical Theology." *Theology and Science* 18.2 (2020): 258–78.

Dawkins, Richard. *The Blind Watchmaker*. London: Penguin Books, 1991.

———. *The God Delusion*. Boston: Houghton Mifflin, 2006.

———. *The Greatest Show on Earth: The Evidence for Evolution*. New York: Free Press, 2009.

Deane-Drummond, Celia. "In Adam All Die? Questions at the Boundary of Niche Construction, Community Evolution, and Original Sin." In *Evolution and the Fall*, edited by William Cavanaugh and James Smith, 23–47. Grand Rapids, MI: Eerdmans, 2017.

Dembski, William. *The Design Revolution: Answering the Toughest Questions about Intelligent Design*. Nottingham, UK: Inter-Varsity Press, 2004.

Dennett, Daniel. *Darwin's Dangerous Idea: Evolution and the Meaning of Life*. New York: Simon & Schuster, 1995.

Diamond, Jared. *The Third Chimpanzee: The Evolution and Future of the Human Animal*. New York: HarperPerennial, 2006.

Dobzhansky, Theodosius. "Nothing in Biology Makes Sense Except in the Light of Evolution." *The American Biology Teacher* 35.3 (1973): 125–29.

Dodds, Michael. *Unlocking Divine Action: Contemporary Science and Thomas Aquinas*. Washington, D.C.: The Catholic University of America Press, 2017.

Dubay, Thomas. *Faith and Certitude*. San Francisco: Ignatius Press, 1985.

Dunn, James. *Romans 1–8*. Vol. 38A of *Word Biblical Commentary*. Dallas: Word, Incorporated, 1988.

Dunne, John Anthony. "Enuma Elish." In *The Lexham Bible Dictionary*, edited by John D. Barry et al. Bellingham, WA: Lexham Press, 2016.

Ehrman, Terrance. "Anthropogenesis and the Soul." *Scientia et Fides* 8.2 (2020): 173–92.

Elphinstone, Andrew. *Freedom, Suffering and Love*. London: S.C.M. Press, 1976.

Enns, Peter. *Inspiration and Incarnation*. Grand Rapids, MI: Baker Academic, 2005.

———. *The Evolution of Adam: What the Bible Does and Doesn't Say about Human Origins*. Grand Rapids, MI: Brazos, 2012.

———. *The Bible Tells Me So: Why Defending Scripture Has Made Us Unable to Read It*. San Francisco: HarperOne, 2014.

———. *How the Bible Actually Works*. San Francisco: HarperOne, 2019.

Everett, Daniel. *How Language Began: The Story of Humanity's Greatest Invention*. New York: Liveright, 2017.

Fagerberg, David. *Liturgical Mysticism*. Steubenville, OH: Emmaus Academic, 2019.

Farkasfalvy, Denis. *Inspiration and Interpretation: A Theological Introduction to Sacred Scripture*. Washington, D.C.: The Catholic University of America Press, 2010.

Favale, Abigail. "Does Darwinian Evolution Petrify God's Image?" *Church Life Journal*. October 5, 2018. https://churchlifejournal.nd.edu/articles/does-darwinian-evolution-naturally-petrify-the-image-of-god/.

Feingold, Lawrence. *The Natural Desire to See God According to St. Thomas and His Interpreters*. Ave Maria, FL: Sapientia Press, 2004.

Feser, Edward. *The Last Superstition: A Refutation of the New Atheism*. South Bend, IN: St. Augustine's Press, 2008.

Fitzmyer, Joseph. *Romans*. New York: Doubleday, 1993.

Flaman, Paul. "Evolution, the Origin of Human Persons, and Original Sin: Physical Continuity with an Ontological Leap." *The Heythrop Journal* 57 (2016): 568–83.

Foerster, Werner. "Ὄφις." In Vol. 5 of *Theological Dictionary of the New Testament*, edited by Gerhard Kittel, Geoffrey W. Bromiley, and Gerhard Friedrich, 576–79. Grand Rapids, MI: Eerdmans, 1964.

Francis, *Address before the Pontifical Academy of Sciences*. October 27, 2014.

———. *Laudato Si'*. Encyclical Letter. May 24, 2015.

———. *The Name of God Is Mercy*. New York: Random House, 2016.

———. *Scripturae Sacrae Affectus*. Apostolic Letter, September 30, 2020.

———. *Fratelli Tutti*. Encyclical Letter. October 4, 2020.

Francis and Antonio Spadaro, SJ, "A Big Heart Open to God." *America*. September 30, 2013.

Frankfort, Henri. *The Art and Architecture of the Ancient Orient*. Baltimore: Penguin Books, 1955.

Frings, Josef. "Das Konzil und die moderne Gedankenwelt." *Herder Korrespondenz* 16 (1961–1962): 168–74.

Futuyma, Douglas. *Evolution*. Fourth Edition. Sunderland, MA: Sinauer, 2017.

Gaál, Emery de. *The Theology of Pope Benedict XVI: The Christocentric Shift*. New York: Palgrave Macmillan, 2010.

———. *O Lord, I Seek Your Countenance: Explorations and Discoveries in Pope Benedict XVI's Theology*. Steubenville, OH: Emmaus Academic, 2018.

———. "Mariology as Christology and Ecclesiology: Professor Joseph Ratzinger's Only Mariology Course." In *Joseph Ratzinger and the Healing of Reformation-Era Divisions*, edited by Emery de Gaál and Matthew Levering, 93–120. Steubenville, OH: Emmaus Academic, 2019.

Gadamer, Hans-Georg. *Truth and Method*. New York: Seabury, 1975.

Gaine, Simon. "The Teaching of the Catholic Church and the Evolution of Humanity." Forthcoming.

Galileo Galilei, "Letter to the Grand Duchess Christina." In *The Galileo Affair: A Documentary History*, edited by Maurice Finocchiaro, 87–118. Berkeley, CA: University of California Press, 1989.

Ghose, Tia. "'Just a Theory': 7 Misused Science Words." *Scientific American*. April 2, 2013. https://www.scientificamerican.com/article/just-a-theory-7-misused-science-words/.

Girard, René. "Generative Scapegoating: Discussion." In *Violent Origins: Walter Burkert, René Girard, and Jonathan Z. Smith on Ritual Killing and Cultural Formation*, edited by Robert G. Hamerton-Kelly, 106–48. Stanford, CA: Stanford University Press: 1987.

———. *Deceit, Desire and the Novel*. Baltimore: The Johns Hopkins University Press, 1988.

———. *A Theater of Envy: William Shakespeare*. New York: Oxford University Press, 1991.

———. *I See Satan Fall Like Lightning*. Maryknoll, NY: Orbis Books, 2001.

*Gilgamesh*. Translated by David Ferry. New York: Farrar, Straus and Giroux, 1993.

Gilson, Étienne. *From Aristotle to Darwin and Back Again: A Journey in Final Causality, Species, and Evolution*. San Francisco: Ignatius Press, 2009.

Giussani, Luigi. *The Risk of Education: Discovering Our Ultimate Destiny*. Montreal: McGill-Queen's University Press, 2019.

Gorman, Michael. *Kenosis, Justification, and Theosis in Paul's Narrative Soteriology*. Grand Rapids, MI: Eerdmans, 2009.

Gould, Stephen Jay. "Evolution as Fact and Theory." In *Hen's Teeth and Horse's Toes*, 253–62. New York: W.W. Norton & Company, 1994.

———. "Nonoverlapping Magisteria." In *Leonardo's Mountain of Clams and the Diet of Worms*, 269–83. New York: Harmony Books, 1998.

Gregory of Nyssa. *Homilies on the Song of Songs*. Atlanta, GA: Society of Biblical Literature, 2012.

———. *Life of Moses*. New York: Paulist Press, 1978.

Gregory, Brad. "Science v. Religion? The Insights and Oversights of the 'New Atheists,' *Logos: A Journal of Catholic Thought and Culture* 12.4 (2009): 17–55.

Grisez, Germain. "The Inspiration and Inerrancy of Scripture." In St. Paul Center for Biblical Theology, *For the Sake of Our Salvation: The Truth and Humility of God's Word*, 181-90. Steubenville, OH: Emmaus Road Publishing, 2010.

Guardini, Romano. *The Lord*. Washington, D.C.: Gateway, 2016.

Guerriero, Elio. *Benedict XVI: His Life and Thought*. San Francisco: Ignatius Press, 2018.

Haarsma, Deborah. "Response from Evolutionary Creation," in *Four Views on Creation, Evolution, and Intelligent Design*, edited by J.B. Stump, 124–53. Grand Rapids, MI: Zondervan, 2017.

Haddad, Jordan. "Modern Biology's Contribution to Our Understanding of Christ's Sufferings." *Church Life Journal*. August 08, 2018. https://churchlifejournal.nd.edu/articles/modern-biologys-contribution-to-our-understanding-of-christs-sufferings/.

Hahn, Scott. *First Comes Love: Finding Your Family in the Church and the Trinity*. New York: Image, 2002.

———. *Kinship by Covenant: A Canonical Approach to the Fulfillment of God's Saving Promises*. New Haven, CT: Yale University Press, 2009.

———. *Romans*. Grand Rapids, MI: Baker Academic, 2017.

Hahn, Scott, and Benjamin Wiker. *Politicizing the Bible: The Roots of Historical Criticism and the Secularization of Scripture, 1300–1700*. New York: Crossroad Publishing Company, 2013.

Hahn, Scott, and Curtis Mitch, *Genesis: With Introduction, Commentary, and Notes*. San Francisco: Ignatius Press, 2010.

Halton, Charles, ed. "Genesis 1–11 as Ancient Historiography," in *Genesis: History, Fiction, or Neither? Three Views on the Bible's Earliest Chapters*. Grand Rapids: Zondervan Academic, 2015.

Hamilton, Victor. *The Book of Genesis, Chapters 1–17*. Grand Rapids, MI: Eerdmans, 1990.

Harrison, Brian. "Restricted Inerrancy and the 'Hermeneutic of Discontinuity.'" In St. Paul Center for Biblical Theology, *For the Sake of Our Salvation: The Truth and Humility of God's Word*, 225–46. Steubenville, OH: Emmaus Road Publishing, 2010.

Hart, David Bentley. *The Experience of God: Being, Consciousness, Bliss*. New Haven, CT: Yale University Press, 2013.

Hartman, Louis. "Etiology (In The Bible)." In vol. 5 of *New Catholic Encyclopedia*, edited by Thomas Carson, 407–409. Second Edition. Washington, D.C.: The Catholic University of America Press, 2002.

Haught, John. *God After Darwin: A Theology of Evolution*. Boulder, CO: Westview Press, 2008.

Hawking, Stephen. *A Brief History of Time: From the Big Bang to Black Holes*. London: Bantam, 1988.

Havel, Vaclav. *The Power of the Powerless: Citizens against the State in Central-Eastern Europe*. London: Routledge, 1985.

Healy, Mary. "Behind, in Front of . . . or Through the Text? The Christological Analogy and the Last Word of Biblical Truth." In *Behind the Text: History and Biblical Interpretation*, edited by Craig Bartholomew, C. Stephen Evens, Mary Healy, and Murray Rae, 181–95. Grand Rapids, MI: Zondervan, 2003.

Heidel, Alexander. *The Babylonian Genesis: The Story of Creation*. Chicago: University of Chicago Press, 1963.

Herron, Jon, and Scott Freeman. *Evolutionary Analysis*. Fifth Edition. Upper Saddle River, NJ: Pearson, 2013.

Hibbs, Thomas. "A Place in the Cosmos," *First Things*. February 2009. https://www.first-things.com/article/2009/02/003-a-place-in-the-cosmos

Hiestand, Gerald. "A More Modest Adam: An Exploration of Irenaeus' Anthropology in Light of the Darwinian Account of Pre-Fall Death" in *Bulletin of Ecclesial Theology* 5.1 (2018): 55–72.

von Hippel, William. *The Social Leap: The New Evolutionary Science of Who We Are, Where We Come From, and What Makes Us Happy*. New York: Harper Wave, 2018.

Hofmann, James. "Catholicism and Evolution: Polygenism and Original Sin." *Scientia et Fides* 8.2 (2020): 95–138.

Holmes, Jeremy. *Cur Deus Verba: Why the Word Became Words*. San Francisco: Ignatius Press, 2021.

Houck, Daniel. *Aquinas, Original Sin, and the Challenge of Evolution*. Cambridge: Cambridge University Press, 2020.

———. "Toward a New Account of the Fall, Informed by Anselm of Canterbury and Thomas Aquinas." *Pro Ecclesia* 29.4 (2020): 429–48.

Howell, Kenneth. *God's Two Books: Copernican Cosmology and Biblical Interpretation in Early Modern Science*. Notre Dame, IN: University of Notre Dame Press, 2002.

Hurowitz, Victor. "The Genesis of Genesis: Is the Creation Story Babylonian?" *Bible Review* 21 (2005): 37–53.

Ignatius of Antioch. *The Epistle of Ignatius to the Romans*. Translated by Alexander Roberts and James Donaldson. Vol. 1 of *Ante-Nicene Fathers*. Edited by Alexander Roberts, James Donaldson, and A. Cleveland Coxe. Buffalo, NY: Christian Literature Publishing Co., 1885.

Imbelli, Robert. "Joseph Ratzinger's 'Spiritual Christology.'" In *Gift to the Church and World: Fifty Years of Joseph Ratzinger's Introduction to Christianity*, edited by John Cavadini and Donald Wallenfang, 218–41. Eugene, OR: Pickwick, 2021.

International Theological Commission. *The Interpretation of Dogma*. 1989.

———. *Memory and Reconciliation: The Church and the Faults of the Past*. 1999.

———. *Communion and Stewardship: Human Persons Created in the Image of God*. 2004.

Jaeger, Andrew. "To-Be or Not-To-Be? The Existence and Non-Existence of God." Lecture at Ashland University, Ashland, OH. October 19, 2020.

Jobling, Mark, Edward Hollox, Matthew Hurles, and Toomas Kivisild. *Human Evolutionary Genetics*. *Second Edition*. New York: Garland Science, 2013.

John Paul II. General Audience. November 7, 1979.

———. *Address to the Pontifical Academy of the Sciences*. October 3, 1981.

———. *Salvifici Doloris*. Encyclical Letter. February 11,1984.

———. *Reconciliatio et Paenitentia*. Apostolic Exhortation. December 2,1984.

———. *Address to the Symposium "Christian Faith and the Theory of Evolution."* April 26, 1985.

————. General Audience. January 29, 1986.

————. General Audience. April 16, 1986. http://inters.org/John-Paul-II-Catechesis-Spiritual-Corporeal.

————. General Audience. June 4, 1986.

————. *Address to Participants in a Colloquium on Science, Philosophy and Theology.* September 5, 1986.

————. *Sollicitudo Rei Socialis.* Encyclical Letter. December 30, 1987.

————. *Letter to George Coyne, SJ, Director of the Vatican Observatory.* June 1, 1988.

————. *Message to the Pontifical Academy of Sciences Plenary Session on "The Origins and Early Evolution of Life."* October 22, 1996.

————. *Fides et Ratio.* Encyclical Letter. September 14, 1998.

————. *Ecclesia de Eucharistia.* Encyclical Letter. April 17, 2003.

Johnston, Mark. *Saving God: Religion after Idolatry.* Princeton, NJ: Princeton University Press, 2011.

Kaiser, Walter, and Duane Garrett, eds. *NIV Archaeological Study Bible.* Grand Rapids, MI: Zondervan, 2005.

Keener, Craig, and John Walton, eds. *NIV Cultural Backgrounds Study Bible: Bringing to Life the Ancient World of Scripture.* Grand Rapids, MI: Zondervan, 2016.

Kelly, Anthony. "Lonergan, Emergent Evolution and the Cosmic Process." *Quodlibet Journal* 8 (2009).

Kemp, Kenneth. "Adam and Eve and Evolution." *Society of Catholic Scientists.* 2020. https://www.catholicscientists.org/idea/adam-eve-evolution.

————. "God, Evolution, and the Body of Adam." *Scientia et Fides* 8.2 (2020): 139–72.

————. *The War That Never Was: Evolution and Christian Theology.* Eugene, OR: Cascade Books, 2020.

Kereszty, Roch. *Jesus Christ: Fundamentals of Christology.* New York: Alba House, 2002.

Khan, Razib. "Conservatives Shouldn't Fear Evolutionary Theory." *National Review.* May 13, 2019.

Kline, Meredith. "Trial by Ordeal." In *Through Christ's Word: A Festschrift for Dr. Philip E. Hughes,* 81–93. Phillipsburg, NJ: Presbyterian and Reformed, 1985.

Knight, Douglas, and Amy-Jill Levine. *The Meaning of the Bible: What the Jewish Scriptures and Christian Old Testament Can Teach Us.* New York: HarperOne, 2012.

Koninck, Charles de. *The Cosmos.* In Vol. 1 of *The Writings of Charles de Koninck,* edited by Ralph McInerny, 278–83. Notre Dame, IN: University of Notre Dame Press, 2016.

————. "La mort et l'Assomption de la sainte Vierge," *Laval théologique et philosophique* 7 (1952): 9–86.

Kromholtz, Bryan. *On the Last Day: The Time of the Resurrection of the Dead, according to Thomas Aquinas.* Fribourg: Academic Press Fribourg, 2010.

Ladaria, Luis. *Teología del pecado original y de la gracia: antropología teológica especial.* Second Edition. Madrid: Biblioteca de Autores Cristianos, 2001.

Lambert, W.G. "Enuma Elish." In *The Anchor Yale Bible Dictionary*, 526–28. New York: Doubleday, 1992.

Lamoureux, Dennis. *Evolutionary Creation: A Christian Approach to Evolution*. Eugene, OR: Wipf & Stock, 2008.

———. "No Historical Adam: Evolutionary Creation View." In *Four Views of the Historical Adam*, 37–65. Grand Rapids, MI: Zondervan, 2013.

Lane, William. *Hebrews 1–8*. Vol. 47A of *Word Biblical Commentary*. Dallas: Word, Incorporated, 1991.

Lear, Jonathan. *Radical Hope: Ethics in the Face of Cultural Devastation*. Cambridge, MA: Harvard University Press, 2006.

Lemna, Keith. *The Apocalypse of Wisdom: Louis Bouyer's Theological Recovery of the Cosmos*. Brooklyn, NY: Angelico Press, 2019.

Leo XIII. *Providentissimus Deus*. Encyclical Letter. November 18, 1893.

Levenson, Jon. *Sinai and Zion*. San Francisco: Harper and Row, 1987.

Levering, Matthew. "'Be Fruitful and Multiply, and Fill the Earth': Was and Is This a Good Idea?" In *On Earth as It Is in Heaven: Cultivating a Contemporary Theology of Creation*, edited by David Meconi, 80–122. Grand Rapids, MI: Eerdmans, 2016.

———. *Engaging the Doctrine of Creation: Cosmos, Creatures, and the Wise and Good Creator*. Grand Rapids, MI: Baker Academic, 2017.

———. *Engaging the Doctrine of Israel A Christian Israelology in Dialogue with Ongoing Judaism*. Eugene, OR: Cascade Books, 2021.

Lewis, C.S. *God in the Dock*. Grand Rapids, MI: Eerdmans, 1998.

———. *The Grand Miracle: And Other Selected Essays on Theology and Ethics from God in the Dock*. New York: Ballantine Books, 1983.

———. *The Last Battle*. New York: HarperCollins, 2005.

———. *Letters to Malcolm: Chiefly on Prayer*. London: Geoffrey Bles, 1964.

———. *The Magician's Nephew*. In *The Chronicles of Narnia*, 7–106. New York: HarperCollins, 2001.

———. *Miracles, a Preliminary Study*. New York: Macmillan, 1978.

———. *The Problem of Pain*. New York: HarperOne, 2001.

———. *Reflections on the Psalms*. London: Harvest Books, 1964. 112.

———. *The Weight of Glory, and Other Addresses*. New York: Macmillan, 1980.

Lohfink, Gerhard. *Jesus of Nazareth: What He Wanted, Who He Was*. Collegeville, MN: Liturgical Press, 2012.

Lombardo, Nicholas. "Evolutionary Genetics and Theological Narratives of Human Origins." *The Heythrop Journal* 59.3 (2018): 523–533.

———. "Evil, Suffering, and Original Sin." In *The Oxford Handbook of Catholic Theology*, edited by Lewis Ayres and Medi Ann Volpe, 139–50. Oxford: Oxford University Press, 2019.

———. "A Voice Like the Sound of Many Waters: Inspiration, Authorial Intention, and Theological Exegesis" *Nova et Vetera* 19.3 (2021): 825–69.

Lonergan, Bernard. *Insight: A Study of Human Understanding.* Vol. 3 of *Collected Works of Bernard Lonergan*, edited by Frederick Crowe and Robert Doran. Toronto: University of Toronto, 1992.

Lubac, Henri de. *Cosmic Liturgy: The Universe according to Maximus the Confessor.* San Francisco: Ignatius Press, 1988.

———. *The Discovery of God.* Grand Rapids, MI: Eerdmans, 1996.

———. *The Drama of Atheist Humanism.* San Francisco: Ignatius Press, 1995.

———. *Further Paradoxes.* Westminster, MD: Newman Press, 1958.

———. *Paradoxes of Faith.* San Francisco: Ignatius Press, 1987.

———. *The Religion of Teilhard de Chardin.* New York, Desclee Co. 1967.

———. *Teilhard de Chardin: The Man and His Meaning.* New York: Hawthorn Books, 1965.

———. *Vatican Council Notebooks.* Vol. 1. San Francisco: Ignatius Press, 2007.

Madden, James. *Mind, Matter, and Nature: A Thomistic Proposal for the Philosophy of Mind.* Washington, D.C.: The Catholic University of America Press, 2013.

Mahoney, Jack. *Christianity in Evolution: An Exploration.* Washington, D.C.: Georgetown University Press, 2011.

Maloney, George. *The Mystery of Christ in You: The Mystical Vision of St. Paul.* New York: Alba House, 1998.

Maritain, Jacques. *The Degrees of Knowledge.* London: Geoffrey Bles, 1937.

Marmion, Columba. *Christ in His Mysteries.* St. Louis, MO: Herder, 1924.

Matthews, Victor, and Don Benjamin. *Old Testament Parallels: Laws and Stories from the Ancient Near East.* New York: Paulist Press, 1991.

Maximus the Confessor. *On the Cosmic Mystery of Jesus Christ.* Crestwood, NY: St. Vladimir's Seminary Press, 2003.

———. *On Difficulties in the Church Fathers: The Ambigua.* Cambridge, MA: Harvard University Press, 2014.

———. *On Difficulties in Sacred Scripture: The Responses to Thalassios.* Washington, D.C.: The Catholic University of America Press, 2018.

McCabe, Herbert. *God Matters.* London: Mowbray, 2000.

Meconi, David. *The One Christ: St. Augustine's Theology of Deification.* Washington, D.C.: The Catholic University of America Press, 2013.

Meyer, Stephen. "DNA and Other Designs." *First Things.* April 1, 2000. https://www.firstthings.com/article/2000/04/dna-and-other-designs

———. *Signature in the Cell: DNA and the Evidence for Intelligent Design.* New York: Harper One, 2009.

———. *Darwin's Doubt: The Explosive Origin of Animal Life and the Case for Intelligent Design.* New York: HarperOne, 2013.

———. "Intelligent Design." In *Four Views on Creation, Evolution, and Intelligent Design*, edited by J.B. Stump, 177–230. Grand Rapids, MI: Zondervan, 2017.

Middleton, J. Richard. "Reading Genesis 3 Attentive to Human Evolution." In *Evolution and the Fall*, edited by William Cavanaugh and James Smith, 67–97. Grand Rapids, MI: Eerdmans, 2017.

Miller, Kenneth. "The Flagellum Unspun: The Collapse of 'Irreducible Complexity.'" In *Debating Design: From Darwin to DNA*, edited by William Dembski and Michael Ruse, 81–97. London: Cambridge University Press, 2004.

———. *Finding Darwin's God: A Scientist's Search for Common Ground Between God and Evolution*. New York: Perennial, 2007.

———. *Only a Theory: Evolution and the Battle for America's Soul*. New York: Penguin, 2008.

———. *The Human Instinct: How We Evolved to Have Reason, Consciousness, and Free Will*. New York: Simon & Schuster, 2018.

Miller, Michael. "Archbishop Gerhard Ludwig Müller and the Virgin Birth." *Homiletic and Pastoral Review*. December 13, 2012. https://www.hprweb.com/2012/12/archbishop-gerhard-ludwig-muller-and-the-virgin-birth/.

Morales, Isaac. "What Kind of Death? Romans 5 and Modern Science." Forthcoming.

Moritz, Berta. "A Patron Saint of Evolution?" *Church Life Journal*. October 16, 2019. https://churchlifejournal.nd.edu/articles/a-patron-saint-of-evolution/

Mounce, Robert. *The Book of Revelation*. Grand Rapids, MI: Eerdmans, 1997.

Müller, Gerhard Ludwig. "Die Jungfräulichkeit Marias in der Geburt." In *Katholische Dogmatik. Für Studium und Praxis der Theologie*, 497–99. Freiburg: Herder, 2003.

Murphy, Francesca. "Touching the Void: Ratzinger's Soteriology." In *Gift to the Church and World: Fifty Years of Joseph Ratzinger's Introduction to Christianity*, edited by John Cavadini and Donald Wallenfang, 242–54. Eugene, OR: Pickwick, 2021.

Newman, John Henry. *Apologia Pro Vita Sua*. New York: Longmans, Green, and Co, 1908.

———. *Discourses on the Scope and Nature of University Education Addressed to the Catholics of Dublin*. Dublin: James Duffy, 1852.

———. *An Essay in Aid of a Grammar of Assent*. Notre Dame, IN: University of Notre Dame Press, 1979.

———. *An Essay on the Development of Christian Doctrine*. Notre Dame, IN: University of Notre Dame Press, 1989.

———. *The Idea of a University*. London: Longmans, Green, and Co., 1907.

———. Letter to E.B. Pusey. In Vol. 25 of *The Letters and Diaries of John Henry Newman*, edited by C.S. Dessain and T. Gornall, 137–38. Oxford: Clarendon Press, 1978.

———. Letter to J. Walker of Scarborough on Darwin's Theory of Evolution. In Vol. 24 of *The Letters and Diaries of John Henry Newman*, edited by C.S. Dessain and T. Gornall, 77–78. Oxford: Clarendon Press, 1973.

———. Letter to William Robert Brownlow. In Vol. 25 of *The Letters and Diaries of John Henry Newman*, edited by C.S. Dessain and T. Gornall, 137–38. Oxford: Clarendon Press, 1978.

Nichols, Aidan. *The Thought of Pope Benedict XVI: An Introduction to the Theology of Joseph Ratzinger*. New York: Burns & Oates, 2007.

North, Robert. *Teilhard and the Creation of the Soul*. Milwaukee, WI: Bruce Pub. Co., 1967.

Novo, Javier. "The Theory of Evolution in the Writings of Joseph Ratzinger." *Scientia et Fides* 8.2 (2020): 323–49.

Oakes, Edward. *A Theology of Grace in Six Controversies*. Grand Rapids, MI: Eerdmans, 2016.

O'Brien, John. *Evolution and Religion*: New York: Century Co., 1932.

O'Callahan, Paul. *God's Gift of the Universe: An Introduction to Creation Theology*. Washington, D.C.: The Catholic University of America Press, 2021.

O'Connor, Flannery. *Mystery and Manners: Occasional Prose*. New York: Farrar, Straus, and Giroux, 1969.

Osborn, Ronald. Death *Before the Fall: Biblical Literalism and the Problem of Animal Suffering*. Downers Grove, IL: IVP Academic, 2014.

Pascal, Blaise. *Pensées*. Translated by Roger Ariew. Indianapolis, IN: Hackett, 2004.

Paul VI. *Ecclesiam Suam*. Encyclical Letter. August 6,1964.

Pew Research Center. "Public's Views on Human Evolution." December 30, 2013. https://www.pewforum.org/2013/12/30/publics-views-on-human-evolution/.

Philo. *The Works of Philo*. Peabody, MA: Hendrickson, 1993.

Pidel, Aaron, "Biblical Inspiration and Inerrancy According to Joseph Ratzinger." Master's Thesis. Boston College. 2011.

———. "Joseph Ratzinger and Biblical Inerrancy." *Nova et Vetera* 12.1 (2014): 307–30.

Pieper, Josef. *In Defense of Philosophy*. San Francisco: Ignatius Press, 1992.

Pitre, Brant. *Jesus and the Jewish Roots of Mary*. New York: Image, 2018.

Pitre, Brant, and John Bergsma. *A Catholic Introduction to the Old Testament*. San Francisco: Ignatius Press, 2018.

Pitre, Brant, Michael Barber, and John Kincaid. *Paul, a New Covenant Jew: Rethinking Pauline Theology*. Grand Rapids, MI: Eerdmans, 2019.

Pius XI. *Mit Brennender Sorge*. Encyclical Letter. March 14,1937.

Pius XII. *Divino Afflante Spiritu*. Encyclical Letter. September 30, 1943.

Pius XII. *Humani Generis*. Encyclical Letter. August 12,1950.

Pontifical Academy of Sciences. "Statement by the Pontifical Academy of Sciences on Current Scientific Knowledge on Cosmic Evolution and Biological Evolution." In *Scientific Insights into Evolution of the Universe and Life*, 586, edited by W. Arber, N. Cabibbo, M. Sánchez Sorondo. Vatican City: Pontificia Academia Scientiarum, 2009.

———. *Evolving Concepts of Nature*. Vatican City: Ex Aedibus Academicis in Civitate Vaticana, 2015.

Pontifical Biblical Commission. *The Historicity of the Gospels*. 1964.

———. *The Interpretation of the Bible in the Church*. 1993.

———. *On the Historicity of Genesis 1–3*. In Dean Béchard, *The Scripture Documents*, 192–194. Collegeville, MN: The Liturgical Press, 2002.

———. *The Inspiration and Truth of Sacred Scripture*. Collegeville, MN: The Liturgical Press, 2014.

Pritchard, James. *The Ancient Near East in Pictures Relating to the Old Testament*. Princeton, NJ: Princeton University Press, 1954.

———. *Archaeology and the Old Testament*. Princeton, NJ: Princeton University Press, 1958.

———. *Ancient Near Eastern Texts: An Anthology and Pictures*. Princeton, NJ: Princeton University Press, 2010.

Rahner, Karl. *Theological Investigations*. Vol. 1. Baltimore: Helicon Press, 1960.

———. *On the Theology of Death*. New York: Herder and Herder, 1961.

———. *Nature and Grace*. New York: Sheed and Ward, 1964.

———. *Hominisation*. New York: Herder and Herder, 1965.

Ramage, Matthew. *Dark Passages of the Bible*. Washington, D.C.: The Catholic University of America Press, 2013.

———. "Benedict XVI on Freedom in Obedience to the Truth: A Key for the New Evangelization." *Homiletic and Pastoral Review*. May 12, 2014. https://www.hprweb.com/2014/05/benedict-xvi-on-freedom-in-obedience-to-the-truth-a-key-for-the-new-evangelization/

———. "How to Read the Bible and Still Be a Christian: The Problem of Divine Violence as Considered in Recent Curial Documents." *Homiletic and Pastoral Review*. July 12, 2015. https://www.hprweb.com/2015/07/how-to-read-the-bible-and-still-be-a-christian/.

———. "In the Beginning: Aquinas, Benedict XVI, and the Book of Genesis." In *Reading Sacred Scripture with Thomas Aquinas: Hermeneutical Tools and New Perspectives*, edited by P. Roszak and J. Vijgen, 481–505. Turnhout, Belgium: Brepols, 2015.

———. "Benedict XVI's Hermeneutic of Reform: Towards a Rapprochement of the Magisterium and Modern Biblical Criticism." *Nova et Vetera* 14.3 (2016): 879–917.

———. "*Extra Ecclesiam Nulla Salus* & the Substance of Catholic Doctrine: Towards a Realization of Benedict XVI's 'Hermeneutic of Reform,'" *Nova et Vetera* 14.1 (2016): 295–330.

———. *Jesus, Interpreted*. Washington, D.C.: The Catholic University of America Press, 2017.

———. *The Experiment of Faith: Pope Benedict XVI on Living the Theological Virtues in a Secular Age*. Washington, D.C.: The Catholic University of America Press, 2020.

———. "Machine or Melody? Joseph Ratzinger on Divine Causality in Evolutionary Creation." *Scientia et Fides* 8.2 (2020): 307–21.

———. "Does Evolution Undermine Christianity? Joseph Ratzinger on the Bible and Humanity's Evolutionary Origins." *Review for Religious: New Series* 1.2 (2021): 159–77.

———. "Putting the Last Adam First: Aquinas, Ratzinger, and Human Origins in Light of Kenotic Christology." In *Thomas Aquinas and the Crisis of Christology*, edited by Michael A. Dauphinais, Andrew Hofer, OP, and Roger W. Nutt, 279–302. Ave Maria, FL: Sapientia Press, 2021.

———. "Ratzinger on Evolution and Evil: A Christological and Mariological Answer to the Problem of Suffering and Death in Creation." *Religions* 12.8 (2021): 583.

Ratzinger, Joseph. *Volk und Haus Gottes in Augustins Lehre von der Kirche*. München: K. Zink, 1954.

————. *Mariologie* (1957). Lecture notes from course on Mariology taught at Freising Seminary.

————. *Schöpfungslehre* (1958). Lecture notes from course on the doctrine of creation taught at Freising Seminary.

————. "Zum Problem der Entmythologisierung Des Neuen Testamentes," *Religionsunterricht an höheren Schulen* 3 (1960): 2–11.

————. *Schöpfungslehre* (1964). Lecture notes from course on the doctrine of creation taught at Bonn University.

————. *Theological Highlights of Vatican II*. New York: Paulist Press, 1966.

————. *Einführung in das Christentum*. München: Kösel, 1968.

————. "The Dignity of the Human Person." In *Commentary on the Documents of Vatican II*, edited by Herbert Vorgrimler, Vol. V, 115–64. New York: Herder and Herder, 1969.

————. *Storia e Dogma*. Milano: Jaca Book, 1971.

————. "Schöpfungsglaube und Evolutionstheorie." In *Dogma Und Verkündigung*. Munich: Erich Wewel Verlag, 1973.

————. *Schöpfungslehre* (1976). Lecture notes from course on the doctrine of creation taught at the University of Regensburg.

————. *Die Tochter Zion*. Einsiedeln: Johannes-Verl,1977.

————. *Eshcatologie: Tod und ewiges Leben*. Regensburg: Pustet, 1977.

————. "Sources and Transmission of the Faith," *Communio* 10 (1983): 17–34.

————. *Schauen auf den Durchbohrten: Versuche zu einer spirituellen Christologie*. Einsiedeln: Johannes Verlag, 1984.

————. *Behold the Pierced One: An Approach to a Spiritual Christology*. San Francisco: Ignatius Press, 1986.

————."Die Ekklesiologie des zweiten Vatikanums." *Communio* 15 (1986): 41–52.

————. *Im Anfang schuf Gott: Vier Münchener Fastenpredigten über Schöpfung und Fall*. München: Wewel, 1986.

————. Preface to *Evolutionismus und Christentum*, edited by Robert Spaemann, R. Löw, and P. Koslowski, vii-ix. Weinheim: Acta Humaniora, 1986.

————. *Principles of Catholic Theology*. San Francisco: Ignatius Press, 1987.

————. *Eschatology: Death and Eternal Life*. Translated by Michael Waldstein. Washington, D.C.: The Catholic University of America Press, 1988.

————. "Biblical Interpretation in Crisis: On the Question of the Foundations and Approaches of Exegesis Today." In *Biblical Interpretation in Crisis: The Ratzinger Conference on Bible and Church*, 1–23. Grand Rapids, MI: Eerdmans, 1989.

————. "Der Mensch zwischen Reproduktion and Schöpfung." *Internationale Katholische Zeitschrift* 1 (1989): 61-71

————. "'You Are Full of Grace': Elements of Biblical Devotion to Mary." *Communio* 16 (1989): 54–68.

————. "Concerning the Notion of Person in Theology," *Communio* 17 (1990): 439–454.

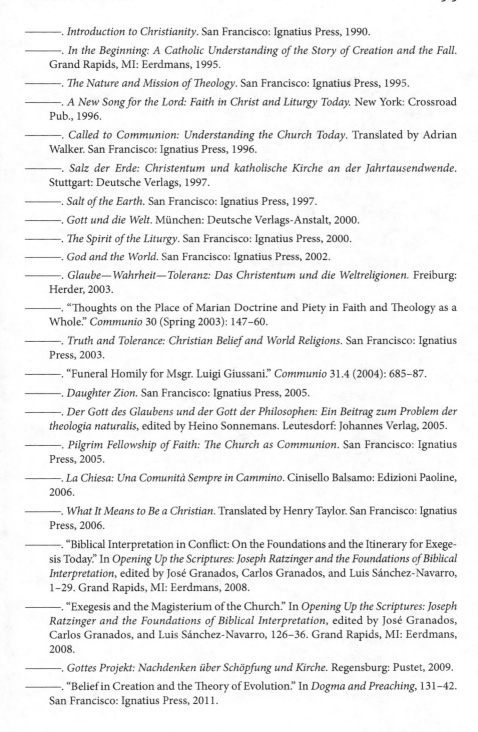

————. *Introduction to Christianity.* San Francisco: Ignatius Press, 1990.

————. *In the Beginning: A Catholic Understanding of the Story of Creation and the Fall.* Grand Rapids, MI: Eerdmans, 1995.

————. *The Nature and Mission of Theology.* San Francisco: Ignatius Press, 1995.

————. *A New Song for the Lord: Faith in Christ and Liturgy Today.* New York: Crossroad Pub., 1996.

————. *Called to Communion: Understanding the Church Today.* Translated by Adrian Walker. San Francisco: Ignatius Press, 1996.

————. *Salz der Erde: Christentum und katholische Kirche an der Jahrtausendwende.* Stuttgart: Deutsche Verlags, 1997.

————. *Salt of the Earth.* San Francisco: Ignatius Press, 1997.

————. *Gott und die Welt.* München: Deutsche Verlags-Anstalt, 2000.

————. *The Spirit of the Liturgy.* San Francisco: Ignatius Press, 2000.

————. *God and the World.* San Francisco: Ignatius Press, 2002.

————. *Glaube—Wahrheit—Toleranz: Das Christentum und die Weltreligionen.* Freiburg: Herder, 2003.

————. "Thoughts on the Place of Marian Doctrine and Piety in Faith and Theology as a Whole." *Communio* 30 (Spring 2003): 147–60.

————. *Truth and Tolerance: Christian Belief and World Religions.* San Francisco: Ignatius Press, 2003.

————. "Funeral Homily for Msgr. Luigi Giussani." *Communio* 31.4 (2004): 685–87.

————. *Daughter Zion.* San Francisco: Ignatius Press, 2005.

————. *Der Gott des Glaubens und der Gott der Philosophen: Ein Beitrag zum Problem der theologia naturalis,* edited by Heino Sonnemans. Leutesdorf: Johannes Verlag, 2005.

————. *Pilgrim Fellowship of Faith: The Church as Communion.* San Francisco: Ignatius Press, 2005.

————. *La Chiesa: Una Comunità Sempre in Cammino.* Cinisello Balsamo: Edizioni Paoline, 2006.

————. *What It Means to Be a Christian.* Translated by Henry Taylor. San Francisco: Ignatius Press, 2006.

————. "Biblical Interpretation in Conflict: On the Foundations and the Itinerary for Exegesis Today." In *Opening Up the Scriptures: Joseph Ratzinger and the Foundations of Biblical Interpretation,* edited by José Granados, Carlos Granados, and Luis Sánchez-Navarro, 1–29. Grand Rapids, MI: Eerdmans, 2008.

————. "Exegesis and the Magisterium of the Church." In *Opening Up the Scriptures: Joseph Ratzinger and the Foundations of Biblical Interpretation,* edited by José Granados, Carlos Granados, and Luis Sánchez-Navarro, 126–36. Grand Rapids, MI: Eerdmans, 2008.

————. *Gottes Projekt: Nachdenken über Schöpfung und Kirche.* Regensburg: Pustet, 2009.

————. "Belief in Creation and the Theory of Evolution." In *Dogma and Preaching,* 131–42. San Francisco: Ignatius Press, 2011.

————. "Farewell to the Devil?" In *Dogma and Preaching*, 197–205. San Francisco: Ignatius Press, 2011.

————. "Gratia Praesupponit Natura: Grace Presupposes Nature." in *Dogma and Preaching*, 143–61. San Francisco: Ignatius Press, 2011.

————. "On the Understanding of 'Person' in Theology." In *Dogma and Preaching*, 181–96. San Francisco: Ignatius Press, 2011.

————. *Progetto di Dio: Meditazioni sulla Creazione e la Chiesa*. Venice: Marcianum Press, 2012.

————. "Man between Reproduction and Creation: Theological Questions on the Origin of Human Life." In Vol. 2 of *Joseph Ratzinger in* Communio: *Anthropology and Culture*, 70–83. Grand Rapids, MI: Eerdmans, 2013.

Ratzinger, Joseph, and Christoph Cardinal Schönborn. *Introduction to the Catechism of the Catholic Church*. San Francisco: Ignatius Press, 1994.

Ratzinger, Joseph, and Hans Urs von Balthasar. *Mary: The Church at the Source*. San Francisco: Ignatius Press, 1997.

Ratzinger, Joseph, and Vittorio Messori. *The Ratzinger Report*. San Francisco: Ignatius Press, 1987.

Rhonheimer, Martin. "Benedict XVI's 'Hermeneutic of Reform' and Religious Freedom." *Nova et Vetera* 9.4 (2011): 1029–54.

Riches, Aaron. "El misterio del origen humano. Para mantener la tensión entre la doctrina de Adán y la ciencia de la evolución." *Facies Domini* 8 (2016): 265–286.

Rolnick, Phillip. *Origins: God, Evolution, and the Question of the Cosmos*. Waco, TX: Baylor University Press, 2015.

Rossano, Matt. *Supernatural Selection: How Religion Evolved*. New York: Oxford University Press, 2010.

Roszak, Piotr. "Imperfectly Perfect Universe? Emerging Natural Order in Thomas Aquinas." Forthcoming.

————. "Life in Paradise. Thomas Aquinas on Original Justice and Its Anthropological Significance." Forthcoming.

Rowland, Tracey. *Ratzinger's Faith: The Theology of Pope Benedict XVI*. Oxford: Oxford University Press, 2008.

————. "Benedict's Intellectual Mentors and Students." *Crisis Magazine*. February 19, 2013.

————. "Reading Scripture within the Horizon of Faith." *Evangelization and Culture* 5 (2020): 88–98.

Rziha, John. *The Christian Moral Life: Directions for the Journey to Happiness*. Notre Dame, IN: University of Notre Dame Press, 2017.

Salkeld, Brett. "René Girard and the Literal Sense of Scripture," *Vox Nova*. November 12, 2015. https://www.patheos.com/blogs/voxnova/2015/11/12/rene-girard-and-the-literal-sense-of-scripture/.

————. "Catholic Creationism as a Conspiracy Theory." *Church Life Journal*. May 13, 2020.

Salzmann, Andrew. "Bonaventure." In *T&T Clark Companion to Atonement*, 409. New York: Bloomsbury T&T Clark, 2017.

Sanz, Santiago. "Joseph Ratzinger y la doctrina de la creación. Los apuntes de Münster de 1964." *Revista Española de Teología* 74 (2014): 31–70.

———. "Joseph Ratzinger y la doctrina de la creación. Los apuntes de Münster de 1964 (y II). Algunos temas fundamentales." *Revista Española de Teología* 74 (2014): 201–48.

———. "Joseph Ratzinger y la doctrina de la creación. Los apuntes de Münster de 1964 (y III). Algunos temas debatidos." *Revista Española de Teología* 74 (2014): 453–96

———. "La dottrina della creazione nelle lezioni del professor Joseph Ratzinger: gli appunti di Freising (1958)." *Annales theologici* 30 (2016): 11–44.

———. "Joseph Ratzinger e il peccato originale: riflessioni a proposito di un libro mancato." *Revista Española de Teología* LXXVIII.3 (2018): 439–57.

———. "The Manuscripts of Joseph Ratzinger's Lectures on the Doctrine of Creation." Translated by Matthew J. Ramage. Forthcoming in *Nova et Vetera*.

———. "Original Sin." Entry in a forthcoming *Joseph Ratzinger Dictionary*.

Schindler, D.C. *A Companion to* Homo Abyssus. Washington, D.C.: The Catholic University of America Press, 2019.

Schönborn, Christoph. "The Reflections of Joseph Ratzinger Pope Benedict XVI on Evolution." In *Scientific Insights into the Evolution of the Universe and of Life*, 12–21. Vatican City: Ex Aedibus Academicis in Civitate Vaticana, 2009.

Schwager, Raymund. *Erbsünde und Heilsdrama: Im Kontext von Evolution, Gentechnologie und Apokalypse.* Münster: LIT Verlag, 1997.

———. *Banished from Eden: Original Sin and Evolutionary Theory in the Drama of Salvation.* Herefordshire: Gracewing Publishing, 2005.

Scruton, Roger. *On Human Nature.* Princeton, NJ: Princeton University Press, 2017.

Seewald, Peter. *Benedict XVI: A Life.* New York: Bloomsbury, 2020.

Sinclair, Upton. *I, Candidate for Governor: And How I Got Licked.* Berkeley, CA: University of California Press, 1994.

Smith, James. "What Stands on the Fall?" In *Evolution and the Fall*, edited by William Cavanaugh and James Smith, 48–66. Grand Rapids, MI: Eerdmans, 2017.

Smith, Mark. *The Genesis of Good and Evil: The Fall(out) and Original Sin in the Bible.* Louisville, KY: Westminster John Knox Press, 2019.

Society of Catholic Scientists. "Did the Catholic Church ever condemn Evolution in the past?" https://www.catholicscientists.org/common-questions/a-does-catholic-church-accept-evolution-b-did-catholic-church-ever-condemn-evolution-in-past.

Sollereder, Bethany. "From Survival to Love: Evolution and the Problem of Suffering." *Christian Century* 131.19 (2014): 22–25.

Sparks, Kenton. *God's Word in Human Words: An Evangelical Appropriation of Critical Biblical Scholarship.* Grand Rapids, MI: Baker Academic, 2008.

———. *Sacred Word, Broken Word: Biblical Authority and the Dark Side of Scripture.* Grand Rapids, MI: Eerdmans, 2011.

Spezzano, Daria. "You Prepared a Body for Me" (Heb 10:5): The Eschatological End of Evolution." Forthcoming.

Spinoza, Baruch. *Theological-Political Treatise*. Cambridge: Cambridge University Press, 2007.

Stallsworth, Paul T. "The Story of an Encounter." In *Biblical Interpretation in Crisis: The Ratzinger Conference on Bible and Church*, 102–90 Grand Rapids, MI: Eerdmans, 1989.

Steinmair-Pösel, Petra. "Original Sin, Grace, and Positive Mimesis," *Journal of Violence, Mimesis, and Culture* 14 (2007): 1–12.

Stinessen, Wilfrid. *Bread That Is Broken*. San Francisco: Ignatius Press, 2020.

Synave, Paul, and Pierre Benoit. *Prophecy and Inspiration: A Commentary on the Summa Theologica II-II, Questions 171–178*. New York: Desclée Co., 1961.

Szathmary, Eörs, and John Maynard Smith. "The Major Evolutionary Transitions." *Nature* 374 (1995): 227–32.

———. *The Origins of Life*. Oxford: Oxford University Press, 2000.

Tabaczek, Mariusz. "What Do God and Creatures Really Do in an Evolutionary Change? Divine Concurrence and Transformism from the Thomistic Perspective." *American Catholic Philosophical Quarterly* (2019): 445–82.

———. "Does God Create through Evolution? The Aristotelian-Thomistic Perspective," Public lecture for the Thomistic Institute at Blackfriars, Oxford, UK. February 5, 2020. https://soundcloud.com/thomisticinstitute/does-god-create-through-evolution-fr-mariusz-tabsczek.

Tanzella-Nitti, Giuseppe. "Il coraggio dell'Intellectus fidei: le 'lezioni carinziane' di Joseph Ratzinger su theologia de la creazione." Introduction to Benedict XVI, *Progetto di Dio. La Creazione: Meditazioni sulla Creazione e la Chiesa*, 7–29. Venezia: Marcianum Press, 2012.

———. "La questione antropologica in prospettiva teologica." In Centro di documentazione interdisciplinare di Scienza e fede, *Conversazioni fra scienza e fede*. Lindau: Torino, 2012.

Tolkien, J.R.R. *Tree and Leaf: Including the Poem Mythopoeia*. Boston: Houghton Mifflin, 1965.

———. *The Silmarillion*. Boston: Houghton Mifflin, 2001.

Torrell, Jean-Pierre. "Nature and Grace in Thomas Aquinas." In *Surnaturel: A Controversy at the Heart of Twentieth-Century Thomistic Thought*, edited by Serge-Thomas Bonino, 155–87. Ave Maria, FL: Sapientia Press, 2007.

Trasancos, Stacy. *Particles of Faith: A Catholic Guide to Navigating Science*. Notre Dame, IN: Ave Maria Press, 2016.

Trent, Council of. "Decree on Original Sin." 1546. https://www.ewtn.com/catholicism/library/decree-concerning-original-sin—decree-concerning-reform-1495.

Ulrich, Ferdinand. *Homo Abyssus: The Drama of the Question of Being*. Washington, D.C.: Humanum Academic Press, 2018.

Vall, Gregory. "Psalm 22: *Vox Christi* or Israelite Temple Liturgy?" *The Thomist* 66 (2002): 175–200.

VanGemeren, Willem, ed. *New International Dictionary of Old Testament Theology and Exegesis*. Grand Rapids, MI: Zondervan, 1997.

Vanhoozer, Kevin. *The Drama of Doctrine: A Canonical-Linguistic Approach to Christian Theology*. Louisville, KY: Westminster John Knox Press, 2005.

———. *Is There a Meaning in This Text? The Bible, the Reader, and the Morality of Literary Knowledge*. Grand Rapids, MI: Zondervan Academic, 2009.

———. *Remythologizing Theology: Divine Action, Passion, and Authorship*. Cambridge: Cambridge University Press, 2010.

Vatican Council I. *Dei Filius* IV, no. 3017. Dogmatic Constitution. April 24, 1870.

Vatican Council II. *Dei Verbum*. November 18, 1965.

———. *Gaudium et Spes*. December 7, 1965.

———. *Lumen Gentium*. November 24,1964.

———. *Nostra Aetate*. October 28, 1965.

Venema, Dennis, and Scot McKnight. *Adam and the Genome: Reading Scripture after Genetic Science*. Grand Rapids, MI: Baker, 2017.

Verschuuren, Gerard. *How Science Points to God*. Manchester, NH: Sophia Institute Press, 2020.

Wainwright, Geoffrey. *Eucharist and Eschatology*. New York: Oxford University Press, 1981.

Waltke, Bruce, and Cathi Fredricks. *Genesis: A Commentary*. Grand Rapids, MI: Zondervan, 2001.

Walton, John. "Genesis." In *Zondervan Illustrated Bible Backgrounds Commentary*, edited by John Walton, 1:10–42. Grand Rapids, MI: Zondervan, 2009.

———. *The Lost World of Genesis One*. Downers Grove, IL: IVP Academic, 2009.

Ward, Maisie. *Gilbert Keith Chesterton*. New York: Sheed and Ward, 1943.

Ware, Kallistos. *The Orthodox Way*. Crestwood, NY: St. Vladimir's Press, 1995.

———. "The Understanding of Salvation in the Orthodox Tradition." In *For Us and Our Salvation*, edited by Rienk Lannoy, 107–31. Utrecht-Leiden: Interuniversitair Instituut voor Missiologie en Oecimenica, 1994.

Weinandy, Thomas. *Jesus Becoming Jesus: A Theological Interpretation of the Synoptic Gospels*. Washington, D.C.: The Catholic University of America Press, 2018.

———. *Jesus Becoming Jesus: A Theological Interpretation of the Gospel according to John: Prologue and the Book of Signs*. Washington, D.C.: The Catholic University of America Press, 2021.

Weinrich, William, ed. *Revelation*. Ancient Christian Commentary on Scripture. Downers Grove, IL: InterVarsity Press, 2005.

Wenham, Gordon. *Genesis 16–50*. Vol. 2 of *Word Biblical Commentary*. Dallas: Word, Incorporated, 1994.

———. *Rethinking Genesis 1-11*. Eugene, OR: Cascade Books, 2015.

White, Thomas Joseph. *The Light of Christ: An Introduction to Catholicism*. Washington, D.C.: The Catholic University of America Press, 2017.

Wicks, Jared. "Six texts by Prof. Joseph Ratzinger as *Peritus* Before and During Vatican Council II." *Gregorianum* 89 (2008): 233–311.

Williams, Rowan. *Christ the Heart of Creation*. London: Bloomsbury, 2018.

Wilson, Jessica Hooten. "The Unoriginal Augustine." *Church Life Journal*. December 04, 2019.

Work, Telford. *Living and Active: Scripture in the Economy of Salvation*. Grand Rapids, MI: Eerdmans, 2002.

———. *Jesus—the End and the Beginning*. Grand Rapids: Baker, 2019.

Wrangham, Richard. *Catching Fire: How Cooking Made Us Human*. New York: Basic Books, 2009.

Wrathall, Mark. "Between the Earth and the Sky: Heidegger on Life after the Death of God." In *Heidegger and Unconcealment: Truth, Language, and History*, 69–87. Cambridge: Cambridge University Press, 2010.

Wright, N.T. "The Challenge of Dialogue." In Christoph Heilig, J. Thomas Hewitt, and Michael Bird, *God and the Faithfulness of Paul*, 711-70. Minneapolis, MN: Fortress Press, 2017.

———. *Jesus and the Victory of God*. Minneapolis, MN: Fortress Press, 1996.

———. *The Resurrection of the Son of God*. Minneapolis, MN: Fortress Press, 2003.

# Index